New Advances and Illustrations in Applied Geochemistry

New Advances and Illustrations in Applied Geochemistry

Editors

Qingjie Gong
Zeming Shi

MDPI • Basel • Beijing • Wuhan • Barcelona • Belgrade • Manchester • Tokyo • Cluj • Tianjin

Editors

Qingjie Gong
China University of
Geosciences
Beijing, China

Zeming Shi
Chengdu University of
Technology
Chengdu China

Editorial Office
MDPI
St. Alban-Anlage 66
4052 Basel, Switzerland

This is a reprint of articles from the Special Issue published online in the open access journal *Applied Sciences* (ISSN 2076-3417) (available at: https://www.mdpi.com/journal/applsci/special_issues/093IB50YT8).

For citation purposes, cite each article independently as indicated on the article page online and as indicated below:

LastName, A.A.; LastName, B.B.; LastName, C.C. Article Title. *Journal Name* **Year**, *Volume Number*, Page Range.

ISBN 978-3-0365-8346-4 (Hbk)
ISBN 978-3-0365-8347-1 (PDF)

Contents

About the Editors

Qingjie Gong

Dr. Qingjie Gong is a professor and doctoral supervisor of geochemistry from China University of Geosciences (Beijing) and acts as the director of the committee of applied geochemistry, Chinese Society for Mineralogy, Petrology and Geochemistry (CSMPG); associate editor of the Applied Geochemistry journal hosted by the International Association of Geochemistry; and on the editorial board of the Acta Geoscientic Sinica journal hosted by Chinese Academy of Geological Sciences. They are an expert at geochemical exploration of metals and experimental geochemistry at high temperatures and pressures. Dr. Gong presents a weathering index of granite (WIG) to assess a sample's weathering degree, an empirical equation to describe trace element behaviors due to rock weathering and trace element backgrounds of normal geological materials, a method called seven levels' classification of geochemical anomaly to determine and classify geochemical anomalies based on backgrounds and cutoff grades of trace element, a promising concept called geochemical gene to discriminate and trace geological materials. Now, Dr. Gong has published nearly 100 papers in domestic and foreign journals and 7 monographs in Chinese and awarded 7 provincial and ministerial awards. In order to calculate geochemical backgrounds and anomaly levels, a software called GBAL was developed by Dr. Gong and another software called GGC to calculate geochemical gene codes and gene similarities of samples was also developed by Dr. Gong.

Zeming Shi

Dr. Zeming Shi, (Post-doctoral) is a Full Professor II and doctoral supervisor. He is currently dean of the School of Earth Sciences at the Chengdu University of Technology (CDUT), China, head of the Applied Nuclear Techniques in Geosciences Key Laboratory of Sichuan Province, Academic and Technical Leader of Sichuan Province, the Tianfu famous teacher of Tianfu Qingcheng Plan, and the executive member of the Society of Chinese Mineralogy, Petrology and Geochemistry. He is mainly engaged in environmental geochemistry and mineral deposit geochemistry research and is responsible for more than 20 provincial and ministerial-level projects such as the National Natural Science Foundation of China (NSFC) and the National Key Research and Development Program of China (subprojects). He has published more than 100 academic papers, compiled 2 textbooks and published 3 monographs, and has been awarded 3 provincial and ministerial science and technology awards.

applied sciences

Editorial

Special Issue on New Advances and Illustrations in Applied Geochemistry in China

Qingjie Gong [1,*] and Zeming Shi [2,*]

1 School of Earth Sciences and Resources, China University of Geosciences, Beijing 100083, China
2 College of Earth Sciences, Chengdu University of Technology, Chengdu 610059, China
* Correspondence: qjiegong@cugb.edu.cn (Q.G.); shizm@cdut.edu.cn (Z.S.)

1. Introduction

The 9th national conference on applied geochemistry in China will be held in Chengdu, Sichuan province, in October 2023, hosted by the committee of applied geochemistry, the Chinese Society for Mineralogy, Petrology and Geochemistry (CSMPG). In order to facilitate the academic exchange on applied geochemistry, this Special Issue is intended for the presentation of new advances and case illustrations in the field of applied geochemistry.

This Special Issue gathers 14 scientific papers that capture various hot and challenging issues in applied geochemistry. These articles belong to three broad groups: (i) new advances and case illustrations in resource exploration; (ii) new advances and case illustrations in environment assessment; and (iii) new advances in the basic theory of geochemistry.

2. Resource Exploration

Geochemical exploration has played an important role in resource prospecting. This issue includes six papers on geochemical exploration. As discoveries of world-class mineral deposits continue to decline, shallow deposits are no longer enough to meet the daily needs of human beings, and exploration in covered areas has received increasing attention. The first paper, authored by J. Li, B. Zhang, Q. Gong, H. Liu, and N. Liu, presents the fine-grained soil-prospecting method in the Jiaojia gold deposit in Shandong province [1], where three lines of evidence on gold concentrations, microscopic morphology, and geochemical lithogenes were illustrated to explain the gold migration from ore to surface soils in a covered area. The second paper introduces the theory of the geoelectrochemical exploration method and presents three case studies on gold prospecting in covered areas [2], authored by M. Kang, H. Guo, W. Zhu, X. Luo, and J. Yang. Unlike the above two papers, the third paper, authored by B. Zhou, Z. Zhang, Z. Shi, H. Song, and L. Yu, focuses on the geochemistry and geochronology of a pluton in western Kunlun orogen [3], where the formation of the pluton and its mineralization potential on polymetallic deposits were illustrated. The paper by T. Dong, L. Kang, Y. Zhang, and Y. Gao presents prospecting on shale oil [4], where shales with higher TOC and lower pore fractal parameters in the Songliao basin, NE China, are favorable reservoirs.

The remaining two papers focus on determining geochemical anomalies in geochemical survey data. The first paper, authored by B. Zhao, D. Zhang, R. Zhang, Z. Li, P. Tang, and H. Wan, describes an advanced workflow of an object-based geochemical graph learning approach [5], where a case study on multiple mineral anomalies was illustrated in Southeastern Inner Mongolia, North China. The other paper illustrates a creative method to determine the tungsten composite anomalies using the geochemical gene technique [6], authored by J. Li, Q. Gong, B. Zhang, N. Liu, X. Wu, T. Yan, X. Li, and Y. Wu. The mineralization similarities of the geochemical metallogene can be viewed as useful integrated indices on geochemical tungsten exploration with the elimination of the lithological influence.

Citation: Gong, Q.; Shi, Z. Special Issue on New Advances and Illustrations in Applied Geochemistry in China. *Appl. Sci.* **2023**, *13*, 8220. https://doi.org/10.3390/app13148220

Received: 11 July 2023
Accepted: 12 July 2023
Published: 15 July 2023

3. Environment Assessment

The soil quality survey and environment assessment are enduring topics in applied geochemistry. This issue includes three papers that focus on the evaluation of soil nutrient status, pollution assessment of heavy metals, and geochemical survey of geoherbs, respectively.

The first paper, authored by J. Zhang, Y. Liu, S. Hong, M. Wen, C. Zheng, and P. Liu, presents the geochemical soil survey of heavy metals in a typical mining area [7], where single and integrated pollution indices were used to assess the environmental quality of soils, and the speciation of heavy metals were analyzed to discover their mobility. The second paper presents a LightGBM model to assess the soil nutrient status, authored by Z. Liang, T. Zou, J. Gong, M. Zhou, W. Shen, and J. Zhang [8], where the tobacco planting soil in Debao County, Guangxi province, was illustrated as an example. Finally, the quality of the top-geoherb in Chengde City, Hebei province, was geochemically surveyed in the paper authored by Z. Sun, W. Shen, W. Fang, H. Zhang, Z. Chen, L. Xiong, and T [9], where the geochemical signatures of trace elements (especially rare earth elements) and medicinal components of Scutellaria baicalensis were described.

4. Basic Theory

In this Special Issue, five papers focus on the basic theory of geochemistry, such as the elemental abundance, the equation of state of multicomponent fluids, geochemical indices and mechanism, and a new geochemical concept.

The successful return of Chang'E-5 (CE5) samples implores the study of the Moon in geochemistry. The paper authored by Z. Hou, Q. Gong, N. Liu, B. Jiang, J. Li, Y. Wu, and J. Huang compiled the reported geochemical data on Moon samples and derived the elemental abundance of Moon samples [10], where the statistical distributions of normal, log-normal, and additive log-ratio transformation methods were used to derive the elemental abundance of major components, trace elements, and rare earth elements, respectively. Furthermore, Moon samples were classified into two types, low-Ca and high-Ca samples.

An equation of state (EOS) of CH_4-N_2 fluid mixtures in terms of Helmholtz free energy is presented in the paper authored by J. Zhang, S. Mao, and Z. Shi [11], which can reproduce the pressure–volume–temperature–composition (PVTx) and vapor–liquid equilibrium (VLE) properties of CH_4-N_2 fluid mixtures. Dendrite is a typical self-similar morphology. The paper authored by N. Liu, Y. He, S. Xu, L. Xiong, Y. Wei, J. Li, P. Li, and Q. Gong presents a dendrite developed along the bedding plane in limestone and dolomite strata in Zhoukoudian, Beijing city [12], where the formation's dynamic mechanism was simulated on the diffusion-limited aggregation method on a model of fractal growth.

Sediment provenance is a main topic in research on soils, sediments, and sedimentary rocks. The paper authored by Z. Dong, L. Zhang, and B. Jin illustrates a case study on sediment provenance along the Subei coast to the Yangtze estuary [13], where the detrital mica composition was used as an efficient approach in sediment provenance analysis and transport tracing. With respect to the provenance and tracing of geological materials, a promising concept, the geochemical gene, has been presented recently [14], which can be used not only to classify geological materials [1,15] but also to determine geochemical anomalies [6]. The last paper, authored by Y. An, X. Yin, Q. Gong, X. Li, and N. Liu, presents an excellent illustration of the classification and provenance of geological materials [16], where the rock–soil–sediment system in the Wangquan area of Zhangjiakou, North China, was investigated and traced on geochemical lithogenes.

Although this Special Issue has been closed, more in-depth research into new advances and illustrations in applied geochemistry are expected to be presented at the national conference on applied geochemistry.

Author Contributions: Q.G.: Conceptualization, Writing—original draft preparation. Z.S.: Methodology, Writing—review and editing. All authors have read and agreed to the published version of the manuscript.

Funding: This research received no external funding.

Acknowledgments: We are grateful to all contributors who made this Special Issue a success. Our thanks and congratulations are extended to all the authors for submitting their work. Our sincere gratefulness is also put forward to all reviewers for their effort and time spent to help the authors improve their papers. We want to express our gratitude to the editorial team of *Applied Sciences* for their effective and untiring editorial support for the success of this issue. We hope this issue serves as an inspiration for future research in applied geochemistry.

Conflicts of Interest: The author declares no conflict of interest.

References

1. Li, J.; Zhang, B.; Gong, Q.; Liu, H.; Liu, N. Microscopic Morphology and Indicative Significance of Nanoscale Au Particles in Soils and Fault Muds: A Case Study of Jiaojia, Shandong Province. *Appl. Sci.* **2023**, *13*, 2126. [CrossRef]
2. Kang, M.; Guo, H.; Zhu, W.; Luo, X.; Yang, J. The Improvement and Application of the Geoelectrochemical Exploration Method. *Appl. Sci.* **2023**, *13*, 2735. [CrossRef]
3. Zhou, B.; Zhang, Z.; Shi, Z.; Song, H.; Yu, L. Geochemistry, Geochronology, and Prospecting Potential of the Dahongliutan Pluton, Western Kunlun Orogen. *Appl. Sci.* **2022**, *12*, 11591. [CrossRef]
4. Dong, T.; Kang, L.; Zhang, Y.; Gao, Y. Pore Fractal Characteristics of Lacustrine Shale of Upper Cretaceous Nenjiang Formation from the Songliao Basin, NE China. *Appl. Sci.* **2023**, *13*, 4295. [CrossRef]
5. Zhao, B.; Zhang, D.; Zhang, R.; Li, Z.; Tang, P.; Wan, H. Delineation and Analysis of Regional Geochemical Anomaly Using the Object-Oriented Paradigm and Deep Graph Learning—A Case Study in Southeastern Inner Mongolia, North China. *Appl. Sci.* **2022**, *12*, 10029. [CrossRef]
6. Li, J.; Gong, Q.; Zhang, B.; Liu, N.; Wu, X.; Yan, T.; Li, X.; Wu, Y. Construction, Test and Application of a Tungsten Metallogene Named MGW11: Case Studies in China. *Appl. Sci.* **2023**, *13*, 606. [CrossRef]
7. Zhang, J.; Liu, Y.; Hong, S.; Wen, M.; Zheng, C.; Liu, P. Speciation Analysis and Pollution Assessment of Heavy Metals in Farmland Soil of a Typical Mining Area: A Case Study of Dachang Tin Polymetallic Ore, Guangxi. *Appl. Sci.* **2023**, *13*, 708. [CrossRef]
8. Liang, Z.; Zou, T.; Gong, J.; Zhou, M.; Shen, W.; Zhang, J.; Fan, D.; Lu, Y. Evaluation of Soil Nutrient Status Based on LightGBM Model: An Example of Tobacco Planting Soil in Debao County, Guangxi. *Appl. Sci.* **2022**, *12*, 12354. [CrossRef]
9. Sun, Z.; Shen, W.; Fang, W.; Zhang, H.; Chen, Z.; Xiong, L.; An, T. The Quality of Scutellaria baicalensis Georgi Is Effectively Affected by Lithology and Soils Rare Earth Elements (REEs) Concentration. *Appl. Sci.* **2023**, *13*, 3086. [CrossRef]
10. Hou, Z.; Gong, Q.; Liu, N.; Jiang, B.; Li, J.; Wu, Y.; Huang, J.; Gu, W. Elemental Abundances of Moon Samples Based on Statistical Distributions of Analytical Data. *Appl. Sci.* **2023**, *13*, 360. [CrossRef]
11. Zhang, J.; Mao, S.; Shi, Z. A Helmholtz Free Energy Equation of State of CO_2-CH_4-N_2 Fluid Mixtures (ZMS EOS) and Its Applications. *Appl. Sci.* **2023**, *13*, 3659. [CrossRef]
12. Liu, N.; He, Y.; Xu, S.; Xiong, L.; Wei, Y.; Li, J.; Li, P.; Gong, Q. Dynamic Mechanism of Dendrite Formation in Zhoukoudian, China. *Appl. Sci.* **2023**, *13*, 2049. [CrossRef]
13. Dong, Z.; Zhang, L.; Jin, B. Detrital Mica Composition Quantitatively Indicates the Sediment Provenance along the Subei Coast to the Yangtze Estuary. *Appl. Sci.* **2022**, *12*, 12653. [CrossRef]
14. Gong, Q.; Yan, T.; Wu, X.; Li, R.; Wang, X.; Liu, N.; Li, X.; Wu, Y.; Li, J. Geochemical gene: A promising concept in discrimination and traceability of geological materials. *Appl. Geochem.* **2022**, *136*, 105133. [CrossRef]
15. Wu, Y.; Gong, Q.; Liu, N.; Wu, X.; Yan, T.; Xu, S.; Li, W. Classification of geological materials on geochemical lithogenes: Illustration on a case study in Gejiu area of Yunnan Province, China. *Appl. Geochem.* **2022**, *146*, 105460. [CrossRef]
16. An, Y.; Yin, X.; Gong, Q.; Li, X.; Liu, N. Classification and Provenance on Geochemical Lithogenes: A Case Study on Rock-Soil-Sediment System in Wanquan Area of Zhangjiakou, North China. *Appl. Sci.* **2023**, *13*, 1008. [CrossRef]

applied sciences

Article

Microscopic Morphology and Indicative Significance of Nanoscale Au Particles in Soils and Fault Muds: A Case Study of Jiaojia, Shandong Province

Jie Li [1,2], Bimin Zhang [1,*], Qingjie Gong [2,*], Hanliang Liu [1] and Ningqiang Liu [2]

1 Key Laboratory of Geochemical Exploration, Institute of Geophysical and Geochemical Exploration, CAGS, Langfang 065000, China
2 School of Earth Sciences and Resources, China University of Geosciences, Beijing 100083, China
* Correspondence: zbimin@hotmail.com (B.Z.); qjiegong@cugb.edu.cn (Q.G.)

Abstract: In recent decades, the human demand for mineral resources has increased dramatically, and the mining of shallow deposits has basically been completed. The prospecting direction has turned to concealed deposits. For this reason, various penetrating geochemical methods have been developed to find concealed minerals and a series of geochemical exploration techniques have been proposed. At the same time, the use of the geochemical gene as a new technique presented in recent years is feasible in discussing component classification and provenance tracing. In this study, we applied these methods for mineral exploration in the Jiaojia gold deposit in Shandong Province, China. The results show that a large number of ore-forming element particles can be observed in ores, fault muds, and soils; compared with Chinese soil, Au has higher enrichment coefficients; according to the LG03 lithogene, the ores belong to a neutral composition, and the fault muds and soils belong to an acidic composition. Based on the above results, it can be found that the ore-forming elements in the Jiaojia gold deposit have migrated. Although this migration cannot change the original lithology, it can provide theoretical support for the fine-grained soil-prospecting method.

Keywords: Shandong Jiaojia gold deposit; metal nanoparticles; migration mechanism; LG03 lithogene

Citation: Li, J.; Zhang, B.; Gong, Q.; Liu, H.; Liu, N. Microscopic Morphology and Indicative Significance of Nanoscale Au Particles in Soils and Fault Muds: A Case Study of Jiaojia, Shandong Province. *Appl. Sci.* **2023**, *13*, 2126. https://doi.org/10.3390/app13042126

Academic Editors: Simone Morais and Mauro Marini

Received: 1 November 2022
Revised: 3 February 2023
Accepted: 5 February 2023
Published: 7 February 2023

1. Introduction

As discoveries of world-class mineral deposits continue to decline, shallow deposits are no longer enough to meet the daily needs of human beings [1], and people turn their attention to the deep formation and pay more and more attention to geochemical exploration technology specially designed for the terrain covered by thick regolith. These techniques include: partial extraction, geogas analysis, electrogeochemistry, biogeochemistry, hydrochemistry, and soil fine particle separation [2–15]. Among the numerous geochemical exploration techniques, soil fine particle separation is an important method with which to find concealed deposits in thickly covered terrain. It is thought that this method mainly believes that in the process of the upward migration of elements from deep minerals, earth gas can carry ultra-fine particles containing metals or metal elements in the form of tiny bubbles or microflows to migrate upward and reach the surface, so the faults above the deep concealed minerals, fault muds, and topsoil contain metallic elements that can reflect anomalies in deep ore bodies. The best way to test this theory is to find ultrafine metal-bearing particles in soils and fault muds that must have come from deep ore bodies. After years of research, metal-bearing ultrafine particles from nanoscale studies have been widely used in soils and fault muds of different types of concealed minerals [7,10,16,17]. Zhang et al. [1] observed the existence of metallogenic metal nanoparticles in the soils and fault muds of the Shenjiayao gold deposit; Han et al. [18] observed mineralization in the ore rocks, fault muds, and soils of the Shanggong gold deposit in Henan, with the presence of metal nanoparticles. Often, the only source of anomalies in fault zones and surface soils surrounding a mine is the deep ore body. In order to explain the formation mechanism of the anomaly, the key is to determine the occurrence state and genesis of the ore-forming elements in the fault zone above the concealed mineral deposits and in the soil.

The geochemical gene is a new developing concept recently proposed in the identification and traceability of geological materials [19,20]. The term "gene" has been adopted in geochemistry from biology for two decades by Xuejin Xie and Xueqiu Wang [21] who proposed that the element is the gene of the earth and the geochemical map is the gene map of the earth surface. This is the "embryo" concept of the geochemical gene. Another term related to genes is the "gene-profile curve of geochemical elements" presented by Zhang et al. (2015, 2016) [22,23] in geochemistry which is like the REE pattern or spider diagram without gene properties [24]. Therefore, this idea can be viewed as the "fetal" stage of the geochemical gene concept. Although those primitive ideas were inspiring, the geochemical gene with tangible properties such as codes, heredity, inheritance, variability, and similarity has been proposed only recently [24–26]. The quantitatively defined geochemical gene was firstly presented by Yan et al. (2018) with an illustration on a geochemical lithogene [25]. It is proposed firstly as a lithogene named LG02 [25], and then followed by lithogenes called LG01 [26] and LG03 [27], gold metallogene (MGAu) [24], tungsten metallogene (MGW) [28], and tungsten metallogene (MGW11) [29], and REE (rare earth element) genes called REEG01 and REEG02 [26]. Therefore, there are a total of eight geochemical genes reported now, which were introduced and reviewed by Gong et al. (2022) [19] and the lithogene named MGW11 was introduced by Li et al. (2023) [29] recently.

These genes all have different codes and can represent the heritance, inheritance, variability, and similarity of different samples. According to the 39 elements or oxides analyzed by the RGNR project [30] and the NMPRGS project [31] in China, the geochemical gene is constructed in five steps.

The first step is to select elements. Generally, 11 kinds of fixed elements and indicator elements that can represent different characteristics are selected. The second step is to determine the reference value. According to the purpose of different genes, we select different data to standardize the data. For example, the element abundances of the upper continental crust (UCC) and acidic rocks and basic rocks compiled by Chi Qinghua and Yan Mingcai are selected for data standardization. The third step is to draw and code gene lines. The spectral line of the gene is like a spider map on the normalized value of the initial sequence. The length of the gene code is set to 11 because 11 elements are selected. The first digit of the code is set to 1, and then the next digit will be 0, 1, or 2 according to the decrease, stability, or rise of the next normalized value on the spectral line. We use the 0.1 logarithmic unit (base 10) value to evaluate the difference between two adjacent elements on the log-normalized value, marked as Δ, calculated as

$$\Delta_i = \lg(C_i)_N - \lg(C_{i-1})_N \quad (1)$$

where i is the sequence number from 2 to 11 of the elements in the spectral line, and the subscript N represents the normalized value. In addition to the first number set to 1, another number in the code is labeled g_i and set as

$$g_i = \begin{cases} 2, & \Delta_i > 0.1 \\ 1, & -0.1 \le \Delta_i < 0.1 \\ 0, & \Delta_i < -0.1 \end{cases} \quad (2)$$

where i is from 2 to 11, and the value of g_i in gene coding is only 0, 1, or 2. According to the coding method, the gene of one sample can be 11011020011, and the gene of the other sample can be 12210202120. How to evaluate the similarity between two genes is the fourth step in constructing geochemical genes. The similarity of g_i is marked as R_i and set as

$$R_i = \begin{cases} 1, \text{ Values of } g_i \text{ ar the same} \\ 0.5, \text{ Values of } g_i \text{ are similar (1 and 0, or 1 and 2)} \\ 0, \text{ Values of } g_i \text{ are different (2 and 0, or 0 and 2)} \end{cases} \quad (3)$$

Then, the similarity between the two genes is labeled as R and calculated as

$$R = \frac{\sum_{i=2}^{n} R_{g_i}}{n-1} \times 100\% \quad (4)$$

where n is 11 and the value of R is limited between 0% and 100%. For example, the similarity between Gene A and Gene B is calculated as

Gene A: 1 1 0 1 1 0 2 0 0 1 1

Gene B: 1 2 2 1 0 2 0 2 1 2 0

R_{g_i}: 0.5 0 1 0.5 0 0 0 0.5 0.5 0.5

$$R = \frac{0.5+0+1+0.5+0+0+0+0.5+0.5+0.5}{10} \times 100\% = 35\%$$

The last step in constructing geochemical genes is to adjust the sequence of elements in the spectral lines. According to the different research objects of genes, the most obvious differentiation can be achieved by adjusting the sequence of elements. For example, the element sequence of the lithogene LG03 is to effectively distinguish acidic rock and basic rock to maximize their genetic similarity. By repeatedly adjusting the initial element sequence in step 3, the positions of Ni and Cr are exchanged, and then the positions of V and Cr are exchanged to form the final sequence.

With respect to the lithogenes LG01 and LG03, the gene properties of their heredity and inheritance have been tested on many weathering profiles developed over different lithological rocks in different climate zones in China [26,27,32] according to the similar gene criterion of ≥80% on gene similarity by Yan et al. (2018) [25]. Their application in classifying geological materials is useful and suitable for fresh and altered rocks and weathered products such as fresh rocks, sediments, and soils [20].

In this paper, TEM was used to observed the ores, fault muds, and soils in the Jiaojia gold deposit, Shandong Province. Then, the element content of the samples were analyzed to determine the enrichment degree of different elements in the study area and the lithogenes such as LG01 and LG03 were used to determine the lithology of the different samples which provided theoretical support for the migration of elements in soil fine-grained exploration.

2. Regional Settings

The Jiaojia gold deposit is located in the Jiao-xin metallogenic belt in the east and west of Jiaojiao, including the Jiaojia, Wangershan, Matang, and other gold deposits. The Jiaojia gold deposit is a super-large gold deposit, and the overall type of the deposit is the trunk fault of Jiaojia (Figure 1). The Jiaojia-type altered gold deposit is controlled by the fractured alteration zone within its secondary Wangershan branch fault. The main strike of the fault in this area is NNE-NE, and the strike of the ore body is the same as the main strike. The Jiaojia gold deposit is exposed as Neoarchean gabbro on the side of the Jiaojia trunk fault, and on the east side of the fault is the Linglong sheet of biotite monzogranite. There are also diorite porphyrite, diabase porphyry, lamprophyre, and other rocks in the area. The main ore minerals are gold and silver ore, pyrite, siderite, chalcopyrite, galena, sphalerite, and mirror iron ore. Gangue minerals are mainly quartz, sericite, feldspar, and calcite.

The bedrock in the study area is covered by the Quaternary system composed of loose sediments such as gray-brown clay and sandy clay, with a thickness of about 2–40 m [33].

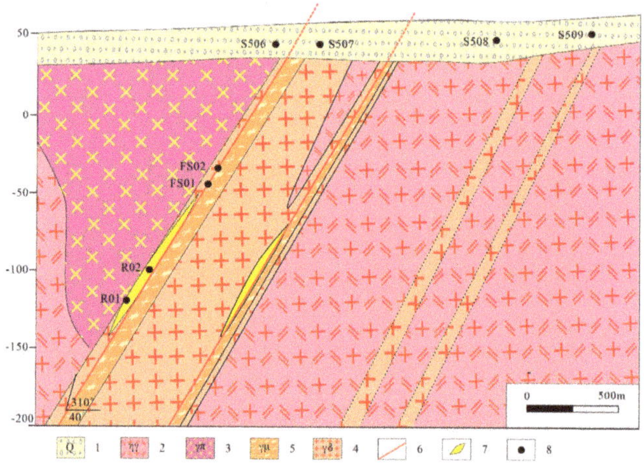

Figure 1. Sampling points profile of Jiaojia gold mine. 1—quaternary clayey coarse sand and fine sand; 2—biotite monzogranite; 3—medium-fine-grained gabbro; 4—pyrite sericite granite; 5—pyrite sericite cataclastic granite; 6—fault; 7—ore body; 8—sampling point.

3. Samples and Methods

3.1. Sample Collection and Pretreatment

This research mainly collects and analyzes the ores, upper fault muds, and soils of the Jiaojia gold deposit in Shandong Province. The samples include two concealed ore body samples (R01, R02), two fault mud samples above the concealed ore body (FS01, FS02), two surface soil samples above the concealed ore body (S506, S507), and two surface soil samples around the concealed ore body (S508, S509). The collected soil samples were dried at 80 °C for 1 h, and sieved to ≤76 μm under the crusher. About 100 g of the fault muds were then dispersed using an electromagnetic vibrating micrometer shaker, which was connected to a concentrator and an air extractor (soil fine particle separation device) (Figure 2). The concentrator contains a 0.45 μm microporous filter membrane and six carbon-coated aluminum TEM (transmission microscope) grid slots, which are used to collect the oscillated nanoparticles. The shaker was turned on for 3 min to adsorb the appropriate amounts of nanoparticles on the aluminum grid, and then the six carbon-coated aluminum TEM (transmission microscope) grids in the concentrator were removed using tweezers and placed in a box for analysis. For the treatment of the fault mud and ore samples, the samples were ground to ≤76 μm using a ceramic grinder and the nanoparticles were separated using the same soil fine particle separation device.

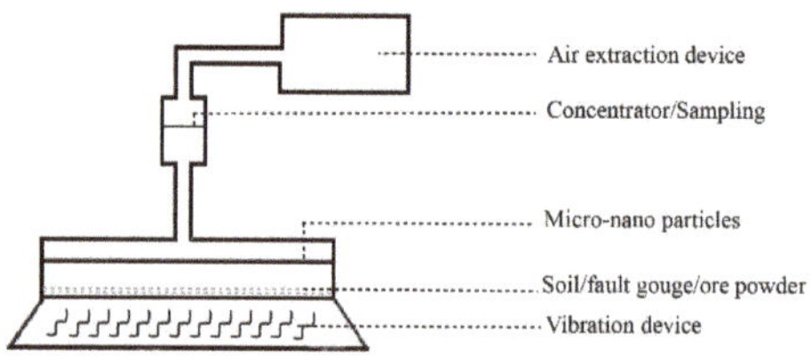

Figure 2. Diagram of soil fine particle separation device.

3.2. TEM Observation

After the pretreatment, the samples to be tested were sent to the Beijing Physical and Chemical Analysis Center to analyze the TEM grid by transmission electron microscopy to observe the particle characteristics (such as size, shape, and composition) of the enriched nanoparticles. The transmission electron microscope (TEM) used for detection has a spot resolution of 0.20 nm, a lattice resolution of 0.1 nm, and a STEM-HAADF resolution of 0.17 nm, of which the minimum spot diameter is 0.8 nm. The transmission electron microscope is equipped with an X-ray energy dispersive spectrometer (EDS) with an accelerating voltage of 300 kV, and the samples observed under the microscope obtained in this study were all carried out in this environment. In the study, the composition of the particles was determined using EDS in the absence of reference substances; therefore, we cannot report the exact mass percentage of each chemical composition. When observing, we set the spot radius to <0.2 μm. The relative content of a specific element or component in the particle is expressed in mass percent. Two points were selected to study the background composition of the Al grid. The results show that the aluminum mesh is mainly composed of C, O, Al, and Si. One contains C (94.21%), O (3.55%), Al (1.61%), and Si (0.63%); the other contains C (92.68%), O (3.76%), Al (2.85%), and Si (0.71%) [18].

3.3. Chemical Analysis

The samples of soil, fault mud, and ore were sent to China University of Geosciences (Wuhan) for trace elements analysis. Inductively coupled plasma mass spectrometry (ICP-MS) was used for the determination of V, Co, Ni, Nb, Ti, Th, U, La, Y, Cu, Pb, Zn, Zr, Mn, Li, Ba, W, Ag, and Au concentrations. Atomic absorption spectrometry (AAS) was used to obtain the Cr and Ag concentrations (Table 1).

Table 1. Analytical detection limits of elements.

Elements	**V**	**Cr**	**Co**	**Ni**	**Nb**	**Ti**	**Th**	**U**	**La**	**Y**
Detection limit	2.0	3.0	0.2	1.0	0.01	3.0	0.8	0.003	0.01	0.01
Elements	**Cu**	**Pb**	**Zn**	**Zr**	**Au**	**Ag**	**Mn**	**Li**	**Ba**	**W**
Detection limit	0.2	59	2.0	0.05	0.1	3.0	0.5	1.0	0.5	0.05

Note: Unit is μg/g except Au in ng/g.

4. Results and Discussion

4.1. Metal Particles Observed Using TEM

Complex micro-/nanoscale metal particles composed of Au, Cu, and other elements were observed in carriers (Al grids), which captured particles from soils, fault muds, and ores above the ore body, as shown in Figure 3. Nanoscale Au particles were found in the near-ore surface soils above the deposit (Figure 3a,b), the fault muds (Figure 3e,f), and the ores (Figure 3g,h), but nanoscale Au particles were not found in the near-ore surface soils above the background area (Figure 3c,d).

The characteristics of the particles in soils, fault muds, and ores are as follows: (1) the radii of metal particles are mainly in the order of several hundred or several tens of nm, with some several nm in size; (2) single metal particles are always ellipsoidal or polygonal, and may form clusters or aggregates (Figure 3e–h); (3) the EDS analysis shows that the metal particles are composed of metal complexes with Au, Cu–Co–Fe, Cu, and Fe–Co. Particles collected from background areas mainly contain Fe, Mn, Zn, Al, and Cu (Figure 3c,d). No Au- or Ag-bearing particles were observed in the background samples.

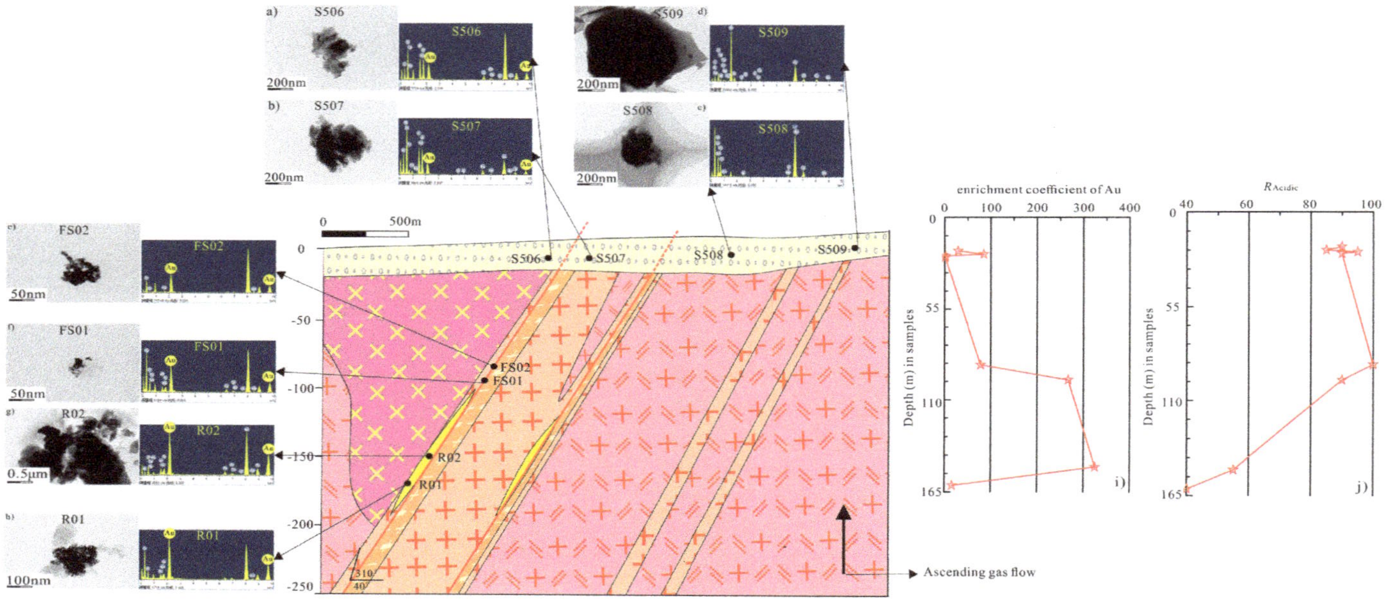

Figure 3. Schematic diagram of the migration model of the metal-bearing nanoparticles. (**a**,**b**)—the TEM image of Au particles and the energy spectrum of the soils S506, S507 above the ore body; (**c**,**d**)—the TEM image and the energy spectrum of the soil samples S508, S509 away from the ore body; (**e**,**f**)—the TEM image of Au particles and the energy spectrum of the fault muds FS02, FS01 above the ore body; (**g**,**h**)—the TEM image of Au particles and the matching energy spectrum of ores R02, R01; (**i**)—enrichment coefficients of Au in different samples; (**j**)—gene similarities of different samples.

4.2. Elemental Composition

The concentrations of trace elements of the samples are listed in Table 2. The average concentration of Au in soils above the concealed ore body (S506, S507) was 74.8 ppm; relative to Chinese soil, the enrichment coefficient of S506 is 28.6 and S507 is 84.7; the overall enrichment coefficient of the two samples is 56.6 (Figure 3i). The average concentration of Au in soils around the concealed ore body (S508, S509) was 1.86 ppm; the enrichment coefficient of S508 and S509 is 1.4; the overall enrichment coefficient of the two samples is 1.4 (Figure 3i). The average concentration of Au in fault muds is 227.61 ppm; the enrichment coefficient of FS01 is 78 and FS02 is 267; the overall enrichment coefficient of the two samples is 172 (Figure 3i). The average concentration of Au in ores is 224.34 ppm; the enrichment coefficient of R01 is 324 and R02 is 15.7; the overall enrichment coefficient of the two samples is 170 (Figure 3i).

Table 2. Trace element in surface soils, fault muds, and ores.

Element	S508	S509	S506	S507	FS01	FS02	R01	R02	Chinese Soil
Samples Type	Soil Outside Orebody		Soil Above Orebody		Fault Mud		Ore		
Co	12.61	11.59	12.7	15.4	3.76	2.29	23.9	20.7	12.1
Ni	15.1	14.7	15.7	16.8	2.16	0.3	15.8	64.5	25
Cu	22.2	29.2	51.2	29.4	69.5	50.9	7.1	22.4	22
Zn	64.81	67.38	121.2	69.15	256	161	106	129	70
Mn	615	661	707	717	156	82	1620	3979	670
Cr	75.8	66.5	72.9	81.5	18.3	13.1	180	166	59
V	85.2	84.8	87.0	105.7	18.2	14.1	220	132	80
Ti	5019	5223	5029	5173	1351	1199	7925	3697	4105
Li	31.5	27.7	31.3	32.1	43.8	20.7	18.3	79.6	32
Zr	447	502	417	516	136	135	228.1	139.6	270
Ba	827	830	799	837	214	193	210	121	490
Pb	35.3	50.1	58.3	34.2	443	289	16.2	20.2	24
W	1.84	1.95	1.91	1.89	9.63	8.98	4.68	7.23	1.8
Th	7.37	7.8	7.21	7.81	3.82	2.99	16.4	8.7	11.9
U	1.94	2.07	2.17	2.21	1.52	1.23	3.35	4.73	2.45
Y	27.2	29.6	30.8	27.8	9.02	8.58	29.7	26.7	25
La	42.1	45.0	37.6	40.9	30.1	23.4	205	32	39
Nb	15.4	15.0	15.1	14.6	10.4	9.1	11.9	7.6	16
Au	1.9	1.8	37.8	111.8	103	352	428	20.7	1.32
Ag	63.8	261.1	97.7	166.5	359	402	1044	3027	77

Note: unit in μg/g.

Moreover, the average concentrations of Au were significantly higher than those reported for soil from China by Chi et al. (2007) [34], and other elements, such as W, Pb, Zn, and Cu are not significantly enriched in this area. At the same time, the enrichment coefficient of the ore-forming element Au decreases from ores to fault muds to soils.

4.3. Geochemical Lithogene (LG03)

The geochemical gene is a new technique presented in recent years [19]. Although the term "gene" has been adopted in geochemistry from biology for two decades by Xuejin Xie and Xueqiu Wang [21,24,34,35] who proposed that the element is the gene of the earth and the geochemical map is the gene map of the earth surface, and another term related to genes is the "gene profile curve of geochemical elements" presented by Zhang et al. (2015, 2016) [22,23] in geochemistry which is like the REE pattern or spider diagram without gene properties [20,24], the above two studies do not have the essential connotation of genes, such as codes, heredity, inheritance, variability, similarity, and other characteristics, only the geochemical characteristics of elements. Therefore, it can be regarded as the germination and gestation stage of the geochemical gene. Geochemical genes with these characteristics have just been proposed only recently [24,25,28].

This technique combines the concept of biological gene with geochemistry, and proposes a complete geochemical gene construction process, including gene sequence, gene coding, and gene similarity calculation methods. Gong et al. (2020) proposed that the acidic similarities of genes can be used to classify the composition of rocks, soils, and stream sediment samples according to the characteristics of lithogenes [26]. In recent years, with the development of lithogenes, great achievements have been made in composition classification and provenance tracing [20,23,27,32,36–39].

According to the construction steps of a geochemical gene, Li et al. (2021) proposed a new lithogene labelled LG03 [27]. The gene eliminates the influence of the addition of aeolian sand, organisms, and other media on lithology determination, and is feasible in discussing component classification and provenance tracing. Gene coding and acidic similarities of soils, fault muds, and ores using LG03 lithogene calculate the following (Table 3):

Table 3. Gene similarities of 8 samples with different sampling points.

Sample	S508	S509	S506	S507	FS01	FS02	R01	R02
LG03	11202020202	12202020202	11201020202	12201020202	10202020202	10202020211	12022001202	12120111200
LG03_R_{Acidic} (%)	95	90	90	85	100	90	55	40

It can be seen from Table 3 that the acidic similarities of ores are 40–55, the fault muds are 90–100, and the soils are 85–90 (Figure 3j). The proposed lithogene LG02 not only gives a clear meaning to the gene, but also stipulates the division of gene similarity. Yan et al. (2018) determined that the gene of acidic rock in China is 11012020211, the gene of neutral rock in China is 11210002110, and the gene of basic rock in China is 10210102200. According to the above gene similarity calculation method, the similarity to the other two rocks of a rock is calculated, respectively. Compared with acidic rock, the genetic similarity of neutral rock is 50%, and the genetic similarity of basic rock is 40%. Compared with intermediate rocks, the genetic similarity of basic rocks is 80% [25]. This indicates that the lithologic gene LG02 can significantly distinguish acidic rocks from the other two rocks. However, for the two kinds of rocks, neutral rock and basic rock, their differentiation is relatively low. In order to make up for the deficiency that the lithologic gene LG02 cannot effectively distinguish basic rock from neutral rock, Gong et al. [26] proposed that the ideal acidic rock in China (a virtual rock sample represented by the elemental abundance of acidic rock in China compositionally) has the same gene code of 10202020202 on LG01 and LG03, and the ideal basic rock in China also has the same gene code of 12020202020 on these two lithogenes. The gene similarity of a sample relative to the ideal acidic rock is called the sample's acidic similarity and can be labeled as R_{Acidic}. This also makes up for the fact that the genetic code of the lithogene LG02 is not easy to remember when expressing lithology. According to this definition, the R_{Acidic} of the ideal acidic rock in China is 100%, while the R_{Acidic} of the ideal basic rock in China is 0%. Geological materials can be classified into three groups: acidic-like composition with $R_{Acidic} \geq 80\%$ labeled 1, intermediate-like composition with RAcidic between 75% and 25% labeled 2, and basic-like composition with $R_{Acidic} \leq 20\%$ labeled 3. Therefore, according to the acidic similarities, the ores belong to neutral components, and fault muds and soils belong to acidic components. Three types of samples were clearly divided into two different components.

In summary, TEM observation and energy spectrum analysis showed that Au nanoparticles were found in the ores, fault muds, and soils above the concealed ore body, but not in the soils around the concealed ore body. At the same time, the element composition also proves that Au is much higher in the soils above the concealed ore body than in the soils around the concealed ore body. The LG03 lithogene shows that the ores are neutral components, and the fault muds and soils are acidic components; their sources are different, thus excluding the possibility that the soils above the concealed ore body are formed by ore weathering. This also provides an explanation for the source of the high concentration of

Au in the top soil of the ore, that is, by the migration of the bottom ore, which also provides a basis for soil fine-grained prospecting (Figure 3).

5. Conclusions

(1) The nanoscale Au particles were found in ores, fault muds, and soils above the concealed ore body, but not in the soils around the concealed ore body by TEM observation.
(2) The concentration of nanoscale Au particles in ores, fault muds, and soil above the concealed ore body are much higher than that in Chinese soil and has a higher enrichment coefficient. On the contrary, the concentration of nanoscale Au particles in the soils around the concealed ore body are almost the same as that in Chinese soil.
(3) The LG03 lithogene divides the ores into neutral components, and fault muds and soils into acidic components, which proved that they have different substrates. It is proven that the high concentration of nanoscale Au particles in soils above the concealed ore body migrate from ore to soil, which also provides a basis for soil fine-grained prospecting.

Author Contributions: J.L.: Conceptualization, data curation, and writing—original draft. B.Z.: Conceptualization, data curation, and writing—review and editing. Q.G.: Conceptualization, methodology, and writing—review and editing. H.L.: Conceptualization and data curation. N.L.: Conceptualization and formal analysis. All authors have read and agreed to the published version of the manuscript.

Funding: This work was financially supported by the National Natural Science Foundation of China (41573044, 41903071), the State Key Research & Development Project (2016YFC0600602) and the National Nonprofit Institute Research Grant of IGGE(AS2022P03).

Institutional Review Board Statement: Not applicable.

Data Availability Statement: Not applicable.

Acknowledgments: We greatly appreciate the comments from the anonymous reviewers and editors for their valuable suggestions to improve the quality of this manuscript.

Conflicts of Interest: The authors declare that they have no known competing financial interests or personal relationships that could have appeared to influence the work reported in this paper.

References

1. Zhang, B.M.; Han, Z.X.; Wang, X.Q.; Liu, X.Q.; Wu, H.; Feng, H. Metal-Bearing Nanoparticles Observed in Soils and Fault Gouges over the Shenjiayao Gold Deposit and Their Significance. *Minerals* **2019**, *9*, 414. [CrossRef]
2. Malmqvist, L.; Kristiansson, K. Microflow of geogas—A possible formation mechanism for deep-sea nodules. *Mar. Geol.* **1981**, *40*, M1–M8. [CrossRef]
3. Malmqvist, L.; Kristiansson, K. Experimental evidence for an ascending microflow of geogas in the ground. *Earth Planet. Sci. Lett.* **1984**, *70*, 407–416. [CrossRef]
4. Bradshaw, P.M.D.; Thomson, I.; Smee, B.W.; Larsson, J.O. The application of different analytical extractions and soil profile sampling in exploration geochemistry. *J. Geochem. Explor.* **1974**, *3*, 209–225. [CrossRef]
5. Clark, R.J.; Meier, A.L.; Riddle, G. Enzyme leaching of surficial geochemical samples for detecting hydromorphic trace-element anomalies associated with precious-metal mineralized bedrock buried beneath glacial overburden in northern Minnesota. In Proceedings of the Gold '90 Symposium—Gold '90, Salt Lake City, UT, USA, 26 February–1 March 1990; pp. 189–207.
6. Mann, A.W.; Birrell, R.D.; Gay, L.M.; Al, E. Partial extraction and mobile metal ions. In Proceedings of the 17th International Geochemical Exploration Symposium (IGES), Townsville, Australia, 15–19 May 1995; pp. 31–34.
7. Clark, R.J. Innovative Enzyme Leach Provides. In Proceedings of the Exploration 97: Fourth Decennial International Conference on Mineral Exploration, Toronto, ON, Canada, 14–18 September 1997; pp. 371–374.
8. Wang, X.Q.; Cheng, Z.Z.; Lu, Y.X.; Xie, X.J. Nanoscale metals in Earthgas and mobile forms of metals in overburden in wide-spaced regional exploration for giant deposits in overburden terrains. *J. Geochem. Explor.* **1997**, *58*, 63–72. [CrossRef]
9. Mann, A.W.; Birrell, R.D.; Mann, A.T.; Humphreys, D.B.; Perdrix, J.L. Application of the mobile metal ion technique to routine geochemical exploration. *Geochem. Explor.* **1998**, *61*, 87–102. [CrossRef]
10. Cohen, D.R.; Shen, X.C.; Dunlop, A.C.; Rutherford, N.F. A comparison of selective extraction soil geochemistry and biogeochemistry in the Cobar area, New South Wales. *J. Geochem. Explor.* **1998**, *61*, 173–189. [CrossRef]

11. Chunhan, O.; Juchu, I.; Liangquan, E.; Fenggen, A. Experimental observation of the nano-scale particles in geogas matters and its geological significance. *Sci. China (Ser. D Earth Sci.)* **1998**, *41*, 325–329. [CrossRef]
12. Wang, X.Q. Leaching of mobile forms of metals in overburden: Development and application. *J. Geochem. Explor.* **1998**, *61*, 39–55.
13. Kelley, D.L. The use of partial extraction geochemistry for copper exploration in northern Chile. *Geochem. Explor. Environ. Anal.* **2003**, *3*, 85–104. [CrossRef]
14. Cameron, E.M.; Hamilton, S.M.; Leybourne, M.I.; Hall, G.E.M.; McClenaghan, M.B. Finding deeply buried deposits using geochemistry. *Geochem. Explor. Environ. Anal.* **2004**, *4*, 7–32. [CrossRef]
15. Leybourne, M.I.; Cameron, E.M. Groundwater in geochemical exploration. *Geochem. Explor. Environ. Anal.* **2010**, *10*, 99–118. [CrossRef]
16. Kristiansson, K.; Malmqvist, L.; Persson, W. Geogas prospecting: A new tool in the search for concealed mineralizations. *Endeavour* **1990**, *14*, 28–33. [CrossRef]
17. Tong, C.H.; Li, J.C. A New Method Searching for Concealed Mineral Resources: Geogas Prospecting Based on Nuclear Analysis and Accumulation Sampling. *J. China Univ. Geosci.* **1999**, *10*, 329–332.
18. Han, Z.X.; Zhang, B.M.; Wu, H.; Liu, H.L.; Qiao, Y.; Zhang, S.K. Microscopic characterisation of metallic nanoparticles in ore rocks, fault gouge and geogas from the Shanggong gold deposit, China. *J. Geochem. Explor.* **2020**, *217*, 106562. [CrossRef]
19. Gong, Q.J.; Yan, T.T.; Wu, X.; Li, R.K.; Wang, X.Q.; Liu, N.Q.; Li, X.L.; Wu, Y.; Li, J. Geochemical gene: A promising concept in discrimination and traceability of geological materials. *Appl. Geochem.* **2022**, *136*, 105133. [CrossRef]
20. Wu, Y.; Gong, Q.J.; Liu, N.Q.; Wu, X.; Yan, T.T.; Xu, S.C.; Li, W.J. Classification of geological materials on geochemical lithogenes: Illustration on a case study in Gejiu area of Yunnan Province, China. *Appl. Geochem.* **2022**, *146*, 105460. [CrossRef]
21. Wang, X.Q. Geochemistry of Exploration on Giant Ore Deposit and Large Mineral Camp. In *Geochemistry of Exploration on Mineral Resources towards the 21st Century*; Xie, X., Shao, Y., Wang, X., Eds.; Geological Publishing House: Beijing, China, 1999; pp. 35–47. (In Chinese with English abstract)
22. Zhang, Y.F.; Yuan, J.M.; Wu, D.W.; Lü, W.Y.; Zhang, J.L. Basic principle and technical framework of analysis on geochemical elements sequence structure. *Miner. Explor.* **2015**, *6*, 39–746. (In Chinese with English abstract)
23. Zhang, Y.F.; Zhang, J.L.; Wu, D.W.; Yuan, J.M.; Lü, W.Y. A preliminary study of gene profile curve of geochemical elements and its geological significance: A case study of the central-south part of Da Hinggan mountains metallogenic belt, Inner Mongolia. *Geophys. Geochem. Explor.* **2016**, *40*, 235–242. (In Chinese with English abstract)
24. Li, R.K.; Liu, N.Q.; Gong, Q.J.; Wu, X.; Yan, T.T.; Li, X.L.; Liu, M.X. Construction, test and application of a geochemical gold metallogene: Case studies in China. *Geochem. Explor.* **2019**, *204*, 1–11. [CrossRef]
25. Yan, T.T.; Wu, X.; Quan, Y.K.; Gong, Q.J.; Li, X.L.; Wang, P.; Li, R.K. Heredity, inheritance and similarity of element behaviors among parent rocks and their weathered products: A geochemical lithogene. *Geoscience* **2018**, *32*, 453–467. (In Chinese with English abstract)
26. Gong, Q.J.; Wu, X.; Yan, T.T.; Liu, N.Q.; Li, X.L.; Li, R.K.; Liu, M.X. Construction and test of geochemical genes: Case studies in China. *Geoscience* **2020**, *34*, 865–882. (In Chinese with English abstract)
27. Li, J.; Liu, N.Q.; Gong, Q.J.; Wu, X.; Yan, T.T. Construction and test of a geochemical lithogene based on trace elements: Case studies on weathering profiles in China. *Geoscience* **2021**, *35*, 1459–1470. (In Chinese with English abstract)
28. Gong, Q.J.; Liu, N.Q.; Wu, X.; Yan, T.T.; Fan, T.Q.; Li, X.L.; Liu, M.X.; Li, R.K.; Albanese, S. Using regional geochemical survey data to trace anomalous samples through geochemical genes: The Tieshanlong tungsten deposit area (Southeastern China) case study. *Geochem. Explor.* **2020**, *219*, 106637. [CrossRef]
29. Li, J.; Gong, Q.J.; Zhang, B.M.; Liu, N.Q.; Wu, X.; Yan, T.T.; Li, X.L.; Wu, Y. Construction, Test and Application of a Tungsten Metallogene Named MGW11: Case Studies in China. *Appl. Sci.* **2023**, *13*, 606. [CrossRef]
30. Xie, X.J.; Cheng, H.X. Sixty years of exploration geochemistry in China. *Geochem. Explor.* **2014**, *139*, 4–8. [CrossRef]
31. Li, M.; Xi, X.H.; Xiao, G.Y.; Cheng, H.X.; Yang, Z.F.; Zhou, G.H.; Ye, J.Y.; Li, Z.H. National multipurpose regional geochemical survey in China. *Geochem. Explor.* **2014**, *139*, 21–30. [CrossRef]
32. Wu, Y.; Li, X.L.; Gong, Q.J.; Wu, X.; Yao, N.; Peng, C.; Chao, Y.D.; Wang, X.Y.; Pu, X.L. Test and application of the geochemical lithogene on weathering profiles developed over granitic and basaltic rocks in China. *Appl. Geochem.* **2021**, *128*, 104958. [CrossRef]
33. Cheng, H.Y. *Comparative Study on Geochemical Characteristics of Linglong Gold Deposit and Jiaojia Gold Deposit in Jiaodong*; China University of Geossciences: Beijing, China, 2019; pp. 1–72.
34. Chi, Q.H.; Yan, M.C. *Handbook of Elemental Abundance for Applied Geochemistry*; Geological Publishing House: Beijing, China, 2007; pp. 1–148.
35. Shi, J.; Ma, H. Xie Xuejin: Drawing the gene map of the earth. *Chin. Natl. Geograp.* **2007**, *6*, 96–101. (In Chinese)
36. Kong, L. *Testing and Application of Geochemical Lithogene: A Case Study in Lianyang Area, Guangdong Province*; China University of Geosciences: Beijing, China, 2020; pp. 1–60.
37. Wang, X.Y.; Yao, N.; Gong, Q.J.; Chao, Y.D.; Peng, C.; Wu, Y. Properties of geochemical genes due to granite weathering in the Yunmengshan area of Beijing, China. *Earth Sci. Front.* **2021**, *28*, 363–374. (In Chinese with English abstract)

38. Wang, X.Y. *Geochemical Genes Related to Granite Weathering in the Yunmengshan Area of Beijing, China;* China University of Geosciences: Beijing, China, 2021; pp. 1–67.
39. Peng, C. *Testing and Application of Geochemical Gene: A Case Study in Tieling Area, Liaoning Province;* China University of Geosciences: Beijing, China, 2021; pp. 1–69.

applied sciences

MDPI

Article

The Improvement and Application of the Geoelectrochemical Exploration Method

Ming Kang [1,*], Huanzhao Guo [1], Wende Zhu [2], Xianrong Luo [3] and Jianwen Yang [4]

1 School of Earth Science and Resources, Chang'an University, 126 Yanta Road, Xi'an 710054, China
2 Geologic Team 212 of Shanxi Provincial Geological Prospecting Bureau, Changzhi 046000, China
3 College of Earth Sciences, Guilin University of Technology, Guilin 541006, China
4 Department of Earth and Environmental Sciences, University of Windsor, 401 Sunset Avenue, Windsor, ON N9B 3P4, Canada
* Correspondence: kangmin@chd.edu.cn

Abstract: The anionic and cationic species of elements from deeply buried deposits migrate to the near surface driven by various geological forces. The geoelectrochemical exploration method (GEM), derived from CHIM, consists of the application of an electric field to collect these active ions at the designated electrode. Prospecting effects have been investigated by researchers since the coming up of CHIM. However, the cumbersome technical equipment, complex techniques and low production efficiency have restricted its potential application in field geological survey. This paper presents the newly developed CHIM that is electrified by a low voltage dipole. The improved technique allows both anionic and cationic species of elements to be extracted simultaneously in an anode and in a cathode. Compared with the conventional CHIM method, the innovative techniques called dipole geoelectrochemical method are characterized by simple instrumentation, low cost and easy operation in field, and in particular enables simultaneous extraction of anionic and cationic species of elements, from which more information can be derived with higher extraction efficiency. The dipole geoelectrochemical method was proposed and applied in the experiments of the Yingezhuang gold ore from Zhaoyuan, Shandong Province, the 210 gold ore from Jinwozi, Xinjiang Province, and the Daiyinzhang gold polymetallic deposit from Wutaishan, Shanxi Province. There are clearly anomalies above the gold ore body, indicating the effectiveness and feasibility of the improved dipole geoelectrochemical method in both scientific research and mineral exploration. The results of anode extraction in several mining areas have shown good results, indicating that gold may be mainly negatively charged. In fact, many metal nanoparticles, clay minerals, or complexes of metal ions are negatively charged, so they migrate to the anode electrode and enrich.

Keywords: geoelectrochemical method; dipole; low voltage; technique improvement; concealed deposit

Citation: Kang, M.; Guo, H.; Zhu, W.; Luo, X.; Yang, J. The Improvement and Application of the Geoelectrochemical Exploration Method. *Appl. Sci.* **2023**, *13*, 2735. https://doi.org/10.3390/app13042735

Academic Editors: Qingjie Gong and Zeming Shi

Received: 2 December 2022
Revised: 13 February 2023
Accepted: 15 February 2023
Published: 20 February 2023

1. Introduction

The geoelectrochemical exploration method (GEM), derived from CHIM (Chastichnoe Izvlechennye Metallov), was invented by Leningrad researchers in the late 1960s to early 1970s, and the method refers to partial extraction of metals. The systematic theory and field techniques, together with some practical results, were first published by Ryss and Goldberg (1973) [1]. The laboratory results upon which the method is based, some additional field conditions, equipment parameters, and speed of coverage of the method were described in several other papers [1–3].

In the 1970s and 1980s, the CHIM method was extensively applied in Russia in exploration for base and precious metals, W, U, Be, and oil and gas [4]. In the early 1980s, experimental research was carried out in China [5,6], and in the late 1980s, geoelectrochemical experimentation was started in India [7]. In the 1990s, this method was applied on a trial basis in the USA [8] and Canada [9], and then widely applied to search for concealed ore deposits [10,11]. Since the 2000s, a large amount of research on the halo-forming mechanism of this method has been performed, and great progress has been made for its technique improvement [12–15]. Excellent results of searching hidden ore deposits of Cu, Pb, Zn, Au, Ag, Sn, As and Sb have been obtained with this method [16]. Meanwhile, application studies have been carried out for different stages of mineral exploration, with great success [17,18].

The CHIM method has been improved since it was put forward. MDI (Method of Diffusion Extraction) was first proposed for exploration of buried ore bodies by Milkov et al. (1981) [19], "Dipole" CHIM was proposed by Levitski (1993) [20], and NEOCHIM was set up by Leinz and Hoover (1993) [21]. More recently, the adsorption–electric extraction method was developed by Fei (1992) [22], Liu et al. (1997) [14], Luo (1994) [23] and Tan and Cai (2000) [15]. However, there are still many disadvantages as follows:

(1) Formerly, researchers [1–11] intended to extract metal ions, under the influence of electric current, from a buried deposit through hundreds of meters of overburden into the element-collectors (ECs) on the surface. To achieve this, a large power generator is required, and each measurement point is connected with the generator by long wires. Procedures are complex, and the operation is inconvenient in field, e.g., the power is easily broken off by accidental factors, such as cars passing by, animal actions, and people walking, etc.

(2) Element-collectors (ECs) filled with solution may leak, to a greater or lesser degree, so that the remaining amount of the solution is very different when the work is finished, which may have an influence on identifying anomalies.

(3) Element-collectors (ECs) of the adsorption–electric extraction method have some advantages over the liquid-type ECs. Previous work, however, only employed a single cathode to extract ions that are in positively charged forms of elements. Levitski (1993) [20] proposed the "Dipole" CHIM method, which enables a simultaneous extraction of anionic and cationic species of elements, and the ECs have been improved greatly as well. However, it is difficult to use in field owing to its weight, complicated operation procedures, high cost and relatively low production rate.

(4) The improvement of method has received only minimal attention in the English-language literature. Kang et al. (2003) [12] and Kang et al. (2006) [13] gave a brief overview of the development and application of the improved method in Chinese, with an English abstract.

On the improvement of the CHIM method, the authors have carried out some exploration in China and made some progress [12,13], and other researchers [24] also conducted related research. In order to carry out the research and further improve the technology of this method on a global scale, the authors systematically summarized the previous research results and wrote this paper.

Firstly, the development history of geoelectrochemical exploration method (GEM) was introduced in this paper. Secondly, the halo-forming mechanism was illustrated on mineral exploration. Then, the basic and the improved geoelectrochemical methods including equipment and sampling were described, respectively. Finally, three case studies on concealed gold deposits in China were illustrated to show the applications of the improved geoelectrochemical method developed.

2. Halo-Forming Mechanism

Deeply concealed ore deposits are dissolved in many forms, such as electrochemical dissolution. Metal anionic and cationic species of elements from concealed deposits migrate to near the surface driven by various geological forces, and they are enriched therein [21,25–28]. Ions with a negative charge go to the anode and positive to the cathode under the influence of an artificial electric field. The man-made electric field can activate and change the forms of occurrence of elements in the soil. Firstly, it can bring about decomposition of a great number of complex anions and other stable or sub-stable form of elements; secondly, it can make anions and cations move to the extraction electrodes, and hence accelerate ionic movement [1,17]. The metal ions of electromobile forms are extracted in either anodes or cathodes under the influence of a man-made electric field, which are called GEM anomalies (Figure 1). There are electrically active fine-grained clay mineral particles in the soil, and charged ions or electrically active ultrafine-grained clay mineral particles can migrate to the designated electrode and be adsorbed in the foam sample under the action of an external electric field [29]. GEM ionic halos are in mobile forms, and they are dynamically related to concealed deposits [7,22,26]. The element composition of the halos is normally correlated with that of the ores, and the halos occur typically directly over the deposits [30]. Therefore, GEM ionic halos can be used to search for concealed deposits.

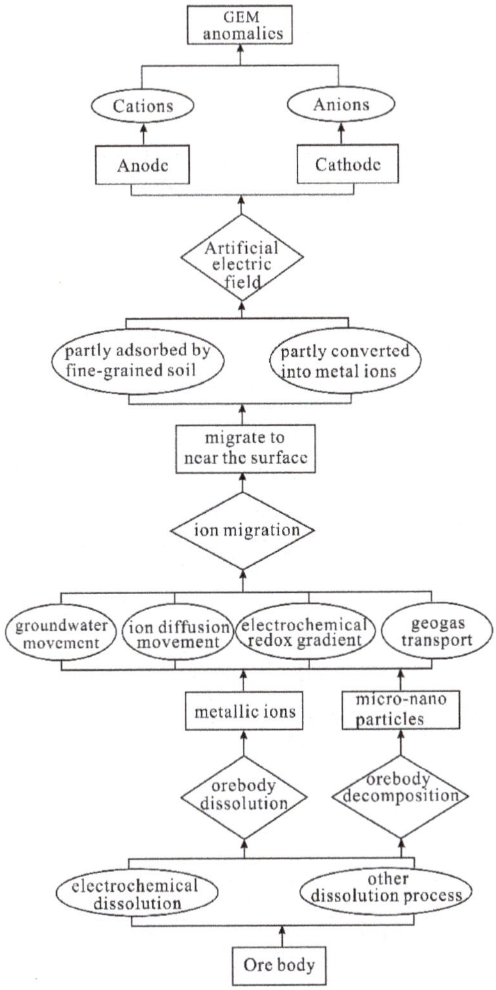

Figure 1. The formation of geoelectrochemical ionic halos.

3. Materials and Methods

The GEM is a prospecting technique that combines geochemical and geophysical exploration. That is, ions or charged complexes of the electromobile forms of elements in soils and rocks are extracted, under the influence of an artificial electric field, into the specially designed element-collectors (ECs). The ECs are analyzed by ICP-MS for indicator elements related to ore deposits.

3.1. Basic GEM-CHIM

The ECs are embedded in the surface sediments along a profile to be explored and are connected to a DC current source as either anodes or cathodes. The collectors comprise cylindrical polyethylene vessels with a semi-permeable diaphragm as a base, filled with specific electrolyte in which a solid electrode is dipped. A common auxiliary electrode is positioned at "infinity" and is represented by a metal or graphite bar(s). The extraction of electromobile forms of occurrence of metals is made with an applied current of 100–200 mA, usually for a duration of 10 or 20 h [7,30–33]. However, the basic CHIM field procedure is complicated and of high cost. As such, some improvements have been made recently, as introduced in this paper.

3.2. Improved GEM—"Dipole CHIM" Electrified by a Low Voltage Dipole (Abbreviated as DL-CHIM)

3.2.1. Theoretical Basis

Both cationic and anionic species may bear useful information, and many metals may form anionic complexes, especially in the presence of chlorides, particularly in surface soils. Such complexes include $[CuI]^-$, $[CuCl_2]^-$, $[Cd(NH_3)_2\,Cl_4]^{2-}$, $[HgCl_4]^{2-}$, etc. [34]. Recognizing that anionic as well as cationic species may provide useful information [33], the "Dipole CHIM" technique electrified by a low voltage dipole was then proposed.

3.2.2. Method Setting and Field Procedures

The element-collectors comprise a graphite bar wrapped foam electrode pairs connected by a 9-volt alkaline battery (Figure 2). The electrodes were embedded in a rectangular sampling area with a length of 40 cm, a width of 20 cm and a depth of 30 cm, and were placed parallel at the bottom of the sampling area at an interval of 30 cm, and then they were covered with soil while watering and pouring a dilute nitric acid solution of 15% HNO_3. Generally, water is in the anode area for one liter, and dilute nitric acid solution is in the cathode area for one liter. These were left for about 24 h, after which time the electrodes were exhumed (depending on the DC power supply and local geological controls). The electrodes need cleaning before using again.

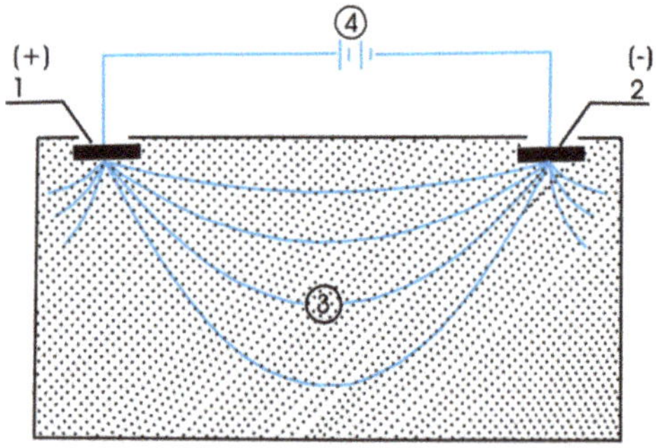

Figure 2. Simplified profile of the DL-CHIM. 1—Anion collector; 2—Cation collector; 3—Current flow lines; 4—Disposable DC power supply.

Soil samples were collected at each sampling point to compare the application effects between the DL-CHIM method with the conventional geochemical soil survey (CGS).

3.3. Sample Testing

Acid digestion in pretreating foam samples was made, and the contents of Au were determined by Inductively Coupled Plasma-Mass Spectrometry (ICP-MS), and the analytical work was carried out at Institute of Geophysical and Geochemical Exploration, Langfang, China and Guilin Research Institute of Geology for Mineral Resources, Guilin.

4. Results and Discussion

4.1. Case Study on Yingezhuang Gold Deposit

The DL-CHIM method was applied at Yingezhuang gold deposit from Shandong, 210 gold deposit from Xinjiang, and Daiyinzhang gold polymetallic deposit from Shanxi, China. The Yingezhuang gold deposit is located in the East of China, whose ore body is situated at a depth of between 100 m and 600 m. The average grade of the ore body is 4.03 g/t with a thickness ranging from 2 m to 10 m [13]. Figure 3a,b show the results obtained using the DL-CHIM method. It can be seen from Figure 3 that the DL-CHIM method identifies distinct anomalies of Au over the gold ore bodies, and that cationic species anomalies of Au have highest values (41.05 ppb) above the buried ore bodies, and anion anomalies of Au have high intensity and good continuity, which corresponds closely to ore body. Anionic species anomalies and cationic species anomalies of Au are much wider and have better continuity (sample numbers from 18 to 54), which can give anomalous responses from deep-seated mineralization. Anionic and cationic species anomalies of Au enable the identification of the position of the deeply buried ore bodies. The maximum anomalous value in cationic species anomalies of Au clearly corresponds to the gold-rich ore body of Yingezhuang gold deposit. In the thick transported covered terrains (sample numbers from 18 to 36), and anion anomalies of Au can show better results for concealed gold deposits in depth because gold may mainly exist as micro–nano particles in surface soils, which are negatively charged and can migrate to the designated electrode and be adsorbed in the foam sample under the action of an artificial electric field. The analytical results of this field work are tabulated in Table 1.

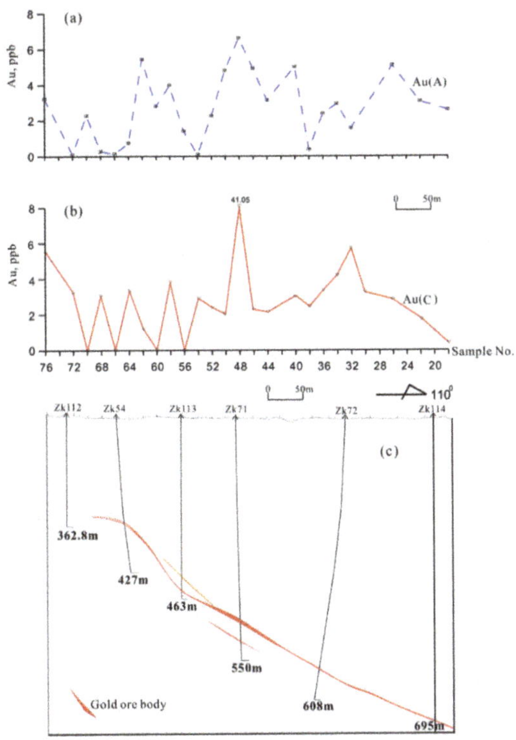

Figure 3. Results obtained by employing the DL-CHIM method over Yingezhuang gold deposit from Shandong, China. (**a**) Anion anomalies of Au (Anode extraction); (**b**) Cation anomalies of Au (Cathode extraction); (**c**) geological base map [13].

Table 1. Analytical data of the samples obtained using the DL-CHIM at the Yingezhuang gold deposit.

Sample No.	Anion-Collectors	Cation-Collectors
	Au (ppb)	Au (ppb)
18	2.59	0.39
22	3.09	1.81
26	5.10	2.84
30		3.28
32	1.56	5.68
34	2.95	4.23
36	2.38	3.36
38	0.38	2.49
40	5.03	3.05
44	3.15	2.18
46	4.94	2.31
48	6.63	41.05
50	4.81	2.06
52	2.25	2.43
54	0.10	2.88
56	1.40	0.10
58	3.99	3.80
60	2.80	0.10
62	5.46	1.20
64	0.73	3.30
66	0.14	0.10
68	0.28	3.08
70	2.28	0.10
72	0.1	3.26
76	3.24	5.60
80	1.64	2.14

4.2. Case Study on 210 Gold Deposit

The 210 gold deposit from Xinjiang is located in the Northwest of China, where arid residual regolith is about 10 m thick. The ore bodies are hosted in a mylonite belt at depths between 20 m and 60 m, whose grade varies between 3 g/t and 10 g/t with an average of 4.11g/t [13]. Figure 4 shows the results obtained using the DL-CHIM method along line I at the 210 gold deposit. It can be seen from Figure 4 that there are obvious anionic species anomalies of Au above the ore body, and the anomalies of Au have a certain continuity, indicating that gold may mainly exist as micro–nano particles, clay minerals, or complexes of metal ions in surface soils, which is negatively charged. Figure 4 indicates that the cation anomaly of Au only shows a single anomalous point. Thus, it suggests that the DL-CHIM method is a great improvement over the previous monopole extraction. The analytical results of this field work are tabulated in Table 2.

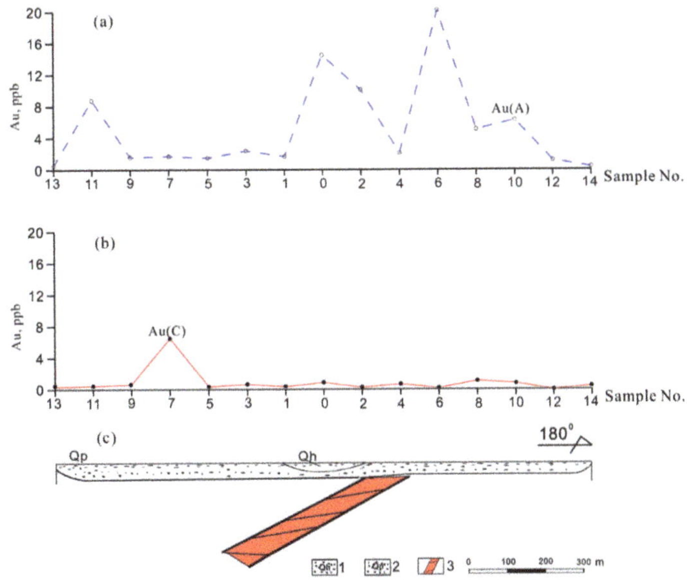

Figure 4. Results obtained by employing the DL-CHIM method over 210 gold deposit from Xinjiang, China. 1—Quaternary System Holocene; 2—Quaternary System Pleistocene; 3—Gold ore body; (**a**) Anion anomalies of Au (Anode extraction); (**b**) Cation anomalies of Au (Cathode extraction); (**c**) geological base map [13].

Table 2. Analytical results of the samples obtained using DL-CHIM method at the 210 gold deposit.

Sample No.	Anion-Collectors	Cation-Collectors
	Au (ppb)	Au (ppb)
0	0.9	14.5
1	0.4	1.7
2	0.3	10.1
3	0.7	2.4
4	0.7	2.1
5	0.4	1.5
6	0.2	20.2
7	6.5	1.7
8	1.1	5.1
9	0.7	1.6
10	0.8	6.3
11	0.5	8.8
12	0.0	1.2
13	0.4	0.5
14	0.5	0.4

4.3. Case Study on Daiyinzhang Gold Deposit

The Daiyinzhang gold polymetallic deposit is located in the midwestern section of Wutaishan area from Shanxi, in the middle-high mountainous area. The terrain in the area is high in the east and low in the west, with developed valleys and severe topography, where exposed strata mainly consist of the chlorite schist and sericite schist of the Baizhiyan Formation of the Neoarchean Wutai Group. The alteration phenomena of pyrite mineralization, silicification, tourmaline, sericitization, and carbonation are obvious. The intrusive rocks are mainly dominated by Wutai plagioclase granite and Lvliang metamorphic diabase [35,36]. The ore body, with strike length 450 m, has a burial depth of 0 m to 558 m and a thickness of 0.53 m to 2.44 m; its Au average grade is 2.97 g/t. It can be seen from Figure 5 that the cation anomalies of Au mainly occur at measurement points from 11 to 18, and the anomalous values are in the range from 6.21 ppb to 11.21 ppb, with an average intensity of 8.83 ppb, which basically corresponds to the ore bodies near the surface; in addition, the extreme values of the anomalies are relatively continuous, which is basically consistent with the distribution of gold ore bodies. The anion anomalies of Au occur at measurement points from 5 to 11, and the anomalous values are in the range from 4.65 ppb to 16.98 ppb, with an average intensity of 9.47 ppb, corresponding to the buried ore bodies. In the geochemical soil survey, the soil anomalies of Au occur at measurement points from 15 to 19, and the anomalous values are in the range from 4.86 ppb to 481.62 ppb, with an average intensity of 121.02 ppb, which has some displacement with the ore bodies near the surface; for buried ore bodies, the soil anomalies of Au are weak, basically showing the background characteristics. In general, in the thick transported covered terrains (measurement points from 1 to 10), the geochemical soil survey shows only background characteristics; however, DL-CHIM method shows obvious anion and cation anomalies of Au at measurement points for 5, 6 and 8. The analytical results of this field work are tabulated in Table 3.

Table 3. Analytical results of the samples obtained using DL-CHIM method at the Daiyinzhang gold polymetallic deposit.

Sample No.	Anion-Collectors	Cation-Collectors	Geochemical Soil Survey
	Au (ppb)	Au (ppb)	Au (ppb)
1	5.34	13.57	2.76
2	5.25	5.49	1.58
3	7.65	4.78	2.42
4	5.74	5.79	1.57
5	16.98	8.28	1.38
6	4.65	10.37	2.13
7	5.14	4.72	2.81
8	9.70	4.68	1.29
9	4.93	6.09	1.28
10	13.14	4.63	1.48
11	11.75	11.21	4.55
12	6.34	9.07	2.90
13	5.73	9.87	9.28
14	5.31	9.01	8.43
15	5.07	7.60	38.55
16	4.78	9.79	4.86
17	7.57	7.86	481.62
18	4.81	6.21	53.16
19	6.67	8.01	26.90
20	4.08	7.34	1.94

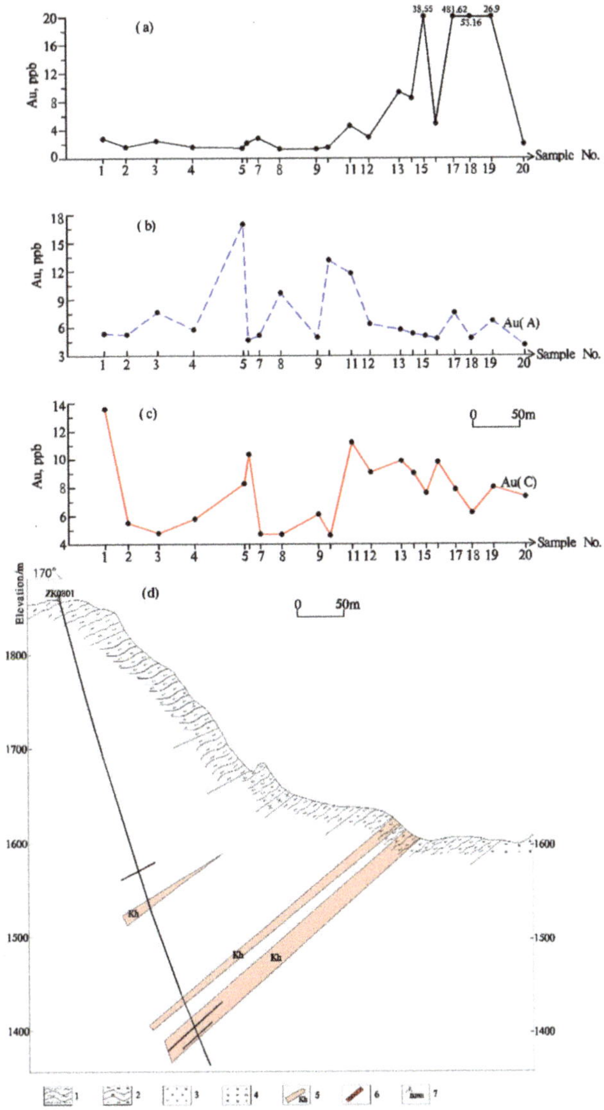

Figure 5. Results obtained by employing the DL-CHIM method and geochemical soil survey over Daiyinzhang gold deposit from Shanxi, China. 1—Chlorite schist; 2—Sericite schist; 3—Metamorphic diabase; 4—Plagioclase granite; 5—Gold mineralization; 6—Gold ore body; 7—Drill hole; (**a**) Soil geochemical anomalies; (**b**) Anion anomalies of Au (Anode extraction); (**c**) Cation anomalies of Au (Cathode extraction); (**d**) geological base map [35,36].

5. Conclusions

(1) The DL-CHIM method, characterized by simple equipment, easy operation and low cost, is therefore suitable particularly for field surveys.

(2) The DL-CHIM method enables a simultaneous extraction of anionic and cationic species of pathfinder elements, from which more information can be derived with a higher extraction efficiency.

(3) In thick overburden areas, deep-seated concealed ore bodies are difficult to identify by conventional geochemical exploration methods, such as geochemical soil survey. However, the DL-CHIM method can detect obvious anomalies of pathfinder elements for anionic or cationic species. Additionally, anion anomalies of elements can show better results for concealed gold deposits in depth because gold may mainly exist as micro–nano particles in surface soils, which are negatively charged.

(4) The prospecting depth of this technique is much greater than that of conventional geochemical exploration methods because the detecting objects of this technique are those mobile forms of elements and ions.

Author Contributions: M.K., conceptualization, methodology, data curation, writing—original draft, investigation, project administration; H.G., investigation, data curation; W.Z., investigation, funding acquisition; X.L., supervision; J.Y., writing—review and editing. All authors have read and agreed to the published version of the manuscript.

Funding: This work was financially supported by the National Natural Science Foundation of China (Grant No. 40743018).

Institutional Review Board Statement: Not applicable.

Informed Consent Statement: Not applicable.

Data Availability Statement: Not applicable.

Conflicts of Interest: The authors declare no conflict of interest.

References

1. Ryss, Y.S.; Goldberg, I.S. Sposob chastichnogo izvlecheniya metallov (CHIM) dlya poiskov rudnykh mestorozhdeniy (The partial extraction of metals (CHIM) method in mineral exploration). In *Metodika I Tekhnika Razvedki*; Earth Science Translation Services, Translator; ONTI VITR: Saint Petersburg, Russia, 1973; pp. 5–19.
2. Ryss, Y.S.; Antropova, L.V.; Goldberg, I.S. Using of electrochemical method for search, evaluation and determination of reserves of deep-seated deposits. *Sov. Geol.* **1977**, *6*, 139–144.
3. Shmakin, B.M. The method of partial extraction of metals in a constant current electrical field for geochemical exploration. *J. Geochem. Explor.* **1985**, *23*, 27–33. [CrossRef]
4. Ryss, Y.S.; Goldberg, I.S.; Vasilyeva, V.I.; Voroshilov, N.A. Vozmojnosti primenenia geoelectrochimicheskih metodov dlja poiskov neftegazovyh mestorojdenij (A feasibility of electrogeochemical technique application in exploration for oil and gas). *Sov. Geol.* **1990**, *6*, 28–33. (In Russian)
5. Fei, X.Q. The experimental results of the electrogeochemical extraction method in several mining districts. *Geophys. Geochem. Explor.* **1984**, *8*, 162–165. (In Chinese with English Abstract)
6. Xu, B.L.; Fei, X.Q.; Wang, H.P. Electrogeochemical extraction technique in the prospecting of buried gold deposits. *J. Geochem. Explor.* **1989**, *33*, 99–108.
7. Talapatra, A.K.; Talakdar, R.C.; De, P.K. Electrochemical technique for exploration of base-metal sulphides. *J. Geochm. Explor.* **1986**, *25*, 389–396. [CrossRef]
8. Smith, D.B.; Hoover, D.B.; Sanzolone, R.F. Development and testing of the CHIM electrogeochemical exploration method. In *USGS Research on Mineral Resources, Program and Abstracts*; U.S. Geological Survey Circular 1062; U.S. Geological Survey: Reston, VA, USA, 1991; pp. 74–75.
9. Ryss, Y.S.; Siegel, H.O. *Some Results of Applying Russian Geoelectrochemical Methods in Canada*; Scintrex Ltd.: Vaughan, ON, Canada, 1992; 16p.
10. Hoover, D.B.; Smith, D.B.; Leinz, R.W. *CHIM—An Electrogeochemical Partial Extraction Method: A Historical Review*; US Geological Survey Open File Report 97-92; U.S. Geological Survey: Reston, VA, USA, 1997; 35p.
11. Leinz, R.W.; Hoover, D.B.; Fey, D.L.; Smith, D.B. Electrogeochemical sampling with NEOCHIM—Results of tests over buried gold deposits. *J. Geochem. Explor.* **1998**, *61*, 57–86. [CrossRef]
12. Kang, M.; Luo, X.R. Improvement and applied results of geoelectrochemical methods. *Geol. Prospect.* **2003**, *39*, 63–66. (In Chinese with English Abstract)
13. Kang, M.; Cen, K.; Luo, X.R. Application of "dipole CHIM" electrified by low voltage dipole. *Geol. Prospect.* **2006**, *42*, 81–85. (In Chinese with English Abstract)
14. Liu, Z.Y.; Liu, J.M.; Cui, A.M. A discussion on the action conditions of CHIM process. *Geophys. Geochem. Explor.* **1997**, *21*, 115–122. (In Chinese with English abstract)
15. Tan, K.R.; Cai, X.P. Field absorption-electricity extraction experiments. *Geotecton. Metallog.* **2000**, *24*, 189–192. (In Chinese with English Abstract)

16. Luo, X.R.; Kang, M.; Ou, Y.F.; Wen, M.L.; Hou, B.H. *Halo-Forming Mechanism, Methodology and Application of Geoelectrochemical Technology in Exploration for Mineral Deposits*; Geological Publishing House: Beijing, China, 2007; p. 193. (In Chinese with English Abstract)
17. Kang, M.; Ma, M.H. The role of artificial electric field in formation of geoelectrochemical ionic halos. *Geophys. Geochem. Explor.* **2008**, *32*, 534–536, 548. (In Chinese with English Abstract)
18. Kang, M. Experiment and application of improved CHIM in mineral exploration. *Geol. Bull. China* **2009**, *28*, 250–256. (In Chinese with English Abstract)
19. Milkov, G.V.; Chvanov, B.F.; Vinogradov, V.N.; Goldberg, I.S.; Alexeev, S.G.; Dukhanin, A.S. Sposob Poiskov Mestorojdeniy Poleznyh Iskopaemyh (Mineral Exploration Technique). USSR Patent No. 894660, 19 March 1981. (In Russian)
20. Levitski, A. A new version of geoelectrochemical exploration technology. In Proceedings of the GSI Annual Meetings, Dubna, Russia, 10–15 May 1993.
21. Leinz, R.W.; Hoover, D.B. The Russian CHIM method—Electrically or diffussion-driven collection of ions? *Explore* **1993**, *79*, 5–9.
22. Fei, X.Q. *Electro-Extraction Ions Method*; Geological Publishing House: Beijing, China, 1992; pp. 80–102. (In Chinese)
23. Luo, X.R. Secondary discussion on prospecting buried ore by geoelectrochemical method. *J. Guilin Coll. Geol.* **1994**, *14*, 295–302. (In Chinese with English Abstract)
24. Liu, P.F.; Luo, X.R.; Wen, M.L.; Zhang, J.L.; Zheng, C.J.; Gao, W.; Ouyang, F. Geoelectrochemical anomaly prospecting for uranium deposits in southeastern China. *Appl. Geochem.* **2018**, *97*, 226–237. [CrossRef]
25. Cao, J.J.; Hu, R.Z.; Liang, Z.R.; Peng, Z.L. TEM observation of geogas-carried particles from the Changkeng concealed gold deposit, Guangdong Province, South China. *J. Geochem. Explor.* **2009**, *101*, 247–253. [CrossRef]
26. Kang, M.; Guo, L. The formation of halos CHIM. *Bull. Mineral. Petrol. Geochem.* **2008**, *27*, 195–199. (In Chinese with English Abstract)
27. Wang, X.Q.; Zhang, B.M.; Lin, X.; Xu, S.F.; Yao, W.S.; Ye, R. Geochemical challenges of diverse regolith-covered terrains for mineral exploration in China. *Ore Geol. Rev.* **2016**, *73*, 417–431.
28. Wang, X.Q.; Zhang, B.M.; Ye, R. Comparison of nanoparticles from soils over concealed gold, copper-nickel and silver deposits. *J. Nanosci. Nanotechnol.* **2017**, *17*, 6014–6025. [CrossRef]
29. Sun, B.B.; Zhang, X.J.; Liu, Z.Y.; Zhou, G.H.; Zhang, B.M.; Chen, Y.D. A preliminary study of the formation mechanism of the geoelectric chemistry anomaly. *Geophys. Geochem. Explor.* **2015**, *39*, 1183–1187. (In Chinese with English Abstract)
30. Alekseev, S.G.; Dukhanin, A.S.; Veshev, S.A.; Voroshilov, N.A. Some aspects of practical use of electrogeochemical methods of exploration for deep-seated mineralization. *J. Geochem. Explor.* **1996**, *56*, 79–86. [CrossRef]
31. Antropova, L.V.; Goldberg, I.S.; Voroshilov, N.A.; Ryss, Y.S. New methods of regional exploration for blind mineralisation: Application in the USSR. *J. Geochem. Explor.* **1992**, *43*, 157–166. [CrossRef]
32. Bloomstein, E. *Selected Translations of the Russian Literature on the Electrogeochemical Sampling Technique Called CHIM (Chastichnoe Izvlechenie Metallov)*; US Geological Survey Open File Report 90-462; U.S. Geological Survey: Reston, VA, USA, 1990; 172p.
33. Levitski, A.; Filanovski, B.; Bourenko, T.; Tannenbaum, E.; Bar-Am, G. "Dipole" CHIM: Concept and application. *J. Geochem. Explor.* **1996**, *57*, 101–114. [CrossRef]
34. Grinberg, A.A. *Vvedenie v Chimiju Kompleksnyh Soedinenij (The Bases of the Chemistry of Complex Compounds)*; Chimia: Saint Petersburg, Russia, 1971; 631p. (In Russian)
35. Tian, Y.Q.; Yu, K.R.; Miao, P.S. A simple analysis of metallogenic geologic features and ore-control factors of Dongyaozhuang gold deposite in Wutaishan greenstone belt. *Prog. Precambrian Res.* **2000**, *23*, 88–97. (In Chinese with English Abstract)
36. Jiang, F.X. Metallogenic geological characteristics and genesis of Dongyaozhuang gold deposit in Wutai, Shanxi. *Geol. Prospect.* **2006**, *42*, 24–29. (In Chinese with English Abstract)

applied sciences

MDPI

Article

Geochemistry, Geochronology, and Prospecting Potential of the Dahongliutan Pluton, Western Kunlun Orogen

Bing Zhou [1,2,*], Zhixue Zhang [3], Zeming Shi [1], Hao Song [1] and Linsong Yu [1,4,*]

1 College of Earth Sciences, Chengdu University of Technology, Chengdu 610059, China
2 Sichuan Development Holding Co., Ltd., Chengdu 610041, China
3 Sichuan Institute of Nuclear Industry Geology, Chengdu 610061, China
4 Shandong Institute of Geophysical and Geochemical Exploration, Jinan 250013, China
* Correspondence: zhoubing_sdh@163.com (B.Z.); sean_yls@163.com (L.Y.)

Abstract: Triassic granitoids are abundant on the northwestern margin of the Tibetan Plateau. The Dahongliutan pluton, located in the eastern Western Kunlun orogen, formed in the Late Triassic.Previous field studies have identified potential mixing of crustal and mantle magmas. In this study, we used zircon U–Pb ages and major and trace elemental analyses to investigate the tectonic evolution of the pluton, and to determine whether any exchange of mantle-derived material occurred between the pluton and the source area. We found that the pluton has relatively high SiO_2 contents, and the aluminum saturation index is consistent with peraluminous high-K calc-alkaline granite. The pluton is enriched in light rare earth elements; both light and heavy rare earth elements are highly fractionated. The magma that formed the pluton was predominantly derived from the crust; however, a small amount of upper mantle material was involved in the early stages of magma formation. The pluton underwent composite emplacement as a result of tectonic extension and magmatic emplacement, which may have occurred in the late Triassic post-collisional orogenic stage. Late Triassic magmatism provided heat and ore-forming material for Pb–Zn, Cu, Fe, and rare metal mineralization, which is of considerable importance for geological prospecting.

Keywords: zircon U–Pb dating; geochemistry; late Triassic; Paleo-Tethys Ocean; syn-collisional; Dahongliutan pluton; western Kunlun orogen

Citation: Zhou, B.; Zhang, Z.; Shi, Z.; Song, H.; Yu, L. Geochemistry, Geochronology, and Prospecting Potential of the Dahongliutan Pluton, Western Kunlun Orogen. *Appl. Sci.* **2022**, *12*, 11591. https://doi.org/10.3390/app122211591

Academic Editors: Nikolaos Koukouzas and Andrea L. Rizzo

Received: 7 October 2022
Accepted: 14 November 2022
Published: 15 November 2022

1. Introduction

The Western Kunlun orogenic belt is located in the northwestern Qinghai–Tibet Plateau at the junction of the Paleo-Asian and Tethys tectonic domains. Magmatic activity has occurred frequently throughout this region, producing granitoid rocks. The Western Kunlun orogen was accompanied by evolution of the Paleo-Tethys Ocean during the Indosinian period. As collisional compressive conditions changed to a collisional extension setting, strong intermediate-acid magmatism occurred along the Mazha–Kangxiwa suture zone [1]. Determining the characteristics, genesis, and evolution of the emplaced granitoids is crucial for investigating the evolution of continental orogenic belts.

The Dahongliutan pluton is one of the main plutons of the Sanshiliyingfang Qitaidaban granite belt [2]; it is located in the northern Tianshuihai–Karakoram terrane, on the southern side of the Mazha–Kangxiwa suture zone, and is bounded by the Dahongliutan Fault to the north. Based on geochronological data, the Bureau of Geology and Mineral Resources of Xinjiang suggested that the Dahongliutan pluton formed during the late Cretaceous. Based on petrography, petrochemistry, and chronology, Qiao, et al. [3] suggested that the Dahongliutan monzogranite is a Late Triassic, highly differentiated S-type granite that experienced crustal source contamination in a collisional setting. Wei, et al. [4] suggested that the Dahongliutan pluton is a compound pluton produced during a single period of tectonomagmatic activity that included partial melting of crustal material in a collisional setting after the closure of the Paleo-Tethys Ocean. Zhang, et al. [5] measured an emplacement age of ~217.5 Ma for the Dahongliutan pluton and determined that the pluton was the product of partial melting of crustal material in a post-collisional setting. Ding, et al. [6] measured the emplacement age of the Dahongliutan biotite monzogranite to be 214 ± 1.8 Ma, which indicates that the pluton was produced by late Indosinian magmatism; they postulated that the magma that formed the Dahongliutan pluton contained mantle and Mesoproterozoic crustal components [6,7]. The Dahongliutan rare metal pegmatite deposit is located south of the Mazha-Kangxiwa Fault in the eastern part of the Western Kunlun orogen and is a large Li-Be-Nb-Ta deposit [8]. More than 400,000 tons of Li_2O resources have been explored, and many of the pegmatite veins have not yet been evaluated; thus, this deposit has great metal prospecting potential [9].

Exploration data indicate that the Dahongliutan belt has large- and super large-scale rare metal prospecting potential. The Dahongliutan rare metal pegmatite deposit, a large Li–Be–Nb–Ta deposit, is located south of the Mazha–Kangxiwa Fault in the eastern Western Kunlun orogen [8]. More than 400,000 t of Li_2O resources have been explored; however, many of the pegmatite veins have not yet been evaluated and this deposit has great metal prospecting potential [9]. The pegmatite dikes that surround Triassic rocks in this area suggest ideal conditions for rare metal mineralization [10]. However, it remains unclear whether the emplacement ages of the different lithofacies in the Dahongliutan pluton are consistent. Moreover, it is unclear whether the pluton formed over multiple magmatic stages. Previous research has suggested that the magmatic source of the Dahongliutan pluton was crustal; however, this does not account for dioritic enclaves developed in the samples. The Muztagata pluton (located to the north), Shangqimugan pluton, and Dahongliutan pluton all formed under similar regional geologic settings and exhibit similar emplacement ages. They contain dark inclusions, which previous field studies attributed to mixing of crustal and mantle magmas. Thus, it is important to determine whether any exchange of mantle-derived material occurred between the Dahongliutan pluton and the source area.

In this study, we used data obtained by a 1:50,000 mineral prospective survey and 1:50,000 regional geological survey, along with previous research results, to investigate the petrology, geochemistry, genesis, and tectonic setting of the Dahongliutan pluton and its geodynamic setting in the Late Triassic. The findings of this study provide important data for systematic studies on tectonomagmatic events related to the Western Kunlun orogeny.

2. Geologic Setting

The Western Kunlun orogen, which is located at the junction of the northwestern margin of the Qinghai–Tibet Plateau and the Tarim Block, comprises a composite orogenic belt formed by multiple arc-continent collisions (Figure 1a). The evolution of the Western Kunlun orogen is complex and includes three tectonic units: the northwestern Kunlun, southwestern Kunlun, and Tianshuihai–Karakoram terranes [7,11].

The Dahongliutan pluton is located ~150 km southwest of Hotan County, Xinjiang Uygur Autonomous Region; the Xinjiang–Tibet highway passes through the north bank of the Karakash River on the northern side of the study area. The tectonic setting is the northern Tianshuihai–Karakoram of the Western Kunlun orogen, which lies to the south of the Mazha–Kangxiwa suture zone. To the north, it is adjacent to the Dahongliutan Fault. The rocks surrounding the Dahongliutan granite are from the Triassic Bayanhar and Paleoproterozoic Kangxiwa groups. The pluton, which forms a linear/oval feature (Figure 1) with its long axis trending NW–SE, was emplaced parallel to the Dahongliutan fault zone [3]. According to the intrusive relationships, rock types, intrusion sequence, and genetic types, the intrusive rocks can be divided into seven different types: muscovite monzogranites (first intrusion, Figure 2a), mica monzogranites (second intrusion, Figure 2b), biotite granodiorites (third intrusion, Figure 2c), biotite monzogranites (fourth intrusion), biotite quartz diorites (fifth intrusion, Figure 2d), tonalites (sixth intrusion), and mica granites (seventh intrusion). These intrusions underwent homologous magmatic and spatial evolutions and belong to a relatively complete magmatic evolution sequence. All the rock types contain gray-black deep-sourced diorite inclusions that are predominantly elliptical; however, the long axes of inclusions near the edges of the pluton are roughly parallel to the contact boundary with the surrounding rock. The pluton has experienced regional or dynamic metamorphism to different degrees, and local sections exhibit flaky and gneissic structures. The rocks generally contain feldspar phenocrysts, which have evolved from neutral to acidic (early to late) and form a relatively complete homologous magmatic sequence. There is a pulsating contact with rocks adjacent to each intrusion in the sequence, with the presence of condensation edges.

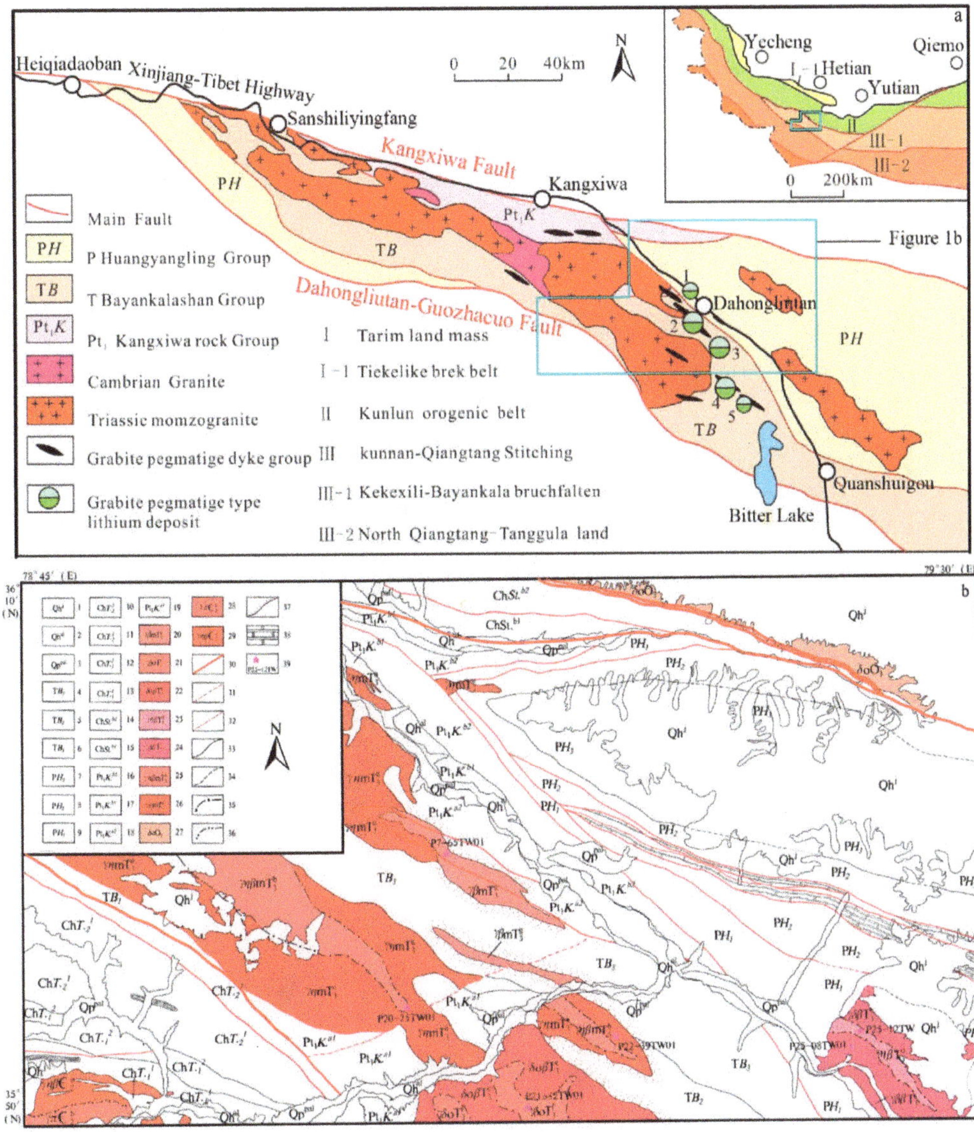

Figure 1. (**a**) Geologic map of the Kangxiwa–Dahongliutan area (base map according to [10]), and (**b**) a simplified geologic map of the study area (1. Modern snow cover; 2. Holocene alluvium; 3. Pleistocene

alluvial diluvium; 4. Upper formation of the Bayankala Mountain Group; 5. Middle formation of the Bayankala Mountain Group; 6. Lower formation of the Bayankala Mountain Group; 7. Upper formation of the Huangyangling Group; 8. Middle formation of the Huangyangling Group; 9. Lower formation of the Huangyangling Group; 10. Second member of the upper formation of the Tianshuihai Group; 11. First member of the upper formation of the Tianshuihai group; 12. Second member of the lower formation of the Tianshuihai group; 13. First member of the lower formation of the Tianshuihai Group; 14. Second member of formation B of the Saitula Group; 15. First member of formation B of the Saitula Group; 16. Second member of formation B of the Kangxiwa Group; 17. First member of formation B of the Kangxiwa Group; 18. Second member of formation A of the Kangxiwa Group; 19. First member of formation A of the Kangxiwa Group; 20. Late Triassic seventh intrusive secondary biotite monzogranite; 21. Late Triassic sixth intrusive secondary tonalite; 22. Late Triassic fifth intrusive secondary biotite quartz diorite; 23. Late Triassic fourth intrusive secondary biotite monzogranite; 24. Late Triassic third intrusive secondary biotite granodiorite; 25. Late Triassic second intrusive secondary biotite monzogranite; 26. Late Triassic first intrusive secondary muscovite monzogranite; 27. Late Ordovician quartz diorite; 28. Middle Cambrian second intrusive secondary biotite granite; 29. Middle Cambrian first intrusive secondary granite porphyry; 30. Fault; 31. Inferred fault; 32. Remote sensing interpreted fault; 33. Geological boundary; 34. Inferred geological boundary; 35. Pulsating contact boundary; 36. Surging contact boundary; 37. Hornization; 38. Marble; 39. Sample locations and numbers).

Figure 2. (**a**) Rock surrounding a xenolith in muscovite monzogranite. (**b**) Joints developed inmica monzogranite. (**c**) Dark inclusions developed in biotite granodiorite. (**d**) Tonalite in pulsating contact with biotite quartz diorite.

3. Analytical Methods

3.1. Major and Trace Elemental Analyses

We analyzed the major and trace elemental contents of 23 rock samples from the study area. Sample analyses were performed at the Urumqi Supervision and Inspection Center of Mineral Resources, Ministry of Land and Resources. Major elements were analyzed using X-ray fluorescence (model # Axios, manufacturer:Panaco Netherlands, country of origin: The Netherlands); the analytical accuracy was better than 1–5%. Trace elements and rare earth elements (REEs) were analyzed using inductively coupled plasma mass spectrometry (ICP–MS; model # NexION 300x ICP-MS iCAP6300 Simultaneous spectrometer, manufacturer: PerkinElmer, country of origin: the United States). Detailed descriptions of the analytical methods and analyses can be found in Liu, et al. [12].

3.2. Zircon U–Pb Dating

Zircon U–Pb dating was performed using laser ablation ICP–MS (LA–ICP–MS) on six samples (P22-39TW01, P20-25TW01, P25-08TW01, P25-12, P21-32TW01, and P7-65TW01). Zircon sorting and analyses were performed at the Shared Collaboration (Beijing) Analysis and Testing Center. The rock samples were first mechanically crushed, then washed and sorted using conventional flotation and electromagnetic separation methods. Zircon grains were carefully chosen using a binocular microscope to ensure grains with good crystal form and transparency, and without inclusions or cracks. The number of zircon grains sorted from each sample ranged from 500 to >1000; these grains were then fixed in a colorless and transparent epoxy resin. Transmitted light, reflected light, and cathodoluminescence (CL) photography were performed to select analytical spots on zircon grains. The selected analytical points avoided the locations of internal cracks and inclusions in order to obtain accurate age values.

Zircon age dating was performed using LA–ICP–MS (Neptune, Finnigan) and a Newwave UP 213 laser ablation system. The spot beam diameter used for laser ablation was 25 μm, the frequency was 10 Hz, and the energy density was ~2.5 J/cm^2; He was used as the carrier gas. The ^{206}Pb, ^{207}Pb, ^{204}Pb ($^{+204}$Hg), and ^{202}Hg signals were received by ion counters, while ^{208}Pb, ^{232}Th, and ^{238}U signals were received by the Faraday cup, allowing for the simultaneous reception of all target isotopic signals. The analytical accuracy of ^{207}Pb/^{206}Pb, ^{206}Pb/^{238}U, and ^{207}Pb/^{235}U was ~2%. Denudation of the sample was measured using the point denudation method, and GJ-1 was used to debug the instrument before analysis. Zircons CJ-1 and M12 were used as external standards. Zircon GJ-1 was analyzed twice before and after every 10 samples for calibration, and one plesovice zircon standard was measured simultaneously.

Data processing of isotope ratios and elemental contents were performed using ICPMS-DataCal 8.0. The age calculations and harmonic maps were completed using lsoplot ver. 3.0. Samples with ^{206}Pb/^{204}Pb ages of ≥1000 Ma were excluded from the calculation because they contained a large amount of radiogenic Pb. For samples with ages of <1000 Ma, the more reliable ^{206}Pb/^{238}U surface age was used. Detailed descriptions of the experimental procedures can be found in Hou, et al. [13].

4. Results

4.1. Petrographic Characteristics

We collected 23 samples from the northern, central, southern, southwestern, and southeastern parts of the pluton. The muscovite monzogranites (samples P22-55 GS, P22-71 GS, P20-15 GS, and D3801GS01) are gray-white with fine-grained hypidiomorphic-granular and massive structures. Euhedral plagioclase (30–35%) crystals have dimensions of 0.1 × 0.25–1 × 2.3 mm; some are replaced by sericite. Interstitial microcline (30%; 0.1–2 × 4.5 mm) is associated with biotite, plagioclase, and quartz. Fine albite stripes are distributed within coarse microcline grains. Quartz grains (25–30%; 0.05–1 × 0.5 mm) are xenomorphic-granular and exhibit strong wavy extinction. Muscovite (5%; 0.05 × 0.2–0.4 × 1.1 mm) is flaky. Flaky biotite (1–5%) is sometimes replaced by chlorite. Small amounts of apatite and white titanium were also observed.

The mica monzogranites (samples P22-39XT01, P26-88 GS, P20-19 GS, P20-03 GS, and P11-15GS01) are gray-white, with fine-grained hypidiomorphic-granular and massive structures. Mineral grain sizes are 0.05–1.7 × 3.5 mm; however, samples are predominantly composed of fine-grained minerals. Plagioclase (30–35%) is euhedral and ranges in size; potassium feldspar (20–25%) exhibits irregular shapes; inclusions of microcline and striped feldspar often replaced interstitial plagioclase. Quartz (25%) is allotriomorphic-granular and exhibits strong wavy extinction. Muscovite (10–15%) is flaky, variable in size, and has an uneven distribution. Biotite (5%) is flaky and commonly replaced by chlorite, with residual visible crystals. A small amount of apatite is also present, along with sericite exhibiting strong wavy extinction. Reticular cracks are filled a small amount of calcite.

The biotite granodiorite (samples P25-08XT01, P25-1-05 GS, and D259GS) is gray-white, with medium to fine-grained hypidiomorphic and massive structures. The main mineral components are plagioclase (45%), microcline (20–25%), quartz (25–30%), biotite (5%), and amphibole (1%). Mineral grains are 0.1–4.5 × 5 mm in size; medium-grained minerals (>2 mm) account for ~45% of the total. Some euhedral plagioclase are replaced by sericite, which has a random distribution. Microcline is irregular and interstitial, and is associated with plagioclase and biotite. Quartz is irregular, exhibits strong wavy extinction, and is associated with plagioclase and biotite. Biotite is flaky, and some grains are replaced by chlorite. Other minerals include small amounts of euhedral amphibole, epidote, sphene, and apatite. Samples are jointed and the surface is locally affected by spherical weathering.

The biotite monzogranite (sample P25-12GS) is gray-white with medium–fine-grained hypidiomorphic-granular and massive structures. The main mineral components are plagioclase (30–35%), microcline (25%), quartz (30–35%), biotite (10–15%), and amphibole (1%). Plagioclase crystals are elongate and exhibit ring structures; some grains are replaced by sericite and zoisite. Microcline is interstitial to plagioclase and biotite. Quartz is irregular and exhibits strong wavy extinction. Biotite is flaky, and some grains are replaced by chlorite. Some amphibole grains are associated with biotite. Epidote, apatite, sphene, and a small number of other minerals are also present. Samples are jointed and the surface is locally affected by alteration.

The biotite quartz diorite (samples P21-20GS and P23-01GS01) is gray with medium–fine-grained hypidiomorphic-granular and massive structures. The mineral grains are 0.1–2.1 × 3.1 mm in size; medium-grained minerals (>2 mm) account for 20–25% of the total. Plagioclase (50%) is tabular with variable grain sizes; some grains are replaced by sericite (1–5%). Hornblende (15%) ranges from euhedral to irregular in shape, and is associated with biotite. Biotite (15–20%) is flaky and randomly distributed. Quartz (15–20%) is interstitial, exhibits strong wavy extinction, and has an uneven distribution. Epidote, sphene, apatite, tourmaline, and small amounts of other minerals are also present.

The tonalite (samples P21-32XT01 and P21-08GS) is light gray-white with fine-grained hypidiomorphic-granular and massive structures. The main mineral components are quartz (25%), plagioclase (40–45%), biotite (20–25%), and amphibole (10%). The mineral grains are predominantly 0.1–2.6 mm in size. Plagioclase exhibits a hypidiomorphic plate strip shape, and some sericite replacement is observed. Biotite is flaky and exhibits weak alteration.

The mica granite (samples P7-65XT03, P9-32GS, and P10-01GS) is gray-white, medium grained, and exhibits hypidiomorphic-granular and massive structures. The main mineral components are plagioclase, potassium feldspar, biotite, muscovite, and quartz. Plagioclase is semi-idiomorphic and columnar; crystals are cloudy and some are extremely undeveloped bicrystals. Potassium feldspar is xenomorphic-granular, and the crystals are clean. Quartz is allomorphic-granular, and the crystals are smaller than those of feldspar. Biotite and muscovite are hypidiomorphic shaped wafers with low degrees of hypidiomorphism. Alteration is less pronounced than in other rock types, with only plagioclase kaolinization and sericitization; however, samples are weathered and the surfaces are broken.

4.2. Major Element Contents

Major elemental analyses (Table 1) indicate that the Dahongliutan pluton is silica-rich (SiO_2 =53.91–73.95 wt.%; average = 68.33 wt.%). The Al_2O_3 content is 12.81–17.41 wt.% (average = 15.08 wt.%), and the aluminum saturation index (A/CNK) ranges from 1.01 to 1.43, indicating peraluminous rocks (Figure 3a). The Na_2O content is 2.06–3.39 wt.% (average = 2.72). The K_2O content is 1.76–6.60 wt.% (average = 3.98 wt.%) and the K_2O/Na_2O ratio is 0.53–2.73 (average = 1.49). The total alkali content (K_2O + Na_2O) ranges from 4.24 wt.% to 9.02 wt.% (average = 6.7). The alkali aluminum index (AI) is 0.24–0.63 (average = 0.45) and the Rittman Portfolio Index (σ) ranges from 0.96 to 3.18, with all values < 3.3 (average = 1.82), thereby exhibiting typical calc-alkaline characteristics. On an SiO_2-K_2O diagram (Figure 3b), the samples fall in the high-potassium calc-alkaline series region. The CaO and TiO_2 contents are low (0.82–6.47 wt.% and 0.13–0.87 wt.%, respectively). The MgO content is 0.21–3.75 wt.% (average = 1.22 wt.%). The total iron (TFeO) content is 1.28–9.49 wt.% (average = 4.07 wt.%), and the TfeO/MgO ratio ranges from 2.53 to 8.19 (average = 4.12), indicating the pluton is Fe-rich and Mg-poor. According to the calculated CIPW norms, corundum (0.16–4.58 wt.%) is present, indicating peraluminous characteristics. The differentiation index (DI) ranges from 40.3 to 90.51 (average = 75.69), indicating a high degree of magmatic differentiation. The consolidation index (SI) ranges from 1.97 to18.21 (average = 7.96), indicating that the magma underwent a high degree of fractional crystallization and was highly acidic. On a total alkali vs. silica (TAS) diagram (Figure 4), 17 samples plot in the granite region. In summary, the Dahongliutan pluton is therefore characterized by high silica, alkali, and potassium contents, but low MgO, TiO_2, MnO, and P_2O_5 contents. These characteristics indicate that the pluton underwent strong fractional crystallization and is a peraluminous granite of the potassium-rich calc-alkaline series.

Table 1. Major element (wt.%) and CIPW norm (wt.%) contents of Dahongliutan granite samples.

Sample	P19-01XT01	P20-25XT01	P6-06XT01	P22-55 GS	P22-71 GS	P20-15 GS	D3801GS01	P22-39XT01	P26-88 GS	P20-19 GS	P20-03 GS	P11-15GS01
Component	1	2	3	4	5	6	7	8	9	10	11	12
SiO_2	73.22	64.68	73.4	73.05	70.74	72.39	72.47	72.16	71.92	73.82	57.01	73.95
TiO_2	0.18	0.58	0.16	0.24	0.63	0.18	0.19	0.24	0.17	0.19	0.83	0.13
Al_2O_3	15.02	15.43	14.41	14.22	12.81	15.02	15.11	15.07	15.01	13.93	16.45	14.55
Fe_2O_3	0.86	2.96	1.06	1.31	2.62	1.1	1.07	1.21	1.64	1.17	4.77	0.77
FeO	1.04	5.2	1.26	1.65	4.31	1.35	1.24	1.46	2.22	1.47	7.15	0.95
MnO	0.03	0.12	0.03	0.05	0.07	0.04	0.03	0.11	0.05	0.04	0.16	0.04
MgO	0.36	1.78	0.21	0.5	1.51	0.45	0.33	0.31	0.46	0.46	3.32	0.33
CaO	0.84	4.05	0.83	0.98	1.86	1.2	0.82	0.96	1.4	1.02	3.31	1.23
Na_2O	2.71	2.17	2.67	3.1	3.39	3.05	3.25	3.18	2.6	3.14	2.06	3.35
K_2O	5.42	2.73	5.48	4.49	1.78	4.92	5.19	4.9	4.4	4.41	4.63	4.44
P_2O_5	0.28	0.12	0.44	0.36	0.14	0.28	0.26	0.35	0.06	0.32	0.15	0.23
LOI	0.82	0.93	0.9	0.9	0.77	1.13	0.71	0.88	1.3	0.6	2.1	0.98
Total	100.78	100.75	100.85	100.85	100.63	101.11	100.67	100.83	101.23	100.57	101.94	100.95
Qz	34.74	27.70	35.50	35.27	36.17	32.76	31.68	32.72	35.31	36.27	11.90	34.56
An	2.34	19.35	1.25	2.51	8.33	4.13	2.37	2.48	6.56	2.24	15.47	4.60
Ab	22.94	18.40	22.60	26.24	28.73	25.81	27.51	26.92	22.02	26.52	17.46	28.36
C	3.84	1.83	3.63	3.34	2.26	3.17	3.28	3.63	3.57	3.16	2.39	2.55
Hy	1.86	10.97	1.75	2.90	8.71	2.47	1.96	2.26	3.69	2.64	16.67	1.79
Mt	1.25	4.21	1.54	1.90	3.75	1.60	1.55	1.76	2.37	1.69	6.78	1.12
Ap	0.65	0.28	1.02	0.83	0.32	0.65	0.60	0.81	0.14	0.74	0.35	0.53
DI	89.73	62.26	90.51	88.06	75.43	87.65	89.88	88.61	83.34	88.81	56.77	89.16
SI	3.46	12.00	1.97	4.52	11.10	4.14	2.98	2.80	4.06	4.32	15.15	3.35
$Mg^{\#}$	0.55	0.47	0.36	0.50	0.50	0.52	0.49	0.41	0.37	0.50	0.56	0.53
A/NK	1.45	2.36	1.40	1.43	1.71	1.45	1.38	1.43	1.66	1.40	1.96	1.41
A/CNK	1.34	1.13	1.34	1.31	1.21	1.27	1.28	1.32	1.31	1.29	1.17	1.21
AI	0.54	0.32	0.57	0.53	0.40	0.53	0.56	0.54	0.47	0.54	0.41	0.54
K_2O + Na_2O	8.13	4.90	8.15	7.59	5.17	7.97	8.44	8.08	7.00	7.55	6.69	7.79
K_2O/Na_2O	2.00	1.26	2.05	1.45	0.53	1.61	1.60	1.54	1.69	1.40	2.25	1.33
CaO/Na_2O	0.31	1.87	0.31	0.32	0.55	0.39	0.25	0.30	0.54	0.32	1.61	0.37
TFeO/MgO	3.92	3.43	8.19	4.40	3.43	4.04	5.19	6.39	6.24	4.26	2.68	3.87
σ	2.19	1.11	2.18	1.92	0.96	2.16	2.42	2.24	1.69	1.85	3.18	1.96
R1	2622.00	2816.00	2630.00	2677.00	3014.00	2556.00	2428.00	2496.00	2794.00	2731.00	1848.00	2675.00
R2	403.00	826.00	382.00	409.00	526.00	445.00	401.00	414.00	467.00	404.00	843.00	434.00

Table 1. *Cont.*

Sample	P25-08XT01	P25-1-05 GS	D259 GS	P25-12 GS	P21-20 GS	P23-01GS01	P21-32XT01	P21-08 GS	P7-65XT03	P9-32 GS	P10-01 GS
Component	13	14	15	16	17	18	19	20	21	22	23
SiO_2	65	69.09	66.88	65.35	60.91	57.78	53.91	64.69	72.32	73.93	72.96
TiO_2	0.43	0.33	0.36	0.46	0.67	0.75	0.87	0.5	0.2	0.24	0.17
Al_2O_3	15.97	13.87	15.35	15.32	15.26	16.23	17.41	16.91	14.33	13.93	15.12
Fe_2O_3	2.86	2.31	2.45	2.91	3.78	3.97	4.16	2.36	1.12	1.2	1.02
FeO	4.32	3.53	3.7	4.35	7.11	7.58	8.46	4.04	1.22	1.53	1.34
MnO	0.1	0.08	0.08	0.1	0.12	0.13	0.16	0.07	0.05	0.04	0.04
MgO	1.5	1.25	1.42	1.64	2.66	3.05	3.75	1.5	0.32	0.48	0.47
CaO	3.3	3.36	3.33	3.32	4.64	5.61	6.47	4.42	1.06	0.9	1.23
Na_2O	2.53	2.37	2.61	2.61	2.37	2.34	2.48	3.27	2.42	2.6	2.37
K_2O	3.7	3.61	3.56	3.67	2.09	2.13	1.76	1.9	6.6	4.83	4.87
P_2O_5	0.16	0.11	0.14	0.15	0.15	0.17	0.21	0.22	0.33	0.28	0.36
LOI	1.04	1.09	0.76	0.71	0.57	0.85	0.99	0.82	1.24	0.74	1.18
Total	100.91	101	100.64	100.59	100.33	100.59	100.63	100.7	101.21	100.7	101.13
Qz	24.95	30.84	27.25	24.68	21.45	15.44	8.80	25.13	30.68	37.80	37.59
An	15.35	15.97	15.63	15.51	22.10	26.80	30.84	20.52	3.11	2.64	3.75
Ab	21.44	20.07	22.11	22.11	20.10	19.85	21.06	27.70	20.48	22.01	20.06
C	2.19	0.22	1.48	1.38	1.02	0.28	0.16	1.97	2.07	3.46	4.58
Hy	8.91	7.35	7.95	9.23	15.97	17.60	20.66	8.61	1.88	2.70	2.58
Mt	4.09	3.32	3.51	4.15	5.34	5.59	5.89	3.37	1.62	1.74	1.48
Ap	0.37	0.25	0.32	0.35	0.35	0.39	0.49	0.51	0.76	0.65	0.83
DI	68.28	72.26	70.42	68.51	53.94	47.91	40.30	64.07	90.18	88.36	86.45
SI	10.06	9.57	10.34	10.81	14.78	16.00	18.21	11.48	2.74	4.51	4.67
$Mg^{\#}$	0.49	0.49	0.51	0.51	0.48	0.50	0.52	0.50	0.49	0.51	0.52
A/NK	1.96	1.78	1.88	1.85	2.48	2.64	2.91	2.27	1.29	1.47	1.65
A/CNK	1.16	1.02	1.11	1.10	1.07	1.02	1.01	1.13	1.17	1.33	1.43
AI	0.39	0.43	0.40	0.41	0.29	0.28	0.24	0.31	0.63	0.53	0.48
$K_2O + Na_2O$	6.23	5.98	6.17	6.28	4.46	4.47	4.24	5.17	9.02	7.43	7.24
K_2O/Na_2O	1.46	1.52	1.36	1.41	0.88	0.91	0.71	0.58	2.73	1.86	2.05
CaO/Na_2O	1.30	1.42	1.28	1.27	1.96	2.40	2.61	1.35	0.44	0.35	0.52
TFeO/MgO	3.57	3.49	3.23	3.30	3.07	2.84	2.53	3.19	5.41	4.23	3.73
σ	1.76	1.37	1.59	1.76	1.11	1.34	1.63	1.23	2.77	1.78	1.75
R1	2487	2852	2628	2487	2623	2410	2183	2635	2382	2836	2850
R2	742	694	729	738	930	1073	1224	880	411	394	452

Note: 1–7, Damourite Adamellite; 8–12, Two-mica Adamellite; 13–15, Biotite Granodiorite; 16, Biotite adamellite; 17–18, Biotite Quartz Diorite; 19–20, Tonalite; 21–23, Two-Mica Granite; Qz, quartz; An, anorthite; Ab, albite; Or, orthoclase; C, corundum; Hy, hypersthene; Ilm, ilmenite; Mt, magnetite; Ap, apatite; Zr, zircon; Chr, chromite. (1) $Mg^{\#} = 100 \times Mg^{2+}/(Mg^{2+} + Fe^{2+})$, in which Mg^{2+} and Fe^{2+} are molar fractions; (2) $A/NK = Al_2O_3/(Na_2O + K_2O)$ (mol); (3) $A/CNK = Al_2O_3/(CaO + Na_2O + K_2O)$ (mol); (4) $AI = (Na_2O + K_2O)/Al_2O_3$ (mol); (5) $\sigma = (Na_2O + K_2O)^2/(SiO_2 - 43)$ (wt.%); (6) DI = Qz + Or + Ab + Ne + Le + Kp.

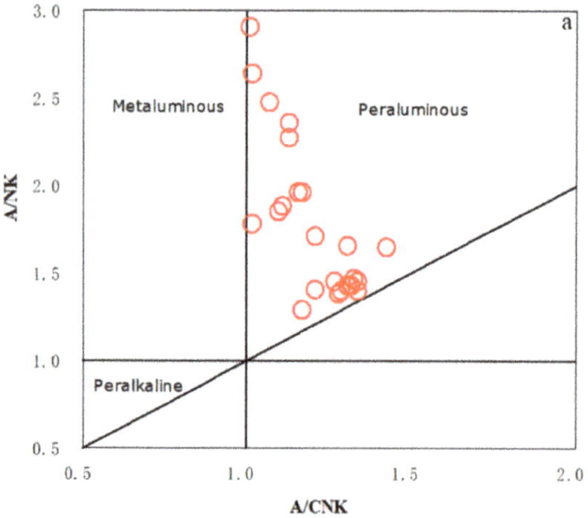

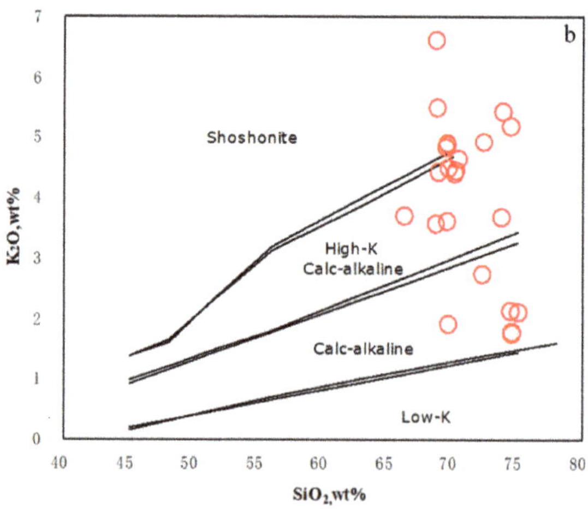

Figure 3. (**a**) A/NK vs. A/CNK (according to Maniar, et al. [14]) and (**b**) K_2O wt.% vs. SiO_2 wt.% plots for the Dahongliutan pluton (according to Peccerillo, et al. [15]).

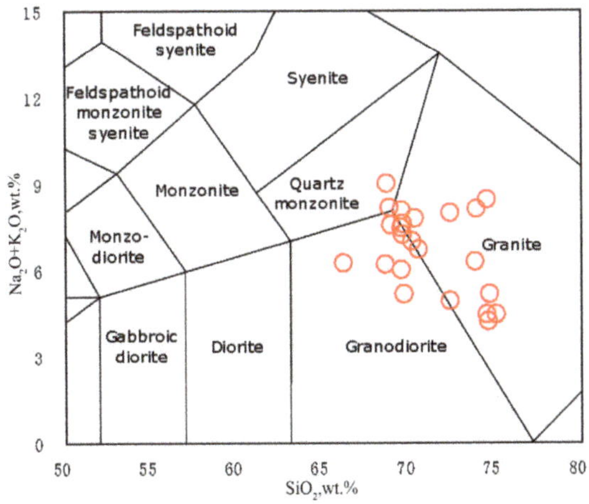

Figure 4. Total alkali vs. silica (TAS) plot of the Dahongliutan pluton samples (according to Middlemost, et al. [16]).

4.3. Trace Element Contents

Table 2 lists the trace element compositions of the samples. Among the large ion lithophile elements (LILEs), Rb is enriched and Sr is depleted (Figure 5a). Among the high field strength elements (HFSEs) Th is enriched, while Ta and Nb are depleted. The observed Sr depletion may be related to the fractional crystallization of plagioclase. HFSE depletion indicates that the magma source was predominantly crustal material.

Table 2. Trace ($\times10^{-6}$) and rare earth element ($\times10^{-6}$) contents of Dahongliutan granite samples.

Sample	P19-01XT01	P20-25XT01	P6-06XT01	P22-55 GS	P22-71 GS	P20-15 GS	D3801GS01	P22-39XT01	P26-88 GS	P20-19 GS	P20-03 GS	P11-15GS01
Component	1	2	3	4	5	6	7	8	9	10	11	12
Rb	194	76.3	179	267	98.99	218	229	331	142	263	173	196
Ta	1.66	1.34	1.2	4.62	1.89	1.89	1	2.07	2.83	3.28	3.23	1.05
Th	9.07	11.32	12.74	17.48	14.63	8.68	9.84	12.9	11.86	11.83	28.84	6.62
Nb	13.96	15.67	12.74	14.89	14.89	14.52	11.2	15.47	12.8	13.59	22.71	12.9
Sr	101	166	69.19	60.98	250	104	118	79.02	152	87.99	143	78.21
Zr	72.3	140	133	106	354	98.42	85.32	110	73.15	86.74	180	65.51
Hf	2.19	7.16	2.62	3.18	9.51	2.47	2.13	2.23	3.3	2.43	6.6	1.93
V	10	118	7.04	16.49	79.22	9.03	8.21	13.02	10.48	9.3	147	4.86
Cr	2.59	27.27	11.54	8.45	63.05	4.44	9.84	15.07	7.5	6.4	86.43	3.66
La	17.8	28.4	20.3	21.5	46.1	17	21.6	25.4	16	27.6	54.8	15.1
Ce	34.5	55.1	42.9	43.4	78.9	32	48.1	54.2	27	54	142	34
Pr	4.11	6.6	5.1	5.57	10.1	3.83	5.16	6.4	3.39	6.47	12.6	3.68
Nd	14.6	24.9	19.1	21	37.2	13.9	18.5	23.7	12.4	23.6	46.8	13.2
Sm	3.46	5.1	4.7	4.76	6.45	3.17	4.1	5.4	2.3	5.16	8.53	3.08
Eu	0.66	1.2	0.57	0.53	1.33	0.7	0.76	0.62	0.73	0.82	1.79	0.39
Gd	3.01	4.5	3.7	3.79	5.66	2.68	3.1	4.2	1.82	4.18	7.97	2.37
Tb	0.46	0.74	0.56	0.56	0.88	0.4	0.41	0.57	0.22	0.56	1.28	0.36
Dy	1.99	3.8	2.3	2.16	4.6	1.61	1.53	2.2	0.87	2.07	6.92	1.57
Ho	0.28	0.75	0.34	0.31	0.91	0.22	0.19	0.3	0.13	0.28	1.39	0.21
Er	0.66	2	0.72	0.72	2.49	0.51	0.44	0.7	0.33	0.66	3.95	0.46
Tm	0.09	0.32	0.1	0.09	0.37	0.07	0.06	0.08	0.04	0.08	0.63	0.06
Yb	0.51	2.2	0.59	0.53	2.23	0.38	0.32	0.55	0.23	0.46	3.83	0.36
Lu	0.07	0.32	0.07	0.07	0.34	0.06	0.05	0.07	0.04	0.07	0.6	0.05
Y	8.20	19.60	12.00	8.60	23.50	6.60	5.40	8.40	3.90	8.00	34.40	6.00
T_{Zr} (°C)	738	770	786	765	872	757	747	768	740	748	780	724
Sr/Y	12.32	8.47	5.77	7.09	10.64	15.76	21.85	9.41	38.97	11.00	4.16	13.04
Rb/Sr	1.92	0.46	2.59	4.38	0.40	2.10	1.94	4.19	0.93	2.99	1.21	2.51
Nd/Th	1.61	2.20	1.50	1.20	2.54	1.60	1.88	1.84	1.05	1.99	1.62	1.99
Nb/Ta	8.41	11.69	10.62	3.22	7.88	7.68	11.20	7.47	4.52	4.14	7.03	12.29
Zr/Hf	33.01	19.55	50.76	33.33	37.22	39.85	40.06	49.33	22.17	35.70	27.27	33.94
La/Nb	1.28	1.81	1.59	1.44	3.10	1.17	1.93	1.64	1.25	2.03	2.41	1.17
∑REE	82.20	135.93	101.05	104.99	197.56	76.53	104.32	124.39	65.50	126.01	293.09	74.89
LREE	75.13	121.30	92.67	96.76	180.08	70.60	98.22	115.72	61.82	117.65	266.52	69.45
HREE	7.07	14.63	8.38	8.23	17.48	5.93	6.10	8.67	3.68	8.36	26.57	5.44
LREE/HREE	10.63	8.29	11.06	11.76	10.30	11.91	16.10	13.35	16.80	14.07	10.03	12.77

Table 2. *Cont.*

Sample	P19-01XT01	P20-25XT01	P6-06XT01	P22-55 GS	P22-71 GS	P20-15 GS	D3801GS01	P22-39XT01	P26-88 GS	P20-19 GS	P20-03 GS	P11-15GS01
La_N/Yb_N	25.04	9.26	24.68	29.10	14.83	32.09	48.42	33.13	49.90	43.04	10.26	30.09
δEu	0.63	0.77	0.42	0.38	0.67	0.73	0.65	0.40	1.09	0.54	0.66	0.44
δCe	0.99	0.99	1.03	0.97	0.90	0.97	1.12	1.04	0.90	0.99	1.32	1.12
Sample	**P25-08XT01**	**P25-1-05 GS**	**D259 GS**	**P25-12 GS**	**P21-20 GS**	**P23-01GS01**	**P21-32XT01**	**P21-08 GS**	**P7-65XT03**	**P9-32 GS**	**P10-01 GS**	
Component	13	14	15	16	17	18	19	20	21	22	23	
Rb	123	132	136	160	119	95.6	53.8	105	164	264	138	
Ta	1.81	2.81	2.32	2.99	1.6	1.4	1.12	1.97	0.99	5.47	1.21	
Th	23.66	27.7	20.74	18.31	8.74	12.64	7.65	7.27	11.26	19.39	13.48	
Nb	13.75	10.62	11.5	13.96	15.27	15.85	15.27	16.38	14.26	15.82	9.5	
Sr	161	188	219	216	264	294	262	316	95.72	76.55	118	
Zr	133	110	137	144	156	156	163	258	79.43	104	113	
Hf	5.31	5.36	6.06	6.45	8.74	5.4	4.38	7.29	1.77	3.11	3.42	
V	83.38	58.11	67.25	85.96	120	120	169	53.36	5.81	12.63	14.62	
Cr	7.82	15.15	11.54	18.55	30.86	55.25	37.19	18.66	0.076	4.54	7.53	
La	30.5	25.3	38	30.2	23.9	45.3	34.1	31.2	23.4	33.3	23.7	
Ce	57.9	45.4	67.8	55.5	44	89.6	64.7	38.8	48.4	65.5	44.7	
Pr	6.9	6.12	8.52	6.76	5.83	9.82	7.4	6.02	6	8.2	5.4	
Nd	25.8	23.3	31.4	25.4	23.4	36.6	28.4	22.8	22.8	30.4	19.5	
Sm	5.4	4.94	6.18	5.4	4.88	6.48	5.1	4.01	5.9	6.48	4.4	
Eu	1.2	0.9	1.13	1.14	1.44	1.53	1.8	1.46	0.77	0.63	0.89	
Gd	4.6	4.41	5.3	4.94	4.49	5.62	4.5	3.6	5.1	5.05	3.99	
Tb	0.81	0.76	0.83	0.86	0.77	0.91	0.71	0.54	0.87	0.65	0.72	
Dy	4.3	4.13	4.46	4.9	4.4	5.08	3.7	2.73	3.7	2.48	3.76	
Ho	0.86	0.81	0.85	0.94	0.88	0.96	0.75	0.52	0.54	0.33	0.63	
Er	2.3	2.33	2.35	2.71	2.43	2.59	2.1	1.38	1.3	0.75	1.48	
Tm	0.39	0.38	0.37	0.44	0.39	0.41	0.34	0.2	0.2	0.1	0.2	
Yb	2.5	2.42	2.3	2.75	2.43	2.69	2.2	1.18	1.2	0.51	1.01	
Lu	0.38	0.38	0.36	0.44	0.39	0.45	0.33	0.18	0.17	0.07	0.14	
Y	24.5	26.7	23.1	26.4	23.5	23.8	18.9	13.9	15.7	9.5	17.4	
T_{Zr} (°C)	767	746	768	769	766	753	746	821	733	768	778	
Sr/Y	6.57	7.04	9.48	8.18	11.23	12.35	13.86	22.73	6.10	8.06	6.78	
Rb/Sr	0.76	0.70	0.62	0.74	0.45	0.33	0.21	0.33	1.71	3.45	1.17	
Nd/Th	1.09	0.84	1.51	1.39	2.68	2.90	3.71	3.14	2.02	1.57	1.45	
Nb/Ta	7.60	3.78	4.96	4.67	9.54	11.32	13.63	8.31	14.40	2.89	7.85	
Zr/Hf	25.05	20.52	22.61	22.33	17.85	28.89	37.21	35.39	44.88	33.44	33.04	
La/Nb	2.22	2.38	3.30	2.16	1.57	2.86	2.23	1.90	1.64	2.10	2.49	
∑REE	143.84	121.58	169.85	142.38	119.63	208.04	156.13	114.62	120.35	154.45	110.52	
LREE	127.70	105.96	153.03	124.40	103.45	189.33	141.50	104.29	107.27	144.51	98.59	
HREE	16.14	15.62	16.82	17.98	16.18	18.71	14.63	10.33	13.08	9.94	11.93	
LREE/HREE	7.91	6.78	9.10	6.92	6.39	10.12	9.67	10.10	8.20	14.54	8.26	
La_N/Yb_N	8.75	7.50	11.85	7.88	7.05	12.08	11.12	18.97	13.99	46.84	16.83	
δEu	0.74	0.59	0.60	0.67	0.94	0.78	1.15	1.17	0.43	0.34	0.65	
δCe	0.98	0.89	0.92	0.95	0.91	1.04	1.00	0.69	1.00	0.97	0.97	

Note: 1–7, Damourite Adamellite; 8–12, Two-mica Adamellite; 13–15, Biotite Granodiorite; 16, Biotite adamellite; 17–18, Biotite Quartz Diorite; 19–20, Tonalite; 21–23, Two-Mica Granite. The calculation method for zircon saturation temperature (TZr) was based on [17,18]. Zircon LA-ICP-MS U-Pb dating (Table 3) was performed on six samples: P22-39TW01, P20-25TW01, P25-08TW01, P25-12, P21-32TW01, and P7-65TW01.

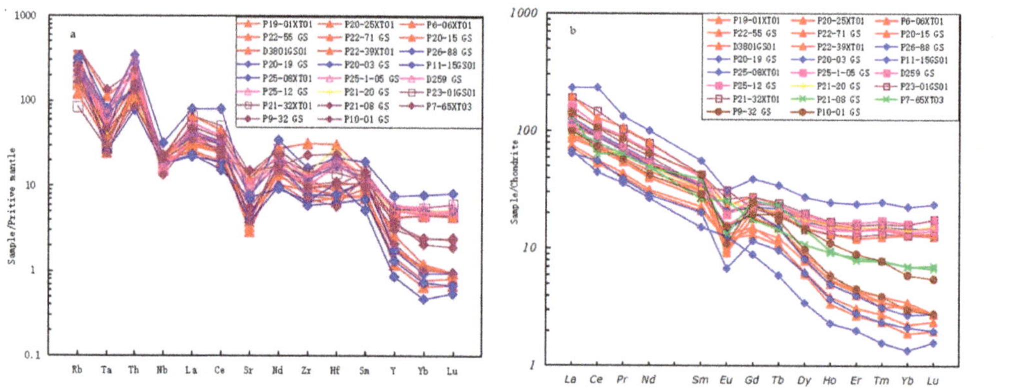

Figure 5. (**a**) Primitive mantle-normalized multi-elemental plots (normalizing values from [17]) and(**b**) chondrite-normalized rare earth element (REE) patterns for the Dahongliutan pluton samples (normalizing values from [18]).

Table 3. Zircon LA–ICP–MS U– Pb isotope analysis results of the Dahongliutan pluton.

Spot No.	Concentration ($\times 10^{-6}$)			Th/U	Isotopic Ratio						Age (Ma)						Concordant
	Pb	Th	U		$^{207}Pb/^{206}Pb$	1σ	$^{207}Pb/^{235}U$	1σ	$^{206}Pb/^{238}U$	1σ	$^{207}Pb/^{206}Pb$	1σ	$^{207}Pb/^{235}U$	1σ	$^{206}Pb/^{238}U$	1σ	
P22-39TW01 Muscovite monzogranite																	
−1	302.12	852.83	1976.09	0.4316	0.0698	0.0013	1.4002	0.0258	0.1446	0.0013	924.07	39.66	889.02	10.90	870.68	7.32	97%
−2	23.03	14.53	621.58	0.0234	0.0697	0.0047	0.3490	0.0226	0.0365	0.0009	920.37	138.89	304.01	17.05	231.16	5.54	72%
−3	140.30	68.74	1522.85	0.0451	0.0903	0.0018	1.1781	0.0280	0.0942	0.0016	1431.79	39.97	790.43	13.04	580.41	9.30	69%
−4	180.20	132.04	576.03	0.2292	0.1590	0.0026	6.3589	0.1086	0.2885	0.0029	2455.55	27.47	2026.62	14.98	1634.21	14.45	78%
−5	50.44	57.90	1580.11	0.0366	0.0501	0.0014	0.2314	0.0066	0.0335	0.0003	211.19	66.66	211.33	5.44	212.27	1.93	99%
−6	127.94	132.19	1494.01	0.0885	0.1225	0.0024	1.5223	0.0467	0.0878	0.0019	1992.28	30.55	939.42	18.79	542.81	11.05	46%
−7	84.97	92.33	2564.62	0.0360	0.0529	0.0055	0.2451	0.0268	0.0332	0.0007	324.13	232.38	222.58	21.84	210.28	4.54	94%
−8	137.01	31.23	4078.24	0.0077	0.0513	0.0016	0.2435	0.0074	0.0343	0.0004	253.77	70.36	221.31	6.07	217.42	2.41	98%
−9	41.04	258.88	1208.14	0.2143	0.0499	0.0023	0.2274	0.0102	0.0332	0.0004	190.82	109.24	208.09	8.40	210.83	2.61	98%
−10	38.51	138.15	837.89	0.1649	0.0561	0.0019	0.3353	0.0113	0.0434	0.0005	457.45	69.44	293.61	8.61	274.10	2.84	93%
−11	25.15	83.18	736.78	0.1129	0.0513	0.0032	0.2376	0.0152	0.0338	0.0008	253.77	142.57	216.48	12.45	214.57	4.82	99%
−12	135.18	73.41	4142.90	0.0177	0.0513	0.0016	0.2382	0.0076	0.0335	0.0004	253.77	65.73	216.93	6.21	212.39	2.57	97%
−13	79.88	27.76	2443.36	0.0114	0.0486	0.0013	0.2315	0.0065	0.0343	0.0003	127.87	61.11	211.40	5.33	217.48	2.13	97%
−14	96.17	21.68	2981.31	0.0073	0.0493	0.0014	0.2306	0.0067	0.0339	0.0004	164.90	66.66	210.66	5.49	215.06	2.51	97%
−15	60.47	21.46	1866.72	0.0115	0.0495	0.0035	0.2306	0.0154	0.0337	0.0005	172.31	155.53	210.72	12.73	213.36	3.28	98%
−16	118.40	25.53	3671.23	0.0070	0.0503	0.0012	0.2351	0.0054	0.0339	0.0003	205.63	51.84	214.43	4.41	214.86	1.72	99%
−17	87.58	21.67	2738.73	0.0079	0.0490	0.0012	0.2282	0.0056	0.0338	0.0003	150.09	54.62	208.74	4.66	214.10	1.72	97%
−18	139.54	31.90	4376.51	0.0073	0.0512	0.0013	0.2385	0.0064	0.0337	0.0004	255.62	59.25	217.17	5.21	213.41	2.21	98%
−19	82.24	34.41	2584.66	0.0133	0.0485	0.0014	0.2262	0.0065	0.0339	0.0003	124.16	70.36	207.07	5.41	214.65	2.10	96%
−20	96.28	26.93	3096.95	0.0087	0.0531	0.0014	0.2436	0.0065	0.0333	0.0004	344.50	59.25	221.38	5.31	210.90	2.42	95%
P20-25TW01 Mica monzogranite																	
−1	45.30	52.33	1317.43	0.0397	0.0501	0.0015	0.2338	0.0069	0.0338	0.0003	198.23	66.66	213.32	5.72	214.16	1.95	99%
−2	15.76	269.95	388.84	0.6942	0.0528	0.0024	0.2425	0.0109	0.0341	0.0004	316.73	105.55	220.50	8.90	215.96	2.78	97%
−3	46.52	488.85	1294.04	0.3778	0.0510	0.0019	0.2416	0.0095	0.0345	0.0005	238.96	87.02	219.75	7.79	218.64	3.23	99%
−4	45.13	784.04	1156.44	0.6780	0.0523	0.0018	0.2460	0.0086	0.0341	0.0004	298.21	79.62	223.35	7.05	216.09	2.23	96%
−5	72.95	9.06	2155.72	0.0042	0.0515	0.0020	0.2426	0.0095	0.0341	0.0004	261.18	88.88	220.58	7.79	216.07	2.35	97%
−6	74.21	472.44	2100.50	0.2249	0.0512	0.0014	0.2429	0.0066	0.0342	0.0003	250.07	61.10	220.76	5.37	216.76	2.05	98%
−7	17.97	372.01	455.73	0.8163	0.0610	0.0058	0.2743	0.0239	0.0332	0.0009	638.91	203.68	246.14	19.06	210.49	5.53	84%
−8	98.08	940.34	2656.71	0.3540	0.0521	0.0014	0.2474	0.0067	0.0343	0.0004	287.10	59.25	224.42	5.42	217.67	2.58	96%
−9	68.00	795.69	1836.14	0.4334	0.0495	0.0016	0.2368	0.0075	0.0346	0.0004	172.31	78.69	215.81	6.19	219.41	2.39	98%
−10	111.50	754.07	3143.51	0.2399	0.0515	0.0018	0.2432	0.0079	0.0343	0.0005	264.88	78.69	221.05	6.46	217.44	3.28	98%

Table 3. *Cont.*

Spot No.	Concentration ($\times 10^{-6}$)			Th/U	Isotopic Ratio						Age (Ma)						Concordant
	Pb	Th	U		$^{207}Pb/^{206}Pb$	1σ	$^{207}Pb/^{235}U$	1σ	$^{206}Pb/^{238}U$	1σ	$^{207}Pb/^{206}Pb$	1σ	$^{207}Pb/^{235}U$	1σ	$^{206}Pb/^{238}U$	1σ	
P25-08TW01 Biotite granodiorite																	
−1	67.66	524.81	1851.05	0.2835	0.0514	0.0014	0.2360	0.0063	0.0332	0.0003	261.18	62.95	215.13	5.21	210.69	1.84	97%
−2	66.19	475.55	1834.40	0.2592	0.0517	0.0013	0.2377	0.0060	0.0333	0.0003	333.39	59.25	216.52	4.91	211.35	1.85	97%
−3	80.01	531.24	2201.39	0.2413	0.0497	0.0012	0.2326	0.0056	0.0338	0.0003	188.97	55.55	212.37	4.63	214.09	1.68	99%
−4	69.20	587.07	1879.92	0.3123	0.0507	0.0013	0.2380	0.0062	0.0339	0.0003	233.40	59.25	216.74	5.11	215.20	1.87	99%
−5	69.56	618.05	1897.15	0.3258	0.0492	0.0013	0.2301	0.0061	0.0339	0.0003	166.75	62.95	210.29	5.00	214.61	1.82	97%
−6	71.80	612.23	1991.11	0.3075	0.0526	0.0017	0.2417	0.0076	0.0332	0.0003	309.32	76.85	219.85	6.18	210.72	2.02	95%
−7	91.41	625.58	2570.97	0.2433	0.0500	0.0014	0.2345	0.0063	0.0339	0.0003	194.53	62.95	213.91	5.16	214.83	1.96	99%
−8	65.00	464.68	1831.99	0.2536	0.0497	0.0014	0.2310	0.0065	0.0336	0.0003	188.97	66.66	211.01	5.34	213.27	1.63	98%
−9	41.02	291.35	1174.06	0.2482	0.0499	0.0018	0.2281	0.0078	0.0335	0.0004	190.82	85.17	208.64	6.43	212.52	2.50	98%
−10	45.50	314.71	1299.59	0.2422	0.0503	0.0015	0.2348	0.0071	0.0338	0.0003	209.33	39.81	214.17	5.87	214.13	2.05	99%
−11	25.77	188.60	748.27	0.2520	0.0526	0.0036	0.2376	0.0154	0.0337	0.0006	322.28	157.39	216.48	12.64	213.93	3.45	98%
−12	102.61	896.42	2892.67	0.3099	0.0482	0.0014	0.2259	0.0065	0.0339	0.0003	109.35	68.51	206.83	5.39	214.82	1.93	96%
−13	56.53	462.55	1630.22	0.2837	0.0516	0.0016	0.2395	0.0073	0.0336	0.0003	333.39	73.14	218.04	5.97	213.27	1.94	97%
−14	56.95	479.68	1662.06	0.2886	0.0521	0.0017	0.2395	0.0079	0.0333	0.0003	300.06	75.92	217.98	6.44	211.02	1.99	96%
−15	44.84	421.17	1280.93	0.3288	0.0520	0.0018	0.2399	0.0078	0.0336	0.0003	287.10	77.77	218.35	6.39	212.86	2.08	97%
−16	62.86	492.51	1852.86	0.2658	0.0498	0.0014	0.2286	0.0065	0.0332	0.0003	187.12	66.66	209.06	5.36	210.84	1.84	99%
−17	82.07	649.69	2436.01	0.2667	0.0510	0.0015	0.2316	0.0067	0.0330	0.0003	238.96	68.51	211.50	5.51	209.19	1.85	98%
−18	50.79	452.43	1455.21	0.3109	0.0509	0.0020	0.2372	0.0090	0.0339	0.0004	235.25	90.73	216.09	7.35	214.65	2.41	99%
−19	64.26	542.27	1910.07	0.2839	0.0506	0.0016	0.2313	0.0071	0.0332	0.0003	233.40	72.21	211.23	5.82	210.30	2.14	99%
−20	80.62	819.07	1581.40	0.5179	0.0546	0.0019	0.3415	0.0125	0.0453	0.0007	398.20	76.85	298.34	9.48	285.36	4.16	95%
P25-12TW Biotite monzogranite																	
−1	13.42	175.20	288.28	0.6078	0.0535	0.0019	0.2920	0.0100	0.0396	0.0004	350.06	47.22	260.12	7.90	250.22	2.45	96%
−2	10.04	129.48	255.23	0.5073	0.0509	0.0021	0.2372	0.0104	0.0340	0.0004	235.25	63.88	216.15	8.54	215.26	2.77	99%
−3	59.45	408.14	1627.03	0.2508	0.0506	0.0009	0.2390	0.0043	0.0343	0.0003	233.40	37.96	217.62	3.55	217.36	2.05	99%
−4	31.76	388.16	819.08	0.4739	0.0503	0.0013	0.2342	0.0056	0.0341	0.0004	209.33	93.51	213.69	4.63	216.28	2.73	98%
−5	25.93	223.03	686.87	0.3247	0.0498	0.0012	0.2365	0.0056	0.0345	0.0003	187.12	55.55	215.53	4.63	218.41	2.08	98%
−6	13.97	139.68	372.02	0.3755	0.0488	0.0018	0.2269	0.0083	0.0340	0.0004	200.08	88.88	207.65	6.85	215.36	2.41	96%
−7	65.25	418.79	1813.81	0.2309	0.0494	0.0008	0.2318	0.0043	0.0339	0.0003	168.60	37.03	211.72	3.56	215.03	1.83	98%
−8	61.06	400.61	1695.06	0.2363	0.0507	0.0009	0.2354	0.0044	0.0337	0.0003	227.85	74.99	214.62	3.64	213.46	1.89	99%
−9	51.08	327.85	1409.27	0.2326	0.0507	0.0009	0.2377	0.0042	0.0340	0.0003	233.40	38.88	216.52	3.44	215.71	2.05	99%
−10	56.86	392.45	1578.61	0.2486	0.0487	0.0006	0.2278	0.0035	0.0339	0.0003	200.08	31.48	208.38	2.86	214.77	1.86	96%
−11	48.33	280.82	1311.08	0.2142	0.0497	0.0009	0.2342	0.0036	0.0346	0.0004	188.97	16.66	213.64	2.99	219.49	2.28	97%
−12	39.57	233.66	1107.89	0.2109	0.0492	0.0009	0.2282	0.0046	0.0337	0.0003	166.75	44.44	208.75	3.78	213.56	2.07	97%
−13	8.74	114.47	226.01	0.5065	0.0499	0.0022	0.2290	0.0102	0.0332	0.0004	190.82	108.32	209.40	8.43	210.36	2.50	99%
−14	27.27	256.85	724.63	0.3545	0.0518	0.0014	0.2381	0.0069	0.0333	0.0004	275.99	65.73	216.85	5.69	211.37	2.50	97%
−15	47.44	350.45	1284.03	0.2729	0.0501	0.0014	0.2361	0.0074	0.0341	0.0006	211.19	32.40	215.26	6.09	216.29	3.48	99%
−16	51.65	292.57	1450.63	0.2017	0.0507	0.0009	0.2320	0.0042	0.0332	0.0003	227.85	73.14	211.82	3.47	210.71	2.13	99%

Table 3. *Cont.*

Spot No.	Concentration ($\times10^{-6}$)			Th/U	Isotopic Ratio						Age (Ma)						Concordant
	Pb	Th	U		^{207}Pb/^{206}Pb	1σ	^{207}Pb/^{235}U	1σ	^{206}Pb/^{238}U	1σ	^{207}Pb/^{206}Pb	1σ	^{207}Pb/^{235}U	1σ	^{206}Pb/^{238}U	1σ	
P25-12TW Biotite monzogranite																	
−17	18.58	155.09	496.61	0.3123	0.0516	0.0022	0.2385	0.0106	0.0338	0.0005	333.39	99.99	217.19	8.66	214.33	3.16	98%
−18	57.96	310.12	1584.64	0.1957	0.0521	0.0013	0.2417	0.0058	0.0339	0.0004	300.06	55.55	219.78	4.78	214.72	2.76	97%
−19	57.57	379.31	1576.35	0.2406	0.0517	0.0012	0.2372	0.0052	0.0336	0.0004	272.29	53.70	216.10	4.24	213.07	2.73	98%
−20	38.59	205.86	1066.73	0.1930	0.0508	0.0012	0.2363	0.0060	0.0337	0.0004	231.55	53.69	215.38	4.92	213.66	2.57	99%
P21-32TW01 Tonalite																	
−1	17.94	228.03	509.74	0.4473	0.0555	0.0042	0.2506	0.0182	0.0328	0.0008	431.53	166.65	227.04	14.80	208.11	4.76	91%
−2	24.05	294.05	665.85	0.4416	0.0524	0.0025	0.2395	0.0109	0.0336	0.0005	305.62	109.25	218.03	8.92	213.04	3.13	97%
−3	19.88	402.45	531.17	0.7577	0.0560	0.0050	0.2425	0.0208	0.0324	0.0009	453.75	199.98	220.49	17.03	205.29	5.31	92%
−4	20.78	473.04	547.15	0.8646	0.0551	0.0030	0.2426	0.0118	0.0326	0.0005	416.72	156.46	220.56	9.63	206.67	2.98	93%
−5	18.08	316.03	487.07	0.6488	0.0513	0.0041	0.2380	0.0208	0.0330	0.0008	253.77	185.16	216.74	17.04	209.08	4.78	96%
−6	7.87	112.97	214.98	0.5255	0.0880	0.0050	0.3865	0.0196	0.0326	0.0006	1383.34	108.80	331.78	14.34	206.73	3.77	53%
−7	5.35	80.67	148.36	0.5437	0.1234	0.0079	0.4840	0.0242	0.0329	0.0007	2005.87	114.97	400.79	16.58	208.36	4.39	36%
−8	12.48	203.27	318.20	0.6388	0.0552	0.0072	0.2484	0.0285	0.0334	0.0014	420.42	295.18	225.31	23.16	211.75	8.70	93%
−9	14.72	204.39	399.41	0.5117	0.0558	0.0033	0.2467	0.0141	0.0330	0.0006	455.60	133.32	223.87	11.46	209.06	3.48	93%
−10	23.06	317.26	620.04	0.5117	0.0538	0.0029	0.2452	0.0137	0.0333	0.0006	364.87	122.21	222.64	11.14	211.29	3.95	94%
P7-65TW01 Mica granite																	
−1	164.18	692.74	5157.81	0.1343	0.0498	0.0014	0.2227	0.0056	0.0326	0.0004	187.12	64.80	204.18	4.68	206.83	2.62	98%
−2	158.23	492.13	5001.14	0.0984	0.0501	0.0011	0.2269	0.0052	0.0327	0.0003	211.19	49.99	207.67	4.28	207.53	1.95	99%
−3	73.61	176.23	2391.58	0.0737	0.0500	0.0022	0.2195	0.0091	0.0323	0.0005	194.53	99.99	201.48	7.54	204.70	3.14	98%
−4	146.11	362.61	4667.11	0.0777	0.0503	0.0010	0.2259	0.0045	0.0327	0.0003	205.63	43.51	206.84	3.70	207.54	1.78	99%
−5	160.03	477.05	5115.07	0.0933	0.0500	0.0011	0.2247	0.0046	0.0325	0.0003	194.53	48.14	205.81	3.85	206.42	1.68	99%
−6	80.97	254.96	2570.38	0.0992	0.0496	0.0016	0.2231	0.0072	0.0327	0.0003	176.01	78.69	204.49	5.95	207.34	2.13	98%
−7	57.84	177.80	1843.11	0.0965	0.0480	0.0017	0.2163	0.0075	0.0327	0.0003	98.24	87.96	198.80	6.25	207.39	1.96	95%
−8	143.57	542.75	4583.03	0.1184	0.0480	0.0008	0.2153	0.0038	0.0323	0.0002	98.24	40.74	197.96	3.22	205.17	1.32	96%
−9	128.81	358.66	4094.73	0.0876	0.0479	0.0012	0.2170	0.0052	0.0327	0.0003	100.09	57.40	199.37	4.33	207.62	1.81	95%
−10	140.97	20.06	4652.68	0.0043	0.0489	0.0009	0.2184	0.0042	0.0322	0.0002	142.68	46.29	200.58	3.47	204.54	1.35	98%
−11	106.11	357.47	3393.57	0.1053	0.0478	0.0011	0.2135	0.0045	0.0323	0.0002	100.09	51.85	196.46	3.81	205.06	1.53	95%
−12	71.65	155.28	2273.56	0.0683	0.0485	0.0017	0.2186	0.0076	0.0327	0.0003	124.16	87.95	200.77	6.37	207.27	1.85	96%
−13	151.02	691.05	4729.54	0.1461	0.0500	0.0010	0.2244	0.0045	0.0324	0.0002	194.53	48.14	205.58	3.76	205.52	1.24	99%
−14	138.84	478.89	4420.51	0.1083	0.0505	0.0010	0.2260	0.0043	0.0324	0.0002	216.74	44.44	206.91	3.57	205.68	1.51	99%
−15	52.30	152.66	1673.73	0.0912	0.0510	0.0017	0.2277	0.0075	0.0325	0.0003	238.96	74.99	208.28	6.16	206.18	1.82	98%
−16	171.93	392.78	5537.23	0.0709	0.0500	0.0012	0.2244	0.0058	0.0323	0.0004	194.53	27.77	205.57	4.85	204.93	2.41	99%
−18	69.02	55.40	2280.80	0.0243	0.0494	0.0015	0.2187	0.0065	0.0324	0.0004	164.90	67.58	200.82	5.39	205.72	2.25	97%
−19	106.39	366.79	3372.65	0.1088	0.0495	0.0012	0.2228	0.0054	0.0325	0.0003	172.31	52.77	204.24	4.49	206.18	1.84	99%
−20	97.36	302.10	3096.41	0.0976	0.0520	0.0013	0.2317	0.0056	0.0323	0.0003	287.10	57.40	211.58	4.59	205.08	1.69	96%

4.4. REE Contents

The total REE contents (Table 2) range from 65.5×10^{-6} to 293.09×10^{-6} and the pluton is enriched in light REEs (LREEs) and depleted in heavy REEs (HREEs), indicating pronounced fractionation between the two groups. There is no pronounced Ce anomaly. The δEu is >1 for three samples (P26-88 GS, P21-32XT01, and P21-08 GS), and from 0.34 to 0.94 for the other 20 samples, with relatively pronounced negative Eu anomalies. This indicates that the fractional crystallization of plagioclase occurred during magmatic differentiation. The chondrite standardized REE distribution patterns are all right-inclined (Figure 5b). Eu is depleted, and the distribution curves all exhibit pronounced Eu depletion, indicating that all samples shared the same source material and formation mechanism.

4.5. Zircon U–Pb Ages

Table 3 lists the zircon U–Pb isotopic results. Among the light gray-white, fresh, unaltered granites and diorites (P22-39TW01, P20-25TW01, P25-08TW01, P25-12TW, P21-32TW01, and P7-65TW01), zircons are predominantly elongate (100–300 μm in length with aspect ratios concentrated between 2:1 and 3:1) and transparent to light yellow in color. The crystal surfaces are bright and clear, with straight edges and pronounced rhythmic bands, consistent with the characteristics of magmatic zircons.

The muscovite monzogranite (P22-39TW01) has $^{232}Th/^{238}U$ ratios of 0.0070–0.4316 (average = 0.0741; <0.1), with an abnormal Th/U ratio, indicating that these magmatic zircons crystallized in a magma with a special composition [19–21]. The weighted average age obtained from 14 points is 214.0 ± 1.2 Ma (MSWD = 0.79, n = 14; Figure 6a).

The mica monzogranite (P20-25TW01) has $^{232}Th/^{238}U$ ratios of 0.0042–1.0226 (average = 0.4486; >0.4). A strong positive correlation is present between Th and U, indicating that they are typical magmatic zircons [19–21]. The weighted average age obtained from nine points is 216.6 ± 1.6 Ma (MSWD = 0.47, n = 9; Figure 6b).

The biotite granodiorite (P25-08TW01) has $^{232}Th/^{238}U$ ratios of 0.2413–0.5179 (average = 0.2913), indicating that the Th/U ratios are related to the Th and U contents of the magma and the distribution coefficient between the zircon and magma [19–21]. CL images show clearly developed oscillating bands (Figure 7a), which are characteristic of magmatic zircons. The weighted average age obtained from 19 points is 212.71 ± 0.89 Ma (MSWD = 0.93, n = 19; Figure 6c).

The biotite monzogranite (P25-12TW) has $^{232}Th/^{238}U$ ratios of 0.1930–0.6078 (average = 0.3095), indicating that the Th/U ratios are related to the Th and U contents of the magma and the distribution coefficient between the zircon and magma [19–21]. CL images show oscillating bands (Figure 7b) typical of magmatic zircons. The weighted average age obtained from 19 points is 214.7 ± 1.0 Ma (MSWD = 1.10, n = 19; Figure 6d).

The tonalite (P21-32TW01) has $^{232}Th/^{238}U$ ratios of 0.4416–0.8648 (average = 0.5938; >0.4), with a strong positive correlation between Th and U, indicating that they reflect magmatic crystallization [19–21]. The weighted average age obtained from eight points is 209.3 ± 2.8 Ma (MSWD = 0.45, n = 8; Figure 6e).

The mica granite (P7-65TW01) has $^{232}Th/^{238}U$ ratios of 0.0043–0.1461 (average = 0.0897; <0.1), with an abnormal Th/U ratio, indicating that these zircons crystallized in a magma with a special composition [19–21]. The weighted average ages obtained from 19 points is 205.99 ± 0.79 Ma (MSWD = 0.36, n = 19; Figure 6f).

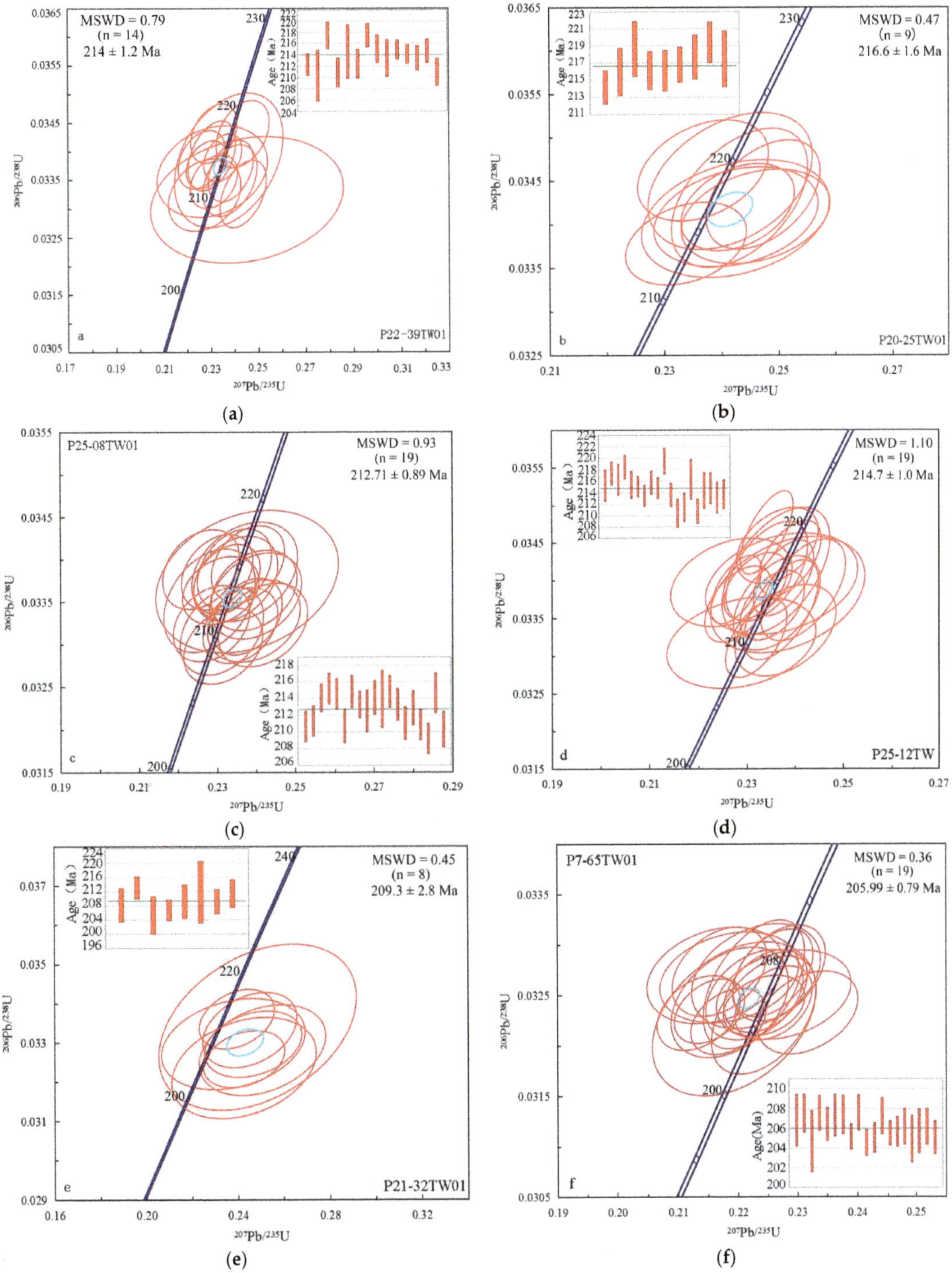

Figure 6. Concordia diagrams for granite samples from the Dahongliutan pluton. (**a**) P22-39TW01, (**b**) P20-25TW01, (**c**) P25-08TW01, (**d**) P25-12TW, (**e**) P21-32TW01, and (**f**) P7-65TW01.

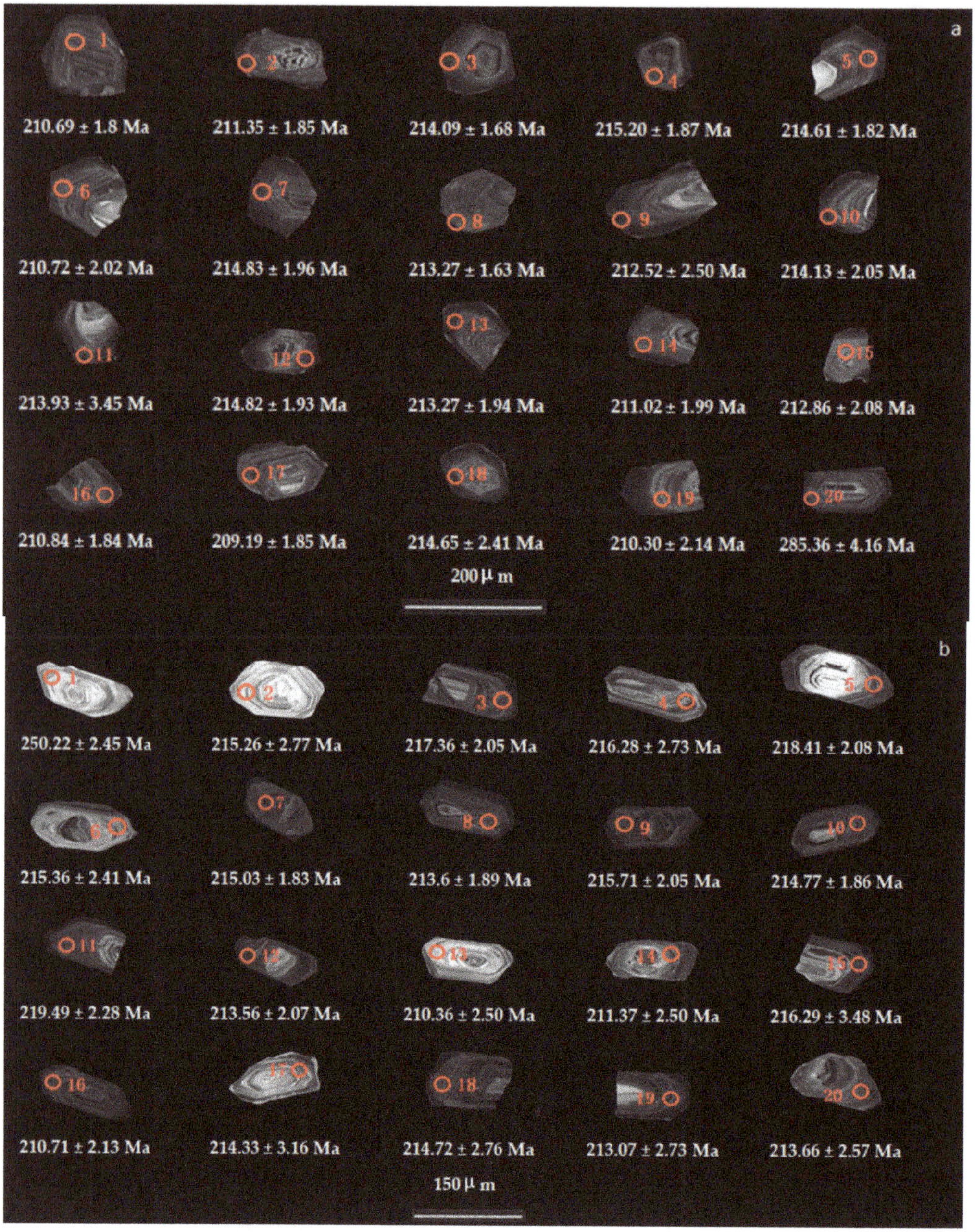

Figure 7. Cathodoluminescence images of selected (**a**) biotite granodiorite (sample P25-08TW01) and (**b**) biotite monzogranite zircons (sample P25-12TW). Solid circles indicate analytical spots used for U–Pb dating.

5. Discussion

5.1. Chronological Significance

Granitoids occur throughout the Western Kunlun region and existing emplacement age data are predominantly concentrated along the China–Pakistan and Xinjiang–Tibet highways [22–28]. The main body of the Dahongliutan pluton is located above the snow line at an altitude of 6000 m. The terrain is relatively steep and the natural environment is harsh, inhibiting systematic field studies. In recent years, chronological studies of granitoids have indicated that the Western Kunlun orogen is a multi-stage intrusive composite batholith [3]. Although early Paleozoic–Mesozoic granites are exposed the region, the late Variscan Indosinian and early Yanshanian periods contained the peak magmatic activity [29]. The Mesozoic Indosinian granitic belt is the largest tectonomagmatic belt in the region [30]. According to the emplacement ages of different rock bodies in the Western Kunlun region (Table 4), the 258–200 Ma granitic bodies form a large-scale magmatic belt that reflects different periods of magmatism under a compressive extensional setting. Chronological studies of Indosinian granitoids provide an important basis for understanding the spatiotemporal distribution, alteration, and mineralization of Indosinian granites in the Western Kunlun orogen.

Table 4. Isotopic ages of Indosinian intrusive rocks in the Western Kunlun region.

Serial Number	Location	Rock Type	Analytical Method	Age/Ma	Data Source
1	Bulun Village	Gnei ss granite	LA-ICP-MS	245	[1]
2	Weizide rock mass	Quartz diorite	LA-ICP-MS	(257.5 ± 4.3)	[31]
3	Korzrov rock body No.9	Gneiss quatz diorite	LA-ICP-MS	253	[32]
4	Gneiss quatz diorite	Gneiss two-mica granite	SHRIMP	(242.9 ± 2.6)	[32]
5	Kayinglik rock mass No.11	Garnet-bearing biotite adamellite	SHRIMP	(240.5 ± 2.6)	[33]
6	Sanshiliyingfang	Granite	Rb-Sr isochron	215	[34]
7	Mustag-Gonger	Granodiorite	LA-ICP-MS	213	[35]
8	Suyingdi	Diorite-porphyrite	LA-ICP-MS	213–210	[35]
9	Bayankala terrane	Adakite	LA-ICP-MS	221–212	[34]
10	Akazi	Granite	LA-ICP-MS	208	[36]
11	Sou Kudi	Granite	SHRIMP	215	[23]
12	Mazha	Granite	SHRIMP	209	[23]
13	Shengliqiao	Biotite	Ar-Ar	(211.2 ± 2.6)	[24]
14	North rock body of Heika station	Biotite	K-Ar	207.8	[32]
15	Thal rock mass	Granodiorite	SHRIMP	(234.2 ± 2.8)	[37]
16	Bandier heath	Granodiorite	LA-ICP-MS	(239.8 ± 1.5)	[38]
17	Kegang	Amphibole granite	TIMS	(228.2 ± 1.5)	[1]
18	Saturasi	Granodiorite	Rb-Sr isochron	215	[1]
19	Keliyang	Lamprophyre	Ar-Ar	237	[23]
20	Pishan	Lamprophyre	Ar-Ar	(228.5 ± 0.3)	[23]
21	Dahongliutan	Monzogranite	SHRIMP	(220 ± 2.2)–(217.4 ± 2.2)	[3]
22	Dahongliutan	Two-mica granite	LA-ICP-MS	(209.6 ± 1.5)	[4]
23	Dahongliutan	Granite	TIMS	(217.5 ± 2.8)	[5]
24	Dahongliutan	Biotite adamellite	LA-ICP-MS	(213 ± 2.1)	[39]
25	Dahongliutan	Damourite Adamellite	LA-ICP-MS	(214.0 ± 0.63)	This study
26	Dahongliutan	Two-mica Monzogranit	LA-ICP-MS	(216.7 ± 0.82)	This study
27	Dahongliutan	Biotitized Granodiorite	LA-ICP-MS	(212.71 ± 0.89)	This study
28	Dahongliutan	Biotite Adamellite	LA-ICP-MS	(214.7 ± 1.0)	This study
29	Dahongliutan	Biotite Quartz Diorite	LA-ICP-MS	(209.3 ± 2.8)	This study
30	Dahongliutan	Two-mica Granite	LA-ICP-MS	(205.90 ± 0.41)	This study

The Dahongliutan pluton is located in the eastern Western Kunlun orogen. Previous studies [3–6] have obtained isotopic ages of 220 ± 2.2–209.6 ± 1.5 Ma. This is consistent with the zircon isotopic ages obtained for the six intrusive units in this study (214.0 ± 1.2,

216.6 ± 1.6, 212.71 ± 0.89, 214.7 ± 1.0, 209.3 ± 2.8, and 205.99 ± 0.79 Ma). Therefore, the emplacement age of the Dahongliutan pluton is 220 ± 2.2 to 205.99 ± 0.79 Ma, indicating that the pluton was likely the product of Late Triassic magmatism.

5.2. Genetic Types and Source Material

The LILE contents of the Dahongliutan pluton indicate Rb enrichment and Sr depletion. The HFSE contents indicate Th enrichment and strongly indicate Ta and Nb depletions. The total REE contents are 65.5×10^{-6} to 293.09×10^{-6} and zircons have inherited cores that share similarities with Himalayan leucogranites [40]. Leucogranites are metasedimentary rocks formed by the dehydration and melting of hydrous minerals [41,42] and are regarded as representative S-type and syn-collisional granites [40]. The Zr contents of the Dahongliutan pluton are relatively low (65.51×10^{-6} to 354×10^{-6}). Even at low temperatures, zircon crystallization also requires Zr contents of ~100×10^{-6} [26]. Therefore, the pluton has experienced zircon fractional crystallization. Only four samples (D3801GS01, P6-06XT01, P22-39XT01, and P7-65XT03) have Zr/Hf ratios of >40; the other 19 samples have low Zr/Hf ratios (17.85–39.85), which supports this conclusion, as zircons have high Zr/Hf ratios (>40). The fractional crystallization of zircon leads to lower Zr/Hf ratios in the residual magma. The presence of inherited cores indicates that the initial magma was Zr-saturated during the formation of the pluton. According to Zr-saturation thermometer calculations, the zircon saturation temperature of the Dahongliutan pluton was 724–872 °C [43,44]. This is similar to the emplacement temperature of I-type granites (750–850 °C). Among the sample, two (P22-71 GS and P21-08 GS) had Zr-saturation temperatures of >800 °C; the remaining 21 samples had Zr-saturation temperatures that were substantially lower than the emplacement temperature of A-type granite (>800 °C), which is the upper limit for the initial magma temperature [45]. However, given that zircon fractional crystallization requires higher temperatures and lower viscosity, the actual temperature of the magma may have been higher [40].

On an S- and I-type granite discrimination diagram (Figure 8) most of the Dahongliutan pluton samples plot in the S-type granite region, and some plot in the I-type granite region. The A/CNK of the pluton is 1.01–1.43 (average = 1.21), which is greater than 1.1 and belongs to the peraluminous granite region. The presence of biotite and Al-rich minerals such as muscovite and garnet is consistent with S-type granites. Dark elliptical or irregular diorite xenoliths of different sizes are common, but are unevenly distributed. The boundaries between the xenoliths and the surrounding rock are clear. Some boundaries have clear condensation edges, indicating that the xenoliths had a magmatic origin. Such boundaries are the result of mixing between relatively more basic and acidic magmas. In summary, the magma that formed the Dahongliutan pluton mainly originated from the crust and was an S-type granite. However, a small amount of upper mantle material was involved in the early stages of magma formation, as reflected by the I-type granite characteristics.

The Dahongliutan pluton samples are enriched in LREEs and depleted in HREEs (La/Yb_N = 7.05–49.9), except for three samples (P26-88 GS, P21-32XT01, and P21-08 GS). One sample has an δEu value of >1, with a pronounced negative Eu anomaly, low Y (~34.4×10^{-6}) and Yb (~3.83×10^{-6}) contents, and a high Sr/Y ratio (~38.97). This is similar to adakite, and indicates that garnet was present during magma formation. The other 20 samples have δEu values of 0.34–0.94, relatively pronounced negative Eu anomalies, and insignificant Sr losses, which indicates that no plagioclase residue was present in the source. Given the lower pressure limit of rutile stability (1.5 GPa), the formation pressure of the Dahongliutan pluton was likely 1–1.5 GPa. Biotite and polysilicon muscovite have stronger affinities for Nb than Ta [46] in granitic magmas. In a low pressure environment (<2 GPa), the melting temperature of polysilicon muscovite is lower than that of biotite. At 1–1.5 GPa, the melting temperature of polysilicon automica is 760 °C, while that of biotite is 820 °C [47]. The Nb/Ta ratios of the Dahongliutan samples are high, which also suggests that dehydration and melting of polysilicon muscovite and biotite may have occurred during magma formation. Thus, the Dahongliutan pluton may have formed via the partial melting of crustal rocks at 1–1.5 GPa.

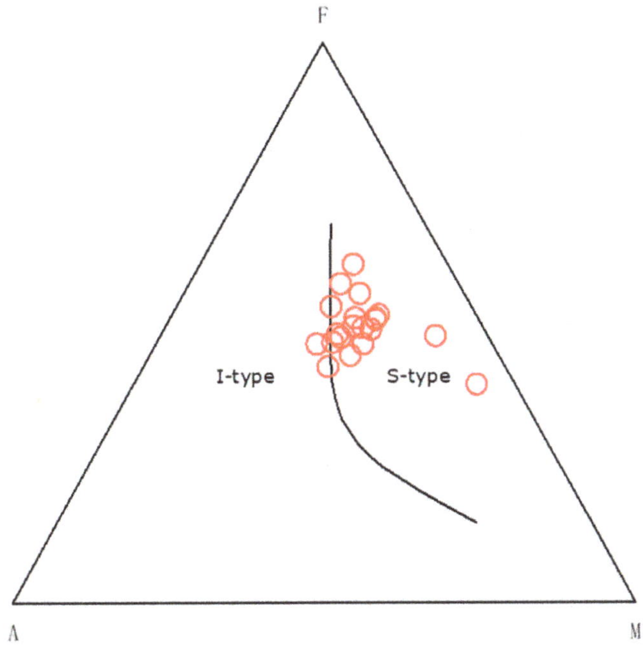

Figure 8. S- and I-type granite discrimination diagram for the Dahongliutan pluton samples (according to Nakada, et al. [48]). A = n (Al_2O_3 − Na_2O − K_2O); C = n (CaO − 3.33 P_2O_5); F = n (FeO + MgO + MnO).

The relative enrichment of LREEs, flat HREE contents, and weak Eu depletion of the Late Triassic granitoids suggests that the magma may have had mixed crustal and mantle sources [49]. The granitoids also have pronounced negative Nb, Ta, and Sr anomalies, which also indicates that their source was predominantly crustal material, and that contamination by mantle-derived magma may have occurred. The Rb/Sr value of a mantle-derived magma is <0.05, that of a mixed crustal and mantle source is 0.05–0.5, and that of a crustal source is >0.5. Four samples have Rb/Sr ratios of 0.21–0.46, indicating a mixed crustal and mantle source. The other samples have Rb/Sr ratios of 0.62–4.38, indicating magma with a dominant crustal source. The Nd/Th values of the samples are 0.84–3.71 (average value = 1.88), which is close to the value of a crustal source (~3) [50], but inconsistent with a mantle source (>15) [51]. The Nb/Ta values of the samples are 2.89–14.40 (average = 8.05), which is close to the crustal Nb/Ta value (11) [52]. The Zr/Hf values range from 17.85 to 50.76 (average = 32.32), which is close to the crustal value (33) [52]. The La/Nb values range from 1.17 to 3.30 (average = 1.99), which is close to the average crustal value (2.58) [52]. Thus, the Dahongliutan pluton predominantly formed as the result of the partial melting of crustal material, but included some mantle-derived material.

5.3. Tectonic Setting and Geological Significance

Many Middle and late Triassic granites [3,24,25,53] in the Western Kunlun orogen are predominantly distributed along both sides of the Mazha–Kangxiwa Fault. The Late Triassic granite belt of the Western Kunlun area is related to the closure of the Paleo-Tethys Ocean. An LA–ICP–MS zircon U–Pb age of 231.4 Ma was previously obtained for the Mushitage pluton [25], while the SHRIMP age was 230.3 Ma [53]. This pluton was the product of a transition from a mainly collisional compressive tectonic setting to a back arc extensional setting [40], and of the detachment of the subducted slab in a post-collisional tectonic setting [53]. Isotopic ages ranging from 213 to 225 Ma have been obtained for the Akaraz Shan granite [22–24,26], which has been postulated to have formed in post-collisional, subduction, and syn-collisional settings [23,24,26]. Studies of the Middle and Late Triassic Yuqikapa, Taer, Mazha, Shengliqiao, and Qitaidaban plutons indicate that they are related to the subduction and closure of the Paleo-Tethys Ocean and subsequent continental collisional orogeny [22,27,28,53].

Zircon U–Pb dating of metamorphic rocks in the Kangxiwa Fault zone and fission track dating of detrital zircons in areas adjacent to the Western Kunlun region indicate that strong compressive uplift occurred between 235 and 267 Ma in the Western Kunlun region. This uplift was closely related to the subduction and collision of the Paleo-Tethys Ocean [1,7,54]. Kang, et al. [55] also found that the Western Kunlun region lacks sedimentary records from the late Permian to the Middle Triassic, which is likely related to the orogenic event that occurred during this period. Before the late Permian, predominantly marine sedimentation occurred; after the Middle Triassic, sediment was composed of continental material, which may indicate the end of the collisional event [55]. Thus, as the Paleo-Tethys Ocean retreated northward until it closed in the Late Triassic [30,56], continental collision occurred along both sides of the Kangxiwa Fault zone. This collision resulted in crustal thickening and large-scale re-melting under a compressive setting, which led to strong magmatism that formed the Dahongliutan pluton on the southern edge of the Kangxiwa Fault zone.

The Dahongliutan pluton is located in the Hoh Xil–Songpan foreland basin, and its long axis trends NW–SE. The pluton is controlled by fault structures consistent with the regional tectonic direction. The steep surrounding rocks were affected by the lateral compression of the pluton, indicating that magma actively expanded and pushed the surrounding rock outward during emplacement. The pluton then expanded further through structural expansion and magmatic encroachment. During the Late Triassic, the study area underwent large-scale crustal uplift, and heat flow values increased accordingly. The melting layer moved upwards and Al-rich granitic magma was produced through the partial melting of the crust. The pluton was emplaced and along a structurally weak zone in the uplift. As the magma ascended through the crust, the viscosity increased, owing to crystallization, and the speed of ascent slowed. When ascent stopped, the magma expanded laterally through tectonic expansion (i.e., along the fault zone). Magma encroachment occurred into the surrounding rock and produced xenoliths in the pluton. The Dahongliutan pluton therefore had a composite emplacement mechanism that was dominated by active expansion supplemented by tectonic expansion and magma intrusion mechanisms.

On a R1–R2 diagram (Figure 9), the data are predominantly in Zone 6 during the same collision period. On an Rb − Y + Nb diagram (Figure 10a), the data fall into the volcanic arc granite and syn-collisional granite areas, but are closer to the syn-collisional area. On an Rb − Yb + Ta diagram (Figure 10b), most data fall into the syn-collisional granite area. Thus, the Dahongliutan pluton may have formed in a syn-collisional tectonic setting. The Late Triassic tectonic setting was the extensional post-collisional orogenic stage of the Paleo-Tethys Ocean [57]. Peak magmatism occurred during the late Hercynian–early Yanshanian period in the Western Kunlun region. However, there is no chronological evidence of magmatic activity from 230 to 250 Ma [56], which may be because the strong compressive stress was not conducive to magmatism [58]. When the tectonic stress changes to post-collisional extension, decompression melting and magmatic upwelling are more likely to occur [58], leading to intense magmatism. With the development of extension and collapse of the orogenic belt, a substantial amount of heat was generated, thereby causing the partial melting of crustal material that ascended and was emplaced. With continuous extension and lithospheric thinning, large-scale magma upwelling formed the Late Triassic intrusive rocks in the Western Kunlun region.

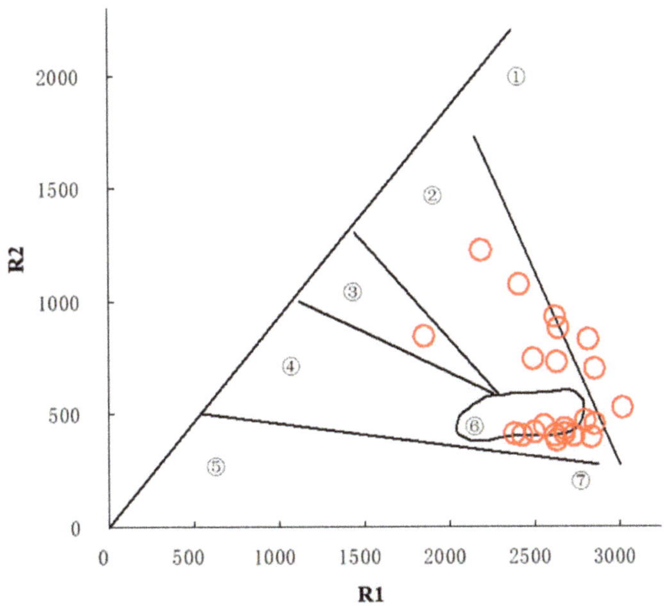

Figure 9. R1–R2 diagram for the Dahongliutan pluton (according to Batchelor, et al. [59]). ① R1: 4Si-11(Na + K) − 2(Fe + Ti); R2: 6Ca + 2Mg + Al; Mantle anorthosite granite; ② Destructive active plate edge (before plate collision) granite; ③ Granite from the uplift stage after plate collision; ④ Late tectonic granite; ⑤ Non-orogenic A-type granite; ⑥ Syn-collisional (S-type) granite; ⑦ Post-orogenic A-type granite.

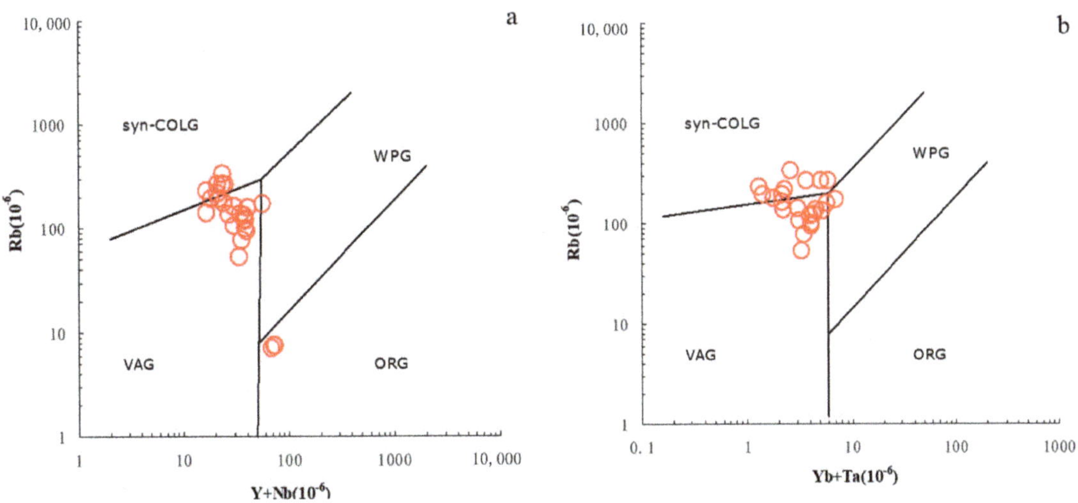

Figure 10. (**a**) Y + Nb vs. Rb and (**b**) Yb + Ta vs. Rb diagrams for the Dahongliutan pluton (according to Pearce, et al. [17]) (WPG: within-plate granite; VAG: volcanic arc granite; syn-COLG: syn-collisional granite, ORG: ocean ridge granite).

5.4. Implications for Geologic Prospecting

Magmatism in the study area not only provided metallogenic hydrothermal fluids, but also promoted the activation, migration, and enrichment of metallogenic elements in the surrounding rock, which is often accompanied by mineralization. Minerals often form in or around plutons. Spatially, most mineralized areas are concentrated in the internal and external contact zones between the Late Triassic pluton and the surrounding rock. Compared with their average crustal abundances, the elements enriched in the Late Triassic pluton include Pb, Zn, W, Sn, Mo, Ag, and Bi. Elements with variation coefficients of >1 include Pb, Zn, As, Sb, Ni, and Ag. The Pb and Zn contents are 1.24–24.37 and 1.03–5.28 times the average value of the Western Kunlun region, respectively. The enrichment of other elements is less pronounced. The Kangxiwanan Ag–Pb, Kalakashihenan Pb–Ag, Ahelangan Pb–Ag, Fulugouxiayoubei Pb–Zn, Fulugou Pb–Zn, and Dahongliutanxi Pb ore deposits are all located in the outer contact zones of Late Triassic rocks. These findings are consistent with geochemical and remote sensing anomalies observed in the study area.

Rare metal mineralization is closely related to the Late Triassic intrusive rocks. The granite pegmatites in the study area were derived from the differentiation of these rocks and provided rare metals, a heat source, and ore-forming materials. The Dahongliutan and Ahelangan Li–Be ore deposits occur in granite pegmatites. Mineralization in the study area is predominantly hydrothermal, and was controlled by NW–SE structures. Mineralization is also mainly distributed in the high strain zones of the regional structures. The orebodies are controlled by a group of joints that are consistent with the overall strike, and exhibit contemporaneous mineralization characteristics. In Triassic strata, Li and Be deposits formed as a result of the intrusion of Indosinian magmatic hydrothermal fluids. The metallogenic mode of these deposits was predominantly crystalline metasomatism. The host rock was granite pegmatite and the surrounding rock was anorthosite biotite quartz schist. The strikes of the orebodies are consistent with those of the regional tectonic trend. The orebodies exhibit discontinuous, lenticular, and vein distributions that are often accompanied by strong albitization. The orebodies are controlled by the pegmatite veins, which have ore bearing properties that are related to the distance between plutons. Poor ore-bearing properties occur near the pluton, while good ore-bearing properties occur further from the pluton [10].

6. Conclusions

Based on analyses of the isotopic ages, mineralogy, and geochemistry of the Dahongliutan pluton in the Western Kunlun orogen, the following conclusions were drawn:

(1) Combined with the zircon CL images and U and Th data, zircon U–Pb dating indicates that the emplacement age of the Dahongliutan pluton is 220 $\pm$ 2.2 to 205.99 $\pm$ 0.79 Ma, and was the result of Late Triassic magmatism.

(2) The Dahongliutan pluton is enriched in silica, alkali elements, and potassium. The A/CNK ranges from 1.01 to 1.43, indicating a strongly peraluminous rock type. LREEs and HREEs are highly fractionated. The negative Eu anomalies of 20 samples are relatively pronounced. The pluton is enriched in HFSEs (e.g., Th) and LILEs (e.g., Rb); however, it is depleted in Sr, Ta, and Nb. Thus, the pluton belongs to the high potassium calc-alkaline peraluminous rock series.

(3) The Dahongliutan pluton is an S-type granite; however, a small amount of upper mantle material was involved during early magma formation. The pluton also exhibits I-type granite characteristics. The negative Eu anomalies, low Y and Yb contents, high Sr/Y ratios, low Nb, Ta, and Sr contents, and high Nb/Ta ratios (2.89–14.40) indicate that garnet and rutile residue were present in the source. Thus, the Dahongliutan pluton may have formed via the partial melting of crustal rocks at 1–1.5 GPa, with the contribution of some mantle-derived material.

(4) The U–Pb ages and regional geology indicate that the Dahongliutan pluton had a composite emplacement mechanism that was dominated by tectonic expansion and magma intrusion, which may have occurred in the same collisional tectonic setting. During

the Late Triassic, the Western Kunlun region entered the post-collisional stage of the orogeny and intrusive rocks formed in an extensional setting.

(5) Late Triassic magmatism provided important heat and ore-forming materials for the mineralization of Pb–Zn, rare metals, Cu, Fe, and other minerals in the study area. Mineralization in this region is closely related to magmatism, which is important for geologic prospecting.

Author Contributions: Conceptualization, B.Z., Z.Z. and Z.S.; methodology, B.Z., Z.Z., Z.S. and H.S.; writing—original draft preparation, B.Z., and Z.Z.; writing—review and editing, B.Z., Z.Z. and H.S.; visualization, B.Z. and Z.Z.; supervision, Z.S., H.S. and L.Y.; funding acquisition, B.Z. and Z.Z. All authors have read and agreed to the published version of the manuscript.

Funding: This research was supported by the China Geological Survey Project (Grant No. 1212011220655) and the Xinjiang Uygur Autonomous Region Geological Exploration Fund Project Management Center Project (Grant No. K15-1-LQ04).

Institutional Review Board Statement: Not applicable.

Informed Consent Statement: Not applicable.

Data Availability Statement: Not applicable.

Acknowledgments: We would like to thank the editor and reviewers for valuable comments and suggestions, which have greatly improved this manuscript.

Conflicts of Interest: The authors declare no conflict of interest.

References

1. Zhang, C.L.; Lu, S.N.; Yu, H.F.; Ye, H.M. Tectonic evolution of the West Kunlun orogenic belt on the northern margin of the Qinghai-Xizang Plateau: Evidence from zircon SHRIMP and LA-ICP-MS dating. *Chin. Sci.* **2007**, *37*, 145–154. [CrossRef]
2. Zhang, Z.; Liang, T.; Feng, Y.G.; Yang, X.Q.; Li, K.; Ding, K.; Wang, Y.Q. Geological feature and chronology study of Kangxiwa berylbearing Muscovite pegmatite in West Kunlun orogenic belt, Xinjiang. *N. West. Geol.* **2019**, *52*, 75–88. [CrossRef]
3. Qiao, G.B.; Zhang, H.D.; Wu, Y.Z.; Jin, M.S.; Du, W.; Zhao, X.J.; Chen, D.H. Petrogenesis of the Dahongliutan Monzogranite in Western Kunlun:Constraints from SHRIMP Zircon UPb Geochronology and Geochemical Characteristics. *Acta Geol. Sin.* **2015**, *89*, 1180–1194. [CrossRef]
4. Wei, X.P.; Wang, K.; Hu, J.; Mu, S.L.; Qiu, Z.W.; Yan, Q.H.; Li, P. Geochemistry and geochronology of the Dahongliutan two-mica granite pluton in western Kunlun orogen: Geotectonic implications. *Geochemistry* **2017**, *46*, 66–80. [CrossRef]
5. Zhang, Q.C.; Liu, Y.; Wu, Z.H.; Huang, H.; Li, K.; Zhou, Q. Late Triassic granites from the northwestern margin of the Tibetan Plateau, the Dahongliutan example: Petrogenesis and tectonic implications for the evolution of the Kangxiwa Palaeo-Tethys. *Int. Geol. Rev.* **2019**, *61*, 175–194. [CrossRef]
6. Ding, K.; Liang, T.; Zhou, Y.; Feng, Y.G.; Zhang, Z.; Ding, L.; Li, K. Petrogenesis of Dahongliutan Biotite Monzogranite in Western Kunlun Orogen:Evidence from Zircon U-Pb Age and Li-Hf Isotope. *Northwest Geol.* **2020**, *53*, 24–34. [CrossRef]
7. Xu, Z.Q.; Qi, X.X.; Yang, J.S.; Ji, S.C.; Li, H.B.; Chen, F.Y. Two types of shear direction, formation time and tectonic significance of Kangxiwa ductile strike-slip shear zone in WestKunlun. *Geol. Bull. China* **2007**, *18*, 1252–1261.
8. Yan, Q.H.; Wang, H.; Qiu, Z.W.; Wei, X.P.; Li, P. Geochronology and Geological Significance of Cassiterite and niobium-tantalum Iron Deposits in Dahongliutan Rare Metalpegmatite Deposit, Western Kunlun. In Proceedings of the Ninth National Congress and 16th Annual Academic Conference of China Mineral and Petrological Geochemistry Society; 2017; pp. 802–803. Available online: http://ir.gig.ac.cn/handle/344008/35548 (accessed on 1 November 2022).
9. Li, K.; Teng, J.X.; Gao, Y.B.; Jin, M.S. Metallogenic characteristics of granitic pegmatite-type rare metal deposits in Dahongliutan area, Xinjiang. *Northwestern Geol.* **2017**, *52*, 206–221.
10. Tu, Q.J.; Han, Q.; Li, P.; Wang, D.H.; Li, J.K. Basic characteristics and exploration progress of thespodumene ore deposit in the Dahongliutan area, West Kunlun. *Acta Geol. Sin.* **2019**, *93*, 2862–2873. [CrossRef]
11. Liu, H.; Wang, G.C.; Cao, K.; Meng, Y.N.; Wang, A.; Zhang, K.X. The detrital zircon fission track ages constraint to tectonic processes in west Kunlun and adjacent regions. *Earth Sci. Front.* **2010**, *17*, 64–78.
12. Liu, Y.S.; Hu, Z.C.; Gao, S.; Günther, D.; Xu, J.; Gao, C.G.; Chen, H.H. In situ analysis of major and trace elements of anhydrous minerals by LA-ICP-MS without applying an internal standard. *Chem. Geol.* **2008**, *257*, 34–43. [CrossRef]
13. Hou, K.J.; Li, Y.H.; Tian, Y.R. In situ U-Pb zircon dating using laser ablation-multi ion counting-ICP-MS. *Miner. Depos.* **2009**, *28*, 481–492. [CrossRef]
14. Piccoli, P. Tectonic discrimination of granitoids. *Geol. Soc. Am. Bull.* **1989**, *101*, 635–643. [CrossRef]
15. Peccerillo, A.; Taylor, S.R.; Peccerillo, R.; Taylor, S.R. Geochemistry of eocene calc-alkaline volcanic rocks from the Kastamonu area, Northern Turkey. *Contrib. Mineral. Petrol.* **1976**, *58*, 63–81. [CrossRef]

16. Middlemost, E.A.K. Naming materials in the magma/igneous rock system. *Earth Sci. Rev.* **1994**, *37*, 215–224. [CrossRef]
17. Pearce, J.A.; Harris, N.B.; Tindle, A.G. Trace-element discrimination diagrams for the tectonic interpretation of graniticrocks. *J. Petrol.* **1984**, *25*, 956–983. [CrossRef]
18. Sun, S.S.; McDonough, W.F. Chemical and isotopic systematics of oceanic basalts: Implications for mantle compositions and processes. *Geol. Soc. Spec. Public Lond.* **1989**, *42*, 313–345. [CrossRef]
19. Wu, Y.B.; Zheng, Y.F. Zircon genetic mineralogy and its constraints on U-Pb age interpretation. *Sci. Bull.* **2004**, *49*, 1589–1604. [CrossRef]
20. Li, C.M. A Review on the Minerageny and Situ Microanalytical Dating Techniques of Zircons. *Geol. Surv. Res.* **2009**, *3*, 161–174. [CrossRef]
21. Zhong, Y.F.; Ma, C.Q.; She, Z.B. Geochemical Characteristics of Zircon and Its Applications. *Geol. Sci. Technol. Inf.* **2006**, *25*, 27–34. [CrossRef]
22. Liu, Z. *Petrogemesis of Early Mesozoic Granites in Western Kunlun Orogen and its Implications for Paleo-Tethys Tectonic Evolution*; Nanjing University: Nanjing, China, 2015; (In Chinese with English abstract).
23. Zhang, Y.; Niu, Y.L.; Hu, Y.; Liu, J.J.; Ye, L.; Kong, J.J.; Duan, M. The syncollisional granitoid magmatism and continental crust growth in the West Kunlun Orogen, China-Evidence from geochronology and geochemistry of the Arkarz pluton. *Lithos* **2016**, *245*, 191–204. [CrossRef]
24. Liu, Z.; Jiang, Y.H.; Jia, R.Y.; Zhao, P.; Zhou, Q. Origin of Late Triassic high-K calc-alkaline granitoids and their potassic microgranular enclaves from the western Tibet Plateau, northwest China: Implications for Paleo-Tethys evolution. *Gondwana Res.* **2015**, *27*, 326–341. [CrossRef]
25. Kang, L.; Xiao, P.X.; Gao, X.F.; Dong, Z.C.; Guo, L.; Xi, R.G. LA-ICP-MS U-Pb Dating of the Zircon from Muztagata Pluton in Western Kunlun Orogenic Belt: Constraints on the Time of Paleotethys Collision. *Geol. Rev.* **2012**, *58*, 763–774. [CrossRef]
26. Yuan, C.; Sun, M.; Li, J.L. Two granitic plutons inCentral Western Kunlun Belt: Their ages and possible sources. *Chin. Sci. Bull.* **1999**, *44*, 1807–1810. [CrossRef]
27. Li, D.P.; Zhao, Y.; Hu, J.M.; Li, X.L.; Zhou, X.K.; Wang, X.L.; Du, S.X.; Xiao, A.F. Zircon TIMS U-Pb dating of the Qitaidaban granite in the westKunlun Mountains and its thermal evolution history. *Geol. China* **2007**, *34*, 1013–1021. [CrossRef]
28. Liao, S.Y.; Jiang, Y.H.; Zhou, Q.; Yang, W.Z.; Jin, G.D.; Zhao, P. Geochemistry and geodynamic implications of the Triassicbimodal magmatism from western Kunlun Orogen, northwest China. *Int. J. Earth Sci.* **2012**, *101*, 555–577. [CrossRef]
29. Kang, L.; Xiao, P.X.; Gao, X.F.; Xi, R.G.; Guo, L.; Dong, Z.C. Geochemical characteristics and petrogenesis of Muztagata intrusion in Western Kunlun orogenic belt and their tectonic significance. *Gelogical Rev.* **2012**, *58*, 763–774. [CrossRef]
30. Han, F.L. Evolution and Metallogenic Background of the West Kunlun Orogenic Belt. Ph.D. Thesis, China University of Geosciences, Beijing, China, 2006; pp. 41–160.
31. Mattern, F.; Schneider, W. Suturing of the Proto- and Paleo-Tethys oceans in the western Kunlun (Xinjiang, China). *J. Asian Earth Sci.* **2000**, *18*, 637–650. [CrossRef]
32. Zhang, C.L.; Yu, H.F.; Wang, A.G.; Guo, K.Y. Dating of Triassic Granites in the Western Kunlun Mountains and Its Tectonic Significane. *Acta Geol. Sin.* **2005**, *79*, 645–652. [CrossRef]
33. Liao, S.Y.; Jiang, Y.H.; Jiang, S.Y.; Yang, W.Z.; Zhou, Q.; Jin, G.D.; Zhao, P. Subducting sediment-derived arc granitoids: Evidence from the Datong pluton and its quenched enclaves in the western Kunlun orogen, northwest China. *Mineral. Petrol.* **2010**, *100*, 55–74. [CrossRef]
34. Du, H.X. The Study of Ore Forming Characters and Prospecting Onientation of Lead-Zinc Deposits from Chalukou to Tianshuihai Ranges in West Kunlun, Xinjiang. Ph.D. Thesis, China University of Geosciences, Beijing, China, 2014. (In Chinese).
35. Song, Y.; Wang, J.; Liu, J.L.; Bao, Z.Y. Chronology, Geochemistry, Hafnium Isotope Characteristics and Tectonic Implications of Muztag Kongur Indosinian Intrusive Rocks. *J. Jilin Univ.* **2015**, *5*, 1418–1435. [CrossRef]
36. Robinson, A.C. Geologic offsets across the northern Karakorum fault. Implications for its role and terrane corelations in the western Himalayan-Tibetan orogen. *Earth Planet. Sci. Lett.* **2009**, *279*, 123–130. [CrossRef]
37. Lu, J.Y.; Yu, X.F.; Sun, F.Y.; Chen, J.; Li, B.L.; Qian, Y. A study of zircon U-Pb dating and ore-forming fluid in the Bandiersirehong iron-copper polymetallic deposit, West Kunlun orogenic belt. *Acta Petrol. Sin.* **2015**, *31*, 2696–2706.
38. Duchesne, J.C.; Berza, T.; Liegeois, J.P.; Vander, A.J. Shoshonitic liquid line of descent from diorite to granite: The Late Precambrian post-collisional Tismana pluton (South Carpathians, Romania). *Lithos* **1998**, *45*, 281–303. [CrossRef]
39. Ding, K.; Liang, T.; Yang, X.Q.; Zhou, Y.; Feng, Y.G.; Li, K.; Teng, J.X.; Wang, R.T. Geochronology, petrogenesis and tectonic significance of Dahongliutan pluton in Western Kunlun orogenic belt, NW China. *J. Cent. South Univ.* **2019**, *26*, 3420–3435. [CrossRef]
40. Wu, F.Y.; Liu, Z.C.; Liu, X.C.; Ji, W.Q. Himalayan leucogranite: Petrogenesis and implications to orogenesis and plateau uplift. *Acta Pet. Sin.* **2015**, *31*, 1–36.
41. Huang, C.M.; Zhao, Z.D.; Zhu, D.C.; Liu, D.; Huang, Y.; Dong, M.C.; Hu, Z.C.; Zheng, J.P. Geochemistry, zircon U-Pb chronology and Hf isotope of Luozha leucogran ite, southern Tibet: Implication for petrogenesis. *Acta Pet. Sin.* **2013**, *29*, 3689–3702.
42. Guo, S.S.; Li, S.G. Petrological and geochemical constraints on the origin of leucogranites. *Earth Sci. Front.* **2007**, *14*, 290–298. [CrossRef]
43. Watson, E.B.; Harrison, T.M. Zircon saturation revisited: Temperature and composition effects in a variety of crustal magma types. *Earth Planet Sci. Lett.* **1983**, *64*, 295–304. [CrossRef]

44. Miller, C.F.; Mcdowell, S.M.; Mapes, R.W. Hot and cold granites?Implications of zircon saturation temperatures and preservation of inheritance. *Geology* **2003**, *31*, 529–532. [CrossRef]
45. Zhao, Z.H. Trace element geochemistry of accessory minerals and its applications in petrogenesis and metallogenesis. *Earth Sci. Front.* **2010**, *17*, 267–286.
46. Stepanov, A.; Hermann, J. Fractionation of Nb and Ta by biotite and phengite: Implications for the \"missing Nb paradox\". *Geology* **2013**, *41*, 303–306. [CrossRef]
47. Hermann, J.; Green, D.H. Experimental constraints on high pressure melting in subducted crust. *Earth Planet Sci. Lett.* **2001**, *188*, 149–168. [CrossRef]
48. Nakada, S.; Takahashi, M. Regional variation in chemistry of the Miocene intermediate to felsic magmas in the Outer Zone and the Setouchi Province of Southwest Japan. *Geol. Soc. Jpn.* **1979**, *85*, 571–582. [CrossRef]
49. Xiao, Q.H.; Deng, J.F.; Ma, D.S. *The Ways of Investigation on Granitoids*; Geological Publishing House: Beijing, China, 2002.
50. Jiang, C.F.; Wang, Z.Q.; Li, J.Y. *The Opening and Closing Tectonics in Central Orogenic Belt, China*; Geological Publishing House: Beijing, China, 2000. (In Chinese)
51. Bea, F.; Arzamasbsev, A.; Montero, P.; Arzamastseva, L. Anomalous alkaline rocks of Soustov, Kola: Evidence of mantle-derived metasomatic fluids affecting crustal materials. *Contrib. Mineral. Petrol.* **2001**, *140*, 554–566. [CrossRef]
52. Gibbs, A.K.; Stuart, R.T.; Scott, M.M. The continental crust: Its Composition and evolution. *J. Geol.* **1986**, *94*, 632–633. [CrossRef]
53. Jiang, Y.H.; Jia, R.Y.; Liu, Z.; Liao, S.Y.; Zhao, P.; Zhou, Q. Origin of Middle Triassic high-K calc-alkaline granitoids and their potassic microgranular enclaves from the western Kunlun orogen, northwest China: A record of the closure of Paleo-Tethys. *Lithos* **2013**, *156*, 13–30. [CrossRef]
54. Xu, Z.; Qi, X.; Liu, F.; Yang, J.; Wu, C. The Kangxiwar Caledonian Khondalite Series in West Kunlun, China, and Its Geological Significance. *Acta Geol. Sin.* **2004**, *78*, 733–743. [CrossRef]
55. Kang, L.; Xiao, P.X.; Gao, X.F.; Dong, Z.C.; Guo, L.; Xi, R.G. LA-ICP MS zircon U-Pb dating of garnet-bearing muscovite-biotite plagioclase gneiss in western Kangxiwar fault of Western Kunlun and its tectonic significance. *Geol. Bull. China* **2012**, *31*, 1244–1250. [CrossRef]
56. Bi, H.; Wang, Z.G.; Wang, Y.L.; Zhu, X.Q. Tectonic magmatic evolution history of the West Kunlun orogenic belt. *Sci. China* **1999**, *37*, 145–154. [CrossRef]
57. Kang, L.; Xiao, P.X.; Gao, X.F.; Xi, R.G.; Yang, Z.C. Neopaleczoic and Mesozoic granitoid magmat ism and teclonic evolution of the westem West Kunlun Mountains. *Geol. China* **2015**, *42*, 533–552. [CrossRef]
58. Wu, F.Y.; Li, X.H.; Yang, J.H.; Zheng, Y.F. Discussions on the petrogenesis of granites. *Acta Petrol. Sin.* **2007**, *23*, 1217–1238. [CrossRef]
59. Batchelor, R.A.; Bowden, P. Petrogenetic interpretation of granitoid rock series using multicationic parameters. *Chem. Geol.* **1985**, *48*, 43–55. [CrossRef]

applied sciences

MDPI

Article

Pore Fractal Characteristics of Lacustrine Shale of Upper Cretaceous Nenjiang Formation from the Songliao Basin, NE China

Tian Dong [1], Lei Kang [2,*], Yifan Zhang [1] and Yuan Gao [1,3]

1 School of Earth Science and Resources, China University of Geosciences (Beijing), Beijing 100083, China
2 College of Mechanical and Electronic Engineering, Dalian Minzu University, Dalian 116600, China
3 State Key Laboratory of Biogeology and Environmental Geology, China University of Geosciences (Beijing), Beijing 100083, China
* Correspondence: kanglei@dlnu.edu.cn

Abstract: The evaluation of pore characteristics in lacustrine shales is of significance for shale oil and gas exploration in terrestrial sedimentary basins. However, due to the complex depositional environments, there have been few reports on the quantitative evaluation of lacustrine pores. In this study, we carry out experiments, e.g., scanning electron microscopy (SEM), nitrogen adsorption, X-ray diffraction (XRD), and rock pyrolysis, on sixteen lacustrine shale core samples of the Late Cretaceous Nenjiang Formation (K_2n^{1+2}) in the Songliao Basin. At the same time, we bring in the fractal dimensions to quantitatively characterize the pores of shale samples in K_2n^{1+2}. The kerogen type of shales in the Nenjiang Formation is mainly type I. The shales of K_2n^{1+2} develop a large number of mineral intergranular pores and a small number of organic pores and mineral intragranular pores. The primary minerals of the samples are clay minerals and quartz. The total organic carbon (TOC) has a correlation with the pore physical parameters, whereas the content of minerals does not correlate significantly with pore development. The average pore fractal dimensions obtained from the analysis of nitrogen adsorption data are D1 = 2.5308 and D2 = 2.6557. There is a significant negative correlation between the fractal dimensions (D1 and D2) and the TOC content: the lower the fractal dimensions, the higher the TOC, and the more the free oil. In low maturity shales with higher TOC content, due to hydrocarbon generation, larger pores with a regular shape (small fractal parameters) can be produced, which can store more free oil. The shale reservoir evaluation of K_2n^{1+2} in the Songliao Basin should be focused on shales with higher TOC and lower pore fractal parameters. Our work provides a reference for the shale oil evaluation of K_2n^{1+2} in the Songliao Basin and complements studies on lacustrine pore characteristics.

Keywords: shale oil; pore structure; fractal dimension; lacustrine; Songliao Basin

Citation: Dong, T.; Kang, L.; Zhang, Y.; Gao, Y. Pore Fractal Characteristics of Lacustrine Shale of Upper Cretaceous Nenjiang Formation from the Songliao Basin, NE China. *Appl. Sci.* **2023**, *13*, 4295. https://doi.org/10.3390/app13074295

Academic Editor: Eduardo Ferreira da Silva

Received: 22 February 2023
Revised: 23 March 2023
Accepted: 27 March 2023
Published: 28 March 2023

1. Introduction

With the increasing demand for oil and gas resources, shale oil, as a kind of unconventional resource, has become a research focus [1–5]. Different from conventional oil and gas reservoirs, shale reservoirs tend to have a more complex pore structure, diverse pore morphology, and stronger heterogeneity [6–9]. The study of shale pore characteristics and heterogeneity is of great significance for oil and gas storage, migration, and exploration [1–5].

Previous studies on pore characteristics have been focused on marine shales, such as the Barnet Shale in the Fort Worth Basin, the Eagle Ford Shale in the Western Gulf Basin, and the Bakken Shale in the Williston Basin in the United States [10–13]. China has also made breakthroughs in the exploitation of shale oil and gas resources, especially with the recent development in the marine shale Ordovician Longmaxi Formation and Cambrian Qiongzhusi Formation in the Sichuan Basin [14–21]. Compared to marine shales, the pore systems of lacustrine shales are less known due to more complex depositional environments and lithofacies in lacustrine shales, which may cause different pore structure characteristics and different influences on shale oil/gas enrichment and production. Therefore, the quantitative evaluation of lacustrine pores is significant but has been seldom reported [18–22].

Shale contains a large number of nano-micron pores and has a very strong heterogeneity. The traditional technical methods for pore structure studies have limitations and cannot effectively describe the pore structure and surface morphology. In this regard, the characterization of shale pore structure requires a multi-technology, multi-scale, and multi-faceted method [2,3,8,23–32]. Mandelbrot proposed the fractal geometry theory to characterize the special structure of many objects with complex shapes in nature; the geometry of shale pores is a typical example of such shapes [33–35]. Pfeifer et al. were the first to demonstrate the fractal characteristics of reservoir pores by molecular adsorption [36]. Pape et al. used SEM to observe rock samples and found that pores in the range of 0.2 to 5.0 μm in sandstones, shales, and carbonates have good fractal properties [35]. Katz and Thompson also supported the theory by confirming the fractal characteristics of several sandstones [37]. With the research on the pore structures of shale, fractal theory has become an effective method to characterize the complexity of pore structures in shale [38–40].

The Songliao Basin in northeast China is a large Cretaceous terrestrial basin and a petroleum-bearing sedimentary basin [41–45]. There are two sets of shales as source rocks and shale oil reservoirs: the Qingshankou Formation (K_2q) and the Nenjiang Formation (K_2n) [42,44,46,47]. Multiple methods have been used to characterize the shale pore structure in K_2q and K_2n of the Songliao Basin, including the application of fractal dimensions. Zhang et al. analyzed the geochemical, pore structural, and fractal characteristics of the K_2n samples from an outcrop section located at the junction zone of the Central Depression and Southeastern Uplift and showed that the fractal dimension of the K_2n shale is positively correlated with the organic matter, clay content, total pore volume, and specific surface area [47]. Liao et al. measured the content and proportion of retained hydrocarbons at different stages of maturity for outcrop samples from K_2n and found that the K_2n shale in Songliao Basin has the strongest retention capacity but the weakest expulsion capacity compared to shales in other basins [48]. He et al. showed variation in the permeability of the low-maturity shale of K_2n with increasing temperatures [49]. Similar to the previous study, Zhang et al. analyzed the shale pore structures of samples from multiple boreholes and inferred a positive correlation between the fractal dimension and the organic matter content [50]. On the contrary, Wang et al. analyzed the pore structure parameters and the fractal dimension of the K_2q shale in the Songliao Basin and found a U-shaped relationship between the fractal dimensions and the TOC content [51]. The different findings on the relationship between the pore structure and shale composition may be due to different studied intervals and discontinuous or weathered samples from multiple cores and outcrop sections.

The SK-1 scientific drilling project, under the International Continental Scientific Drilling Program framework, has recovered ~165 m continuous cores of lacustrine shales from the Nenjiang Formation in Songliao Basin. In this study, we collected 16 samples of shale in the first and second members of the Nenjiang Formation (K_2n^{1+2}) of the SK-1(S) well and conducted scanning electron microscopy, nitrogen adsorption, X-ray diffraction (XRD), and rock pyrolysis analysis. The primary objectives of this study were: (1) to study the pore morphology and pore structure of lacustrine shales, (2) to analyze the relationship between the mineral content and pore space, and (3) to introduce fractal dimensions to characterize the pore structure and analyze its relationship with TOC. Our research complements the vertical variation in the pore characteristics of continuous shale samples and provides a reference for shale oil evaluation of the Nengjiang Formation in the Songliao Basin.

2. Geological Setting

The Songliao Basin, which covers roughly 26 × 10^4 km^2, is a large terrestrial basin in Northeastern China [42–44] (Figure 1). Three tectonic stages are recognized in the Songliao Basin: the syn-rift stage (Late Jurassic), the post-rift stage (Early to Middle Cretaceous), and the structural inversion stage (Late Cretaceous) [44,45]. After the structural inversion stage, according to the topographical characteristics, the basin was divided into six structural units: the northern dipping area, the northeast uplift area, the southeast uplift area, the southwest uplift area, the western slope area, and the central depression area [46,47]. K_2n was deposited in the post-rift stage, with a development of gray-black lacustrine mudstone, oil shale, marl, and tuff [45,46]. At the beginning of the K_2n deposition, the deposition rate accelerated, and the lake expanded rapidly to cover the whole basin. In the later stage, thick gray and black mudstones developed in the deep lacustrine environment until the basin was gradually uplifted, resulting in a shallow lake and the deposition of lighter-color shales [45,46].

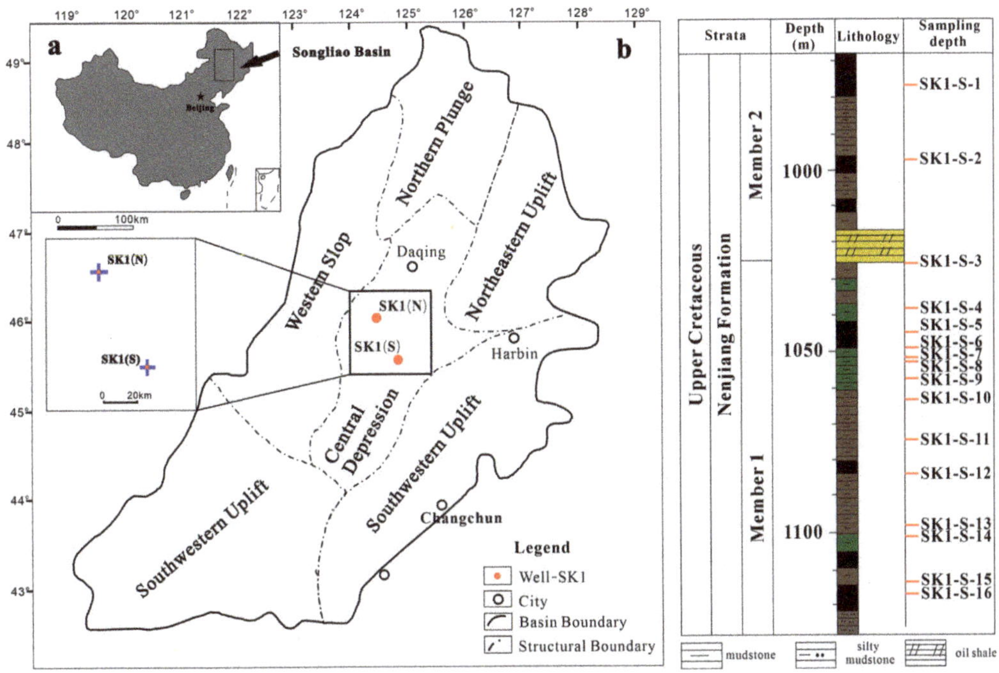

Figure 1. (**left**): (**a**) Location of the Songliao Basin in China; (**b**) the main structural divisions of Songliao Basin and drilling sites of SK-1(S) and SK-1(N). (**right**): Lithology and sampling depth of K_2n^{1+2} in SK-1(S).

The SK-1 scientific drilling site is located in the central depression area (Figure 1) and composed of two boreholes—the south borehole (SK1(S)) and the north borehole (SK1(N)) [52,53]. The coring ratio of SK-1 is as high as 96.46% [46]. The two cores are correlated by a basin-wide oil shale layer of the Nenjiang Formation (Fm) [46]. The coring layer of the south borehole of SK-1 is from the top of the third member of the Quantou Formation to the bottom of the second member of K_2n. This paper focuses on the first and second members of the Nenjiang Formation in the south borehole of SK-1. The oil shale at the bottom of the second member of K_2n represents a lake-level peak during the evolution of the Songliao Basin, with a sedimentary range far beyond the present basin boundary. The lithology of K_2n^{1+2} is mainly black and gray shale and mudstone (Figure 1) [41–46].

3. Samples and Methods

Sixteen lacustrine shale samples were obtained from K_2n^{1+2} with a depth range of 972.26–1128.17 m in the south borehole of SK-1 (Figure 1), and scanning electron micro-scopy, nitrogen adsorption, X-ray diffraction (XRD), and rock pyrolysis analysis were conducted.

Field emission scanning electron microscope (FE-SEM) was used to observe the 2D structure of the pores. Before the samples were observed under the microscope, argon ion polishing technology (Ar-BIB) was used to etch the surface of the samples (Leica RES102 Ion Milling System of Leica company, Wetzlar, Germany). The cross-sections of the samples were bombarded by three independent argon ion beams under a voltage of 7.0 kV and current of 2.6 mA. The polishing time was 5–7 h for each sample. The polished surface was crescent-shaped with an area of about 2 mm^2. For SEM analysis (Apreo FE-SEM of FEI company, Hillsboro, USA, 5.0 kV, 0.40 nA), the samples were treated by carbon plating to make the surface conductive. Then the samples were placed in the electron microscope instrument, the distance between the SEM lens and the top of the sample table was adjusted to about 4 mm, and the backscattering mode (BSE) was used to observe the rock surface. Using a high-resolution electron microscope, the distribution of the organic matter, pore size, shape, contact relationship between the pores and organic matter was clearly observed. At the same time, the plane distribution of inorganic minerals, such as pyrite, and their contact relationship with the organic matter and pores were also observed [54–56] (Figure 2).

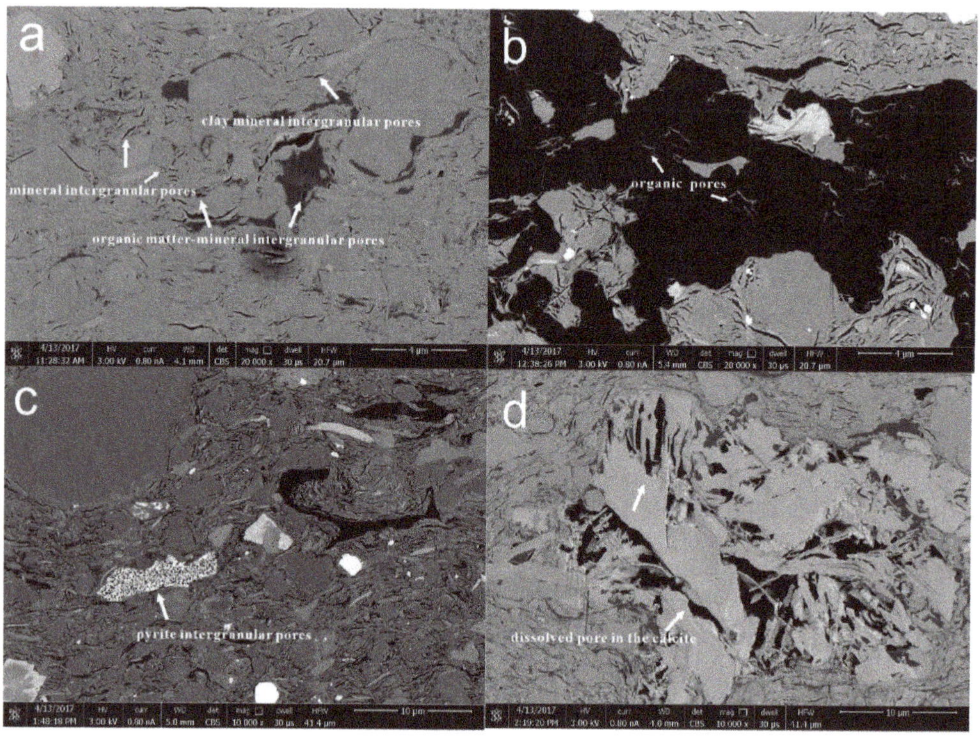

Figure 2. Pore types of shales by SEM in K_2n^{1+2}, Songliao Basin. (**a**) Mudstone sample at 1082.4 m; (**b**) shale sample at 978.2 m; (**c**) mudstone sample at 1052.1 m; (**d**) mudstone sample at 1127.8 m.

Low-pressure N_2 adsorption is an effective method to analyze the nanopore of shale [55,57–62]. The samples were ground to a 40–80 mesh powder (~178–425 μm particle size) and dried at 110 °C for 8 h to remove any adsorbed moisture and volatiles. An

N_2 adsorption experiment was carried out on the ultra-high performance automatic gas adsorption system ASAP 2020 produced by the Micromeritics Company (Georgia State, USA). The range of the pore size distribution was 1.7 to 300 nm. The equivalent surface areas were determined with the Brunauer–Emmett–Teller (BET) method. The pore volumes were calculated using the density functional theory (DFT) model. The average pore diameters were calculated using the adsorption branch of the Barrette–Joyner–Halenda (BJH) model [54,57–66].

The whole rock mineral composition of shale was analyzed by an X-ray diffractometer produced by Rigaku Motor Co., Ltd., Tokyo, Japan. The test conditions were carried out with reference to industry standard SY/T 5163-2010. The whole rock mineral analysis was carried out on samples of 300 mesh powder. With reference to the K value of the international standard sample, the mass percentage of each mineral was calculated using MDI JADE software (6.5, Central South University, Hunan, China).

The analysis of the total organic carbon content (TOC) was carried out in accordance with the national standard GB/T 19145-2003. The Leco CS230 carbon and sulfur instrument was used to analyze the TOC. In the first step, a sample powder of ~10 mg was weighed by electronic balance and put into the porous porcelain crucible (which was heated in a muffle furnace to 1000 °C for 2 h). In the second step, a sufficient amount of 12.5% HCl was added to the electric heating plate at 60 °C for 2 h until the reaction was complete. In the third step, the crucible was put into the filter container and washed with distilled water every half an hour to one hour for three days. In the fourth step, the crucible was dried in a furnace at 60 °C and cooled, and the TOC was determined.

A Rock-Eval 6 pyrolyzer, manufactured by Vinci Technologies, was used for pyrolysis. The samples were crushed into 0.07–0.15 mm, and then weighed and loaded onto sample crucibles, which were put into a pyrolysis oven. The pyrolyzed samples were put into an oxidation oven. Determination parameters: free hydrocarbon (S1) was analyzed at 300 °C for 3 min to detect the free hydrocarbon content in the sample (mg/g); pyrolysis hydrocarbon (S2) was detected at a temperature rate of 25 °C/min between 300 and 650 °C to detect the pyrolysis hydrocarbon content in the sample (mg/g). T_{max} is the pyrolysis temperature corresponding to the highest point of the S2 peak (°C). S3 is the amount of CO_2 produced by the pyrolysis of organic matter (mg CO_2/g Rock), which is generally used to calculate the oxygen index. The pyrolyzable carbon (PC; from the pyrolysis stage), residual carbon (RC; from the oxidation stage), total organic (TOC; sum of RC and PC), hydrogen index [HI; (S2/TOC) × 100], oxygen index [OI; (S3/TOC) × 100], oil saturation index [OSI; (S1/TOC) × 100] were determined and calculated. The analysis and calculation procedures were carried out in accordance with the national standard GB/T 18602-2012.

Correlations among the variables were evaluated by the R^2, the F-test, the T-test, and the *p*-value. In general, the degree of the variables' statistical correlation (R^2) was judged by the magnitude of the correlation coefficient (1.0–0.8: very strong correlation, 0.8–0.6: strong correlation, 0.6–0.4: moderate correlation, 0.4–0.2: weak correlation, 0.2–0.0: very weak or no correlation); the F-test was used for the overall regression equation significance test; the T-test was used to determine the significance of the coefficient of variation; and the *p*-value was used as a measure of the T-test and F-test [67–70]. In simple linear regression, the square of the T-statistic of the T-test for the explanatory variables is equal to the F-test for the overall significance of the equation of the F-statistic, and the two tests are equivalent [63–68]. We measured the correlation and significance of the regression equation using the T-statistic, *p*-value, and R^2: T-absolute value > 1.65, $p < 0.10$ regression coefficient is significant at the 10% level; T-absolute value > 1.96, $p < 0.05$ regression coefficient is significant at the 5% level; T-absolute value > 2.58, $p < 0.01$ regression coefficient is significant at the 1% level [67–70].

4. Results

4.1. 2D Pore Structure

4.1.1. SEM Analysis

Under the scanning electron microscope, the types of pores observed in the SK1-S-2, SK1-S-4, SK1-S-5, SK1-S-6, SK1-S-9, and SK1-S-11 samples were intergranular pores and intragranular pores, but no organic pores were observed. The pores were mainly intergranular pores, including mineral intergranular pores, organic-mineral intergranular pores, and clay mineral intergranular pores. Most of the mineral intergranular pores and organic–mineral intergranular pores were narrow or acicular, and a few were round or sub-circular. The pore diameters observed under the microscope were about 0.1–1 μm. The intergranular pores of the clay minerals were mostly in the shape of long strips, and the pore size was about 0.1 μm (Figure 2a).

Under the scanning electron microscope, the pore types of samples SK1-S-1, SK1-S-8 and SK1-S-12 were observed as mineral intergranular pores, organic–mineral intergranular pores, mineral intragranular pores, and organic pores. Mineral intergranular pores were mainly observed in SK1-S-12 with a few organic pores. The pores of SK1-S-1 and SK1-S-8 were mostly circular or subcircular, and their sizes were between 0.1 and 0.5 μm (Figure 2b).

The pore types observed in SK1-S-3, SK1-S-13, and SK1-S-7 were mainly intergranular pores and mineral intragranular pores, but no organic pores were observed. Intergranular pores of pyrites have developed, which were in the form of microspheres with a pore size of less than 0.1 μm (Figure 2c).

Intragranular dissolution pores are those formed by dissolution inside of the particles of feldspar, carbonate, and other soluble minerals. They are formed by port-like dissolution of the particles around the pores. Intergranular dissolution pores are larger than intra-grain dissolution pores. The intragranular pores observed in the SK1-S-16 sample were developed in the calcite (Figure 2d).

In summary, the shale of K_2n^{1+2} in SK-1(S) has mainly developed intergranular pores, including mineral intergranular pores, organic–mineral intergranular pores, and clay mineral intergranular pores. A small number of mineral intragranular pores have developed, including calcite intragranular dissolution pores. The distribution of the organic pores was uneven, and the number of organic pores was small, which shows that K_2n^{1+2} in Songliao Basin has oil generation potential.

4.1.2. PCAS Analysis

The pore (particle) and fracture image identification and analysis system (PCAS) is professional software for the quantitative analysis of the pore system and fracture system. The software can automatically obtain geometric and statistical parameters and calculate the depth, area, and fractal dimensions of individual pores. The pores are identified by importing the SEM pictures of the core samples into the software and adjusting the grayscale threshold of the pictures. In the SEM pictures, the areas with pores have a darker color compared to other areas, and the adjustment process can make the darker parts of the pictures appear darker and the brighter parts appear brighter, thus identifying the physical parameters of the pores [63].

In this study, the probability entropy and shape factor obtained were mainly calculated by PCAS software [63]. The probability entropy is mainly used to describe the directionality of the 2D structure of the pores, which is calculated as follows (Equation (1)):

$$H = -\sum_{i=1}^{n} P_i \log_n P_i \tag{1}$$

where H is the probability entropy; P_i denotes the percentage of pores in a specific range, for example, between 0° and 10° when i = 1, in the 2D direction ranging from 0° to 180°, and divided into eighteen parts, i.e., n = 18, the probability entropy has values between 0 (all pores are arranged in the same orientation) and 1 (pores have random orientation).

The shape factor (*ff*) is a descriptor of the characteristic shape and reflects the roundness and roughness of the hole edges. It has a maximum value of 1.0 (for a circle) or 0.785 (for a square). Its calculation formula is as follows (Equation (2)):

$$ff = 4\pi S/C^2 \quad (2)$$

where S is the area of the pore, and C is the perimeter of the pore.

The scanning electron microscope images of the shale samples from K_2n^{1+2} were imported into PCAS software, and the organic and inorganic pores could be identified by adjusting the gray level of the images. Taking SEM images of sample SK1-S-1 as an example, the gray level of the SEM images was adjusted to identify the organic pores. Each organic pore was colored with different colors, and the other inorganic pores were eliminated. Then some parameters of each organic pore with different colors were obtained by further calculation in the software (Figure 3) [63].

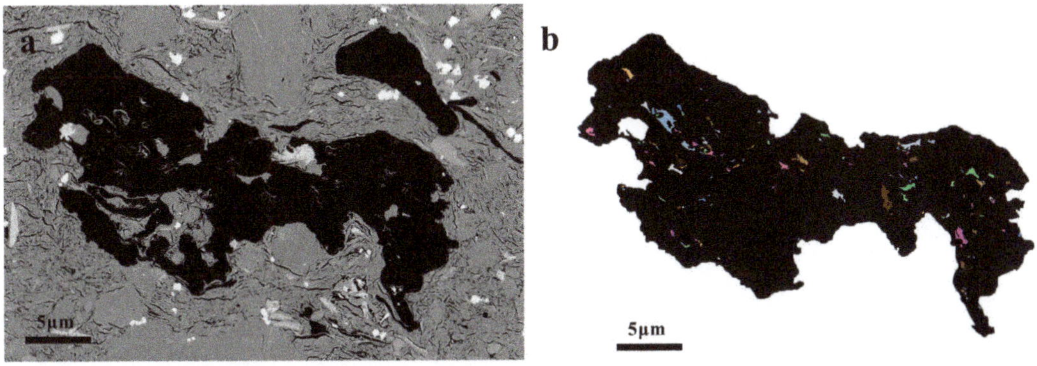

Figure 3. Original (**a**) and colorized (**b**) images of organic pores in sample SK1-S-1 using PCAS software processing.

Using PCAS software, the scanning electron microscope images were divided into organic and inorganic pores, the probability entropy and shape factors of different types of pores were analyzed separately, and the distribution of the pore size were analyzed at the same time (Table 1). By processing 31 scanned images of K_2n^{1+2} with PCAS software, and rejecting the unqualified images and obtaining each parameter of the pores, the following results were obtained by comprehensive analysis: (i) The shape factor of the organic pores was mainly concentrated between 0.3 and 0.7. The average shape factor was 0.56. The average probability entropy of the organic pores was ~0.6 (Table 2). (ii) The shape factor of the inorganic pores was mainly concentrated between 0.5 and 0.6. The average shape factor was 0.54. The average probability entropy of the inorganic pores was ~0.9 (Table 2). (iii) As a whole, the number of inorganic pores was much larger than the number of organic pores.

The use of backscattered electron imaging is beneficial to observe the shape, size, and distribution pattern of nanoscale pores on the smooth and flat surface of the sample after argon ion polishing [10,15–18]. SEM analysis and PCAS analysis showed the 2D pore structure characteristics. As image-processing tests on the number of pores have some limitations, these were specific analyses of typical micro-regions, aiming to complement the information on pore characteristics. To identify the pore types and quantitatively characterize the pore structures, nitrogen adsorption and desorption experiments were applied and are described in the following section.

Table 1. Parameters of each organic pore obtained from sample SK1-S-1 after PCAS software processing. Length: longest diameter; width: shortest diameter; average pore size: average diameter (longest+ shortest)/2.

Pore	Length (μm)	Width (μm)	Average Pore Size (nm)
1	0.245308312	0.160560518	202.9344146
2	0.55289136	0.387186408	470.0388843
3	0.320037996	0.275904161	297.9710785
4	0.191697886	0.081227918	136.4629019
5	0.141878096	0.084477035	113.1775655
6	0.14810557	0.104242495	126.1740323
......	......	......	......

Table 2. Average pore parameters of organic pores and inorganic pores obtained from K_2n^{1+2} by PCAS software.

Porosity	Number	Pore Size (nm)			Average Shape Factor	Average Probability Entropy
		Max	Min	Average		
Inorganic pores	6321	3083	103	225	0.54	0.926294
Organic pores	161	1616	112	329	0.56	0.628375

4.2. N_2 Adsorption and Desorption Isotherms

According to IUPAC classification, there are four types of N_2 adsorption isotherms [61,62]. In this study, there were obvious hysteresis loops in the samples, and all of the hysteresis loops were closed. The existence of a hysteresis loop shows that evaporation from the pores is obviously different from condensation in the pores, and that capillary condensation occurs in mesoporous pores [71]. Useful information about the pore structure can be obtained from the shape of the hysteresis loop. The hysteresis loops of 16 samples were analyzed and it was found that there was only one type of hysteresis loop: type H3 (Figure 4). H3 hysteresis occurs with the accumulation of plate-like particles that produce slit-shaped pores, which corresponds to the slit-shaped and acicular intergranular pores of clay minerals observed under a scanning electron microscope (SEM) (Figure 2).

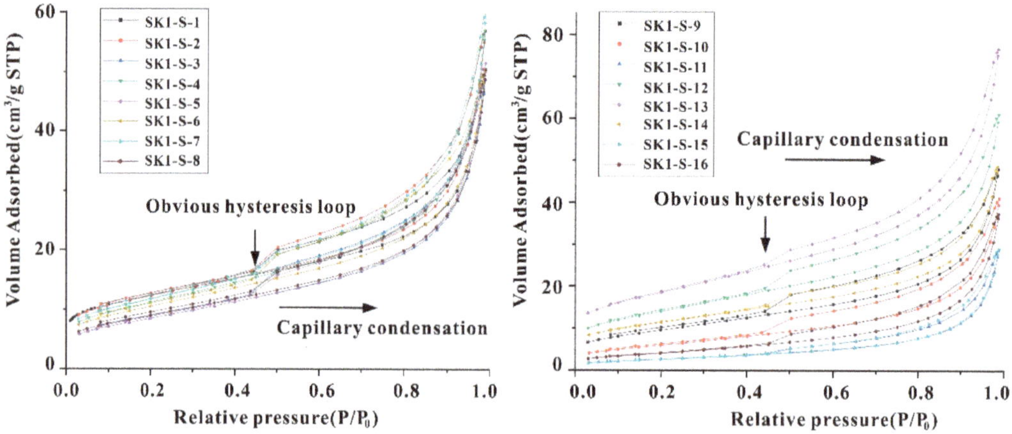

Figure 4. Nitrogen adsorption–desorption isotherms of K_2n^{1+2} samples.

The sample crush size may have an influence on the behavior of low-pressure gas adsorption and desorption. Through experimental analysis, Hazra et al. showed that the macro-pore volume in N_2 adsorption and desorption increased if the particle-crush size was too small [71]. In this study, the crushed size of the samples was in the range of 178–425 μm, which was chosen to take into account the shale matrix and the particle size distribution within the mineral. This size range falls into the medium particle size range in the study of Hazra et al. (2018), which showed no significant influence on the N_2 adsorption and desorption results [71]. At the same time, the surface chemistry of the sample also affects the results of the pore characterization by nitrogen adsorption [72]. The presence of a catalyst on the sample surface attracts the adsorption of nitrogen molecules, resulting in a decrease in the ability of gas molecules to enter the pores and a shift in the measured pore size distribution curve toward smaller pore sizes [72]. The adsorption behavior of nitrogen molecules is also affected by the hydrophilicity or hydrophobicity of the sample surface. The hydrophilic surface attracts nitrogen molecules, resulting in a high measured specific surface area, while the hydrophobic surface repels nitrogen molecules, resulting in a low measured specific surface area [72]. This effect was minimized in the pre-treatments of the experiments to accurately characterize the pore structure.

Some useful information about the surface area, pore volume, and pore size distribution (PSD) can be provided by N_2 adsorption experiments. The equivalent surface area was calculated by the multi-point BET equation (equation describing the theory of adsorption of multilayers based on the Langmuir equation, proposed by Brunauer, Emmet and Teller), and the BET repeat calculation was corrected using "BET Surface Identification" (BETSI) software [23]. The range of the BET surface area of the samples was 9.69–65.91 m^2/g. The pore volume and average pore size were estimated by the Kelvin equation and the Barret–Joyner–Halenda (BJH) model. The pore volume range was 0.0444–0.1187 cm^3/g (average 0.0768 cm^3/g), and the average pore diameter was 8.22–15.40 nm (average 10.10 nm), which is slightly larger than that of K_2q in the Songliao Basin [51] (Table 3).

Table 3. Pore parameters of K_2n^{1+2} by low-pressure N_2 adsorption.

Sample	Average Pore Diameter (nm)	BET Surface Area (m^2/g)	Total Pore Volume (cm^3/g)	Hysteresis Loop Type
SK1-S-1	8.73	44	0.0750	H3
SK1-S-2	9.80	44	0.0881	H3
SK1-S-3	9.58	31	0.0756	H3
SK1-S-4	9.21	40	0.0883	H3
SK1-S-5	10.01	31	0.0798	H3
SK1-S-6	8.74	38	0.0776	H3
SK1-S-7	9.62	42	0.0935	H3
SK1-S-8	9.77	32	0.0781	H3
SK1-S-9	8.84	35	0.0743	H3
SK1-S-10	10.52	22	0.0636	H3
SK1-S-11	14.61	10	0.0444	H3
SK1-S-12	8.26	50	0.0944	H3
SK1-S-13	8.22	66	0.1187	H3
SK1-S-14	8.51	41	0.0752	H3
SK1-S-15	15.03	10	0.0450	H3
SK1-S-16	12.25	16	0.0580	H3

4.3. Fractal Dimensions

At present, several methods to calculate the fractal dimension based on the gas adsorption method have been proposed, including the BET model method, the PSD model method, and the Frenkel–Halsey–Hill (FHH) model method [64,65], but the FHH model qA the most widely used and the most effective method [39,65–67]. In this study, the fractal dimensions of the 16 shale samples of K_2n^{1+2} in the Songliao Basin were calculated by the FHH model. The calculation formula (Equation (3)) is as follows:

$$ln\left(\frac{v_n}{v_{n_0}}\right) = A\left[\ln\left(\ln\left(\frac{P_0}{P}\right)\right)\right] + \beta \quad (3)$$

where v_n is the volume of adsorbed gas at pressure equilibrium P; v_{n_0} is the volume of the saturated adsorption of the monolayer; A is a power-law exponent related to the fractal dimension; β is the intercept; P_0 is the saturated vapor pressure of the gas. The value A can be calculated by plotting the $ln\left(\frac{v_n}{v_{n_0}}\right)$ and $\ln\left(\ln\left(\frac{P_0}{P}\right)\right)$ of the gas adsorption isotherm data, and the slope of the straight line is equal to A. The method for calculating the fractal dimension D_n (Equation (4)) is as follows:

$$D_n = A + 3 \tag{4}$$

Figure 5 shows the FHH diagram of the sample SK1-S-2. At the relative pressures $\frac{P}{P_0}$ of 0–0.5 (R^2 = 0.9999) and 0.5–1 (R^2 = 0.9971), there are two different linear segments because the gas adsorption mechanism was different at different relative pressures (Appendix A) [63,72–77]. The characteristics of the pores were also different. Considering the difference in the gas adsorption behavior between $\frac{P}{P_0}$ < 0.5 and $\frac{P}{P_0}$ > 0.5, the fractal dimensions of the samples were calculated in these two regions, which are defined as D1 and D2. D1 is monolayer–multilayer adsorption controlled by van der Waals forces, and D2 represents the adsorption behavior controlled by capillary condensation at a higher $\frac{P}{P_0}$ [73–77].

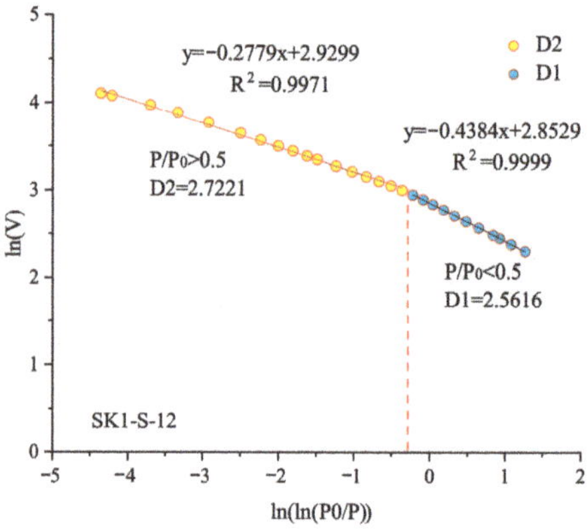

Figure 5. Fractal calculation results (intercept: A of Equation (4)) from FHH model (Equation (3)) of N_2 adsorption at low temperature for sample SK1-S-12 from K_2n^{1+2} of the Songliao Basin, NE China.

The general fractal dimension was between 2 and 3, which was determined by the geometric irregularity and roughness of the surface. The larger value of D represents a more complex and irregular surface (with a value close to 2, the surface is smoother and flatter; with a value close to 3, the surface is rougher and the heterogeneity is stronger) [35–37]. The fractal dimension D1 indicates the irregularity of the sample surface (the larger the fractal dimension D1, the more irregular and rougher surface) [65]. The fractal dimension D2 indicates the irregularity of the pore structure (the larger the fractal dimension D2, the higher the heterogeneity of the pore distribution, the smaller the pore size, the higher the liquid/gas surface tension, and the lower the gas adsorption capacity) [65]. Fractal dimensions D1 and D2 represent the pore surface fractal dimensions and pore structure fractal dimensions, respectively (Figure 5, Appendix A).

The range of the fractal dimension D1 was 2.4406 to 2.6174, and the average value was 2.5308. The fractal dimension D2 ranged from 2.5036 to 2.7197, and the average value was 2.6556. The fractal dimension D values were all higher than 2.5 (Table 4). These results indicate that the shale pores have good fractal properties in both their internal structure and surface. The D2 values were larger than the D1 values of the K_2n^{1+2} shale samples, demonstrating that the pore internal structure has stronger complexity and heterogeneity than the pore surface, while the smaller pores have stronger complexity and heterogeneity than the larger pores. There was a positive correlation (R^2 = 0.7372, T = 6.56, p = 0.00001) between D1 and D2 of K_2n^{1+2} in the Songliao Basin, indicating that these two fractal dimensions can be used to characterize the pore structure and pore surface of the shale [51] (Figure 6).

Table 4. Fractal dimensions calculated by the FHH model.

Sample	$P/P_0 < 0.5$			$P/P_0 > 0.5$		
	Fitting Equation	R^2	D1	Fitting Equation	R^2	D2
SK1-S-1	y = −0.3826x + 2.6889	0.9983	2.6174	y = −0.2818x + 2.6962	0.9991	2.7182
SK1-S-2	y = −0.3904x + 2.6925	0.9998	2.6096	y = −0.3156x + 2.6975	0.9988	2.6844
SK1-S-3	y = −0.4956x + 2.3775	0.9999	2.5044	y = −0.3411x + 2.4528	0.9961	2.6589
SK1-S-4	y = −0.4541x + 2.6328	0.9998	2.5459	y = −0.3229x + 2.6938	0.9978	2.6771
SK1-S-5	y = −0.4915x + 2.3774	0.9998	2.5085	y = −0.353x + 2.4526	0.9963	2.647
SK1-S-6	y = −0.4544x + 2.5658	0.9997	2.5456	y = −0.3038x + 2.6377	0.9969	2.6962
SK1-S-7	y = −0.436x + 2.6787	0.9999	2.564	y = −0.3181x + 2.733	0.9972	2.6819
SK1-S-8	y = −0.4724x + 2.4215	0.9999	2.5276	y = −0.332x + 2.4910	0.9969	2.668
SK1-S-9	y = −0.4883x + 2.4726	0.9999	2.5117	y = −0.3145x + 2.5566	0.9972	2.6855
SK1-S-10	y = −0.5229x + 2.0487	0.9995	2.4771	y = −0.365x + 2.1397	0.9952	2.635
SK1-S-11	y = −0.5476x + 1.2553	0.9991	2.4524	y = −0.4832x + 1.3124	0.9978	2.5168
SK1-S-12	y = −0.4384x + 2.8529	0.9999	2.5616	y = −0.2779x + 2.9299	0.9971	2.7221
SK1-S-13	y = −0.4069x + 3.1168	0.9998	2.5931	y = −0.2803x + 3.1884	0.9962	2.7197
SK1-S-14	y = −0.4129x + 2.6306	0.9997	2.5872	y = −0.2907x + 2.676	0.9996	2.7093
SK1-S-15	y = −0.5594x + 1.2352	0.9988	2.4406	y = −0.4964x + 1.2921	0.9953	2.5036
SK1-S-16	y = −0.5533x + 1.6927	0.9979	2.4467	y = −0.4323x + 1.8071	0.993	2.5677

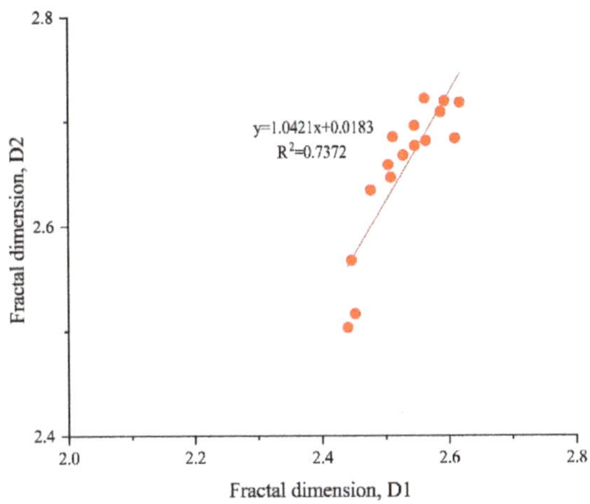

Figure 6. Relationship between fractal dimensions D1 and D2 of K_2n^{1+2} shale.

4.4. Mineralogy

All samples contained clay, quartz, feldspar, calcite, pyrite, and other minerals. Clay minerals were the most abundant, with a content between 40.2 wt.% and 56.1 wt.% and an average of 48.92 wt.%. The second most abundant mineral was quartz, which accounted for 17 wt.% to 35.6 wt.% of the samples (average 27.79 wt.%). The content of carbonate (calcite and dolomite) was between 3.4 and 24.3 wt.%, and the content of feldspar was between 6.5 wt.% and 15.1 wt.%. The content of pyrite was low, not more than 5.5 wt.% (Table 5).

Table 5. Mineral composition of K_2n^{1+2} by XRD (unit: wt.%).

Sample	Quartz	Potash Feldspar	Plagioclase	Calcite	Dolomite	Siderite	Pyrite	Clay
SK1-S-1	35.5	2.2	8.1	2.3	3.4	/	0.5	48
SK1-S-2	35.6	1.5	5.1	2.2	1.3	/	1.9	52.4
SK1-S-3	21.8	2	6.5	8.4	8.3	/	4.3	48.7
SK1-S-4	17.8	1.8	5.1	3.4	0	/	2.4	47.2
SK1-S-5	21.7	1.7	4.8	11.2	8.6	/	3.6	48.4
SK1-S-6	18.9	1.7	6.1	8.8	8.2	7.1	2.8	46.4
SK1-S-7	19.3	1.8	5.5	12.8	3.5	4.5	0.6	52
SK1-S-8	17	1.8	5.2	3.8	20.5	/	0.1	51.6
SK1-S-9	21.5	2.6	7.1	6.8	2.8	5.7	1.4	52.1
SK1-S-10	20.6	1.7	6.7	11.2	4.9	/	2.9	52
SK1-S-11	28.4	1.5	8.1	1.6	14.9	/	1.9	43.6
SK1-S-12	21.1	1.7	7.3	5.8	7.7	/	4.2	52.2
SK1-S-13	19.7	1.9	7.7	8.3	5.9	/	0.4	56.1
SK1-S-14	24.9	2.8	11.3	9	4.2	/	2.9	44.9
SK1-S-15	20.5	1.8	13.3	3.5	8.5	/	5.5	46.9
SK1-S-16	20.3	1.5	12	17.1	4.3	/	4.6	40.2

4.5. Organic Geochemistry

The hydrocarbon generation potential of shale can be evaluated according to the TOC content and hydrogen enrichment. Although the crushed particle size has an effect on the rock analysis results, the rock pyrolysis and the total organic carbon content (TOC) were analyzed more than twice in parallel strictly according to the national standards GB/T 18602-2012 and GB/T 19145-2003 [78] so as to guarantee analytical precision. Flame ionization detector (FID) saturation during pyrolysis is a common source of error found in the analysis of organic-rich rocks, especially those that generate large quantities of hydrocarbons from kerogen during pyrolysis (large S2 yields). FID saturation usually occurs when analyzing type II kerogen with thermal evolution in the immature-to-medium oil window range or with high TOC samples. Considering the TOC content of the samples and the type of kerogen, the experimental results would not have FID saturation [79–82].

The S2 value of the K_2n^{1+2} shale in the Songliao Basin varied greatly, with an average of 24.43 mg HC/g rock, ranging from 0.39 to 75.41 mg HC/g rock. The content of TOC ranged from 0.3 to 8.74 wt.%, with an average of 3.21 wt.% (Table 4). The S2-TOC diagram shows that there is type I kerogen in the shale of K_2n^{1+2} [45] (Figure 7). S2 and the TOC had a good linear correlation, and the correlation coefficient was $R^2 = 0.9781$ (Figure 7). The slope (S2/TOC) indicates that the trend-based HI (hydrogen index) had a value of about 980 mg HC/g TOC (Slope $\times$ 100 = HI = 980 mg HC/g TOC), and the sample was of type I kerogen oil-prone.

The value of free hydrocarbon (S1) was between 0.04 and 3.38 mg HC/g rock, with an average of 0.79 mg HC/g rock. S1 had a positive correlation ($R^2 = 0.8973$, $T > 2.58$, $p < 0.01$) with the TOC (Figure 7). The range of HI was 131 to 975 mg HC/g TOC, and the average was 600.8 mg HC/g TOC. The value of the oil saturation index (OSI) ranged from 7.87 to 43.9 mg HC/g TOC, and the average was 18.62 mgHC/g TOC. The T_{max} value represents the temperature at which the S2 peak reached its maximum, ranging from 434 °C to 443 °C, with an average of 439 °C (Table 6).

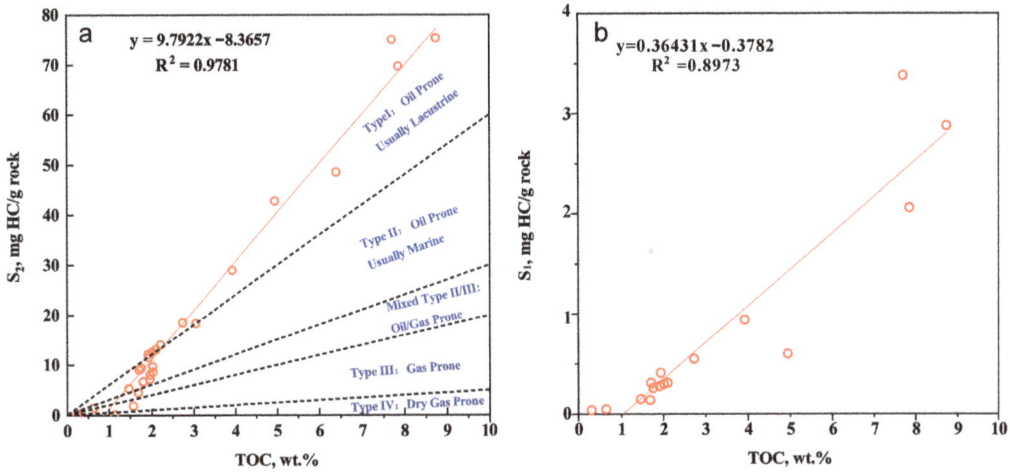

Figure 7. Relationship between TOC content and hydrocarbon generation potential of K_2n^{1+2} shale. (**a**) S2 versus TOC plot showing the quantity and quality of the organic matter, kerogen type, trend HI (HIL), and dead carbon content. (**b**) Relationship between TOC content and S1.

Table 6. Rock-Eval data of K_2n^{1+2} shale, Songliao Basin.

Sample	TOC (%)	T_{max} (°C)	S1 (mg/g)	S2 (mg/g)	HI (mg/g TOC)	OSI (mg/g TOC)
SK1-S-1	1.68	435	0.14	4.59	273	8.33
SK1-S-2	1.46	438	0.15	5.41	371	10.27
SK1-S-3	4.94	442	0.60	42.83	867	12.15
SK1-S-4	1.70	436	0.31	9.16	539	18.24
SK1-S-5	2.73	439	0.55	18.58	681	20.15
SK1-S-6	1.91	439	0.28	12.18	638	14.66
SK1-S-7	2.10	441	0.31	13.22	630	14.76
SK1-S-8	2.01	438	0.30	12.70	632	14.93
SK1-S-9	1.93	434	0.41	11.57	599	21.24
SK1-S-10	3.92	439	0.94	29.05	741	23.98
SK1-S-11	8.74	441	2.88	75.41	863	32.95
SK1-S-12	1.75	439	0.26	9.48	542	14.86
SK1-S-13	0.30	439	0.04	0.39	131	13.42
SK1-S-14	0.64	441	0.05	1.55	244	7.87
SK1-S-15	7.70	441	3.38	75.05	975	43.90
SK1-S-16	7.85	443	2.06	69.78	889	26.24

5. Discussion

As both the generation and storage of shale oil and gas occur in shales, understanding the pore characteristics, e.g., the distribution of pore spaces, the fractal dimensions of the pores, etc., could assist in the study of shale reservoirs. Below, we discuss the relationships among the mineral composition (quartz, clay minerals, etc.), organic geochemical parameters (TOC content, free oil content S1, etc.), and shale pore parameters (e.g., BET surface area, average pore diameter, and pore volume), analyze the trends of pore evolution and the shale oil exploitation potentials of the K_2n^{1+2} shales in the Songliao Basin, and make comparisons with similar pore shales.

5.1. Relationships between Fractal Dimensions and Pore Structure Parameters

The average shape factor was 0.56 for organic pores and 0.54 for inorganic pores (Table 1). These indicate that both the organic pores and inorganic pores in the shale of K_2n have similar near-square pore shapes. The average probability entropy was about 0.6 for the organic pores and about 0.9 for the inorganic pores (Table 2). These indicate that more than half of the pores in the shale of K_2n have same directional property. This is consistent with the fracture pores shown by the hysteresis loop of the nitrogen adsorption isotherm.

The fractal dimension D1 ranged from 2.4406 to 2.6174, with a mean value of 2.5308. The fractal dimension D2 ranged from 2.5036 to 2.7197, with a mean value of 2.6556. The fractal dimensions indicate that the shale pores have good fractal properties in both internal structure and surface, the internal structure of the pores has stronger complexity and non-homogeneity than the surface of the pores, and the smaller pores have stronger complexity and non-homogeneity than the larger ones. The BET specific surface area of the samples ranged from 9.69 to 65.91 m^2/g, the pore volume ranged from 0.0444 to 0.1187 cm^3/g (average 0.0768 cm^3/g), and the average pore size was 8.22–15.40 nm (average 10.10 nm). The average pore diameter of the shale of K_2n was negatively correlated with the fractal dimensions D1 (R^2 = 0.5948, T > 2.58, $p < 0.01$) and D2 (R^2 = 0.9716, T > 2.58, $p < 0.01$), indicating that the fractal dimension increases with the decrease in the average pore diameter (Figure 8). This trend is consistent with the shale data of the Qingshankou Formation recorded by Wang et al. and Cao et al. [51,78]. The lacustrine shale samples with higher D2 values had a more complex pore structure, which may be due to the fact that the shale samples with a smaller average pore size also contained more micropores.

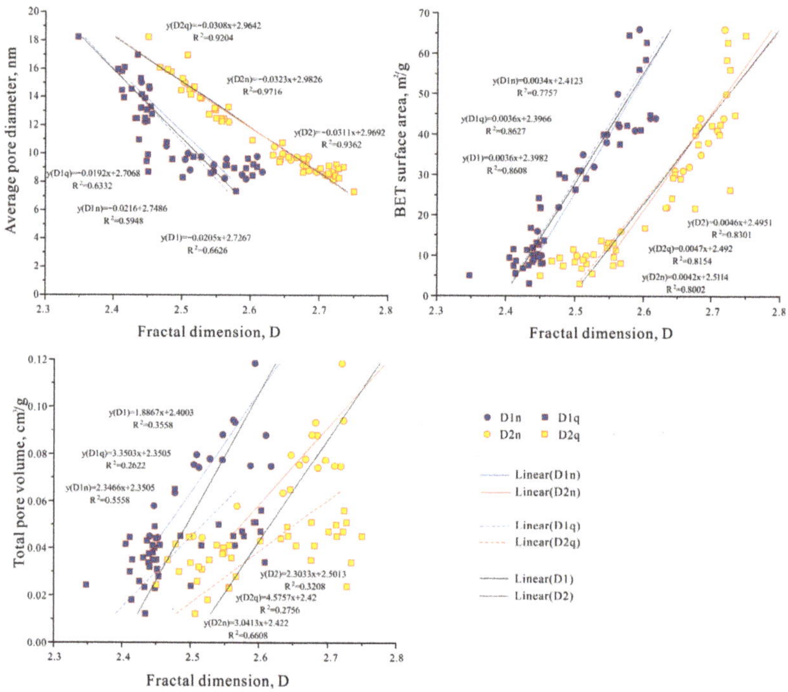

Figure 8. Relationship between fractal dimensions and total pore structure parameters of K_2n^{1+2} and K_2q shale. The K_2q compared to [78].

The fractal dimensions D1 and D2 increased with the increase in the BET surface area. The correlation coefficient between D2 and the BET surface area (R^2 = 0.8002, T > 2.58, $p < 0.01$) was slightly higher than that between D1 and the BET surface area (R^2 = 0.7757, T > 2.58, $p < 0.01$, Figure 8). This correlation indicates that the irregularity of the shale pore structure and the roughness of the surface make the pore surface area increase, and the complex pore structure provides a greater contribution to the pore surface area than the pore roughness itself. The fractal dimensions (D1 and D2) also had a good positive correlation ($R^2 > 0.5$, $T > 2.58$, $p < 0.01$, $R^2_{D2} > R^2_{D1}$) with the total pore volume of the lacustrine shale samples, indicating that the irregularity of the pores further increases the total pore volume (Figure 8). This trend is consistent with the shale data of the Qingshankou Formation recorded by Cao et al. (Figure 8) [78].

5.2. Relationships among the Sedimentary Environment, Fractal Dimensions, and Mineral Compositions

The minerals comprising the K_2n^1 shale in the Songliao Basin are clay minerals (50.2%), quartz (35.6%), calcite (2.3%), and dolomite (2.4%); the K_2n^2 shale consists of clay minerals (48.7%), quartz (21%), calcite (8%), and dolomite (7.3%) (Tables 1 and 5). Compared to the K_2n^2 shale, the K_2n^1 shale consists of more quartz, less calcite, and comparable clay content. During the evolution of the Songliao Basin, K_2n^1 followed the trend of rapid lake development by the end of the Yaojia Formation, and the semi-deep lacustrine sedimentation covered the central depression of the basin [51]. Strong input from terrestrial sources may have caused the higher quartz content but less authigenic calcite. The basin area was further expanded during the K_2n^2 deposition period, and the whole basin was in a deep lacustrine environment with rich organic matter [51], consistent with a decrease in the quartz content and increases in the calcite and dolomite contents.

Through a comparison of the mineral content and the fractal dimensions, it was found that there was no correlation between the quartz and the fractal dimensions. Although the fracturing of quartz could further induce development of the pore space and gain more storage space, quartz may not be the main factor affecting pore development in the samples of this study. There was also no clear correlation between the clay minerals and fractal dimensions, indicating little or no correlation between the clay minerals and fractal dimension D1 ($R^2 < 0.2$, $T > 1.96$, $p > 0.05$) and weak correlation between the clay minerals and D2 ($R^2 > 0.2$, $T > 1.96$, $p < 0.05$, Figure 9). It is interpreted that the contribution of clay minerals to the pore structure complexity of K_2n^{1+2} shale is limited. This is consistent with the Qingshankou formation results (Figure 9).

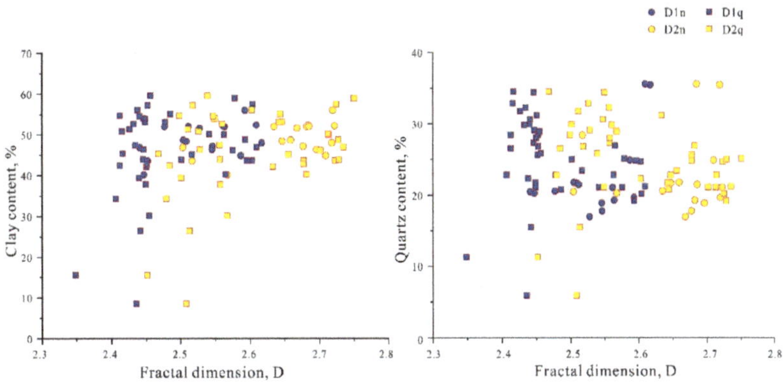

Figure 9. Relationships between mineral compositions and fractal dimensions of K_2n^{1+2} and K_2q shale. The K_2q compared to [78].

5.3. Relationships between TOC Content and Fractal Dimensions of Shale Pores

The fractal dimensions (D1 and D2) show a clear negative correlation with the total organic carbon content, indicating that the fractal dimension decreases significantly with the increase in the TOC content (Figure 10a). This phenomenon is not consistent with the findings of previous studies on the Qingshankou and the Nenjiang Formations [46,50,51,65,78], which are discussed below.

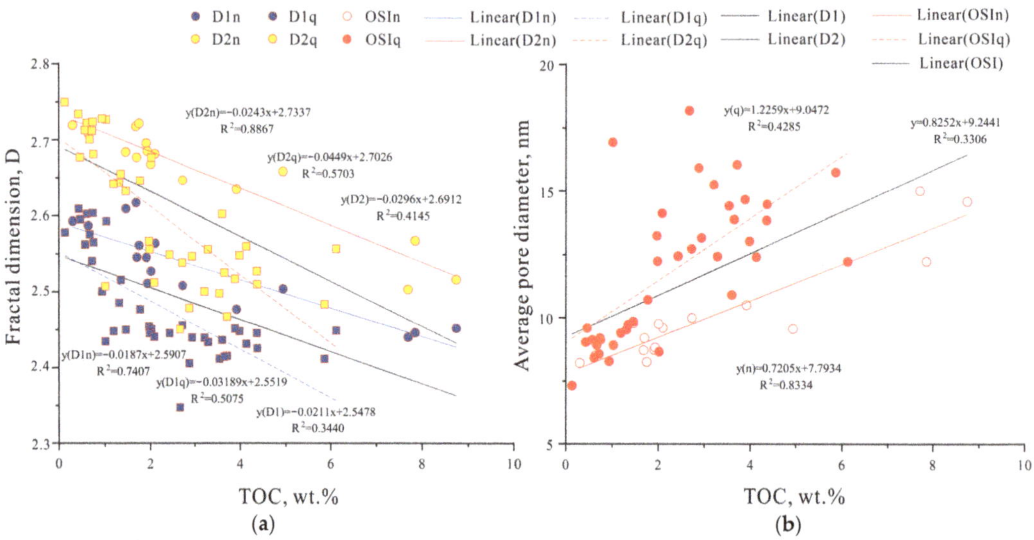

Figure 10. (**a**) Relationship between TOC content and fractal dimensions D1 and D2 of K_2n^{1+2} and K_2q shale samples. (**b**) Relationship between TOC content and average pore diameter of K_2n^{1+2} and K_2q shale samples. The K_2q compared to [78].

For the shales of the Qingshankou Formation within a depth range of 500–2300 m and a T_{max} range of 427–460 °C, Wang et al. found that D1 and D2 decreased rapidly with increasing TOC content when the TOC content was less than 2.5~3.0 wt.% [51]. This is interpreted as the result of hydrocarbon generation and expansion in low-maturity shale to create more uniform mesopores, which further lead to lower D1 and D2 and a higher average pore size [51]. When the TOC value is greater than 2.5 to 3.0%, D1 and D2 increase with the increase in the TOC content [51]. This indicates that the organic pores may collapse due to higher TOC levels, burial, and thermal maturation, leading to more complex and smaller pores.

For the shales of the Nenjiang Formation, previous studies have indicated a positive correlation between the fractal dimensions and the organic matter content [49,51]. However, in the present study, we found a negative correlation between the fractal dimensions and the organic matter content (Figure 10). One possible explanation is that previous studies have selected discontinuous samples from multiple cores and/or outcrop sections. The analysis of our 16 continuously distributed shale samples from the SK-1(S) core indicates that, although the T_{max} is low, the limited maturation process may still cause expansion of hydrocarbons to some extent, thus increasing the pore sizes of the K_2n^{1+2} shale and decreasing the fractal dimensions (Figure 10b). The results of the study by Cao et al. support our explanation (Figure 10).

5.4. Relationships between Fractal Dimensions and Free Oil Content

There was an obvious linear negative correlation between S1, OSI, and the fractal dimensions of the shale of K_2n^{1+2}. The correlation between S1 and D2 ($R^2 = 0.9464$, $T > 2.58$, $p < 0.01$) was better than that of S1 and D1 ($R^2 = 0.6603$, $T > 2.58$, $p < 0.01$), indicating that D2 can be used to characterize the oil content of shale (Figure 11). This is consistent with the negative correlation shown between the Qingshankou Formation S1 and the fractal dimensions (Figure 11, $R^2_{D2q} > R^2_{D1q}$). Shale samples with higher free oil levels always have a lower fractal dimension D2 value, which may be due to the fact that free oil is mainly stored in large pores, and these pores have lower D2 values. Contrary to shale gas adsorption, the molecular diameter of shale oil is much larger than that of shale gas.

Therefore, shale oil is intelligently stored in pores with larger diameters, which causes the phenomenon that shale with higher free oil content usually has lower D2 [51]. As a result, combining the influence of the TOC content on the fractal dimensions and the relationship between the free oil and fractal dimensions, we conclude that the best area for exploitation in the low maturity shales of the Nengjiang Formation in the Songliao Basin would be the area with lower pore fractal dimensions and higher TOC content.

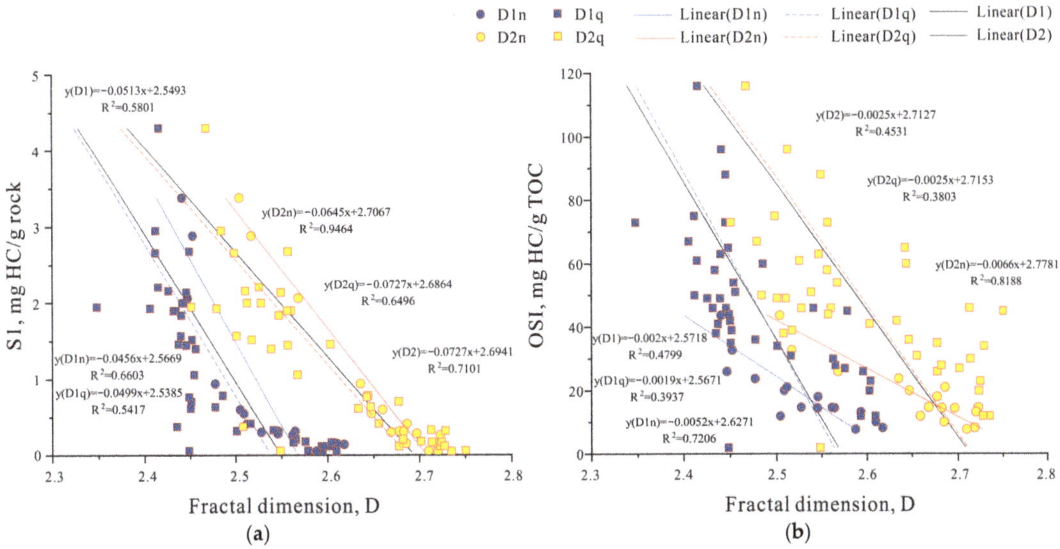

Figure 11. Relationship between fractal dimensions and oil content of K_2n^{1+2} and K_2q shale samples, (**a**) for S1; (**b**) for OSI. The K_2q compared to [78].

6. Conclusions

In this study, based on experiments using scanning electron microscopy, XRD, rock pyrolysis, and nitrogen adsorption, the shale pores of K_2n^{1+2} in the Songliao Basin were studied, and the following conclusions are addressed based on the advantages of the fractal dimensions in characterizing pores.

(1) The samples of K_2n^{1+2} mainly had mineral intergranular pores and small numbers of organic pores and mineral intragranular pores. The pores were mainly wedge-shaped. The inorganic pores were much larger than the organic pores. The clay mineral and quartz contents had no clear control on the pore development in the K_2n^{1+2} shales.

(2) The negative correlation between the fractal dimensions (D1 and D2) and the TOC content may be due to expansion of hydrocarbon, which was generated more in high-TOC intervals. Therefore, when extracting oil resources in the low-maturity shales of K_2n^{1+2} in the Songliao Basin, it would be beneficial to find the area with higher TOC contents, smaller fractal dimensions, and larger pore size. This provides a reference for the shale oil evaluation of K_2n^{1+2} in the Songliao Basin and complements the lacustrine pore characteristics, which provides a reference value for oil and gas exploration and development in the Songliao Basin and a quantitative evaluation of continuous lacustrine pore characteristics.

Author Contributions: Conceptualization, L.K. and Y.G.; methodology, T.D.; software, L.K.; investigation, T.D. and L.K.; writing—original draft preparation, T.D., L.K. and Y.G.; writing—review and editing, T.D., L.K., Y.G. and Y.Z.; funding acquisition, Y.G. All authors have read and agreed to the published version of the manuscript.

Funding: This research was funded by the China Geological Survey Program (DD20190502).

Institutional Review Board Statement: Not applicable.

Informed Consent Statement: Not applicable.

Data Availability Statement: All data needed to evaluate the conclusions in the paper are present in the paper. Additional data related to this paper are available from the authors upon request.

Acknowledgments: We deeply appreciate the Research Institute of Petroleum Exploration and Development for the analytical equipment and help with the experiments.

Conflicts of Interest: The authors declare no conflict of interest.

Appendix A

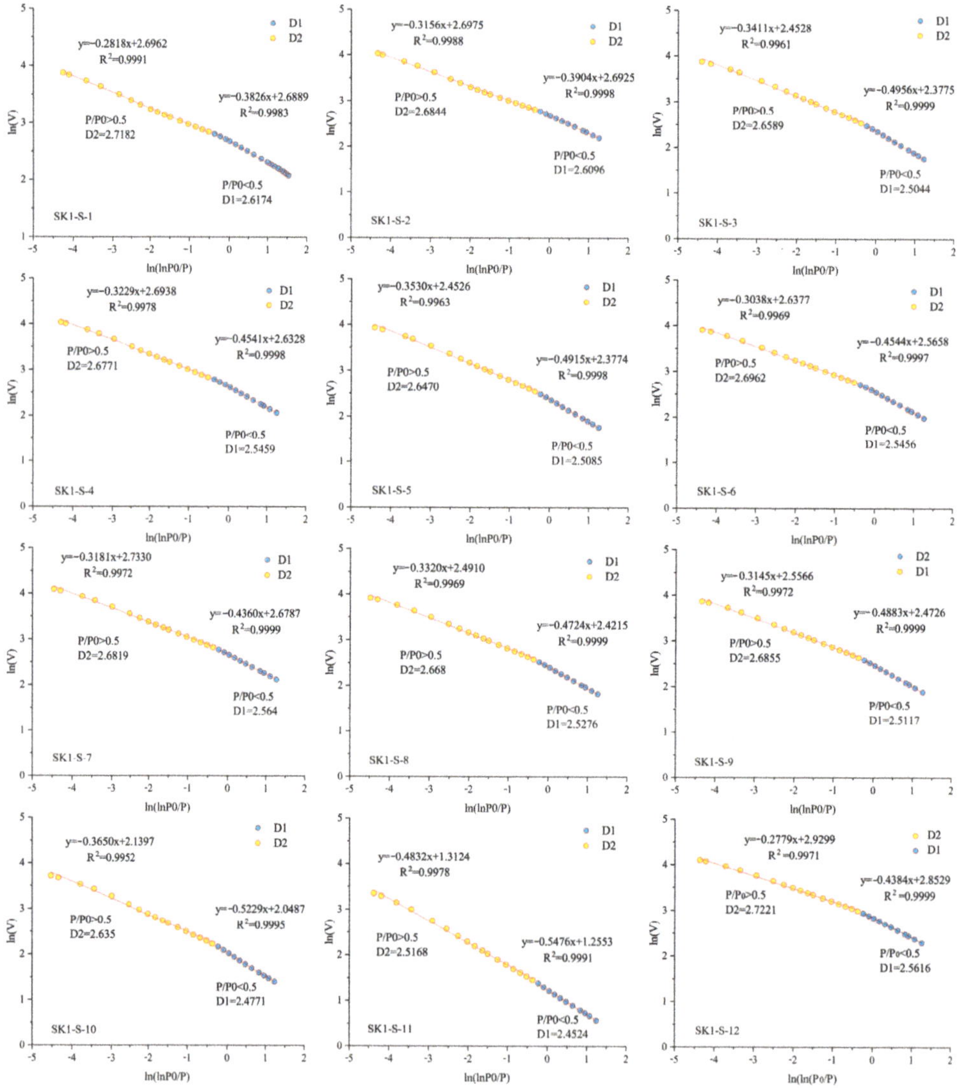

Figure A1. *Cont.*

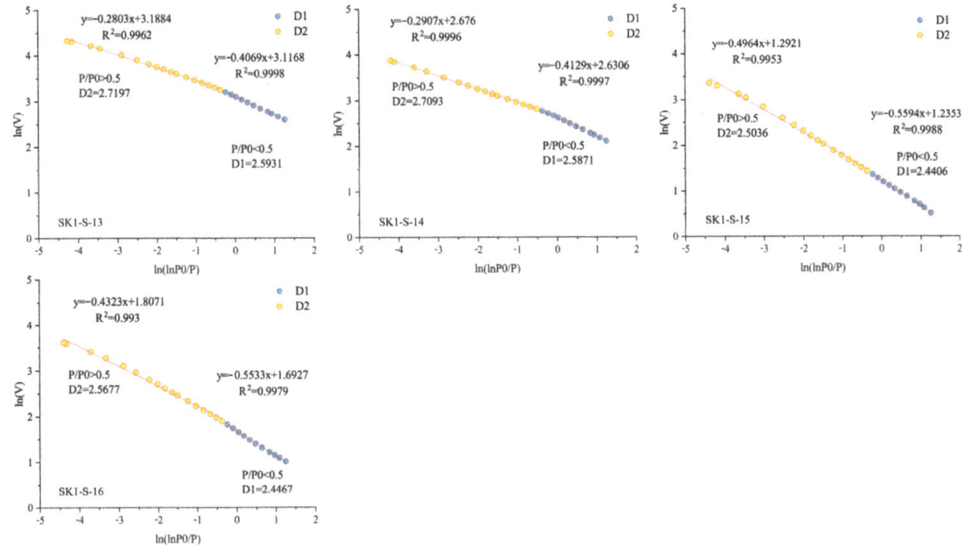

Figure A1. Fractal calculation results from FHH model of N^2 adsorption at low temperature for all samples.

References

1. Curtis, J.B. Fractured shale-gas systems. *AAPG Bull.* **2002**, *86*, 1921–1938. [CrossRef]
2. Jarvie, D.M.; Hill, R.J.; Ruble, T.E.; Pollastro, R.M. Unconventional shale-gas systems: The Mississippian Barnett Shale of north-central Texas as one model for thermogenic shale-gas assessment. *AAPG Bull.* **2007**, *91*, 475–499. [CrossRef]
3. Jarvie, D.M. Shale Resource Systems for Oil and Gas: Part 2: Shale-oil Resource Systems. In *Shale Reservoirs—Giant Resources for the 21st Century*; AAPG Memoir; Breyer, J.A., Ed.; American Association of Petroleum Geologists: Tulsa, OK, USA, 2012; Volume 97, pp. 89–119. [CrossRef]
4. Lv, D.W.; Chen, J.T.; Li, Z.X.; Zheng, G.Q.; Song, C.Y.; Liu, H.Y.; Meng, Y.R.; Wang, D.D. Controlling Factors, Accumulation Model and Target Zone Prediction of the Coal-bed Methane in the Huanghebei Coalfield, North China. *Resour. Geol.* **2014**, *64*, 332–345. [CrossRef]
5. Lv, D.W.; Li, Z.X.; Wang, D.D.; Li, Y.; Liu, H.Y.; Liu, Y.; Wang, P.L. Sedimentary Model of Coal and Shale in the Paleogene Lijiaya Formation of the Huangxian Basin: Insight from Petrological and Geochemical Characteristics of Coal and Shale. *Energy Fuels* **2019**, *33*, 10442–10456. [CrossRef]
6. Reynolds, D.B.; Umekwe, M.P. Shale-Oil Development Prospects: The Role of Shale-Gas in Developing Shale-Oil. *Energies* **2019**, *12*, 3331. [CrossRef]
7. Jia, B.; Tsau, J.S.; Barati, R. Investigation of Shale-Gas-Production Behavior: Evaluation of the Effects of Multiple Physics on the Matrix. SPE Reservoir Eval. *SPE Res. Eval. Eng.* **2020**, *23*, 68–80. [CrossRef]
8. Liang, Z.K.; Li, Z.; Jiang, Z.X.; Gao, F.L.; Zhang, Y.H.; Xiao, L.; Yang, Y.D.; Hou, Y.F.; Wang, L.W. Characteristics of Pore Structure and Fractal Dimension in Continental Shale Based on NMR Experiments and SEM Image Analyses-A Case Study of Shahezi Formation Shale in Changling Fault Depression of Songliao Basin, China. *JEES* **2020**, *42*, 313–328. [CrossRef]
9. Zhu, R.K.; Wu, S.T.; Su, L.; Cui, J.W.; Mao, Z.G.; Zhang, X.X. Problems and Future Works of Porous Texture Characterization of Tight Reservoirs in China. *Acta Pet. Sin.* **2016**, *37*, 1323–1336. [CrossRef]
10. Ross, D.J.K.; Bustin, R.M. The importance of shale composition and pore structure upon gas storage potential of shale gas reservoirs. *Mar. Pet. Geol.* **2009**, *26*, 916–927. [CrossRef]
11. Cui, J.W.; Zou, C.N.; Zhu, R.K.; Bai, B.; Wu, S.T.; Wang, T. New advances in shale porosity research. *Adv. Earth Sci.* **2012**, *27*, 319–325.
12. Chen, Z.H.; Osadetz, K.G.; Jiang, C.Q.; Li, M.W. Spatial variation of Bakken or Lodgepole oils in the Canadian Williston Basin. *AAPG Bull.* **2009**, *93*, 829–851. [CrossRef]
13. Jarvie, D.M. Williston Basin Petroleum Systems: Inferences from Oil Geochemistry and Geology. *Mt. Geol.* **2001**, *38*, 19–41. Available online: https://www.researchgate.net/publication/279546481 (accessed on 25 December 2022).
14. Treadgold, G.; Campbell, B.; Mclain, B.; Sinclair, S.; Nicklin, D. Eagle Ford shale prospecting with 3D seismic data within a tectonic and depositional system framework. *Lead. Edge* **2011**, *30*, 48. [CrossRef]

15. Zhao, J.H.; Jin, Z.Z.; Hu, Q.H.; Jin, Z.K.; Barber, T.J.; Zhang, Y.X.; Bleuel, M. Integrating SANS and fluid-invasion methods to characterize pore structure of typical American shale oil reservoirs. *Sci. Rep.* **2017**, *7*, 15413. [CrossRef] [PubMed]
16. Yan, C.; Jin, Z.; Zhao, J.; Zhao, J.W.; Liu, Q. Influence of sedimentary environment on organic matter enrichment in shale: A case study of the Wufeng and Longmaxi Formations of the Sichuan Basin, China. *Mar. Pet. Geol.* **2018**, *92*, 880–894. [CrossRef]
17. Ter Heege, J.; Zijp, M.; Nelskamp, S.; Douma, L.; Verreussel, R.; Ten Veen, J.; de Bruin, G.; Peters, R. Sweet spot identification in underexplored shales using multidisciplinary reservoir characterization and key performance indicators: Example of the Posidonia Shale Formation in the Netherlands. *J. Nat. Gas. Sci. Eng.* **2015**, *27*, 558–577. [CrossRef]
18. Pu, B.L.; Jiang, Y.L.; Wang, Y.; Bao, S.J.; Liu, X.J. Reservoir-forming conditions and favorable exploration zones of shale gas in Lower Silurian Longmaxi Formation of Sichuan Basin. *Acta Pet. Sin.* **2010**, *32*, 225–230. [CrossRef]
19. Fan, Y.C.; Liu, K.Y.; Yu, L.J.; Liu, J.; Regenauer-Lieb, K. Assessment of multi-scale pore structures and pore connectivity domains of marine shales by fractal dimensions and correlation lengths. *Fuel* **2022**, *330*, 125463. [CrossRef]
20. Cao, T.T.; Song, Z.G.; Wang, S.B.; Xia, J. Characterization of pore structure and fractal dimension of Paleozoic shales from the northeastern Sichuan Basin, China. *J. Nat. Gas Sci. Eng.* **2016**, *35*, 882–895. [CrossRef]
21. Zhao, D.; Guo, Y.; Zhu, Y.; Wang, G.; Chong, X.; Hu, X. Micropore heterogeneity of marine shale reservoirs and its quantitative characterization. *J. China Univ. Min. Technol.* **2018**, *47*, 1–12. [CrossRef]
22. Li, M.; Pang, X.Q.; Xiong, L.; Hu, T.; Chen, D.; Zhao, Z.; Hui, S.S.; Liu, Y.; Zhang, S.Y. The main controlling factors on shale gas occurrence characteristics in deep and high-over mature shales: A case study of Silurian Longmaxi Formation in the Sichuan Basin, southern China. *Energy Rep.* **2022**, *8*, 6901–6913. [CrossRef]
23. Osterrieth, J.W.M.; Rampersad, J.; Madden, D.; Rampal, N.; Skoric, L.; Connolly, B.; Allendorf, M.D.; Stavila, V.; Snider, J.L.; Ameloot, R.; et al. How Reproducible are Surface Areas Calculated from the BET Equation? *Adv. Mater.* **2022**, *34*, 2201502. [CrossRef] [PubMed]
24. Zou, C.N.; Yang, Z.; He, D.B.; Wei, Y.S.; Li, J.; Jia, A.L.; Chen, J.J.; Zhao, Q.; Li, Y.L.; Li, J.; et al. Theory, Technology and Prospects of Conventional and Un conventional Natural Gas. *Pet. Explor. Dev.* **2018**, *45*, 575–587. [CrossRef]
25. Yang, C.; Zhang, J.C.; Tang, X. Microscopic pore types and its impact on the storage and permeability of continental shale gas, Ordos Basin. *Earth Sci. Front.* **2013**, *20*, 240–250.
26. Nie, H.K.; Zhang, J.C. Types and characteristics of shale gas reservoir: A case study of Lower Paleozoic in and around Sichuan Basin. *Pet. Geol. Exp.* **2011**, *33*, 219–225.
27. Yang, F.; Ning, Z.F.; Kong, D.T.; Liu, H.Q. Pore structure of shales from high pres sure mercury injection and nitrogen adsorption method. *Nat. Gas Geosci.* **2013**, *24*, 450–455.
28. Tian, H.; Zhang, S.C.; Liu, S.B.; Zhang, H. Determination of organic rich shale pore features by mercury injection and gas adsorption methods. *Acta Pet. Sin.* **2012**, *33*, 419–427.
29. Chalmers, G.R.L.; Bustin, R.M. The organic matter distribution and methane capacity of the Lower Cretaceous strata of North eastern British Columbia, Canada. *Int. J. Coal Geol.* **2007**, *70*, 223–239. [CrossRef]
30. Bustin, R.M.; Bustin, A.; Ross, D.; Chalmers, G.; Murthy, V.; Chikatamarla, L.; Cui, A. Shale gas opportunities and challenges. *Search Discov. Artic.* **2009**, *1*, 20–23.
31. Medina-Rodriguez, B.X.; Alvarado, V. Use of Gas Adsorption and Inversion Methods for Shale Pore Structure Characterization. *Energies* **2021**, *14*, 2880. [CrossRef]
32. Mandelbrot, B.B. *Les Objects Fractals: Forme, Hasard et Dimension*; Flammarion: Paris, France, 1975.
33. Hansen, J.P.; Skjeltorp, A.T. Fractal pore space and rock permeability implications. *Phys. Rev. B* **1988**, *38*, 2635–2638. [CrossRef] [PubMed]
34. Krohn, C.E. Sandstone fractal and Euclidean pore volume distributions. *J. Geophys. Res. Earth Planets* **1988**, *93*, 3286–3296. [CrossRef]
35. Pape, H.; Clauser, C.; Iffland, J. Permeability prediction based on fractal porespacegeometry. *Geophysics* **1999**, *64*, 1447–1460. [CrossRef]
36. Pfeifer, P.; Avnir, D. Chemistry in noninteger dimensions between two and three. I. Fractal theory of heterogeneous surfaces. *J. Chem. Phys.* **1983**, *79*, 3558–3565. [CrossRef]
37. Katz, A.J.; Thompson, A.H. Fractal sandstone pores: Implications for conductivity and pore formation. *Phys. Rev. Lett.* **1985**, *54*, 1325–1328. [CrossRef] [PubMed]
38. Yang, F.; Ning, Z.F.; Liu, H.Q. Fractal characteristics of shales from a shale gas reservoir in the Sichuan Basin, China. *Fuel* **2014**, *115*, 378–384. [CrossRef]
39. Hazra, B.; Wood, D.A.; Vishal, V.; Varma, A.K.; Sakha, D.; Singh, A.K. Porosity controls and fractal disposition of organic-rich Permian shales using low-pressure adsorption techniques. *Fuel* **2018**, *220*, 837–848. [CrossRef]
40. Pan, S.X.; Zha, M.; Gao, C.H.; Qu, J.X.; Ding, X.J. Pore structure and fractal characteristics of organic-rich lacustrine shales of the Kongdian Formation, Cangdong Sag, Bohai Bay Basin. *Front. Earth Sci.* **2021**, *9*, 760583. [CrossRef]
41. Gao, Y.; Wang, C.S.; Wang, P.J.; Gao, Y.F.; Huang, Y.J.; Zou, C.C. Progress on Continental Scientific Drilling Project of Cretaceous Songliao Basin (SK-1 and SK-2). *Sci. Bull.* **2019**, *64*, 73–75. [CrossRef]
42. Wang, C.S.; Feng, Z.G.; Zhang, L.M.; Huang, Y.J.; Cao, K.; Wang, P.J.; Zhao, B. Cretaceous paleogeography and paleoclimate and the setting of SKI borehole sites in Songliao Basin, northeast China. *Palaeogeogr. Palaeoclimatol. Palaeoecol.* **2013**, *385*, 17–30. [CrossRef]

43. Feng, Z.Q.; Jia, C.Z.; Xie, X.N.; Zhang, S.; Feng, Z.H.; Cross, T.A. Tectonostratigraphic units and stratigraphic sequences of the nonmarine Songliao basin, northeast China. *Basin Res.* **2010**, *22*, 79–95. [CrossRef]
44. Wang, P.J.; Mattern, F.; Didenko, N.A.; Zhu, D.F.; Singer, B.; Sun, X.M. Tectonics and cycle system of the Cretaceous Songliao Basin: An inverted active continental margin basin. *Earth-Sci. Rev.* **2016**, *159*, 82–102. [CrossRef]
45. Gao, Y.; Wang, C.S.; Liu, Z.F.; Du, X.J.; Ibarra, D.E. Diagenetic and Paleoenvironmental Controls on Late Cretaceous Clay Minerals in the Songliao Basin, Northeast China. *Clays Clay Miner.* **2015**, *63*, 469–484. [CrossRef]
46. Feng, Z.Q.; Wang, C.S.; Graham, S.; Koeberl, C.; Dong, H.L.; Huang, Y.J.; Gao, Y. Continental Scientific Drilling Project of Cretaceous Songliao Basin: Scientific objectives and drilling technology. *Palaeogeogr. Palaeoclimatol. Palaeoecol.* **2013**, *385*, 6–16. [CrossRef]
47. Zhang, L.; Zhang, X.J.; Chai, H.; Li, Y.C.; Zhou, Y.J. Pore structure characterization for a continental lacustrine shale parasequence based on fractal theory. *Fractals* **2019**, *27*, 1940006. [CrossRef]
48. Liao, L.L.; Wang, Y.P.; Chen, C.S.; Pan, Y.H. Application of the Grain-Based Rock-Eval Pyrolysis Method to Evaluate Hydrocarbon Generation, Expulsion, and Retention of Lacustrine Shale. *Front. Earth Sci.* **2022**, *10*, 921806. [CrossRef]
49. He, W.Y.; Meng, Q.A.; Lin, T.F.; Wang, R.; Liu, X.; Li, X.; Yang, F.; Sun, G.X. Evolution of in-situ permeability of low-maturity shale with the increasing temperature, Cretaceous Nenjiang Formation, northern Songliao Basin, NE China. *Pet. Explor. Dev.* **2022**, *49*, 453–464. [CrossRef]
50. Zhang, J.Z.; Tang, Y.J.; He, D.X.; Sun, P.; Zou, X.Y. Full-scale nanopore system and fractal characteristics of clay-rich lacustrine shale combining FE-SEM, nano-CT, gas adsorption and mercury intrusion porosimetry. *Appl. Clay Sci.* **2020**, *196*, 105758. [CrossRef]
51. Wang, M.; Xue, H.T.; Tian, S.S.; Wilkins, R.W.T.; Wang, Z.W. Fractal characteristics of Upper Cretaceous lacustrine shale from the Songliao Basin, NE China. *Mar. Pet. Geol.* **2015**, *67*, 144–153. [CrossRef]
52. Gao, Y.F.; Wang, P.J.; Cheng, R.H.; Wang, G.D.; Wan, X.Q.; Wu, H.Y.; Wang, S.X.; Liang, W.L. Centimeter-scale sedimentary sequence description of Upper Cretaceous Nenjiang Formation (lower numbers 1&2): Lithostratigraphy, facies and cyclostratigraphy, based on the scientific drilling (SK1) borehole in the Songliao Basin. *Earth Sci. Front.* **2011**, *18*, 195–217.
53. Gao, Y.; Ibarra, D.E.; Wang, C.; Caves, J.K.; Chamberlain, C.P.; Graham, S.A.; Wu, H. Mid-latitude terrestrial climate of East Asia linked to global climate in the Late Cretaceous. *Geology* **2015**, *43*, 287–290. [CrossRef]
54. Bernard, S.; Wirth, R.; Schreiber, A.; Schulz, H.M.; Horsfield, B. Formation of nanoporous pyrobitumen residues during maturation of the Barnett Shale (Fort Worth Basin). *Int. J. Coal. Geol.* **2012**, *103*, 3–11. [CrossRef]
55. Clarkson, C.R.; Freeman, M.; He, L.; Agamalian, M.; Melnichenko, Y.B.; Mastalerz, M.; Bustin, R.M.; Radlinski, A.P.; Blach, T.P. Characterization of tight gas reservoir pore structure using USANS/SANS and gas adsorption analysis. *Fuel* **2012**, *95*, 371–385. [CrossRef]
56. Loucks, R.G.; Reed, R.M.; Ruppel, S.C.; Jarvie, D.M. Morphology, Genesis, and Distribution of Nanometer-Scale Pores in Siliceous Mudstones of the Mississippian Barnett Shale. *J. Sediment. Res.* **2009**, *79*, 848–861. [CrossRef]
57. Milliken, K.L.; Rudnicki, M.; Awwiller, D.N.; Zhang, T.W. Organic matter-hosted pore system, Marcellus Formtion (Devonian), Pennsylvania. *Am. Assoc. Pet. Geol. Bull.* **2013**, *97*, 177–200. [CrossRef]
58. Clarkson, C.R.; Solano, N.; Bustin, R.M.; Bustin, A.M.M.; Chalmers, G.R.L.; He, L.; Melnichenko, Y.B.; Radlinski, A.P.; Blach, T.P. Pore structure characterization of North American shale gas reservoirs using USANS/SANS, gas adsorption, and mercury intrusion. *Fuel* **2013**, *103*, 606–616. [CrossRef]
59. Chen, J.; Xiao, X. Evolution of nanoporosity in organic-rich shales during thermal maturation. *Fuel* **2014**, *129*, 173–181. [CrossRef]
60. Mastalerz, M.; He, L.L.; Melnichenko, Y.B.; Rupp, J.A. Porosity of Coal and Shale: Insights from Gas Adsorption and SANS/USANS Techniques. *Energy Fuels* **2012**, *26*, 5109–5120. [CrossRef]
61. Schmitt, M.; Fernandes, C.P.; Neto, J.A.B.D.; Wolf, F.B.; dos Santos, V.S.S. Characterization of pore systems in seal rocks using nitrogen gas adsorption combined with mercury injection capillary pressure techniques. *Mar. Pet. Geol.* **2013**, *39*, 138–149. [CrossRef]
62. Tian, H.; Pan, L.; Xiao, X.M.; Wilkins, R.W.T.; Meng, Z.P.; Huang, B.J. A preliminary study on the pore characterization of Lower Silurian black shales in the Chuandong Thrust Fold Belt, southwestern China using low pressure N-2 adsorption and FE-SEM methods. *Mar. Pet. Geol.* **2013**, *48*, 8–19. [CrossRef]
63. Liu, C.; Shi, B.; Zhou, J.; Tang, C.S. Quantification and characterization of microporosity by image processing, geometric measurement and statistical methods: Application on SEM images of clay materials. *Appl. Clay Sci.* **2011**, *54*, 97–106. [CrossRef]
64. Cai, Y.; Liu, D.; Pan, Z.; Yao, Y.B.; Li, J.Q.; Qiu, Y.K. Pore structure and its impact on CH_4 adsorption capacity and flow capability of bituminous and subbituminous coals from Northeast China. *Fuel* **2013**, *103*, 258–268. [CrossRef]
65. Yao, Y.B.; Liu, D.M.; Tang, D.Z.; Tang, S.H.; Huang, W.H. Fractal characterization of adsorption-pores of coals from North China: An investigation on CH4 adsorption capacity of coals. *Int. J. Coal Geol.* **2008**, *73*, 27–42. [CrossRef]
66. Liu, J.Z.; Zhu, J.F.; Cheng, J.; Zhou, J.H.; Cen, K.F. Pore structure and fractal analysis of Ximeng lignite under microwave irradiation. *Fuel* **2015**, *146*, 41–50. [CrossRef]
67. Wang, B.X. *Medical Statistics and SAS Application*; Shanghai Jiao Tong University Press: Shanghai, China, 2009; Volume 95, p. 135, ISBN 978-7-313-04844-8.
68. Wilson, E.B. Statistical Inference. *Science* **1926**, *63*, 289–296. [CrossRef]
69. Bishop, T.F.A.; Lark, R.M. The geostatistical analysis of experiments at the landscape-scale. *Geoderma* **2006**, *133*, 87–106. [CrossRef]

70. Sing, K.S.W.; Everett, D.H.; Haul, R.A.W.; Moscou, L.; Pierotti, R.A.; Rouquerol, J.; Siemieniewsha, T. Reporting physisorption data for gas/solid systems with special reference to the determination of surface area and porosity. *Pure Appl. Chem.* **1985**, *57*, 603–619. [CrossRef]
71. Hazra, B.; Wood, D.A.; Vishal, V.; Singh, A.K. Pore Characteristics of Distinct Thermally Mature Shales: Influence of Particle Size on Low-Pressure CO_2 and N_2 Adsorption. *Energy Fuels* **2018**, *32*, 8175–8186. [CrossRef]
72. Liu, L.H.; Gu, M.; Xian, X.F. Effect of pore structure and surface chemical properties on adsorption properties of activated carbon. *Chin. J. Environ. Eng.* **2012**, *4*, 1299–1304.
73. Tang, X.L.; Jiang, Z.X.; Li, Z.; Gao, Z.Y.; Bai, Y.Q.; Zhao, S.; Feng, J. The effect of the variation in material composition on the heterogeneous pore structure of high-maturity shale of the Silurian Longmaxi formation in the southeastern Sichuan Basin, China. *J. Nat. Gas Sci. Eng.* **2015**, *23*, 464–473. [CrossRef]
74. Qi, H.; Ma, J.; Wong, P.Z. Adsorption isotherms of fractal surfaces. *Colloids Surf. A* **2002**, *206*, 401–407. [CrossRef]
75. Pyun, S.I.; Rhee, C.K. An investigation of fractal characteristics of mesoporous carbon electrodes with various pore structures. *Electrochim. Acta* **2004**, *49*, 4171–4180. [CrossRef]
76. Zhao, D.; Guo, Y.; Wang, G.; Guan, X.; Zhou, X.; Liu, J. Fractal Analysis and Classification of Pore Structures of High-Rank Coal in Qinshui Basin, China. *Energies* **2022**, *15*, 6766. [CrossRef]
77. Rigby, S.P. Predicting surface diffusivities of molecules from equilibrium adsorption isotherms. *Colloid Surf. A* **2005**, *262*, 139–149. [CrossRef]
78. Cao, X.M.; Gao, Y.; Cui, J.W.; Han, S.B.; Kang, L.; Song, S.; Wang, C.S. Pore Characteristics of Lacustrine Shale Oil Reservoir in the Cretaceous Qingshankou Formation of the Songliao Basin, NE China. *Energies* **2020**, *13*, 2027. [CrossRef]
79. Singh, D.P.; Wood, D.A.; Singh, V.; Hazra, B.; Singh, P.K. Impact of Particle Crush-Size and Weight on Rock-Eval S2, S4, and Kinetics of Shales. *J. Earth Sci. China* **2022**, *33*, 513–524. [CrossRef]
80. Hazra, B.; Dutta, S.; Kumar, S. TOC calculation of organic matter rich sediments using Rock-Eval pyrolysis: Critical consideration and insights. *Int. J. Coal. Geol.* **2017**, *169*, 106–115. [CrossRef]
81. Carvajal-Ortiz, H.; Gentzis, T. Critical considerations when assessing hydrocarbon plays using Rock-Eval pyrolysis and organic petrology data: Data quality revisited. *Int. J. Coal Geol.* **2017**, *152*, 113–122. [CrossRef]
82. Cornford, C.; Gardner, P.; Burgess, C. Geochemical truths in large data sets. I: Geochemical screening data. *Org. Geochem.* **1998**, *29*, 519–530. [CrossRef]

applied sciences

MDPI

Article

Delineation and Analysis of Regional Geochemical Anomaly Using the Object-Oriented Paradigm and Deep Graph Learning—A Case Study in Southeastern Inner Mongolia, North China

Bo Zhao [1], Dehui Zhang [2,*], Rongzhen Zhang [2,3,*], Zhu Li [2,4], Panpan Tang [1] and Haoming Wan [1]

1 Research Center of Big Data Technology, Nanhu Laboratory, Jiaxing 314000, China
2 School of Earth Sciences and Resources, China University of Geosciences, Beijing 100086, China
3 Henan Institute of Geology, Zhengzhou 450001, China
4 Inner Mongolian Geological Engineering Co., Ltd., Hohhot 010010, China
* Correspondence: zhdehui@cugb.edu.cn (D.Z.); zrzyang@126.com (R.Z.)

Abstract: This research describes an advanced workflow of an object-based geochemical graph learning approach, termed OGE, which includes five key steps: (1) conduct the mean removal operation on the multi-elemental geochemical data and then normalize them; (2) data gridding and multiresolution segmentation; (3) calculate the Moran's I value and construct the geochemical topology graph; (4) unsupervised deep graph learning; (5) the within-object statistical analysis. The final product of OGE is an object-based anomaly score map. The performance of OGE was demonstrated by a case study involving eighteen ore-forming elements (Cu, Pb, Zn, W, Sn, Mo, F, Au, Fe_2O_3, etc.) in stream sediment samples in the Bayantala-Mingantu district, North China. The results showed that the OGE analysis performed at lower levels of scale greatly improved the quality of anomaly recognition: more than 80% of the known ore spots, no matter what their scales and mineral species, were predicted in less than 45% of the study area, and most of the ore spots falling outside the delineated anomalous regions occur nearby them. OGE can extract both the spatial features and compositional relationships of geochemical variables collected at irregularly distributed centroids in irregularly shaped image objects, and it outperforms other convolutional autoencoder models such as GAUGE in anomaly detection.

Keywords: object-based image analysis; graph neural network; geochemical anomalies; fractal dimension

Citation: Zhao, B.; Zhang, D.; Zhang, R.; Li, Z.; Tang, P.; Wan, H. Delineation and Analysis of Regional Geochemical Anomaly Using the Object-Oriented Paradigm and Deep Graph Learning—A Case Study in Southeastern Inner Mongolia, North China. *Appl. Sci.* **2022**, *12*, 10029. https://doi.org/10.3390/app121910029

Academic Editors: Zeming Shi and Qingjie Gong

Received: 1 September 2022
Accepted: 3 October 2022
Published: 6 October 2022

1. Introduction

Regional geochemical surveys are an important part of geoscience investigations in both environmental and mineral exploration studies [1]. By discrete data gridding, the original X-Y-Z (longitude–latitude-element content) regional geochemical data can be converted into a big matrix, which is analogous to a remote sensing (RS) image: e.g., a matrix element vs. an image pixel, element content vs. the reflectance value or digital number [2], a multi-element dataset vs. a multiband image, delineating geochemical anomalies vs. classifying ground objects, etc. Intuitively, some algorithms developed for processing the remotely sensed data may be equally applicable to geochemical data analysis. The object-based image analysis (OBIA) [3] is such an example.

In the RS field, there has been a very rapid growth in the use of OBIA ever since its documented introduction in late 1990s [3]. The first step of this method is the grouping of spatially contiguous pixels with similar spectral/textural characteristics into meaningful image objects, which is a process often termed "segmentation". An object is usually composed of a group of pixels that are spatially continuous and have high spectral homogeneity, and the shape of an adaptive object is usually consistent with the shape of a ground target [4]. Once the objects are formed, the next step is to assign appropriate labels to them by using a supervised or unsupervised classifier [5]. The object-based approach is a widely accepted solution to process high spatial resolution RS data [6], and obviously, it applies as well to analyzing regional geochemical dataset if the X-Y-Z matrix is plotted as an image. However, current geochemical data analysis conducted in the literature is still on a per-point basis [7], and every sampling point (matrix element) is treated as an individual unit and is processed without any textural, contextual, neighborhood, and shape consideration. Therefore, except identification and separation of the anomalies from background, traditional geochemical analysis rarely contributes new insight [7–9]. In practice, the geological object, e.g., sedimentary stratum, tectonic line, igneous intrusion, etc., is usually the minimum mapping unit required for regional geological analysis [9]. Likewise, it is feasible and better to use the geochemical objects produced by OBIA to do regional geochemical analysis.

According to [10], OBIA can be carried out in two ways: (1) the object-level analysis: most of the current object-oriented analysis approaches rely on object-level summary statistics, such as median, mean, and standard deviation of the pixel values within each segment. Such summary measures provide one value per band for each segment to describe its data central tendency or dispersion [11]. (2) The within-object analysis. The pixel values within an object usually have their own distribution pattern—unimodal Gaussianity or multiple peaks [3], and it reflects the internal structure characteristics of the object. In theory, these data-analysis/-mining techniques apply as well to analyzing regional geochemical datasets characterized by multi-source, multi-stage and multi-genesis [7], and a large amount of geological information can thus be rediscovered, not just anomaly and background. Moreover, OBIA is often performed at multiple levels of scale to capture variably sized image objects, which may help with discriminating between classes that are differentiable by size (for example buildings versus forests) [12]. At a given scale parameter, homogeneous areas (background) result in larger objects, and heterogeneous areas (targets/anomalies) result in smaller objects. The larger the segmentation scale, the larger the segmented objects grow, and vice versa. Obviously, such a multi-scale design will help to establish a better understanding of the regional geochemical processes at different scales.

In OBIA-based image analysis, the standard practice is to conduct "multiresolution segmentation + machine learning-based classification" [5]. Actually, over the last few years, machine learning techniques have become an essential tool to advance different branches of science and engineering, including geochemical anomaly recognition. For example, a hybrid machine learning method was proposed in [13], which is based on combining K-Nearest Neighbor Regression and Random Forest Regression to predict Pb and Zn grades in the Irankuh Mining District (IMD), Iran. Reference [14] goes deeper: it trained four regression machine learning algorithms, i.e., K neighbor regressor, support vector regressor, gradient boosting regressor, and random forest regressor, to build a hybrid model to predict Pb and Zn grades of IMD. After that, the multifractal model [15] was used to classify Pb-Zn anomalies. Despite the success of the examples in the literature, few studies have explored the advantages of introducing traditional machine learning algorithms into OBIA-based geochemical prospecting.

At the same time, over past years, deep learning has yielded impressive results in image analysis, e.g., the land cover mapping. In particular, neural networks with FCN (fully convolution networks) structures are widely used in image analysis tasks [16]. In recent years, there has become an increased focus on the combination of OBIA and FCN. For example, in [17], the object-based convolutional neural network (OCNN) was proposed for urban land use classification using high-resolution RS images. Rather than pixel-wise convolutional processes, OCNNs rely on segmented objects as their functional units, and then, FCNs were used to analyze and label objects such as to partition within-object and between-object variation [10]. Reference [18] presented a multiscale OCNN framework for large-scale RS land cover classification, in which FCNs pretrained at multiple scales were applied for final classification. Additional examples which adopt OCNN as the basic image analyzer can be found in [19–22]. Although OCNN approaches have achieved astonishing performance, they require an enormous amount of training data [23]. In fact, supervised OCNN are unsuitable for regional geochemical exploration because we cannot have a priori knowledge to make per-point or per-object annotations for multi-element geochemical data. Unsupervised learning methods, on the other hand, do not rely on labeled samples, and have become the mainstream methodology in geochemical anomaly recognition [24,25]. GAUGE (i.e., recognition of Geochemical Anomalies Using Graph Learning) [24], One-class Support Vector Machine [25], and Autoencoders [26] are recent examples. However, there is still a research gap regarding the combination of OBIA and unsupervised deep learning, and we wonder if such a combination could produce even more exploration geochemical information and provide new insights into regional geologic process.

This study mainly follows the idea of GAUGE [24]. GAUGE is a three-step procedure including: (1) building up a multi-elemental geochemical topology graph at a group of randomly located sampling points. (2) constructing a symmetric GAT (Graph Attention Network) autoencoder, namely an attributed graph encoder combined with an attributed reconstruction decoder [27]. The former is used to model both the spatial structure and compositional relationships of geochemical variables simultaneously, and the latter is responsible for reconstructing the input variables with the obtained node embeddings. (3) conduct the anomaly detection. To be specific, the Euclidean distance between pairs of original multi-elemental content values and the reconstructed background values at each sampling point are calculated as the anomaly score, and on this basis, the anomaly map is created [24]. Inspired by the success of GAUGE, in this article we present a novel object-based graph learning architecture (OGE) for geochemical anomaly recognition and analysis, and there are three main differences between GAUGE and OGE: (1) the OGE approach involves a three-step pre-processing procedure, which is (i) grid the multi-element geochemical sampling data, and generate a multi-channel image in "Geo-Tiff" format; (ii) segment the original image into homogeneous objects; and (iii) extract the centroids of each object, and transform them into topology graphs according to their adjacency relations, while GAUGE does not. (2) The autoencoder of OGE comprises a GAT-based encoder and a GCN (Graph Convolution Network)-based decoder [28], while GAUGE involves a symmetric GAT-based autoencoder. (3) the OGE approach involves post-processing and post-analysis. For example, the nodal anomaly scores must be assigned back to the corresponding image objects as the summary statistics. And then, the within-object anomaly analysis can be conducted. To the best of our knowledge, we are the first to introduce in the OBIA tasks the unsupervised GNN (Graph Neural Network).

The remainder of this work is organized as follows: Section 2 reviewed the geological settings of the study area and described the data materials; Section 2 also gave the detailed methodology of OGE; Section 3 described and analyzed the experiment results; in Section 4, we discussed the implications and extensions of the results of Section 3; and we concluded the research in Section 5.

2. Materials and Methods

2.1. Materials

2.1.1. Geological Settings

The study area is located in Eastern Inner Mongolia, North China, and its regional geology is shown in Figure 1. It can be seen from Figure 1 that: (1) the study area is heavily covered with Neogene and Quaternary sedimentary layers [29], especially N_2b—red purple variegated mudstone and clay rock. In addition, J_3mk (acid volcanic rocks), J_3mn (tuff), P_1sm (limestone, tuff, greywacke, and fine sandstone), and P_1e (andesite) are also sparsely distributed. (2) The igneous intrusive rocks are widely developed in the study area, dominated by intermediate and acidic granitoids, and their rock-forming ages extend mainly from Permian to Cretaceous, with a few Neoarchean and Paleozoic intrusive rocks. Note that there are both I-type (formed by the igneous) and S-type (formed by melting of metasedimentary rocks) granitoids in this area. Therein, S-type magmas are in general more evolved chemically than I-types, are relatively reduced, and when highly fractionated, are related to Sn-W mineralization; I-types are opposite and are related to Cu-Mo mineralization [30]. (3) The geological structure in this area is very complex, including NE- and NW-trending fault zones, NE-trending folds (anticline and syncline), etc. However, due to the large magmatic events and the widely distributed Cenozoic sedimentary layers, it is difficult to identify the characteristics of geological structure occurring before the Mesozoic.

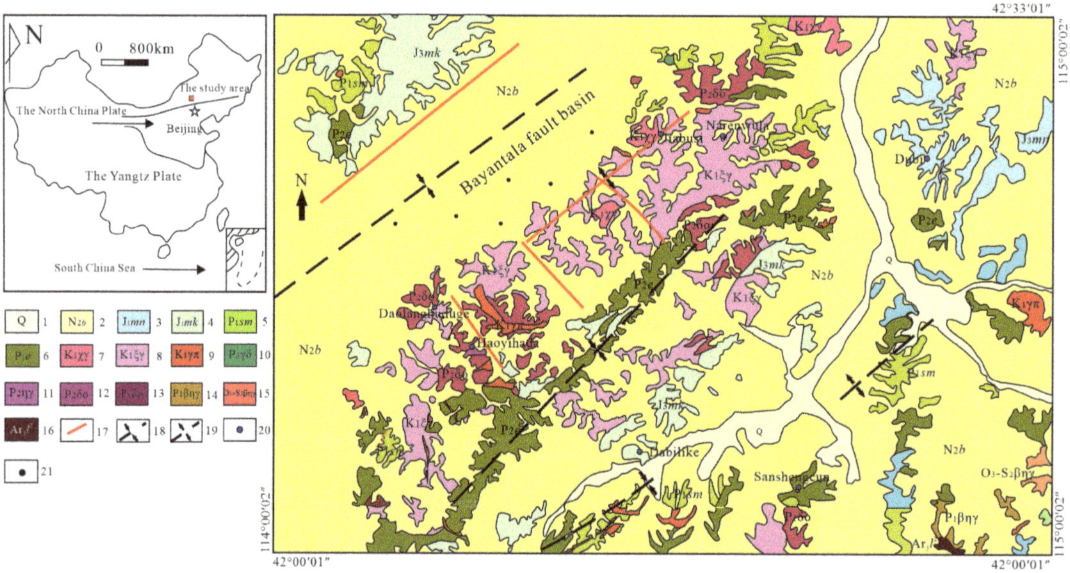

Figure 1. Generalized geologic map of the study area. Note: 1. Quaternary; 2. Baogedawula Formation, Pliocene Series, Neogene; 3. Manitu Formation, Upper Jurassic Series; 4. Manketouebo Fromation, Upper Jurassic Series; 5. Sanmianjing Formation, Lower Permian Series; 6. Elitu Formation, Upper Permian Series; 7. Early Cretaceous alkali-feldspar granite; 8. Early Cretaceous syenogranite; 9. Early Cretaceous granite porphyry; 10. Late Permian granodiorite; 11. Middle Permian monzonitic granite; 12. Middle Permian quartz diorite; 13. Early Permian quartz diorite; 14. Early Permian monzonitic granite; 15. Late Ordovician-Middle Silurian monzonitic granite; 16. Neo-Archean Liushugou Formation; 17. fault zone; 18. syncline; 19. anticline; 20. W-Nb-Ta-F deposit; 21. U-mineralized deposit. The study area is located in Inner Mongolia, North China, as shown in the overview.

2.1.2. Data Materials

We collected a set of 1:200,000 stream sediments survey data matching the study area shown in Figure 1, which were provided by China Geological Survey. As the study area is situated in arid and semiarid regions, the sampling media include soil and stream sediments (10–40 mesh). The surface organic layer was avoided during the sampling process. There were 0.25 to 1 sampling points per km^2, and samples collected within 4 km^2 were combined into one composite testing sample. If the stream-sediment samples cannot be easily collected, the soil samples will be used instead. The sample collection, preparation, storage, chemical tests, quality control and data preprocessing adhered strictly to the "criterion of regional geochemical exploration" released by the Ministry of Land and Resources of China in 2006. For example, the general quality control flow involved the following steps: (i) analyses of the Geochemical-Standard-Drainage sediment samples; (ii) analyses of the coded Geochemical-Reference-Drainage sediment samples developed by the provincial laboratory; (iii) duplicate analyses of the randomly selected and coded samples; (iv) rechecked analyses of the samples with anomalous values; and (v) rechecked analyses conducted by external laboratories, if necessary.

Finally, we got 1325 composite samples, and 39 elements were accurately analyzed by multiple methods, including 32 elements and 7 oxides. In this article, we mainly focus on eighteen main ore-forming elements, which are Ag, As, Au, B, Be, Bi, Cu, F, Hg, Mo, Nb, Pb, Sb, Sn, U, W, Zn, and Fe_2O_3. Elemental contents of each composite sample are determined mainly by the ICP-MS (i.e., inductively coupled plasma mass spectrometry) method [7]. The statistical parameters of them are given in Table 1.

Table 1. Statistical parameters of 17 main ore-forming elements.

Element	Ag	As	Au	B	Be	Bi	Cu	F	Hg
Maximum	4500	248.7	93.5	660	12	272.34	287.8	24,600	5511
Minimum	10	1.24	0.2	2.9	0.7	0.036	0.8	80	4.5
Median	60	8.60	0.8	38	2.1	0.24	13.3	340	16
Average	71.22	9.83	1.24	42.05	2.25	0.53	14.01	380.05	21.44
CV	1.87	0.97	2.43	0.92	0.36	14.36	0.88	1.89	7.08
Element	**Mo**	**Nb**	**Pb**	**Sb**	**Sn**	**U**	**W**	**Zn**	**Fe_2O_3**
Maximum	5.64	4468	220.50	13.41	260	4.80	1299.20	841	7.91
Minimum	0.28	0.7	0.90	0.10	0.10	0.15	0.30	9.10	0.53
Median	0.8	10.1	14.6	0.56	2.5	1.5	1.36	43.6	3.18
Average	0.90	14.19	16.76	0.65	2.99	1.57	2.57	48.30	3.17
CV	0.47	8.64	0.70	0.95	2.44	0.32	13.90	0.78	0.31

CV: coefficient of variation; Unit of elemental concentration: Ag/Au/Hg: 10^{-9}; Fe_2O_3: %, others: 10^{-6}.

Previous studies [29] have indicated that the mineralization of Nb, Ta, Li, Be, REE, U, etc. in the study area is most related to highly fractionated peraluminous granitoids (S-type); while the mineralization of W, Pb, Zn, Ag, fluorite, tourmaline (B), Au, Cu, etc. is mainly of quartz-vein type, often occurring within the syenogranitic wall rocks (highly fractionated I-type) surrounding the peraluminous granitoids. Based on these facts and according to the metallogenic specialization of granitoids [31], the relevant ore-forming elements can be divided into two groups: (1) Ag, Au, As, B, Cu, Hg, Mo, Pb, U, Zn, and Fe_2O_3, which are closely related to magnetite series granites (I-type); and (2) Be, Bi, F, Mo, Nb, Pb, Sb, Sn, U, W, and Fe_2O_3, which are closely related to ilmenite series granites (S-type) [29]. At the same time, in consideration of the extensive development of granitic complexes in this area and the complex mineral paragenesis [30] such as Cu-Mo versus W-Mo, Pb-Zn versus W, Sn-Pb, U-Pb versus Th-U, and pyrite versus Fe_2O_3, we make Mo, Pb, U, and Fe_2O_3 appear in both groups.

2.2. Methodology

The proposed algorithm is a complex multi-step procedure, which involves several different methodologies and datasets, and the details of each step are given below. At the center of this algorithm is OGE—a graph network-based autoencoder, and other sub-algorithms can be regarded as the pre-processing and post-processing for OGE.

2.2.1. Data Pre-Processing

(1) Pre-Processing of Original Geochemical Data

First, based on Python, a mean removal operation was conducted on the original X-Y-Z geochemical data of the ore-forming elements to remove the background noise, that is, subtracting the mean values from each value in the X-Y-Z dataset. And then, normalized them into the range [0, 1]. After that, based on Surfer v11.0 and using the Kriging interpolation algorithm, the normalized data of each element were expanded into a matrix of size 405 × 500, and then it was saved as a single-band image in "Info ASCII Grid

(*.grd)" format, so that it is readable for the eCognition Developer and Python platforms. Finally, these *.grd files were concatenated along the dimension of channels and saved as a multi-band *.geotif image, termed Image I.

(2) Multiresolution Segmentation

Using the business image processing software eCognition, the FNEA (Fractal Net Evolution Approach) multiresolution segmentation was conducted on Image I. The scale parameter is empirically set as 3.0, the shape parameter is set as 0.1, and the compactness as 0.5. Finally, we got 663 segmented objects as shown in Figure 2. Note that the Fe_2O_3-band in Image I was not involved in the segmentation process. This is because: as the only major element (or say rock-forming element), the incorporation of Fe_2O_3 may misguide FNEA to pay more attention to regional diagenesis, rather than metallogenesis.

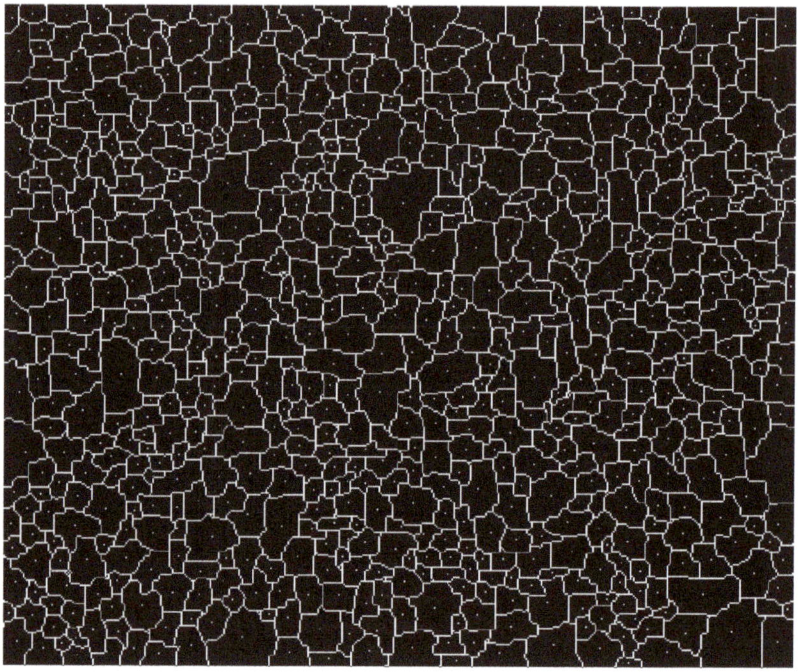

Figure 2. The multiresolution segmentation result and the centroids within each image object.

(3) Find the Centroid of Each Object

First, draw the minimum enclosing rectangle (MER) for each image object, and the centroids of the MERs will act as the centroids of the corresponding objects, see Figure 2. However, if the centroid falls on or outside the boundary of an image object, it will be recalculated in the following way: (i) generating the skeleton lines for each object; (ii) removing the suspension lines along the main skeleton line; and (iii) finding the midpoint of the main skeleton line, and taking it as the centroid of the corresponding object. Thanks to the skimage.morphology, numpy, and other Python packages, these processing steps can be easily implemented on a computer.

Finally, we note that image segmentation is the process by which an original image is partitioned into some homogeneous regions/objects [6], so the spectral features of the centroids can be used to represent the spectral features of the corresponding image objects. Our proposed algorithm is developed based on this assumption.

2.2.2. Constructing the Geochemical Topology Graph

As shown in Figure 2, the geochemical dataset can be collected as a group of centroids in an area. At the suggestion of [24], for regional geochemical exploration, only capturing the multivariable (multi-elemental) geochemical anomalies may be insufficient because their spatial distribution also reflects complex geological processes such as mineralization. To achieve this, the undirected graph (G) [24] which is used to connect closely related centroids to represent the spatial structure from point data is constructed as:

$$X = \{\vec{X_1}, \vec{X_2}, \ldots, \vec{X_N}\}, \vec{X_i} \in R^F \quad (1)$$

$$A = \{A_{1,1}, A_{1,2}, \ldots, A_{N,N}\}, A_{i,j} = \begin{cases} 1, & d_{i,j} \le K \\ 0, & d_{i,j} > K \end{cases} \quad (2)$$

where X and A represent the set of nodes/centroids, and edges, respectively; N represents the number of nodes in the graph; F denotes the number of features, namely geochemical variables (elements), of each node; $d_{i,j}$ denotes the spatial distance between node j and i; K represents the distance threshold when constructing the geochemical topology graph, and generally, the smaller the distance between these two centroids is, the more related they are [24]; 1—connected edge and 0—disconnected.

In our case, $N = 663$; $F = 11$, which means there are 11 I-series or S-series ore-forming elements; and K is determined by the global Moran's I analysis according to [24].

Global Moran's I is a measure of the overall clustering of the spatial data. Figure 3 gives the global Moran's I values versus different distance bands of all the geochemical variables. According to [32], if the Moran's I value decreases rapidly as the distance band increases, there is a strong dependency relationship between the spatial structure and distance; on the contrary, if the Moran's I value decreases slowly as the distance band increases, this indicates a stable spatial structure [32]. Obviously, the inflection point of the curve can act as the optimal threshold K to balance partial heterogeneity (i.e., anomaly) and the background features. An edge connects two adjacent centroids when the distance between them is less than K, and remains disconnected otherwise.

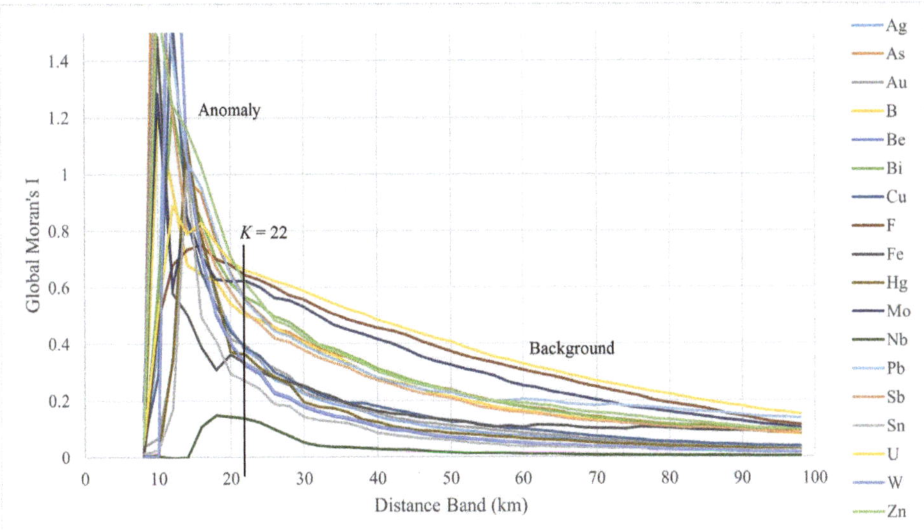

Figure 3. Variation in global Moran's I index with different distance bands (namely K).

It can be seen from Figure 3 that there is a clear turning point at about 20 km for most of the ore-forming elements. For insurance purposes, here we use $K = 22$ as the distance threshold to construct the geochemical topology graph for subsequent network training and anomaly detection. Figure 4 is the generated topology graph, and each node of it corresponds to $F = 11$ features or geochemical variables [33]. Obviously, such a topology graph integrates both the spatial structural features and multi-elemental concentrations for a group of centroids in a given area.

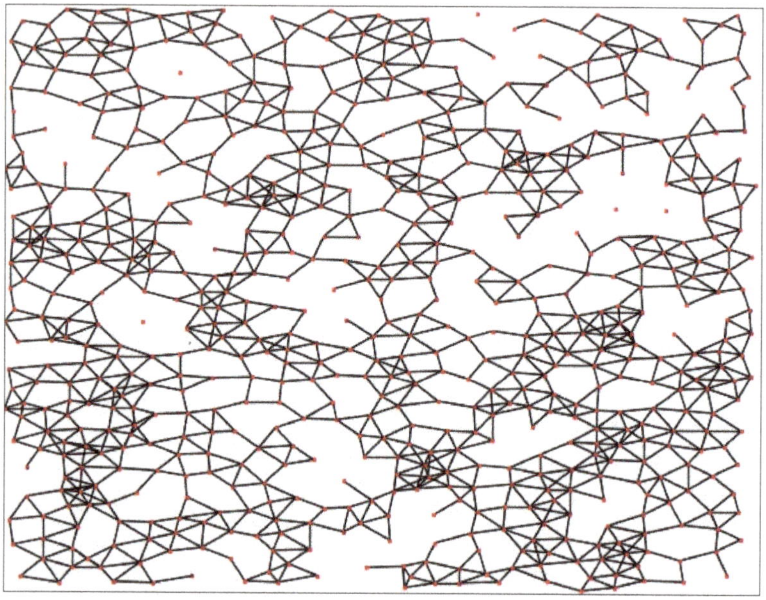

Figure 4. The geochemical topology graph in the study area. Red dot—the graph node; black line—edge.

2.2.3. The Graph Network Architecture

Figure 5 gives the pipeline of the OGE architecture. Its basic components include a GAT-dominated encoder, a GCN-dominated decoder, the loss function, and so on. A detailed description of them is provided below.

(1) The GAT-Dominated Encoder.

GAT is one of the most popular GNN (Graph Neural Network) architectures and is considered as the state-of-the-art architecture for representation learning with graphs [33]. As illustrated in Figure 6, GAT is a two-step procedure: first, it calculates the attention coefficients (or say weights) of each graph edge according to the masked attention mechanism; afterwards, it aggregates the neighboring node features according to their weights [27].

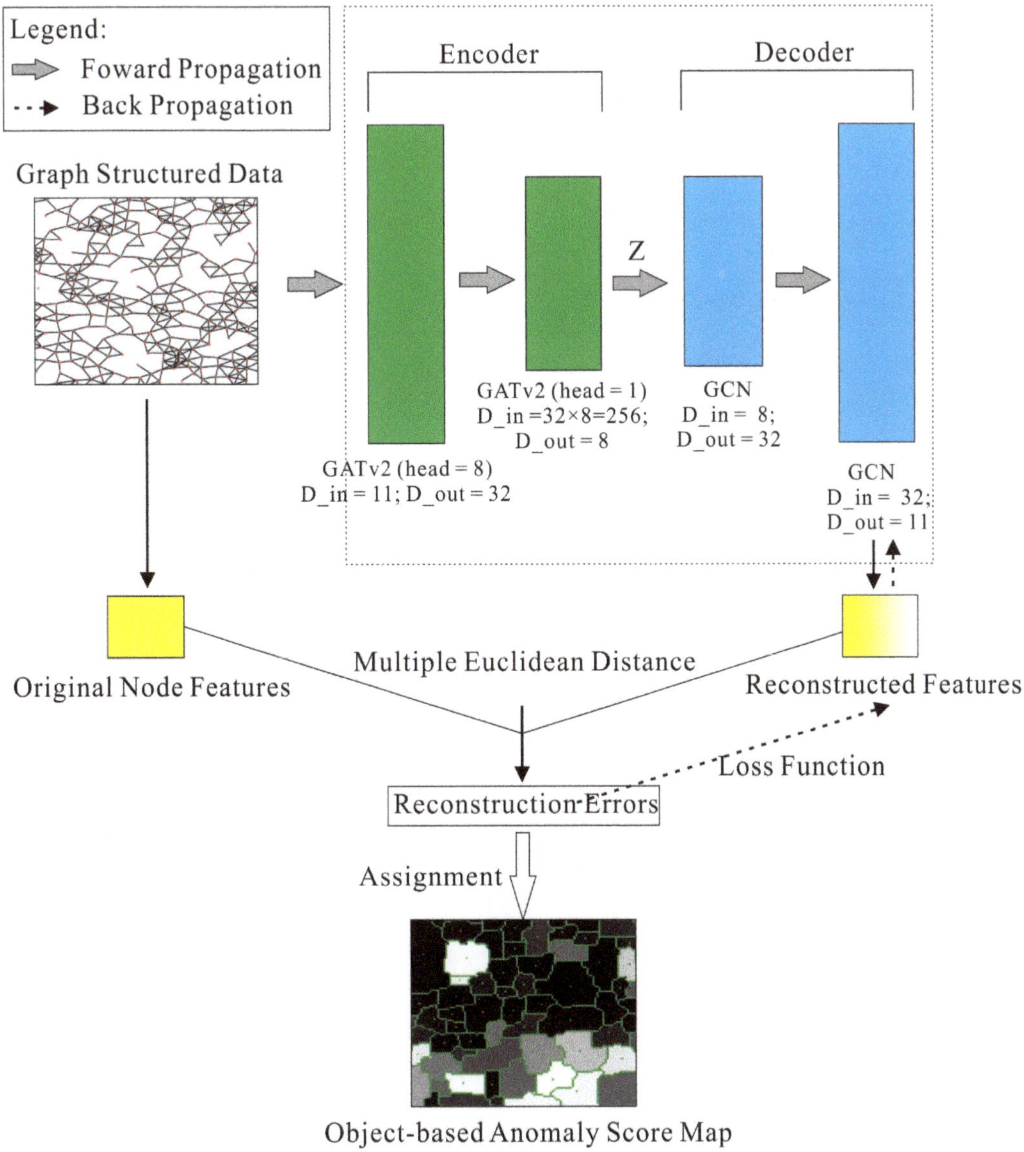

Figure 5. The overall OGE framework for geochemical anomaly identification. GATv2: Graph Attention Networks (Version 2); GCN: Graph Convolution Networks; D_in/D_out: Number of input/output channels.

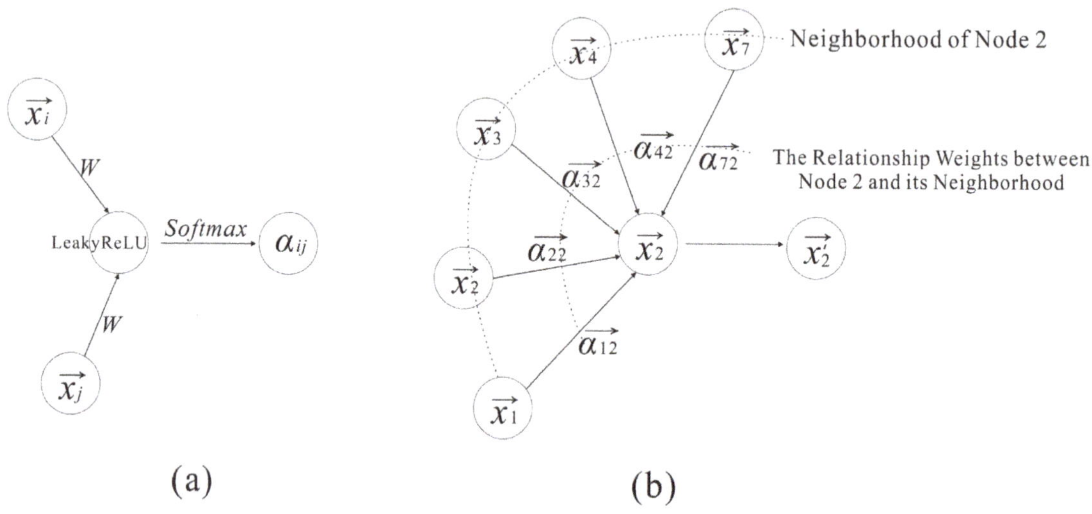

Figure 6. Illustration of the GAT layer (Modified after [24]): (**a**) how to determine the attention coefficient, corresponding to the Formula (3); (**b**) aggregating features of the node 2-based attention mechanism, with neighborhood {1,3,4,7}, corresponding to the Formula 4.

Given an input topology graph $G\ (X, A)$ containing N nodes/centroids, each node has a feature vector $\vec{x_i}$ and dimension F. The attention coefficients α_{ij} between nodes i and j is calculated as:

$$\begin{aligned}\alpha_{ij} &= softmax\left(attention\left(W\cdot\vec{x_i},\ W\cdot\vec{x_j}\right)\right) \\ &= softmax\left(LeakyReLU\left(\vec{a}^{T}\left[W\cdot\vec{x_i}\,||\,W\cdot\vec{x_j}\right]\right)\right)\end{aligned} \tag{3}$$

where *attention*() represents a single-layer feedforward neural network with a weight vector $\vec{a}$; W represents the weight matrix for transforming the input features into higher-level features; ^{T} and $||$ represent the transposition and concatenation operations, respectively; LeakyReLU is a non-linear activation function; and *softmax*() is used to normalize the neighbors of node i between 0 and 1.

After that, GAT aggregates each neighboring node and obtains the embedded features as follows:

$$\vec{x_i}' = \sigma\left(\sum_{j\in N_i}\alpha_{ij}\cdot W\cdot\vec{x_j}\right)\vec{x_i} \in N_i \tag{4}$$

where $\vec{x_i}$ and $\vec{x_i}'$ represent the input data and embedded features, respectively; σ-*sigmoid*() is used to normalize the output between 0 and 1; N_i denotes the neighbors of node i. From the geological point of view, the geochemical signatures of mineralization-favored spaces inherited from multiple geochemical processes are often anisotropic [7], and Formula (4) indicates that the anisotropy of the node i in terms of geochemical signatures can be characterized by the relationship weights α_{ij} of node i's neighborhood points $\{x_j, j = 1, 2, \ldots, N_i\}$, including itself, see Figure 6b.

Authors in [34] further pointed out that: in GAT, every node attends to its neighbors given its own representation as the query, but for any query, the neighbor-scoring is monotonic with respect to per-node scores. This could be problematic in real-world applications. To remove this limitation, they proposed GATv2 by just modifying the order of operations in GAT. Their experiments demonstrated that GATv2 outperforms GAT in all benchmarks while having the same parametric cost. Inasmuch, as shown in Figure 5, this study used two GATv2 layers to construct the encoder of OGE, and then, the input geochemical topology graph is learned and mapped to a low-dimensional vector space Z. Our encoder can seamlessly learn the compositional relationships of eleven geochemical variables (i.e., nodal attributes) and their spatial structural features. On the contrary, traditional encoders (backbone networks) based on convolutional layers or self-attention can only process data with regular spatial arrangements, and they cannot be applied to extract features from graph structured data.

(2) The GCN-Dominated Decoder.

GCN is a type of convolutional neural network that can work directly on graphs and take advantage of their structural information [33]. To put it simply, for each node, first we get the feature information from all its neighbors including itself, and then, we take the average of all its neighbors (assuming we use the *average*() function), after that, these average values will be feed into a fully connected neural network [33]. Note that in practice, we usually use more sophisticated aggregate functions rather than *average*(). In Figure 5, a GCN-based decoder, which is symmetric to the encoder architecture, was proposed to reconstruct the nodal attributes from the encoded latent representations Z. Finally, we use the *sigmoid*() function to restrict the reconstructed background values within the range of [0, 1].

Maybe it is better to use GAT layers to construct the decoder structurally symmetric to the encoder. If so, D_out of the second GAT layer in the decoder must be divisible by the number of nodal features (11), or say D_out * 8 (the number of heads) must be equal to 11 and D_out must be an integer, but it is obviously not possible in our case. So instead, GCN was applied to obtain the nodal reconstructed features.

(3) The Loss Function.

Our OGE is an unsupervised machine learning approach, so its loss function does not involve manually annotated labels. At the suggestion of Guan et al. [24], here we use the unsupervised SPRE (i.e., sampling point reconstruction error) function as our loss function, which is formulized as:

$$L_{SPRE} = \frac{1}{N}\sum_{i=1}^{N} A_i \tag{5}$$

$$A_i = \sqrt{\sum_{k=1}^{F}\left(x_i^k - x'^k_i\right)^2} \tag{6}$$

where x_i^k and x'^k_i represent the kth original and reconstructed nodal features of ith node, respectively; N and F denote the number of nodes/centroids and variable categories, respectively; A_i denotes the reconstruction error (or say the anomaly score) for each centroid, namely the multivariate Euclidean distance between the original geochemical values and the reconstructed background values.

By minimizing the Formula (5), OGE can continuously learn the spatial structural features and compositional relationship from the input graph structured data by back propagation, and then approximate iteratively the input attributed graph with encoded latent features until the L_{SPRE} function converges [24]. After that, we input the original geochemical topology data into the trained model to obtain the reconstructed geochemical background values for each node or centroid. And then, we calculate the reconstruction error (namely A_i) for each node. Finally, the geochemical anomaly score map is generated by assigning the nodal reconstruction errors back to the corresponding image objects as the summary statistics. This process is summarized and pictured in Figure 5.

2.2.4. Data Post-Processing

After obtaining the object-oriented anomaly score map, we need a binarization threshold defining whether a given image object is anomalous or not. In this article, the threshold value is empirically set as the 50% quantile (median) of the object-oriented anomaly score matrix, which is 0.089434 for the I-type elemental association, 0.091733 for the S-type association, and 0.12807 for all the ore-forming elements.

In addition, as the anomaly score is an object-level summary statistics, so our post-processing operations will focus on the within-object statistical analysis as mentioned in the Introduction. From the geological perspective, differentiation-dominant processes are believed to be the pivotal cause of metallogenesis [30], and the fractal dimension (*D*) [15] is introduced here to describe the differentiation degree of each anomalous patch. As a within-object statistical parameter, *D* is used to quantify the power-law relationship between multi-elemental contents and their cumulative summation in a given image object. It can be computed and interpreted in the following way:

$$N(\geq r) = Cr^{-D}\ (r > 0) \tag{7}$$

where r is the multi-elemental content value within an image object, and $N(\geq r)$ denotes the summation of content values larger than or equal to a given r; $C > 0$ is a proportionality coefficient, and the exponent D is known as the fractal dimension.

Mathematically, a number of straight-line segments (namely scaleless intervals) can be derived from Formula (7) on the log-log paper. It aims to cluster a dataset into most similar groups in the same segment and most dissimilar groups in different segments [15]. For two adjacent straight lines with different slopes, D_n & D_{n+1}, the inflection point (*T*) is routinely determined by RSS:

$$\text{RSS} = \sum_{i=1}^{i_0}[\ln N(r_i) + D_1 \ln r_i - \ln C_1]^2 + \sum_{i=i_0+1}^{N}[\ln N(r_i) + D_2 \ln r_i - \ln C_2]^2 \rightarrow \text{Min} \tag{8}$$

where RSS denotes the "residual sum of squares", and r_{i_0} is the dividing threshold (namely T_n, n = 1, 2,. . .). In a similar fashion, the slopes of several scaleless segments, as well as the thresholds between them, can be quantitatively determined.

As shown in Figure 7, in this step, they are customarily classified into two segments, D_1 and D_2. According to Zhao et al. [15], the dimension D can be used to measure the clustering degree of a dataset, which is a diagnostic spatial distribution pattern for ore-related geological objects. The larger the D value, the steeper is the line, the greater is the rate of change in elemental content, the lower is the degree of clustering, and vice versa. Note that D_1 usually represents the low-content background information, and it does not change much over different image objects, so we use D_2 as an indicator to quantify the multi-elemental clustering. Suppose there are L pixels in an image object, and each object has F data layers representing different geochemical variables, and then, all of the $L \times F$ content values will be fed into the fractal algorithm aforementioned. As the selected elements are paragenetically associated with each other, and their content values are normalized to [0, 1] by subtracting the mean values, so if the metallogenesis or differentiation occurs, the content values of these elements within a given object will become more clustered, which corresponds to a smaller D_2; otherwise, they remain scattered because of the weak feature of elemental association, which corresponds to a larger D_2 value. In addition, we do not have to make a strict assumption that the multi-elemental contents follow a multi-fractal distribution when conducting the within-object statistical analysis, for the algorithm can adaptively process or yield new insights for those non-fractal data [35]. Finally, every image object will be assigned a dimension value that can be used to modify the anomalous regions delineated by OGE.

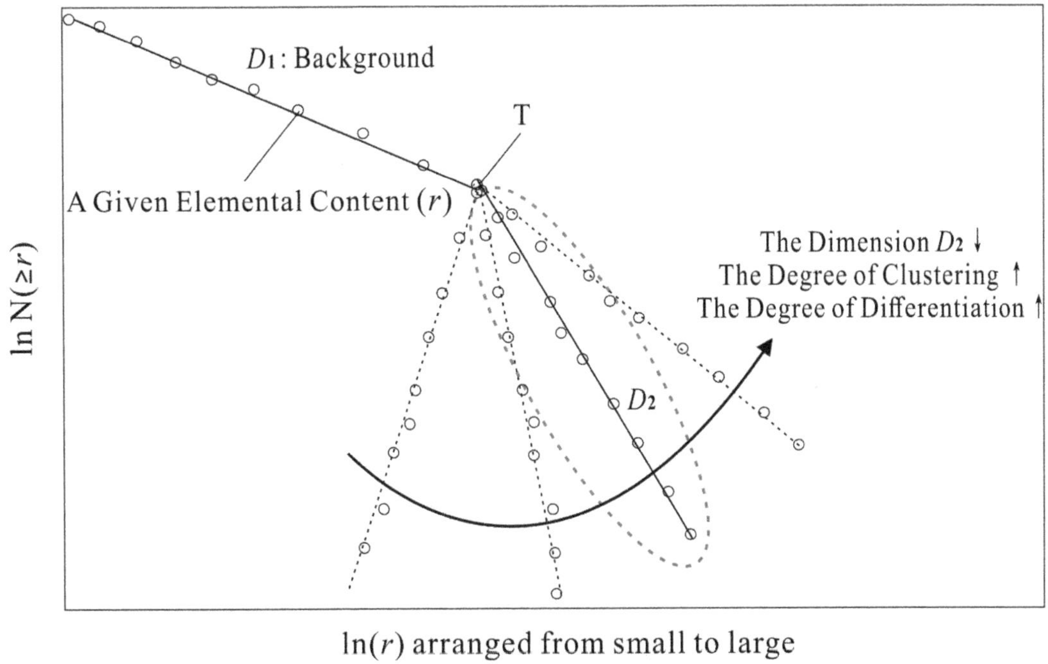

Figure 7. The fractal schema ln N(≥r) versus ln r.

3. Results

3.1. Implementation Details

We implement the proposed OGE model as well as the relevant pre- and post- processing using the Python framework which is open source. The most important packages involved in the programming experiments include but not limited to Pytorch, Pytorch Geometric, Numpy, Networkx, and so on. OGE was conducted on a single NVIDIA Tesla V100 with 32 GB of GPU memory and train for 2000 epochs to make the model converge. We use the Adam optimizer to train our models from scratch, and the initial learning rate is set to 0.005, and the weight decay coefficient is set to 0.0005 By the way, the primary purpose of regional geochemical exploration is to delimit areas of interest for further exploration, and thus, the performance of OGE can be evaluated or described from two perspectives: the percentage of discovered mineral deposits to the total mineral deposits—the recognition rate, and the size of the anomalous area.

For a better illustration, taking the I-series elemental association as example, Figure 8 gives the recognition rate versus loss curves during the training phase. As can be seen, before completing 160 epochs, both the recognition rate and the training loss decrease sharply. And then, the decreasing trend of loss become slow, eventually stabilizing at 0.124 or so; meanwhile, the growth of the recognition rate rises and became oscillating, centered at 0.837. So, in order to jump over the oscillation area, here we set the training epoch as 2000.

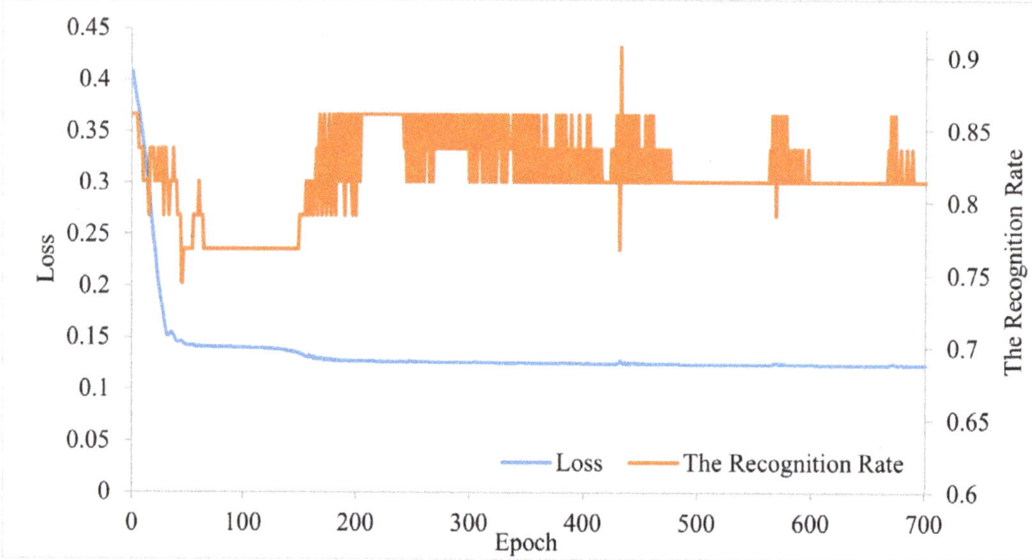

Figure 8. Variation in loss and the recognition rate with number of training epochs. Note that: here we set the threshold of the anomaly score map as median, and the recognition rate is calculated as the ratio of the number of ore spots falling within the anomalous areas to the total number of known ore spots.

3.2. The Object-Based Anomaly Score Map

For the I-series elements, it can be seen from Figure 9 that: (1) most of the known ore spots/deposits, no matter what their scales and mineral species, fall within the image objects having higher anomaly scores (brighter colored areas). (2) Using the median value as the threshold, there are 30 ore spots falling within the delineated anomalous regions, and 13 spots falling outside. The recognition rate is 69.767%. (3) Using the 60th percentile value as the threshold, there are 26 ore spots falling within the Level I anomalies, and the recognition rate is 60.465%. (3) The Level II anomalous area accounts for 49.778% of the total area, and the Level I area accounts for 40.079%. (4) Many of the anomalous objects are barren, especially those on the northwest corner of the study area. (5) Most of the mineral spots except Au falling outside the anomalous regions occur nearby the anomalous boundaries. If we create a 4-pixel buffer zone around the Level II anomalous objects, there are only 4 ore spots falling outside, and the ore-spot recognition rate comes up to 90.70%. (6) If we create a buffer zone around the Level I anomalies, the recognition rate increases to 74.419%.

For the S-series elements, it can be seen from Figure 10 that: (1) there are 40 ore spots falling within the Level II anomalous regions, and only 7 spots falling outside. The recognition rate is 85.106%. (2) there are 33 ore spots falling within the Level I anomalies, and the recognition rate is 70.213% (3) most of the ore spots falling outside the anomalous regions occur nearby the anomalous boundaries, and relevant anomaly scores fluctuate between 0.030 and 0.070. If we create a 4-pixel buffer zone around the Level II anomalous patches, there are only one fluorite ore-spot falling outside, and the recognition rate comes up to 97.87%. (4) If we create a buffer zone around the Level I anomalies, the recognition rate increases to 78.723%. (5) The Level II anomalous area without the buffer zone accounts for 50.054% of the total area, and the buffered anomalous area accounts for 68.24%. (6) The spatial distribution of the anomalous regions in Figure 10 is generally consistent with that in Figure 9.

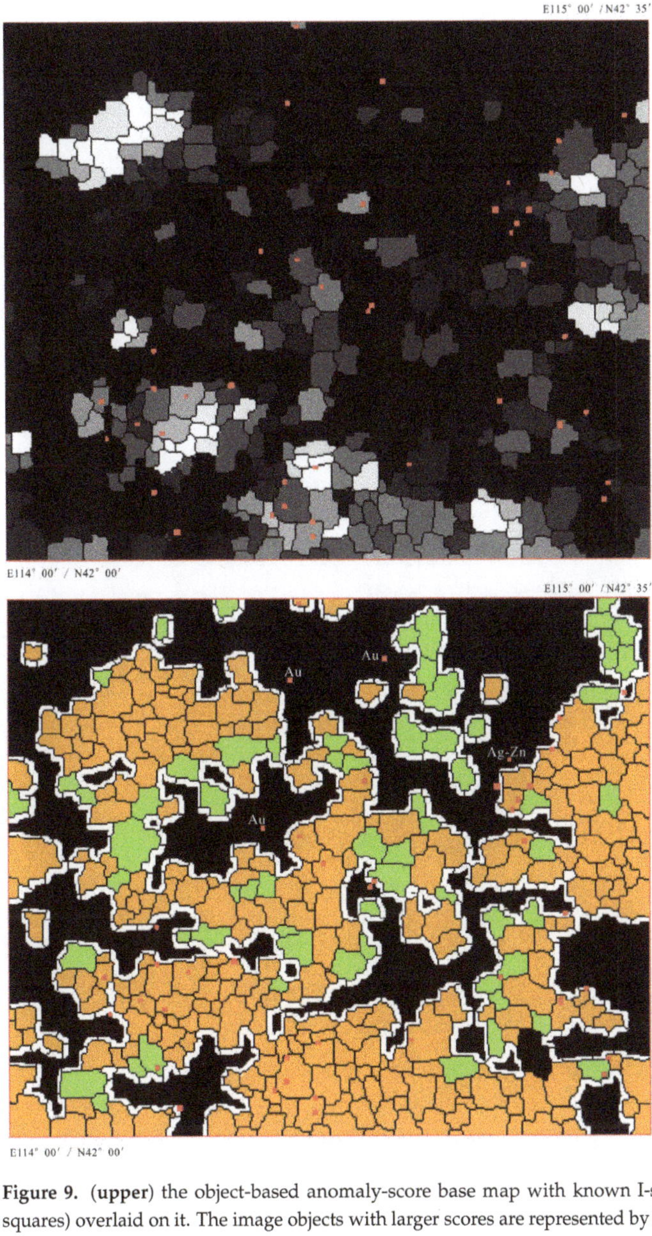

Figure 9. (**upper**) the object-based anomaly-score base map with known I-series ore spots (red squares) overlaid on it. The image objects with larger scores are represented by brighter tones, while image objects with smaller scores are represented by darker tones. (**lower**) the delineated anomalous regions (green-colored patches—Level II anomalies, orange-colored patches—Level I anomalies, delineated by the 60% quantile) with ore spots overlaid on it. We also created a 4-pixel buffering zone (white colored belts) around the known anomalous regions. Note: the mineral species include Cu, Au, Fe, Mo, Hg, Ag-Pb-Zn-Fe, Ag-Pb-Zn, Pb-Zn, Cu-Zn, Ag-Pb, Pb, Zn, and U. In the lower picture, the ore spots not falling in the anomalous objects are labelled with their mineral species. The size of the ore spots is proportional to the mineralized scale ranging from mineralized spots to small- and medium-scaled ore deposits. Actually, most of the ore spots shown in Figure 9 are mineralized spots, namely micro-mineralization outcrops. The ore-spot data are provided by reference [29].

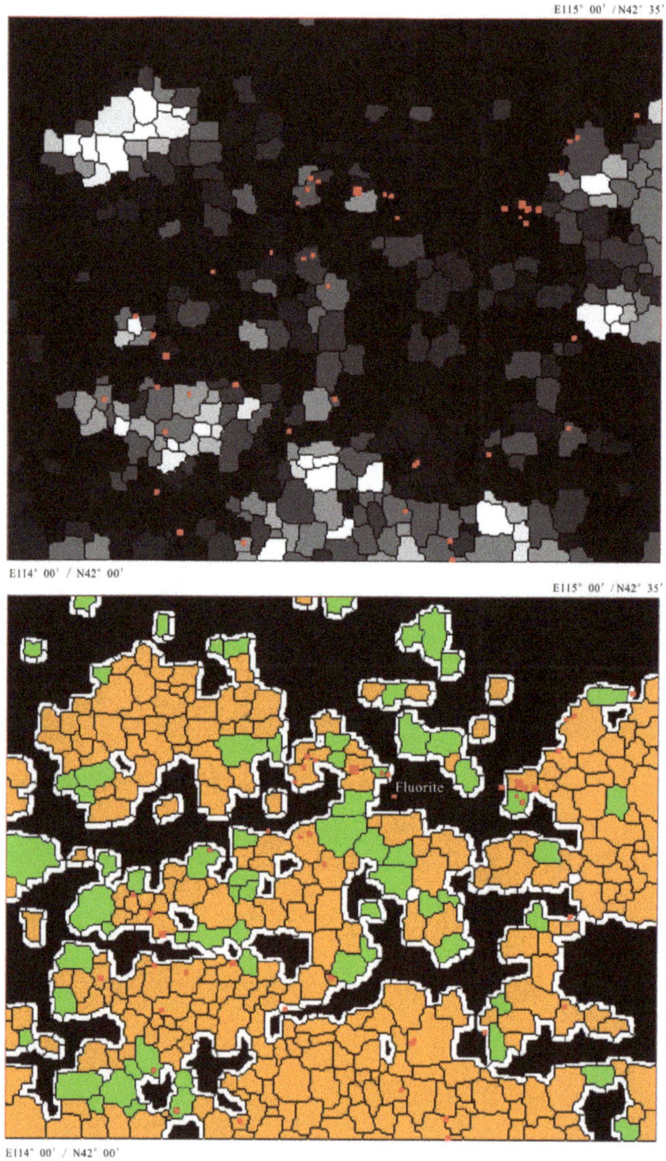

Figure 10. (**upper**) the object-based anomaly-score base map with known S-series ore spots (red squares) overlaid on it; (**lower**) the delineated anomalous regions (green-colored patches—Level II anomalies, orange-colored patches—Level I anomalies, delineated by the 60% quantile) with mineral spots overlaid on it. We also created a 4-pixel buffering zone (white colored belts) around the known anomalous regions. Note: the mineral species include Fe, Mo, Ag-Pb-Zn-Fe, Ag-Pb-Zn, Pb-Zn, Ag-Pb, Pb, W, Nb-Ta, Rb-Nb-Ta, Fluorite, W-Mo, Beryl, U, and etc. Other legends in this figure are consistent with those in Figure 9 if not specified.

Figure 11 gives the anomaly score map of all the ore-forming elements, and we can observe that: (1) The Level II anomalous area accounts for 49.881% of the total area. (2) There are 50 ore spots falling within the Level II anomalous regions, and 18 ore spots falling outside. (3) The recognition rate of the Level I anomalies is 66.176%. (4) In the buffered anomalous area, only 8 mineral spots falling outside, and the recognition rate increases to 88.24%. (3) Only a few ore spots fall within the image objects with the brightest tone, namely with the largest anomaly scores.

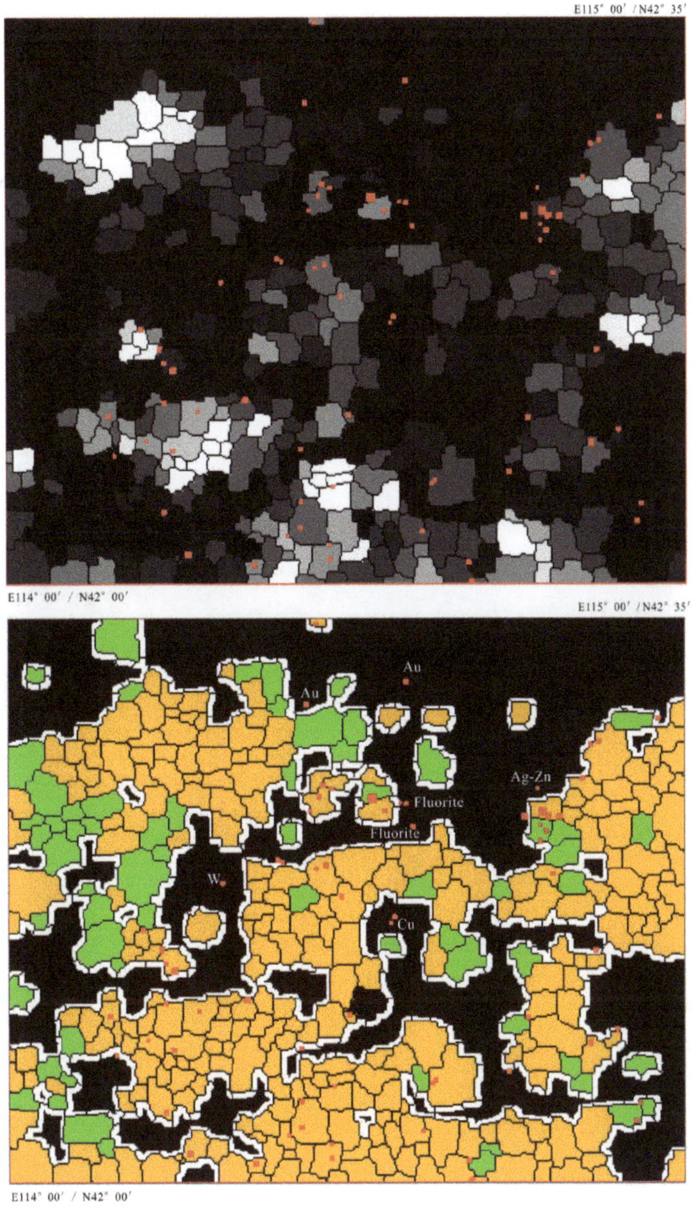

Figure 11. (**upper**) the object-based anomaly-score base map with all the known ore spots (red squares) overlaid on it; (**lower**) the buffered anomalous regions (green- and orange- colored patches edged with white) with ore spots overlaid on it. Note: the mineral species of the ore spots include Cu, Au, Fe, Mo, Hg, Ag-Pb-Zn-Fe, Ag-Pb-Zn, Pb-Zn, Cu-Zn, Ag-Pb, Pb, Zn, W, Nb-Ta, Rb-Nb-Ta, Fluorite, W-Mo, Beryl, U, etc. Other legends in this figure are consistent with those in Figure 9 if not specified.

Given the above, OGE's performance on S-series elements is even better than that on I-Series elements. The main drawback of our methodology is that the delineated anomalous area is too large and many of the anomalous patches are barren, which is not helpful for guiding the follow-up anomaly verification. As stated before, these results may demonstrate the possible pitfalls of using object-level anomaly scores due to their possible misrepresentation of the within-object geochemical characteristics [10]. That is to say, the anomalies delineated by OGE must be further modified through the within-object multi-elemental statistical analysis.

3.3. Elemental Within-Object Separability

Figure 12 gives the object-based map of dimension (D_2) for the I-series and S-series elemental associations, respectively. We note that as the geochemical behaviors of the I-series elements are quite different from those of the S-series elements [30], so the object-based D_2 map for all elements was not calculated here. From Figures 12 and 13, we have delivered three important observations as follows:

(1) The D_2 values of the image objects containing the known ore spots vary in a wide range. For the I-series ore spots, the relevant dimension values fluctuate between 2 and 116 with a peak at 18 (The original D_2 values were normalized to [0, 255]), and if we set $D_2 = 116$ as the binarization threshold, the obtained anomalous area accounts for 98.63% of the total area. For the S-series ore spots, the relevant dimension values fluctuate between 1 and 32 with a peak at 14, and if we set $D_2 = 32$ as the threshold, the obtained anomalous area will account for 78.93%.

(2) As the histogram of the D_2 map is usually right-skewed, so we empirically set the binarization threshold as the mode value + 1 × standard deviation (for a standard normal distribution, 68.3% of data falls within one standard deviation of the mean, so we suppose that most, if not all, of the ore-spots would fall within the objects with the D_2 value $\leq$ mode + 1 × standard deviation). For I-series elements, the threshold is 36, and for S-series, it is 34. Our purpose of image binarization is not to delineate the anomalous regions like Figures 9–11 do, but to delineate some highly confident non-anomalous objects. That is why in Figure 12, very few ore-spots fall in the colored patches. Naturally, by removing these non-anomalous objects from Figures 9 and 10, we can obtain a moderately reduced prospecting-target-area as shown in Figure 13.

(3) In Figure 13 (upper), the anomalous area of I-series elements decreases to 43.045% of the total area, and the buffered anomalous area decreases to 61.608%. Only 5 ore-spots fall outside the reduced anomalous target area, which are Au, Pb-Zn, and Ag-Zn mineral spots. In Figure 13 (lower), the anomalous area of S-series elements decreases to 43.172% of the total area, and the buffered area decreases to 61.534%. Only 2 ore-spots fall outside the target area, which are fluorite and Pb-Zn spots.

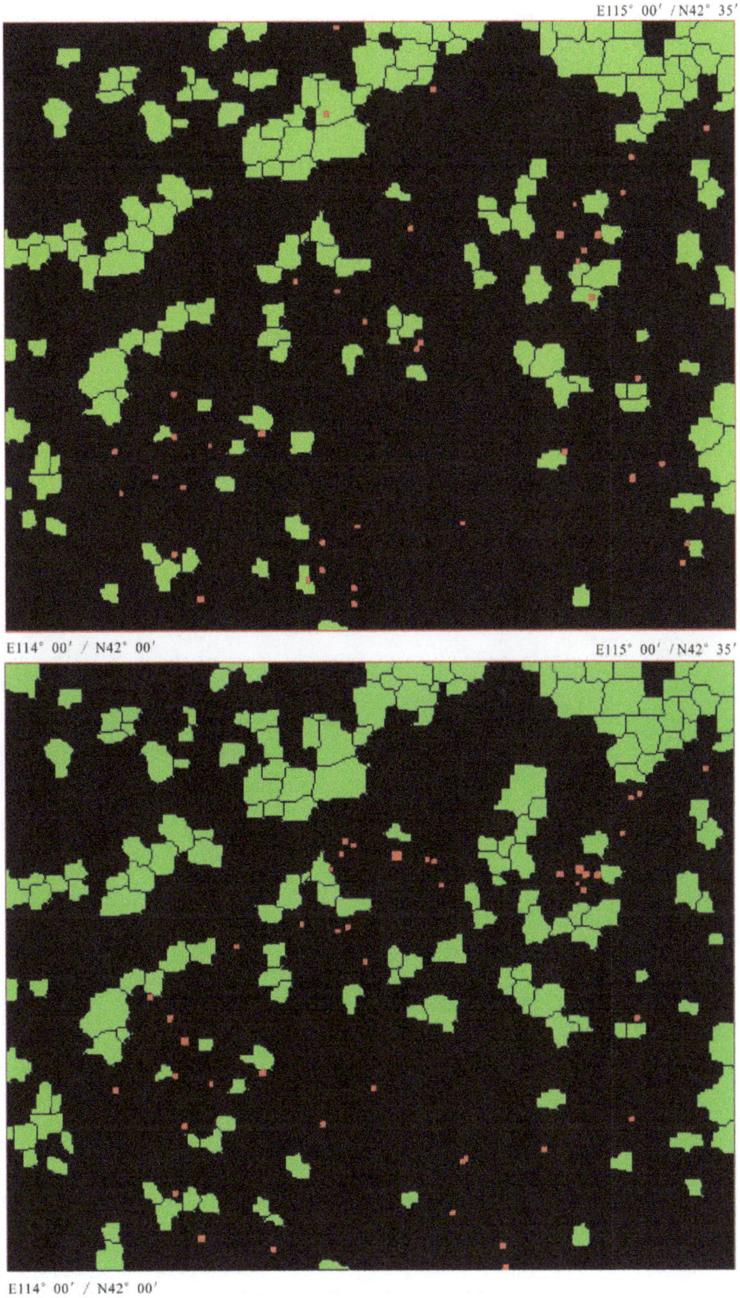

Figure 12. (**upper**) the object-based D_2 map for I-series elements with relevant ore spots (red squares) overlaid on it. (**lower**) the D_2 map for S-series elements with relevant ore spots overlaid on it. The green colored patches represent the delineated non-anomalous regions.

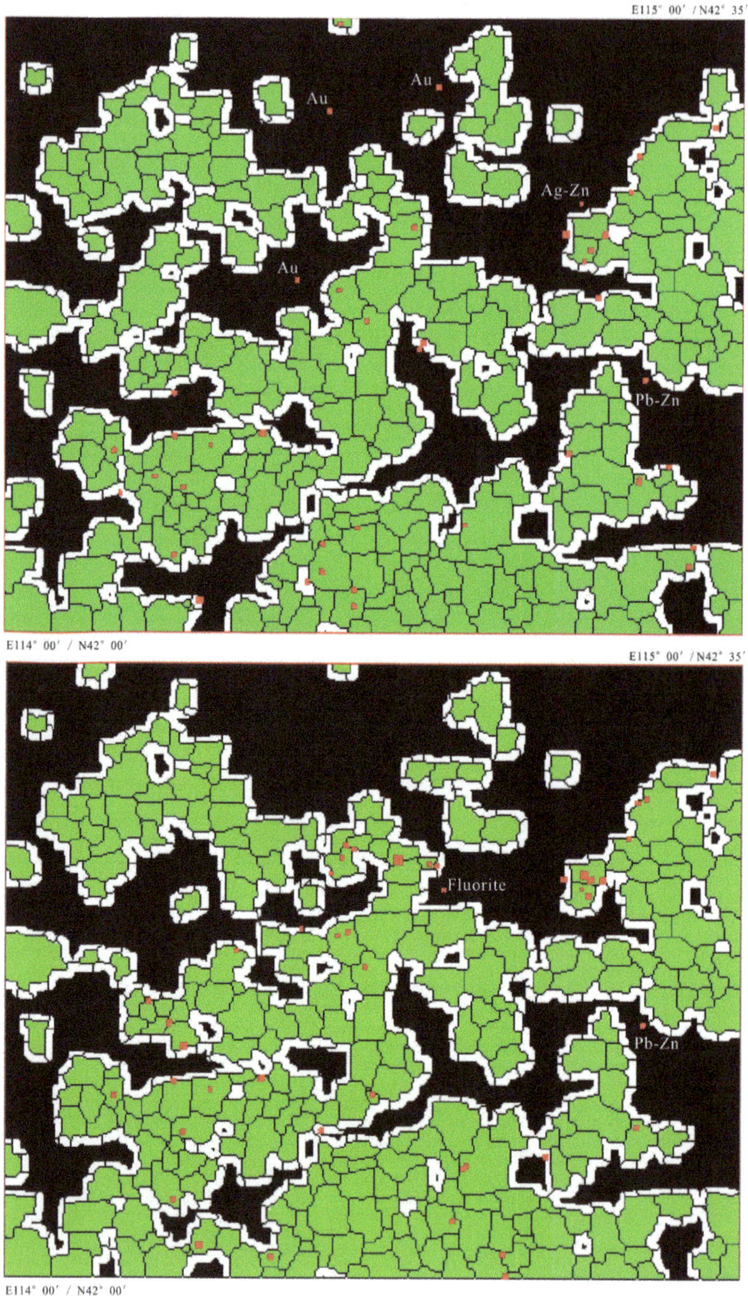

Figure 13. (**upper**) the buffered anomalous regions (green colored patches edged with white, delineated by the 50% quantile) for I-series elements with relevant ore spots overlaid on it. (**lower**) the buffered anomalous regions for S-series elements with relevant ore spots overlaid on it. The ore spots not falling in the anomalous regions are labelled with their mineral species. Other legends in this figure are consistent with those in Figures 9 and 10.

3.4. Comparison and Validation by Factor Analysis

The best way to validate the effectiveness of our OGE algorithm is to observe how many ore spots can fall into the anomalous image objects, but this is not enough because most of the anomalous patches in Figure 13 are barren. Comparing Figure 13 to Figure 1, we also discover that the presence of ore spots and anomalies is not completely controlled by the spatial distribution of the outcropped bedrocks and known geological structure. For example, over a third of the known ore spots occur within the N_2b and Quaternary-covered areas with less geological exposure. Inasmuch, it is difficult to directly validate the anomalies from the perspective of regional geology. In this Section, the factor analysis is used to do so. As we know, factor analysis is a well-validated technique that is widely used to reduce a large number of variables into fewer numbers of factors [32]. Although irrespective of the spatial structure of geochemical patterns, it facilitates the identification of multivariate geochemical anomalies. This is consistent with the major aim of OGE. So, supposing the results of factor analysis are tenable and close to truth, we can cross-validate the correctness and robustness of our model's outputs by observing if the factor-score anomalies overlap considerably with the anomalies delineated in Figure 13.

We can make the following observations from Figure 14: (1) Nearly all the factor-score anomalies, no matter what the elemental association each factor represents, reside within the OGE-derived anomalous areas, and occupy most of the interior space. This result strongly supports the basic correctness of our model's outputs. (2) Our OGE model is advantageous since quite a few ore spots that cannot be identified by the factor-score anomalies are well-identified by OGE. (3) The I-series elemental association can be further divided into five factors: Factor 1: As-Pb-Zn, Factor 2: Ag-B-Cu, Factor 3: Au-Hg, Factor 4: Mo-U, and Factor 5: Fe_2O_3. Likewise, the S-series elements can be divided into: Factor 1: Bi-W, Factor 2: Pb-Sb-Sn, Factor 3: Mo-U, Factor 4: Nb-Fe_2O_3, and Factor 5: Be-F. These divisions improve the interpretability of the extracted anomalies and facilitate the mineral species-specific geochemical exploration.

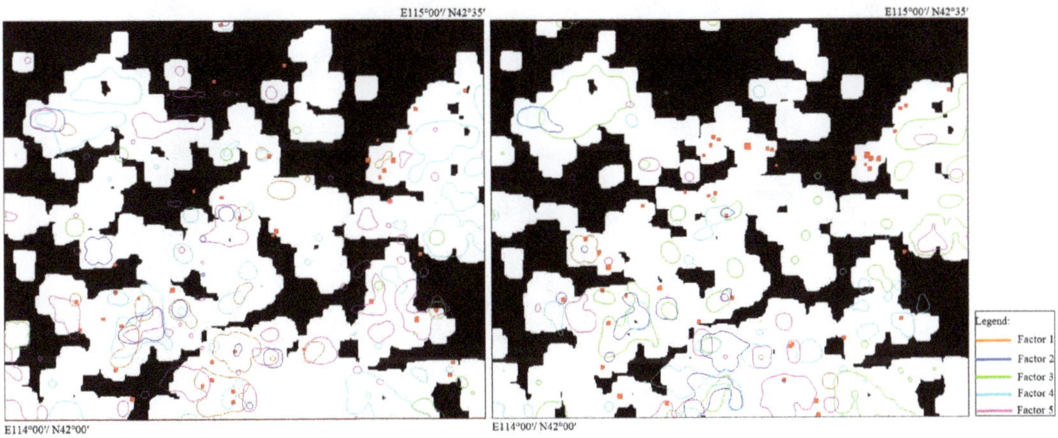

Figure 14. The geochemical anomalous areas (white) delineated in Figure 13 with relevant factor-score anomalies (colored polygons) overlaid on them. (**Left**): the I-series elements. (**Right**) the S-series elements. Note that: the factor-score anomalies were obtained by setting the binarization threshold as mean + 1 × standard deviation. Other legends in this figure are consistent with those in Figures 9 and 10.

Given the above, by calculating the ore-spot recognition rate and conducting factor analysis, the OGE-derived anomalies in Figure 13 get validated.

4. Discussion

In our opinion, there are six meaningful aspects around the proposed network architecture worth to discuss, which are listed in the following paragraphs.

First, many factors, e.g., steep topography, the weathering and transportation of chemical compositions in stream sediment samples, surface hydrological processes, etc., can cause displacement of geochemical anomalies from the source area [7], and that is why most of the mineral spots falling outside the delineated anomalous regions occur nearby them. Inasmuch, it is highly necessary to create buffer zones for the known anomalous regions, although the total anomalous area increases accordingly.

Second, Figure 15 gives the anomalous score map using the geochemical dataset consisting of seven major rock-forming elements (Fe_2O_3, Al_2O_3, SiO_2, MgO, Na_2O, K_2O, and CaO) as input to OGE. Here we suppose that the anomalies delineated in Figure 15 reflect the regional diagenesis. It can be seen from Figure 15 that only 6 ore-spots fall outside the anomalous regions, and the ore-spot recognition rate is as high as 91.176%, exceeding Figure 11's 88.24%. The spatial distribution of the anomalous regions in Figure 15 is also consistent with that in Figures 9–11. Obviously, owing to the strong control of bedrock geology may exert on the chemical composition of stream sediments or soil samples, the determination of geochemical anomalies can be heavily affected by the lithology background in areas with variable lithologies. That is to say, the mineralization is attached to the diagenesis, and the delineated anomalies in Figures 9–11 primarily reflects the regional diagenesis, and, to a lesser extent, the mineralization. Zhao et al. [36] further pointed out that, due to the lower spatial resolution, the 1:200,000 geochemical data cannot directly link to small-/medium-scaled ore occurrences, especially the micro-mineralization outcrops. Worse still, taking the image objects as basic analysis units tends to accentuate these trends rather than mitigate them. These explained why our delineated anomalous area is so large and is largely controlled by the outcropped bedrocks as displayed in Figure 1.

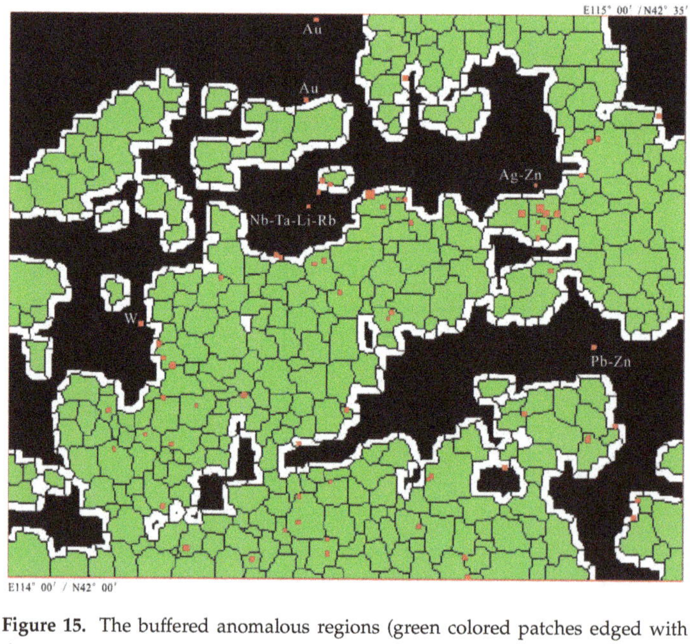

Figure 15. The buffered anomalous regions (green colored patches edged with white) with all the known ore spots overlaid on it. Note that the anomalous regions are generated by using the geochemical dataset consisting of the major rock-forming elements as input to OGE. We set the binarization threshold as the 50% quantile: 0.66982. Other legends in this figure are consistent with those in Figure 11 if not specified.

Third, in the within-object analysis stage, we use fractal dimension D_2 to measure the degree of multi-elemental clustering, but its performance in terms of reducing the prospecting-target-area is not as good as expected. We also observed that: the overall distribution pattern of the multi-elemental contents of the "pixels" in an object is usually right-skewed, thus it can be approximately modelled by a bimodal Gaussian distribution: one population deals with the normally distributed part, and the other one deals with the long right tail—although sometimes it is multi-peaked. And then, we can separate them and obtain their shape parameters, namely m_1 and m_2: the mean values of two adjacent Gaussian distributions, respectively, and $m_1 < m_2$; σ_1 and σ_2: the corresponding standard deviations. On this basis, the separability (J) [37] is calculated as:

$$J = 2(1 - e^{-B}), J \in [0, 2], \tag{9}$$

$$B = \frac{1}{8}(m_1 - m_2)^2 \frac{2}{\sigma_1^2 + \sigma_2^2} + \frac{1}{2}\ln\left[\frac{\sigma_1^2 + \sigma_2^2}{2\sigma_1\sigma_2}\right] \tag{10}$$

If the metallogenesis or differentiation occurs, the multi-elemental content values within an image object will have a small separability because of the strong feature of elemental association; otherwise, they will have a larger J value.

Unfortunately, like the case in Figure 13, only a moderately reduced prospecting-target-area was generated based on the object-oriented J map. These experiments imply that: D_2, J, as well as other manually designed features may not be a good indicator to separate multi-elemental anomalies from background, and alternatively, deep features produced by, e.g., OGE usually perform well in this case.

Fourth, the delineated anomalous area can be dramatically reduced by increasing the binarization threshold. For example, for the S-series elements, when setting the binarization threshold as the 60% quantile (0.10562), the anomalous area decreases to 40.005% of the total area, but 6 ore-spots are excluded from the buffered anomalous regions; when setting the threshold as the 70% quantile (0.12625), the anomalous area decreases to 29.872%, but 14 ore-spots are excluded; when setting the threshold as the 80% quantile (0.16079), the anomalous area decreases to 20.157%, but 22 ore-spots are excluded; when setting the threshold as 0.2202 – the 90% quantile, the anomalous area decreases to 10.022%, but 34 ore-spots fall outside the buffered anomalous regions, and only 13 ore-spots fall within. The case is similar for the I-series elements. That is to say, the anomaly scores of the ore-containing image objects vary in a wide range, from the 50% quantile to 100%. In our opinion, this can be mainly attributed to the low resolution of the geochemical data in use and its weak ability in detecting the micro-mineralization outcrops. To prove this, Figure 16 further gives the anomalous regions extracted by 1:50,000 soil/stream-sediment survey data, which is generated using the geochemical dataset consisting of 12 ore-forming elements (Ag, As, Au, Bi, Cu, Hg, Mo, Pb, Sb, Sn, W, and Zn) as input to OGE. In Figure 16, we raise the binarization threshold from the 50% quantile (median) to the 60% quantile, and the anomalous area decreases to 38.11% of the total area accordingly. Comparing to Figure 11, a 11.77% reduction in anomalous area has been achieved without affecting the recognition rate: only 7 ore-spots fall outside the buffered anomalous area. If we raise the threshold to the 70% quantile, the anomalous area decreases to 29.54%, and only 11 ore-spots fall outside (the recognition rate remains above 80%). Obviously, due to the improved spatial resolution, our OGE model is guided to focus more on regional mineralization, rather than diagenesis.

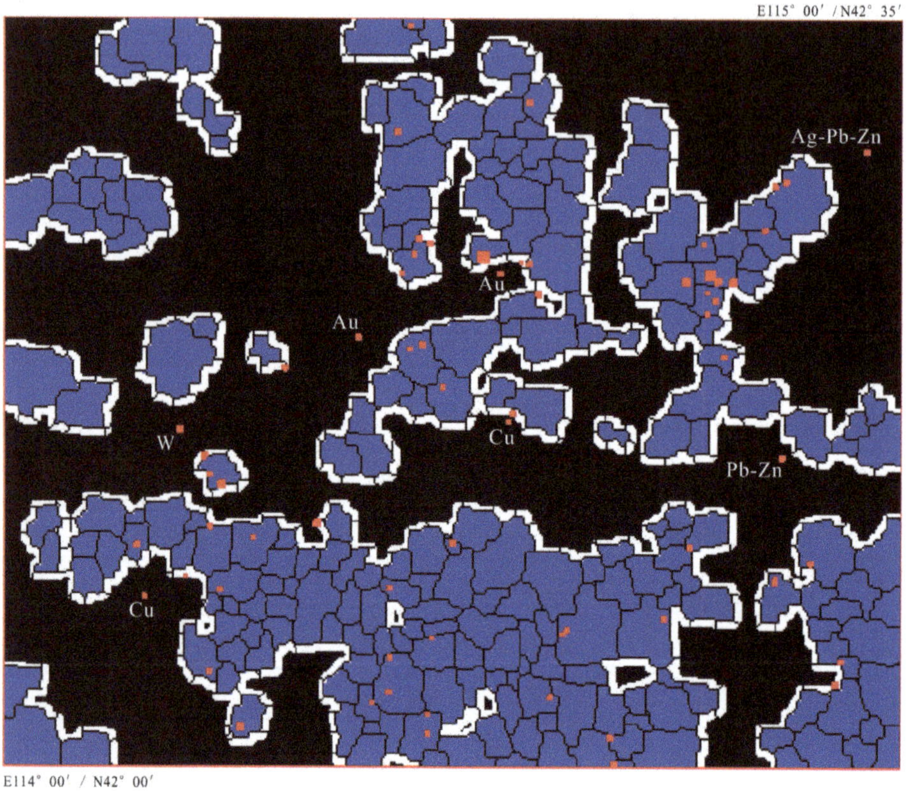

Figure 16. The buffered anomalous regions (blue colored patches edged with white) with all the known ore spots overlaid on it. Note that the anomalous regions are generated by using the 1:50,000 geochemical dataset consisting of 12 ore-forming elements (Ag, As, Au, Bi, Cu, Hg, Mo, Pb, Sb, Sn, W, and Zn) as input to OGE. We set the binarization threshold as the 60% quantile: 0.10515. Some ore spots, e.g., fluorite, Nb-Ta, etc., are removed from this figure because of the absence of relevant geochemical data. The 1:50,000 soil/stream-sediment geochemical data was provided by the Development Research Center, China Geological Survey. To ensure consistency, the 1:200,000 multiresolution segmentation result shown in Figure 2 is reused to generate the 1:50,000 anomaly score map. Other legends in this figure are consistent with those in Figure 11 if not specified.

Fifth, in the pre-processing stage, first we interpolate sampled point data into raster grids, and then, they are aggregated into different image objects, which inevitably introduces uncertainties into the data. Naturally, people may question if a reduced segmentation scale can help improve the anomaly-detection performance. To answer this question, we use the scale parameter 2.0 to segment the input geochemical image, and finally we get 2465 objects as displayed in Figure 17. Taking the S-series elements as example, comparing to Figure 10 (upper), more details about the anomalies have emerged, but their spatial distribution patterns are generally consistent with those in Figure 10. We still have to set the binarization threshold as median to keep the ore-spot recognition rate greater than 90%, whereas if we raise the threshold to the 70% quantile, only 9 mineral spots fall outside the buffered anomalous area, and the recognition rate remains greater than 80%. Figure 18 gives the big picture: when we set the threshold smaller than or equal to the 60% quantile, the OGE analysis performed at higher levels of scale has higher recognition rate; whereas when we set the threshold greater than the 60% quantile, lower levels of scale may perform better. Figure 17 is such an example: when the threshold is set as the 70% quantile and the scale parameter is set as 2, 81.4% of the I-series mineral spots can fall within the corresponding buffered-anomalous-area which accounts for <45% of the study area, and 80.9% of the S-series ore spots can be included. By contrast, if the scale parameter increases to 3, only 72% of the I-series ore spots and 70% of the S-series ore spots can be included in the relevant anomalous areas. Given the above, in order to balance the recognition rate and anomalous area, it is better to use a smaller scale parameter to segment the multivariable geochemical image.

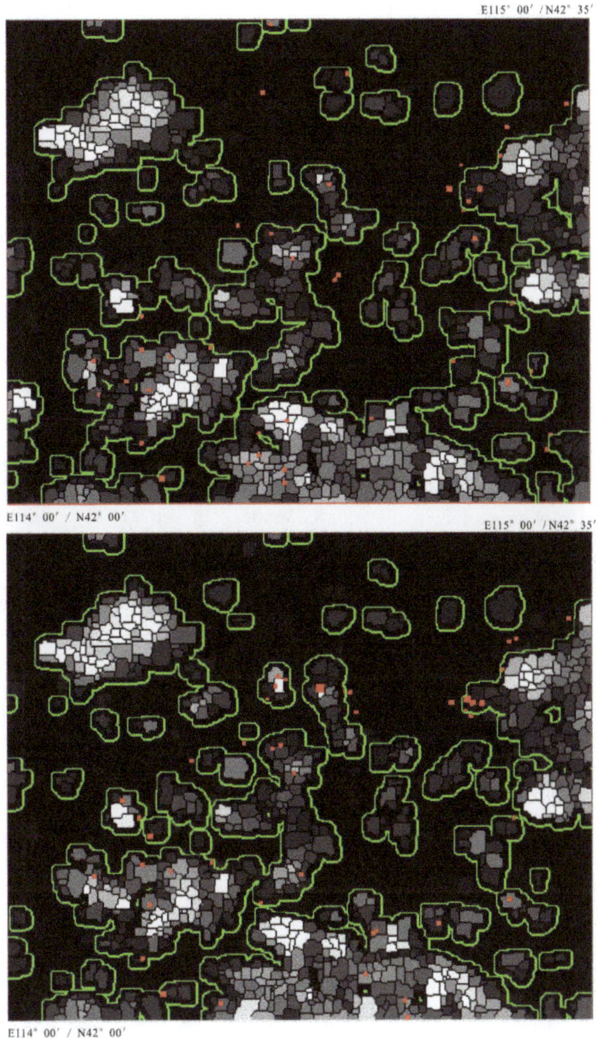

Figure 17. (**upper**) the object-based anomaly score map for I-series elements with relevant ore spots (red squares) overlaid on it. (**lower**) the object-based anomaly score map for S-series elements with relevant ore spots overlaid on it. The image objects with larger scores are represented by brighter tones, while the image objects with smaller scores are represented by darker tones. Here we set the binarization threshold as the 70th percentile value, and the regions delineated by green lines are the anomalous regions with a 3-pixel buffer zone, which account for approximately 44.375% of the total area.

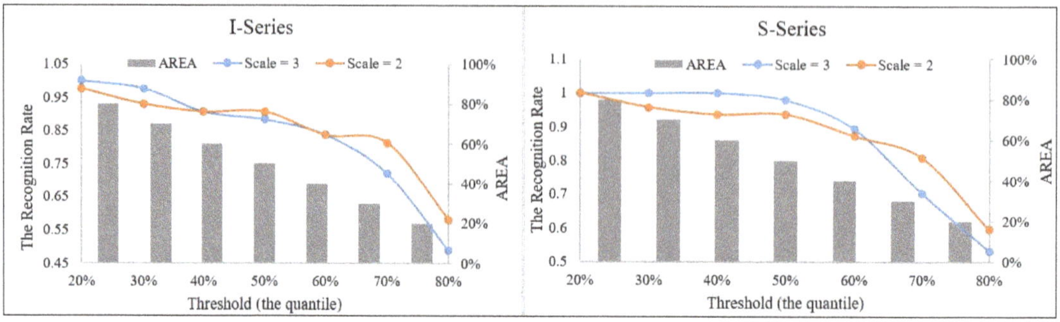

Figure 18. Plot of the recognition rate versus threshold and anomalous area. (**left**): the I-series elements; (**right**): the S-series elements.

Sixth, as our OGE architecture was developed as an updated version of GAUGE by combining OBIA and GNN (GAT & GCN) into a singular network, so it is necessary to compare the performance between them. As shown in Figure 19, which is generated by using the geochemical dataset consisting of all 18 ore-forming elements as input to GAUGE, we found that the spatial distribution patterns of the anomalous areas are generally accorded with those in Figure 11, but more details have emerged; if setting the binarization threshold as the 50% quantile, there are more than 19 ore-spots falling outside but being close to the anomalous regions; if setting the threshold as the 70% quantile, there are 25 missed ore-spots. As far as the recognition rate is concerned, the performance of GAUGE is no better than OGE. Nevertheless, even the threshold is set as the 70% quantile, most of the missed ore spots could fall within the 2 km (i.e., the controlling distance of one sampling point) buffered anomalous regions, and the ore- spot recognition rate approaches 100%. However, the resulting anomalous area will increase to >75% of the total area. In addition, the within-object statistical analysis is not supported by GAUGE. Given the above, our OGE performed better in anomaly detection: in Figure 17, more than 80% of the known ore spots were predicted in the buffered anomalous area accounting for less than 45% of the total area. In fact, both GAUGE and OGE were designed to extract both the spatial features and compositional relationships of geochemical variables collected at irregularly distributed locations. For OGE, such irregularity is implemented by the multiresolution segmentation whose output is a series of irregularly distributed centroids in irregularly shaped image objects [6], which may reflect the variation of geochemical background across the space. On the other hand, as shown in Figure 19, the sampling grid is relatively regular, and very few geochemical sampling points are missing in this area. This implies that GAUGE could not capture the practical spatial distribution characteristics of geochemical variables, which reflects complex geologic processes (i.e., mineralization). That is why the visual performance of GAUGE is not as good as expected. Other convolutional autoencoder models available in the literature, such as SCMA (Spatially Constrained Multi-Autoencoder) [38], were not discussed here because they cannot be applied to an irregular area for anomaly identification.

From the above, it is still difficult for us to reduce the anomalous area to below 30% of the study area. However, previous studies on separation of geochemical anomalies in the literature mainly focus on a singular mineral species, while our study seeks to delineate the all-mineral-species anomalies. In this sense, a relatively large anomalous-target-area may be necessary.

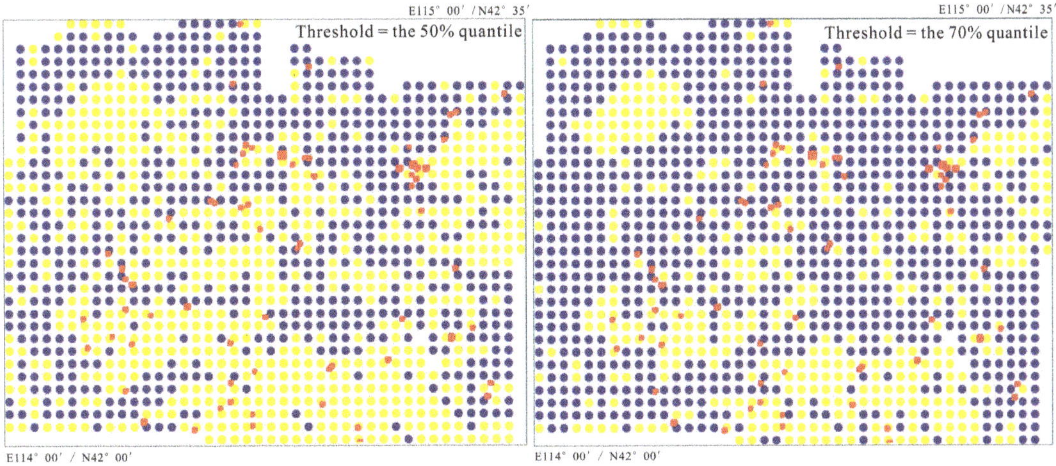

Figure 19. Anomaly map obtained by GAUGE. (**left**): threshold = the 50% quantile; (**right**) threshold = the 70% quantile. Note: the colored dots represent different geochemical sampling points; yellow dots denote anomalies and blue dots denote the background. All the known ore-spots (red squares), no matter what their scales and mineral species, are overlaid on the anomaly maps. The anomaly score maps are generated by using the geochemical dataset consisting of all 18 ore-forming elements as input to GAUGE.

5. Conclusions

The main contribution of this article is fourfold as follows: (1) to the best of our knowledge, this is the first time that the OBIA framework has been applied in regional geochemical prospecting; (2) a novel GNN architecture (OGE) has been designed to extract multi-elemental geochemical anomalies which can locate most of the known ore spots, no matter what their scales and mineral species; (3) for the first time the within-object multi-elemental statistical analysis has been conducted to modify the anomalous regions delineated by object-level summary statistics; and (4) most studies on separation of geochemical anomalies in the literature focus on a singular mineral species, while our study attempts to delineate the all-mineral-species anomalies.

Taking the 1:200,000 stream-sediment geochemical survey data in the Bayantala-Mingantu district, North China as case study, our findings indicated that:

(1) Most of the ore spots falling outside the delineated anomalous regions occur nearby them. (2) Due to the low resolution of the geochemical data at hand and its weak ability in detecting the micro-mineralization outcrops, the anomalous area produced by OGE is relatively large and mainly reflects the regional diagenesis. (3) The within-object statistical analysis based on handcrafted features, e.g., D2 and J, has a limited effect on reducing the anomalous target area. (4) OGE can be guided to focus more on regional mineralization, rather than diagenesis, by using fine-scale geochemical data as input. (5) Smaller segmentation scales can greatly improve the application of OGE. Finally, more than 80% of the known ore spots were predicted in less than 45% of the study area. (6) OGE is designed to extract both the spatial features and compositional relationships of geochemical variables collected at irregularly distributed centroids in irregularly shaped image objects, and it performs slightly better in anomaly detection than other convolutional autoencoder models such as GAUGE.

Future research will focus on improving the OGE in the following respects: (1) to alleviate the spatial heterogeneity of geochemical backgrounds, it is better to conduct the mean removal operation within every image object, rather than removing the global mean values for each element. (2) The optimal segmenting scale can be determined by using the ESP (estimation of scale parameter) tool proposed in [39]. (3) The possible approaches of integrating multiple datasets (e.g., remote sensing data and geophysical data) in the framework of OGE will also be explored. (4) Improve the within-object statistical analysis method, so that those strong but false or meaningless anomalies can be eliminated, while retaining those weak but important or meaningful anomalies.

Author Contributions: Conceptualization, B.Z. and D.Z.; methodology, B.Z. and R.Z.; software, B.Z.; validation, P.T. and H.W.; formal analysis, B.Z., H.W. and P.T.; investigation, B.Z. and Z.L.; resources, Z.L.; data curation, Z.L.; writing—original draft preparation, B.Z.; writing—review and editing, D.Z. and R.Z.; visualization, B.Z.; supervision, D.Z.; project administration, R.Z. and Z.L.; funding acquisition, D.Z. All authors have read and agreed to the published version of the manuscript.

Funding: This work was financially supported by the project of "Study of the Ore-Forming Regularity and Ore Prediction for Key Metallic Deposits in the Bayantala-Mingantu District, Inner Mongolia, China" under Grant 2020-KY03.

Institutional Review Board Statement: Not applicable.

Informed Consent Statement: Not applicable.

Data Availability Statement: The 1:50,000 and 1:200,000 geochemical data used in this study were provided by the Development Research Center, China Geological Survey.

Acknowledgments: Constructive criticism and helpful review comments on this manuscript were provided by several anonymous reviewers, and the authors would like to thank them here.

Conflicts of Interest: The authors declare no conflict of interest.

References

1. Grunsky, E.C.; Drew, L.J.; Sutphin, D.M. Process recognition in multi-element soil and stream-sediment geochemical data. *Appl. Geochem.* **2009**, *24*, 1602–1616. [CrossRef]
2. Cheng, Q.; Li, Q. A fractal concentration–area method for assigning a color palette for image representation. *Comput. Geosci.* **2002**, *28*, 567–575. [CrossRef]
3. Zhao, B.; Gou, P.; Yang, F.; Tang, P. Improving object-oriented land use/cover classification from high resolution imagery by spectral similarity-based post-classification. *Geocarto. Int.* **2021**, *37*, 7065–7088. [CrossRef]
4. Van den Bergh, M.; Boix, X.; Roig, G.; Van Gool, L. Seeds: Superpixels extracted via energy-driven sampling. *Int. J. Comput. Vision.* **2015**, *111*, 298–314. [CrossRef]
5. Kavzoglu, T.; Erdemir, M.Y.; Tonbul, H. Classification of semiurban landscapes from very high-resolution satellite images using a regionalized multiscale segmentation approach. *J. Appl. Remote Sens.* **2017**, *11*, 035016. [CrossRef]
6. Li, X.; Shao, G. Object-based land-cover mapping with high resolution aerial photography at a county scale in midwestern USA. *Remote Sens.* **2014**, *6*, 11372–11390. [CrossRef]
7. Chinese Academy of Geological Sciences. *Application of Geophysical and Geochemical Analysis Methods Specific for Prospecting Typical Metallic Mineral Deposits in China*; Geological Publishing House: Beijing, China, 2011; (In Chinese with English abstract).
8. Liu, Y.; Cheng, Q.; Xia, Q.; Wang, X. Identification of REE mineralization-related geochemical anomalies using fractal/multifractal methods in the Nanling belt, South China. *Environ. Earth Sci.* **2014**, *72*, 5159–5169. [CrossRef]
9. Daya, A.A.; Afzal, P. A comparative study of concentration-area (CA) and spectrum-area (SA) fractal models for separating geochemical anomalies in Shorabhaji region, NW Iran. *Arab. J. Geosci.* **2015**, *8*, 8263–8275. [CrossRef]
10. Sridharan, H.; Qiu, F. Developing an object-based hyperspatial image classifier with a case study using Worldview-2 data. Photogramm. *Eng. Rem. S.* **2013**, *79*, 1027–1036.
11. Geneletti, D.; Gorte, B.G.H. A method for object-oriented land cover classification combining Landsat TM data and aerial photographs. *Int. J. Remote Sens.* **2003**, *24*, 1273–1286. [CrossRef]
12. Kucharczyk, M.; Hay, G.J.; Ghaffarian, S.; Hugenholtz, C.H. Geographic object-based image analysis: A primer and future directions. *Remote Sens.* **2020**, *12*, 2012. [CrossRef]
13. Afzal, P.; Farhadi, S.; Shamseddin Meigooni, M.; Boveiri Konari, M.; Daneshvar Saein, L. Geochemical Anomaly Detection in the Irankuh District Using Hybrid Machine Learning Technique and Fractal Modeling. *Geopersia.* **2022**, *12*, 191–199.
14. Farhadi, S.; Afzal, P.; Boveiri Konari, M.; Daneshvar Saein, L.; Sadeghi, B. Combination of Machine Learning Algorithms with Concentration-Area Fractal Method for Soil Geochemical Anomaly Detection in Sediment-Hosted Irankuh Pb-Zn Deposit, Central Iran. *Minerals.* **2022**, *12*, 689. [CrossRef]
15. Zhao, B.; Wu, J.J.; Yang, F.; Pilz, J.; Zhang, D.H. A novel approach for extraction of Gaoshanhe-Group outcrops using Landsat Operational Land Imager (OLI) data in the heavily loess-covered Baoji District, Western China. *Ore Geol. Rev.* **2019**, *108*, 88–100. [CrossRef]

16. Zhao, B.; Luo, X.; Tang, P.; Liu, Y.; Wan, H.; Ouyang, N. STDecoder-CD: How to Decode the Hierarchical Transformer in Change Detection Tasks. *Appl Sci-Basel.* **2022**, *12*, 7903. [CrossRef]
17. Zhang, C.; Sargent, I.; Pan, X.; Li, H.; Gardiner, A.; Hare, J.; Atkinson, P.M. An object-based convolutional neural network (OCNN) for urban land use classification. *Remote Sens. Environ.* **2018**, *216*, 57–70. [CrossRef]
18. Martins, V.S.; Kaleita, A.L.; Gelder, B.K.; da Silveira, H.L.; Abe, C.A. Exploring multiscale object-based convolutional neural network (multi-OCNN) for remote sensing image classification at high spatial resolution. *ISPRS J. Photogramm.* **2020**, *168*, 56–73. [CrossRef]
19. Zhao, W.; Du, S.; Emery, W.J. Object-based convolutional neural network for high-resolution imagery classification. *IEEE J-STARS.* **2017**, *10*, 3386–3396. [CrossRef]
20. Li, H.; Zhang, C.; Zhang, S.; Ding, X.; Atkinson, P.M. Iterative Deep Learning (IDL) for agricultural landscape classification using fine spatial resolution remotely sensed imagery. *Int. J. Appl. Earth Obs.* **2021**, *102*, 102437. [CrossRef]
21. Zhang, C.; Yue, P.; Tapete, D.; Shangguan, B.; Wang, M.; Wu, Z. A multi-level context-guided classification method with object-based convolutional neural network for land cover classification using very high-resolution remote sensing images. *Int. J. Appl. Earth Obs.* **2020**, *88*, 102086. [CrossRef]
22. Lv, X.; Shao, Z.; Ming, D.; Diao, C.; Zhou, K.; Tong, C. Improved object-based convolutional neural network (IOCNN) to classify very high-resolution remote sensing images. *Int. J. Remote Sens.* **2021**, *42*, 8318–8344. [CrossRef]
23. Hobley, B.; Arosio, R.; French, G.; Bremner, J.; Dolphin, T.; Mackiewicz, M. Semi-supervised segmentation for coastal monitoring seagrass using RPA imagery. *Remote Sens.* **2021**, *13*, 1741. [CrossRef]
24. Guan, Q.; Ren, S.; Chen, L.; Yao, Y.; Hu, Y.; Wang, R.; Feng, B.; Gu, L.; Chen, W. Recognizing Multivariate Geochemical Anomalies Related to Mineralization by Using Deep Unsupervised Graph Learning. *Nat. Resour. Res.* **2022**, *31*, 2225–2245. [CrossRef]
25. Chen, Y.; Wu, W. Application of one-class support vector machine to quickly identify multivariate anomalies from geochemical exploration data. *Geochem-Explor. Env. A* **2017**, *17*, 231–238. [CrossRef]
26. Xiong, Y.; Zuo, R. Recognition of geochemical anomalies using a deep autoencoder network. *Comput. Geosci.* **2016**, *86*, 75–82. [CrossRef]
27. Veli, V.C.; Kovi, C.P.; Cucurull, G.; Casanova, A.; Romero, A.; Lio, P.; Bengio, Y. Graph attention networks. *arXiv* **2017**, arXiv:1710.10903.
28. Kipf, T.N.; Welling, M. Semi-supervised classification with graph convolutional networks. *arXiv* **2016**, arXiv:1609.02907.
29. Dibo Mining Co. *LTD of Inner Mongolia Nonferrous Geology and Mining (Group). Overall Design of the Project of "Study of the Ore-Forming Regularity and Ore Prediction for Key Metallic Deposits in the Bayantala-Mingantu District, Inner Mongolia, China"*; Dibo Mining Co., Ltd.: Hohhot, China, 2020; pp. 1–69. (In Chinese)
30. Pirajno, F. *Hydrothermal Processes and Mineral Systems*; Springer: Berlin/Heidelberg, Germany, 2008; pp. 1–527.
31. Kigai, I.N. Redox problems in the "metallogenic specialization" of magmatic rocks and the genesis of hydrothermal ore mineralization. *Petrology* **2011**, *19*, 303–321. [CrossRef]
32. Smith, M.; Goodchild, M.F.; Longley, P.A. *Geospatial Analysis—A Comprehensive Guide to Principles, Techniques and Software Tools, 2. ed.*; Troubador Publishing Ltd.: Market Harborough, UK, 2007; pp. 32–200.
33. Zhang, Z.; Cui, P.; Zhu, W. Deep learning on graphs: A survey. *IEEE T. Knowl. Data Eng.* **2022**, *34*, 249–270. [CrossRef]
34. Brody, S.; Alon, U.; Yahav, E. How attentive are graph attention networks. *arXiv* **2021**, arXiv:2105.14491.
35. Myint, S.W. Fractal approaches in texture analysis and classification of remotely sensed data: Comparisons with spatial autocorrelation techniques and simple descriptive statistics. *Int. J. Remote Sens.* **2003**, *24*, 1925–1947. [CrossRef]
36. Zhao, B.; Han, L.; Pilz, J.; Wu, J.J.; Khan, F.; Zhang, D.H. Metallogenic efficiency from deposit to region–A case study in western Zhejiang Province, southeastern China. *Ore Geol. Rev.* **2017**, *86*, 957–970. [CrossRef]
37. Zhao, B.; Yang, F.; Zhang, R.; Shen, J.; Pilz, J.; Zhang, D.H. Application of unsupervised learning of finite mixture models in ASTER VNIR data-driven land use classification. *J. Spatial Sci.* **2019**, *66*, 89–112. [CrossRef]
38. Chen, L.; Guan, Q.; Xiong, Y.; Liang, J.; Wang, Y.; Xu, Y. A spatially constrained multi-autoencoder approach for multivariate geochemical anomaly recognition. *Comput. Geosci.* **2019**, *125*, 43–54. [CrossRef]
39. Drăguţ, L.; Csillik, O.; Eisank, C.; Tiede, D. Automated parameterization for multi-scale image segmentation on multiple layers. *ISPRS J. Photogramm. Remote Sens.* **2014**, *88*, 119–127. [CrossRef] [PubMed]

applied sciences

Article

Construction, Test and Application of a Tungsten Metallogene Named MGW11: Case Studies in China

Jie Li [1], Qingjie Gong [1,*], Bimin Zhang [2], Ningqiang Liu [1], Xuan Wu [3], Taotao Yan [2], Xiaolei Li [3] and Yuan Wu [1]

1 School of Earth Sciences and Resources, China University of Geosciences, Beijing 100083, China
2 Key Laboratory of Geochemical Exploration, Institute of Geophysical and Geochemical Exploration, CAGS, Langfang 065000, China
3 Center for Development and Research, China Geological Survey, Beijing 100037, China
* Correspondence: qjiegong@cugb.edu.cn

Abstract: Geochemical gene is a new promising concept proposed recently in the discrimination and traceability of geological materials and is also a useful tool to recognize geochemical anomalies in mineral exploration. Based on the lithogenes of LG01 and LG03, geological materials can be classified into nine types of LG_CR compositionally. With respect to geological materials with 11 types of LG_CR, in order to eliminate the lithological influence and to further narrow the prospecting target area, a tungsten metallogene named MGW11 is proposed for geochemical tungsten exploration after the tungsten metallogene MGW. Six weathering profiles of 11 types of LG_CR developed on granitic intrusions in different areas in China are selected to test the stable properties such as heredity and inheritance of MGW11 and MGW. The results indicate that MGW11 and MGW metallogenes illustrate stable properties during rock weathering regardless of weathering degrees, although gene variations of MGW11 and MGW are also observed during extreme weathering. Based on the regional geochemistry survey data in the Lianyang area in south China, where stream sediments are mostly 11 types of LG_CR compositionally, geochemical maps of mineralization similarities of MGW11 and MGW are contoured, and the anomaly areas are determined on the mineralization similarity value of ≥40%. Comparing the tungsten deposits and anomaly areas determined on MGW11 and MGW metallogenes spatially, a total of six polymetallic W deposits recognized in the study area are all located in the anomaly areas. Therefore, mineralization similarities of MGW11 and MGW can be viewed as useful integrated indices on geochemical tungsten exploration. In areas with 11 types of LG_CR compositionally, anomaly areas determined on the MGW11 are smaller than those on the MGW, which indicates that MGW11 is more efficient than MGW in targeting W deposits during tungsten prospecting because of the elimination of the lithological influence.

Keywords: geochemical gene; MGW; LG_CR; mineralization similarity; Lianyang

Citation: Li, J.; Gong, Q.; Zhang, B.; Liu, N.; Wu, X.; Yan, T.; Li, X.; Wu, Y. Construction, Test and Application of a Tungsten Metallogene Named MGW11: Case Studies in China. *Appl. Sci.* **2023**, *13*, 606. https://doi.org/10.3390/app13010606

Academic Editor: Ricardo Castedo

Received: 6 December 2022
Revised: 29 December 2022
Accepted: 30 December 2022
Published: 2 January 2023

1. Introduction

Geochemical gene is a new promising concept proposed recently in the discrimination and traceability of geological materials [1,2] and is also a useful tool to recognize geochemical anomalies in mineral exploration [3,4]. Geochemical gene is proposed and illustrated firstly as a lithogene [5] named LG02, then followed by lithogenes called LG01 [6] and LG03 [7], gold metallogene (MGAu) [3], and tungsten metallogene (MGW) [4], and REE (rare earth elements) genes called REEG01 and REEG02 [6]. Therefore, there are a total of seven geochemical genes reported till now, which were introduced and reviewed by Gong et al. [1] recently.

With respect to lithogenes LG01 and LG03, their gene properties of heredity and inheritance during weathering have been tested on lots of weathering profiles developed over different lithological rocks in different climate zones in China [6–8] according to the similar gene criterion of ≥80% on gene similarity [1]. Their application in classifying geological materials is useful and suitable for fresh and altered rocks and weathered products such as soils and sediments [2]. The classification method is introduced here briefly. The ideal acidic rock in China (a virtual rock sample represented by the elemental abundance of acidic rock in China compositionally) has the same gene code of 10202020202 on LG01 and LG03, and the ideal basic rock in China also has the same gene code of 12020202020 on these two lithogenes [6,7]. The gene similarity of a sample relative to the ideal acidic rock is called the sample's acidic similarity and can be labeled as R_{Acidic}. According to this definition, the R_{Acidic} of the ideal acidic rock in China is 100%, while the R_{Acidic} of the ideal basic rock in China is 0%. Geological materials can be classified into three groups acidic-like composition with $R_{\text{Acidic}} \geq 80\%$ labeled 1, intermediate-like composition with R_{Acidic} between 75% and 25 labeled 2, and basic-like composition with $R_{\text{Acidic}} \leq 20\%$ labeled 3. In order to integrate the classification results of LG01 and LG03, LG_CR (classification results of lithogenes) with a double-digit is proposed by Wu et al. [2]. The classification result of LG01 is put as the first digit, and the result of LG03 is the second digit. There is a total of nine types theoretically of LG_CR classified based on LG01 and LG03 as 11, 12, 13, 21, 22, 23, 31, 32, and 33 types. The 11 types of LG_CR of a sample indicates that the values of R_{Acidic} of LG01 and LG03 of the sample are all $\geq$80%. Therefore, the result of LG_CR can be used to classify geological materials [2].

With respect to the metallogenes of MGAu and MGW, their gene properties of heredity and inheritance during weathering have also been tested in China [3,4]. The ideal geochemical background samples (all indicator elements are clearly lower than their immobile elements in gene spectral lines) have the same metallogene code of 10202020202 on MGAu and MGW. In contrast, the ideal ore samples (in which indicator elements are enriched clearly in gene spectral lines) will have the same metallogene code of 12020202020 on these two metallogenes. Like the above mentioned on lithogenes, the gene similarity of a sample relative to the ideal ore sample is called the sample's mineralization similarity and can be labeled as R_{IdealOre}. According to this definition, the R_{IdealOre} of the ideal ore sample is 100%, while the R_{IdealOre} of the ideal background sample is 0%. The application of metallogenes is that their R_{IdealOre} can be viewed as an integrated index of recognizing geochemical anomalies for mineral prospecting, and the mineralization similarity (R_{IdealOre}) value of 40% can be viewed as the criterion to discriminate samples with or without mineralization [1,3,4]. Although the metallogenes have been used well in geochemical exploration [4,9], the anomaly area determined on the R_{IdealOre} is commonly too large than deposit areas, which is unfavorable to targeting deposits promptly and precisely during prospecting. This large anomaly area determined on R_{IdealOre} resulted from the elemental reference values during the metallogenes' construction. The reference values are determined by the elemental abundances of acidic, intermediate, and basic rocks in China. Therefore, the R_{IdealOre} index is applicable to geological materials ignoring the lithology of basic-like, intermediate-like, or acidic-like compositions. If the target deposits, such as tungsten deposits, are located in the acidic-like composition area, such as the 11 types of LG_CR area, the determined anomaly areas on the R_{IdealOre} of MGW are certainly larger than the target area. Therefore, a tungsten metallogene aiming at 11 types of LG_CR materials should be constructed to substitute the MGW to determine anomaly areas more efficiently.

In this paper, a tungsten metallogene named MGW11 aiming at 11 types of LG_CR materials is constructed firstly. Then the heredity and inheritance properties of MGW11 are tested on lots of weathering profiles developed over 11 types of LG_CR rocks in different climate zones in China. Finally, the R_{IdealOre} of MGW11 is used to determine geochemical anomaly areas in the Lianyang area of south China, and the results are compared with those derived from the MGW.

2. Construction of MGW11

A geochemical gene is commonly constructed on five steps as a selection of elements, determination of reference values, spectral line and codes, calculation of similarity, and sequence of elements [1,3]. On the basis of the MGW metallogene proposed by Gong et al. [4], the selected elements and their sequences of MGW can be adopted to construct the new tungsten metallogene named MGW11 here. In addition, the methods of coding spectral lines and calculating gene similarities are also adopted during the construction of the MGW11. Therefore, the main task or key step to construct the MGW11 is the determination of reference values for each selected element.

In MGW and MGAu metallogenes, reference values are determined on the abundances of five geological materials in China, which are acidic rock, intermediate rock, basic rock, soil, and stream sediment [10]. The reference values of the six immobile elements, Ti, Th, Nb, Zr, La, and Y, were calculated as

$$C_{ref} = 10^{(\lg C_{min} - 0.1)} \tag{1}$$

where C_{ref} is the reference value and C_{min} is the minimum abundance of each element in the five materials [3]. While references values of the five indicator elements as Cu, W, Sn, Zn, Mo in MGW were calculated as

$$C_{ref} = 10^{(\lg C_{max} + 0.1)} \tag{2}$$

where C_{max} is the maximum abundance of each element in the five materials [4]. The spectral lines of MGW of the five materials are listed in Figure 1a. The gene codes of the five materials are the same as 10202020202, which is the ideal background material's metallogene code.

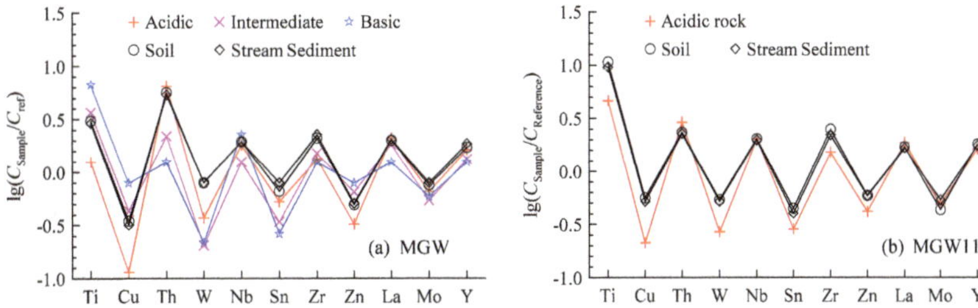

Figure 1. Spectral lines of MGW (**a**) and MGW11 (**b**) metallogenes for geological materials in China. Sample data in (**a**) are from Chi and Yan [10] and data in (**b**) are from Chi and Yan [10], Hou et al. [11], Xiang et al. [12] respectively.

With respect to the MGW11, reference values are determined on elemental abundances of a total of 190 geological materials in China, including 85 records of acidic rocks from Chi and Yan [10], 48 records of soils from Hou et al. [11], and 57 records of stream sediments from Xiang et al. [12] which are all 11 types of LG_CR compositionally. The reference values of the six immobile elements, Ti, Th, Nb, Zr, La, and Y, were calculated as

$$C_{ref} = 10^{(\lg C_{min} + 0.1)} \tag{3}$$

The references values of the five indicator elements, Cu, W, Sn, Zn, and Mo, in MGW, were calculated as

$$C_{ref} = 10^{(\lg C_{max} - 0.1)} \tag{4}$$

where C_{ref} is the reference value and C_{min} and C_{max} are the minimum and maximum abundances of each element in the 190 materials in China. The spectral lines of MGW11 of the three materials are listed in Figure 1b with the same gene code of 10202020202, which is the ideal background material's gene code. The elemental sequence and reference values of MGW and MGW11 are listed in Table 1.

Table 1. Reference values for tungsten metallogenes of MGW and MGW11.

Gene Elements	Ti	Cu	Th	W	Nb	Sn	Zr	Zn	La	Mo	Y	References
Sequence No.	1	2	3	4	5	6	7	8	9	10	11	–
MGW	1406	69.2	2.22	2.27	8.26	3.78	119	138	19.1	1.06	13.5	Gong et al. [4]
MGW11	378	37.4	4.94	3.13	7.4	6.95	105	107	21.3	1.43	13.5	This study

Note: Unit in μg/g.

If a sample of 11 types of LG_CR is mineralized during tungsten ore-forming processes, indicator elements will be enriched relative to the other six immobile elements. If the five indicator elements were all enriched clearly, the sample would have the MGW11 code of 12020202020 and is called the ideal ore sample. Therefore, the MGW11 similarity between the ideal ore and the ideal background sample is 0%. As aforementioned, the genetic similarity between a sample and the ideal ore is called the sample's mineralization similarity labeled as R_{IdealOre}, which can be used as an index to discriminate a geological material as an anomaly or background sample. The 40% value of the R_{IdealOre} was suggested as the criterion to discriminate samples with or without mineralization or to classify anomaly or background samples [3,4] which is also adopted here to the MGW11 gene.

3. Test of MGW11

3.1. Materials

The test of a geochemical gene focuses on stable properties such as heredity and inheritance during rock weathering [1]. Here six weathering profiles of 11 types of LG_CR are selected from literature to test the properties of the MGW11. The six weathering profiles are labeled as DH31, TL19D04, LHK55, and LC19 from northeast to southwest in China and LY18D13 and LY18D06 in Liangyang area of south China (Figure 2, Table 2).

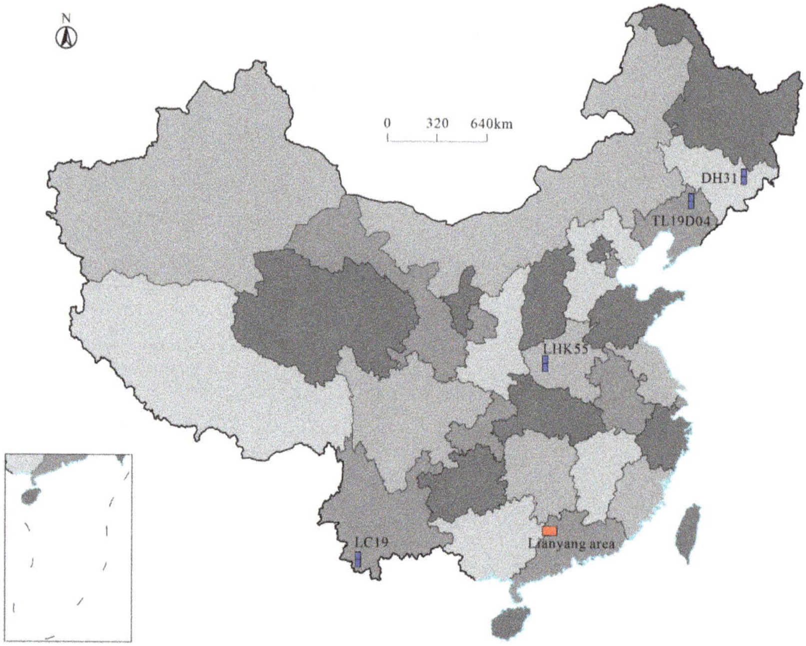

Figure 2. Locations of weathering profiles and Lianyang area in China. LY18D13 and LY18D06 weathering profiles are located in Lianyang area.

Table 2. Information on weathering profiles.

Profiles	Parent Rock	Longitude	Latitude	Depth (m)	Sample Count	References
DH31	Monzogranite	E 128°22′22″	N 43°18′44″	11	13	[8]
TL19D04	Monzogranite	E 123°56′44″	N 42°26′16″	6	9	[13]
LHK55	Granite	E 112°07′09″	N 33°49′06″	5.2	11	[14]
LC19	Granite	E 100°18′05″	N 22°12′24.2″	14	20	[15]
LY18D13	Granite	E 112°15′57.6″	N 24°23′00″	14.6	23	[16]
LY18D06	Granite	E 112°4′26.76″	N 24°9′39.96″	25	29	[17]

The DH31 profile (E 128°22′22″, N 43°18′44″) developed over the Dunhua monzogranite in a temperate monsoon climate. The depth of DH31 profile is ca. 11 m, and 13 samples are collected sequentially from the topsoil downward to the monzogranite. Details, including descriptions, elemental concentrations, and the analytical qualities of these samples, can be found in Reference [8]. The TL19D04 profile (E 123°56′44″, N 42°26′16″) formed on the Tieling monzogranite in a temperate continental monsoon climate. The depth of TL19D04 profile is ca. 6 m, and 9 samples are collected sequentially from the topsoil downward to the monzogranite. Details of these samples can be found in Reference [13]. The LHK55 profile (E 112°07′09″, N 33°49′06″) developed over the Taishanmiao granite in a warm temperate continental monsoon climate. The depth of LHK55 profile is ca. 5.2 m, and 11 samples are collected sequentially from the topsoil down to the granite. Details of these samples can be found in Reference [14]. The LC19 profile (E 100°18′05″, N 22°12′24.2″) formed on the Lincang granite in a subtropical monsoon climate. The depth of LC19 profile is ca. 14 m, and 20 samples are collected sequentially from the topsoil down to the granite. Details of these samples can be found in Reference [15].

The LY18D13 profile (E 112°15′57.6″, N 24°23′), developed over the Lianyang granite in a subtropical monsoon climate. The depth of LY18D13 profile is ca. 14.6 m, and 23 samples are collected sequentially from the topsoil down to the granite. Details of these samples can be found in Reference [16]. The LY18D06 profile (E 112°4′26.76″, N 24°9′39.96″), also developed over the Lianyang granite, is ca. 25 m, and 29 samples are collected sequentially from the topsoil down to the granite, which details including descriptions, elemental concentrations, and their analytical qualities can be found in Reference [17].

3.2. Results

Based on the reported elemental concentrations of samples from each weathering profile, weathering indices including CIA and WIG, acidic similarities (R_{Acidic}) of LG01 and LG03 lithogenes, samples' similarities relative to the top soil and the bottom bedrock, mineralization similarities ($R_{IdealOre}$) of MGW and MGW11 metallogenes are calculated for each weathering profile and illustrated in Figures 3 and 4.

The CIA (chemical index of alteration) was developed by Nesbit and Young [18] in reconstructing paleoclimate from Early Proterozoic sediments, and the WIG (weathering index of granite) was proposed by Gong et al. [19] to describe the weathering degrees of weathered granitic products in the absence of CO_2 contents. The calculation methods used here were detailed and described by Wu et al. [8]. The calculation methods on gene codes and similarities used here can be found in Reference [1]. Acidic similarities (R_{Acidic}) of LG01 and LG03 in each profile were calculated firstly to check whether their products are 11 types of LG_CR or not. The gene similarity (R) of samples is calculated relative to their bedrock (heredity property) labeled as $R_{Bedrock}$, their top soil (inheritance property) labeled as $R_{Topsoil}$, and the ideal ore (mineralization similarity) labeled as $R_{IdealOre}$ respectively in each weathering profile (Figures 3 and 4).

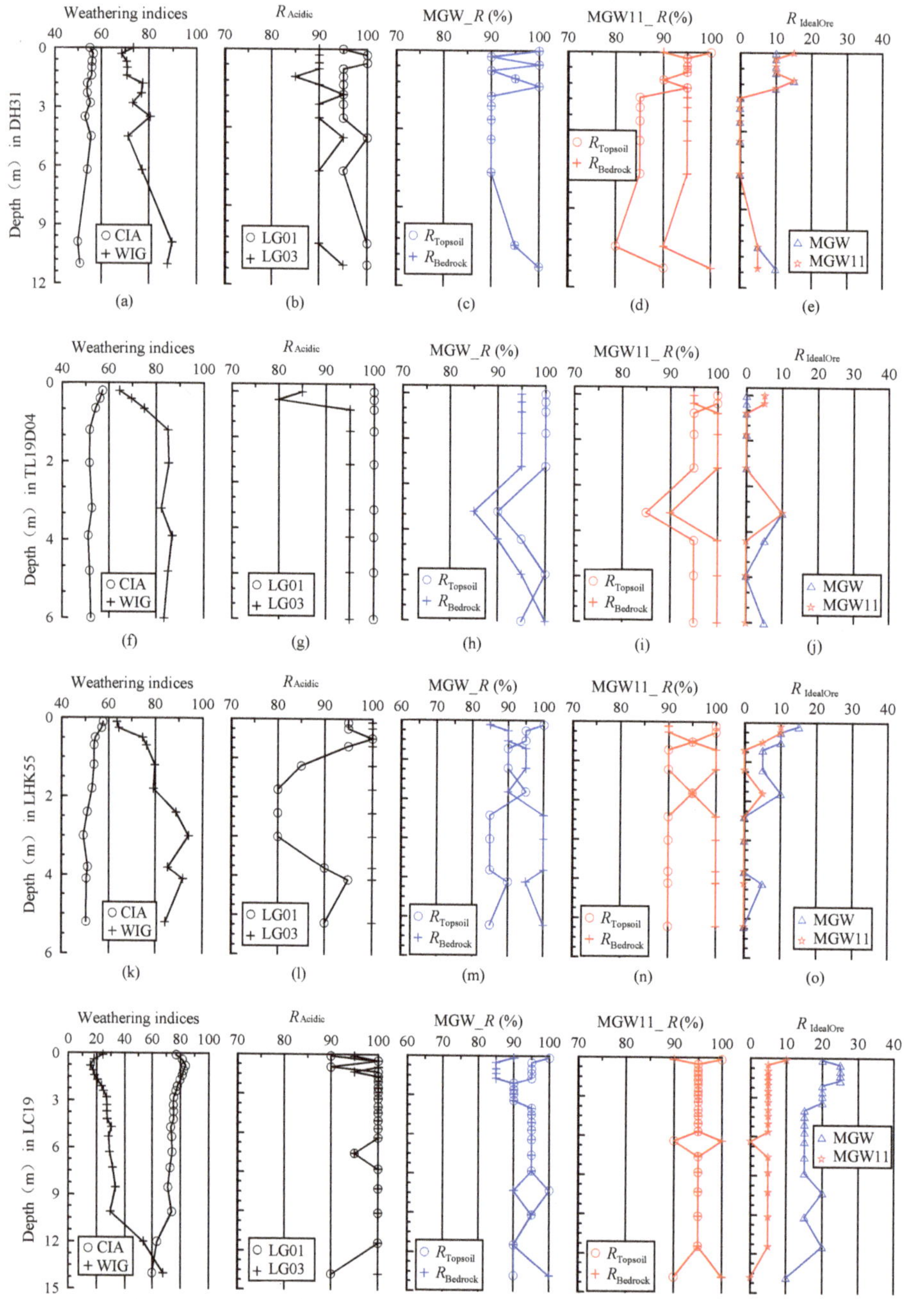

Figure 3. Weathering indices and gene similarities of samples from weathering profiles of DH31, TL19D04, LHK55, and LC19. (**a–e**) are the weathering indices, acidic similarities, similarities of MGW, similarities of MGW11, and mineralization similarities respectively in profile DH31. (**f–j**) are those in profile TL19D04, (**k–o**) are those in LHK55, and (**p–t**) are those in LC19.

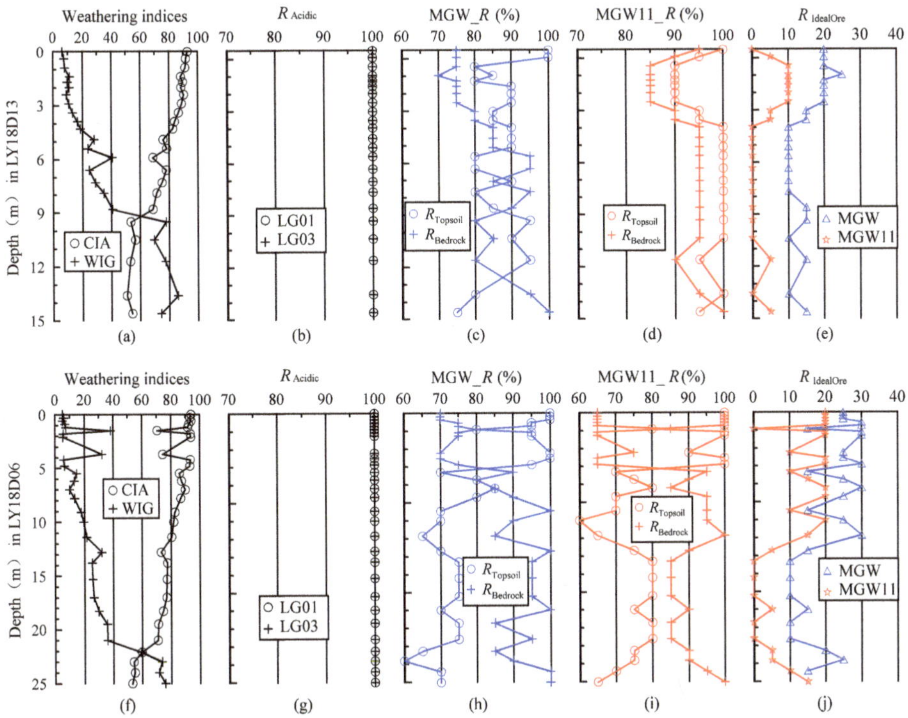

Figure 4. Weathering indices and gene similarities of samples from weathering profiles of LY18D13 and LY18D06 in Lianyang area. (**a–e**) are the weathering indices, acidic similarities, similarities of MGW, similarities of MGW11, and mineralization similarities respectively in profile LY18D13. (**f–j**) are those in profile LY18D06.

The CIA values of samples from DH31, TL19D04, and LHK55 profiles range from 49.8 to 56.6, from 50.9 to 57.4, and from 49.2 to 57.6, respectively (Figure 3a,f,k). The WIG values of samples from these three profiles range from 68.5 to 89.8, from 64.6 to 86.9, and from 63.6 to 94.3, respectively (Figure 3a,f,k). According to the classification values of 60 and 80 on CIA [20] and values of 20 and 60 on WIG [6,8], these three profiles have undergone incipient weathering. While CIA values of samples from LC19, LY18D13, and LY18D06 profiles in south China range from 53.0 to 94.1, from 59.8 to 83.6, and from 50.7 to 93.1, respectively (Figures 3p and 4a,f). The WIG values from these three profiles in south China range from 5.2 to 76.0, from 15.6 to 67.8, and from 6.3 to 86.1, respectively (Figures 3p and 4a,f). These values indicate that the profiles in south China have undergone extreme weathering.

The R_{Acidic} of samples from all profiles vary from 80% to 100% on LG01 and LG03 (Figures 3b,g,l,q and 4b,g). According to the classification method proposed by Wu et al. [2], which is also introduced above, samples from the six weathering profiles are all 11 types of LG_CR compositionally.

In Figure 3, all values of $R_{Bedrock}$ and $R_{Topsoil}$ of MGW and MGW11 in the four profiles of DH31, TL19D04, LHK55, and LC19 are $\geq$80% which indicates good heredity and inheritance of MGW and MGW11 metallogenes in each profile (Figure 3c,d,h,i,m,n,r,s). Values of $R_{IdealOre}$ on MGW are all $\leq$25%, and values of $R_{IdealOre}$ on MGW11 are all $\leq$15% (Figure 3e,j,o,t). This indicates that all samples from these four profiles are background samples (rather than anomaly samples) according to the discrimination criterion of 40% of $R_{IdealOre}$.

In Figure 4, values of $R_{IdealOre}$ on MGW are all $\leq$30%, and values of $R_{IdealOre}$ on MGW11 are all $\leq$20% (Figure 4e,j). This indicates that all samples from weathering profiles in the Lianyang area are also background samples according to the discrimination criterion of 40% of $R_{IdealOre}$.

In the LY18D13 profile, values of $R_{Bedrock}$ and $R_{Topsoil}$ of MGW11 (Figure 4d) are all ≥85% which indicates stable heredity and inheritance of MGW11. Except for some upper soil samples, values of $R_{Bedrock}$ of MGW are higher than 80% (Figure 4c), which indicates good heredity of MGW except for some variations in the upper soils with extreme weathering degrees. On the other hand, values of $R_{Topsoil}$ of MGW are higher than 80% except for only the bottom bedrock sample (Figure 4c), which indicates a good inheritance of MGW, excluding the bottom bedrock sample.

In the LY18D06 profile, values of $R_{Bedrock}$ of MGW and MGW11 are ≥80% except in some upper soil samples (Figure 4h,i) with extreme weathering degrees, which indicates good heredities of MGW and MGW11 except in some variations in the upper soils. However, values of $R_{Topsoil}$ of MGW and MGW11 are higher than 80% only in the upper soils (Figure 4h,i), which indicates good inheritance of MGW and MGW11 only in upper soils and gene variations appear relative to the lower or parent samples in this profile.

In summary, stable properties such as heredity and inheritance of MGW11 and MGW are verified in six weathering profiles which are all 11 types of LG_CR compositionally and are all geochemical background samples with different weathering degrees. However, gene variations of MGW11 and MGW are also observed in some extremely weathered samples. With respect to the MGW, MGW11 shows better stability in the 11 types of LG_CR geological materials.

4. Application of Geochemical Exploration in Lianyang Area

The main aim of constructing the tungsten metallogenes such as MGW and MGW11 is to determine geochemical anomalies using their mineralization similarities ($R_{IdealOre}$) as an integrated index for tungsten exploration. With respect to the MGW, MGW11 should be more precise on anomaly determination in the tungsten mineralized area with geological materials of 11 types of LG_CR compositionally on its construction. Therefore, the Lianyang area in south China is selected here to test or illustrate the applications of MGW and MGW11, where some tungsten deposits have been found, and geological materials such as stream sediments are most 11 types of LG_CR compositionally.

4.1. Geographical and Geological Settings

The Lianyang area is located in south China with an area of ca. 5400 km^2 ranging from E 111°47′24″ to E 112°40′12″ with a distance of 90 km from west to east and N 24°02′24″ to N 24°34′48″ with a distance of 60 km from north to south (Figure 5a), which is situated in a typical subtropical monsoon zone with a humid climate. The mean annual temperature is ca. 15.5~20.4 °C. The annual rainfall is ca. 1500~2200 mm, most of which falls in summer, according to the public network data. The topography in the Lianyang area is characterized by foothills, and the elevation is low in the middle, high in the north and south, and with a value of 50 to 1900 m a.s.l. Soils are thickly developed, and the regolith thickness commonly varies from 10 to 25 m depending on the relief. The land is commonly covered by crops or arbors.

The strata in the study area belong to Cambrian, Devonian, Carboniferous, Permian, Triassic, Jurassic, and Quaternary periods, respectively, which petrological descriptions are illustrated briefly in Figure 5a as notes. Faults are mainly trending N-S in the center and NE-SW in the northwestern, and NW-SE in the northeastern. The main intrusion in the study area is the Lianyang granitic complex in which two types of lithology can be recognized gradationally: the medium-grained biotite granite as the main body and the medium-coarse-grained porphyritic-like biotite granite outcropped locally [21].

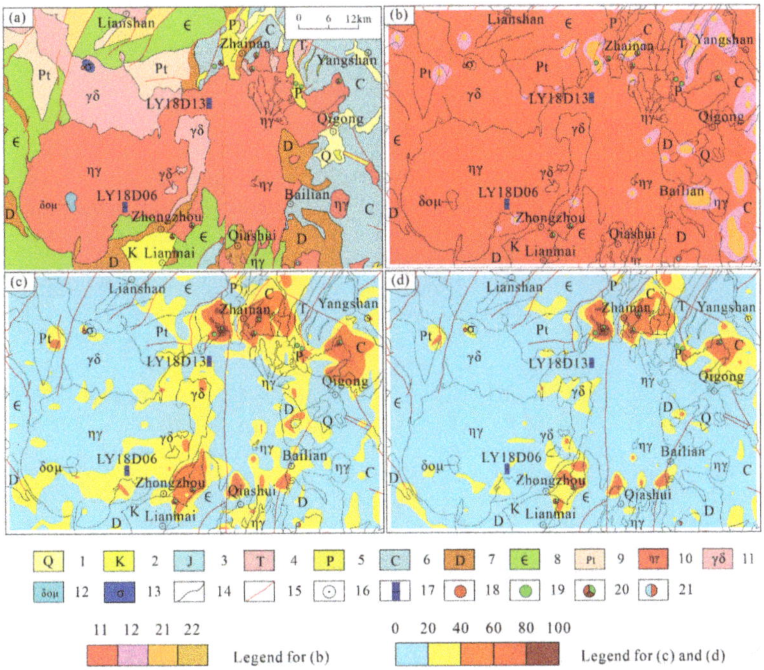

Figure 5. Geological map of Lianyang area (**a**) and geochemical maps of the LG_CR (**b**), R_{IdealOre} of MGW (**c**), and R_{IdealOre} of MGW11 (**d**). Figure 5a is modified after the G49 with a scale of 1:1000,000 from China Geological Survey with notes are as the followings. 1—Quaternary sand and gravel mixed with clay silty sand; 2—Cretaceous sandy conglomerate, pebbled sandstone and siltstone; 3—Jurassic sandstone, siltstone, grit stone and mudstone; 4—Triassic limestone and mudstone; 5—Permian limestone and mudstone; 6—Carboniferous dolomitic limestone and dolomite; 7—Devonian sandstone and dolomitic limestone; 8—Cambrian sandstone, slate and siltstone; 9—Proterozoic sandstone, siltstone and slate; 10—Monzogranite; 11—Granodiorite; 12—Quartz-dioritic porphyrite; 13—Peridotite; 14—Petrological boundary; 15—Fault; 16—Main residential place; 17—Locations of LY18D13 and LY18D06 weathering profiles; 18—Au deposit; 19—Cu deposit; 20—Polymetallic W deposit; 21—Mo-Fe deposit.

Six polymetallic W deposits have been recognized in the study area [22], although they have not been receiving much attention [23]. The polymetallic W deposits are mainly distributed around the Lianyang granitic complex contacting with strata and faults (Figure 5a). Among the six polymetallic W deposits, three deposits are located in the north margin of the Lianyang granitic complex near the Zhainan town, two deposits in the south margin of the Lianyang granitic complex near the Zhongzhou town, and one in the northeast margin of the Lianyang granitic complex near the Yangshan town. In addition, three Cu deposits, one Au deposit, and one Mo-Fe deposit are also recognized in this area [16,24].

4.2. Materials, Results and Discussion

In the Lianyang area, a total of 1393 geochemical records (or samples) of stream sediments were retrieved from the database of the RGNR (Regional Geochemistry–National Reconnaissance) project [12]. In this project or database, stream sediment is the sampling media with a scale of 1:200,000 and was analyzed with 10 major components (SiO_2, Al_2O_3, Fe_2O_3 or TFe_2O_3, K_2O, Na_2O, CaO, MgO, Ti, P, and Mn) and 29 trace elements (W, Sn, Mo, Bi, Cu, Pb, Zn, Cd, Au, Ag, As, Sb, Hg, Li, Be, Sr, Ba, B, F, V, Cr, Co, Ni, Zr, Nb, Th, U, Y, and La) [25].

Based on the geochemical data of each record which represents an area of four square kilometers, the gene codes and their acidic similarities (R_{Acidic}) of LG01 and LG03 are calculated on the GGC software [1] firstly. Then the LG_CR results of the 1393 samples are derived according to the method proposed by Wu et al. [2]. The geochemical map of the LG_CR in the Lianyang area is illustrated in Figure 5b. Although nine types of LG_CR can be classified theoretically on double-digit numbers based on the acidic similarities of LG01 and LG03 lithogenes, only four types are recognized in the Lianyang area as 11, 12, 21, and 22 types. The 11 types of LG_CR are dominant in the whole study area, and the other types of 12, 21, and 22 are located sporadically in the east and north of the area. Therefore, the Lianyang area can be viewed as an area of 11 types of LG_CR compositionally by and large.

Based on the geochemical data of the 1393 records, the gene codes and their mineralization similarities ($R_{IdealOre}$) of MGW and MGW11 are calculated. The geochemical maps of the $R_{IdealOre}$ of MGW and MGW11 in the Lianyang area are illustrated in Figure 5c,d. In these maps, the blue areas with $0 \leq R_{IdealOre} \leq 20$ can be viewed as the normal background area, the yellow area with $20 < R_{IdealOre} < 40$ can be viewed as the higher background area, and the red area with $40 \leq R_{IdealOre} \leq 100$ are the anomaly areas for tungsten exploration. Furthermore, the anomaly areas can be divided into three zones; the outer zone with $40 \leq R_{IdealOre} < 60$, the middle zone with $60 \leq R_{IdealOre} < 80$, and the inner zone with $80 \leq R_{IdealOre} \leq 100$ (Figure 5c,d).

By comparing the deposits and the anomaly areas spatially in the Lianyang area, we can find that a total of six polymetallic W deposits in the study area are all located in the anomaly areas determined on the $R_{IdealOre}$ of MGW (Figure 5c) and MGW11 (Figure 5d). This indicated that the mineralization similarities of MGW and MGW11 can be viewed as useful integrated indices on geochemical tungsten exploration.

With respect to the three Cu deposits in the study area, one is located in the anomaly area, one is near the anomaly area, and one is in the background area determined on MGW (Figure 5c) and MGW11 (Figure 5d). With respect to the Au deposit and the Mo-Fe deposit in the study area, the Au deposit is located in the higher background areas determined on MGW and MGW11 (Figure 5c,d), and the Mo-Fe deposit is located in the background areas (or higher background area determined on the MGW in Figure 5c and normal background area determined on the MGW11 in Figure 5d. This indicates that the mineralization similarities of MGW and MGW11 are invalid in Cu, Au, and Mo (Fe) geochemical exploration.

By comparing the anomaly areas locating the six tungsten deposits, we can find that the areas determined on the MGW11 are all smaller than the anomaly areas determined on the MGW, especially in the south and northeast margins of the Lianyang granitic complex. This is helpful in targeting the tungsten deposits efficiently in geochemical exploration and is consistent with the aim of this study. Therefore, the mineralization similarity of MGW11 is an integrated index for recognizing the tungsten anomalies, which eliminates not only the closure effect of compositional data such as the spider diagrams [26] and elemental correlations [27] but also the weathering and lithology influences during geochemical exploration.

In addition, two anomaly areas are determined in the south margin of the Lianyang granitic complex near the Qiashui town, both on the MGW (Figure 5c) and on the MGW11 (Figure 5d) with outer and middle anomaly zones (or $R_{IdealOre} \geq 60\%$) which may be potential targets for further tungsten prospecting.

5. Conclusions

(1) A tungsten metallogene named MGW11 is proposed for geochemical tungsten exploration in areas with 11 types of LG_CR compositionally.

(2) The MGW11 and MGW metallogenes illustrate stable properties such as heredity and inheritance during weathering of rocks with 11 types of LG_CR compositionally regardless of weathering degrees. However, gene variations of MGW11 and MGW are also observed during extreme weathering.

(3) The mineralization similarities of MGW11 and MGW can be viewed as useful integrated indices on geochemical tungsten exploration. In areas with 11 types of LG_CR compositionally, anomaly areas determined on the MGW11 are all smaller than those on the MGW because the MGW11 eliminates the lithological influence on recognizing tungsten anomalies during tungsten prospecting.

Author Contributions: J.L.: Conceptualization, Data curation, Writing—original draft. Q.G.: Conceptualization, Methodology, Writing—review and editing. B.Z.: Conceptualization, Data curation. N.L.: Methodology, Formal analysis, Data curation. X.W.: Conceptualization, Data curation. T.Y.: Conceptualization, Formal analysis. X.L.: Data curation. Y.W.: Data curation. All authors have read and agreed to the published version of the manuscript.

Funding: This research was financially supported by the Fund from the Key Laboratory of Geochemical Ex-ploration, Ministry of Natural Resources (IGGEW2021030).

Institutional Review Board Statement: Not applicable.

Informed Consent Statement: Not applicable.

Data Availability Statement: Not applicable.

Acknowledgments: We greatly appreciate the comments from the anonymous reviewers and editors for their valuable suggestions to improve the quality of this manuscript.

Conflicts of Interest: The authors declare that they have no known competing financial interest or personal relationships that could have appeared to influence the work reported in this paper.

References

1. Gong, Q.J.; Yan, T.T.; Wu, X.; Li, R.K.; Wang, X.Q.; Liu, N.Q.; Li, X.L.; Wu, Y.; Li, J. Geochemical gene: A promising concept in discrimination and traceability of geological materials. *Appl. Geochem.* **2022**, *136*, 105133. [CrossRef]
2. Wu, Y.; Gong, Q.J.; Liu, N.Q.; Wu, X.; Yan, T.T.; Xu, S.C.; Li, W.J. Classification of geological materials on geochemical lithogenes: Illustration on a case study in Gejiu area of Yunnan Province, China. *Appl. Geochem.* **2022**, *146*, 105460. [CrossRef]
3. Li, R.K.; Liu, N.Q.; Gong, Q.J.; Wu, X.; Yan, T.T.; Li, X.L.; Liu, M.X. Construction, test and application of a geochemical gold metallogene: Case studies in China. *J. Geochem. Explor.* **2019**, *204*, 1–11. [CrossRef]
4. Gong, Q.J.; Liu, N.Q.; Wu, X.; Yan, T.T.; Fan, T.Q.; Li, X.L.; Liu, M.X.; Li, R.K.; Albanese, S. Using regional geochemical survey data to trace anomalous samples through geochemical genes: The Tieshanlong tungsten deposit area (Southeastern China) case study. *J. Geochem. Explor.* **2020**, *219*, 106637. [CrossRef]
5. Yan, T.T.; Wu, X.; Quan, Y.K.; Gong, Q.J.; Li, X.L.; Wang, P.; Li, R.K. Heredity, inheritance and similarity of element behaviors among parent rocks and their weathered products: A geochemical lithogene. *Geoscience* **2018**, *32*, 453–467. (In Chinese with English Abstract)
6. Gong, Q.J.; Wu, X.; Yan, T.T.; Liu, N.Q.; Li, X.L.; Li, R.K.; Liu, M.X. Construction and test of geochemical genes: Case studies in China. *Geoscience* **2020**, *34*, 865–882. (In Chinese with English Abstract)
7. Li, J.; Liu, N.Q.; Gong, Q.J.; Wu, X.; Yan, T.T. Construction and test of a geochemical lithogene based on trace elements: Case studies on weathering profiles in China. *Geoscience* **2021**, *35*, 1459–1470. (In Chinese with English Abstract)
8. Wu, Y.; Li, X.L.; Gong, Q.J.; Wu, X.; Yao, N.; Peng, C.; Chao, Y.D.; Wang, X.Y.; Pu, X.L. Test and application of the geochemical lithogene on weathering profiles developed over granitic and basaltic rocks in China. *Appl. Geochem.* **2021**, *128*, 104958. [CrossRef]
9. Zuo, Y.S.; Gong, Q.J.; Jiang, B.; Zhang, T.; Wu, X.; Yan, T.T. Regional Geochemical Survey in the Area of Shuangjianzishan Ag-polymetallic Deposit in Inner Mongolia, China. *Geoscience* **2021**, *35*, 1411–1424. (In Chinese with English Abstract)
10. Chi, Q.H.; Yan, M.C. *Handbook of Elemental Abundance for Applied Geochemistry*; Geological Publishing House: Beijing, China, 2007; pp. 1–148.
11. Hou, Q.Y.; Yang, Z.F.; Yu, T.; Xia, X.Q.; Cheng, H.X.; Zhou, G.H. *Statistical Parameters of Elemental Concentration of Soils in China*; Geological Publishing House: Beijing, China, 2020; pp. 1–3172.
12. Xiang, Y.C.; Mu, X.Z.; Ren, T.X.; Ma, Z.D.; Liu, R.M.; Gong, Q.J.; Wang, M.Q.; Gong, J.Z.; Yang, W.Z.; Yang, Y.; et al. *Application of Geochemical Survey Data on Potential Evaluation of Mineral Resources in China*; Geological Publishing House: Beijing, China, 2018; pp. 1–445.
13. Peng, C. *Testing and Application of Geochemical Gene: A Case Study in Tieling Area, Liaoning Province*; China University of Geosciences: Beijing, China, 2021; pp. 1–69.
14. Zhang, M.T. *Source Rock Tracing of Weathering Products by Geochemical Lithogene—A Case Study of Taishan Temple Area in Xionger Mountain, Western Henan Province*; China University of Geosciences: Beijing, China, 2019; pp. 1–60.
15. Si, C. *Geochemical Genes in the Weathering of Lincang Granite, Yunnan Province, China*; China University of Geosciences: Beijing, China, 2020; pp. 1–54.

16. Kong, L.L. *Testing and Application of Geochemical Lithogene: A Case Study in Lianyang Area, Guangdong Province*; China University of Geosciences: Beijing, China, 2020; pp. 1–60.
17. Liu, M.X. *Behavior of Elements during Weathering of Granite—A Case Study in Lianyang, Guangdong Province*; China University of Geosciences: Beijing, China, 2020; pp. 1–49.
18. Nesbitt, H.W.; Young, G.M. Early Proterozoic climates and plate motions inferred from major element chemistry of lutites. *Nature* **1982**, *299*, 715–717. [CrossRef]
19. Gong, Q.J.; Deng, J.; Wang, C.M.; Wang, Z.L.; Zhou, L.Z. Element behaviors due to rock weathering and its implication to geochemical anomaly recognition: A case study on Linglong biotite granite in Jiaodong peninsula, China. *J. Geochem. Explor.* **2013**, *128*, 14–24. [CrossRef]
20. Fedo, C.M.; Nesbitt, H.W.; Young, G.M. Unraveling the effects of potassium metasomatism in sedimentary rocks and paleosols, with implications for paleoweathering conditions and provenance. *Geology* **1995**, *23*, 921–924. [CrossRef]
21. Ma, X.H.; Chen, B.; Wang, Z.Z.; Gao, L.; Sun, K.K. Pelrogenesis of the lianyang composite granite, Nanling region; U-Ph zircongeochronology, geochemistry and Nd-Hf isotopes constraints. *Earth Sci. Front.* **2014**, *21*, 264–280. (In Chinese with English Abstract)
22. Ma, X.H.; Wang, Z.Q.; Chen, B. Petrogenesis of the Early Cretaceous Lianyang Granitic Complex, South China: Tectonic and Metallogenic Implications. *Acta Geol. Sin.* **2014**, *88*, 24–25. [CrossRef]
23. Wang, R.C.; Xie, L.; Chen, J.; Yu, A.P.; Wang, L.B.; Lu, J.J.; Zhu, J.C. Titanite as an Indicator Mineral of Tin Mineralizing Potential of Granites in the Middle Nanling Range. *Geol. J. China Univ.* **2011**, *17*, 368–380. (In Chinese with English Abstract) [CrossRef]
24. You, Z.M.; Zhang, Y.; Shi, X. Discussion on the genesis of iron polymetallic deposit (point) in the northeast margin of Lianyang rock mass in northwest Guangdong. *Miner. Resour.* **2019**, 49–50. (In Chinese with English Abstract)
25. Xie, X.; Cheng, H. Sixty years of exploration geochemistry in China. *Geochem. Explor.* **2014**, *139*, 4–8. [CrossRef]
26. Hou, Z.G.; Gong, Q.J.; Liu, N.Q.; Jiang, B.; Li, J.; Wu, Y.; Huang, J.X.; Gu, W.X. Elemental abundances of moon samples based on statistical distributions of analytical data. *Appl. Sci.* **2023**, *13*, 360. [CrossRef]
27. Zhang, B.; Jiang, Z.; Chen, Y.; Cheng, N.; Khan, U.; Deng, J. Geochemical association rules of elements mined using clustered events of spatial autocorrelation: A case study in the Chahanwusu river area, Qinghai province, China. *Appl. Sci.* **2022**, *12*, 2247. [CrossRef]

applied sciences

MDPI

Article

Speciation Analysis and Pollution Assessment of Heavy Metals in Farmland Soil of a Typical Mining Area: A Case Study of Dachang Tin Polymetallic Ore, Guangxi

Jiali Zhang [1], Yinghong Liu [1], Songtao Hong [1], Meilan Wen [1], Chaojie Zheng [2] and Panfeng Liu [1,*]

[1] College of Earth and Sciences, Guilin University of Technology, Guilin 541006, China
[2] School of Resources and Environmental Engineering, Hefei University of Technology, Hefei 230009, China
* Correspondence: panfengliu@glut.edu.cn

Abstract: To explore the distribution characteristics and degree of pollution of heavy metals in the farmland soil around the Dachang tin polymetallic mining area in Guangxi, a total of 140 soil samples were collected around the mining area in this study. The total amount and various forms of seven heavy metals (Cu, Pb, Cd, Cr, Zn, As, and Ni) were analyzed by inductively coupled plasma mass spectrometry, and the improved continuous extraction method of heavy metal speciation analysis in the soil, the potential ecological risk index (*RI*), the and Nemerow evaluation index (P_N) were used to evaluate pollution characteristics of the soil and the bioavailability of heavy metals. Corresponding remediation suggestions were given according to the pollution degree. The results show that the whole soil in the study area is acidic, reducing, and the content of organic matter is low. The average content of heavy metal elements is higher than the background value of Guangxi, among which Cd, Pb, and As exceed the control value and are the main elements of pollution. The speciation analysis of heavy metals in soil shows that Cd is dominated by the ion exchange form; Cu is mainly residual and in a humic acid combined form; and the rest of the elements are mainly in residual form. Among the seven heavy metals, Cd has the strongest mobility, biological toxicity, and ecological risk, followed by As, Ni, and Zn. The overall pollution level of the soil in the study area is heavily polluted (P_N = 39.6), which is a very strong ecological risk level (*RI* = 2196.9), and the main pollutants are Pb, As, and Cd; Cd pollution is the most serious. Correlation (CA) and principal component analysis (PCA) indicate that the pollution sources of Pb, Cu, Zn, Cd, and As among the seven elements were mainly controlled by tailings accumulation, mining, and transportation, and the sources of Cr and Ni were controlled by soil-forming parent materials. Furthermore, according to the actual situation of the farmland around the mining area, two remediation suggestions are put forward: (1) use stabilization remediation technology to clean up the pollution source, such as calcium dihydrogen phosphate to reduce the bioavailability of the most polluted elements, Cd and Pb, in the soil; (2) under the concept of green environmental protection, use *Typha orientalis* Presl to repair the industrial and mining wasteland and some unused land.

Keywords: heavy metal; existing form; bioavailability; risk assessment; Dachang mining area

Citation: Zhang, J.; Liu, Y.; Hong, S.; Wen, M.; Zheng, C.; Liu, P. Speciation Analysis and Pollution Assessment of Heavy Metals in Farmland Soil of a Typical Mining Area: A Case Study of Dachang Tin Polymetallic Ore, Guangxi. *Appl. Sci.* **2023**, *13*, 708. https://doi.org/10.3390/app13020708

Academic Editors: Qingjie Gong and Zeming Shi

Received: 10 December 2022
Revised: 28 December 2022
Accepted: 30 December 2022
Published: 4 January 2023

1. Introduction

The exploitation of mineral resources has greatly promoted the development of regional economies, but long-term mining and the stacking of tailings have also become the source of environmental hazards under economic prosperity [1,2]. In particular, the release, migration, and transformation of heavy metals in the environmental medium have a great impact, causing serious pollution to the surrounding soil, water bodies, and habitats, threatening the ecological balance and human security [3–5], and restricting the construction of an ecological civilization. Soil is the most important medium to maintain balance and stability of an ecosystem, especially the soil quality of agricultural land [6,7].

The content of heavy metals in soil is mainly controlled by soil-forming parent materials and human activities. Human activities such as sewage irrigation, mining and smelting of metal ores, and combustion of industrial wastes and fossil fuels have been proven to be the main causes of heavy metal pollution in the soil of China [8–10]. Among them, the mining of metals, beneficiation, and smelting activities are the main human activities that cause heavy metal pollution in soil, water, and the biosphere [11]. It is reported that the area of polluted soil is increasing at a rate of 46,700 hm^2 every year due to mining in China [12]. Therefore, the phenomenon of heavy metal pollution in soil related to mining activities has always been a research hotspot.

In recent years, studies have shown that mining activities cause soil heavy metal pollution [13]. In many parts of the world, heavy metals produced by mining activities cause serious environmental problems, especially when they pollute the surrounding farmland [14]. Concerns and research surrounding heavy metal polluted soil caused by mining are increasing all over the world. Redwan et al. evaluated the environment quality of the Barramiya gold mine area in the eastern desert of Egypt and found that there are 318–500 t tailings in the area, which cause serious heavy metal pollution to the surrounding environment due to erosion, weathering, and surface runoff [15]. Akoto et al. analyzed the heavy metals of different solid mine wastes in a Ghana mining area and found that the degree of ecological risk varies with the type of wastes: tailings > sulfide > oxide [16]. Yun et al. studied heavy metals in farmland around an abandoned gold mine in South Korea and found that farmland types have an impact on the spatial distribution of heavy metals in soil [17]. The geochemical characteristics of ore samples and of stream-sediment samples from the Tri-State district indicated that past mining activities and leaded gasoline have had significant effects on lead concentrations in river sediments [18]. Taylor et al. investigated heavy metals (Cd, Cu, Pb, and Zn) from the Pb–Zn–Ag and Cu mines at Mount Isa, Queensland, Australia, and showed that the heavy metal content in the surface soil near the mining area (within 2 km) was obviously higher than that far away and that the ecological risk level of lead was very high [19].

Dachang Town in Guangxi is an important tin polymetallic production area in China. It is known as "China's Cenozoic tin capital" and has long-term mining history. However, in the process of early development and utilization, large amounts of tailings were not fully utilized and accumulated on the surface due to the constraints of technical conditions and production concepts. The tailing dumps have been under the action of oxidation for a long time, and the heavy metal elements (e.g., Cu, Pb, Zn, and Cd) have been gradually activated, invading the surrounding soil through rainwater leaching, atmospheric dust, and other ways, threatening the ecological environment of farmland soil and endangering the health of residents through food chain enrichment. Therefore, it is urgent to carry out research on heavy metal pollution of soil in the area. By collecting soil samples from farmland in natural villages around the mining area, analyzing the content of typical heavy metal elements, organic matter, and pH value, and extracting the occurrence form using the improved Tessier seven-step continuous method, we thereby reveal the spatial variation characteristics, migration laws, and pollution sources of heavy metals and comprehensively evaluate the pollution degree and environmental risk effects of heavy metals. This provides a scientific basis for the treatment and restoration of heavy metals in soil of the area and effectively promotes the protective environmental mining of metal mines in the area.

2. Materials and Methods

2.1. Study Site

Dachang mining area is situated in Dachang Town in southwestern Nandan county, Guangxi (Figure 1a–d). It is the main mineral concentration area in the county. The total coverage area of the town is 283 km^2, and the total urban population is more than 30,000, of which 18,000 are mining workers and their family members alone. It is a typical mining town. The study area involves 22 natural villages. The geographical coordinates are $107°33'44''$~$107°38'21''$ E and $24°48'36''$~$24°52'25''$ N. The study area is north of the Tropic of Cancer and belongs to the northern climate zone of the middle subtropical zone. It has the climate characteristics of a plateau mountain area. The annual mean precipitation is approximately 1400 mm, and the annual mean temperature is 17.2 °C. The natural soil in the area is mainly loam, followed by sandy loam; the soil color is mainly black, gray-black, and yellow-brown; and the parent material of the soil is mainly sand shale, followed by sandstone and shale [20].

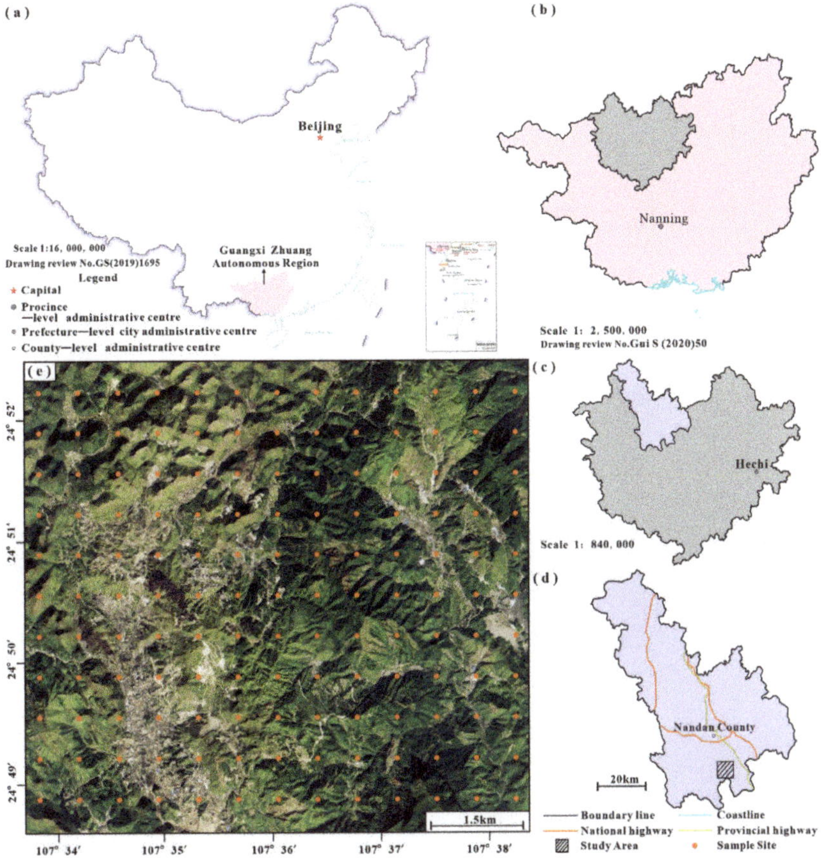

Figure 1. Location diagram of the study area in China and Guangxi (**a–d**) and distribution diagram of soil sampling (**e**).

2.2. Sample Collection and Chemical Analysis

Using geographic information system technology and the grid method, the sample points are evenly distributed in the whole study area. During the sampling process, accessibility and safety were carefully considered, and 140 sampling points were determined in combination with the actual topography around the Dachang mining area (Figure 1e). Each sample was collected from a 0–20 cm thick layer of soil. To maximize the representativeness of the samples, five subsamples collected from each square were mixed into a comprehensive soil sample on site. We removed impurities such as stones and debris from the samples. The weight of each composite sample was about 1 kg. After being crushed with a wooden mallet, all the samples were passed through 100 mesh sieves, were fully mixed and weighed, and were put into a polyethylene sample bottle before chemical analysis.

The sample pretreatment for the determination of the total amount of heavy metals in soil was in accordance with the Ministry of Ecology and Environment of the People's Republic of China (HJ832-2017) [21]. After the sample was digested by HNO_3–HCl–HF–$HClO_4$ (Mars 6 classic, CEM) it was determined by inductively coupled plasma mass spectrometry (ICP-MS). The pH value and organic matter content of the soil were determined by the potentiometric method and the potassium dichromate oxidation colorimetric method, and the EH value was analyzed by an OPR-422 redox potentiometer. The speciation analysis of heavy metals in soil was extracted step-by-step in strict accordance with the technical standard for evaluation and analysis of eco-geochemical samples (DD2005-03) [22]. The reagents used for analysis were superior grade pure. We simultaneously analyzed the total amount, weak acid extraction form, reducible form, and oxidizable form of the reagent blank and sediment reference material BCR701 to reduce errors. The recovery of heavy metals (As, Cd, Cr, Cu, Ni, Pb, and Zn) in the reference materials was 118%, 86%, 88%, 120%, 87%, 109%, and 97%, respectively, which met quality control standards.

2.3. *Risk Assessment and Data Processing*

2.3.1. Single Factor Pollution Index (SFPI)

The SFPI is one of the most effective methods to evaluate heavy metal pollution degree. The equation is as follows; however, its results do not reflect the level of pollution in the whole area:

$$P_i = \frac{C_i}{B_i} \tag{1}$$

where P_i is the pollution index of element i, C_i is the measured data for metal i, and B_i is the soil background value. The heavy metal content of the soil in Guangxi measured in 1990 was used as the background value of the study. The values of Cd, As, Cu, Pb, Zn, Cr, and Ni are 0.27, 20.5, 27.8, 24.0, 75.6, 72.1, and 26.6 mg/kg, respectively.

2.3.2. Nemerow Integrated Pollution Index (NIPI)

The NIPI is a perfect supplement to the shortcomings of the SFPI. It can comprehensively evaluate the overall pollution level of the study area and make comparisons between different areas [23,24]. The index is calculated using the following equation:

$$P_N = \sqrt[2]{\left(\frac{(Pi)_{ave}{}^2 + (Pi)_{max}{}^2}{2}\right)} \tag{2}$$

where P_N is the soil pollution index and $(P_i)ave$ and $(P_i)max$ are the average and maximum values of the pollution element i within a specific area, respectively. The classification criteria for assessment of the soil heavy metal pollution index are shown in Table 1 [25].

Table 1. Classification criteria for heavy metal pollution in soil.

Class	Pollution Index of Element i	Pollution Index of Soil	Pollution Class	Pollution Level
1	$P_i \leq 0.7$	$P_N \leq 0.7$	Secure	Clean
2	$0.7 < P_i \leq 1$	$0.7 < P_N \leq 1$	Alert	Unpolluted
3	$1 < P_i \leq 2$	$1 < P_N \leq 2$	Mild	Began to be polluted
4	$2 < P_i \leq 3$	$2 < P_N \leq 3$	Moderate	Moderately polluted
5	$P_i > 3$	$P_N > 3$	Heavy	Extremely polluted

2.3.3. Potential Ecological Risk Index (PERI)

The PERI has been proposed by Swedish scientist Hakanson. It is a method to evaluate heavy metal pollution in soil or sediment from the perspective of sedimentology according to the properties and environmental behavior characteristics of heavy metals. The method not only considers the content of heavy metals in soil, but also comprehensively considers the synergistic effect of multiple elements, toxicity level, pollution degree, and environmental sensitivity to heavy metal pollution, so it has been widely used in environmental risk assessment [26]. The expression is as follows:

$$RI = \sum_i^k E_r^i = \sum_i^k T_n^i \times \frac{C_i}{B_i} \quad (3)$$

where *RI* represents the PERI of various heavy metals in soil; $E_r{}^i$ is the potential ecological risk coefficient of type *i* heavy metal; C_i is the concentration of type *i* heavy metal (mg/kg); B_i is the parameter ratio of type *i* heavy metal (mg/kg); $T_n{}^i$ is the toxicity coefficient of type *i* heavy metal. In this study, the toxicity coefficients of As, Ni, Cd, Cr, Cu, Pb, and Zn are 10, 5, 30, 2, 5, 5, 5, and 1, respectively [27]. Table 2 shows the corresponding values of ecological risk levels and different indexes.

Table 2. Corresponding range of ecological risk level in soil.

E_r^i	*RI*	Potential Ecological Risk
$E_r^i \leq 40$	$RI \leq 150$	Light ecological hazards
$40 < E_r^i \leq 80$	$150 < RI \leq 300$	Moderate ecological hazards
$80 < E_r^i \leq 160$	$300 < RI \leq 600$	Relatively strong ecological hazards
$160 < E_r^i \leq 320$		Strong ecological hazards
$E_r^i > 320$	$RI > 600$	Extremely strong ecological hazards

2.3.4. The Migration Coefficient (MC) and Bioavailability Coefficient (BC)

Among the seven forms of heavy metals, the water-soluble form and the ion exchange form are the most easily exchanged by other ions, and easy to be directly used by plants [28]. They have a strong migration ability and are sensitive to environmental changes. These two forms are usually used to calculate the mobility of heavy metals and are important indicators for evaluating soil heavy metal pollution. The carbonate-combined form can be extracted by mild acid, which is easily absorbed and utilized by organisms. Therefore, the bioavailability of heavy metals in soil is calculated by the sum of the water-soluble form, the ion exchange form, and the carbonate combined form [7]. The MC and BC are calculated as follows:

$$\text{Migration coefficient (MC)} = \frac{(F1 + F2)}{(F1 + F2 + F3 + F4 + F5 + F6 + F7)} \quad (4)$$

$$\text{Bioavailability coefficient (BC)} = \frac{(F1 + F2 + F3)}{(F1 + F2 + F3 + F4 + F5 + F6 + F7)} \quad (5)$$

where *F*1 and *F*2 represent the water-soluble form and the ion exchange form, *F*3 and *F*4 represent the carbonate combined form and the humic acid combined form, *F*5 and *F*6 represent the iron–manganese oxide combined form and strong organic combined form, and *F*7 represents the residual form.

2.3.5. Data Processing

Arithmetic mean and range were used to analyze the concentration of heavy metals in the study area. The Pearson's correlation analysis (CA) and principal component analysis (PCA) were used to explore the sources of metal elements and establish the relationships between heavy metals and other variables in the soil. All analyses were carried out using SPSS 26.0 Origin Pro 2021, and Excel. ArcGIS 10.8 and CorelDRAW 2020 were used for drawing.

3. Results

3.1. Content Characteristics of Heavy Metal in Soil

Table 3 shows the descriptive statistical data of physical and chemical properties and heavy metal content in the soil around the mining area. The overall soil is acidic, with the pH value ranging from 3.7 to 7.7 and an average value of 5.9. Among them, 86% of the soil is acidic and 34% is strongly acidic. The range of organic matter content is 0.5–10.5 g/kg, with an average of 4.3 g/kg, which indicates that organic matter content in soil is small and might affect the activity of heavy metals. The content ranges of heavy metals (Cr, Ni, Cu, Pb, Zn, As, and Cd) were 32.7–169.2 mg/kg, 9.1–151.7 mg/kg, 13.4–328.7 mg/kg, 1.8–7104.5 mg/kg, 16.8–20,075 mg/kg, 1.2–4097.9 mg/kg, and 0.2–255.9 mg/kg, respectively. The average content shows a change in the trend of Zn (2422.0 mg/kg) > Pb (730.0 mg/kg) > As (307.1 mg/kg) > Cu (86.5 mg/kg) > Cr (66.9 mg/kg) > Ni (42.7 mg/kg) > Cd (16.4 mg/kg). Except for Cr and Ni, the average contents of the other five elements are higher than background values in Guangxi, indicating that the heavy metal elements in the soil are enriched to different degrees. Among them, Cd and Zn reach 61.4 times and 32.0 times their background values, respectively. Pb reaches 30.4 times the background value, and As and Cu are 5.3 times and 3.1 times higher than their background values, respectively. The results show that the mining and smelting of non-ferrous metals can obviously lead to the accumulation of some heavy metals (e.g., Cd, Zn, Pb) [29,30]. According to the Soil Environmental Quality Risk Control Standard for Soil Contamination of Agricultural Land (GB15618-2018) [31], Cd, As, Pb, and Zn exceed the risk screening values, and Cd, As, and Pb even exceed the risk intervention values, indicating that Cd, As, Pb, and Zn are obviously enriched and the main pollution elements in the soil, a fact that needs special attention.

3.2. Speciation Characteristics of Heavy Metals

The speciation characteristics of heavy metal in the soil around the mining area are presented in Table 4 and Figure 2. Cr is mainly in residual form, with an average content of 58.67 mg/kg, accounting for 82.04% of the 7 forms, followed by humic acid combined form of 9.52%. Arsenic is mainly in residual form, with an average content of 172.02 mg/kg, accounting for 69.15% of the 7 forms. Ni, Pb, and Zn are mainly in residual form, accounting for 59.85%, 57.34%, and 61.11%, respectively, followed by iron–manganese oxide combined form, of which Pb accounts for the highest proportion, reaching 22.86%. Some studies show that Pb in air dust is mainly in iron–manganese oxide form [32]. Cu is mainly in residue form and humic acid combined form, followed by iron–manganese oxide combined form and strong organic combined form. Cd is mainly in ion exchange form, with an average content of 26.72 mg/kg, accounting for 24.12%, and the proportions of other forms are in the following order: strong organic combined form > humic acid combined form > iron–manganese oxide combined form > residual form > carbonate combined form > water-soluble form.

Table 3. Statistical parameters of pH value, organic matter, and heavy metal content of the farmland soil around Dachang mining area.

	Maximum	Minimum	Average	Reference Background *	Risk Screening Values	Risk Intervention Values
pH	7.7	3.7	5.9		5.5 < pH ≤ 6.5	5.5 < pH ≤ 6.5
organic matter	10.5	0.5	4.3			
Cr	169.2	32.7	66.9	82.1	150	850
Ni	151.7	9.1	42.7	26.6	70	
Cu	328.7	13.4	86.5	27.8	50	
Pb	7104.5	1.8	730	24.0	90	500
Zn	20,075	16.8	2422	75.6	200	
As	4097.9	1.2	307.1	20.5	40	150
Cd	255.9	0.2	16.4	0.27	0.3	2.0

* Refers to China National Environmental Monitoring Center [33].

Table 4. Contents of different forms of heavy metals in soil around Dachang mining area.

Element	Water-Soluble Form	Ion Exchange Form	Carbonate Combined Form	Humic Acid Combined Form	Iron–Manganese Oxide Combined Form	Strong Organic Combined Form	Residual Form
Cr *	0.16	0.41	0.56	6.81	1.35	3.55	58.67
Ni *	0.36	0.44	1.44	2.36	6.02	5.01	23.30
Cu *	0.40	0.49	2.85	62.38	25.93	20.29	76.84
Pb *	4.26	0.60	61.50	625.74	1017.02	188.54	2551.00
Zn *	115.21	93.73	387.57	546.96	1253.83	959.23	5273.57
As *	7.01	0.97	6.43	43.51	7.27	11.55	172.02
Cd *	4.72	26.72	10.53	17.64	16.08	20.03	15.04

* Represents the arithmetic mean contents of different speciation.

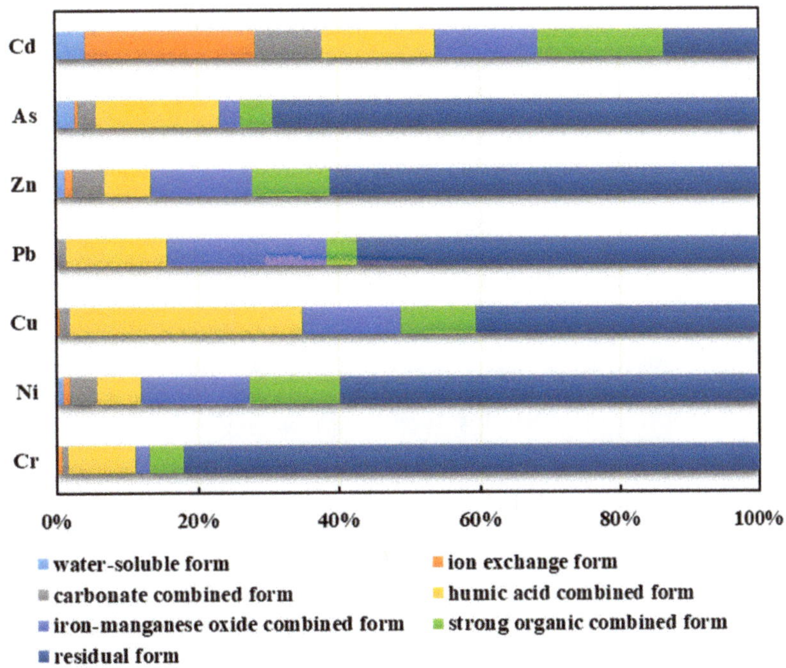

Figure 2. The proportion chart of different forms of heavy metals in the farmland soil around the Dachang mining area.

Figure 3 shows that the migration ability of each heavy metal element in farmland soil with the change in environmental conditions is in the following order: Cd > As > Ni > Zn > Cr > Cu > Pb; the order of the biological availability of each heavy metal element with the change in environmental conditions is: Cd > Zn > As > Ni > Cu > Cr > Pb. Compared with other elements, the absolute content of water-soluble, ion exchange, and carbonate combined forms of Cd is higher. Cd is the most active and easily absorbed and utilized by plants, thus accumulating toxicity in organisms, followed by As, Ni, and Zn. The residual form of Cr, Cu, and Pb elements are higher, and the biological activity and mobility of these heavy metals are poor.

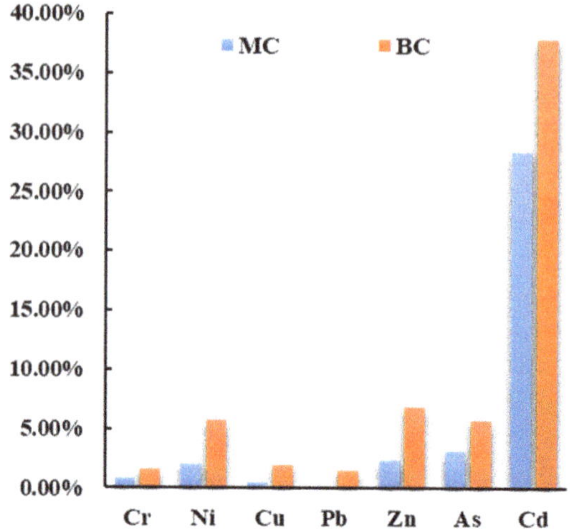

Figure 3. Column diagram of mobility coefficient and bioavailability coefficient of heavy metal.

3.3. Ecological Hazard Assessment

According to the measured data and Equations (1) and (2), corresponding values (the P_i and P_N) can be obtained. The single pollution index range of each pollutant is 0.3–0.6 for P_{Cr}, 0.3–1.5 for P_{Ni}, 0.4–4.2 for P_{Cu}, 0.7–32.5 for P_{Pb}, 2.0–44.9 for P_{Zn}, 0.5–17.4 for P_{As}, and 3.3–258.3 for P_{Cd}. The level of P_i in the farmland soils around the Dachang mining area can be ordered as: P_{Cd} (54.7) > P_{Zn} (12.1) > P_{Pb} (8.1) > P_{As} (7.7) > P_{Cu} (1.7) > P_{Ni} (0.6) > P_{Cr} (0.4). In the whole study area, the soil is not polluted by Cr and Ni, is slightly polluted by Cu, and is extremely polluted by the other four elements (Cd, Zn, Pb, and As) [18,19]. The Nemerow integrated pollution index (P_N) is 39.6, and the pollution level is extremely polluted. Notably, Cd contributes the most to the comprehensive pollution index, with a contribution rate ranging from 33% to 89%, and its contribution rate is as high as 68% in the whole study area.

According to Equation (3), the PERI of soil samples can be calculated, and the results are as follows. The level of E_i heavy metals in the farmland soils around the Dachang mining area can be ordered as: E_{Cd} (1842.6) > E_{Pb} (152.1) > E_{As} (150.0) > E_{Zn} (12.1) > E_{Cu} (1.7) > E_{Ni} (0.6) > E_{Cr} (0.4). The risk of Cd is the most significant, which belongs to the extremely strong ecological hazard level, followed by As and Pb, which belong to the relatively strong ecological hazard level. Zn, Cu, Ni, and Cr belong to the slight ecological risk level. The potential ecological hazard index (RI) of the study area is 2196.9, which belongs to the extremely strong ecological hazard level. The contribution rate of Cd is as high as 84%, which is the main pollution element. This result is highly consistent with the evaluation result of the Nemerow integrated pollution index.

3.4. Source Identification

3.4.1. Correlation Analysis (CA)

The correlation analysis between heavy metals can reflect whether they have homology and provide rich information for judging the source of substances. Table 5 shows that Cr is positively correlated with the other 6 elements, but the correlation is not significant. Ni is significantly correlated with Cu ($p < 0.01$) and negatively correlated with Pb ($p < 0.05$). There is a significant positive correlation between Cu and Zn, Cd, Pb, and As ($p < 0.01$). The correlation coefficients of Zn, Cd, Pb, and As are Zn/Pb, (0.758), Zn/As (0.815), Zn/Cd (0.964), Pb/As (0.839), Pb/Cd (0.785), and As/Cd (0.831), which are all greater than 0.75, indicating a significant positive correlation, meaning they have similar formation causes or common influence factors. The content of organic matter in soil is negatively correlated with Cr and Ni ($p < 0.05$) and positively correlated with Pb and As. The correlation is significant, which is in line with the law that the content of Pb and As increases when the soil changes from acid to neutral. The Eh value is significantly negatively correlated with Ni, Cu, Pb, Zn, As, and Cd ($p < 0.01$), indicating that, the lower the Eh value, the stronger the soil reduction ability and the higher the content of heavy metals.

Table 5. Correlation coefficients among heavy metals, pH, Eh, and organic matter.

Item	Cr	Ni	Cu	Zn	Cd	Pb	As	Organic Matter	pH	Eh
Cr	1									
Ni	0.113	1								
Cu	0.148	0.358 **	1							
Zn	0.174	0.086	0.712 **	1						
Cd	0.160	−0.570 *	0.631 **	0.964 **	1					
Pb	0.037	−0.058	0.633 **	0.758 **	0.785 **	1				
As	0.072	−0.047	0.596 **	0.815 **	0.831 **	0.839 **	1			
organic matter	−0.560 **	−0.338 **	0.129	0.301	0.211	0.266 **	0.385 **	1		
pH	−0.083	0.369 **	0.443 **	0.547 **	0.628 **	0.518 **	0.512 **	0.248	1	
Eh	0.132	−0.338 *	−0.449 **	−0.507 **	−0.581 **	−0.482 **	−0.498 **	−0.206	−0.945 **	1

Notes: ** Correlation is significant at the 0.01 level (double-tailed), * Correlation is significant at the 0.05 level (double-tailed).

3.4.2. Principal Component Analysis (PCA)

To identify and quantify the sources of the seven heavy metals in soil, PCA was used to further analyze the sources of heavy metals in soil more accurately. Firstly, the data were tested by KMO and Bartlett sphere, and the KMO value of the test result was 0.886. Therefore, the dataset was suitable for PCA. The analysis results are shown in Tables 6 and 7. The cumulative variance percentage contribution of the front three principal components is 87.137%, which basically represents the indicators of heavy metal in the study area. The variance contribution rate of the first principal component is 54.72%. The load values of Cu, Pb, Zn, Cd, and As are relatively large among the 7 elements, all of which are greater than 0.6. Meanwhile, they are significantly correlated with each other in the CA. Field investigation also found that they are high in the farmland soil near the mining area and along the road, and the mining of tin polymetallic ore produces a large number of tailings containing a certain amount of Cd, Pb, and Cu. The oxides and sulfides of the above elements may enter the environment through the weathering process and cause serious pollution to the surrounding soil [34,35]. Therefore, it is speculated that the first principal component is enriched by the influence of tailings accumulation, mining, and transportation. The contribution rate of PC2 (the second principal component) is 17.82%, and the highest load value is Ni. Ni has a significant positive correlation with Cu, but not with other elements. It is speculated that it may be related to sewage irrigation, pesticides, and soil-forming parent materials. The load value of Cr is the highest in the third principal component, with a contribution rate of 14.60%. The correlation between Cr and the other six elements is not significant. It is considered that Cr is related to the soil–forming parent materials.

Table 6. Total variance explained and component matrices for heavy metals.

Components	Extraction Sums of Squared Loadings			Rotation Sums of Squared Loadings		
	Eigenvalues	% of Variance	Cumulative %	Eigenvalues	% of Variance	Cumulative %
PC1	3.943	56.327	56.327	3.83	54.720	54.720
PC2	1.233	17.619	73.946	1.247	17.816	72.536
PC3	0.923	13.191	87.137	1.022	14.601	87.137
PC4	0.379	5.414	92.552			

Table 7. Composition matrix of heavy metals.

Elements	Principal Components Factor Load			Rotated Principal Components Factor Load		
	PC1	PC2	PC3	PC1	PC2	PC3
Cr	0.184	0.488	0.852	0.065	0.063	0.994
Ni	0.132	0.866	−0.396	−0.039	0.959	0.052
Cu	0.750	0.365	−0.199	0.664	0.538	0.069
Zn	0.953	−0.044	0.039	0.941	0.107	0.119
Cd	0.963	−0.039	0.014	0.951	0.125	0.100
Pb	0.843	−0.255	−0.016	0.877	−0.070	−0.036
As	0.884	−0.208	0.009	0.908	−0.034	0.012

3.5. Suggestions for Pollution Remediation

Remediation of heavy metal contamination in soil refers to the process of removing heavy metals from soil or immobilizing them in soil to reduce their mobility and bioavailability, thereby reducing the health and environmental risks of heavy metals. Common methods include physical, chemical, and biological methods. According to the heavy metal pollution elements and the pollution degree of the soil around the mining area, combined with the actual situation, the following two suggestions are given:

(1) Clean up the pollution source by using stabilization repair technology. The pollution in the Dachang mining area and its surrounding areas is related to the discharge of waste slag, wastewater, and exhaust gas in the early stage. Therefore, the remediation of the soil in this area must start with cleaning up the pollution sources. Due to the large area of contamination, the guest soil and soil replacement methods are obviously not economically feasible. Considering the advantages and disadvantages of various remediation technologies and the actual situation in the field, it is recommended that stabilization reagents be added in the soil to reduce the mobility and bioavailability of heavy metals in the soil and prevent the transfer of heavy metals to the food chain. Referring to the study results of [36], it is suggested to use calcium dihydrogen phosphate to reduce the bioavailability of Pb and Cd in the soil. After soil remediation is completed, it is useful to plant Pb and Cd resistant crops, such as corn.

(2) There are serious Cd, As, and Pb pollution issues in the industrial and mining wasteland and some unused land in the study area. Studies have shown that *Typha orientalis* Presl can absorb As, Cd, and Pb in the soil, accumulate, and fix them in the root [37]. Therefore, it is suggested to plant *Typha orientalis* Presl in these regions to achieve the goal of remediating and beautifying the environment.

4. Conclusions

(1) The study concludes that the mean concentrations of heavy metals in the farmland soil around Dachang mining area are in the decreasing order of Zn (2422.0 mg/kg) > Pb (730.0 mg/kg) > As (307.1 mg/kg) > Cu (86.5 mg/kg) > Cr (66.9 mg/kg) > Ni (42.7 mg/kg) > Cd (16.4 mg/kg). The soil is generally acidic, in a reduced state, with low organic matter content. Cd, As, and Pb even exceed the risk intervention values, indicating that Cd, As, and Pb are significantly enriched and that they are the main pollution elements of soil.

(2) Speciation analysis of heavy metals shows that Cd in soil is mainly in ion-exchange form, Cu is mainly in residual form and humic acid combined form, and the other elements are mainly in residual form. Among the seven heavy metal elements, Cd has the strongest mobility and biological toxicity, followed by As, Ni, and Zn; Cr, Cu, and Pb have poor biological activity and mobility.

(3) The assessment results show that the overall pollution level of the study area is heavy, which means a very strong ecological risk level. The main pollutants are Pb, As, and Cd; Cd is the most serious pollution. CA and PCA showed that the pollution sources of Cu, Pb, Zn, Cd, and As are mainly affected by tailings accumulation, mining and transportation, while Cr and Ni sources are controlled by soil-forming parent materials.

(4) According to the actual situation of the farmland around the mining area, it is proposed to clean up the pollution source by using stabilization remediation technology, such as using calcium dihydrogen phosphate to reduce the bioavailability of the most polluted elements, Pb and Cd, in the soil. In the industrial and mining wasteland and some unused land, *Typha orientalis* Presl can be used for repair in order to achieve the goal of green governance and beautification of the environment.

Author Contributions: Writing—original draft preparation, J.Z., S.H. and P.L.; Writing—review and editing, M.W. and Y.L.; Collecting the samples, Y.L. and S.H.; Software and data processing, C.Z. and P.L.; Funding acquisition, P.L. and M.W. All authors have read and agreed to the published version of the manuscript.

Funding: This work was supported by the National Natural Science Foundation of China (42203067) and the Natural Science Foundation of Guangxi (2022GXNSFBA035548 and 2021JJA150037). This work was supported by the Basic Ability Enhancement Program for Young and Middle-aged Teachers of Guangxi (2022KY0261).

Institutional Review Board Statement: Not applicable.

Informed Consent Statement: Not applicable.

Data Availability Statement: Not applicable.

Conflicts of Interest: The authors declare no conflict of interest.

References

1. Amuno, S.; Niyogi, S.; Amuno, M.; Attitaq, J. Heavy metal bioaccumulation and histopathological alterations in wild Arctic hares (*Lepus arcticus*) inhabiting a former lead-zinc mine in the Canadian high Arctic: A preliminary study. *Sci. Total Environ.* **2016**, *556*, 252–263. [CrossRef] [PubMed]
2. Ghayoraneh, M.; Qishlaqi, A. Concentration, distribution and speciation of toxic metals in soils along a transect around a Zn/Pb smelter in the northwest of Iran. *J. Geochem. Explor.* **2017**, *180*, 1–14. [CrossRef]
3. Cai, L.M.; Wang, Q.S.; Luo, J.; Wang, S.; Tang, C.H.; Yan, Z. Contamination characteristics and health risk for heavy metals via consumption of vegetables grown in regions affected by tonglvshan mine in Hubei, China. *Resour. Environ. Yangtze Basin* **2018**, *27*, 873–881.
4. Esmaeili, A.; Moore, F.; Keshavarzi, B.; Jaafarzadeh, N.; Kermani, M. A geochemical survey of heavy metals in agricultural and background soils of the Isfahan industrial zone, Iran. *Catena* **2014**, *121*, 88–98. [CrossRef]
5. Kuang, J.L.; Huang, L.N.; Chen, L.X.; Hua, Z.S.; Li, S.J.; Hu, M.; Li, J.T.; Shu, W.S. Contemporary environmental variation determines microbial diversity patterns in acid mine drainage. *ISME J.* **2013**, *7*, 1038–1050. [CrossRef]
6. China Geological Survey. *Investigation Report on Cultivated Land Geochemistry in China: Beijing*; Ministry of Natural Resources of the People's Republic of China: Beijing, China, 2015.
7. Yang, W.; Gao, Y.L.; Kang, Z.Y.; LI, R.F.; Wang, S.; Wu, H.Y. Chemical Forms and Bioavailability of Heavy Metals in Soil of Scenic Adjacent to Iron Ore. *Environ. Sci. Technol.* **2010**, *33*, 82–86.
8. Anju, M.; Banerjee, D.K. Multivariate statistical analysis of heavy metals in soils of a Pb-Zn mining area, India. *Environ. Monit. Assess.* **2012**, *184*, 4191–4206. [CrossRef]
9. Chakraborty, S.; Man, T.; Paulette, L.; DebB, S.; Li, B.; Weindorf, D.C.; Frazier, M. Rapid assessment of smelter/mining soil contamination via portable X-ray fluorescence spectrometry and indicator kriging. *Geoderma Int. J. Soil Sci.* **2017**, *306*, 108–119. [CrossRef]
10. Chen, K.; Huang, L.; Yan, B.Z.; Li, H.B.; Sun, H.; Jun, B. Effect of Lead Pollution Control on Environmental and Childhood Blood Lead Level in Nantong, China: An Interventional Study. *Environ. Sci. Technol.* **2014**, *48*, 12930. [CrossRef]
11. Liu, H.Y.; Probst, A.; Liao, B.H. Metal contamination of soils and crops affected by the Chenzhou lead/zinc mine spill (Hunan, China). *Sci. Total Environ.* **2005**, *339*, 153–166. [CrossRef]
12. Zhuang, P.; McBride, M.B.; Xia, H.P.; Li, N.Y.; Li, Z. Health risk from heavy metals via consumption of food crops in the vicinity of Dabaoshan mine, South China. *Sci. Total Environ.* **2009**, *407*, 1551–1561. [CrossRef] [PubMed]
13. Zhao, L.; Liang, Y.P.; Xu, Q.; Jing, W.H. Spatial Distribution, Contamination Assessment, and Sources of Heavy Metals in the Urban Green Space Soils of a City in North China. *Environ. Sci.* **2020**, *41*, 5552–5561.
14. Wang, R.; Deng, H.; Jia, Z.M.; Wang, J.B.; Yu, F.; Zeng, Q.Q. Spatial Distribution Characteristics, Pollution, and Ecological Risk Assessment of Soil Heavy Metals Around Mercury Mining Areas. *Environ. Sci.* **2021**, *42*, 3018–3027.
15. Redwan, M.; Bamousa, A.O. Characterization and environmental impact assessment of gold mine tailings in arid regions: A case study of Barramiya gold mine area, Eastern Desert, Egypt. *J. Afr. Earth Sci.* **2019**, *160*, 103644. [CrossRef]
16. Akoto, R.; Anning, A.K. Heavy Metal Enrichment and Potential Ecological Risks from Different Solid Mine Wastes at a Mine Site in Ghana. *Environ. Adv.* **2020**, *3*, 100028. [CrossRef]

17. Yun, S.W.; Kim, D.H.; Kang, D.H.; Son, J.; Lee, S.Y.; Lee, C.K.; Lee, S.H.; Ji, W.H.; Baveye, P.C.; Yu, C. Effect of farmland type on the transport and spatial distribution of metal(loid)s in agricultural lands near an abandoned gold mine site: Confirmation of previous observations. *J. Geochem. Explor.* **2017**, *181*, 129–137. [CrossRef]
18. Potra, A.; Dodd, J.W.; Ruhl, L.S. Distribution of trace elements and Pb isotopes in stream sediments of the Tri-State mining district (Oklahoma, Kansas, and Missouri), USA. *Appl. Geochem.* **2017**, *82*, 25–37. [CrossRef]
19. Taylor, M.P.; Mackay, A.K.; Hudson-Edwards, K.A.; Holz, E. Soil Cd, Cu, Pb and Zn contaminants around Mount Isa city, Queensland, Australia: Potential sources and risks to human health. *Appl. Geochem.* **2010**, *25*, 841–855. [CrossRef]
20. Xie, C.W. Soil types and characteristics in Karst area of Guangxi. *J. Guangxi Agric. Univ.* **1982**, *1*, 83–93.
21. *HJ 832-2017*; Soil and Sediment-Digestion of Total Metal Elements—Microwave Assisted Acid Digestion Method. Ministry of Ecology and Environment of The People's Republic of China: Beijing, China, 2017.
22. *DD 2005-03*; Technical Requirements for Sample Analysis of Ecological Geochemical Evaluation (Trial). China Geological Survey: Beijing, China, 2005.
23. Fan, S.X.; Gan, Z.T.; Li, M.J.; Zhang, Z.Q.; Zhou, Q. Progress of Assessment Methods of Heavy Metal Pollution in Soil. *Chin. Agric. Sci. Bull.* **2010**, *26*, 310–315.
24. Nemerow, N.L. *Scientific Stream Pollution Analysis*; ScriptaBookCo: Washington, DC, USA, 1974.
25. *NY/T 395-2012*; Technical Rules for Monitoring of Environmental Quality of Farmland Soil. China Agriculture Press: Beijing, China, 2012.
26. Huang, F. Study on the Removal of Cd(II) from Aqueous Solutions by Bacillus Cereus RC-1: Biosorption Characteristics and Mechanism. Ph.D. Thesis, South China University of Technology, Guangzhou, China, 2013.
27. Xu, Z.Q.; Ni, S.J.; Tuo, X.G.; Zhang, C.J. Calculation of heavy metals' toxicity coefficient in the evaluation of potential ecological risk index. *Environ. Sci. Technol.* **2008**, *2*, 112–115.
28. Hu, M.H.; Yuan, J.H.; Huang, H.P. Fraction Distributions and Availabilities of Heavy Metals in Fraction Distributions and Availabilities of Heavy Metals in Municipal Sludge of Nanchang City. *Bull. Soil Water Conserv.* **2010**, *30*, 63–67.
29. Li, X.D.; Liu, P.S.; Poon, C.S. Heavy metal contamination of urban soils and street dusts in Hong Kong. *Appl. Geochem.* **2001**, *16*, 1361–1368. [CrossRef]
30. Yang, W.L.; Bi, X.Y.; Han, Z.X. Dust lead contamination in rural households of several provinces in China. *Chin. J. Ecol.* **2011**, *30*, 1246–1250.
31. *GB 15618-2018*; Soil Environmental Quality Risk Control Standard for Soil Contamination of Agricultural Land. China Environment Publishing Group: Beijing, China, 2018.
32. Wang, W.H.; Wong, M.H.; Leharne, S.; Fisher, B. Fractionation and Biotoxicity of Heavy Metals in Urban Dusts Collected from Hong Kong and London. *Environ. Geochem. Health* **1998**, *20*, 185–198. [CrossRef]
33. China National Environmental Monitoring Centre. *The Element Background Values of Chinese Soil*; China Environment Publishing Group: Beijing, China, 1990.
34. Pan, H.J.; Cheng, Z.Z.; Yang, R.; Zhou, G.H. Geochemical survey and assessment of tailings of the Gejiu tin-polymetallic mining area, Yunnan Province. *Geol. China* **2015**, *42*, 1137–1150.
35. Wang, F. Prediction and Evaluation of Acidification and Heavy Metal Pollution of Tin-Polymetallic Sulfide Mine Tailings in Dachang, Guangxi. Master's Thesis, Guilin University of Technology, Guilin, China, 2010.
36. Wang, B.L.; Xie, Z.M.; Sun, Y.F.; Li, J.; Tian, Z.J.; Chen, Y.X. Effects of phos phorus fertilizers on remediation of lead toxicity in a soil contaminated by lead and zinc mining. *Acta Sci. Circumstantiae* **2005**, *25*, 1189–1194.
37. Wang, F.Y.; Guo, C.H.; Miao, X.F.; Xiao, X.Y. Tolerance and accumulation characteristics of Typha orientalis Presl for As, Cd and Pb in heavily contaminated soils. *J. Agro-Environ. Sci.* **2011**, *30*, 1966–1971.

applied sciences

Article

Evaluation of Soil Nutrient Status Based on LightGBM Model: An Example of Tobacco Planting Soil in Debao County, Guangxi

Zhipeng Liang [1], Tianxiang Zou [1], Jialin Gong [1], Meng Zhou [1], Wenjie Shen [1,2,3,*], Jietang Zhang [4], Dongsheng Fan [5] and Yanhui Lu [5]

1 School of Earth Science and Engineering, Sun Yat-sen University, Zhuhai 519000, China
2 Guangdong Key Laboratory of Geological Process and Mineral Resources Exploration, Zhuhai 519000, China
3 Guangdong Provincial Key Laboratory of Geodynamics and Geohazards, Zhuhai 519000, China
4 Guangdong Vcarbon Testing Technology Co., Ltd., Qiangyuan 511500, China
5 China National Tobacco Corporation Guangxi Corporation, Nanning 530022, China
* Correspondence: shenwjie@mail.sysu.edu.cn

Abstract: Soil nutrient status is the foundation of agricultural development. Exploring the features of soil nutrients and status evaluation can provide a reference for the development of modern agriculture. LightGBM is an optimization algorithm based on the boosting framework, which uses histograms to improve the accuracy of the model. Based on the construction of the LightGBM model, the main nutrient features and status of tobacco planting soil were analyzed in seven towns in Debao County, Guangxi Province, namely Yantong Town, Longguang Town, Najia Town, Zurong Town, Du'an Town, Dongling Town and Jingde Town. The confusion matrix results show the accuracy of the LightGBM model is 94.2%, and the eigenvalue analysis shows that the available potassium (K) contributes the most to the nutrient status. The pH value of soil ranging from 6.1 to 7.8 is favorable for tobacco growth, and the contents of soil organic matter, total nitrogen (N), available phosphorus (P), exchangeable calcium (Ca) and exchangeable magnesium (Mg) are at the appropriate level. Available potassium (K) and available zinc (Zn) are at a high level, but available boron (B) is slightly insufficient. The nutrient status of 10% of soil is at an extremely high level, and about 81.03% of soil is medium level or above. The LightGBM model has high reliability in the automatic evaluation of soil nutrient status, which not only can accurately monitor the soil nutrient status but also reflects the correlation and importance of nutrient factors. Therefore, the LightGBM model is significant for guiding soil cultivation and agricultural production.

Keywords: LightGBM model; tobacco planting soil; confusion matrix; eigenvalue analysis; nutrient features; nutrient status

Citation: Liang, Z.; Zou, T.; Gong, J.; Zhou, M.; Shen, W.; Zhang, J.; Fan, D.; Lu, Y. Evaluation of Soil Nutrient Status Based on LightGBM Model: An Example of Tobacco Planting Soil in Debao County, Guangxi. *Appl. Sci.* **2022**, *12*, 12354. https://doi.org/10.3390/app122312354

Academic Editors: Dibyendu Sarkar and Andrea L. Rizzo

Received: 21 September 2022
Accepted: 23 November 2022
Published: 2 December 2022

1. Introduction

Soil, as a basic environment for crop growth and an important means of agricultural production, is the primary guarantee for the sustainable development of the biosphere [1,2]. The abundance or shortage of soil nutrients greatly affects the quality of crops, which is one of the important factors for the development of planting agriculture [3]. Influenced by landform, climate, altitude and so on, soil nutrients are diverse in different regions [4]. The level of soil nutrients is not only affected by the independent role of nutrient factors but also depends on the comprehensive coordination of various nutrient factors [5]. Therefore, exploring the comprehensive evaluation of soil nutrient status can lead to a deeper understanding of the current nutrient features of soil, which has important guiding significance for farming and fertilization in agricultural areas.

According to previous studies, the evaluation of soil nutrient features and status is mainly based on the comprehensive evaluation of nutrient factors in the study area [6,7]. However, due to the different locations, soil texture, hydrological conditions and suitable crop types of various cultivated land soils, there are no standard methods to evaluate the soil nutrient status [8]. The commonly used methods include principal component analysis, cluster analysis, the fuzzy mathematical model membership function, Nemero comprehensive index and gray correlation analysis [9].

In recent years, machine learning as a new subject has received wide attention in various fields. As an extension of applied statistics, machine learning is very suitable for the application and research of agronomy and geosciences [10]. For example, random forest and XGBoost in integrated algorithms are often used to solve classification and regression problems in geochemical research due to their good performance [11,12]. Tian et al. [13] established a random forest model for automatic evaluation of soil nutrient status, and the results are objective and accurate. Tong et al. [14] found that the results of risk assessment and prediction are more accurate than the traditional research methods in the risk assessment of waterlogging in the central cities of the Yangtze River Delta based on the XGBoost model. LightGBM is the Microsoft's latest developed source framework, which uses the histogram decision-tree algorithm and is regarded as an improved version of XGBoost. Compared with previous models, LightGBM has the advantages of fast training speed, high accuracy, less memory and more objective training results, which are mainly used to deal with the classification and regression problems of data analysis [15,16]. Therefore, applying the LightGBM model to the research of soil nutrient status can obtain more objective and accurate evaluation results.

Debao County is one of the main tobacco planting areas in Baise City, which is the largest tobacco planting area in Guangxi Province, with an area of about 8167 ha, accounting for 78% of the tobacco planting area in the province [17,18]. At present, there are few in-depth studies on the evaluation of soil nutrient status and the status of soil nutrient dynamics in Debao County, and the main research methods are traditional and lack innovation. The application and research of the new method of machine learning can evaluate the nutrient abundance and deficiency of local tobacco planting soil more accurately and objectively, which is conducive to a better local understanding of the current tobacco planting soil nutrient status and provides the corresponding method reference for regional soil nutrient status evaluation research, so as to promote the development of agriculture.

In this study, the data of nine nutrient factors were preprocessed through principal component analysis in tobacco planting soil of seven towns in Debao County, namely Yantong Town, Longguang Town, Najia Town, Zurong Town, Du'an Town, Dongling Town and Jingde Town, and then used as test set to build the LightGBM model. The feasibility of the LightGBM model was proved using the confusion matrix, and the important differences between diverse soil nutrient factors were obtained with eigenvalue analysis. Through the classification and prediction of the LightGBM model, the nutrient status of tobacco planting soil was evaluated automatically in the study area. Therefore, using the LightGBM model to study the nutrient status of tobacco planting soil can provide some scientific reference for the improvement of soil fertility in the local tobacco industry and the rational layout of tobacco planting.

2. Materials and Methods

2.1. Experimental Sites

The Debao County (106°10′–107°00′ E, 23°00′–23°40′ N) is located in the southwest of Baise City, Guangxi Province, with an altitude of 200–1000 m. Its climate is warm and wet, and the hydrothermal and sunshine conditions are good across four seasons, which is very suitable for producing high quality tobacco. The local average annual rainfall is about 1462.5 mm, the average annual temperature is about 19.5 °C and the average annual sunshine duration is about 1325 h [19]. The soil texture types are mainly clay and loam in the study. The vast area of cultivated land is conducive to agricultural development [20].

2.2. Data Source

According to the planting situation of the tobacco planting industry in the study area, 290 soil samples were collected from seven towns in Debao County, namely Yantong Town, Longguang Town, Najia Town, Zurong Town, Du'an Town, Dongling Town and Jingde Town (Figure 1). The samples were collected according to the *Technical Specification for Soil Testing and Formulated Fertilization* [21]. Among them, every 50 acres of contiguous tobacco fields was taken as a sampling unit, and the 's' shape distribution method was adopted for sampling. The isolated and small tobacco fields that are not connected were used as sampling units, and the 'plum blossom' point distribution method was adopted for sampling. During soil collection, the topsoil of 0–20 cm in the tillage layer was selected, and each sampling unit had 5–8 sampling points. After natural air drying, impurity removal, grinding, screening and other steps, the nutrient factor indexes were determined and analyzed.

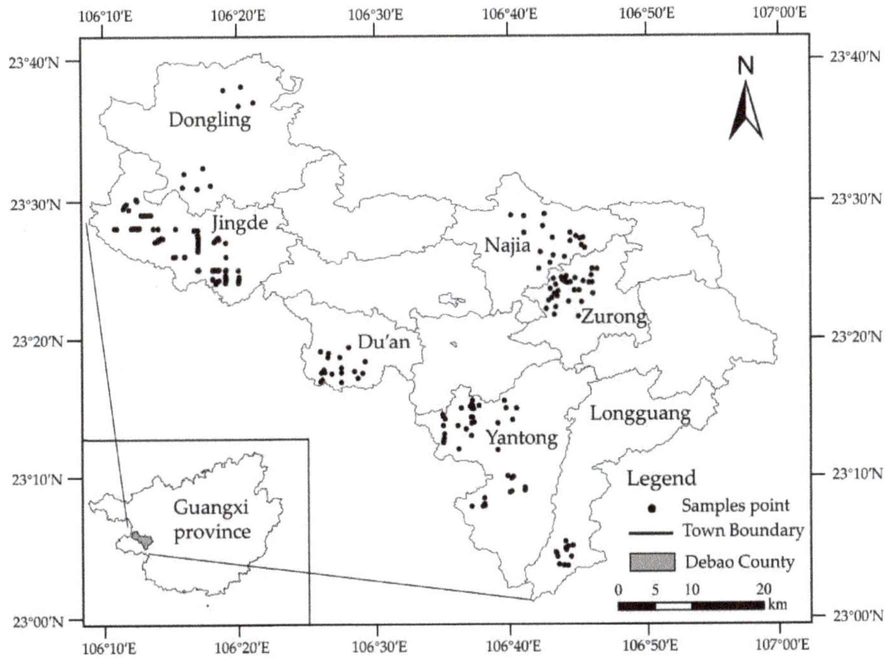

Figure 1. Spatial distribution of tobacco planting soil sampling location in Debao County.

2.3. Evaluation Index and Measurement

Based on the commonly used indicators for soil nutrient status evaluation, nine nutrient factors were selected in this study to assess the soil of Debao County, namely pH value, organic matter, total N, available K, available P, exchangeable Ca, exchangeable Mg, available B and available Zn, for content detection and analysis. All indicators were determined in strict accordance with standard methods (Table 1). According to the *Integrated Management of Tobacco Planting Soil and Tobacco Nutrients in China* [22], the grading standard of abundance and deficiency of different nutrient factors is shown in Table 2.

Table 1. Determination indexes and methods of soil nutrients.

Measurement Index	Determination Method
pH value	pH meter electrode method [23]
Organic matter	Potassium dichromate titration [24]
Total N	Kjeldahl method [25]
Available K, P	Combined extraction colorimetric method [26]
Exchangeable Ca, Mg	Ammonium acetate exchange atomic absorption spectrophotometry [27]
Available B	Boiling water extraction methylimine-H colorimetric method [28]
Available Zn	DTPA extraction atomic absorption spectrophotometry [29]

Table 2. Evaluation criteria of abundance and deficiency for nutrients in tobacco planting soil.

Evaluation Index	Grade				
	Very Low	Low	Moderate	High	Very High
pH value	<4.5	4.5–5.5	5.5–7.0	7.0–7.5	7.5<
Organic matter (g/kg)	<10	10–20	20–30	30–40	>40
Total N (mg/kg)	<500	500–1000	1000–2000	2000–2500	>2500
Available K (mg/kg)	<80	80–150	150–220	220–350	>350
Available P (mg/kg)	<10	10–15	15–30	30–40	>40
Available B (mg/kg)	0.3<	0.3–0.5	0.5–1.0	1.0–3.0	>3.0
Available Zn (mg/kg)	0.3<	0.3–0.5	0.5–1.0	1.0–3.0	>3.0
Exchangeable Ca (cmol/kg)	<2	2–4	4–6	6–10	>10
Exchangeable Mg (cmol/kg)	<0.4	0.4–0.8	0.8–1.6	1.6–3.2	>3.2

2.4. *Research Methods*

2.4.1. LightGBM

LightGBM is a new optimization model algorithm based on the GBDT framework launched by Microsoft in 2017. It is an upgraded version of XGBoost, with more efficient parallel training, lower memory consumption and more accurate results [30]. LightGBM adopts the histogram decision-tree algorithm, which can convert a weak learner into a strong learner. In the continuous combination of multiple groups of tree models, the calculation complexity is reduced by making use of histogram difference so that the result is a high-quality tree, which can be used as a classification and prediction model [31].

2.4.2. LightGBM Model Construction

The LightGBM model training is divided into five steps, namely data collection, feature engineering, model training, cross validation and accuracy evaluation [32]. The data collection is mainly the experimental data of nine nutrient factors, namely pH value, organic matter, total N, available K, available P, exchangeable Ca, exchangeable Mg, available B and available Zn in the soil of the tobacco growing area. The data were preprocessed, and the model database was established after screening and eliminating the abnormal values.

Feature engineering is an important part of the LightGBM model (Figure 2) construction. It is mainly used to classify sample data through feature values that can reflect the nature of classification. In addition, model training and cross validation mainly optimize the model through continuous learning and training. After that, the accuracy of the sample set and the test set was evaluated, and the results were output.

The comprehensive analysis of nine nutrient factors, namely pH value, organic matter, total N, available K, available P, exchangeable Ca, exchangeable Mg, available B and available Zn, in 1038 sample points in Baise, Hechi and Hezhou City of Guangxi Zhuang Province was carried out. The data were preprocessed with principal component and cluster analysis and were used as the training data of the model. The 290 samples in the study area are the test data. Since the original data were divided into five grades according to the nutrient status of tobacco planting soil based on the class average method in cluster analysis during preprocessing, the class labels of the confusion matrix are also displayed as five grades during model training [33].

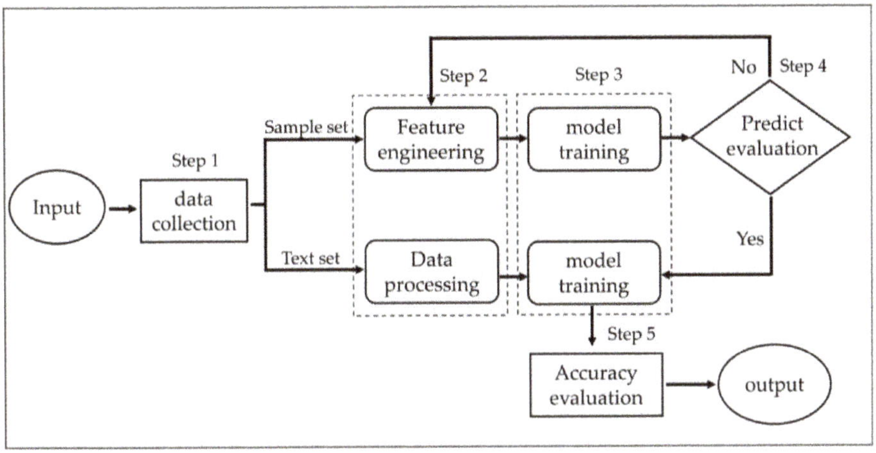

Figure 2. The LightGBM modeling process framework.

3. Results and Analysis

3.1. Analysis of Nutrient Features

In Table 3, the pH of tobacco planting soil in seven towns of Debao County is generally between 6.1 and 7.8, with an average value of about 6.9, which is generally weak acidity. The content of soil organic matter is between 12.1 and 49.3 g/kg, with an average value of 27.5 g/kg, which is moderate, while the average content of organic matter in Najia Town, Zurong Town and Du'an Town is 38.0, 33.5 and 32.5 g/kg, respectively, which is within the high range. The average contents of soil total N, available K and available P are 1250, 270.5 and 23.0 mg/kg. Among them, the content of soil total N and available P is in a moderate state, and available K is in a high state.

Figure 3 shows that the exchangeable Ca content in the tobacco planting soil in seven towns of Debao County is relatively high, with more than 47% of the soil samples containing >4 cmol/kg and 22% of the soil samples containing >10 cmol/kg, which is extremely high. The exchangeable Mg content of soil is good, and the content of most samples is between 0.8 and 1.6 cmol/kg, which is basically within the suitable range for planting high-quality tobacco. The number of soil samples with available B content lower than the B deficiency threshold (0.5 mg/kg) [34] accounted for about 35%, and the number of samples with available Zn content higher than the enrichment threshold (1.0 mg/kg) accounted for about 99.5%. Therefore, the soil available Zn content is very high, but the available B content is slightly insufficient.

Table 3. Soil pH values, organic matter, total N, available K, available P content in seven tobacco planting towns of Debao County.

Nutrient Factors	Town	Range Value	Average	Standard Deviation	Variation Coefficient (%)
pH value	Yantong	6.4–7.2	6.8	0.19	2.84
	Longguang	6.3–7.1	6.8	0.22	3.32
	Najia	6.6–7.4	7.2	0.21	2.99
	Zurong	6.6–7.5	7.2	0.22	3.03
	Du'an	7.4–7.8	7.6	0.10	1.27
	Dongling	7.0–7.6	7.4	0.19	2.55
	Jingde	6.1–7.3	6.7	0.26	3.87
	Total	6.1–7.8	6.9	0.35	4.99
Organic matter (g/kg)	Yantong	12.8–57.0	25.2	8.14	32.34
	Longguang	23.0–39.4	28.8	5.64	19.58
	Najia	29.2–49.3	38.0	4.492	11.83
	Zurong	20.6–48.8	33.5	7.72	23.06
	Du'an	26.9–41.7	32.3	4.12	12.78
	Dongling	14.2–44.1	24.0	9.32	38.89
	Jingde	12.1–39.0	25.1	5.0	19.97
	Total	12.1–49.3	27.5	7.37	24.99
Total nitrogen (mg/kg)	Yantong	50–2020	930	460	49.03
	Longguang	530–2560	1420	519	36.64
	Najia	990–3380	1730	671	38.68
	Zurong	610–2620	1680	500	30.28
	Du'an	7601520	1170	177	15.20
	Dongling	190–1860	840	532	63.65
	Jingde	100–3210	970	356	36.51
	Total	50–3380	1120	516	41.31
Available K (mg/kg)	Yantong	37.3–472.5	231.1	96.38	41.71
	Longguang	48.1-298.2	171.2	78.09	45.61
	Najia	91.8–298.2	183.4	53.32	29.07
	Zurong	57.8–298.0	206.7	63.29	30.61
	Du'an	222.3–364.8	299.0	47.32	15.82
	Dongling	206.8–379.7	287.0	60.20	20.98
	Jingde	49.4–504.8	308.8	81.89	26.86
	Total	37.3–504.8	270.5	93.60	38.84
Available P (mg/kg)	Yantong	3.8–82.3	31.1	20.21	64.96
	Longguang	4.6–44.1	22.5	11.52	51.28
	Najia	6.6–60.9	25.8	17.35	67.38
	Zurong	9.8–62.5	26.1	12.38	47.46
	Du'an	14.8–41.9	25.1	7.75	30.89
	Dongling	9.8–32.1	19.6	7.18	36.68
	Jingde	4.2–60.0	19.4	10.88	56.01
	Total	3.8–62.5	23.0	14.03	57.97

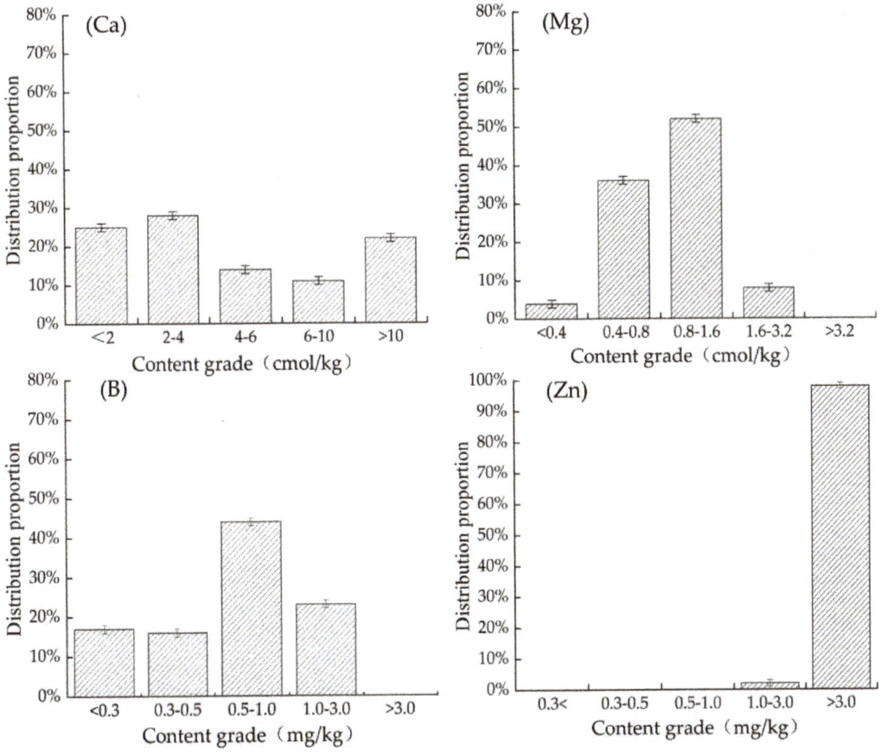

Figure 3. Distribution of exchangeable Ca, exchangeable Mg, available B and available Zn in tobacco growing soil.

3.2. Pearson Correlation Analysis

The quality of soil nutrient status is a comprehensive reflection of various nutrient factors, and there is a certain correlation between different soil nutrient factors [8,35]. Pearson correlation analysis of soil nutrient factors of the nine tobacco planting areas can lead to a better understanding of the relationship between nutrient factors. The results (Table 4) show that there is a significant positive correlation between pH value and organic matter, total N, exchangeable Ca and exchangeable Mg and a significant negative correlation with available B. Among them, the correlation coefficient between pH value and exchangeable Ca reached 0.613. It can be seen that the acidity and alkalinity of soil significantly affected the concentration of calcium ions. Where the pH value is high, the exchangeable calcium content is high.

In addition, the positive correlation coefficient between soil organic matter and total N is 0.588, and there is a significant positive correlation between the two. The main reason is that the N content in the soil mainly exists in the form of organic N, and the organic N mainly comes from the inorganic degradation of organic matter.

Table 4. Correlation analysis of tobacco planting soil.

Nutrient Factors	Ph Value	Organic Matter	Total N	Available K	Available P	Exchangeable Ca	Exchangeable Mg	Available B	Available Zn
pH value	1								
Organic matter	0.341 **	1							
Total N	0.323 **	0.588 **	1						
Available K	−0.107	−0.133 *	−0.182 **	1					
Available P	0.092	0.201 **	0.031	0.042	1				
Exchangeable Ca	0.631 **	0.525 **	0.411 **	−0.198 **	0.078	1			
Exchangeable Mg	0.479 **	0.387 **	0.316 **	0.052	0.099	0.563 **	1		
Available B	−0.356 **	−0.005	−0.002	0.031 **	0.075	−0.330 **	−0.082	1	
Available Zn	0.078	0.204 **	0.213 **	−0.051	0.237 **	0.099	0.041	0.060	1

Note: * $p < 0.05$, ** $p < 0.01$.

3.3. *Evaluation of Soil Nutrient Status by LightGBM Model*

3.3.1. Confusion Matrix

A confusion matrix, also known as an error matrix, is a standard format for expressing accuracy evaluation in integrated algorithm model and is also a method for judging the classification of algorithm model [36]. It is a matrix in which rows represent actual classes and columns are prediction classes. In the calculation process of the LightGBM model, 1038 samples and 9 nutrient factors in Baise, Hechi and Hezhou City were taken as a data set, and 70% of the samples were taken as the training sample set and 30% as the validation sample set according to the ratio of 7:3, for multi-classification prediction.

As shown in Figure 4, 127 of 134 samples in the class I nutrient state were predicted to be true, with a validation rate of 94.8%. 34, 37, 61 and 35 samples in class II, III, IV and V were predicted to be true, with a validation rate of 91.9%, 92.5%, 92.4% and 94.6%, respectively. Of the 312 validation sample sets in the five nutrient status levels, 294 were verified as true categories, with an overall accuracy of 94.2%. The model has a small calculation error and high classification accuracy.

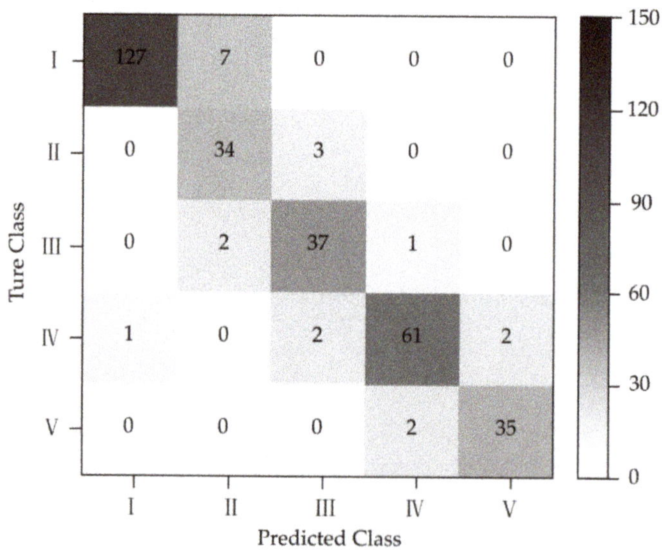

Figure 4. Prediction results of the LightGBM model confusion matrix.

3.3.2. Eigenvalue Analysis

Eigenvalue analysis is an important part of the feature engineering operation in the LightGBM model, and it can directly reflect the own features of the independent variables in classifying the samples. Through its own weight calculation, it can obtain its own importance to the classification results, which is called the importance of the independent variables [32]. In the process of the LightGBM model operation, the eigenvalue is the independent variable, that is, the nine nutrient factors in the nutrient status evaluation. The importance ranking is shown in Figure 5. The larger the value, the higher the importance.

In Figure 5, the eigenvalue score of available K is more than 1000, which is much higher than the other eight nutrient factors, indicating that it has the strongest importance and the greatest contribution to the evaluation and grading of the nutrient status of tobacco planting soil. The contribution degree from high to low is available K, available P, organic matter, total N, available B, pH value, available Zn, exchangeable Ca and exchangeable Mg, which indicates that these nutrient factors have certain differences in the evaluation of the nutrient status of tobacco planting soil and that it is easy to identify and classify the models. The top six characteristic values, available K, available P, organic matter, total N, available B and pH value, are also important nutrient factors for the comprehensive evaluation of nutrient status of tobacco planting soil. For example, when Guo [37] studied the nutrient status of tobacco planting soil in the Erhai Lake Basin, the nutrient factors selected were available K, available P, organic matter, total N and pH value. Mu [38] showed that available B is one of the trace elements necessary for crop growth, and its abundance affects the development and quality of tobacco growth. Therefore, according to the above, the LightGBM model is consistent with the actual research results.

In addition, the contribution rate of available Zn, exchangeable Ca and exchangeable Mg is low, and the characteristic score is lower than 200. The quality of soil nutrient status is a comprehensive reflection of various nutrient factors in the soil. The LightGBM model is reasonable because of the common existence and mutual influence of nine soil nutrient factors and can obtain more accurate and objective evaluation results of nutrient status.

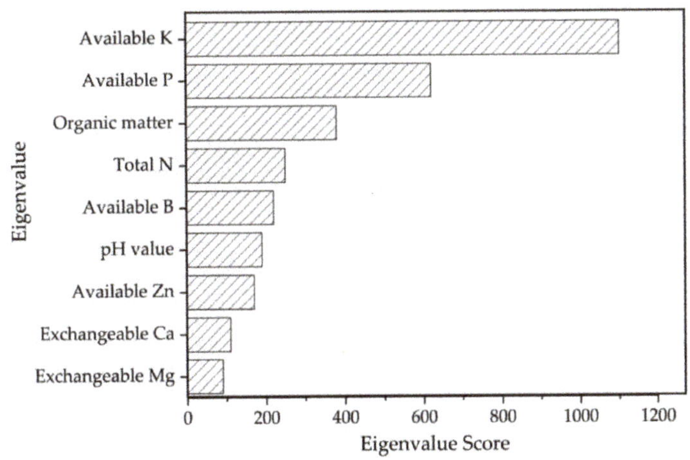

Figure 5. Eigenvalue score of LightGBM model.

3.3.3. Nutrient Status Evaluation

A total of 290 tobacco planting soil samples including nine nutrient factors in Debao County were taken as the test sample sets to conduct automatic classification of nutrient status evaluation in the LightGBM model. The classification level was consistent with that of model training and was divided into five classes (Table 5). As shown in Table 5, Grade I indicates that the nutrient status of tobacco planting soil is at a very high level, accounting for 10%. Grade II and III indicate that the nutrient status is high and relatively high, accounting for 7.24% and 17.59%. Grade IV indicates that the nutrient status of tobacco planting soil is at the medium level, accounting for 46.2%, which is the largest part of the nutrient status of tobacco planting soil in the town. Grade V indicates that the nutrient status of tobacco planting soil is at the general level, accounting for 18.97%.

Based on the evaluation results of nutrient status applied by the LightGBM model, the distribution of soil nutrient status in seven tobacco planting towns in Debao County can be obtained using the kriging analysis method (Figure 6). In Table 5 and Figure 6, the nutrient status of tobacco planting soil in Yantong Town and Jingde Town among the seven tobacco planting towns in Debao County are at a extremely high level, accounting for 0.69% and 9.31%. The nutrient status of Yantong Town, Du'an Town, Dongling Town and Jingde Town in the county are at a medium level or above, while Longguang Town, Najia Town and Zurong Town are at medium and low level. In general, the soil nutrient status of the seven tobacco planting towns in Debao County is basically at the medium level or above, accounting for 81.03%, and the low level of nutrient status accounts for 18.97%.

Table 5. Evaluation of nutrient status based on the LightGBM model.

Town	Proportion of Different Nutrient Grade (%)				
	I Extremely High	II High	III Relatively High	IV Medium	V Low
Yantong	0.69	1.04	4.14	3.79	6.9
Longguang	0	0	0	1.72	2.41
Najia	0	0	0	3.45	2.76
Zurong	0	0	0	8.28	3.79
Du'an	0	1.03	1.72	3.1	0
Dongling	0	0.34	1.04	1.72	0
Jingde	9.31	4.83	10.69	24.14	3.11
Total	10	7.24	17.59	46.2	18.97

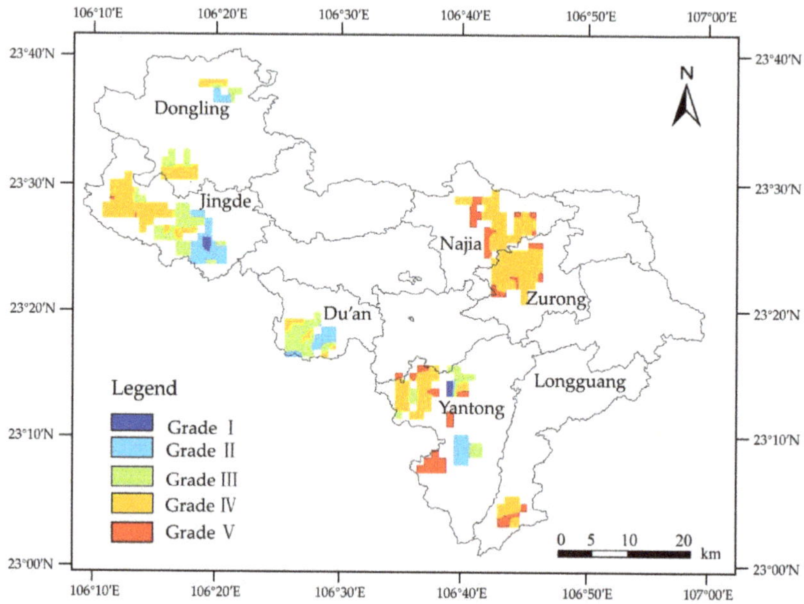

Figure 6. Spatial distribution of soil fertility.

4. Discussion

Soil pH directly affects the growth of plants, and the soil with weak acidity is more suitable for the growth of tobacco [39,40]. The pH of tobacco planting soil in seven towns of Debao County is generally at an appropriate level, which is conducive to the development of tobacco agriculture. The contents of soil organic matter, total N, available P, exchangeable Ca and exchangeable Mg and other nutrient factors are moderate. The average content of soil available K (270.5 mg/kg) is almost five times the average level of the national tobacco planting soil (57.5 mg/kg). As tobacco is a typical K-loving crop, K has an important impact on the growth, development and quality of flue-cured tobacco [41]. Compared with the national tobacco planting soil, the high soil K in the tobacco area of Debao County is more conducive to producing high-quality tobacco. The effective zinc content of the tobacco planting soil in the town is at a very high level, and the effective B content is slightly insufficient. The application of trace element fertilizer B can be slightly increased to improve the effective B content of the local tobacco planting soil.

Based on the LightGBM model, the nutrient status of tobacco planting soil is evaluated. The accuracy of the model is 94.2%, the classification accuracy is high and the reliability is strong. The feature value of available K is the largest, its contribution rate to the evaluation of soil nutrient status is the largest and its importance is the strongest in the tobacco planting area. This also corresponds to the high content of available K in the tobacco planting soil in the study area. In the evaluation of nutrient status, Yantong Town, Du'an Town, Dongling Town and Jingde Town have good nutrient status, and the county is generally at or above the medium level, accounting for 81.03%, which has good tobacco planting value and is conducive to the development of tobacco industry. Some soil nutrients are slightly insufficient. In the future, we can improve the soil nutrients by formulating reasonable and scientific fertilization measures to provide more fertile soil conditions for the planting of tobacco crops.

Applying the integrated algorithm to the evaluation of soil nutrient status, the multi-classification nonlinear mapping relationship between nutrient factors and nutrient status can be established. The regular and clear evaluation indexes improve the sorting performance of training samples and make the final sorting prediction more scientific. In this study, LightGBM, as an upgraded and improved version of XGBoost, obtained more accurate classification and recognition ability through its own full training. Automatic data processing can make the evaluation results of nutrient status of tobacco planting soil in the study area more objective and accurate. In addition, due to the reliability and flexibility of the LightGBM model, it can be widely used in the evaluation of various types of soil nutrient status and fertility, in order to provide more innovative research methods and means for the development of new agriculture in the 21st century. At the same time, the LightGBM model also provides a new and innovative method for the research of other issues outside the agricultural field.

5. Conclusions

There is weak acidity in the tobacco planting soil in Debao County. The content of soil organic matter, total N, available P, exchangeable Ca and exchangeable Mg are at the appropriate level, and available K and Zn are at a high level, but the available B is slightly insufficient. Therefore, the content of soil available B can be adjusted by artificial means such as fertilization.

The rate of the contribution of available K to the evaluation of the soil nutrient status of tobacco planting is the largest in the Debao County. The nutrient status of tobacco planting soil is at a great level in Yantong Town, Du'an Town, Dongling Town and Jingde Town, while Longguang Town, Najia Town and Zurong Town are at a medium or low level. In general, the whole county has reached a medium level and above, which is conducive to the planting of tobacco crops.

The application of the LightGBM model to the evaluation of soil nutrient status is accurate, reliable and objective. Due to the good stability and wide adaptability of the model, the LightGBM can be widely used to solve other problems in agriculture and geosciences so that researchers can obtain more accurate and realistic results.

Author Contributions: Z.L.: Writing, editing and figure preparation; T.Z., M.Z. and J.G.: Table preparation; W.S.: Funding acquisition, review and supervision; J.Z., D.F. and Y.L.: Review and editing. All authors have read and agreed to the published version of the manuscript.

Funding: This research was funded by the Science and Technology Program of Guangzhou, grant numbers 202002030184 and 201804010190, the National Key Research and Development Program of China, grant number 2022YFF0801201 and the National Natural Science Foundation of China, grant numbers 42072229 and U1911202.

Conflicts of Interest: The authors declare no conflict of interest.

References

1. Kibblewhite, M.G.; Ritz, K.; Swift, M.J. Soil health in agricultural systems. *Philos. Trans. R. Soc. B.* **2008**, *363*, 685–701. [CrossRef] [PubMed]
2. Lu, M.Z.; Yang, M.Y.; Yang, Y.R.; Wang, D.; Sheng, L.X. Soil carbon and nutrient sequestration linking to soil aggregate in a temperate fen in Northeast China. *Ecol. Indic.* **2019**, *98*, 869–878. [CrossRef]
3. Yageta, Y.; Osbahr, H.; Morimoto, Y.; Clark, J. Comparing farmers' qualitative evaluation of soil fertility with quantitative soil fertility indicators in Kitui County, Kenya. *Geoderma* **2019**, *344*, 153–163. [CrossRef]
4. Meng, B.; Zhou, Y.F.; Yang, L.S.; Peng, G.Z.; Li, J.Q.; Deng, Y. Nutrient Spatial Distribution and Fertility Evaluation of Sugarcane Soils in Menghai County. *Soils* **2022**, *54*, 277–284. (In Chinese)
5. Shen, J.G.; Wang, Z.; Li, D.; Fei, J.H.; Lou, L.; Ma, W.H. The Quality Evaluation of Newly Reclaimed Red Soils in Yuhang District, Hangzhou. *Chin. J. Soil Sci.* **2018**, *49*, 55–60. (In Chinese)
6. Chen, J.; Qu, M.K.; Zhang, J.L.; Xie, E.Z.; Huang, B.; Zhao, Y.C. Soil fertility quality assessment based on geographically weighted principal component analysis (GWPCA) in large-scale areas. *Catena* **2021**, *201*, 105197. [CrossRef]
7. Huang, J.; Jiang, D.H.; Deng, Y.S.; Ding, S.W.; Cai, C.F.; Huang, Z.G. Soil Physicochemical Properties and Fertility Evolution of Permanent Gully during Ecological Restoration in Granite Hilly Region of South China. *Forests* **2021**, *12*, 510. [CrossRef]
8. Dai, S.X.; Ren, W.J.; Teng, Y.; Chen, M.; Ma, W.T. Basic Physico-chemical Properties and Fertility Comprehensive Evaluation of Main Paddy Soils in Anhui Province. *Soils* **2018**, *50*, 66–72. (In Chinese)
9. Yang, W.X.; Ren, J.X.; Li, Z.Y.; Xu, Y.; Li, Z.L.; He, B.H. Soil Fertility in Karst Regions with Analysis of Principal Component and Fuzzy Synthetic Evaluation. *Southwest China J. Agric. Sci.* **2019**, *32*, 1307–1313. (In Chinese)
10. Hengl, T.; Leenaars, J.G.B.; Shepherd, K.D.; Walsh, M.G.; Heuvelink, G.B.M.; Mamo, T.; Tilahun, H.; Berkhout, E.; Cooper, M.; Fegraus, E.; et al. Soil nutrient maps of Sub-Saharan Africa: Assessment of soil nutrient content at 250 m spatial resolution using machine learning. *Nutr. Cycl. Agroecosyst.* **2017**, *109*, 77–102. [CrossRef] [PubMed]
11. Wu, C.; Fang, C.; Wu, X.; Zhu, G. Health-risk Assessment of Arsenic and Groundwater Quality Classifcation Using Random Forest in the Yanchi Region of Northwest China. *Expo. Health* **2020**, *12*, 761–774. [CrossRef]
12. Ma, M.; Zhao, G.; He, B.; Li, Q.; Dong, H.; Wang, S.; Wang, Z. XGBoost-based method for flash flood risk assessment. *J. Hydrol.* **2021**, *598*, 126382. [CrossRef]
13. Tian, Y.C.; Xu, M.D. Application of Random forest Pattern Recognition in Soil Fertility Assessment. *J. North Univ. China (Nat. Sci. Ed.)* **2019**, *40*, 464–469. (In Chinese)
14. Tong, J.P.; Zhang, H.Y.; Liu, H.; Huang, J.; Hao, Y. XGBoost model-based risk assessment and influencing factors analysis of waterlogging in core cities of Yangtze River Delta. *Water Resour. Hydropower Eng.* **2021**, *52*, 1–11. (In Chinese)
15. Yan, J.; Xu, Y.T.; Cheng, Q.; Jiang, S.Q.; Wang, Q.; Xiao, Y.J.; Ma, C.; Yan, J.B.; Wang, X.F. LightGBM: Accelerated genomically designed crop breeding through ensemble learning. *Genome Biol.* **2021**, *22*, 271. [CrossRef]
16. Shehadeh, A.; Alshboul, O.; Mamlook, R.E.A.; Hamedat, O. Machine learning models for predicting the residual value of heavy construction equipment: An evaluation of modified decision tree, LightGBM, and XGBoost regression. *Autom. ConStruct.* **2021**, *129*, 103827. [CrossRef]
17. Li, Z.L.; Lu, Y.C.; Zhao, L.F.; Fan, D.S.; Wei, Z.; Zhou, W.L.; Huang, L.G.; Huang, Y.; Huang, J.P.; Gu, X.Q.; et al. Evaluation on Tobacco-planting Soil Fertility in Longlin County of Guangxi. *Chin. J. Soil Sci.* **2020**, *51*, 1042–1048. (In Chinese)
18. Gao, H.J.; Wei, Z.; Luo, G.; Lin, B.S. Status and Conservation and Remediation Technology of Tobacco-growing Soils in Baise City. *Crop. Res.* **2016**, *30*, 736–740. (In Chinese)
19. Li, L.Y.; Su, B.L. Present situation and Countermeasures of silkworm production and development in Debao County, Guangxi. *South China Agric.* **2018**, *12*, 116–117. (In Chinese)
20. Li, Q.X. Analysis on climatic conditions of flue-cured tobacco planting in Nandan county. *Mid-Low Latit. Mt. Meteorol.* **2006**, *S1*, 29–31. (In Chinese)
21. *NY/T 1118-2006*; Technical Specification for Soil Testing and Formulated Fertilization. The Ministry of Agriculture of the People's Republic of China: Beijing, China, 2006. (In Chinese)

22. Chen, J.H.; Liu, J.L.; Li, Z.H. Soil and Nutrient Status of Tobacco Growing in China. In *Integrated Management of Tobacco Planting Soil and Tobacco Nutrients in China*; Science Press: Beijing, China, 2008; pp. 39–55. (In Chinese)
23. *NY/T 1377-2007*; Determination of pH in Soil. The Ministry of Agriculture of the People's Republic of China: Beijing, China, 2007. (In Chinese)
24. *NY/T 1121.6-2006*; Soil Testing Part 6: Method for Determination of Soil Organic Matter. The Ministry of Agriculture of the People's Republic of China: Beijing, China, 2006. (In Chinese)
25. *LY/T 1228-2015*; Nitrogen Determination Methods of Forest Soils. The State Forestry Administration of the People's Republic of China: Beijing, China, 2015. (In Chinese)
26. *NY/T 1848-2010*; Method for Determination of Ammonium Nitrogen, Available Phosphorus and Rapidly-Available Potassium in Neutrality or Calcareous Soil. The Ministry of Agriculture of the People's Republic of China: Beijing, China, 2010. (In Chinese)
27. *LY/T 1245-1999*; Determination of Exchangeable Calcium and Magnesium in Forest Soil. The State Forestry Administration of the People's Republic of China: Beijing, China, 1999. (In Chinese)
28. *NY/T 1121.8-2006*; Soil Testing Part8: Method for Determination of Soil Available Boron. The Ministry of Agriculture of the People's Republic of China: Beijing, China, 2006. (In Chinese)
29. *NY/T 890-2004*; Determination of Available Zinc, Manganese, iron, Copper in Soil-Extraction with Buffered DTPA Solution. The Ministry of Agriculture of the People's Republic of China: Beijing, China, 2004. (In Chinese)
30. Tang, Y.F. Research on Loan Default Prediction Model Based on XGBoost Algorithm and LightGBM Algorithm. *Mod. Comput.* **2021**, *27*, 33–37. (In Chinese)
31. Liang, W.Z.; Luo, S.Z.; Zhao, G.Y.; Wu, H. Predicting hard rock pillar stability using GBDT, XGBoost, and LightGBM algorithms. *Mathematics* **2020**, *8*, 765. [CrossRef]
32. Liu, X.W.; Huang, W.B.; Jiang, Y.S.; Guo, R.X.; Huang, Y.X.; Song, Q.; Yang, Y. Study of the Classified Identification of the Strong Convective Weathers Based on the LightGBM Algorithm. *Plateau Meteorol.* **2021**, *40*, 909–918. (In Chinese)
33. Song, Q.F.; Niu, S.Z.; Chen, Z.G.; Yin, J.; Zhou, S.J.; Cen, C.J. Evaluation of nutrient status in site soil of ancient tea trees in Huaxi on principal component analysis. *Acta Agric. Zhejiangensis* **2017**, *29*, 1844–1853. (In Chinese)
34. Hu, H.Z.; Wang, H.J.; Liu, B.F.; Yao, Z.D.; Liu, X.M.; Jiang, C.G.; Niu, Z.X.; Qu, H.F.; Fang, T. Comprehensive Evaluation of Soil Fertility in Panxian Tobacco-Growing Areas of Guizhou Province. *Chin. Agric. Sci. Bull.* **2012**, *28*, 109–116. (In Chinese)
35. Song, D.P.; Li, H.; Liu, S.J.; Zou, G.Y.; Liu, D.S. A geostatistic investigation of the comprehensive evaluation of fertility and spatial heterogeneity of forest soil nutrients in hilly and mountainous regions of southern China. *Arab J. Geosci.* **2019**, *12*, 292. [CrossRef]
36. Caelen, O. A Bayesian interpretation of the confusion matrix. *Ann. Math. Artif. Intel.* **2017**, *81*, 429–450. [CrossRef]
37. Guo, Y.X.; Chen, Y.L.; Miao, Q.; Fan, Z.Y.; Sun, J.W.; Cui, Z.L.; Li, J.Y. Spatial-Temporal Variability of Soil Nutrients and Assessment of Soil Fertility in Erhai Lake Basin. *Sci. Agric. Sin.* **2022**, *55*, 1987–1999. (In Chinese)
38. Mu, T.; Lu, X.Q.; Xu, Z.C.; Xie, Y.; Fang, X.; Zhang, S. The relationship between the contents of available boron and available molybdenum in soil with the contents of boron and molybdenum of tobacco leaf in Luoping. *Soil Fertil. Sci. China* **2017**, 44–50. (In Chinese)
39. Yin, Y.Q.; Wei, Z.Y.; He, M.X.; Chen, D.K.; Kong, F. Analysis of soil nutrient status in tobacco planting areas of Nandan County, Guangxi. *J. South. Agric.* **2010**, *41*, 147–152. (In Chinese)
40. Jiang, C.Q.; Dong, J.J.; Xu, J.N.; Shen, J.; Xue, B.Y.; Zu, C.L. Effects of Soil Amendment on Soil pH, Plant Growth and Heavy Metal Accumulation of Flue-Cured Tobacco in Acid Soil. *Soils* **2015**, *47*, 171–176. (In Chinese)
41. Zhang, C.S.; Kong, F.Y. Isolation and identification of potassium-solubilizing bacteria from tobacco rhizospheric soil and their effect on tobacco plants. *Appl. Soil Ecol.* **2014**, *82*, 18–25. [CrossRef]

applied sciences

MDPI

Article

The Quality of *Scutellaria baicalensis* Georgi Is Effectively Affected by Lithology and Soil's Rare Earth Elements (REEs) Concentration

Zijian Sun [1,2], Wei Shen [1], Weixuan Fang [3,*], Huiqiong Zhang [2], Ziran Chen [2], Lianghui Xiong [2] and Tianhao An [2]

1 School of Earth Sciences and Resources, China University of Geosciences (Beijing), Beijing 100083, China
2 Beijing Institute of Geology for Mineral Resources Co., Ltd., Beijing 100012, China
3 China Non-Ferrous Metals Resource Geological Survey, Beijing 100012, China
* Correspondence: weixuanfang123@163.com

Abstract: The top-geoherb "Rehe *Scutellaria baicalensis*" was naturally distributed on Yanshan Mountain in Chengde city, Hebei Province, China. Exploring the influences of parent materials on the quality of the top-geoherbs in terms of micronutrient elements is of great significance for the protection of origin and for optimizing replanting patterns of *Scutellaria baicalensis*. In this study, three habitats of *Scutellaria baicalensis* with contrasting geopedological conditions, i.e., naturally grown habitats (NGHs), artificial planting habitats (APHs), and biomimetic cultivation habitats (BCHs), are taken as objects to probe the influences of parent materials on the quality of *Scutellaria baicalensis* in terms of rare earth elements (REEs) by testing on REEs concentrations in the weathering profiles, rhizosphere soil and growing *Scutellaria baicalensis*, as well as their flavonoid compound contents. Hornblende-gneiss was the parent rock in NGHs, whose protolith was femic volcanic rock. Loess was the parent rock in APHs and BCHs. REEs were more abundant in hornblende-gneiss than loess, and therefore, soils developed in NGHs contained higher REE concentrations than those in APHs, which was lower than BCHs after REE-rich micro-fertilizers application. The coefficient of variation (CV) of REEs concentrations in the rhizosphere soils of hornblende-gneiss was higher than that in loess. It possibly was attributed to the complicated minerals compositions and various minerals' grain sizes of hornblende-gneiss, resulting in the variety of weathering intensity involving eluviation, leaching, adsorption, etc., as well as weathering productions, dominated by clay minerals and Fe-(hydro)oxide, and ultimately the remarkable differences in the migrations, enrichments and fractionations within REEs. The biological absorption coefficients (BACs) of REEs for *Scutellaria baicalensis* decreased in the order of NGHs > APHs > BCHs. Roots of *Scutellaria baicalensis* contained similar ΣREE in NGHs (2.02 mg·kg^{-1}) and BCHs (2.04 mg·kg^{-1}), which were higher than that in APHs (1.78 mg·kg^{-1}). Soils developed in hornblende-gneiss were characterized by lower clay fraction content and overall alkalinity with a pH value of 8.06. The absorption and utilization efficiency of REEs for *Scutellaria baicalensis* in NGHs was higher than in APHs and BCHs. Flavonoid compounds, effective constituents of *Scutelleria baicalensis*, showed more accumulations in NGHs than APHs and BCHs, implying their optimal quality of *Scutellaria baicalensis* in NGHs. Flavonoid compounds were remarkably correlated with REEs in the roots, suggesting the influence of REEs concentrations on the quality of *Scutellaria baicalensis*. It can be concluded that high REEs and micronutrient element concentrations of hornblende-gneiss favored the synthesis and accumulation of flavonoid compounds in *Scutellaria baicalensis* after the activation of endocytosis induced by REEs.

Keywords: parent materials; weathering; geoherbs; gneiss; flavonoid compounds

Citation: Sun, Z.; Shen, W.; Fang, W.; Zhang, H.; Chen, Z.; Xiong, L.; An, T. The Quality of *Scutellaria baicalensis* Georgi Is Effectively Affected by Lithology and Soil's Rare Earth Elements (REEs) Concentration. *Appl. Sci.* **2023**, *13*, 3086. https://doi.org/10.3390/app13053086

Academic Editor: José A. González-Pérez

Received: 9 December 2022
Revised: 21 January 2023
Accepted: 1 February 2023
Published: 27 February 2023

1. Introduction

Geoherb is a term used by ancient Chinese to describe the inter-species variation of Chinese medicines relevant to the geographical variation, and top-geoherb (Dao-di Herbs) is the population of a geoherb growing in habitats with natural conditions and ecological environment, featuring proverbial superior qualities, better curative effect and popularly used in traditional Chinese medicine clinical practice [1–3], such as *Lycium barbarum* L. from Ningxia, *Radix Angelicae* from Hangzhou, *Radix Rehmanniae* from Henan and *Scutellaria baicalensis* from Rehe in China [4]. Biological factors, e.g., species and intrinsic nature, and geo-environmental factors, e.g., physical and chemical characteristics of parent rock and weathering productions, jointly exert a crucial control on the formation of top-geoherbs' traits. As one of the critical material bases of traditional Chinese medicines, micronutrient elements significantly regulated and controlled the activity of many biological molecules (proteins, enzymes, and hormones) by taking part in enzymatic structures, constructing electron transport systems as carriers, and participating in the synthesis of hormones and vitamins, which ultimately influenced the metabolic activities and accumulation of effective constituents in medicines [5,6]. Therefore, micronutrient element assemblages played a decisive role in forming top-geoherbs' traits [5–8].

Rare earth elements (REEs) are a group of chemically similar elements behaving coherently in nature and consist of lanthanide elements from La to Lu (International Union of Pure and Applied Chemistry, 2005) [9]. REEs can be divided into light rare earth elements (LREEs; La–Eu) and heavy rare earth elements (HREEs; Gd–Lu). Although Y did not belong to REEs, it was studied together because of its chemically similar behavior to REEs. As significant components of micronutrient elements for plant growth, REEs can activate the endocytosis of plant cells [10]. It was demonstrated in previous studies that during the cultivation of Chinese medicines, e.g., *Ginseng, Coix lachryma-jobi, and Eucommia Land wolfberry,* adding moderate concentrations of rare earth fertilizer notably improved yield, quality and the accumulation of effective constituents [11–14]. These discoveries have led to the large-scale application of rare earth micro-fertilizers to medicines production. In order to enable the development of more sustainable rare earth utilization practices, it is significant to conduct research on their sources, migrations, enrichments, fractionations and transformations in the soil–root environments. Bedrock and its weathering production were the parent materials of soil on which plants survived, which was the natural mineral–nutrition elements pools and primary source of REEs for plants [5,15]. In general, the micronutrient element concentrations in the soils that developed in the mountain terrain were primarily inherited from parent materials. Therefore, the latter controlled the background characteristics of micronutrient elements concentrations in the former [16–18] and, ultimately, the adsorption and enrichments of micronutrient elements in Chinese medicines.

The root of the labiate *Scutellaria baicalensis* was initially documented in *Shennong's Classic of Materia Medica* and in *Collective Notes to the Canon of Materia Medica* as traditional Chinese medicines, which were characterized by a cold property and bitter taste. It is a commonly used Chinese medicine recorded in *The Pharmacopoeia of the People's Republic of China* (2015 version) [19], which is beneficial for clearing away hot and toxic substances, promoting diuresis, cooling blood, preventing miscarriage, and relieving cough [20,21]. Chengde city, Hebei Province, China, has been verified to be one of the top-geoherbs habitats for *Scutellaria baicalensis*. It was claimed in *Differentiation of drug production* that *Scutellaria baicalensis* has been widespread around Zhili and Rehe in Hebei Province for a long time, featuring a thick and long root, solid texture, golden-yellow rind, and extra low impurity, and it has been entitled "Rehe *Scutellaria baicalensis*" [22]. According to a field survey, gneiss was confirmed to be the dominant rock type inhabiting Rehe *Scutellaria baicalensis. Scutellaria baicalensis* was also observed being planted in loess locations, and REE-rich micro-fertilizers applications were conducted in parts of these habitats. In order to explore the effect of parent materials on the geoherbalism and quality of *Scutellaria baicalensis* in terms of REEs, three habitats of *Scutellaria baicalensis* with contrasting geo-pedological conditions, i.e., naturally grown habitat (NGHs), artificial planting habitats (APHs) without fertilization, and biomimetic cultivation habitats (BCHs) under field management and fertilization were studied. This study focused on the enrichments and fractionations of REEs during bedrock weathering and micronutrients adsorption by *Scutellaria baicalensis* and further on the controlling mechanism based on field eco-geological investigation and systematical sampling on roots of *Scutellaria baicalensis* and corresponding rhizosphere soil, and in weathering crust from the bottom of bedrock up to soil. REEs test for all samples and flavonoid compound tests for roots of *Scutellaria baicalensis* were conducted.

2. Physical Geography and Distribution of *Scutellaria baicalensis*

The study area is located in Yanshan Mountain, geographically in Chengde city, Hebei Province, China, where Rehe *Scutellaria baicalensis* is regionally widespread. A warm temperate semi-humid continental monsoon climate characterizes the region, with annual precipitation from 500 to 800 mm, frost-free days from 92 to 180 d, an annual effective accumulative temperature from 2800 to 3980 °C, and annual sunshine duration from 2500 to 3100 h [23]. The characteristics of the three comparable habitats of *Scutellaria baicalensis* (NGHs, APHs, and BCHs) were as follows (Figure 1).

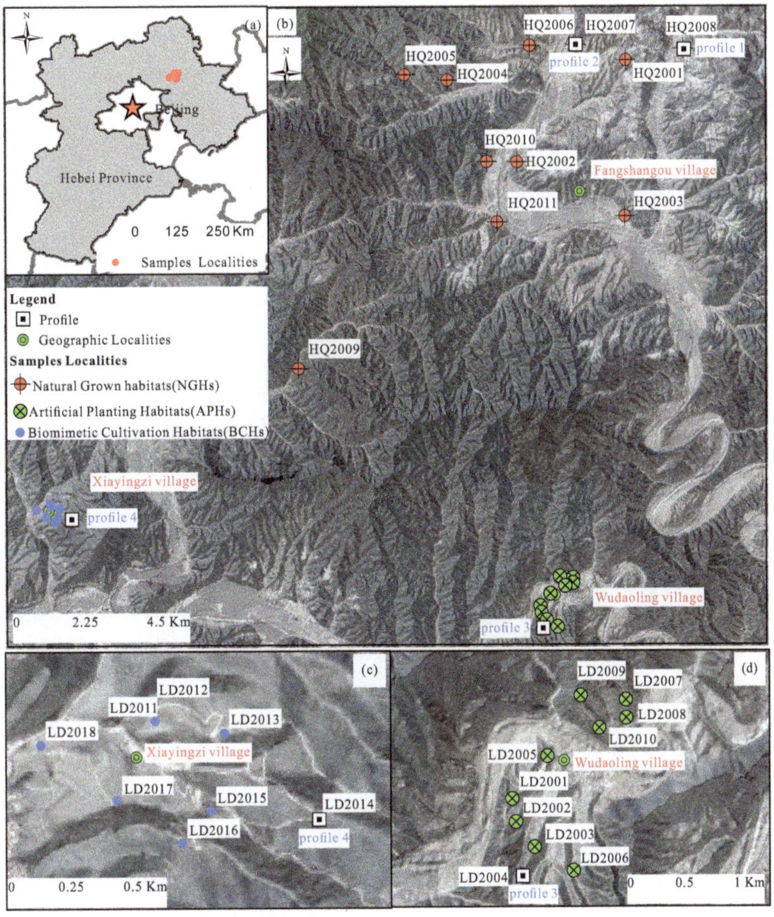

Figure 1. (**a**) Geographical location map; (**b**) Distribution map of sampling in three habitats; (**c**) Distribution map of sampling in biomimetic cultivation habitats (BCHs); (**d**) Distribution map of sampling in artificial planting habitats (APHs).

(1) It was documented that NGHs were concentrated in southern Chengde, such as Luanping County, Xinglong County and Kuanchen County, China. Based on our field survey, NGHs in Hongqi, Luanping County, were selected for sampling (Figure 2a–c).

The lithology was dominated by hornblende-gneiss, which were strongly weathered and had intensive fractures along weathering profiles, resulting in thick saprolite and soil with a thickness of 1 m.

(2) Sample plots of APHs were concentrated in Wudaoling village, Luanping County, whose parent materials were loess. *Scutellaria baicalensis* was planted in artificial terraced fields without fertilization (Figure 2d,e).

(3) Sample plots of BCHs were chosen in a Chinese herbal medicine plantation in Xiayingzi Villiage, Luanping County, whose parent materials were also loess, mingled with a small amount of weathering residues of andesitic volcanic and pyroclastic rocks. *Scutellaria baicalensis* was planted along turnover hillside fields under field management by biomimetic cultivation and adding a certain amount of REE-rich micro-fertilizers to replenish the soil nutrient contents (Figure 2f).

Figure 2. Field photos of *Scutellaria baicalensis* in various habitats; (**a–c**) Natural grown habitats (NGHs); (**d**,**e**) Artificial planting habitats (APHs); (**f**) Biomimetic cultivation habitats (BCHs).

3. Materials and Methods

3.1. Sampling Strategy

For research on the migrations and enrichments of REEs in the soil–roots environment, the sampling numbers of rhizosphere soils and corresponding roots of *Scutellaria baicalensis* in NGHs, APHs, and BCHs were 11, 10 and 8, respectively. Soil samples were collected in the topsoil layer extending 20 cm down from the surface. In addition, two weathering profiles in the close vicinity of field plots (HQ2007 and HQ2008) in NGHs were systemically sampled from the fresh parent rock (bedrocks) through the semi-weathered and highly weathered horizons (regoliths) to the fully weathered horizons (soils). Both profiles were distributed in the second stage of Fenghuangzui formation in the Neoarcjean Dantazi group, whose rock type was dominated by migmatite hornblende-gneiss, amphibolite and biotite-plagioclase-fels. In our study, the rock type of both profiles was hornblende-gneiss; however, their mineralogical compositions were slightly different: the bedrock in profile 1 was mainly composed of medium- and coarse-grained hornblende, plagioclase, quartz and a small amount of fine-grained biotite, while in profile 2, the bedrock was mainly composed of fine-grained plagioclase, biotite, quartz, and a small amount of hornblende. Weathering extended to a depth of 3.6 m in profile 1. The soil layer was 20 cm thick, and its texture was dominated by gravel. The regolith layer extended for a further 340 cm below soil layers with the chemical index of alteration (CIA) values ranging from 65.0 to 71.1. Bedrock extended to a depth of 5.6 m. Weathering extended to a depth of 5.8 m in profile 2. The soil layer was 50 cm thick, with the humus horizon being 10 cm. The soil texture was dominated by gravel. The regolith layer extended for a further 530 cm below soil layers with the CIA values ranging from 51.1 to 67.2. Bedrock extended to a depth of 7.6 m in which alteration zones, e.g., chloritization, occurred, extending 1 m upwards from the bottom. About 1–2 samples were collected per subhorizon. A total of 8 samples from profile 1 and 10 samples from profile 2 were collected, and each one soil profile was collected per habitats in APHs and BCHs in the close vicinity of field plots (LD2004 and LD2014), respectively. The topsoil layer extending 20 cm downwards from the surface and the loess layer extending for a further 20 cm were sampled, and a total of 2 samples from profile 3 and also 2 samples from profile 4 were collected.

3.2. Analytical Methods

For REE analyses, the prepared samples were first dried at 70 °C, and then both the dried soil, regolith and fresh bedrock were crushed, pulverized by an agate mortar and sieved through a 200 mesh into powder. The powder was baked at 105 °C to remove adsorbed water before analysis. REEs were measured using inductively coupled plasma-mass spectrometry (ICP–MS). For soil samples, approximately 50 mg of soil sample was digested with 0.5 mL HNO_3 and 1 mL HF in screw-top, PTFE-lined stainless steel bombs at 185 °C for 24 h. The inner Teflon was removed from the hot plate after cooling, and the solution was evaporated to dryness. The solution was then drained and evaporated to dryness with 0.5 mL HNO_3. This procedure was repeated twice. The final residue was redissolved by adding 1.5 mL HNO_3 and 1.5 mL deionized water. Subsequently, the bomb was resealed and heated at 130 °C for 3 h. After cooling to room temperature, the final solution was diluted to 50 mL by adding distilled deionized water. For regolith and bedrock samples, approximately 50 mg of powdered samples was digested with 100 mL APS, which was followed by mechanical shaking for 2 h and standing for 30 min. After filtration at medium speed, 2 mL of filterable solution was diluted to 100 mL by adding distilled deionized water. Subsequently, 10 mL of the solution was diluted to 100 mL by adding 1 mL indium (In) solution, 1 mL HNO_3 and deionized water. The *Scutellaria baicalensis* samples were washed with tap water and deionized water successively and then oven-dried at 75 °C until the dry weight reached a constant value. Due to the dominant distributions of flavonoid compounds in roots, roots were used for an REE and flavonoid compound test. The dry root samples were ground to a fine powder. Approximately 200 mg of powdered sample was digested with 5 mL HNO_3 in a high-pressure digestion tank for 1 h, which was followed by cooling and removing HNO_3 at 140 °C. After cooling to room temperature, the solution was diluted to 10 mL by adding deionized water. The reagent blanks of soil, regolith, bedrock, and roots were treated following the same procedures as the corresponding samples. The total analytical errors for REEs in this study were within ±6.

High-Performance Liquid Chromatography (HPLC–DAD) was applied to test the six flavonoid compounds, including baicalin, oroxylin A glycoside, wogonoside, baicalein, wogonin, and oroxylin A. First, the reference substances of the six flavonoid compounds were dissolved in chromatographic methanol and shaken to prepare the reference solution. Second, root powder samples were placed in a volumetric flask with 70% ethanol and shaken. The supernatant was extracted for filtration through a 0.22 μm filter membrane after ultrasonic extraction for 40 min and cooling to room temperature. Finally, a high-performance liquid chromatograph Water E2695 was utilized to test the flavonoid compounds of the reference solutions and our specimens. Methanol-0.1% phosphoric acid solution was applied to gradient elute the mobile phase. The accuracy was controlled by adding 10% of blank samples and parallel samples during testing according to the specification requirement.

3.3. Parameters on the REE Distribution Characteristics

ΣREE, ΣLREE and ΣHREE were calculated as the sum of REEs, LREEs and HREEs, respectively. LREE/HREE was the ratio of ΣLREE to ΣHREE and La_N/Yb_N was the ratio of La_N and Yb_N, where La_N and Yb_N represent the chondrite normalized values of La and Yb.

Eu anomaly values are quantifed as (1):

$$\delta \text{Eu} = \frac{\text{Eu}_\text{N}}{\sqrt{\text{Sm}_\text{N} \times \text{Gd}_\text{N}}}, \tag{1}$$

where Eu_N, Sm_N, and Gd_N represent the chondrite normalized values of Eu, Sm, and Gd, respectively.

Ce anomalies were calculated by formula (2):

$$\delta \text{Ce} = \frac{\text{Ce}_\text{N}}{\sqrt{\text{La}_\text{N} \times \text{Pr}_\text{N}}}, \tag{2}$$

where Ce_N, La_N, and Pr_N represent the chondrite normalized values of Ce, La, and Pr, respectively.

The normality of the parameters in various habitats was confirmed using the Shapiro–Wilkes test, and probability (p value) lower than 0.05 showed their abnormal distribution. The normal distribution test was conducted in SPSS 26.0.

4. Results

4.1. REE Concentrations in the Weathering Crust

4.1.1. REE Concentrations of Rhizosphere Soils

The concentrations of REEs and several parameters on the REEs distribution characteristics of rhizosphere soils in various habitats are listed in Table 1. According to the Shapiro–Wilkes test, ΣREE, ΣLREE and ΣHREE in the rhizosphere soils were normally distributed in NGHs and APHs ($p > 0.05$) but not in BCHs ($p < 0.05$), and therefore, the median represents the statistical characteristic of REE concentrations in various habitats. Rhizosphere soils in NGHs contained REE concentrations with the median ΣREE values being 173 $\mu g \cdot g^{-1}$ and the median ΣLREE values being 157 $\mu g \cdot g^{-1}$, which were higher than that in APHs with the median ΣREE values being 149 $\mu g \cdot g^{-1}$ and the median ΣLREE values being 133 $\mu g \cdot g^{-1}$. However, ΣHREE exhibited the opposite feature that rhizosphere soils in APHs with higher HREE concentrations. The median LREE/HREE and La_N/Yb_N of rhizosphere soils in NGHs were 9.76 and 7.86, respectively, which were higher than that in APHs with a median of 11.4 and 8.82, respectively, suggesting greater fractionations with LREEs and HREEs in NGHs. After micro-fertilizers application, it exhibited remarkable enrichments of REEs in the rhizosphere soils of BCHs with the median ΣREE, ΣLREE and ΣHREE values being 187 $\mu g \cdot g^{-1}$, 166 $\mu g \cdot g^{-1}$ and 20.2 $\mu g \cdot g^{-1}$, respectively, which were also higher than that in NGHs. Additionally, LREE/HREE and La_N/Yb_N in the rhizosphere soils of BCHs increased, with the median LREE/HREE and La_N/Yb_N being 8.36 and 9.53, respectively. The chondrite-normalized REE patterns exhibited an obvious right-inclined style that all the rhizosphere soils were enriched in LREEs (Figure 3a,c,e) with moderately to slightly negative Eu anomalies, especially in APHs and BCHs. However, the Ce anomaly was not apparent. The coefficients of variation (CVs) of ΣREE, ΣLREE and ΣHREE of rhizosphere soils in APHs were 6.84%, 6.88% and 8.84%, respectively, which were much lower than those in NGHs and BCHs, indicating that the REEs concentrations of soils developed in loess without fertilization were relatively homogeneous.

4.1.2. REE Concentrations in the Weathering Profile

Two weathering profiles were distributed in hornblende-gneiss locations. The ΣREE values of bedrock were 233 $\mu g \cdot g^{-1}$ and 264 $\mu g \cdot g^{-1}$, respectively, in profiles 1 and 2, indicating their similar REEs concentrations. Both weathering profiles in NGHs showed similar chondrite-normalized REE patterns from the bottom of bedrock up to regolith, and onto the soil, with enrichment of LREEs and moderately negative Eu anomalies (Table 2, Figure 4), which is in accordance with the weathering characteristics in mountain terrain that bedrock was in-situ weathered to the soil, and the latter has inherited REE concentrations from the former. However, different enrichments and fractionations within REEs have occurred during weathering. As shown in profile 1 (Figure 4a), the ΣREE was overall higher in the regoliths in which HREEs were deficient, but LREEs were enriched as compared to bedrock, while topsoil was deficient in both LREEs and HREEs. Regoliths contained higher REE concentrations with ΣREE values ranging 242–289 $\mu g \cdot g^{-1}$, and that of soil was 169 $\mu g \cdot g^{-1}$. LREE/HREE varied in the range of 8.28–11.2 and La_N/Yb_N varied in the range of 9.24–13.8, which were slightly different with bedrock (LREE/HREE = 8.56, La_N/Yb_N = 9.48). However, profile 2 exhibited that the ΣREE was overall lower in the regoliths and soils, and that LREEs were more deficient than HREEs in both regolith and soil as compared to bedrock, while topsoil was more enriched in REEs than regolith (Figure 4b). Regoliths contained lower REE concentrations with ΣREE values ranging 142–238 $\mu g \cdot g^{-1}$, and that of topsoil was 238 $\mu g \cdot g^{-1}$. LREE/HREE varied in the range of 6.08–10.7 and La_N/Yb_N varied in the range of 5.83–14.3, which were different with bedrock (LREE/HREE = 20.6, La_N/Yb_N = 35.8).

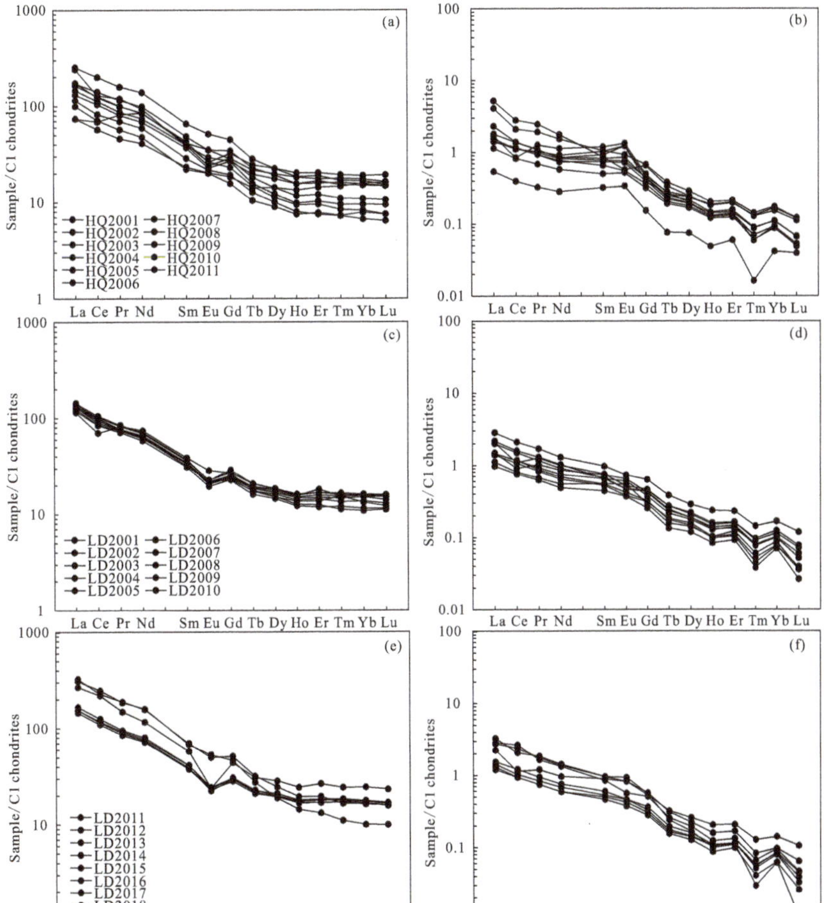

Figure 3. Chondrite-normalized REE patterns of rhizosphere soils and roots of *Scutellaria baicalensis*. (**a**) Rhizosphere soils in NGHs; (**b**) Roots in NGHs; (**c**) Rhizosphere soils in APHs; (**d**) Roots in APHs; (**e**) Rhizosphere soils in BCHs; (**f**) Roots in BCHs.

Table 1. Parameters on REE distribution characteristics of rhizosphere soils in various habitats, Hebei Province.

Parameters	Habitats	Median (25–75%) (μg·g^{-1})	Average (μg·g^{-1})	Skewness	CV/%	p Value
ΣREE	NGHs (n = 11)	174 (127–212)	173	0.754	33.9	0.541
	APHs (n = 10)	149 (140–156)	149	0.231	6.84	0.753
	BCHs (n = 8)	187 (177–337)	238	0.726	34.4	0.007
ΣLREE	NGHs (n = 11)	154 (115–194)	157	0.765	35.1	0.673
	APHs (n = 10)	133 (124–139)	133	0.120	6.88	0.791
	BCHs (n = 8)	166 (158–311)	216	0.761	36.8	0.009
ΣHREE	NGHs (n = 11)	15.2 (12.1–19.9)	16.2	0.131	29.7	0.802
	APHs (n = 10)	16.7 (15.3–18.1)	16.6	−0.158	8.84	0.701
	BCHs (n = 8)	20.2 (19.5–24.7)	21.7	1.49	16.3	0.008
LREE\HREE	NGHs (n = 11)	9.76 (7.85–11.5)	9.85	0.156	25.2	0.814
	APHs (n = 10)	7.86 (7.64–8.30)	8.01	1.89	7.00	0.016
	BCHs (n = 8)	8.36 (7.96–11.7)	9.84	1.73	29.8	0.005
$La_N \backslash Yb_N$	NGHs (n = 11)	11.4 (8.49–15.9)	12.4	1.03	46.0	0.315
	APHs (n = 10)	8.82 (8.34–10.1)	9.27	1.37	12.7	0.042
	BCHs (n = 8)	9.53 (8.87–17.6)	13.4	1.96	59.7	0.001
δEu	NGHs (n = 11)	0.900 (0.710–0.970)	0.869	−0.168	14.4	0.385
	APHs (n = 10)	0.719 (0.704–0.791)	0.743	1.31	8.05	0.057
	BCHs (n = 8)	0.686 (0.652–0.793)	0.699	0.032	18.9	0.512
δCe	NGHs (n = 11)	0.950 (0.890–0.970)	0.919	−2.09	8.15	0.002
	APHs (n = 10)	0.910 (0.870–0.935)	0.892	−2.20	7.89	0.003
	BCHs (n = 8)	0.950 (0.935–0.990)	0.959	0.490	5.18	0.510

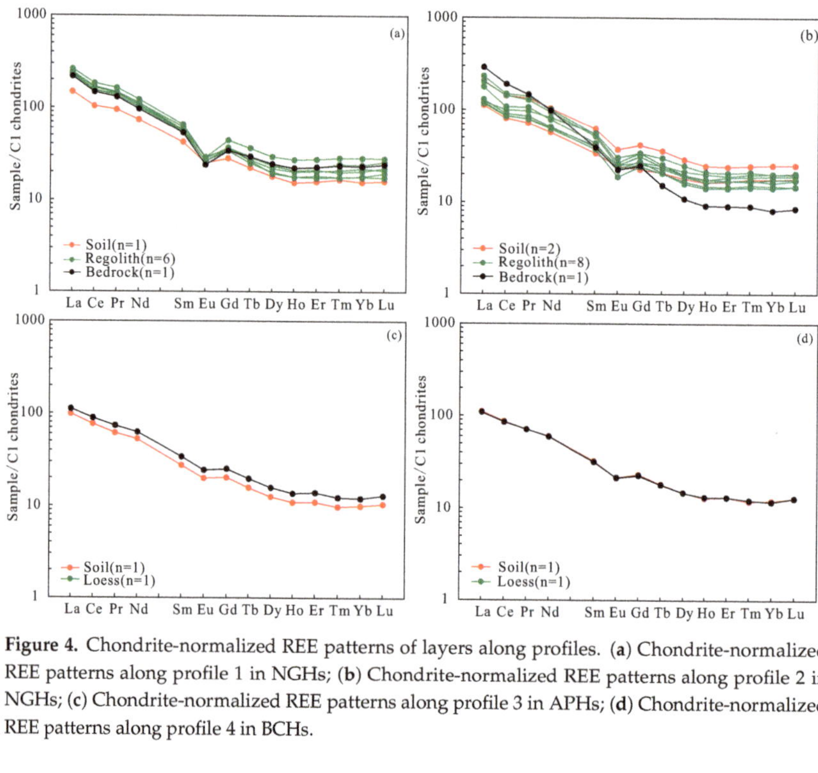

Figure 4. Chondrite-normalized REE patterns of layers along profiles. (**a**) Chondrite-normalized REE patterns along profile 1 in NGHs; (**b**) Chondrite-normalized REE patterns along profile 2 in NGHs; (**c**) Chondrite-normalized REE patterns along profile 3 in APHs; (**d**) Chondrite-normalized REE patterns along profile 4 in BCHs.

Soils developed in loess also showed chondrite-normalized REE patterns similar to those of parent materials with enrichment of LREEs and lightly negative Eu anomalies (Figure 4c,d). It also exhibited the depletion of REEs in topsoil as compared to parent material in APHs. The ΣREE values of parents materials (loess) were similar, 139 and 133 $\mu g \cdot g^{-1}$, whose corresponding soils contained total REE concentrations being 119 and 136 $\mu g \cdot g^{-1}$. LREE/HREE was, respectively, 8.43 and 8.17, which was similar to their parent materials with LREE/HREE being 7.90 and 8.11. La_N/Yb_N was, respectively, 9.87 and 9.23, which was similar to their parent materials, with La_N/Yb_N being 9.32 and 9.26. In general, the REEs of soils and parent material horizons in hornblende-gneiss were more abundant, and they had more substantial variation between LREE and HREE than those in loess.

Table 2. Parameters on REEs distribution characteristics along profiles in various habitats, Hebei Province.

Habitats	Profile	Layer	Depth (cm)	ΣREE ($\mu g \cdot g^{-1}$)	ΣLREE ($\mu g \cdot g^{-1}$)	ΣHREE ($\mu g \cdot g^{-1}$)	LREE/HREE	La_N/Yb_N	δEu	δCe
NGHs (hornblende gneiss)	Profile 1	Soil	0–20	169	150	18.2	8.28	9.52	0.734	0.872
		regolith	20–30	259	235	23.8	9.88	11.6	0.596	0.895
		regolith	50–70	259	237	21.2	11.2	13.8	0.572	0.889
		regolith	260–270	255	231	24.6	9.37	9.9	0.650	0.902
		regolith	280–300	243	220	23.2	9.47	10.5	0.587	0.842
		regolith	310–320	289	259	30.3	8.54	9.24	0.538	0.888
		regolith	340–360	242	221	21	10.5	12.9	0.612	0.883
		bedrock	540–560	233	208	24.4	8.56	9.48	0.563	0.875
	Profile 2	soil	0–10	238	210	28.3	7.4	8.19	0.729	0.852
		soil	20–40	134	117	17.7	6.6	6.31	0.879	0.901
		regolith	60–80	238	218	20.4	10.6	14.3	0.619	0.827
		regolith	110–120	146	126	20.7	6.08	5.83	0.756	0.883
		regolith	210–220	151	132	18.6	7.11	7.36	0.693	0.867
		regolith	230–240	172	149	23.5	6.32	6.11	0.700	0.918
		regolith	290–300	142	126	16.6	7.55	8.01	0.621	0.890
		regolith	510–520	180	163	16.9	9.67	12.4	0.660	0.783
		regolith	560–580	223	202	20.6	9.81	10.6	0.620	0.889
		Bedrock	600	264	252	12.2	20.6	35.8	0.724	0.921
APHs (loess)	profile 3	soil	0–20	119	107	12.6	8.43	9.87	0.841	0.990
		loess	20–40	139	124	15.6	7.90	9.32	0.835	0.982
BCHs (loess)	profile 4	soil	0–20	136	121	14.8	8.17	9.23	0.775	0.981
		loess	20–40	133	118	14.6	8.11	9.26	0.799	0.968

4.2. REE Concentrations in the Roots of *Scutellaria baicalensis*

The concentrations of REEs and several parameters on the REE distribution characteristics for roots of *Scutellaria baicalensis* in various habitats are listed in Table 3. The median was also utilized to represent the statistical characteristic of REE concentrations in the roots of various habitats. Roots of *Scutellaria baicalensis* contained similar ΣREE and ΣLREE in NGHs (ΣREE = 2.02 $mg \cdot kg^{-1}$, ΣLREE = 1.78 $mg \cdot kg^{-1}$) and BCHs (ΣREE = 2.04 $mg \cdot kg^{-1}$, ΣLREE = 1.82 $mg \cdot kg^{-1}$), which are higher than that in APHs (ΣREE = 1.78 $mg \cdot kg^{-1}$, ΣLREE = 1.60 $mg \cdot kg^{-1}$). However, roots in NGHs contained the highest HREE concentrations, with the median ΣHREE being 0.212 $mg \cdot kg^{-1}$, and roots in BCHs contained the lowest HREE concentrations, with the median ΣHREE being 0.183 $mg \cdot kg^{-1}$, which was exactly opposite to the ΣHREE in the soils. LREE/HREE and La_N/Yb_N decreased following the order of BCHs > APHs > NGHs, which was inconsistent with the order in the soils. The considerable variance in REEs adsorption by roots from the rhizosphere soil between various habitats can be speculated. The concentrations of REEs with even atomic numbers were higher than those with odd atomic numbers at HREEs, which conformed to the rule of Oddo-Harkins [24,25]. In general, the chondrite-normalized REE patterns presented an obvious right-inclined style with the enrichment of LREEs (Figure 3b,d,f). Positive Eu anomalies were observed for some samples in all habitats, indicating the adsorption of Eu from soil to some extent. However, the negative Ce anomaly of roots was stronger than that of soil, especially in NGHs, since Ce^{4+} was hard to be adsorbed by roots.

Table 3. Parameters of the REE distribution characteristics of *Scutellaria baicalensis* in various habitats, Hebei Province.

Parameters	Habitats	Median (25–75%) (mg·kg^{-1})	Average (mg·kg^{-1})	Skewness	CV/%	p Value
ΣREE	NGHs (n = 11)	2.02 (1.79–2.3)	2.21	1.14	47.0	0.066
	APHs (n = 10)	1.78 (1.55–2.31)	1.94	1.01	30.3	0.484
	BCHs (n = 8)	2.04 (1.5–3.33)	2.34	0.386	38.0	0.042
ΣLREE	NGHs (n = 11)	1.78 (1.62–2.11)	2.00	1.24	49.2	0.056
	APHs (n = 10)	1.6 (1.4–2.09)	1.76	0.998	30.7	0.491
	BCHs (n = 8)	1.82 (1.36–3.12)	2.15	0.441	39.8	0.039
ΣHREE	NGHs (n = 11)	0.212 (0.175–0.246)	0.209	−0.541	30.3	0.724
	APHs (n = 10)	0.187 (0.146–0.217)	0.187	1.07	28.1	0.376
	BCHs (n = 8)	0.183 (0.148–0.235)	0.189	0.378	25.7	0.580
LREE\HREE	NGHs (n = 11)	8.64 (7.55–10.8)	9.27	1.48	23.7	0.063
	APHs (n = 10)	9.27 (8.57–9.89)	9.38	0.840	11.0	0.536
	BCHs (n = 8)	10.2 (9.13–14.7)	11.27	0.556	26.2	0.283
$La_N \backslash Yb_N$	NGHs (n = 11)	15.2(12.4–20.9)	17.26	1.07	43.4	0.291
	APHs (n = 10)	16 (14.6–18.4)	16.56	1.04	15.0	0.246
	BCHs (n = 8)	19.8 (16.5–32.9)	24.58	1.10	43.6	0.168
δEu	NGHs (n = 11)	1.28 (1.08–1.57)	1.32	−0.109	22.8	0.985
	APHs (n = 10)	0.937 (0.854–1.14)	0.998	0.787	16.0	0.185
	BCHs (n = 8)	1.06 (0.972–1.13)	1.05	−0.357	11.6	0.972
δCe	NGHs (n = 11)	0.9 (0.730–0.950)	0.845	−1.00	15.7	0.192
	APHs (n = 10)	0.935 (0.858–0.963)	0.897	−1.55	12.5	0.009
	BCHs (n = 8)	0.935 (0.835–1.04)	0.933	−0.241	16.7	0.933

4.3. Accumulation of REE in the Roots of *Scutellaria baicalensis*

The biological absorption coefficient (BAC) of REEs provides an estimate of the individual availability of REEs to the plant [26–28]. This was adopted to quantify the natural process of element transfer from the soil to the roots of *Scutellaria baicalensis*. The BAC is defined as follows (3):

$$BAC_i = \frac{CM_i}{CS_i}, \quad (3)$$

where BAC_i is the migration and accumulation rate of element i, and CM_i and CS_i are the concentrations of element i in the plant and soil, respectively. The results were categorized into five groups based on the magnitude of the coefficient: BAC $>$ 3—very strongly accumulated; from 1.5 to 3.0—strongly accumulated; from 0.5 to 1.5—moderate absorption; from 0.1 to 0.5—weak absorption, and BAC $<$ 0.1—very weak absorption [29]. Under normal circumstances, the ratio of the concentrations of REEs in plants to that in the soil is less than 1, even as low as 0.02 [30]. In the study area, all REEs in *Scutellaria baicalensis* had low BACs: less than 0.1.

One-way ANOVA and LSD tests were applied to analyze whether there were remarkable differences in the BACs of REEs between various habitats after the test for normal distribution and homogeneity of variance. In addition, permutation tests, t tests and nonparametric tests were utilized for the BACs that were not normally distributed or had heterogeneity of variance. The statistical analyses were conducted in the R program. In the box plots, various letters (e.g., a and b) imply that there exist statistically remarkable differences between BACs in various habitats ($p < 0.05$); otherwise, differences are not statistically remarkable(e.g., ab and a, ab and b). Almost all HREEs and Y, except for Gd and

Tb, showed statistically remarkable differences in BACs between NGHs with both BCHs and APHs. According to the median (black line in the box), the BACs of all REEs decreased in the order of NGHs > APHs > BCHs (Figure 5), suggesting higher utilization efficiency for REEs with natural source from bedrock, which was attributed to their self-adaption to the environment for a long time in a complicated open system [31]. On the contrary, the utilization efficiency for anthropogenic REEs was relatively low.

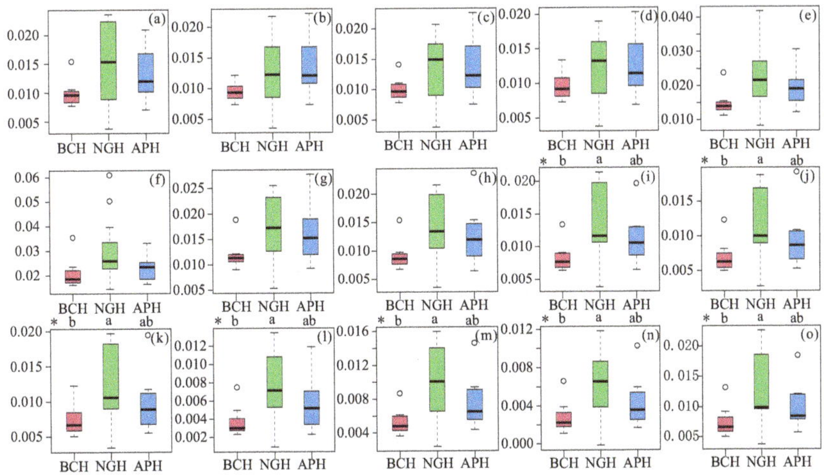

Figure 5. Box plot of biological absorption coefficient (BACs) of REEs Y from soils into roots. (**a**) La; (**b**) Ce; (**c**) Pr; (**d**) Nd; (**e**) Sm; (**f**) Eu; (**g**) Gd; (**h**) Tb; (**i**) Dy; (**j**) Ho; (**k**) Er; (**l**) Tm; (**m**) Yb; (**n**) Lu; (**o**) Y. * $p < 0.1$.

4.4. *Effective Constituent Content of Scutellaria baicalensis*

Flavonoid compounds are the dominant effective constituents of *Scutellaria baicalensis*, which are composed of two polyhydroxy phenolic benzene rings interconnected by three carbon atoms. Flavonoid compounds included baicalin, oroxylin A glycoside, wogonoside, baicalein, wogonin, and oroxylin A, in which baicalin was recognized as the main criterion of quality [32]. Contents of baicalin ranged from 12.8 to 51.7 mg·g^{-1} with an average of 27.5 mg·g^{-1} in the NGHs, which were higher than that in APHs (4.22–13.2 mg·g^{-1}) and BCHs (4.04–17.1 mg·g^{-1}). Almost all the flavonoid compounds were normally distributed ($p > 0.05$) except for oroxylin A in BCHs. According to the average, baicalin and wogonoside decreased in the order of NGHs > BCHs > APHs, and oroxylin A glycoside, baicalein, wogonin, and oroxylin A followed the order of NGHs > APHs > BCHs (Table 4).

Table 4. Statistical characteristics of flavonoid compound contents in the roots of *Scutellaria baicalensis*.

Flavonoids Compounds	Habitats	Average (mg·g^{-1})	Ranges (mg·g^{-1})	Skewness	p Value
Baicalin	NGHs (n = 11)	27.5	12.8-51.7	1.42	0.325
	APHs (n = 10)	8.28	4.22–13.2	0.546	0.911
	BCHs (n = 8)	11.0	4.04–17.1	−0.411	0.273
Oroxylin A glycoside	NGHs (n = 11)	1.85	0.270-4.03	1.06	0.326
	APHs (n = 10)	0.895	0.030–1.83	0.136	0.601
	BCHs (n = 8)	0.724	0.080–1.62	0.633	0.726

Table 4. Cont.

Flavonoids Compounds	Habitats	Average (mg·g^{-1})	Ranges (mg·g^{-1})	Skewness	p Value
Wogonoside	NGHs (n = 11)	5.24	1.96-12.2	1.79	0.099
	APHs (n = 10)	1.81	0.080–3.02	−0.588	0.396
	BCHs (n = 8)	2.69	1.03–4.56	0.031	0.585
Baicalein	NGHs (n = 11)	2.43	0.820–4.68	0.765	0.605
	APHs (n = 10)	1.15	0.550–2.09	1.42	0.356
	BCHs (n = 8)	1.09	0.330–2.43	1.22	0.357
wogonin	NGHs (n = 11)	0.966	0.310–1.75	0.476	0.508
	APHs (n = 10)	0.468	0.200–0.810	0.862	0.598
	BCHs (n = 8)	0.478	0.090–1.19	1.38	0.301
Oroxylin A	NGHs (n = 11)	0.386	0.200–0.560	−0.036	0.61
	APHs (n = 10)	0.23	0.060–0.440	0.378	0.561
	BCHs (n = 8)	0.184	0.030–0.570	1.92	0.031

5. Discussions

5.1. Lithological Influences on the Enrichments and Fractionations of REEs in the Soils

Micronutrient element concentrations in the soils developed in mountain terrain were primarily inherited from parent materials [16–18]. As mentioned, REE distribution patterns of soils developed in different habitats presented a genetic relationship with their corresponding parent materials. According to 1:250,000 reports of regional geologic survey and our field survey, the protolith of hornblende-gneiss in NGHs was femic volcanic rock, whose REEs concentrations were higher than those that developed in loess; therefore, soils developed from hornblende-gneiss contained higher REEs concentrations (ΣREE = 174 ug·g^{-1}) than that from loess (ΣREE = 149 ug·g^{-1}), which is in agreement with the expectations from the different lithologies that soils originating from volcanic rock tend to have higher REE concentrations than soils developed from loess [28,33,34].

Weathering crust in hornblende-gneiss showed great variation of REEs concentrations than loess, resulting in relatively homogeneous REEs concentrations in the soils developed from loess (CV = 6.84%) and notable heterogeneity of REEs concentrations in the soils developed from hornblende-gneiss (CV = 33.9%). The weathering of parent materials profoundly impacted the migrations and enrichments of REEs. The REE concentrations distribution pattern in soils of loess was significantly similar to their parent materials since their weak weathering and indistinctive movement of clay particles. However, the complex mineral compositions and grain sizes in hornblende-gneiss significantly influenced the weathering process, resulting in remarkable discrepancies in migrations and enrichments of REEs during weathering [35,36]. Two weathering profiles in hornblende-gneiss locations exhibited different evolution of REEs. In profile 1, REE concentrations decreased in the order of soils $<$ bedrock $<$ regoliths, while in profile 2, REE concentrations decreased followed the order regoliths $<$ topsoil $<$ bedrock (Figure 6a,b). It can be speculated that in profile 1, as eluviation proceeded, soluble components were greatly leached while sparingly soluble components, including REEs, showed relative enrichments, resulting in the overall REE enrichments of the regoliths [37,38]. REEs in the topsoil penetrated downward to the lower part of the profile, which was accompanied with REE-containing clay minerals [39,40], resulting in depletion in the topsoil compared with the lower parts. However, the minerals grain size in the bedrock of profile 2 was much smaller than that in profile 1. As the mineral grain size decreases and specific surface area increases, fine-grained rock offers a potentially increased area over which water penetration may occur [41,42]. Therefore, the reaction with water in the regolith and soils causes releasing of REE from REE-containing minerals and the leaching of REE, especially LREE. It was observed in the field that the humus horizon was 10 cm thick with a higher content of organic materials in profile 2; therefore, topsoil contained higher REE concentrations since organic matter has a fixed effect on REEs [43–45].

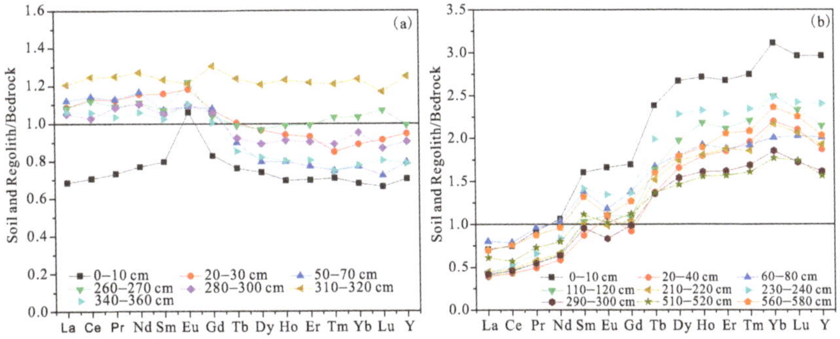

Figure 6. Bedrock-normalized REE patterns in profiles in NGH. (**a**) Profile 1; (**b**) Profile 2.

The clays and iron (hydro) oxide that formed during chemical weathering in hornblende-gneiss locations were notably different, resulting in apparent different fractionations within REEs [46–50], since the mixed speciation of the REEs in clays and Fe-Mn oxyhydroxides is typical for REEs in soils [38,51–53]. Under natural pH, clay minerals with a negative layer charge are effective in the adsorption of REEs through ion exchange, surface complexation, electrostatic attraction and migration into clay structures [54]. The adsorption capacity is largely determined by the surface structure, surface charge of clay minerals and composition [55,56]. In our study area, under alkaline conditions (pH > 7) with abundant Fe^{2+}, Mg^{2+}, and K^+, clay minerals were dominated by smectite, illite or chlorite, especially in profile 2 [46,50,57,58]. Smectite and illite may intrinsically retain HREE more efficiently than LREE [46,58]. As shown in Figure 7a, LREE/HREE had a remarkable positive relationship with $SiO_2/(Al_2O_3+Fe_2O_3)$ in profile 2 according to Pearson correlation analysis. As weathering proceeded, clay minerals were gradually generated from aluminosilicate minerals with the enrichment of Al_2O_3 and depletion of SiO_2. In addition, enhanced oxidation contributed to the enrichment of Fe_2O_3. Therefore, the decrease of the $SiO_2/(Al_2O_3+Fe_2O_3)$ ratio showed the enrichment of clay mineral (smectite and illite) and iron (hydro) oxide, favoring the preferential adsorption of HREE and fractionation within REEs [59]. However, according to CIA, the chemical weathering in profile 1 (CIA = 65.0–71.1) was generally stronger than that in profile 2 (CIA = 51.1–67.2), and a small amount of kaolinite and boehmite with higher maturity was formed from illite/smectite [60]. Therefore, LREEs were preferentially adsorbed by kaolinite in profile 1. In addition, HREEs have a smaller ionic radius and stronger hydrolysis ability than LREEs and therefore have a higher affinity toward iron (hydro) oxide. Previous studies also showed that the chondrite-normalized iron (hydro) oxide fractions are slightly enriched in HREEs via inner-sphere complexation and may play an important role in redistributing HREEs in the weathering crust [61,62]. As shown in Figure 7b, LREE/HREE had a remarkable negative relationship with Fe_2O_3 in profile 2, suggesting the critical control of iron (hydro) oxide on the REE fractionation. In the study area, profile 2 contained more abundant Fe_2O_3 (4.92–9.49%, 7.95%) than those in profile 1 (Fe_2O_3 = 4.40–7.47%, 6.22%). Therefore, in profile 1, HREEs are predominantly dissolved and migrate as bicarbonate and organic complexes in solution in case of the low contents of iron (hydro) oxide, leading to the fractionation of REEs among weathering crust [63–69]. However, the preferential scavenging of HREEs during the precipitation of pedogenetic iron (hydro) oxide resulted in the HREE enrichment in profile 2 instead of being dissolved and migrating as bicarbonate and organic complexes, which is consistent with the conclusion of Land (1999) [51].

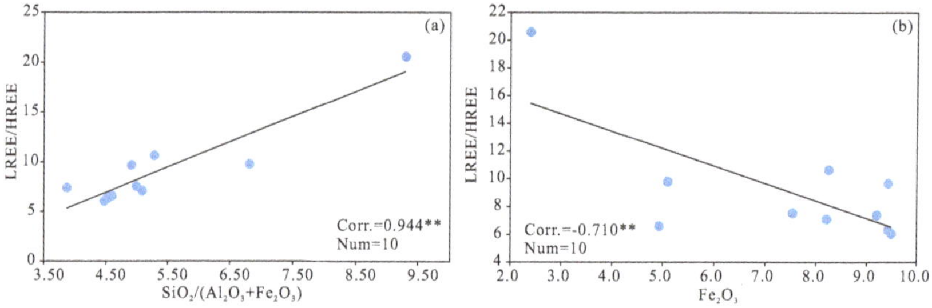

Figure 7. Scatter diagram of (**a**) $SiO_2/(Al_2O_3+Fe_2O_3)$ versus LREE/HREE and (**b**) Fe_2O_3 versus LREE/HREE in profile 2. ** $p < 0.01$.

5.2. Enrichments and Fractionations of REE in the Roots of Scutellaria baicalensis

The soil mineral particles present in the close vicinity of the roots were the primary source of REEs for plants. It exhibited a remarkable positive correlation between ΣREE in the roots and rhizosphere soils with a coefficient of 0.479 ($p < 0.01$), especially the correlation coefficient between ΣLREE in the roots and rhizosphere soils being 0.511 ($p < 0.01$) (Figure 8). Previous research on the distribution of *Scutellaria baicalensis* demonstrated that they were naturally widespread in the fertile sand or loam underlying the humus horizon, especially chestnut soil or sandy loam, with pH values ranging from 5 to 8 [70]. For a type of species, the REEs concentrations in plants are influenced by some complex related factors, including total REEs concentrations and their occurrences in the rhizosphere soils, as well as pH, Eh, clay fraction contents, nutrient features, etc., in the soil–root environment [71–75]. In our study area, the clay fraction contents of soil developed in NGHs range from 18.8 to 66.9 g/kg, and the sand fraction contents range from 884.1 to 940.9 g/kg (our unpublished data), suggesting that soils were classified into sand according to texture classification. Their pH value varied from 7.31 to 8.57, with an average of 8.06. Therefore, NGHs were optimal for the inhabitation of *Scutellaria baicalensis*, and the absence of clay fraction favored the migrations of REEs into plants, resulting in higher biological absorption coefficients (BACs) of REEs. On the contrary, loess in APHs was generally deemed to comprise higher clay fractions than other lithologies. REEs may be preferentially involved in the crystal lattice of clay minerals as isomorphisms or hosted into REE-rich minerals, e.g., Ti oxides or phosphorite, and therefore inhibit the absorption of REEs into plants [37,76], leading to lower BACs of REEs. However, after rare earth micro-fertilizers application, BACs of all REEs in BCHs were still lower than that in APHs, despite both rhizosphere soils and roots in BCH comprised higher REE concentrations. Previous studies have demonstrated that once exogenous REEs enter the soil, more than 99.5% of them are absorbed by the solid phase of the soil, and only a small amount is dissolved in the water present in the soil [10,77]. This means that within a short period, REE fertilization would not notably increase the concentrations of REEs with high bioavailability [78–82], e.g., water-soluble fractions and iron-exchangeable fractions. In contrast, REEs accumulate in the soil as residue fractions, which are difficult for the plant to adsorb [83]. We can conclude that REE fertilization in BCHs contributes to improving REE concentrations in roots to some extent but that utilization efficiency for anthropogenic REEs was relatively low.

The BCAs of LREEs for *Scutellaria baicalensis* were overall higher than those of HREEs. Previous studies showed that the coprecipitation of rare earth ion salts (mostly in the form of insoluble oxalates or phosphates) and the selective absorption of root cell walls (in the form of trivalent cations) were the main mechanisms through which plant roots fix REEs [10,84,85]. In general, the dominant speciation of the LREEs is as free ions, whereas the HREEs are mainly present as dissolved complexes [38,86,87]. Diffusion through ion channels, i.e., passive diffusion, was the dominant movement mechanism of REEs from the soil into the roots [88–90], and LREEs were dominantly adsorbed into root cells in the form of trivalent cations. In this study area, the BACs distribution patterns of REEs in various habitats exhibited an overall right-inclined style to different degrees, with a high biological absorption coefficient of Eu (Figure 9), indicating that *Scutellaria baicalensis* preferentially adsorbed LREEs and thus resulted in fractionation within REEs.

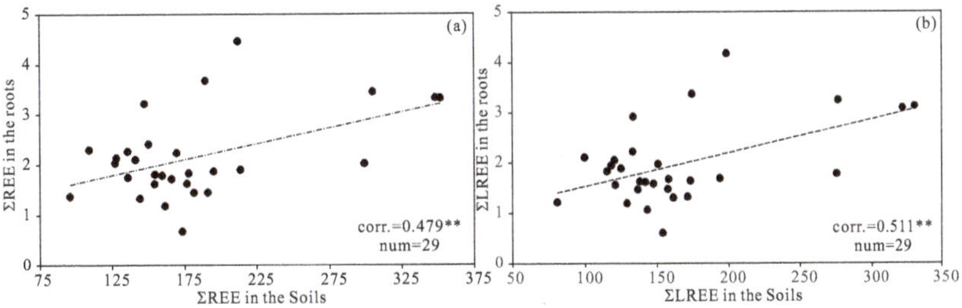

Figure 8. Scatter diagram of (**a**) ΣREE in the rhizosphere soils versus roots and (**b**) ΣLREE in the rhizosphere soils versus roots. ** $p < 0.01$.

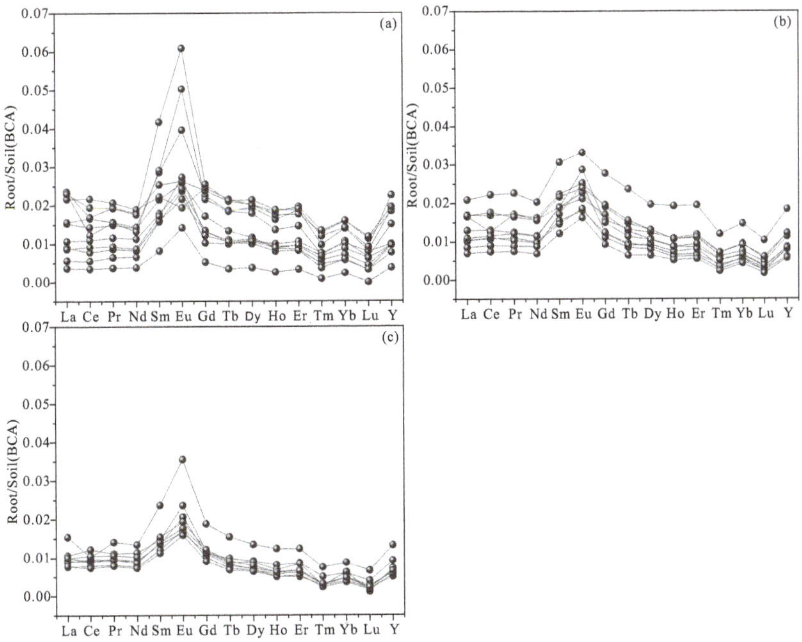

Figure 9. BACs distribution patterns of REEs in roots of *Scutellaria baicalensis*. (**a**) NGHs; (**b**) APHs; (**c**) BCHs.

5.3. Relationships between REE and Effective Constituents of Scutellaria baicalensis

Flavonoid compounds are effective constituents and secondary metabolites of *Scutellaria baicalensis*, which are controlled by the growing conditions, including illumination, temperature, moisture, and nutrients [91]. In our study area, flavonoid compounds were more abundant in NGHs than APHs and BCHs. Previous data have demonstrated that mineral nutrient elements (e.g., REE^{3+}) control the synthesis and accumulation of flavonoid compounds, either as catalysts for secondary compound metabolism [92–96], by involving in their functional structure [97–100] or by contributing to the growth of cells [101–105]. Pearson correlation analysis was applied to check out further the correlations between micronutrient elements with flavonoid compounds in the roots. The results exhibited that micronutrient elements, including REEs, Cu, Zn, Sr, Ge, and Se, had a significant positive correlation with flavonoid compounds to some extent ($p < 0.05$ or $p < 0.01$) (Figure 10), indicating that the micronutrient elements of roots have a significant influence on the medicinal composition of *Scutellaria baicalensis*.

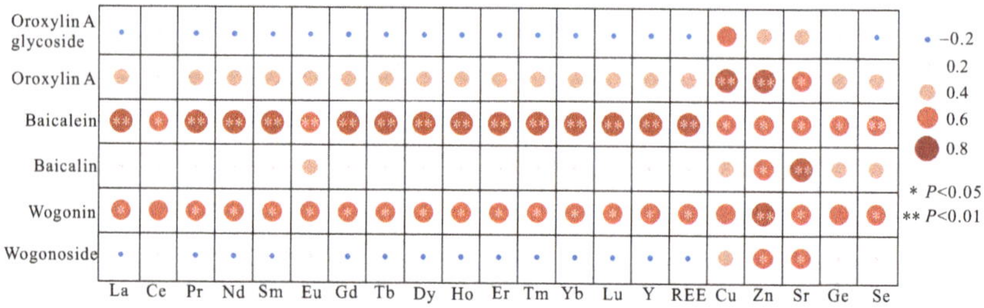

Figure 10. Pearson correlation analysis between flavonoid compounds and micronutrient elements in the roots of *Scutellaria baicalensis*.

It was widely acknowledged that the activation of endocytosis is the primary response of plant cells to REEs [10,106–108], which induces a series of physiological and biochemical responses, affecting the activation of various enzymes, substance synthesis and cell growth [104,107,109,110]. Previous studies have demonstrated that exposure to REEs can affect the absorption of mineral elements by plants [111,112]. In our study area, roots of *Scutellaria baicalensis* in NGHs contained higher micronutrient elements concentrations than BCHs and APHs, e.g., Cu, Zn, Sr, Ge and Se (Table 5). Therefore, high REEs and micronutrient elements concentrations of hornblende-gneiss favored the synthesis and accumulation of flavonoid compounds in Scutellaria baicalensis after the activation of endocytosis induced by REEs [100,113]. In addition, trivalent lanthanum (La(III)) is similar to Ca^{2+} in terms of properties and structures as mentioned above. Therefore, La(III) may substitute for Ca^{2+} and present similar effects as Ca^{2+} in biological systems [105,114,115]. For instance, La(III) may bind to Ca-binding sites in the CaM molecule by electrostatic attraction or coordination [106,116] based on the concentrations of REEs. Hence, the CAM expression level in plants and its molecular structure was therefore affected by REE concentrations, affecting the accumulation of effective constituents [117].

Table 5. Parameters on micronutrient elements distribution characteristics of roots in various habitats, Hebei Province.

Micronutrient Elements	Habitats	Median (25~75%) ($mg \cdot kg^{-1}$)	Average ($mg \cdot kg^{-1}$)	p Value
Cu	NGHs (n = 11)	11 (9.08–14.5)	12.2	0.277
	APHs (n = 10)	10.1 (7.59–11)	9.44	0.190
	BCHs (n = 8)	9.09 (6.85–11.8)	9.24	0.310
Zn	NGHs (n = 11)	15.9 (14.1–16.9)	15.3	0.806
	APHs (n = 10)	11.5 (10.53–13.2)	11.8	0.373
	BCHs (n = 8)	12.4 (11.58–17)	13.6	0.084
Sr	NGHs (n = 11)	48 (28.35–51.3)	48.3	0.039
	APHs (n = 10)	22.2 (20.8–25.7)	22.9	0.873
	BCHs (n = 8)	28.4 (22.26–34.7)	28.4	0.479
Ge	NGHs (n = 11)	1.21 (0.963–1.45)	1.28	0.004
	APHs (n = 10)	0.837 (0.777–0.995)	0.910	0.095
	BCHs (n = 8)	1.15 (0.829–1.57)	1.17	0.929
Se	NGHs (n = 11)	0.064 (0.045–0.069)	0.0592	0.818
	APHs (n = 10)	0.06 (0.045–0.063)	0.0550	0.686
	BCHs (n = 8)	0.045 (0.04–0.069)	0.0510	0.025

As mentioned above, we can conclude that parent materials significantly impact the quality of Scutellaria baicalensis in terms of micronutrient elements involving REEs. Some strategies for management of the habitats of *Scutellaria baicalensis* are as follows:

(1) Hornblende-gneiss locations were confirmed to be the natural top-geoherbs habitats of Rehe *Scutellaria baicalensis* for their relatively higher REEs and other micronutrient elements concentrations and soil property. In order to protect the chemical type of top-geoherbs, it was significant to avoid excessive digging of *Scutellaria baicalensis* to maintain their natural propagation and replacement.
(2) Luanping County and Kuancheng Kuancheng Manchu Nationality Autonomous County was also the main gneiss location in the Luanhe watershed in Chengde City. It can be considered for the large-scale cultivation of *Scutellaria baicalensis* by biomimetic cultivation.
(3) Scientific and reasonable rare earth micro-fertilizers application was optional for optimizing replanting patterns. The conventional principle that high micronutrient concentrations inhibit their absorption while low micronutrient concentrations favor their absorption should not be neglected.

6. Conclusions

This study presented the influences of parent materials on the inhabitation and quality of top-geoherb *Scutellaria baicalensis* in Chengde City, Hebei province, in terms of REEs. It was greatly significant for protecting the origin and optimizing replanting patterns of *Scutellaria baicalensis*. The migrations, enrichments, fractionations and transformations of REEs in the bedrock–regolith–soil–root continuum were studied in three habitats of *Scutellaria baicalensis* with contrasting geopedological conditions. Parent materials and soils in the hornblende-gneiss locations contained higher REE concentrations than loess locations. REE concentrations in loess soils were relatively homogeneous, while various mineral compositions and mineral grain sizes of the hornblende-gneiss resulted in the heterogeneity of REEs concentration in rhizosphere soils, with a coefficient of variation (CV) being 33.9% as weathering proceeded. Weathering, involving eluviation, leaching, absorption, etc., influenced the migrations and enrichments of REEs in weathering crust in hornblende-gneiss, and weathering productions, dominated by clay minerals and iron (hydro) oxide, controlled the fractionations within REEs. Roots of *Scutellaria baicalensis* contained similar ΣREE in NGHs (2.02 $mg \cdot kg^{-1}$) and BCHs (2.04 $mg \cdot kg^{-1}$), which are higher than that in APHs (1.78 $mg \cdot kg^{-1}$). It exhibited a remarkable positive correlation between REE concentrations in the roots and rhizosphere soils with a coefficient of 0.479 ($p < 0.01$). The biological absorption coefficients (BACs) of REEs for *Scutellaria baicalensis* decreased in the order of NGHs > APHs > BCHs. Soils developed in hornblende-gneiss were characterized by high REE concentrations, lower content of clay fraction and overall alkaline with a pH value of 8.06, favoring the inhabitation of Rehe *Scutellaria baicalensis* and adsorption for RREs. Micronutrient elements in the roots, e.g., REEs, Cu, Zn, Sr, Ge and Se, were remarkably correlated with flavonoid compound contents, suggesting their significant impact on the quality of *Scutellaria baicalensis*. The activation of endocytosis induced by REEs favored the adsorption of micronutrient elements and together improved the quality of *Scutellaria baicalensis*. Therefore, *Scutellaria baicalensis* in NGHs, featuring high REEs and other micronutrient elements concentrations, contained higher flavonoid compound content.

Author Contributions: Conceptualization, W.F. and Z.S.; methodology, Z.C. and Z.S.; software, T.A.; validation, L.X.; formal analysis, Z.S.; investigation, Z.C. and Z.S.; resources, H.Z.; data curation, L.X.; writing—original draft preparation, Z.S.; writing—review and editing, Z.S., W.F.; visualization, Z.S.; supervision, W.S. and H.Z.; project administration, Z.C. and H.Z. All authors have read and agreed to the published version of the manuscript.

Funding: This research was funded by the China Geological Survey Program (Grant No. DD20190822).

Institutional Review Board Statement: Not applicable.

Informed Consent Statement: Not applicable.

Data Availability Statement: Not applicable.

Acknowledgments: We would like to thank Wei Liu and Xiaoying Cui from Hebei Huakan Resource Environmental Survey Co., Ltd. for the test of REEs and flavonoid compounds.We thank Xia Li form China Institute of Geo-Environment Monitoring for financial support and Shoulin Zhang from Beijing Institute of Geology for Mineral Resources CO., LTD for valuable suggestions. We also thank editor and three anonymous reviewers for their valuable comments and suggestions

Conflicts of Interest: The authors declare no conflict of interest.

References

1. Hu, S. *Geoherbs in China*; Heilongjiang Science and Technology Press: Haerbin, China, 1989.
2. Xie, W. Discussion about geoherbs. *J. Tradit. Chin. Med.* **1990**, *40*, 43–46.
3. Huang, L.; Zhang, R. Biological essential about geoherbs. *Chin. Pharm. J.* **1997**, *32*, 563–566.
4. Huang, L.; Guo, L.; Ma, C.; Gao, W.; Yuan, Q. Top-geoherbs of traditional Chinese medicine: Common traits, quality characteristics and formation. *Front. Med.* **2011**, *5*, 185–194. [CrossRef] [PubMed]
5. Zhu, Y.G.; Duan, G.L.; Chen, B.D.; Peng, X.H.; Chen, Z.; Sun, G.X. Minerals Weathering and Elemental cycling in the System of Siols-microorganisms-plants. *Sci. Sin.* **2014**, *44*, 1107–1116.
6. Reimann, C.; Englmaier, P.; Fabian, K.; Gough, L.; Lamothe, P.; Smith, D. Biogeochemical plant–soil interaction: Variable element composition in leaves of four plant species collected along a south–north transect at the southern tip of Norway. *Sci. Total. Environ.* **2015**, *506*, 480–495. [CrossRef]
7. Yan, H.; Duan, J.A.; Qian, D.W.; Xiu, S.L.; Song, B.S.; He, Z.Q. Correlation Analysis and Evaluation of Inorganic Elements in Angelica sinensis and Its Correspondence Soil from Different Regions. *J. Chin. Med. Mater.* **2011**, *34*, 512–516.
8. Zhong, X.J.; Tan, Y.F. Research progress of soil factor influences on the quality of genuine medicinal materials. *J. South. Agric.* **2012**, *43*, 1708–1711.
9. Yao, Q.H.; Yan, S.A.; Zhang, B.L.; Su, H.G.; Pan, H.Y.; Lin, Q. Effects of Soil Types in Tea Garden on Distribution and Composition of Rare Earth Elements in Tieguanyin. *J. Trop. Subtrop. Bot.* **2018**, *26*, 644–650.
10. Tao, Y.; Shen, L.; Feng, C.; Qu, J.; Ju, H.; Yang, R.; Zhang, Y. Distribution of rare earth elements (REEs) and their roles in plants growth: A review. *Environ. Pollut.* **2022**, *298*, 118540. [CrossRef]
11. Qi, J.S.; Xu, H.B.; Zhou, J.Y.; Lu, X.H.; Yang, X.L.; Guan, J.H. Studies on the Amount of trace elements and Four Characteristics in Prescriptions of Chinese Medicine. *J. Anal. Sci.* **1998**, *14*, 283–287.
12. Zhang, Z.J.; Song, B. Effect Analyses on Micronutrient or REE Fertilization to Ginseng. *Liaoning Agric. Sci.* **1998**, *1*, 14–16.
13. Liu, C.E.; Ren, S.Y.; Yin, W.Y.; He, M.Y. Application Effect and Technique analyses of REE to the Eucommia ulmoides. *Hunan Agric. Sci.* **1999**, *27*, 29–31.
14. Chen, H.; Liu, H.L.; Dong, Y.Y. Study on the Relationship between Rare Earth Elements (REES)and Traditional Chinese Medicine(TCM). *Guangdong Trace Elem. Sci.* **2001**, *8*, 1–8.
15. Fu, W.; Li, X.; Feng, Y.; Feng, M.; Peng, Z.; Yu, H.; Lin, H. Chemical weathering of S-type granite and formation of rare earth element (REE)-rich regolith in South China: Critical control of lithology. *Chem. Geol.* **2019**, *520*, 33–51. [CrossRef]
16. Brantley, S.L.; Goldhaber, M.B.; Ragnarsdottir, K.V. Crossing disciplines and scales to understand the critical zone. *Elements* **2007**, *3*, 307–314. [CrossRef]
17. Hewawasam, T.; von Blanckenburg, F.; Bouchez, J.; Dixon, J.L.; Schuessler, J.A.; Maekeler, R. Slow advance of the weathering front during deep, supply-limited saprolite formation in the tropical Highlands of Sri Lanka. *Geochim. Cosmochim. Acta* **2013**, *118*, 202–230. [CrossRef]
18. Cheng, H.X.; Pei, M.; Zhao, C.D.; Hna, W.; Wang, H.Y.; Wang, Q.L.; Yang, F.; Zhang, F.G.; Wang, C.W.; Liu, F. Epigenetic geochemical dynamics and driving mechanisms of distribution patterns of chemical elements in soil, Southwest China. *Earth Sci. Front.* **2019**, *26*, 159–191.
19. Chinese Pharmacopoeia Commission. *The Pharmacopoeia of the People's Republic of China*; China Medical Science Press: Beijing, China, 2015.
20. Xie, Y.; Bi, J.H.; Peng, G.Y. Comparative Study on Detoxication between Dao-di Herb and Non Dao-di Herb of Huangqin. *Guid. J. Tradit. Chin. Med. Pharm.* **2015**, *21*, 35–38.
21. Liu, Y.; Li, L.T.; Ji, X.Q.; Kong, L.J.; Gao, Z.H.; Pang, J.; Chen, H.N.; Wang, S.M. Effect of inorganic element in soil on contents of inorganic elements and baicalin in *Scutellaria baicalensis* from different regions. *Chin. Tradit. Herb. Drugs* **2017**, *48*, 1225–1228.
22. Xin, X.J.; Li, Y.C.; Liu, G.J. Scutellaria Baicalensis Georgi Conformation Simulation Cultivation Technology In Daxing'An Mountains. *For. Sci. Technol. Inf.* **2016**, *48*, 20–21.
23. Liu, Y.Y.; Wu, P.P.; Yang, L.B.; Wang, L.M. Analysis of the Climate Characteridtics of thunderstorms in Chengde from 1973 to 2012. *Meteorol. J. Inn. Mong.* **2018**, *2*, 15–17.
24. Chen, D.; Chen, G. *Practical Geochemistry of Rare Earth Elements*; Geological Press: Beijing, China, 1990.
25. Yuan, M.; Guo, M.N.; Liu, W.S.; Liu, C.; van der Ent, A.; Morel, J.L.; Huot, H.; Zhao, W.Y.; Wei, X.G.; Qiu, R.L.; et al. The accumulation and fractionation of Rare Earth Elements in hydroponically grown Phytolacca americana L. *Plant Soil* **2017**, *421*, 67–82. [CrossRef]

26. Wang, J.; Wang, Z.H.; Geng, X.; He, F.P.; Zu, Y.C.; Wang, L. REE Biogeochemistry of Soil-Vegetation System in Dabaoshan Polymetallic Mine. *Earth Sci. J. China Univ. Geosci.* **2014**, *39*, 733–740.
27. Miao, L.; Xu, R.; Ma, Y.; Zhu, Z.; Wang, J.; Cai, R.; Chen, Y. Geochemistry and biogeochemistry of rare earth elements in a surface environment (soil and plant) in South China. *Environ. Geol.* **2008**, *56*, 225–235. [CrossRef]
28. Ryan, S.E.; Snoeck, C.; Crowley, Q.G.; Babechuk, M.G. 87Sr/86Sr and trace element mapping of geosphere-hydrosphere-biosphere interactions: A case study in Ireland. *Appl. Geochem.* **2018**, *92*, 209–224. [CrossRef]
29. Chen, D.; Zou, Z.; Ren, D. Preliminary application of plant exploration in search for Thallium mineral deposits. *Bull. Mineral. Petrol. Geochem.* **2000**, *19*, 397–400.
30. Hu, R.; Beguiristain, T.; De Junet, A.; Leyval, C. Bioavailability and transfer of elevated Sm concentration to alfalfa in spiked soils. *Environ. Sci. Pollut. Res.* **2020**, *27*, 44333–44341. [CrossRef]
31. Huang, L. *Molecular Pharmacognosy*; Peking University Medical Press: Beijing, China, 2006.
32. Xiao, Y.Q.; Jiang, Y.; Li, L.; Zhang, W.T.; Li, M.P.; Zhang, W.S. Relationship between active components in Scutellaria baicalensis and environmental factors in mountainous region of Western Beijing. *Chin. Tradit. Herb. Drugs* **2009**, *40*, 1291–1296.
33. Hu, Z.; Haneklaus, S.; Sparovek, G.; Schnug, E. Rare earth elements in soils. *Commun. Soil Sci. Plant Anal.* **2006**, *37*, 1381–1420. [CrossRef]
34. Loell, M.; Reiher, W.; Felix-Henningsen, P. Contents and bioavailability of rare earth elements in agricultural soils in Hesse (Germany). *J. Plant Nutr. Soil Sci.* **2011**, *174*, 644–654. [CrossRef]
35. Pye, K. Mineralogical and textural controls on the weathering of granitoid rocks. *Catena* **1986**, *13*, 47–57. [CrossRef]
36. Worthington, S.R.; Davies, G.J.; Alexander, E.C., Jr. Enhancement of bedrock permeability by weathering. *Earth-Sci. Rev.* **2016**, *160*, 188–202. [CrossRef]
37. Zhang, L.; Li, X.; Li, D.; Han, Z.; Zhang, G. Rare earth elements distribution and its correlation with microelements and particle-size of basalt-deriver soils in Leizhou Peninsula. *Acta Pedol. Sin.* **2011**, *48*, 1–9.
38. Brioschi, L.; Steinmann, M.; Lucot, E.; Pierret, M.C.; Stille, P.; Prunier, J.; Badot, P.M. Transfer of rare earth elements (REE) from natural soil to plant systems: Implications for the environmental availability of anthropogenic REE. *Plant Soil* **2013**, *366*, 143–163. [CrossRef]
39. Braun, J.J.; Riotte, J.; Battacharya, S.; Violette, A.; Prunier, J.; Bouvier, V.; Candaudap, F.; Maréchal, J.C.; Ruiz, L.; Panda, S.R.; et al. REY-Th-U solute dynamics in the critical zone: Combined influence of chemical weathering, atmospheric deposit leaching, and vegetation cycling (Mule Hole Watershed, South India). *Geochem. Geophys. Geosys.* **2017**, *18*, 4409–4425. [CrossRef]
40. Chang, C.; Song, C.; Beckford, H.O.; Wang, S.; Ji, H. Behaviors of REEs during pedogenetic processes in the karst areas of Southwest China. *J. Asian Earth Sci.* **2019**, *185*, 104023. [CrossRef]
41. Holdren, G.R., Jr.; Berner, R.A. Mechanism of feldspar weathering—I. Experimental studies. *Geochim. Cosmochim. Acta* **1979**, *43*, 1161–1171. [CrossRef]
42. Heckman, K.; Rasmussen, C. Lithologic controls on regolith weathering and mass flux in forested ecosystems of the southwestern USA. *Geoderma* **2011**, *164*, 99–111. [CrossRef]
43. Fu, S.Z.; Yan, C.L.; Wu, S.Q.; Yang, X.K. Content and Distribution Characteristics of Rare Earth Elements In Typical Soils Of Guizhou Province. *Acta Pedol. Sin.* **2000**, *37*, 109–115.
44. Miao, L.; Xu, R.S.; Xu, J.H. Geochemical Characteristics of Rare Earth Elements(REEs) in the Soil-Plant System in West Guangdong Province. *Acta Pedol. Sin.* **2007**, *44*, 54–62.
45. Mihajlovic, J.; Bauriegel, A.; St'ark, H.J.; Roßkopf, N.; Zeitz, J.; Milbert, G.; Rinklebe, J. Rare earth elements in soil profiles of various ecosystems across Germany. *Appl. Geochem.* **2019**, *102*, 197–217. [CrossRef]
46. Coppin, F.; Berger, G.; Bauer, A.; Castet, S.; Loubet, M. Sorption of lanthanides on smectite and kaolinite. *Chem. Geol.* **2002**, *182*, 57–68. [CrossRef]
47. Tertre, E.; Berger, G.; Simoni, E.; Castet, S.; Giffaut, E.; Loubet, M.; Catalette, H. Europium retention onto clay minerals from 25 to 150 C: Experimental measurements, spectroscopic features and sorption modelling. *Geochim. Cosmochim. Acta* **2006**, *70*, 4563–4578. [CrossRef]
48. Galán, E.; Fernández-Caliani, J.; Miras, A.; Aparicio, P.; Márquez, M. Residence and fractionation of rare earth elements during kaolinization of alkaline peraluminous granites in NW Spain. *Clay Miner.* **2007**, *42*, 341–352. [CrossRef]
49. Borst, A.M.; Smith, M.P.; Finch, A.A.; Estrade, G.; Villanova-de Benavent, C.; Nason, P.; Marquis, E.; Horsburgh, N.J.; Goodenough, K.M.; Xu, C.; et al. Adsorption of rare earth elements in regolith-hosted clay deposits. *Nat. Commun.* **2020**, *11*, 4386. [CrossRef]
50. Andrade, G.R.P.; Cuadros, J.; Barbosa, J.M.P.; Vidal-Torrado, P. Clay minerals control rare earth elements (REE) fractionation in Brazilian mangrove soils. *Catena* **2022**, *209*, 105855. [CrossRef]
51. Land, M.; Òhlander, B.; Ingri, J.; Thunberg, J. Solid speciation and fractionation of rare earth elements in a spodosol profile from northern Sweden as revealed by sequential extraction. *Chem. Geol.* **1999**, *160*, 121–138. [CrossRef]
52. Laveuf, C.; Cornu, S. A review on the potentiality of rare earth elements to trace pedogenetic processes. *Geoderma* **2009**, *154*, 1–12. [CrossRef]
53. Steinmann, M.; Stille, P. Rare earth element behavior and Pb, Sr, Nd isotope systematics in a heavy metal contaminated soil. *Appl. Geochem.* **1997**, *12*, 607–623. [CrossRef]

54. Granados-Correa, F.; Vilchis-Granados, J.; Jiménez-Reyes, M.; Quiroz-Granados, L. Adsorption behaviour of La (III) and Eu (III) ions from aqueous solutions by hydroxyapatite: Kinetic, isotherm, and thermodynamic studies. *J. Chem.* **2013**, *2013*, 751696. [CrossRef]
55. Yusoff, Z.M.; Ngwenya, B.T.; Parsons, I. Mobility and fractionation of REEs during deep weathering of geochemically contrasting granites in a tropical setting, Malaysia. *Chem. Geol.* **2013**, *349*, 71–86. [CrossRef]
56. Yang, M.; Liang, X.; Ma, L.; Huang, J.; He, H.; Zhu, J. Adsorption of REEs on kaolinite and halloysite: A link to the REE distribution on clays in the weathering crust of granite. *Chem. Geol.* **2019**, *525*, 210–217. [CrossRef]
57. Jin, P.P.; Ou, C.H.; Ma, Z.G.; Li, D.; Ren, Y.J.; Zhao, Y.F. Evolution of montmorillonite and its related clay minerals and their effects on shale gas development. *Geophys. Prospect. Pet.* **2018**, *57*, 344–355.
58. Alshameri, A.; He, H.; Xin, C.; Zhu, J.; Wei, X.; Zhu, R.; Wang, H. Understanding the role of natural clay minerals as effective adsorbents and alternative source of rare earth elements: Adsorption operative parameters. *Hydrometallurgy* **2019**, *185*, 149–161. [CrossRef]
59. Zhang, Y.; Changan, L.; Xiong, D.; Zhou, Y.; Sun, X. Oxide geochemical characteristics and paleoclimate records of "Wushan loess". *Geol. China* **2013**, *40*, 352–360.
60. Cui, Y.; Luo, C.G.; Xu, L.; Zhang, H.; Deng, M.G.; Gu, H.N.; Meng, Y.; Qin, C.J.; Wen, H.J. Weathering Origin and Enrichment of Lithium in Clay Rocks of the Jiujialu Formation, Central Guizhou Province, Southwest China. *Bull. Mineral. Geochem.* **2018**, *37*, 696–704.
61. Quinn, K.A.; Byrne, R.H.; Schijf, J. Sorption of yttrium and rare earth elements by amorphous ferric hydroxide: Influence of pH and ionic strength. *Mar. Chem.* **2006**, *99*, 128–150. [CrossRef]
62. Huang, J.; Tan, W.; Liang, X.; He, H.; Ma, L.; Bao, Z.; Zhu, J. REE fractionation controlled by REE speciation during formation of the Renju regolith-hosted REE deposits in Guangdong Province, South China. *Ore Geol. Rev.* **2021**, *134*, 104172. [CrossRef]
63. Lee, Y.; Park, E.; Kim, W.; Choi, Y.; Park, J. A case of pelvic paragonimiasis combined with myoma uteri and pelvic inflammatory disease. *Korean J. Parasitol.* **1993**, *31*, 295–297. [CrossRef]
64. Takahashi, Y.; Minai, Y.; Ambe, S.; Makide, Y.; Ambe, F.; Tominaga, T. Simultaneous determination of stability constants of humate complexes with various metal ions using multitracer technique. *Sci. Total Environ.* **1997**, *198*, 61–71. [CrossRef]
65. Luo, Y.R.; Byrne, R.H. Carbonate complexation of yttrium and the rare earth elements in natural waters. *Geochim. Cosmochim. Acta* **2004**, *68*, 691–699. [CrossRef]
66. Sonke, J.E.; Salters, V.J. Lanthanide–humic substances complexation. I. Experimental evidence for a lanthanide contraction effect. *Geochim. Cosmochim. Acta* **2006**, *70*, 1495–1506. [CrossRef]
67. Zhao, Z.Z.; Xu, D.R.; Bi, H.; Tang, S.X. Vertical Distribution Pattern of REE Contents in Latosol in The Eastern Areas of Hainan Island. *Geotecton. Metallog.* **2006**, *30*, 401–407.
68. Pourret, O.; Davranche, M.; Gruau, G.; Dia, A. Competition between humic acid and carbonates for rare earth elements complexation. *J. Colloid Interface Sci.* **2007**, *305*, 25–31. [CrossRef]
69. Wan, Y.; Liu, C. The effect of humic acid on the adsorption of REEs on kaolin. *Colloids Surf. A Physicochem. Eng. Asp.* **2006**, *290*, 112–117. [CrossRef]
70. Li, Z. Study on Herbal Textual Research and Distribution and Change of Authentic Region of Huang Qin. Ph.D. Thesis, China Academy of Chinese Medical Sciences, Beijing, China, 2010.
71. Wyttenbach, A.; Furrer, V.; Schleppi, P.; Tobler, L. Rare earth elements in soil and in soil-grown plants. *Plant Soil* **1998**, *199*, 267–273. [CrossRef]
72. Ozaki, T.; Enomoto, S. Uptake of rare earth elements by Dryopteris erythrosora (autumn fern). *Riken Rev.* **2001**, *1*, 84–87.
73. Cao, X.; Ding, Z.; Hu, X.; Wang, X. Effects of soil pH value on the bioavailability and fractionation of rare earth elements in wheat seedling (Triticum aestivum L.). *Huanjing Kexue* **2002**, *23*, 97–102.
74. Tyler, G. Rare earth elements in soil and plant systems-A review. *Plant Soil* **2004**, *267*, 191–206. [CrossRef]
75. Semhi, K.; Chaudhuri, S.; Clauer, N. Fractionation of rare-earth elements in plants during experimental growth in varied clay substrates. *Appl. Geochem.* **2009**, *24*, 447–453. [CrossRef]
76. Gao, A.G.; Chen, Z.H.; Liu, Y.G.; Sun, H.Q.; Yang, S.Y. REE geochemical characteristics of surficial sediments in chukchi sea. *Sci. China Ser. D* **2003**, *33*, 148–154.
77. Jones, D. Trivalent metal (Cr, Y, Rh, La, Pr, Gd) sorption in two acid soils and its consequences for bioremediation. *Eur. J. Soil Sci.* **1997**, *48*, 697–702. [CrossRef]
78. Iyengar, S.; Martens, D.; Miller, W. Distribution and plant availability of soil zinc fractions. *Soil Sci. Soc. Am. J.* **1981**, *45*, 735–739. [CrossRef]
79. LeClaire, J.P.; Chang, A.; Levesque, C.; Sposito, G. Trace Metal Chemistry in Arid-Zone Field Soils Amended with Sewage Sludge: IV. Correlations between Zinc Uptake and Extracted Soil Zinc Fractions. *Soil Sci. Soc. Am. J.* **1984**, *48*, 509–513. [CrossRef]
80. Sims, J.T. Soil pH effects on the distribution and plant availability of manganese, copper, and zinc. *Soil Sci. Soc. Am. J.* **1986**, *50*, 367–373. [CrossRef]
81. Zhu, W.H.; Yang, Y.G.; Bi, H.; Liu, Q. Progress in Geochemical Research of Rare Earth Element in Soils. *Bull. Mineral. Petrol. Geochem.* **2003**, *23*, 259–264.
82. Ji, H.B.; Wang, L.J.; Dong, Y.S.; Wang, S.J.; Luo, J.M.; Sun, Y.Y. An Overview on the Study of Biogeochemical Cycle for Rare Earth Elements(REEs). *Prog. Geogr.* **2004**, *23*, 51–61.

83. Pang, X.; Xing, X.Y.; Wang, D.H.; Pei, A. Change of Rare-Earth Elements (REEs) Forms Using Them as Fertilizers. *Agro-Environ. Prot.* **2001**, *20*, 319–321.
84. Wang, X.; Liu, D. Integration of cerium chemical forms and subcellular distribution to understand cerium tolerance mechanism in the rice seedlings. *Environ. Sci. Pollut. Res.* **2017**, *24*, 16336–16343. [CrossRef]
85. Ding, S.; Liang, T.; Yan, J.; Zhang, Z.; Huang, Z.; Xie, Y. Fractionations of rare earth elements in plants and their conceptive model. *Sci. China Ser. C Life Sci.* **2007**, *50*, 47–55. [CrossRef]
86. Wang, L.F. Studies on the Photosynthetic Characterizations and Distributions of Rear Earth Elements in Fern Dicranopteris Dichotoma. Ph.D. Thesis, Institute of Botany, Chinese Academy of Sciences, Beijing, China, 2005.
87. Liang, M.X.; Chen, Z.B.; Chen, Z.Q.; Ren, T.J.; Qu, X. Effects of Vegetation Restoration on REEs Migration and Control in Red Soil Erosion Area in Southern China. *Chin. Rare Earths* **2022**, *43*, 64–72.
88. Shan, X.; Wang, H.; Zhang, S.; Zhou, H.; Zheng, Y.; Yu, H.; Wen, B. Accumulation and uptake of light rare earth elements in a hyperaccumulator Dicropteris dichotoma. *Plant Sci.* **2003**, *165*, 1343–1353. [CrossRef]
89. Chen, Z.; Chen, Z.; Bai, L. Rare earth element migration in gullies with different Dicranopteris dichotoma covers in the Huangnikeng gully group, Changting County, Southeast China. *Chemosphere* **2016**, *164*, 443–450. [CrossRef] [PubMed]
90. Khan, A.M.; Yusoff, I.; Abu Bakar, N.K.; Abu Bakar, A.F.; Alias, Y.; Mispan, M.S. Accumulation, Uptake and Bioavailability of Rare Earth Elements (Rees) in Soil Grown Plants from Ex-Mining Area in Perak, Malaysia. *Appl. Ecol. Environ. Res.* **2017**, *15*, 117–133. [CrossRef]
91. Yuan, Y.; Huang, H.L.; Liu, X.W. Influences of inorganic fertilizer on the effective constituent content. *Jiangxi For. Sci. Technol.* **2000**, *2*, 29–30.
92. Zhou, C.Z. Taxonomy and Systematic Research of Asarum Plants and Genuine Medicine. Ph.D. Thesis, Beijing University of Chinese Medicine, Beijing, China, 1994.
93. Lei, W.; Shui, X.; Zhou, Y.; Tang, S.; Sun, M. Effects of praseodymium on flavonoids production and its biochemical mechanism of Scutellaria viscidula hairy roots in vitro. *Pak. J. Bot.* **2011**, *43*, 2387–2390.
94. Zhou, J.; Fang, L.; Li, X.; Guo, L.; Huang, L. Jasmonic acid (JA) acts as a signal molecule in LaCl3-induced baicalin synthesis in Scutellaria baicalensis seedlings. *Biol. Trace Elem. Res.* **2012**, *148*, 392–395. [CrossRef]
95. Zhang, J.; Zhang, Y.; Jia, X.Y.; Sun, B.X.; Zhang, R.R.; Ma, C.G.; Liang, J.P. Nutrient uptake rules of *Polygala tenuifolia* and its relationship with accumulation of bioactive components. *J. Plant Nutr. Fertil.* **2019**, *25*, 1230–1238.
96. Fang, Y.M.; Cui, M.Y.; Liu, J.; Pei, T.L.; Wei, Y.K.; Zhao, Q. Study advance in biosynthesis of flavone from Scutellaria. *China J. Chin. Mater. Med.* **2020**, *43*, 4819–4826.
97. Guo, M.; Wu, Z.L.; Wang, C.G.; Gao, X.Y. Synthesis and anti-tumor activity of baicalin-metal complex. *Acta Pharm. Sin.* **2014**, *49*, 337–345.
98. Wang, Z.L.; Wang, S.; Kuang, Y.; Hu, Z.M.; Qiao, X.; Ye, M. A comprehensive review on phytochemistry, pharmacology, and flavonoid biosynthesis of *Scutellaria baicalensis*. *Pharm. Biol.* **2018**, *56*, 465–484. [CrossRef]
99. Sun, H.Y.; Sun, X.M.; Jia, F.C.; Wang, Y.L.; Li, D.J.; Li, J. The eco-geochemical characteristics of germanium and its relationship with the genuine medicinal material Scutellaria baicalensis in Chengde, Hebei Province. *Geol. China* **2020**, *47*, 1646–1667.
100. Bai, Y.C.; Wei, X.F.; Chen, L.; Wan, R.M.; Hou, Z.X. Multivariate Analysis of Fruit Leaf Mineral Elements, Soil Fertility Factors and Fruit Quality of Vaccinium uliginosum L. *Sci. Agric. Sin.* **2018**, *51*, 170–181.
101. Guo, B.S. Recent Research Advance of Rare Earth in the Field of Biology. *Chin. Rare Earths* **1999**, *20*, 64–68.
102. Hong, F.S.; Fang, N.H.; Gu, Y.H.; Zhao, G.W. Effect of Cerium Nitrate on Seed Vigor and Activitiesof Enzymes during Germination of Rice. *Chin. Rare Earths* **1999**, *20*, 45–47.
103. Jiang, L.; Zhang, W.C.; Wei, Z.L. Effects of micronutrient elements on cell growth and formation of flavonol glycosides of ginkgo callus. *Hubei Agric. Sci.* **1999**, *38*, 45–47.
104. Yuan, X.F.; Wang, Q.; Zhao, B.; Wang, Y.C. Promotion of Cell Growth and Flavonoids Production in Saussurea medusa Cell Suspension Cultures by Rare Earth Elements. *Chin. J. Process. Eng.* **2004**, *4*, 325–329.
105. Wang, J.N.; Huang, Y.H.; Mou, Z.M.; Wang, Y.W. Research Progress on Flavonoid of the Plant Secondary Metabolites. *Sci. Seric.* **2007**, *33*, 499–505.
106. Wang, L.; Cheng, M.; Chu, Y.; Li, X.; Chen, D.D.; Huang, X.; Zhou, Q. Responses of plant calmodulin to endocytosis induced by rare earth elements. *Chemosphere* **2016**, *154*, 408–415. [CrossRef]
107. Wang, L.; Li, J.; Zhou, Q.; Yang, G.; Ding, X.L.; Li, X.; Cai, C.X.; Zhang, Z.; Wei, H.Y.; Lu, T.H.; et al. Rare earth elements activate endocytosis in plant cells. *Proc. Natl. Acad. Sci. USA* **2014**, *111*, 12936–12941. [CrossRef]
108. Ben, Y.; Cheng, M.; Wang, L.; Zhou, Q.; Yang, Z.; Huang, X. Low-dose lanthanum activates endocytosis, aggravating accumulation of lanthanum or/and lead and disrupting homeostasis of essential elements in the leaf cells of four edible plants. *Ecotoxicol. Environ. Saf.* **2021**, *221*, 112429. [CrossRef] [PubMed]
109. Ge, Z.Q.; Li, J.C.; Yuan, Y.J.; Hu, Z.D. Effects of Ce (4+) on DNA Content and PAL Activity of Cell in Suspension Culture of Taxus Chinensis Var.Mairei. *Chin. Rare Earths* **2000**, *21*, 35–37.
110. Fang, Y.; Lv, W.M.; Hu, D.D.; Min, S.Z.; Cao, Z.Q. Interactions between baicalein and La(III), Nd(III), Sm(III), Yb(III) and Y(III). *J. Shaanxi Norm. Univ. (Nat. Sci. Ed.)* **1993**, *21*, 44–48.
111. Hu, Z.; Richter, H.; Sparovek, G.; Schnug, E. Physiological and biochemical effects of rare earth elements on plants and their agricultural significance: A review. *J. Plant Nutr.* **2004**, *27*, 183–220. [CrossRef]

112. Liu, Y.; Yang, Q.; Zhu, M.; Wang, L.; Zhou, Q.; Yang, Z.; Huang, X. Endocytosis in microcystis aeruginosa accelerates the synthesis of microcystins in the presence of lanthanum (III). *Harmful Algae* **2020**, *93*, 101791. [CrossRef]
113. Tang, L.; Lin, J.H.; Nian, G.X.; Li, Y.M.; Lin, Y.L.; Wang, S.; Liu, D.H. Effects of Cu, Zn and Se on contents of total flavonlid, chlorogenic acid and Se in the flower of Chrysanthemum morifolium Ramat. *Plant Nutr. Fertil. Sci.* **2009**, *15*, 1475–1480.
114. Yang, S.H.; Liu, X.F.; Guo, D.A.; Zheng, J.H. Effect of Rare-earth Element Eu (3+) on Callus Growth and Flavonoids Content in *Glycyrrhiza uralensis*. *J. Chin. Med. Mater.* **2005**, *28*, 533–534.
115. Ynag, S.H.; Liu, X.F.; Guo, D.A.; Zheng, J.H. Effects of Different Additives on Accumulation of Flavonoids in *Glycyrrhiza uralensis* Callus. *Chin. Pharm. J.* **2006**, *41*, 96–99.
116. Wang, L.; Lu, A.; Lu, T.; Ding, X.; Huang, X. Interaction between lanthanum ion and horseradish peroxidase in vitro. *Biochimie* **2010**, *92*, 41–50. [CrossRef]
117. Batistič, O.; Kudla, J. Analysis of calcium signaling pathways in plants. *Biochim. Biophys. Acta (BBA) Gen. Subj.* **2012**, *1820*, 1283–1293. [CrossRef]

applied sciences

MDPI

Article

Elemental Abundances of Moon Samples Based on Statistical Distributions of Analytical Data

Zhiguan Hou [1], Qingjie Gong [1,*], Ningqiang Liu [1], Biao Jiang [2,*], Jie Li [1], Yuan Wu [1], Jiaxin Huang [1] and Weixuan Gu [1]

1 School of Earth Sciences and Resources, China University of Geosciences, Beijing 100083, China
2 Institute of Mineral Resources, Chinese Academy of Geological Sciences, Beijing 100037, China
* Correspondence: qjiegong@cugb.edu.cn (Q.G.); jiangbiao334223@163.com (B.J.)

Abstract: The successful return of Chang'E-5 (CE5) samples urges the hot topic of the study of the Moon in geochemistry. The elemental data of the analyzed moon samples reported in the literature were collected to determine the elemental abundances in moon samples. Based on 2365 analytical records of moon samples from ten missions of Apollo, Luna, and CE5, elemental abundances of 11 major oxides including Cr_2O_3, 50 trace elements including Ti, P, Mn, Cr, and 15 rare earth elements (REEs) including Y are derived based on statistical distributions of normal, log-normal, and additive log-ratio transformation, respectively. According to the value of 13.5% CaO content, moon samples are classified into two types, as low-Ca and high-Ca samples, whose elemental abundances are also calculated respectively based on the methods used in the total moon samples. With respect to the mid-ocean ridge basalt (MORB) of the Earth, moon samples (including the Moon, low-Ca, and high-Ca samples) are rich in Cr, REEs, Th, U, Pb, Zr, Hf, Cs, Ba, W, and Be and poor in Na, V, Cu, and Zn in terms of their concentrations, and are enriched in Cr and depleted in Na, K, Rb, P, V, Cu, Zn in spider diagrams. The CE5 sample is a low-Ca type of moon sample and is clearly rich in Ti, Fe, Mn, P, Sc, REEs, Th, U, Nb, Ta, Zr, Hf, Sr, Ba, W, and Be and poor in Mg, Al, Cr, and Ni in terms of their concentrations relative to the moon or the low-Ca samples. If compared with the moon sample, the CE5 sample is also clearly rich in K, REE, and P.

Keywords: lunar samples; CE5; low-Ca; high-Ca; spider diagram

Citation: Hou, Z.; Gong, Q.; Liu, N.; Jiang, B.; Li, J.; Wu, Y.; Huang, J.; Gu, W. Elemental Abundances of Moon Samples Based on Statistical Distributions of Analytical Data. *Appl. Sci.* **2023**, *13*, 360. https://doi.org/10.3390/app13010360

Academic Editors: Dibyendu Sarkar and Andrea L. Rizzo

Received: 30 November 2022
Revised: 22 December 2022
Accepted: 25 December 2022
Published: 27 December 2022

1. Introduction

The successful return of Chang'E-5 (CE5) has marked China as the third country to retrieve moon samples after the United States and the former Soviet Union. Studies on the returned samples have been an interesting and hot topic in geochemistry recently [1–11]. Elemental abundance is a basic topic in geochemistry, such as in the Earth [12–16]; therefore, the elemental composition of CE5 samples and moon samples from the Apollo and Luna missions is very attractive to geochemists.

On the elemental compositions of moon samples, Rose et al. [17–21] proposed the compositions from the Apollo missions. Samples in each Apollo mission were divided into the types of soil and rock, and the average elemental concentrations were used to represent their compositions. However, the analyzed samples or sample count from each mission was mostly less than 30, and items of major oxides, trace elements, and rare earth elements (REEs) were limited, such as 11 major oxides (including Cr_2O_3), 14 trace elements, and 3 REEs (Table 1). In addition, Taylor et al. [22] proposed a set of average elemental compositions in the lunar highland, including 8 major oxides (lack of P_2O_5 and MnO), 16 trace elements, and 14 REEs based on 4 samples from Apollo 17 and 6 samples from Apollo 16 (Table 1). Korotev [23] proposed the compositions of Apollo 16 soils, including 8 major oxides, 12 trace elements, and 8 REEs based on 8 sampling stations with 2~6 samples in each station (Table 1). Warren and Taylor [24] proposed the compositions of mare basalts and highland regolith on the Moon. The compositions of mare basalts include 8 major oxides, 10 trace elements, and 5 REEs derived from the elemental averages of mare basalts from all the Apollo and Luna missions except Apollo 16 and Luna 20. The sample count of the mare basalts is less than 200 from the Apollo missions and less than 20 from the Luna missions. The compositions of highland regolith, including 9 major oxides (lack of P_2O_5), 12 trace elements, and 9 REEs, were derived based on the statistical average of soils from Apollo 16, 2 regolith breccias from Apollo 14, and 7 lunar meteorites (Table 1). Although the elemental data from CE5 samples have been reported recently [1–3,5–7], the elemental compositions or abundances of moon samples are incomplete, which were derived based on only a few analytical samples with limited items (Table 1).

Table 1. Sample counts and element counts of analyzed moon samples.

References	Rose et al. [17–21]	Taylor et al. [22]	Korotev [23]	Warren and Taylor [24]	
Samples	**Apollo Missions**	**Lunar Highland**	**Apollo 16 Soils**	**Mare Basalts**	**Highland Regolith**
Counts of samples/records	<30	10	<50	<220	10
Counts of major oxides	11	8	8	8	9
Counts of trace elements	14	16	12	10	12
Counts of rare earth elements	3	14	8	5	9

In this paper, the analytical data reported in the literature on moon samples from Apollo, Luna, and CE5 missions were compiled firstly. Then the elemental abundances of moon samples were derived based on statistical distributions of the analytical data. Thirdly, the moon samples were classified into two types according to their concentrations of CaO, and the elemental abundances of each type were also calculated. Finally, the elemental compositions of CE5 samples were compared with the newly derived elemental abundances of moon samples.

2. Samples and Analytical Methods

2.1. Samples

The exploration and research of the Moon have been launched since 1957 [25]. In 1969, the Apollo 11 mission realized a manned moon landing and retrieved moon samples, which shifted the research on the Moon from theoretical conception to practical analysis [26–31]. Then in 1970, Luna 16 realized an unmanned moon landing sampling [32–34]. In 2020, Chang'E-5 (CE5) brought back moon samples [35]. So far, humans have retrieved moon samples 10 times, including 6 Apollo missions, 3 Luna missions, and the Chang'E-5 mission (Figure 1). The uppermost few meters of the Moon's crust, from which all the moon samples came, is a layer of loose, highly porous regolith or moon soil [24]. Samples from the Apollo missions contain lumps of rocks, breccias, surface soils, and core soils. The Apollo missions brought back a total of 380.95 kg of samples (Table 2), of which rock and breccia samples were picked up by the astronauts on the surface, and soil samples were mainly extracted by the surface scoop and deep drilling core, with a depth of 2 to 3 m. The Luna missions brought back a total of 0.301 kg of samples (Table 2). The sampling method was mechanical core drilling with a depth of 0.2 to 1.6 m. As for the CE5 mission, it brought back a total of 1.731 kg of lunar samples [1–3,5–7]. The sampling methods were mechanical shovel sampling and drilling sampling, but the drilling samples have not been analyzed or reported until now.

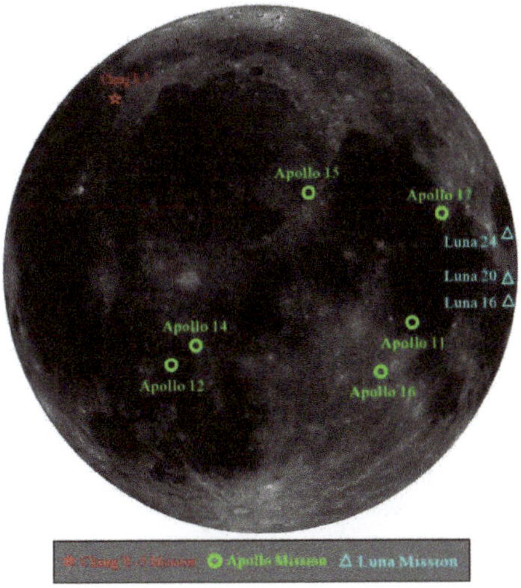

Figure 1. The landing sites of Apollo, Luna, and Chang'E-5 missions.

Table 2. The counts of analyzed records collected in this paper from each mission with other information.

Mission	Longitude	Latitude	Counts of Samples	Weight of Samples (kg)
Apollo 11	23.47297	0.67408	183	21.55
Apollo 12	−23.42157	−3.01239	218	34.30
Apollo 14	−17.47136	−3.6453	272	42.80
Apollo 15	3.63386	26.13222	364	76.70
Apollo 16	15.49812	−8.97301	685	95.20
Apollo 17	30.77168	20.1908	476	110.40
Luna 16	56.3	−0.68	33	0.101
Luna 20	56.5	3.57	34	0.030
Luna 24	62.2	12.75	67	0.170
Chang'E-5	−51.916	43.058	33	1.731
Sum	-	-	2365	382.982

2.2. Analytical Methods

The Apollo samples were first analyzed by the Lunar Sample Preliminary Examination Team of NASA. It reported a few samples' composition data, including major oxides and some trace elements without REEs for each mission [26–31]. Later, other experts and scholars applied to NASA for samples, of which the analytical composition data have been reported one after another [17–21,36,37]. The samples from the Luna missions were first analyzed and tested by the former Soviet Union [32–34]. Then after exchanging with the United States, the composition data was also analyzed and reported [32–34,38–40]. The composition data of CE5 samples have been analyzed and reported only recently [1–3,5–7].

The main analytical methods used to determine the composition data of moon samples are X-ray fluorescence spectrometry (XRF), inductively coupled plasma mass spectrometry (ICP-MS), instrumental neutron activation analysis (INNA), and electron microprobe analysis (EPMA), which can analyze many items such as major oxides, some trace elements, and/or REEs simultaneously [17,36–38]. In addition, other analytical methods such as isotope dilution analyses (IDA), emission spectrography (ES), and radiochemical neutron activation (RCNA) were adopted to analyze the composition of Rb, Sr, Zr, Re, Au, etc. [41–43]. The analytical quality, such as the detection limits, precisions, accuracies, relative errors, and relative standard deviations, were illustrated in the original literature. In general, the relative errors were less than 5% for major oxides and 10% for trace elements, including REEs.

All the analytical data collected in this paper are from moon samples brought back from the Apollo, Luna, and CE5 missions (excluding meteorites found on the Earth) and have been reported in the literature. The analyzed samples are soils, breccias, and rocks, and the counts of analytical samples (or records) in each mission or landing site are listed in Table 2. There are 2365 records of analytical data of moon samples used in this paper in total.

3. Statistical Methods and Results

3.1. Elemental Abundances in Moon Samples

In order to calculate the elemental abundances in moon samples, a total of 2365 records of analytical data were used with equal weight, ignoring the different missions or landing sites, sample types, and analytical methods from the literature.

According to the rule of "The contents of major oxides commonly obey normal distribution", the average of the analytical data excluding outliers was calculated as the abundance for each major oxide here. Firstly, the average (Avg) and standard deviation (Std) of each oxide's data were calculated for all the samples (the count of samples is labeled as n_0). Then, the boundary values of Avg $\pm$ 3Std were used to delete the outliers repeatedly until no outlier data were found. Finally, the average of each oxide's data without outliers (the count of samples is labeled as n) was calculated and viewed as its abundance. The abundances of 11 major oxides (including Cr_2O_3) along with counts of samples (n_0 and n) are listed in Table 3, and statistical histograms of major oxides are illustrated in Figure 2. The sum of the 11 major oxides (or Total in Table 2) is 99.10%, which is close to the closure value of 100%.

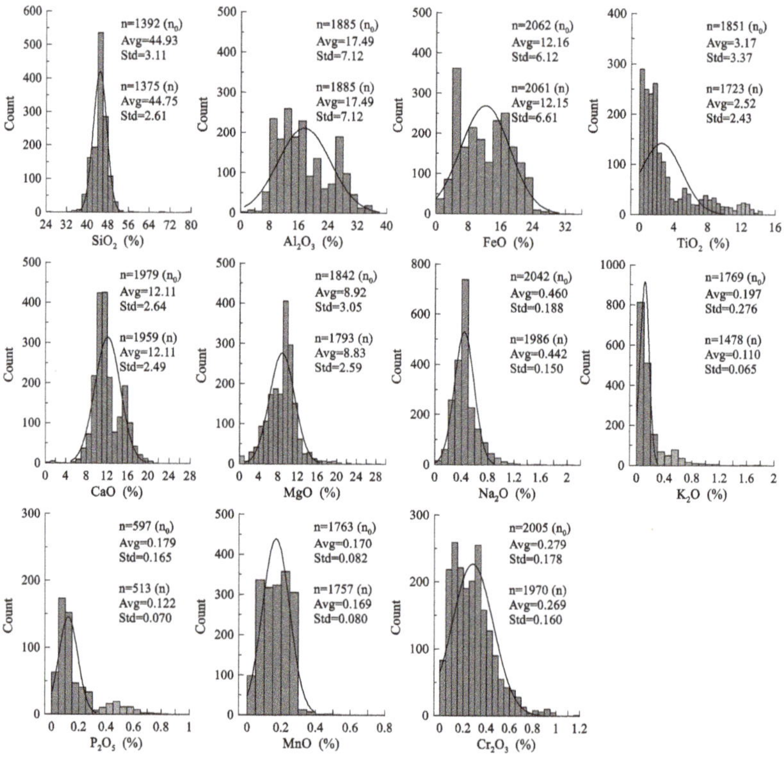

Figure 2. Histograms of major oxides with their counts of samples (n_0 is the count of total analytical data and n is the count of analytical data without outliers). The histogram of K_2O contents is drawn without the three highest values of 5.8, 3.2, and 3.1, and the histogram of P_2O_5 contents is without the two highest values of 1.38 and 1.1.

Table 3. Elemental abundances in moon samples with their counts of samples (n_0 and n).

Oxides/	Moon			Low-Ca			High-Ca			CE5
Elements	Abundance	n_0	n	Abundance	n_0	n	Abundance	n_0	n	Abundance
SiO_2	44.89	1392	1375	44.78	1029	1015	45	346	327	41.51
Al_2O_3	17.49	1885	1885	14.17	1379	1377	27.66	466	447	10.93
FeO	12.15	2062	2061	14.59	1456	1454	4.98	511	464	22.7
TiO_2	2.52	1851	1723	3.98	1383	1379	0.431	444	419	5.43
CaO	12.11	1979	1959	10.93	1468	1440	15.69	511	493	11.36
MgO	8.83	1842	1793	9.77	1359	1302	5.75	462	461	6.21
Na_2O	0.443	2040	1984	0.449	1452	1422	0.458	509	485	0.434
K_2O	0.11	1769	1478	0.171	1277	1181	0.088	409	393	0.175
P_2O_5	0.123	596	512	0.18	476	461	0.106	120	120	0.248
MnO	0.169	1763	1757	0.194	1347	1341	0.061	362	336	0.285
Cr_2O_3	0.269	2012	1974	0.316	1384	1364	0.095	458	445	0.199
Total	99.1	-	-	99.53	-	-	100.32	-	-	99.49
Ag	5.1	112	112	11.1	38	38	12	1	1	-
As	0.054	79	79	0.057	52	52	0.027	14	14	-
Au	3.91	572	528	4.24	366	347	4.46	87	87	8.8
B	3.88	20	19	3.42	19	18	39	1	1	-
Ba	162	1488	1466	202	962	957	106	307	297	388
Be	1.35	186	185	2.03	86	85	1.06	22	22	2.84
Bi	0.0006	95	93	0.0167	5	5	-	0	0	-
Br	0.076	84	84	0.065	38	38	0.09	9	9	-
Cd	12.4	145	144	59.9	32	32	7.2	21	21	-
Cl	13.5	78	78	12	52	52	22.7	13	13	-
Co	32.2	1675	1608	35.1	1096	1062	25.4	322	322	37.7
Cr	1546	1970	1933	2046	1384	1354	607	429	429	1359
Cs	0.136	583	579	0.242	247	247	0.118	152	152	0.205
Cu	9.45	448	437	9.5	238	229	4.77	83	83	12.2
F	67	48	48	86	37	37	29.2	11	11	-
Ga	4.59	613	574	5.55	384	357	3.42	100	100	5.79
Ge	0.08	181	181	0.087	75	75	0.219	15	15	-
Hf	5.5	1401	1372	6.84	960	954	2.95	248	248	13.8
In	0.0054	159	159	0.0081	40	40	0.0043	14	14	-
Ir	8.1	602	559	8.6	367	359	10.2	116	116	3.61
Li	9.5	347	340	12.3	174	174	6.24	65	65	15.4
Mn	1167	1761	1734	1441	1347	1325	490	341	320	2205
Mo	0.119	89	85	0.239	23	23	0.014	2	2	0.033
Nb	12.2	545	537	15.7	333	332	6.67	96	96	35.6
Ni	213	1413	1323	208	837	806	288	330	329	139
Os	1.67	103	103	15.7	12	12	7.5	1	1	-
P	267	840	840	626	476	476	395	115	115	1080
Pb	1.42	215	211	2.44	81	80	2.08	47	47	1.89
Pd	3.53	136	136	7.3	44	44	2.9	2	2	-
Pt	9.3	13	13	9.4	12	12	9	1	1	-
Rb	2.92	854	845	4.34	447	447	1.97	142	139	5.63
Re	0.167	124	124	0.464	30	30	2.31	2	2	-
Rh	16.7	2	2	16.7	2	2	-	0	0	-
Ru	13.7	29	28	10.1	19	18	23.7	10	10	-
S	819	248	235	881	193	189	592	46	45	-
Sb	0.0054	182	182	0.068	25	25	0.0079	16	16	-
Sc	25.6	1613	1600	36.1	1039	1035	8.3	347	334	63.5
Se	0.068	146	142	0.346	32	32	0.204	7	7	-
Sn	0.497	79	79	0.361	23	23	0.074	21	21	-
Sr	150	1337	1305	148	871	857	165	264	261	309
Ta	0.82	1193	1176	1.08	838	827	0.384	220	219	1.81
Te	0.0053	94	93	0.027	1	1	0.5	1	1	-
Th	1.99	1140	1127	2.36	755	752	1.58	262	255	4.98
Ti	11009	1850	1835	17063	1383	1378	2581	429	408	32526
Tl	0.00324	106	106	0.011	14	14	0.0006	1	1	-
U	0.63	986	959	0.88	589	589	0.465	196	185	1.36
V	64	1077	1070	79	763	751	19.8	188	187	93.1
W	0.207	170	170	0.331	92	92	0.229	12	12	0.54
Zn	13	643	640	18.5	341	340	6.6	92	92	14.5
Zr	222	979	961	288	601	598	134	222	222	523
La	12.3	1553	1532	14.7	1050	1041	8.57	284	249	35.6
Ce	35.1	1429	1407	42.7	946	942	22.5	265	246	97.7
Pr	5	196	195	7.25	87	87	2.9	30	26	12.6
Nd	24.6	1102	1081	31.2	752	740	13.7	159	149	59.7
Sm	7.5	1473	1403	9.48	984	944	3.89	261	248	16.9
Eu	1.35	1499	1443	1.52	1004	997	1.07	269	261	2.58
Gd	9.8	346	335	12.5	143	141	4.67	54	52	19.3
Tb	1.67	1315	1268	2.12	886	851	0.8	255	249	3.28
Dy	10.5	1103	1017	13.3	759	689	5.04	163	152	20.4
Ho	2.36	540	490	3.04	346	302	1.13	74	71	4.14
Er	6.5	375	348	8.4	170	157	3.11	43	40	11.2
Tm	0.9	377	314	1.15	256	208	0.458	45	42	1.48
Yb	5.84	1680	1652	7.39	1126	1121	2.88	303	301	9.75
Lu	0.84	1414	1312	1.07	942	855	0.413	263	245	1.36
Y	60	426	407	73	259	243	31.4	67	64	116

Note: The units of major oxides and trace elements (including REEs) are % and μg/g, respectively, except Ag, Au, Cd, Re, Ru, Rh, Pd, Os, Ir, Pt, which are in ng/g.

According to the rule of "The contents of trace elements commonly obey log-normal distributions", the geometric average of analytical data excluding outliers was calculated as the abundance for each trace element. The elemental abundances of 50 trace elements (including Ti, P, Mn, and Cr), along with their counts of samples (n_0 and n), are also listed in Table 3.

REE pattern is a useful tool for traceability or provenance in geochemistry [44,45], and the key signature is the variation trend of the pattern, which is dependent on REE concentrations. Therefore, the covariation of REE abundances needs to be considered. Here, the additive log-ratio (alr) transformation method [46,47] was adopted to calculate the REE (including Y) abundances, and Yb was selected as the denominator to calculate the ratios for other REEs. Yb was selected as the denominator of the alr transformation method because it not only has the largest count of analyzed samples (n_0 = 1680 and n = 1652) but also obeys the log-normal distribution well relative to the other REEs. According to the geometric average of Yb without outliers, 5.84 μg/g was set as its abundance of moon samples and was used to calculate the abundances of the other REEs (including Y). The abundances of 15 REEs (including Y) with their counts of samples (n_0 and n) are also listed in Table 3.

3.2. Elemental Abundances in Moon Samples with Low-Ca and High-Ca

Although elemental abundances in moon samples were derived based on statistical distributions such as normal, log-normal, and alr-normal distributions, some items clearly deviate from their ideal distributions, such as CaO, FeO, Al_2O_3, TiO_2, P_2O_5, Cr_2O_3, etc., as shown in Figure 2. It is worth mentioning that the distribution of CaO contents is near a bimodal distribution (Figure 2). In order to derive more meaningful elemental abundances, moon samples were classified into two types, as low-Ca and high-Ca samples, based on the CaO content boundary of 13.5% used in this paper.

In the total 2365 analyzed moon samples, there were only 1979 records with valid CaO contents. According to the content boundary of 13.5% CaO, there were 1468 records classified as low-Ca samples and 511 as high-Ca samples. Therefore, moon samples with low Ca were about three-quarters of the total moon samples collected in this paper, and samples with high Ca were about one-quarter.

With respect to the low-Ca moon samples and high-Ca moon samples, we used the same statistical methods as adopted for the total moon samples to calculate the elemental abundances of each type separately. The abundances of each type are also listed in Table 3, along with their counts of samples (n_0 and n).

4. Discussion

4.1. Geochemical Signatures of Elemental Abundances

Based on the elemental abundances of the moon, low-Ca, and high-Ca samples in Table 2, we compared their geochemical signatures with the elemental abundances of carbonaceous chondrite CI [12], primitive mantle [13], bulk oceanic crust [14], mid-ocean ridge basalt (including those of Atlantic, India, and Pacific [14]), continental crust (including total continental crust, lower continental crust, middle continental crust, and upper continental crust [15]), and rocks of China (including acidic rock, intermediate rock, and basic rock of China [16]) and found moon samples are more close to the mid-ocean ridge basalt (MORB) of the Earth. Here, only the comparison results with the MORB were illustrated to derive the geochemical signatures of moon samples.

4.1.1. Major Oxides

According to the illustration method of spider diagrams, the 11 major oxides were first sequenced descending on their abundances of moon samples. Then, moon samples were normalized based on the MORB of the Earth. Finally, the spider diagrams of major oxides of moon samples were derived and illustrated in Figure 3.

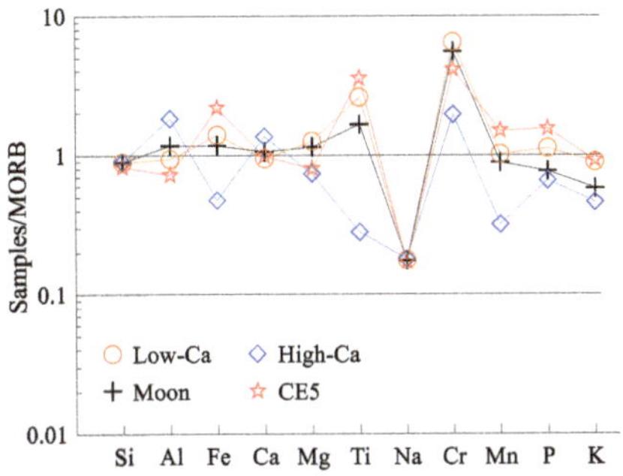

Figure 3. Spider diagrams of major oxides of moon samples normalized based on MORB. Abundances of the MORB are from White and Klein [14]. Elements in the horizontal axis are the abbreviations of their major oxides listed in Table 2.

With respect to the MORB, the moon sample (labeled as Moon in Figure 3) is clearly rich in Cr_2O_3 and TiO_2 and poor in K_2O in terms of their concentrations. The moon sample with low-Ca (labeled as Low-Ca in Figure 3) is also clearly rich in Cr_2O_3 and TiO_2 and poor in K_2O, like the moon sample. While the moon sample with high-Ca (labeled as High-Ca in Figure 3) is clearly rich in Cr_2O_3 and Al_2O_3 and poor in Na_2O, TiO_2, MnO, and FeO in terms of their concentrations. In the three abundances of moon samples, the moon sample with low-Ca is closer to the MORB, except for the clear signature of higher concentrations of Cr_2O_3 and TiO_2 and lower concentrations of K_2O.

With respect to the MORB, the moon samples (including Moon, low-Ca, and high-Ca in Figure 3) are clearly enriched in Cr and depleted in Na in the diagrams. Here, the terms of rich and poor are used for concentrations (comparison between/among samples), and the terms of enriched and depleted are used for diagrams (comparison among elements in the same sample).

4.1.2. REEs

The REE patterns of the three abundances of moon samples (including Moon, low-Ca, and high-Ca) are illustrated in Figure 4.

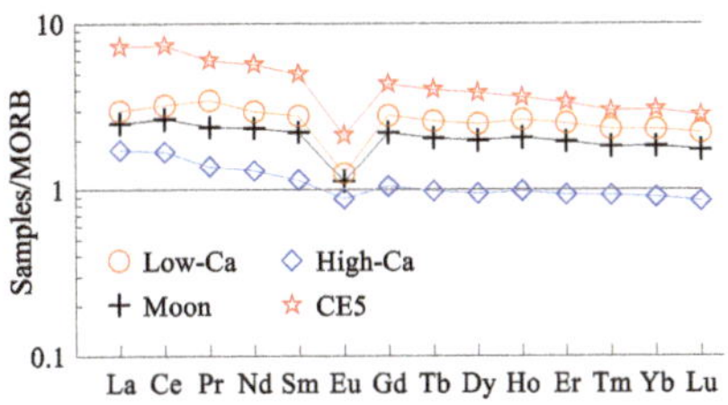

Figure 4. REE patterns of moon samples normalized to the MORB. Abundances of the MORB are from White and Klein [14].

With respect to the MORB, the REE patterns of the Moon and low-Ca samples (Figure 4) are near flat, except for the clear negative Eu anomaly. While the pattern of high-Ca (Figure 4) is tilted right for light REEs and nearly flat for heavy REEs. Therefore, the Moon and low-Ca samples are closer to the MORB than the high-Ca samples in the REE pattern, except for the clear negative Eu anomaly. With respect to the absolute concentrations of REEs, the three abundances of moon samples (including Moon, low-Ca, and high-Ca) are all higher or richer than those of the MORB. The descending sequence of total REE concentrations is (CE5 discussed in the following), low-Ca, Moon, high-Ca, and the MORB (Figure 4).

4.1.3. Trace Elements

Trace elements are illustrated using the spider diagram suggested by Sun and McDonough [48], with 31 elements, including K, P, and Ti. In order to avoid the repetition of REEs, the Ce and Eu were deleted from the spider diagram in which Ce and Eu are following the La and Sm, respectively. Therefore, a total of 29 elements (including K, P, and Ti) were used to draw the spider diagrams of the moon samples, which are illustrated in Figure 5.

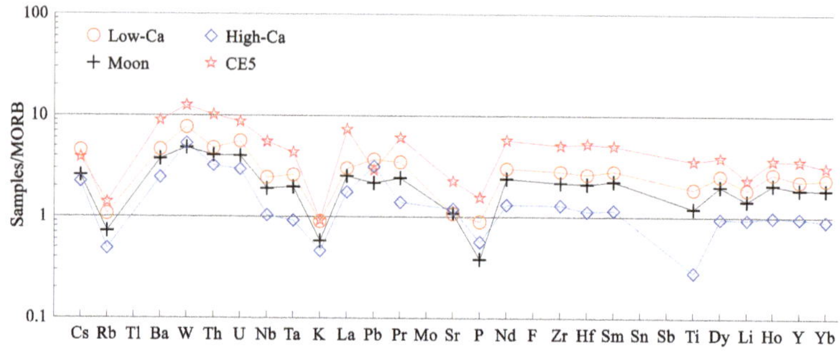

Figure 5. Spider diagrams of moon samples normalized to the MORB. Abundances of the MORB are from White and Klein [14].

With respect to the MORB in terms of their concentrations, the moon samples (including the Moon, low-Ca, and high-Ca) are all clearly rich in Cs, Ba, W, Th, U, and Pb (Figure 5).

With respect to the MORB, spider diagrams of moon samples (including the Moon, low-Ca, and high-Ca) are nearly flat (variations are limited to one order of magnitude), except for the clear depletion in Rb, K, and P (Figure 5). Furthermore, the diagram of high-Ca is also clearly depleted in Ti (Figure 5).

4.1.4. Other Trace Elements

Except for the aforementioned major oxides, REEs, and trace elements, there are only eight remaining elements of Sc, V, Co, Ni, Cu, Zn, Be, and B, which are reported abundances both of moon samples and the MORB. Here we supplement Ti, Cr, Mn, and Fe to the eight elements to form a series of the first transition elements plus Be and B. Therefore, 12 elements were used to form the spider diagrams of the moon samples which are illustrated in Figure 6.

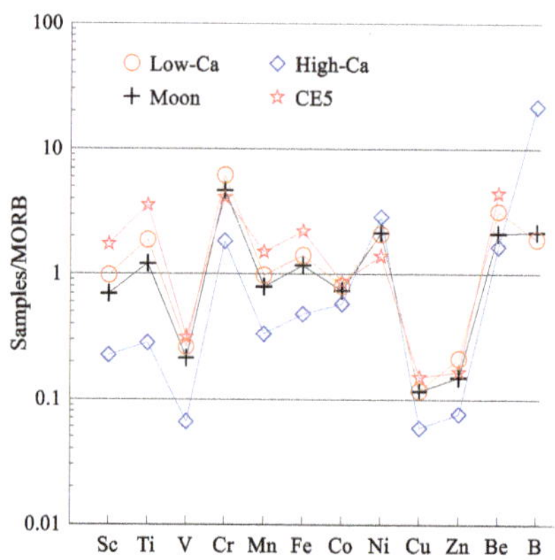

Figure 6. Spider diagrams of moon samples on first transition elements plus Be and B normalized to the MORB. Abundances of the MORB are from White and Klein [14].

With respect to the MORB in terms of their concentrations, the moon samples (including the Moon, low-Ca, and high-Ca) are all clearly rich in Cr, Ni, and Be and poor in V, Cu, and Zn (Figure 6).

With respect to the MORB, the spider diagrams of moon samples (including the Moon, low-Ca, and high-Ca) are nearly flat (variations are limited to one order of magnitude), except for the clear enrichment in Cr and depletion in V, Cu, and Zn (Figure 6). In addition, the diagram for the high-Ca moon sample is also clearly enriched in Ni and B (Figure 6).

In summary, the geochemical signatures of major oxides, REEs, and trace elements in moon samples (including the Moon, low-Ca, and high-Ca) are rich in Cr, REEs, Th, U, Pb, Zr, Hf, Cs, Ba, W, and Be and poor in Na, V, Cu, and Zn in terms of their concentrations, and are enriched in Cr and depleted in Na, K, Rb, P, V, Cu, and Zn in the spider diagrams, relative to the MORB. Among the total moon samples, low-Ca samples, and high-Ca samples, the low-Ca samples are closer to the total moon samples in concentration or patterns (or diagrams), which is not only illustrated in Figure 3 to Figure 6 but also consistent with the counts of analytical data with equal weighting used in this study. Except the 46 elements discussed in this paper, the other 26 elemental abundances in moon samples are not discussed here because of the data lack on the MORB.

4.2. *Chang'E-5 Samples*

4.2.1. Elemental Concentrations

Here we compile the analyzed elemental data of CE5 samples reported recently. The averages are used to represent the elemental concentrations of the CE5 samples which include 33 analyzed records, including two repetitions reported by different authors. If the elemental concentrations were only reported by Zong et al. [7], the suggested concentrations by Zong et al. [7] are used in this paper.

The calculated elemental concentrations of the CE5 samples are also listed in Table 3, including 11 major oxides, 15 REEs (including Y), and 28 trace elements (including Ti, P, Mn, and Cr).

4.2.2. Geochemical Signatures

The content of CaO of CE5 is 11.36%, which is lower than the boundary value of 13.5% for low-Ca and high-Ca moon samples. Therefore, the CE5 sample is the low-Ca type of moon sample. In terms of Ti content, moon samples can be divided into three types: high Ti ($TiO_2 \geq 6\%$), low Ti ($1\% \leq TiO_2 < 6\%$), and very low Ti ($TiO_2 < 1\%$) [11]. The content of TiO_2 of CE5 is 5.43%, which indicates that the CE5 sample is the low Ti type of moon sample.

According to the illustrations of moon samples, the geochemical signatures of the CE sample are also illustrated in Figure 3 to Figure 6.

With respect to the MORB, the CE5 sample is clearly rich in Cr_2O_3, TiO_2, and FeO and poor in Na_2O (Figure 3) in major oxides in terms of their concentrations, and is also enriched in Cr_2O_3, TiO_2, and FeO and depleted in Na_2O in the diagrams. The REE pattern of CE5 is tilted right slowly, except for the clear negative Eu anomaly, and its REE concentrations are clearly higher than those of the MORB (Figure 4). In the spider diagrams (Figures 5 and 6), the CE5 sample is clearly rich in Cs, Ba, W, Th, U, Nb, Ta, Pb, Zr, Hf, Ti, Li, Sr, Cr, and Be and poor in V, Cu, and Zn in terms of their concentrations, and is enriched in Cr and depleted in Rb, K, P, V, Cu, and Zn in the spider diagrams. Among the total moon sample, low-Ca sample, and high-Ca sample, the CE5 sample is closer to the low-Ca sample in concentrations or patterns (or diagrams), which are illustrated in Figure 3 to Figure 6. This is consistent with the low-Ca type of moon samples discriminated on CaO content, as mentioned previously.

With respect to the total moon sample, the CE5 sample is clearly rich in Ti, Fe, Mn, P, Sc, K, REEs, Th, U, Nb, Ta, Zr, Hf, Sr, Ba, W, and Be and poor in Mg, Al, Cr, and Ni in terms of their concentrations. From this view, the CE5 sample is the KREEP type of moon sample [49,50] because it is rich in K, REEs, and P relative to the moon sample. However, the contents of K_2O in the CE5 sample and the low-Ca sample are 0.175% and 0.171%, respectively, which are almost the same within the relative error. From this view, the CE5 sample is the non-KREEP type of moon sample [1] because of the non-enrichment of K relative to the low-Ca moon sample.

Except for the aforementioned studies on the CE5, more and more articles are being published [51–54] on hot and interesting topics, which are very helpful in promoting the research of the Moon. The elemental abundances of the CE5 sample in this paper will be improved on with more studies in the near future.

5. Conclusions

(1) The elemental abundances of moon samples, including the moon sample, the low-Ca moon sample, and the high-Ca moon sample, were derived from statistical distributions of analytical data reported in the literature. The classification criterion of low-Ca and high-Ca types of moon samples was 13.5% CaO content.

(2) With respect to the MORB of the Earth, the moon samples (including the Moon, low-Ca, and high-Ca samples) were rich in Cr, REEs, Th, U, Pb, Zr, Hf, Cs, Ba, W, and Be and poor in Na, V, Cu, and Zn in terms of their concentrations, and were enriched in Cr and depleted in Na, K, Rb, P, V, Cu, and Zn in the spider diagrams.

(3) The CE5 sample is the low-Ca type of moon sample and is clearly rich in Ti, Fe, Mn, P, Sc, REEs, Th, U, Nb, Ta, Zr, Hf, Sr, Ba, W, and Be and poor in Mg, Al, Cr, and Ni in terms of their concentrations relative to the moon and the low-Ca moon samples. If compared with only the moon sample, the CE5 sample is also clearly rich in K, REE, and P.

Author Contributions: Conceptualization, Z.H., Q.G., B.J., J.L. and Y.W.; Methodology, Q.G. and N.L.; Formal analysis, Z.H.; Data curation, Z.H., N.L., B.J., J.L., Y.W., J.H. and W.G.; Writing—original draft, Z.H.; Writing—review & editing, Q.G. and N.L. All authors have read and agreed to the published version of the manuscript.

Funding: This research received no external funding.

Institutional Review Board Statement: Not applicable.

Informed Consent Statement: Not applicable.

Data Availability Statement: Not applicable.

Acknowledgments: We thank the authors who reported the geochemical data of moon samples used in this manuscript. We greatly appreciate the comments from the anonymous reviewers for their valuable suggestions to improve the quality of this manuscript.

Conflicts of Interest: The authors declare that they have no known competing financial interests or personal relationships that could have appeared to influence the work reported in this paper.

References

1. Tian, H.C.; Wang, H.; Chen, Y.; Yang, W.; Zhou, Q.; Zhang, C.; Lin, H.L.; Huang, C.; Wu, T.S.; Jia, L.H.; et al. Non-KREEP origin for Chang'E-5 basalts in the Procellarum KREEP Terrane. *Nature* **2021**, *600*, 59–63. [CrossRef] [PubMed]
2. Li, Q.L.; Zhou, Q.; Liu, Y.; Xiao, Z.Y.; Lin, Y.T.; Li, J.H.; Ma, H.X.; Tang, G.Q.; Guo, S.; Tang, X.; et al. Two-billion-year-old volcanism on the Moon from Chang'e-5 basalts. *Nature* **2021**, *600*, 54–58. [CrossRef] [PubMed]
3. Che, X.C.; Nemchin, A.; Liu, D.Y.; Long, T.; Wang, C.; Norman, M.D.; Joy, K.H.; Tartese, R.; Head, J.; Jolliff, B.; et al. Age and composition of young basalts on the Moon, measured from samples returned by Chang'e-5. *Science* **2021**, *374*, 887–890. [CrossRef] [PubMed]
4. Hu, S.; He, H.C.; Ji, J.L.; Lin, Y.T.; Hui, H.J.; Anand, M.; Tartèse, R.; Yan, Y.H.; Hao, J.L.; Li, R.Y.; et al. A dry lunar mantle reservoir for young mare basalts of Chang'E-5. *Nature* **2021**, *600*, 49–53. [CrossRef] [PubMed]
5. Li, C.L.; Hu, H.; Yang, M.F.; Pei, Z.Y.; Zhou, Q.; Ren, X.; Liu, B.; Liu, D.W.; Zeng, X.G.; Zhang, G.L.; et al. Characteristics of the lunar samples returned by the Chang'E-5 mission. *Natl. Sci. Rev.* **2022**, *9*, nwab188. [CrossRef] [PubMed]
6. Yao, Y.G.; Xiao, C.J.; Wang, P.S.; Li, C.L.; Zhou, Q. Instrumental Neutron Activation Analysis of Chang'E-5 Lunar Regolith Samples. *J. Am. Chem. Soc.* **2022**, *144*, 5478–5484. [CrossRef]

7. Zong, K.Q.; Wang, Z.C.; Li, J.W.; He, Q.; Harry, B.; Hu, Z.C.; He, T.; Cao, K.N.; She, Z.B.; Wu, X.; et al. Bulk compositions of the Chang'E-5 lunar soil: Insights into chemical homogeneity, exotic addition, and origin of landing site basalts. *Geochim. Cosmochim. Acta* **2022**, *335*, 284–296; ISSN 0016-7037. [CrossRef]
8. Zhang, C.Q.; Li, J.H. Non-destructive Identification and Quantification of Ilmenite from a Single Particle of the Chang'E-5 Lunar Soil Sample. *At. Spectrosc.* **2022**, *43*, 284–291.
9. Su, B.; Yuan, J.; Chen, Y.; Yang, W.; Ross, N.M.; Hui, H.J.; Wang, H.; Tian, H.C.; Li, X.H.; Wu, F.Y. Fusible mantle cumulates trigger young mare volcanism on the Cooling Moon. *Sci. Adv.* **2022**, *8*, eabn2103. [CrossRef]
10. Yang, W.; Chen, Y.; Wang, H.; Tian, H.C.; Hui, H.J.; Xiao, Z.Y.; Wu, S.T.; Zhang, D.; Zhou, Q.; Ma, X.H.; et al. Geochemistry of impact glasses in the Chang'e-5 regolith: Constraints on impact melting and the petrogenesis of local basalt. *Geochim. Cosmochim. Acta* **2022**, *335*, 183–196. [CrossRef]
11. Tian, H.C.; Yang, W.; Zhang, D.; Zhang, H.J.; Jia, L.H.; Wu, S.T.; Lin, Y.T.; Li, X.H.; Wu, F.Y. Petrogenesis of Chang'E-5 mare basalts: Clues from the trace elements in plagioclase. *Am. Mineral.* **2022**, *600*, 59–63.
12. Palme, H.; Lodders, K.; Jones, A. Solar system abundances of the elements. In *Treatise on Geochemistry, Volume 1: Meteorites, Comets, and Planets*; Holland, H.D., Turekian, K.K., Eds.; Elsevier: Amsterdam, The Netherlands, 2014; pp. 15–36.
13. Palme, H.; O'Neill, H.S.C. Cosmochemical Estimates of Mantle Composition. In *Treatise on Geochemistry, Volume 3: The Crust*; Holland, H.D., Turekian, K.K., Eds.; Elsevier: Amsterdam, The Netherlands, 2014; pp. 1–39.
14. White, W.M.; Klein, E.M. Composition of the oceanic crust. In *Treatise on Geochemistry, Volume 3: The Crust*; Holland, H.D., Turekian, K.K., Eds.; Elsevier: Amsterdam, The Netherlands, 2014; pp. 457–496.
15. Rudnick, R.L.; Gao, S. Composition of the Continental Crust. In *Treatise on Geochemistry, Volume 3: The Crust*; Holland, H.D., Turekian, K.K., Eds.; Elsevier: Amsterdam, The Netherlands, 2014; pp. 1–64.
16. Chi, Q.H.; Yan, M.C. *Handbook of Elemental Abundance for Applied Geochemistry*; Geological Publishing House: Beijing, China, 2007; pp. 1–148.
17. Rose, H.J.; Cuttitta, F.; Dwornik, E.J.; Carron, M.K.; Christian, R.P.; Lindsay, J.R.; Ligon, D.T.; Larson, R.R. Semimicro chemical and X-ray fluorescence analysis of lunar samples. *Science* **1970**, *167*, 520–521. [CrossRef] [PubMed]
18. Rose, H.J.; Cuttitta, F.; Annell, C.S.; Carron, M.K.; Christian, R.P.; Dwornik, E.J.; Greenland, L.P.; Ligon, D.T. Compositional data for twenty-one Fra Mauro lunar materials. In Proceedings of the 2nd Lunar Science Conference, Houston, TX, USA, 10–13 January 1972; Volume 2, pp. 1215–1229.
19. Rose, H.J.; Cuttitta, F.; Berman, S.; Carron, M.K.; Christian, R.P.; Dwornik, E.J.; Greenland, L.P.; Ligon, D.T. Compositional data for twenty-two Apollo 16 samples. In Proceedings of the 2nd Lunar Science Conference, Houston, TX, USA, 5–8 March 1973; Volume 2, pp. 1149–1158.
20. Rose, H.J.; Cuttitta, F.; Berman, S.; Carron, M.K.; Christian, R.P.; Dwornik, E.J.; Greenland, L.P. Chemical composition of rocks and soils at Taurus-Littrow. In Proceedings of the 2nd Lunar Science Conference, Houston, TX, USA, 18–22 March 1974; Volume 2, pp. 1119–1133.
21. Rose, H.J.; Christian, R.P.; Dwomik, E.J.; Schnepfe, M.M. Major elemental analysis of some Apollo 15, 16, and 17 samples (abs). *Lunar Sci.* **1975**, *6*, 686–688.
22. Taylor, S.R.; Gorton, M.P.; Muir, P.; Nance, W.B.; Rudowski, R.; Ware, N. Composition of the Descartes region, lunar highlands. *Geochim. Cosmochim. Acta* **1973**, *37*, 2665–2683. [CrossRef]
23. Korotev, R.L. Some things we can infer about the Moon from the composition of the Apollo 16 regolith. *Meteorit. Planet. Sci.* **1997**, *32*, 447–478. [CrossRef]
24. Warren, P.H.; Taylor, G.J. The Moon. In *Treatise on Geochemistry, Volume 1: Meteorites, Comets, and Planets*; Holland, H.D., Turekian, K.K., Eds.; Elsevier: Amsterdam, The Netherlands, 2014; pp. 559–599.
25. Crawford, I.A.; Joy, K.H.; Anand, M. Lunar Exploration. In *Encyclopedia of the Solar System, Part V: Earth and Moon as Planets*; Spohn, T., Breuer, D., Johnson, T.V., Eds.; Elsevier: Amsterdam, The Netherlands, 2014; pp. 555–579.
26. LSPET. Preliminary examination of lunar samples from Apollo 11. *Science* **1965**, *165*, 1211–1227.
27. LSPET. Preliminary examination of lunar samples from Apollo 12. *Science* **1970**, *167*, 1325–1339. [CrossRef]
28. LSPET. Preliminary examination of lunar samples from Apollo 14. *Science* **1971**, *173*, 681–693. [CrossRef]
29. LSPET. The Apollo 15 lunar samples: A preliminary description. *Science* **1972**, *175*, 363–375. [CrossRef]
30. LSPET. The Apollo 16 lunar samples: Petrographic and chemical description. *Science* **1973**, *179*, 23–34. [CrossRef]
31. LSPET. Apollo 17 lunar samples: Chemical and petrographic description. *Science* **1973**, *182*, 659–690. [CrossRef] [PubMed]
32. Vinogradov, A.P. Preliminary data on lunar ground brought to Earth by Automatic Probe "Luna 16". In Proceedings of the 2nd Lunar Science Conference, Houston, TX, USA, 11–14 January 1971; Volume 2, pp. 1–16.
33. Vinogradov, A.P. Preliminary data on lunar soil collected by the Luna 20 unmanned spacecraft. *Geochim. Et Cosmochim. Acta* **1973**, *37*, 721–729. [CrossRef]
34. Barsukov, V.L. Preliminary data for the regolith core brought to earth by the automatic lunar station Luna 24. In Proceedings of the 8th Lunar Science Conference, Houston, TX, USA, 14–18 March 1977; Volume 2, pp. 3303–3318.
35. Qian, Y.; Xiao, L.; Wang, Q.; Head, J.W.; Yang, R.; Kang, Y.; van der Bogert, C.H.; Hiesinger, H.; Lai, X.; Wang, G.; et al. China's Chang'e-5 landing site: Geology, stratigraphy, and provenance of materials. *Earth Planet. Sci. Lett.* **2021**, *561*, 116855. [CrossRef]

36. Dickinson, T.; Taylor, G.J.; Keil, K.; Bild, R.W. Germanium abundances in lunar basalts-Evidence of mantle metasomatism? In Proceedings of the 19th Lunar and Planetary Science Conference Proceedings, Houston, TX, USA, 14–18 March 1989; Volume 19, pp. 189–198.
37. Neal, C.R. Interior of the Moon: The presence of garnet in the primitive deep lunar mantle. *J. Geophys. Res. Planets* **2001**, *106*, 27865–27885. [CrossRef]
38. Albee, A.L.; Chodos, A.A.; Gancarz, A.J.; Haines, E.L.; Papanastassiou, D.A.; Ray, L.; Tera, F.; Wasserburg, G.J.; Wen, T. Mineralogy, petrology, and chemistry of a Luna 16 basaltic fragment, sample B-1. *Earth Planet. Sci. Lett.* **1972**, *13*, 353–367, ISSN 0012-821X. [CrossRef]
39. Barsukov, V.L.; Tarasov, L.S.; Dmitriiev, L.V.; Kolesov, G.M.; Shevaleevsky, I.D.; Garanin, A.V. The geochemical and petrochemical features of regolith and rocks from Mare Crisium (preliminary data). In Proceedings of the 8th Lunar Science Conference, Houston, TX, USA, 14–18 March 1977; Volume 2, pp. 3319–3332.
40. Helmke, P.A.; Blanchard, D.P.; Jacobs, J.W.; Haskin, L.A. Rare earths, other trace elements and iron in Luna 20 samples. *Geochim. Cosmochim. Acta* **1973**, *37*, 869–874. [CrossRef]
41. Compston, W.; Berry, H.; Vernon, M.J.; Bruce, W. Rubidium-strontium chronology and chemistry of lunar material from the Ocean of Storms. In Proceedings of the 2nd Lunar and Planetary Science Conference Proceedings, Houston, TX, USA, 11–14 January 1971; Volume 2, p. 1471.
42. Taylor, S.R.; Kaye, M.; Muir, P.; Nance, W.; Rudowski, R.; Ware, N. Composition of the lunar uplands: Chemistry of Apollo 14 samples from Fra Mauro. In Proceedings of the 3rd Lunar and Planetary Science Conference Proceedings, Houston, TX, USA, 10–13 January 1972; Volume 3, p. 1231.
43. Wänke, H.; Palme, H.; Kruse, H.; Baddenhausen, H.; Cendales, M.; Dreibus, G.; Hofmeister, H.; Jagoutz, E.; Palme, C.; Spettel, B.; et al. Chemistry of lunar highland rocks-A refined evaluation of the composition of the primary matter. In Proceedings of the 7th Lunar and Planetary Science Conference Proceedings, Houston, TX, USA, 15–19 March 1976; Volume 7, pp. 3479–3499.
44. Gong, Q.J.; Deng, J.; Yang, L.Q.; Zhang, J.; Wang, Q.F.; Zhang, G.X. Behavior of major and trace elements during weathering of sericite–quartz schist. *J. Asian Earth Sci.* **2011**, *42*, 1–13; ISSN 1367-9120. [CrossRef]
45. Gong, Q.J.; Yan, T.T.; Wu, X.; Li, R.K.; Wang, X.Q.; Liu, N.Q.; Li, X.L.; Wu, Y.; Li, J. Geochemical gene: A promising concept in discrimination and traceability of geological materials. *Appl. Geochem.* **2022**, *136*, 105133. [CrossRef]
46. Aitchison, J. The Single Principle of Compositional Data Analysis, Continuing Fallacies, Confusions and Misunderstandings and Some Suggested Remedies. 2008. Available online: https://hdl.handle.net/10256/706 (accessed on 15 May 2020).
47. Egozcue, J.J.; Pawlowsky-Glahn, V.; Mateu-Figueras, G.; Barcelo-Vidal, C. Isometric logration transformations for compositional data analysis. *Math. Geol.* **2003**, *35*, 279–300. [CrossRef]
48. Sun, S.S.; McDonough, W.F. Chemical and isotopic systematics of oceanic basalts: Implications for mantle composition and processes. *Geol. Soc.* **1989**, *42*, 313–345. [CrossRef]
49. Meyer, C., Jr.; Hubbard, N.J. High potassium, high phosphorus glass as an important rock type in the Apollo 12 soil samples. *Meteoritics* **1970**, *5*, 210–211.
50. Meyer, C., Jr.; Brett, R.; Hubbard, N.J.; Morrison, D.A.; McKay, D.S.; Aitken, F.K.; Takeda, H.; Schonfeld, E. Mineralogy, chemistry, and origin of the KREEP component in soil samples from the Ocean of Storms. In Proceedings of the 2nd Lunar and Planetary Science Conference Proceedings, Houston, TX, USA, 11–14 January 1971; Volume 2, p. 393.
51. Qiao, L.; Chen, J.; Xu, L.Y.; Wan, S.; Cao, H.J.; Li, B.; Li, Z.C. Geology of the Chang'e-5 landing site: Constraints on the sources of samples returned from a young nearside mare. *Icarus* **2021**, *364*, 114480. [CrossRef]
52. He, Q.; Li, Y.H.; Baziotis, I.; Qian, Y.Q.; Xiao, L.; Wang, Z.C.; Zhang, W.; Luo, B.J.; Neal, C.R.; Day, J.M.D.; et al. Detailed petrogenesis of the unsampled Oceanus Procellarum: The case of the Chang'e-5 mare basalts. *Icarus* **2022**, *383*, 115082. [CrossRef]
53. Mitchell, R.N. Chang'E-5 reveals the Moon's secrets to a longer life. *Innovation* **2021**, *2*, 100177. [CrossRef] [PubMed]
54. Du, J.; Fa, W.Z.; Gong, S.X.; Liu, Y.; Qiao, L.; Tai, Y.S.; Zhang, F.; Zou, Y.L. Thicknesses of Mare basalts in the Chang'E-5 landing region: Implications for the late-stage volcanism on the Moon. *J. Geophys. Res. Planets* **2022**, *127*, e2022JE007314. [CrossRef]

applied sciences

MDPI

Article

A Helmholtz Free Energy Equation of State of CO_2-CH_4-N_2 Fluid Mixtures (ZMS EOS) and Its Applications

Jia Zhang [1,*], Shide Mao [2] and Zeming Shi [1]

1 College of Earth Sciences, Chengdu University of Technology, Chengdu 610059, China
2 School of Earth Sciences and Resources, China University of Geosciences, Beijing 100083, China
* Correspondence: jiazhang202211@163.com

Abstract: An equation of state (EOS) of CH_4-N_2 fluid mixtures in terms of Helmholtz free energy has been developed by using four mixing parameters, which can reproduce the pressure-volume-temperature-composition (*PVTx*) and vapor-liquid equilibrium (VLE) properties of CH_4-N_2 fluid mixtures. The average absolute deviation of all the *PVTx* data available up to 673.15 K and 1380 bar from this EOS is 0.38%. Combining this EOS of CH_4-N_2 fluid mixtures and the EOS of CH_4-CO_2 and CO_2-N_2 fluid mixtures in our previous work, an EOS of CO_2-CH_4-N_2 fluid mixtures has been developed, which is named ZMS EOS. The ZMS EOS can calculate all thermodynamic properties of ternary CO_2-CH_4-N_2 fluid mixtures and the average absolute deviation of the *PVTx* data from the ZMS EOS is 0.40% for the CO_2-CH_4-N_2 system. The ZMS EOS can be applied to calculate excess enthalpies of CO_2-CH_4-N_2 fluid mixtures, predict the solubility of CO_2-CH_4-N_2 fluid mixtures in brine and water, and quantitatively estimate the impact of the impurities (CH_4 and N_2) on the CO_2 storage capacity in the CO_2 capture and storage (CCS) processes. The ZMS EOS can also be applied to calculate the isochores of CO_2-CH_4-N_2 system in the studies of fluid inclusions. All Fortran computer codes and Origin drawing projects in this paper can be obtained freely from the corresponding author.

Keywords: CO_2-CH_4-N_2 system; equation of state; CCS; excess enthalpies; fluid inclusion

Citation: Zhang, J.; Mao, S.; Shi, Z. A Helmholtz Free Energy Equation of State of CO_2-CH_4-N_2 Fluid Mixtures (ZMS EOS) and Its Applications. *Appl. Sci.* **2023**, *13*, 3659. https://doi.org/10.3390/app13063659

Academic Editor: Andrea L. Rizzo

Received: 20 January 2023
Revised: 6 March 2023
Accepted: 7 March 2023
Published: 13 March 2023

1. Introduction

The CO_2, CH_4 and N_2 are important natural fluids, and non-aqueous CO_2–CH_4–N_2 mixtures are often reported in the studies of fluid inclusions [1–3]. In recent decades, the amount of greenhouse gas CO_2 in the atmosphere has gradually increased because of the development of industry. Numerous studies have shown that CO_2 capture and storage (CCS) is an effective method to reduce the amount of CO_2 in the atmosphere [4–6]. However, CO_2 in industrial exhaust gases is usually impure, mixing with other components, such as CH_4 and N_2 [7,8]. The impurities can affect the design of the CCS processes [9–11]. Therefore, predicting thermodynamic properties of the CO_2-CH_4-N_2 fluid mixtures, especially the pressure-volume-temperature-composition (*PVTx*) and vapor-liquid equilibrium (VLE) properties at different temperatures and pressures, is of great significance for the related CCS and fluid inclusion studies [12–15].

Although experimental thermodynamic data are the most reliable in the corresponding applications, they are costly and time-consuming to obtain. On the other hand, the predictive EOS is a better choice for us. In the past century, the cubic EOSs (e.g., Peng-Robinson (PR) EOS [16], Soave–Redlich–Kwong (SRK) EOS [17]) originated from the van der Waals EOS [18] are highly preferred for the CCS researchers because of their simplicity. Based on the standard PR EOS, some more accurate EOSs have been presented for the CCS mixtures, such as a model that integrates the classical PR EOS with advanced mixing rules, called the "Peng-Robinson + residual part of excess Helmholtz energy model" [19], and the Enhanced-Predictive-PR78 (E-PPR78) EOS [20]. However, the cubic EOSs cannot well reproduce the *PVTx* properties of fluids under high pressure-temperature conditions, as can be seen in

Section 2. Based on Heyen EOS [21], Heyen et al. [22] simulated the phase equilibria of the CH_4-CO_2 system below 50 °C and 100 bar; Darimont and Heyen [23] predicted the phase equilibria of the CO_2-N_2 system below 20 °C and 90 bar. Because cubic EOSs cannot well reproduce the *PVTx* properties, Thiery et al. [24,25] and Thiery and Dubessy [26] modeled the phase equilibria of the CO_2-CH_4-N_2 system including liquid, vapor and solid by the cubic EOSs and the *PVTx* properties by the Lee–Kesler correlation [27]. However, these models have the disadvantage of using two EOSs that may cause incoherency of various fluid parameters [28].

In recent years, the Statistical Associating Fluid Theory (SAFT) EOS [29] from Wertheim's thermodynamic perturbation theory (TPT) has become popular for CCS fluid mixtures. Because it is based on statistical mechanics and has an explicit physical meaning, it has more reliable extrapolation and more accurate predictive capability than traditional empirical models. Many successful modifications of the SAFT-based EOSs have been presented, such as the EOS of perturbed-chain SAFT (PC-SAFT) [30,31], variable range SAFT (SAFT-VR) [32], and Lennard-Jones SAFT (LJ-SAFT) [33]. However, the SAFT EOSs cannot well reproduce experimental VLE data in the near-critical region of the CO_2-N_2 fluid mixture, as can be seen in the previous work [34]. Up to now, the EOS in terms of Helmholtz free energy is also commonly used to calculate the thermodynamic properties of CCS fluid mixtures [35–39], because the EOS in the form of Helmholtz free energy has high precision, wide temperature-pressure range, and can calculate all thermodynamic properties of the fluids by the derivation from the Helmholtz free energy EOS, such as enthalpy, heat capacity, entropy, etc. The derivation from the Helmholtz free energy EOS is not complex, as can be seen later.

In our previous work [34,40], the EOS in terms of dimensionless Helmholtz free energy for the CH_4-CO_2 and CO_2-N_2 fluid mixtures have been established by using four mixing parameters, which have been applied to the studies of the CH_4-CO_2 and CO_2-N_2 fluid inclusions. In this work, firstly, the EOS in terms of dimensionless Helmholtz free energy of the CH_4-N_2 fluid mixture has been developed by the same approach. The ZMS EOS is obtained by combining the binary interaction parameters of CH_4-CO_2, CO_2-N_2 and CH_4-N_2 systems. Experimental data available for the binary CH_4-N_2 and ternary CO_2-CH_4-N_2 fluid mixtures are used to verify the accuracy of the ZMS EOS. Then the ZMS EOS is applied to calculate the excess enthalpies, the solubility of CO_2-CH_4-N_2 gas mixtures in brine and water, the impact of impurities (CH_4 and N_2) on the CO_2 storage capacity, and the isochores of the CO_2-CH_4-N_2 fluid inclusions.

2. The ZMS EOS

The EOS of the CO_2-CH_4-N_2 mixtures is in terms of dimensionless Helmholtz free energy α, which is represented by

$$\alpha = \alpha^0 + \alpha^r \tag{1}$$

where α^0 and α^r are the ideal-gas part and the residual part of dimensionless Helmholtz free energy. α^0 and α^r are defined by

$$\alpha^0 = \sum_{i=1}^{n} x_i \left[\alpha_i^0 + lnx_i\right] \tag{2}$$

$$\alpha^r = \sum_{i=1}^{n} x_i \alpha_i^r(\delta, \tau) + \alpha^E(\delta, \tau, x) \tag{3}$$

where n is the number of components in the mixture, x_i is the mole fraction of component i in the mixture, the superscripts "0", "r" and "E" denote the ideal-gas part, the residual part, and the excess of dimensionless Helmholtz free energy, respectively. The subscript i denotes the component i. α_i^r can be calculated by the EOSs of pure CO_2, CH_4 and N_2 fluids [41–43], which are in terms of dimensionless Helmholtz free energy and are recommended as the standard EOSs of pure CO_2, CH_4 and N_2 fluids by the National Institute of Standards and Technology (NIST).

δ and τ of Equation (3) are the reduced mixture density ($\delta = \rho/\rho_c$) and the inverse reduced mixture temperature ($\tau = T_c/T$), where ρ and T are the density and temperature of the mixture, and ρ_c and T_c are the pseudo-critical density and temperature of the mixture. ρ_c and T_c are defined by

$$\rho_c = \left[\sum_{i=1}^{n} \frac{x_i}{\rho_{ci}} + \sum_{i=1}^{n-1} \sum_{j=i+1}^{n} x_i x_j \zeta_{ij} \right]^{-1} \tag{4}$$

$$T_c = \sum_{i=1}^{n} x_i T_{ci} + \sum_{i=1}^{n-1} \sum_{j=i+1}^{n} x_i^{\beta_{ij}} x_j \varsigma_{ij} \tag{5}$$

where x_j is the mole fraction of component j in the mixture, ρ_{ci} and T_{ci} are the critical density and temperature of component i, respectively. The critical temperatures and densities of the three components considered in this study are listed in Table 1. ζ_{ij}, β_{ij} and ς_{ij} are binary parameters associated with components i and j.

Table 1. Critical parameters of pure fluids.

Component i	T_{ci} (K)	ρ_{ci} (mol/dm^3)	References
CH_4	90.6941	10.139	Setzmann and Wagner [42]
CO_2	216.592	10.625	Span and Wagner [41]
N_2	63.151	11.184	Span et al. [43]

α^E of Equation (3) takes the general form developed by Lemmon and Jacobsen (LJ-1999 EOS) [35].

$$\alpha^E(\delta, \tau, x) = \sum_{i=1}^{n-1} \sum_{j=i+1}^{n} x_i x_j F_{ij} \sum_{k=1}^{10} N_k \delta^{d_k} \tau^{t_k} \tag{6}$$

where F_{ij} is a binary parameter associated with components i and j, N_k, d_k and t_k are the general parameters independent of fluids, which can be obtained from Lemmon and Jacobsen [35]. There are four binary parameters (ζ_{ij}, β_{ij}, ς_{ij} and F_{ij}) in the above equations. Binary interaction parameters of CH_4-CO_2 and CO_2-N_2 have been determined in previous work [34,40]. In this work, the binary interaction parameters of CH_4-N_2 systems are obtained by the nonlinear regression of selected experimental data. Since experimental *PVTx* data available are much more than experimental VLE data, only part of new and accurate experimental *PVTx* data are selected to fit the parameters to make the *PVTx* and VLE data keep similar weights in the fitting. In this work, the Levenberg–Marquardt algorithm of the nonlinear least squares method is used for fitting, which is an efficient and widely used mathematical optimization technique. The fitting condition is to minimize the weighted sum of squares of the calculation errors of the equation on the selected experimental *PVTx* and VLE data. Compared to Newton's method (e.g., The Newton–Raphson method used in REFPROP [44]), it combines the advantages of two numerical minimization algorithms: the gradient descent method and the Gauss–Newton method, and it has good convergence and robustness. Regressed parameters of the CH_4-N_2 system are listed in Table 2, which also includes the parameters of CH_4-CO_2 and CO_2-N_2 systems from previous studies.

Table 2. Binary interaction parameters of the CO_2-CH_4-N_2 system.

References	Binary Mixtures	F_{ij}	ζ_{ij} (dm^3/mol)	ς_{ij} (K)	β_{ij}
Mao et al. [40]	CH_4-CO_2	0.12844025×10	$0.35751245 \times 10^{-2}$	$-0.43720344 \times 10^{2}$	0.10358865×10
Zhang et al. [34]	CO_2-N_2	0.16671494×10	$0.58411078 \times 10^{-2}$	$-0.22952094 \times 10^{2}$	0.16878787×10
This work	CH_4-N_2	0.63739997	0.3812517×10^{-2}	$-0.17790001 \times 10^{2}$	0.1009001×10

Note: Subscripts i and j refer to the first component and the second component, respectively.

2.1. The Binary CH_4-N_2 Mixture

The calculated deviations of the *PVTx* and VLE properties from each experimental data set [45–66] by this EOS for the CH_4-N_2 fluid mixture are listed in Table 3. Detail calculation method for the *PVTx* and VLE properties can be found in Mao et al. [40]. The deviations of the *PVTx* data are the density deviations, and the temperature and pressure of the experimental *PVTx* data are up to 673.15 K and 1380 bar, respectively. The deviations of VLE property are the deviations of the vapor-liquid phase equilibrium composition, and the experimental VLE composition covers the full range. The average absolute deviation of all *PVTx* data from this EOS is 0.38% for the CH_4-N_2 fluid mixture.

Table 3. Calculated *PVTx* and VLE deviations for the CH_4-N_2 mixture.

References	Number of Data Points		*T-P-x* Range for xCH_4-(1-x) N_2			AAD%
	Styles	Total (Used)	*T* (K)	*P* (bar)	*x*	
Liu and Miller [45]	*PVTx*	7 (0)	91–115	3–12	0.5	0.57
Rodosevich and Miller [46]	*PVTx*	8 (0)	91–115	43–454	0.8–0.95	3.83
Pan et al. [47]	*PVTx*	7 (0)	91–115	1–11	0.5–0.86	0.11
Hiza et al. [48]	*PVTx*	21 (0)	95–140	1–21	0.5–0.95	0.10
Da Ponte et al. [49]	*PVTx*	182 (50)	110–120	15–1380	0.3–0.68	0.12
Straty and Diller [65]	*PVTx*	578 (0)	82–320	6–356	0.32–0.7	0.24
Haynes and McCarty [56]	*PVTx*	85 (85)	140–320	10–164	0.3–0.71	0.09
Seitz et al. [64]	*PVTx*	190 (90)	323–573	99–999	0.1–0.9	0.28
Seitz and Blencoe [63]	*PVTx*	43 (0)	673.15	199–999	0.1–0.9	5.36
Ababio et al. [50]	*PVTx*	83 (83)	308–333	9–120	0.5–0.78	0.12
Chamorro et al. [52]	*PVTx*	242 (56)	230–400	9–192	0.8–0.9	0.23
Janisch et al. [57]	*PVTx*	17 (0)	129–180	15–50	0.4–0.9	2.10
Li et al. [60]	*PVTx*	27 (27)	17–270	1–16	0.9	0.06
Gomez-Osorio et al. [54]	*PVTx*	142 (42)	304–470	100–1379	0.25–0.75	0.07
Brandt and Stroud [51]	VLE	23 (0)	128–179	34	0.05–0.98	1.48
Cheung and Wang [53]	VLE	20 (0)	92–124	0.2–6	0.85–1.0	5.02
Pan et al. [47]	VLE	60 (60)	95–120	0.2–25	0.05–1	5.05
Miller et al. [62]	VLE	11 (0)	112	2–13	0.2–0.97	3.30
Kidnay et al. [59]	VLE	83 (83)	112–180	2–49	0.1–0.99	1.31
McClure et al. [61]	VLE	8 (8)	91	1–3	0.1–0.8	5.60
Jin et al. [58]	VLE	10 (10)	123	4–26	0.1–0.95	2.96
Parrish and Hiza [66]	VLE	48 (43)	95–120	2–20	0.1–0.9	3.14
Janisch et al. [57]	VLE	16 (6)	130–180	0.5–5	0.4–0.96	1.14
Han et al. [55]	VLE	77 (60)	110–123	4–13	0.7–1.0	2.49

Note: Deviations of the PVTx data are the density deviations, and the deviations of VLE data are the equilibrium composition deviations. AAD is the abbreviation of average absolute deviation.

Figure 1 shows the deviations between this EOS and the experimental density data of the CH_4-N_2 mixture [49,52,54,64] at different pressures. It can be seen in Figure 1 that most of the density deviations are within $\pm 1\%$, with or close to experimental accuracy. The comparisons between experimental density and the calculated densities by this EOS are shown in Figure 2, where the calculated densities from the PR and SRK EOSs [67] are also included. The errors of three EOSs are also plotted in Figure 2. Figure 2 shows the PR and SRK EOSs cannot well reproduce the *PVTx* properties, especially under high-pressure conditions. In contrast, the calculated densities from this EOS are in good agreement with experiment data [68].

Figure 3 compares the vapor-liquid phase equilibrium curves calculated from this EOS with experimental data [55,57,59,66] at three temperatures of 170 K, 115 K and 110 K. It can be seen from Figure 3 that the calculated vapor-liquid phase equilibrium curves from this EOS are consistent with experimental data, indicating that this EOS can accurately calculate the vapor-liquid phase equilibrium of CH_4-N_2 mixture.

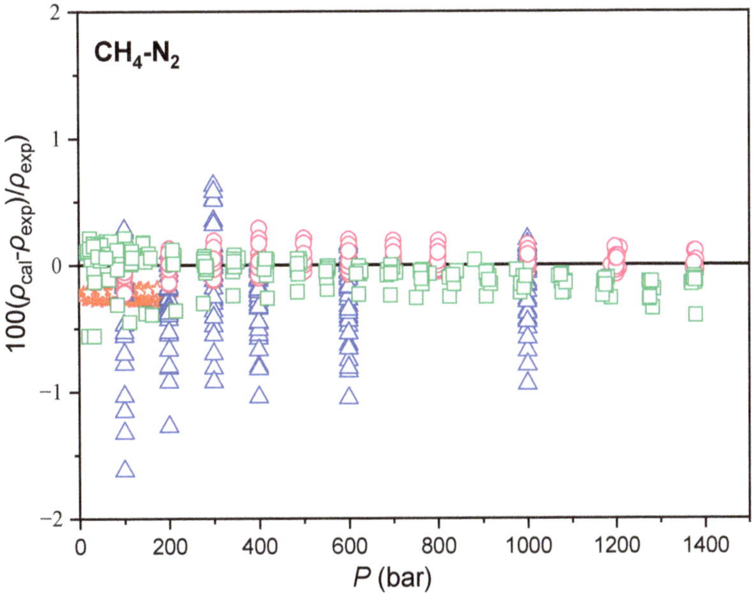

Figure 1. Density deviations for the CH_4-N_2 system at different pressures. Experimental data(triangles [64], stars [52], rounds [54], squares [49]): P is the pressure, ρ_{cal} is the calculated density, and ρ_{exp} is the experimental density.

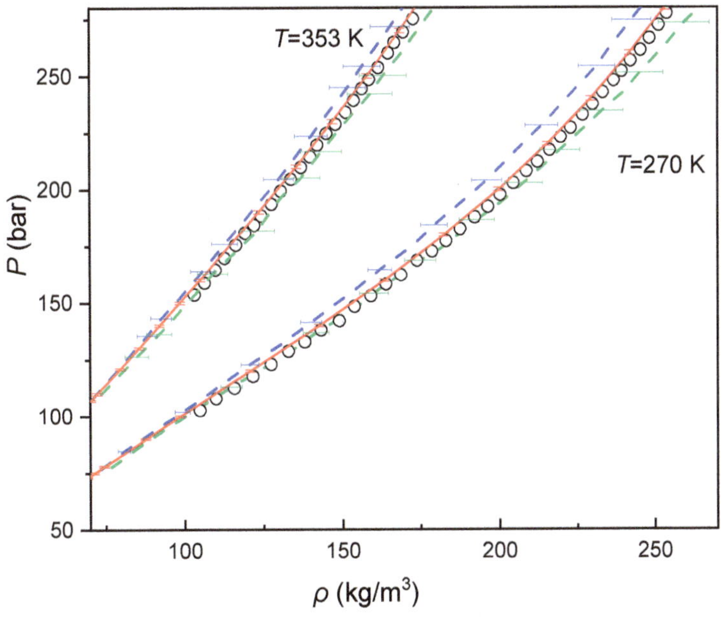

Figure 2. Experimental and calculated densities for the 0.8 mole CH_4 + 0.2 mole N_2 mixture at different temperatures. The experimental density data (rounds) [68], the PR (green dash lines) and SRK (blue dash lines) EOSs [67], this work (red lines): P is the pressure, ρ is the density, and T is temperature.

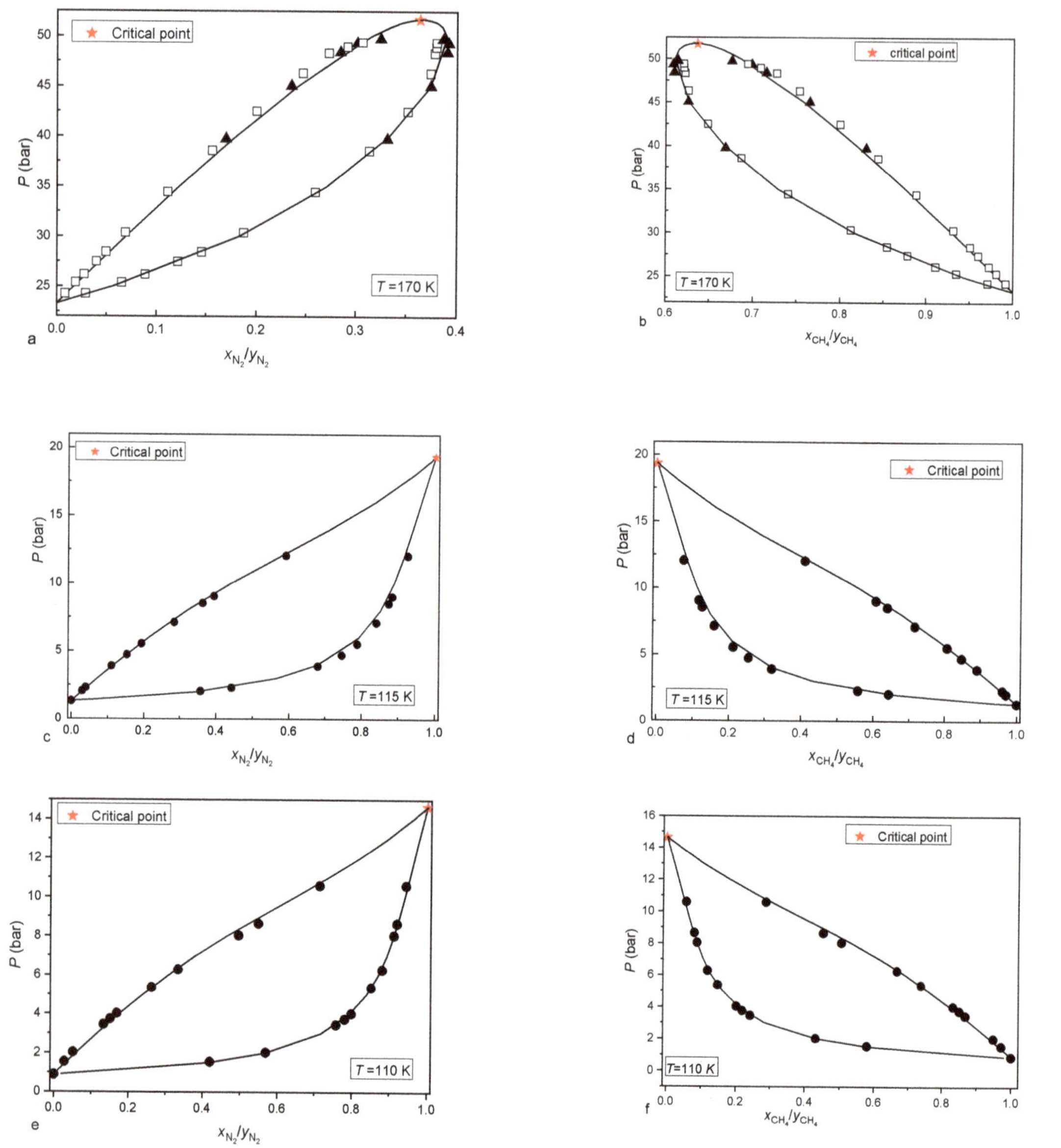

Figure 3. Vapor-liquid phase equilibria of the CH_4-N_2 system at different temperatures, (**a**) P-x_{N_2}/y_{N_2} figure at 170 K; (**b**) P-x_{CH_4}/y_{CH_4} figure for 170 K; (**c**) P-x_{N_2}/y_{N_2} figure for 115 K; (**d**) P-x_{CH_4}/y_{CH_4} figure for 115 K; (**e**) P-x_{N_2}/y_{N_2} figure for 110 K; (**f**) P-x_{CH_4}/y_{CH_4} figure for 110 K. Experimental data (rounds [55], triangles [57], squares [59]), this work (solid lines): x_{N_2} and y_{N_2} are the mole fractions of N_2 in the liquid and vapor phases, respectively x_{CH_4} and y_{CH_4} are the mole fractions of CH_4 in the liquid and vapor phases, respectively.

2.2. The Ternary CO_2-CH_4-N_2 Mixture

Combining binary interaction parameters of the CH_4-CO_2, CO_2-N_2 and CH_4-N_2 systems, the EOS can also predict the thermodynamic properties of the CO_2-CH_4-N_2 mixture. Here, the experimental *PVTx* and vapor-liquid equilibrium data are used to verify the accuracy of this EOS for the ternary mixture.

The calculated *PVTx* deviations for the ternary CO_2-CH_4-N_2 mixture from each experimental data set [1,64,69–71] are given in Table 4, where the temperature and pressure of the *PVTx* data are up to 573.15 K and 1000 bar, and the composition almost covers the full range. The average absolute deviation of all *PVTx* data from this EOS is 0.40% for the CO_2-CH_4-N_2 fluid mixture. Figure 4 shows the comparison between experimental data [71] and calculated densities for the CO_2-CH_4-N_2 mixture at different temperatures. It can be seen from Figure 4 that calculated densities from this EOS are in good agreement with experiment data, indicating that this EOS has a good predictive ability for the CO_2-CH_4-N_2 mixture.

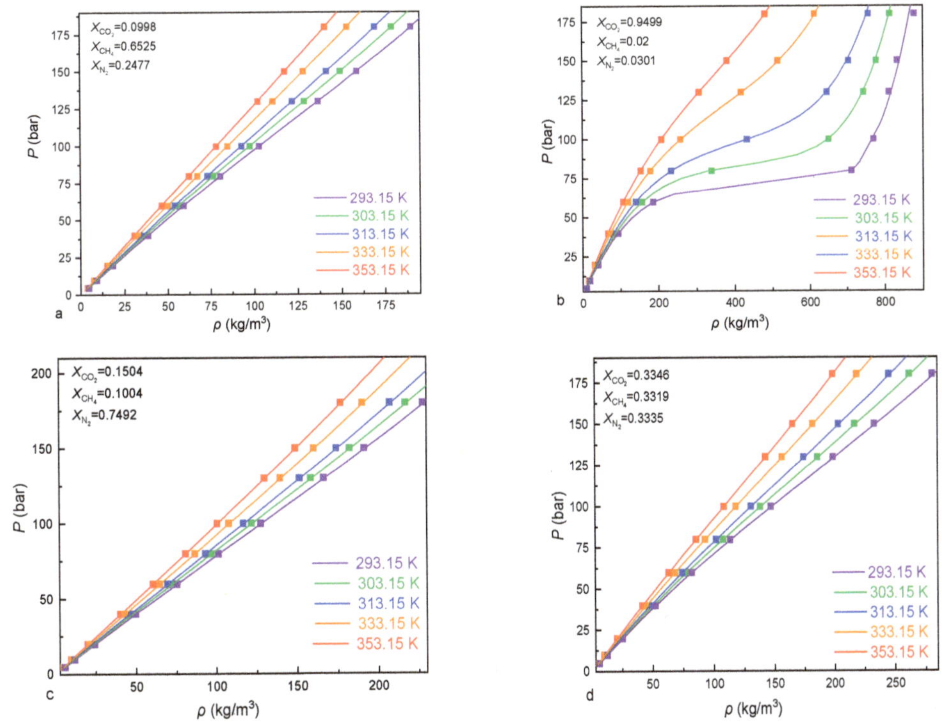

Figure 4. Comparisons between experimental and calculated densities for the CO_2-CH_4-N_2 mixture at different temperatures. (**a**) $X_{CO_2} = 0.0998$, $X_{CH_4} = 0.6625$, $X_{N_2} = 0.2477$; (**b**) $X_{CO_2} = 0.9949$, $X_{CH_4} = 0.02$, $X_{N_2} = 0.0301$; (**c**)$X_{CO_2} = 0.1504$, $X_{CH_4} = 0.1004$, $X_{N_2} = 0.7492$; (**d**) $X_{CO_2} = 0.3346$, $X_{CH_4} = 0.3319$, $X_{N_2} = 0.3335$. Experimental data (squares [71]), this work (solid lines): X_{CO_2} is the mole fraction of CO_2 in the mixture, X_{CH_4} is the mole fraction of CH_4 in the mixture, X_{N_2} is the mole fraction of N_2 in the mixture.

Table 4. Calculated *PVTx* deviations for the ternary CO_2-CH_4-N_2 mixture.

References	N	*T-P-x* Range for xCO_2-yCH_4-$(1-x-y)$ N_2				AAD%
		T (K)	P (bar)	x	y	
McElroy et al. [59]	242	303–333	6–126	0–0.9998	0–0.999	0.45
Seitz et al. [60]	42	474.15	1000	0.0–1.0	0.0–1.0	0.28
Seitz et al. [55]	271	323–573	199–999	0.1–0.8	0.1–0.8	0.28
Zhang et al. [61]	200	293.15–353.25	5–180	0.098–0.9949	0.02–0.6525	0.52
Le et al. [1]	84	305.15	5–600	0.499–0.899	0.0505–0.331	0.82

Note: Deviations of the *PVTx* data are the density deviations. *N* is the Number of data points, AAD is the abbreviation of average absolute deviation.

The vapor-liquid phase equilibrium properties of the ternary CO_2-CH_4-N_2 system are shown in Figure 5, where the curves are calculated from this EOS, and the experimental data are from the literature of [72–74]. As can be seen from Figure 5, all the experimental data points in the non-critical region agree well with this EOS, but in the near-critical region (Figure 5c), the calculated values deviate largely from experimental data [72–74].

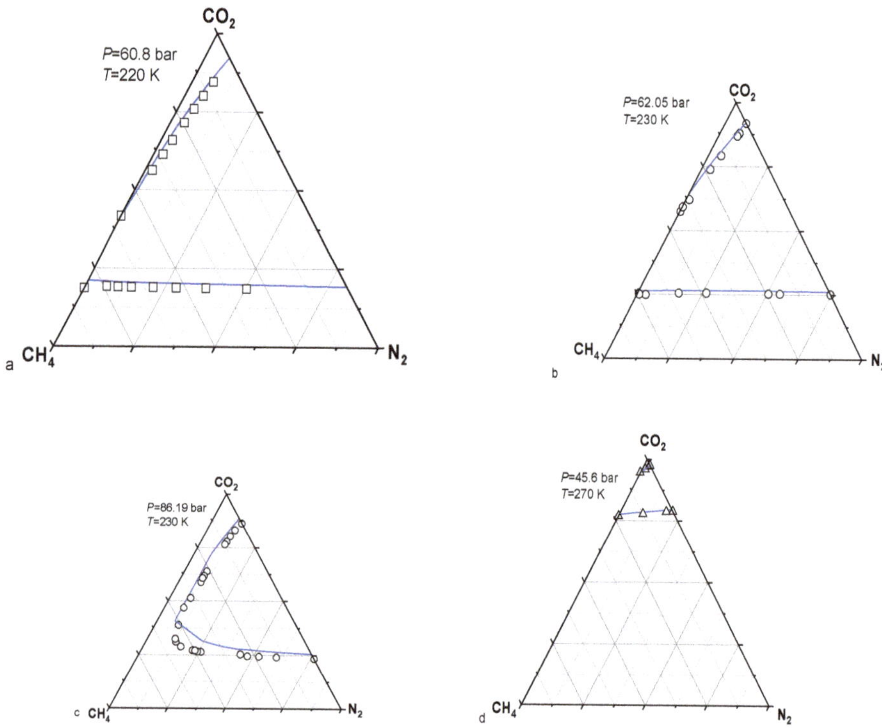

Figure 5. Vapor-liquid phase equilibria for the CO_2-CH_4-N_2 system at different temperatures and pressures, (**a**) T = 220 K, P = 60.8 bar; (**b**) T = 230 K, P = 62.05 bar; (**c**) T = 230 K, P = 86.19 bar; (**d**) T = 270 K, P = 45.6 bar. Experimental data (squares [73], rounds [72], triangles [74]), this work (solid lines).

3. The Applications of the ZMS EOS

3.1. Calculating Excess Enthalpies

The excess enthalpy (H^E) is an important thermodynamic property of the mixture for the mixing and separation processes, which is defined by

$$H^E = \left\{ H_m - \sum_i x_i H_i \right\}_{P,T} \tag{7}$$

where H_m is the enthalpy of the mixture, H_i is the enthalpy of pure component i, and x_i is the mole fraction of component i in the mixture. According to the thermodynamic relationship between Helmholtz free energy and enthalpy, H_m and H_i are given by

$$H_m = RT\left(1 + \tau\left(\alpha_\tau^0 + \alpha_\tau^r\right) + \delta\alpha_\delta^r\right) \tag{8}$$

$$H_i = RT\left(1 + \tau_i\left(\alpha_{\tau i}^0 + \alpha_{\tau i}^r\right) + \delta_i\alpha_{\delta i}^r\right) \tag{9}$$

where $\alpha_\tau^0 = \left(\frac{\partial\alpha^0}{\partial\tau}\right)_\delta$, $\alpha_\tau^r = \left(\frac{\partial\alpha^r}{\partial\tau}\right)_\delta$, $\alpha_\delta^r = \left(\frac{\partial\alpha^r}{\partial\delta}\right)_\tau$, $\alpha_{\tau i}^0 = \left(\frac{\partial\alpha_i^0}{\partial\tau_i}\right)_{\delta i}$, $\alpha_{\tau i}^r = \left(\frac{\partial\alpha_i^r}{\partial\tau_i}\right)_{\delta i}$ and $\alpha_{\delta i}^r = \left(\frac{\partial\alpha_i^r}{\partial\delta_i}\right)_{\tau i}$. δ_i and τ_i are the reduced density and inverse reduced temperature of pure component i, which are defined by

$$\delta_i = \rho_i/\rho_{ci} \tag{10}$$

$$\tau_i = T_{ci}/T \tag{11}$$

where ρ_i is the density of component i. Based on Equations (8)–(11), H_m can be calculated by this EOS of the CO_2-CH_4-N_2 fluid mixtures and H_i can be calculated by the above-mentioned equations of pure CO_2, CH_4 and N_2 fluids.

The calculated excess enthalpy curves of the CH_4-CO_2 and CO_2-N_2 mixtures are, respectively, shown in Figures 6 and 7, where the experimental data [75,76] are included for comparison. The following EOSs are also included for comparison: the standard Peng–Robinson (PR) EOS, either optimized (optimal k_{ij}) or not (k_{ij} = 0); the PR EOS with the residual part of the Wilson excess Helmholtz energy model (PR + EOS/$a_{res}^{E,Wilson}$) [19]. It can be seen from Figures 6 and 7 that this EOS is more accurate than the standard PR EOS, either optimized (optimal k_{ij}) or not (k_{ij} = 0) at most cases. In general, the PR + EOS/$a_{res}^{E,Wilson}$ and this EOS shows a similar predictive capability for the excess enthalpies of the CH_4-CO_2 mixture. However, this EOS is slightly more accurate than the PR + EOS/$a_{res}^{E,Wilson}$ for the CO_2-N_2 mixture at low pressures.

Figure 8 compares the excess enthalpy curves of the CH_4-N_2 mixture calculated from the ZMS EOS with experimental data [77], and enthalpies calculated from the Enhanced-Predictive-PR78 (E-PPR78) EOS [20] are also added for comparison. Figure 8a shows the ZMSEOS are significantly more accurate than the (E-PPR78) EOS at high and middle pressures. Figure 8b shows the enthalpies of mixing calculated from the E-PPR78 EOS are slightly better than those of the ZMS EOS at low and middle pressures, but the enthalpies of mixing calculated from the ZMS EOS are better than those from the E-PPR78 EOS at P = 101.33 bar.

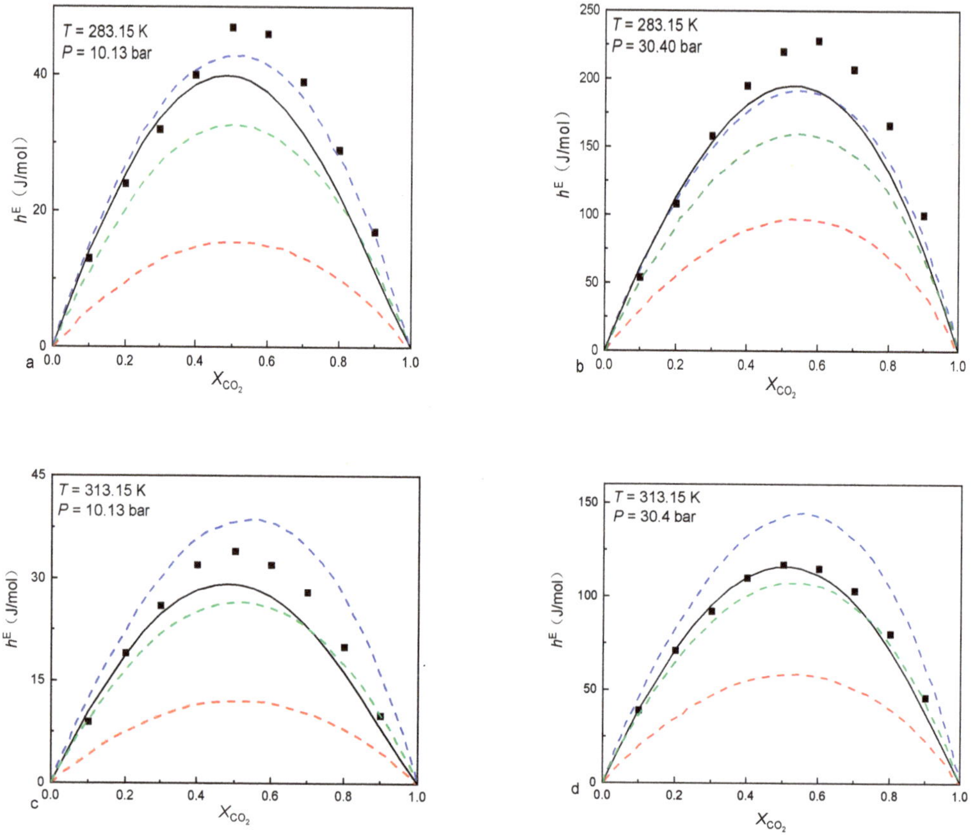

Figure 6. Comparisons between experimental and calculated mixing enthalpies for the CH_4-CO_2 mixture, (**a**) T = 283.15 K, P = 10.13bar; (**b**) T = 283.15 K, P = 30.40 bar; (**c**) T = 313.15 K, P = 10.13 bar; (**d**) T = 313.15 K, P = 30.40 bar. Experimental data (squares [75]). PR(k_{ij} = 0) (red dash curves); PR (optimal k_{ij}) (green dash curves); PR + EOS/$a_{res}^{E,Wilson}$ (blue dash curves); This work (black solid curves): h^E is the mixing enthalpy.

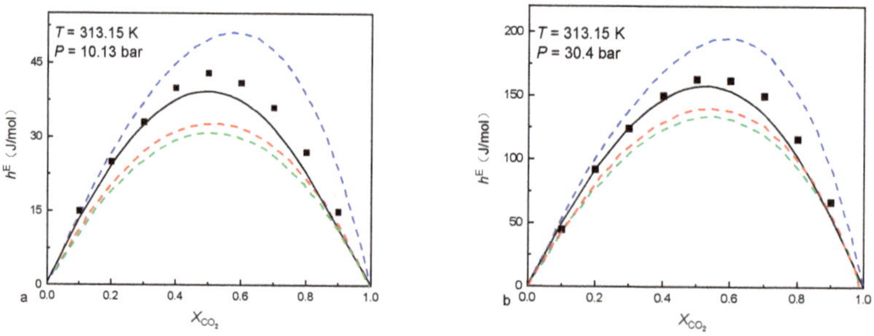

Figure 7. *Cont.*

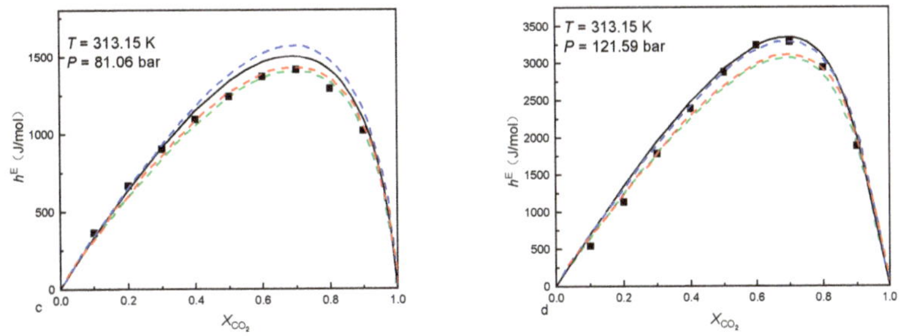

Figure 7. Comparisons between experimental and calculated mixing enthalpies for the CO_2-N_2 mixture, (**a**) T = 313.15 K, P = 10.13bar; (**b**) T = 313.15 K, P = 30.40 bar; (**c**) T = 313.15 K, P = 81.06 bar; (**d**) T = 313.15 K, P = 121.59 bar. Experimental data (black squares [76]). PR (k_{ij} = 0) (red dash curves); PR (optimal k_{ij}) (green dash curves); PR + EOS/$a_{res}^{E,Wilson}$ (blue dash curves); This work (black solid curves).

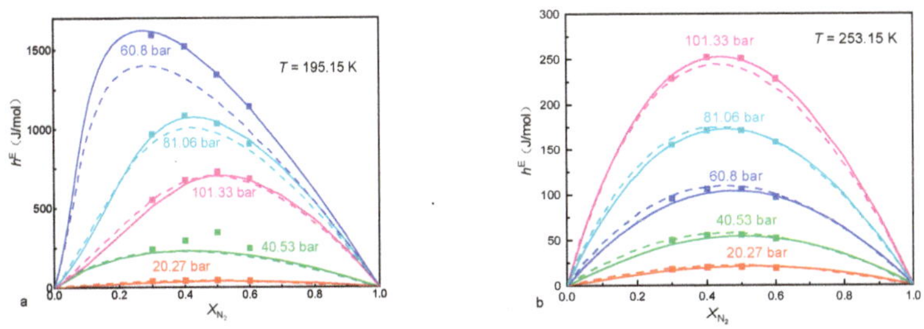

Figure 8. Comparisons between experimental and calculated mixing enthalpies for the CH_4-N_2 mixture at 195.15 K and 253.15 K. (**a**) T = 195.15 K; (**b**) T = 253.15 K. Experimental data (squares [77]), this work (solid curves); the Enhanced-Predictive-PR78 (E-PPR78) EOS (dash curves).

3.2. Calculating the Solubility of CO_2-CH_4-N_2 Mixtures in Aqueous Electrolyte Solution

The solubility of the CO_2-CH_4-N_2 gas mixtures in the electrolyte solutions can provide the quantitative assessment for the storage of CO_2 in deep saline aquifers. According to the thermodynamic principle, when the CO_2-CH_4-N_2 gas mixtures reach dissolution equilibrium in the electrolyte solution, the chemical potential of component i in the liquid phase (μ_i^L) and its chemical potential in the vapor phase (μ_i^V) are equal. The chemical potential can be written in terms of fugacity in the vapor phase and activity in the liquid phase

$$\mu_i^L = \mu_i^{L(0)} + RTlnm_i\gamma_i \tag{12}$$

$$\mu_i^V = \mu_i^{V(0)} + RTln\varphi_i y_i P \tag{13}$$

where i is the gas component in vapor mixtures, and P is the pressure in bar. y_i is the molar fraction of i in the vapor phase, φ_i is the fugacity coefficient of i in the vapor phase and m_i is the solubility of i in the liquid phase in mol/kg. γ_i is the activity coefficient of component i in the liquid phase. $\mu_i^{L(0)}$ and $\mu_i^{V(0)}$ are the standard chemical potential of i in the liquid and vapor phase, respectively.

At the dissolution phase equilibrium, $\mu_i^V = \mu_i^L$. From Equations (12) and (13), we can obtain

$$lnm_i = lny_i P + ln\varphi_i - \frac{\mu_i^{L(0)} - \mu_i^{V(0)}}{RT} - ln\gamma_i \tag{14}$$

Since the water content in the vapor phase at equilibrium is generally small, it has a negligible effect on the fugacity coefficient. When calculating the fugacity coefficient, the water content in the vapor phase can be ignored, the vapor phase can be approximated as the CO_2-CH_4-N_2 system and the mole fraction of gas component *i* in the vapor phase is expressed as y_i. Consequently, φ_i can be calculated from the ZMS EOS developed in this work.

Pitzer activity coefficient model [78] is chosen to calculate γ_i

$$ln\gamma_i = \sum_c 2\lambda_{i-c}m_c + \sum_a 2\lambda_{i-a}m_a + \sum_c\sum_a \zeta_{i-c-a}m_c m_a \tag{15}$$

where λ and ζ are second-order and third-order interaction parameters, respectively; c and *a* refer to cation and anion, respectively. Substituting Equation (15) into Equation (14) yields

$$\begin{aligned} lnm_i = \; & lny_iP + ln\varphi_i - \frac{\mu_i^{L(0)} - \mu_i^{V(0)}}{RT} - \sum_c 2\lambda_{i-c}m_c \\ & - \sum_a 2\lambda_{i-a}m_a - \sum_c\sum_a \zeta_{i-c-a}m_c m_a a \end{aligned} \tag{16}$$

As can be seen from Equation (17), m_i is related to the difference between $\mu_i^{L(0)}$ and $\mu_i^{V(0)}$, and is not related to the specific value of $\mu_i^{L(0)}$ or $\mu_i^{V(0)}$. Therefore, to simplify the model, $\mu_i^{V(0)}$ is assumed to be zero. Equation (16) can be simplified as

$$\begin{aligned} lnm_i = \; & lny_iP + ln\varphi_i - \frac{\mu_i^{L(0)}}{RT} - \sum_c 2\lambda_{i-c}m_c \\ & - \sum_a 2\lambda_{i-a}m_a - \sum_c\sum_a \zeta_{i-c-a}m_c m_a \end{aligned} \tag{17}$$

where $\frac{\mu_i^{L(0)}}{RT}$, λ and ζ are the function of temperature and pressure, and the parameters can be determined by the solubility model of pure gases (CO_2, CH_4, N_2). Since the 1980s, many solubility models for CO_2, CH_4 and N_2 gases in pure water and brine have been developed [79–91], most of which do not exceed 473 K and 1000 bar. Among them, the solubility models of CH_4, CO_2 and N_2 established by Mao and co-workers [83,86,91] are applicable to a wider range of temperature, pressure, and salinity with higher accuracy. They have been chosen as the solubility models of pure CH_4, CO_2 and N_2 gases in this work. Table 5 lists the applicable temperature, pressure, and salinity ranges of these solubility models for pure gases.

Table 5. Ranges of pure gas solubility models.

Pure Gas	T	P	Salinity (m_{NaCl})	References
CH_4	273–523 K	1–2000 bar	0–6 mol/kg	Duan and Mao [83]
CO_2	273.15–723.15 K	1–1500 bar	0–4.5 mol/kg	Mao et al. [91]
N_2	273–590 K	1–600 bar	0–6 mol/kg	Mao and Duan [86]

To verify the accuracy of the predictions, the experimental data for the solubility of the CO_2-CH_4-N_2 gas mixtures are compared with the calculated results. Figure 9 compares the experimental data on the solubility of the CH_4-CO_2 mixture in pure water [92,93] for the temperature range of 324.5–375.5 K and the pressure range of 100–750 bar, and it can be seen that the agreement is very good.

The solubility experimental data of the CO_2-N_2 gas mixture in pure water [94] and the calculated results are compared in Figure 10, where the temperature range is 308.15–318.15 K and the pressure range is 80–160 bar. As can be seen from Figure 10 the predictive results are in good agreement with the experimental data. The average absolute deviations between the calculated N_2 and CO_2 solubility of this model and the experimental data are 6.04% and 1.52%, respectively. Figure 11 compares the solubility experimental data of the CO_2-N_2 gas mixture in saline water. The average absolute deviations between the calculated N_2 and CO_2 solubility and the experimental data are 2.04% and 2.49%, respectively.

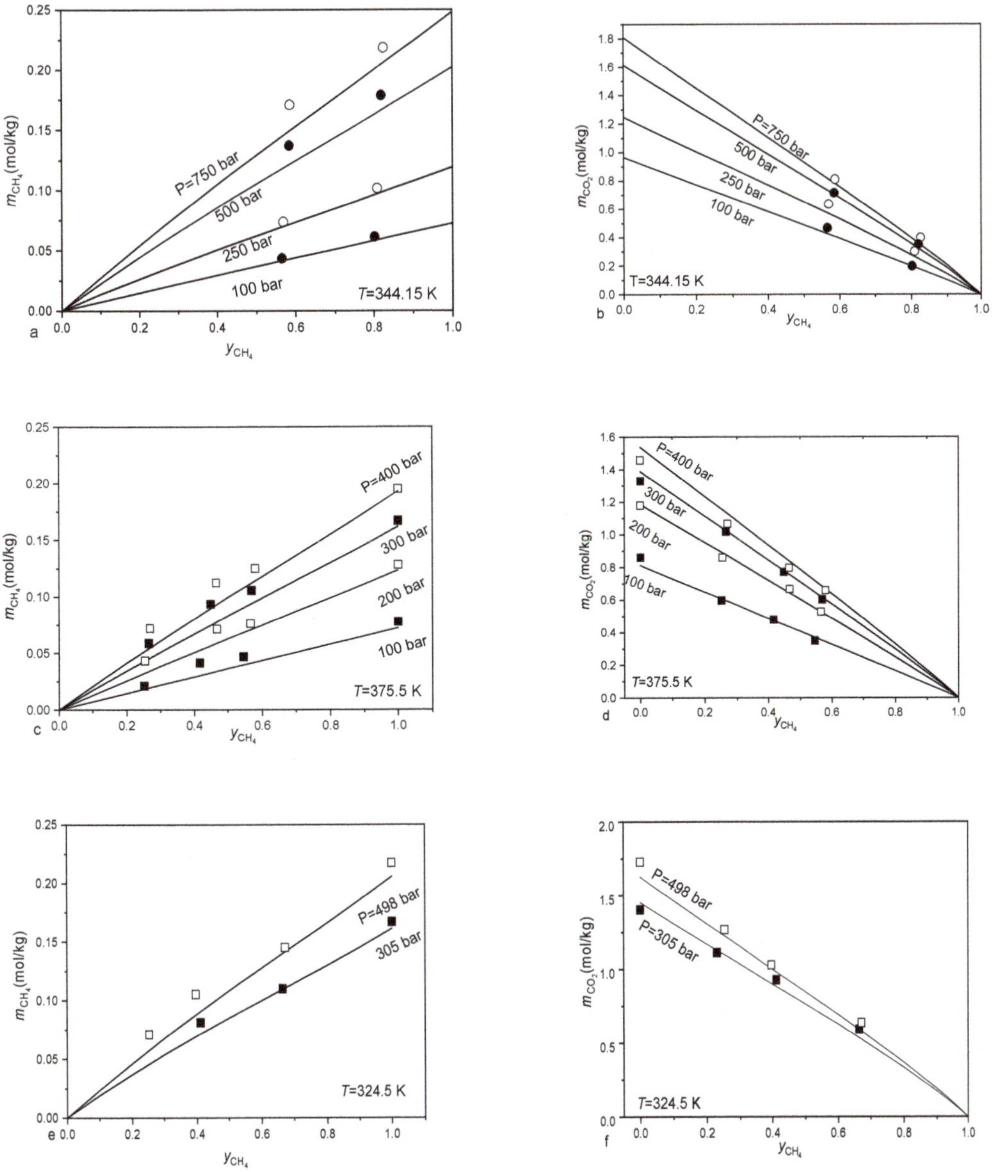

Figure 9. Comparisons between experimental and calculated solubilities for the CH_4-CO_2 mixture in water. (**a**) m_{CH_4}-y_{CH_4} figure at 344.15 K; (**b**) m_{CO_2} - y_{CH_4} figure at 344.15 K;(**c**) m_{CH_4} -y_{CH_4} figure at 373.5 K; (**d**) m_{CO_2} - y_{CH_4} figure at 375.5 K; (**e**) m_{CH_4} -y_{CH_4} figure at 324.5 K; (**f**) m_{CO_2} - y_{CH_4} figure at 324.5 K. Experimental data (rounds [92], squares [93]), this work (solid curves): m_{CO_2} is the solubility of CO_2, m_{CH_4} is the solubility of CH_4.

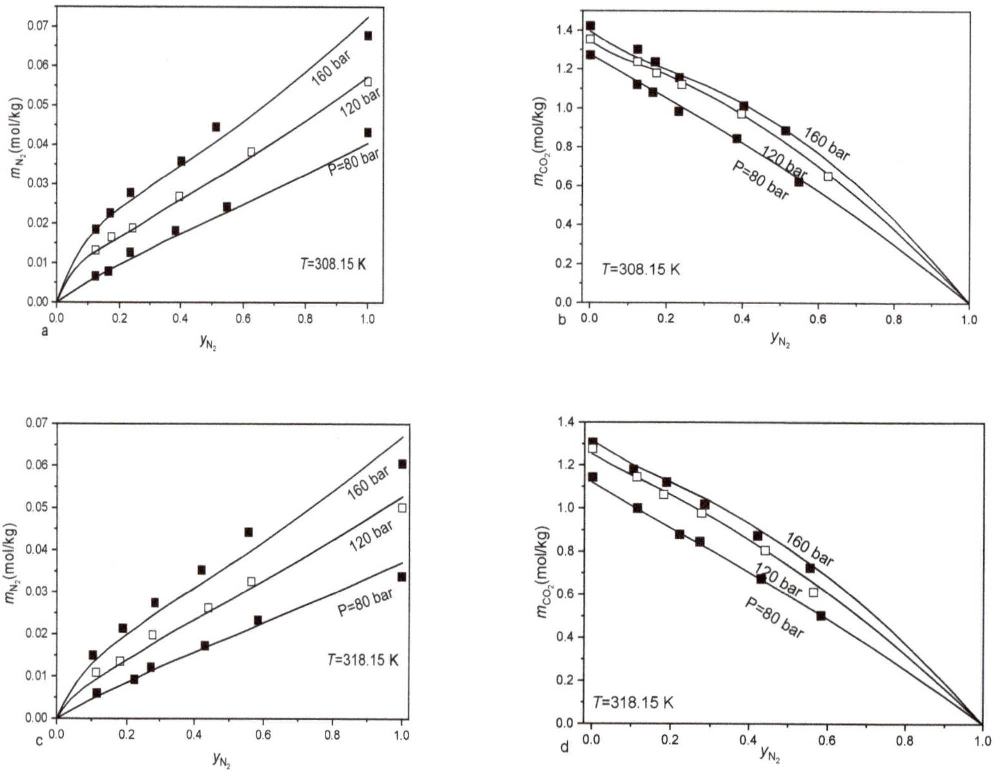

Figure 10. Comparisons between experimental and calculated solubilities for the CO_2-N_2 mixture in water. (**a**) m_{N_2} - y_{N_2} figure at 308.15 K; (**b**) m_{CO_2} - y_{N_2} figure at 308.15 K; (**c**) m_{N_2} - y_{N_2} figure at 318.15 K; (**d**) m_{CO_2} - y_{N_2} figure at 318.15 K. Experimental data (squares [94]), this work (solid curves): m_{N_2} is the solubility of N_2.

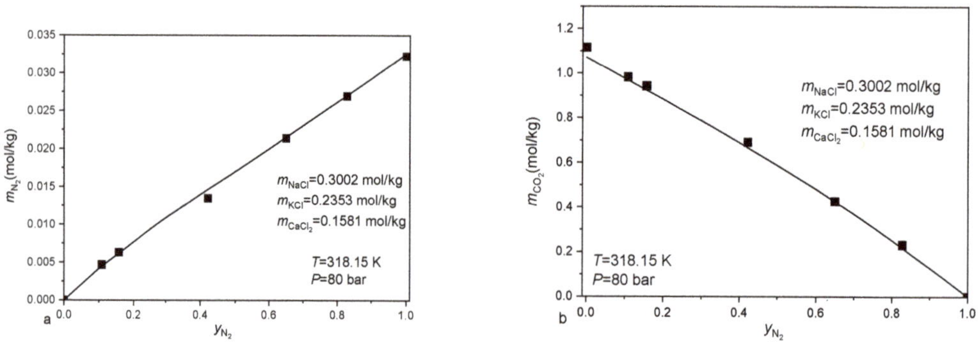

Figure 11. Comparisons between experimental and calculated solubilities for the CO_2-N_2 mixture in saline water. (**a**) m_{N_2} - y_{N_2} figure; (**b**) m_{CO_2} - y_{N_2} figrure. Experimental data (black squares [94]), this work (solid curves).

3.3. The Impact of Impurities (CH_4 and N_2) on the CO_2 Storage Capacity

CH_4 and N_2 are non-condensable impurities, which reduce the CO_2 storage capacity in geological formations. Based on the EOS of the CO_2-CH_4-N_2 fluid mixtures, the impact of CH_4 and N_2 on CO_2 storage capacity can be calculated quantitatively by the normalized storage capacity proposed by Wang et al. [9]. For a certain reservoir with a certain volume, the normalized storage capacity of the CO_2-CH_4-N_2 gas mixtures is shown as

$$\frac{A}{A_{CO_2}} = \frac{\rho}{\rho_{CO_2}(1 + \frac{M_{CH_4}}{M_{CO_2}} + \frac{M_{N_2}}{M_{CO_2}})} \quad (18)$$

where A and A_{CO_2} are the mass of CO_2 in the mixtures and the mass of pure CO_2 under the same volume, respectively. ρ_{CO_2} and ρ are the density of the pure CO_2 and CO_2-CH_4-N_2 gas mixtures, respectively; M_{CH_4}, M_{N_2} and M_{CO_2} are the mass of CH_4, N_2, and CO_2 in the mixture, respectively. A/A_{CO_2} is the ratio of the mass of CO_2 per unit volume in the mixture to that in the pure state. The value of A/A_{CO_2} can be viewed as the normalized storage capacity for CO_2 (i.e., the storage capacity for structural trapping of CO_2). For pure CO_2, the normalized storage capacity (A/A_{CO_2}) is 1. For the CO_2-CH_4-N_2 gas mixtures of a given composition, M_{CH_4}, M_{N_2} and M_{CO_2} are also known. ρ_{CO_2} can be calculated by the above-mentioned equation of pure CO_2 fluid and ρ can be calculated by the ZMS EOS.

The normalized storage capacity of the CO_2-CH_4-N_2 fluid mixture calculated by the ZMS EOS is plotted in Figure 12. Figure 12a shows the normalized storage capacity of a given composition at different temperatures. With the increase in pressure, the normalized storage capacity decreases at first and then increases, and there is a minimum point. When the temperature changes, the pressure corresponding to the lowest point of the normalized storage also changes. Figure 12b shows the normalized storage capacity of different compositions at the same temperature, which indicates that the content of impurities is much larger and the normalized storage capacity is much smaller.

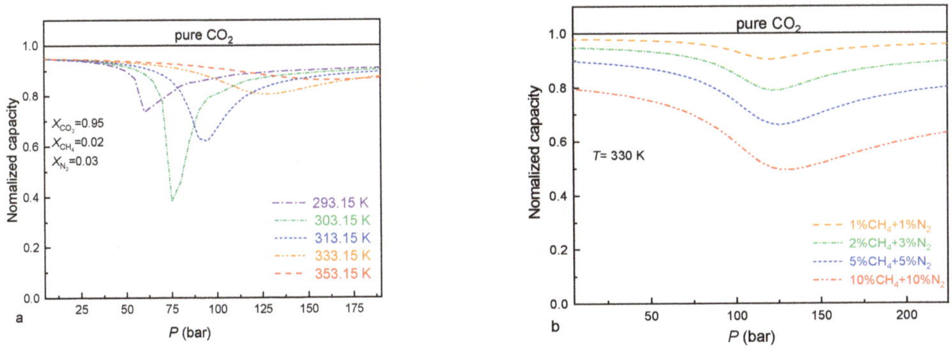

Figure 12. Normalized CO_2 storage capacity calculated by this EOS of CO_2-CH_4-N_2 mixture. (**a**) the Normalized capacity-P figure at different temperatures for the same composition; (**b**) the Normalized capacity-P figure at differents compositions for the same temperatures.

3.4. Isochores of the CO_2-CH_4-N_2 fluid Inclusions

In the studies of fluid inclusions, the isochores (pressure-temperature relation at constant density and composition) are frequently used to estimate the trapping temperatures and pressures.

Based on the EOS of the CO_2-CH_4-N_2 fluid mixtures, isochores of the CO_2-CH_4-N_2 inclusions can be calculated by the following equation:

$$P(\delta, \tau, x) = \rho RT[1 + \delta \alpha^r_\delta] \quad (19)$$

The calculated isochores of the CO_2-CH_4-N_2 inclusions at two different compositions are plotted in Figure 13, from which it can be seen that the isochores of the CO_2-CH_4-N_2 inclusions are a bit curved.

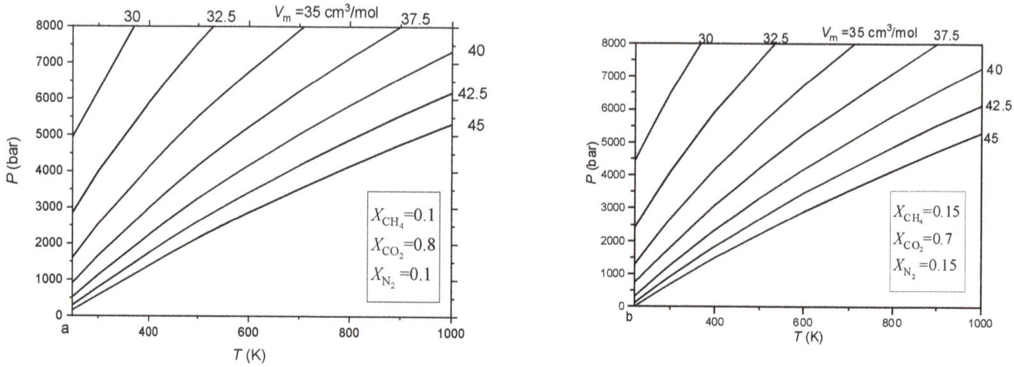

Figure 13. Calculated isochores of the CO_2-CH_4-N_2 mixture by this EOS, (**a**) $X_{CO_2} = 0.8$, $X_{CH_4} = 0.1$, $X_{N_2} = 0.1$; (**b**) $X_{CO_2} = 0.7$, $X_{CH_4} = 0.15$, $X_{N_2} = 0.15$: V_m is the molar volume.

This section may be divided into subheadings. It should provide a concise and precise description of the experimental results, their interpretation, as well as the experimental conclusions that can be drawn.

4. Conclusions

A fundamental EOS for the Helmholtz free energy of the CH_4-N_2 mixture has been developed by using four binary interaction parameters. Comparisons with experimental *PVTx* and VLE data available showed that the EOS can satisfactorily reproduce the experimental volumetric and vapor-liquid phase equilibria data of binary CH_4-N_2 mixtures up to 673.15 K and 1380 bar, with or close to experimental accuracy. Combining this EOS of the CH_4-N_2 fluid mixtures and the EOS of the CH_4-CO_2 and CO_2-N_2 fluid mixtures developed in our previous work, an EOS of ternary CO_2-CH_4-N_2 fluid mixtures has been presented, which is named ZMS EOS. The ZMS EOS can be applied to calculate excess enthalpies, predict the solubility of the CO_2-CH_4-N_2 gas mixtures in water and brine, estimate the impurities CH_4 and N_2 on the CO_2 storage capacity, and calculate the isochores of the CO_2-CH_4-N_2 fluid mixtures.

Author Contributions: J.Z.: Conceptualization, Software, Investigation, Writing—original. S.M.: Supervision, Methodology, Writing—review, and editing. Z.S.: Investigation, Software, Validation. All authors have read and agreed to the published version of the manuscript.

Funding: This research was funded by the National Natural Science Foundation of China (Grant No. 42073056) and Everest Scientific Research Program of Chengdu University of Technology (80000-2021ZF11419).

Institutional Review Board Statement: Not applicable.

Informed Consent Statement: Not applicable.

Data Availability Statement: Not applicable.

Conflicts of Interest: The authors declare that they have no known competing financial interests or personal relationships that could have appeared to influence the work reported in this paper.

References

1. Le, V.H.; Caumon, M.C.; Tarantola, A.; Randi, A.; Robert, P.; Mullis, J. Calibration data for simultaneous determination of *PVX* properties of binary and ternary CO_2-CH_4-N_2 gas mixtures by Raman spectroscopy over 5–600 bar: Application to natural fluid inclusions. *Chem. Geol.* **2020**, *552*, 119783. [CrossRef]
2. Caumon, M.C.; Tarantola, A.; Wang, W. Raman spectra of gas mixtures in fluid inclusions: Effect of quartz birefringence on composition measurement. *J. Raman Spectrosc.* **2020**, *51*, 1868–1873. [CrossRef]
3. Lüders, V.; Plessen, B.; di Primio, R. Stable carbon isotopic ratios of CH_4–CO_2-bearing fluid inclusions in fracture-fill mineralization from the Lower Saxony Basin (Germany)–A tool for tracing gas sources and maturity. *Mar. Pet. Geol.* **2012**, *30*, 174–183. [CrossRef]
4. Gaurina-Međimurec, N.; Mavar, K.N. Carbon capture and storage (CCS): Geological sequestration of CO_2. In *CO2 Sequestration*; IntechOpen: London, UK, 2019; pp. 1–21. [CrossRef]
5. Pires, J.; Martins, F.; Alvim-Ferraz, M.; Simões, M. Recent developments on carbon capture and storage: An overview. *Chem. Eng. Res. Des.* **2011**, *89*, 1446–1460. [CrossRef]
6. Bui, M.; Adjiman, C.S.; Bardow, A.; Anthony, E.J.; Boston, A.; Brown, S.; Fennell, P.S.; Fuss, S.; Galindo, A.; Hackett, L.A. Carbon capture and storage (CCS): The way forward. *Energy Environ. Sci.* **2018**, *11*, 1062–1176. [CrossRef]
7. Chapoy, A.; Burgass, R.; Tohidi, B.; Austell, J.M.; Eickhoff, C. Effect of common impurities on the phase behavior of carbon-dioxide-rich systems: Minimizing the risk of hydrate formation and two-phase flow. *SPE J.* **2011**, *16*, 921–930. [CrossRef]
8. Thoutam, P.; Rezaei Gomari, S.; Chapoy, A.; Ahmad, F.; Islam, M. Study on CO_2 hydrate formation kinetics in saline water in the presence of low concentrations of CH_4. *ACS Omega* **2019**, *4*, 18210–18218. [CrossRef]
9. Wang, J.; Ryan, D.; Anthony, E.J.; Wildgust, N.; Aiken, T. Effects of impurities on CO_2 transport, injection and storage. *Energy Procedia* **2011**, *4*, 3071–3078. [CrossRef]
10. Wetenhall, B.; Aghajani, H.; Chalmers, H.; Benson, S.; Ferrari, M.; Li, J.; Race, J.; Singh, P.; Davison, J. Impact of CO_2 impurity on CO_2 compression, liquefaction and transportation. *Energy Procedia* **2014**, *63*, 2764–2778. [CrossRef]
11. Blanco, S.T.; Rivas, C.; Fernández, J.; Artal, M.; Velasco, I. Influence of methane in CO_2 transport and storage for CCS technology. *Environ. Sci. Technol.* **2012**, *46*, 13016–13023. [CrossRef]
12. Li, H.; Yan, J. Impact of impurities in CO2-fluids on CO2 transport process. In *Turbo Expo: Power for Land, Sea, and Air*; American Society of Mechanical Engineers: Barcelona, Spain, 2006; pp. 367–375.
13. Li, H.; Yan, J. Impacts of equations of state (EOS) and impurities on the volume calculation of CO_2 mixtures in the applications of CO_2 capture and storage (CCS) processes. *Appl. Energy* **2009**, *86*, 2760–2770. [CrossRef]
14. Tenorio, M.J.; Parrott, A.J.; Calladine, J.A.; Sanchez Vicente, Y.; Cresswell, A.J.; Graham, R.S.; Drage, T.C.; Poliakoff, M.; Ke, J.; George, M.W. Measurement of the vapour–liquid equilibrium of binary and ternary mixtures of CO_2, N_2 and H_2, systems which are of relevance to CCS technology. *Int. J. Greenh. Gas Control* **2015**, *41*, 68–81. [CrossRef]
15. Shi, G.U.; Tropper, P.; Cui, W.; Tan, J.; Wang, C. Methane (CH_4)-bearing fluid inclusions in the Myanmar jadeitite. *Geochem. J.* **2005**, *39*, 503–516. [CrossRef]
16. Peng, D.Y.; Robinson, D.B. A new two-constant equation of state. *Ind. Eng. Chem. Fundam.* **1976**, *15*, 59–64. [CrossRef]
17. Soave, G. Equilibrium constants from a modified Redlich-Kwong equation of state. *Chem. Eng. Sci.* **1972**, *27*, 1197–1203. [CrossRef]
18. Van der Waals, J. *On the Continuity of the Gas and Liquid State*; Leiden University: Leiden, The Netherlands, 1873.
19. Lasala, S.; Chiesa, P.; Privat, R.; Jaubert, J.N. Measurement and prediction of multi-property data of CO_2-N_2-O_2-CH_4 mixtures with the "Peng-Robinson+ residual Helmholtz energy-based" model. *Fluid Phase Equilibria* **2017**, *437*, 166–180. [CrossRef]
20. Xu, X.; Lasala, S.; Privat, R.; Jaubert, J.N. E-PPR78: A proper cubic EOS for modelling fluids involved in the design and operation of carbon dioxide capture and storage (CCS) processes. *Int. J. Greenh. Gas Control* **2017**, *56*, 126–154. [CrossRef]
21. Heyen, G. An equation of state with extended range of application. In Proceedings of the Second World Congress of Chemical Engineering, Montreal, QC, Canada, 4–9 October 1981.
22. Heyen, G.; Ramboz, C.; Dubessy, J. Modelling of phase equilibria in the system CO_2–CH_4 below 50 °C and 100 bar. *Appl. Incl. Fluids Fr. Comptes Rendus Acad. Sci. Paris* **1982**, *294*, 203–206.
23. Darimont, A.; Heyen, G. Simulation des équilibres de phases dans le système CO_2-N_2. Application aux inclusions fluides. *Bull. Minéralogie* **1988**, *111*, 179–182. [CrossRef]
24. Thiery, R.; Vidal, J.; Dubessy, J. Phase equilibria modelling applied to fluid inclusions: Liquid-vapour equilibria and calculation of the molar volume in the CO_2-CH_4N2 system. *Geochim. Cosmochim. Acta* **1994**, *58*, 1073–1082. [CrossRef]
25. Thiéry, R.; Van Den Kerkhof, A.M.; Dubessy, J. vX properties of CH_4-CO_2 and CO_2-N_2 fluid inclusions: Modelling for T < 31 °C and P < 400 bars. *Eur. J. Miner.* **1994**, *6*, 753–771.
26. Thiéry, R.; Dubessy, J. Improved modelling of vapour-liquid equilibria up to the critical region. Application to the CO_2-CH_4- N_2 system. *Fluid Phase Equilibria* **1996**, *121*, 111–123. [CrossRef]
27. Lee, B.I.; Kesler, M.G. A generalized thermodynamic correlation based on three-parameter corresponding states. *AIChE J.* **1975**, *21*, 510–527. [CrossRef]
28. Bakker, R.; Diamond, L.W. Determination of the composition and molar volume of H_2O-CO_2 fluid inclusions by microthermometry. *Geochim. Cosmochim. Acta* **2000**, *64*, 1753–1764. [CrossRef]
29. Chapman, W.G.; Gubbins, K.E.; Jackson, G.; Radosz, M. New reference equation of state for associating liquids. *Ind. Eng. Chem. Res.* **1990**, *29*, 1709–1721. [CrossRef]

30. Gross, J.; Sadowski, G. Perturbed-Chain SAFT: An Equation of State Based on a Perturbation Theory for Chain Molecules. *Ind. Eng. Chem. Res.* **2001**, *40*, 1244–1260. [CrossRef]
31. Kouskoumvekaki, I.A.; von Solms, N.; Michelsen, M.L.; Kontogeorgis, G.M. Application of the perturbed chain SAFT equation of state to complex polymer systems using simplified mixing rules. *Fluid Phase Equilibria* **2004**, *215*, 71–78. [CrossRef]
32. Gil-Villegas, A.; Galindo, A.; Whitehead, P.J.; Mills, S.J.; Jackson, G.; Burgess, A.N. Statistical associating fluid theory for chain molecules with attractive potentials of variable. *J. Chem. Phys.* **1997**, *106*, 4168–4186. [CrossRef]
33. Kraska, T.; Gubbins, K.E. Phase Equilibria Calculations with a Modified SAFT Equation of State. 2. Binary Mixtures of n-Alkanes, 1-Alkanols, and Water. *Ind. Eng. Chem. Res.* **1996**, *35*, 4738–4746. [CrossRef]
34. Zhang, J.; Mao, S.; Peng, Q. An improved equation of state of binary CO_2–N_2 fluid mixture and its application in the studies of fluid inclusions. *Fluid Phase Equilibria* **2020**, *513*, 112554. [CrossRef]
35. Lemmon, E.W.; Jacobsen, R. A generalized model for the thermodynamic properties of mixtures. *Int. J. Thermophys.* **1999**, *20*, 825–835. [CrossRef]
36. Gernert, J.; Span, R. EOS-CG: A Helmholtz energy mixture model for humid gases and CCS mixtures. *J. Chem. Thermodyn.* **2016**, *93*, 274–293. [CrossRef]
37. Kunz, O.; Klimeck, R.; Wagner, W.; Jaeschke, M. *The GERG-2004 Wide-Range Reference Equation of State for Natural Gases and Other Mixtures*; GERG Technical Monographs 15; GERG: Düsseldorf, Germany, 2007.
38. Mao, S.; Lü, M.; Shi, Z. Prediction of the PVTx and VLE properties of natural gases with a general Helmholtz equation of state. Part I: Application to the CH_4-C_2H_6-C_3H_8 -CO_2 -N_2 system. *Geochim. Cosmochim. Acta* **2017**, *219*, 74–95. [CrossRef]
39. Herrig, S. *New Helmholtz-Energy Equations of State for Pure Fluids and CCS Relevant Mixtures*; Ruhr-Universität Bochum: Bochum, Germany, 2018.
40. Mao, S.; Shi, L.; Peng, Q.; Lü, M. Thermodynamic modeling of binary CH_4–CO_2 fluid inclusions. *Appl. Geochem.* **2016**, *66*, 65–72. [CrossRef]
41. Span, R.; Wagner, W. A new equation of state for carbon dioxide covering the fluid region from the triple-point temperature to 1100 K at pressures up to 800 MPa. *J. Phys. Chem. Ref. Data* **1996**, *25*, 1509–1596. [CrossRef]
42. Setzmann, U.; Wagner, W. A new equation of state and tables of thermodynamic properties for methane covering the range from the melting line to 625 K at pressures up to 1000 MPa. *J. Phys. Chem. Ref. Data* **1991**, *20*, 1061–1155. [CrossRef]
43. Span, R.; Lemmon, E.W.; Jacobsen, R.T.; Wagner, W.; Yokozeki, A. A reference equation of state for the thermodynamic properties of nitrogen for temperatures from 63.151 to 1000 K and pressures to 2200 MPa. *J. Phys. Chem. Ref. Data* **2000**, *29*, 1361–1433. [CrossRef]
44. Lemmon, E.W.; Huber, M.L.; McLinden, M.O. NIST reference fluid thermodynamic and transport properties–REFPROP. *NIST Stand. Ref. Database* **2002**, *23*, v7.
45. Liu, Y.P.; Miller, R. Temperature dependence of excess volumes for simple liquid mixtures: Ar+ CH_4, N_2+ CH_4. *J. Chem. Thermodyn.* **1972**, *4*, 85–98. [CrossRef]
46. Rodosevich, J.B.; Miller, R.C. Experimental liquid mixture densities for testing and improving correlations for liquefied natural gas. *AIChE J.* **1973**, *19*, 729–735. [CrossRef]
47. Pan, W.; Mady, M.; Miller, R. Dielectric constants and Clausius-Mossotti functions for simple liquid mixtures: Systems containing nitrogen, argon and light hydrocarbons. *AIChE J.* **1975**, *21*, 283–289. [CrossRef]
48. Hiza, M.; Haynes, W.; Parrish, W. Orthobaric liquid densities and excess volumes for binary mixtures of low molarmass alkanes and nitrogen between 105 and 140 K. *J. Chem. Thermodyn.* **1977**, *9*, 873–896. [CrossRef]
49. Da Ponte, M.N.; Streett, W.; Staveley, L. An experimental study of the equation of state of liquid mixtures of nitrogen and methane, and the effect of pressure on their excess thermodynamic functions. *J. Chem. Thermodyn.* **1978**, *10*, 151–168. [CrossRef]
50. Ababio, B.; McElroy, P.; Williamson, C. Second and third virial coefficients for (methane+ nitrogen). *J. Chem. Thermodyn.* **2001**, *33*, 413–421. [CrossRef]
51. Brandt, L.W.; Stroud, L. Phase Equilibria in Natural Gas Systems. Apparatus with Windowed Cell for 800 PSIG and Temperatures to 320° F. *Ind. Eng. Chem.* **1958**, *50*, 849–852. [CrossRef]
52. Chamorro, C.; Segovia, J.; Martín, M.; Villamañán, M.; Estela Uribe, J.; Trusler, J. Measurement of the (pressure, density, temperature) relation of two (methane+ nitrogen) gas mixtures at temperatures between 240 and 400 K and pressures up to 20 MPa using an accurate single-sinker densimeter. *J. Chem. Thermodyn.* **2006**, *38*, 916–922. [CrossRef]
53. Cheung, H.; Wang, D.I.J. Solubility of volatile gases in hydrocarbon solvents at cryogenic temperatures. *Ind. Eng. Chem. Fundam.* **1964**, *3*, 355–361. [CrossRef]
54. Gomez-Osorio, M.A.; Browne, R.A.; Carvajal Diaz, M.; Hall, K.R.; Holste, J.C. Density measurements for ethane, carbon dioxide, and methane+ nitrogen mixtures from 300 to 470 K up to 137 MPa using a vibrating tube densimeter. *J. Chem. Eng. Data* **2016**, *61*, 2791–2798. [CrossRef]
55. Han, X.H.; Zhang, Y.J.; Gao, Z.J.; Xu, Y.J.; Wang, Q.; Chen, G.M. Vapor–liquid equilibrium for the mixture nitrogen (N_2) + methane (CH_4) in the temperature range of (110 to 125) K. *J. Chem. Eng. Data* **2012**, *57*, 1621–1626. [CrossRef]
56. Haynes, W.; McCarty, R. Low-density isochoric (P, V, T) measurements on (nitrogen+ methane). *J. Chem. Thermodyn.* **1983**, *15*, 815–819. [CrossRef]
57. Janisch, J.; Raabe, G.; Köhler, J. Vapor– liquid equilibria and saturated liquid densities in binary mixtures of nitrogen, methane, and ethane and their correlation using the VTPR and PSRK GCEOS. *J. Chem. Eng. Data* **2007**, *52*, 1897–1903. [CrossRef]

58. Jin, Z.; Liu, K.; Sheng, W. Vapor-liquid equilibrium in binary and ternary mixtures of nitrogen, argon, and methane. *J. Chem. Eng. Data* **1993**, *38*, 353–355. [CrossRef]
59. Kidnay, A.; Miller, R.; Parrish, W.; Hiza, M. Liquid-vapor phase equilibria in the N_2+CH_4 system from 130 to 180 K. *Cryogenics* **1975**, *15*, 531–540. [CrossRef]
60. Li, H.; Gong, M.; Guo, H.; Dong, X.; Wu, J. Measurement of the (pressure, density, temperature) relation of a (methane + nitrogen) gaseous mixture using an accurate single-sinker densimeter. *J. Chem. Thermodyn.* **2013**, *59*, 233–238. [CrossRef]
61. McClure, D.; Lewis, K.; Miller, R.; Staveley, L. Excess enthalpies and Gibbs free energies for nitrogen+ methane at temperatures below the critical point of nitrogen. *J. Chem. Thermodyn.* **1976**, *8*, 785–792. [CrossRef]
62. Miller, R.; Kidnay, A.; Hiza, M. Liquid-vapor equilibria at 112.00 K for systems containing nitrogen, argon, and methane. *AIChE J.* **1973**, *19*, 145–151. [CrossRef]
63. Seitz, J.C.; Blencoe, J.G. Volumetric properties for $\{(1-x)\ CO_2+\ xCH_4\}$,$\{(1-x)\ CO_2+\ xN_2\}$, and $\{(1-x)\ CH_4+\ xN_2\}$ at the pressures (19.94, 29.94, 39.94, 59.93, 79.93, and 99.93) MPa and the temperature 673.15 K. *J. Chem. Thermodyn.* **1996**, *28*, 1207–1213. [CrossRef]
64. Seitz, J.C.; Blencoe, J.G.; Bodnar, R.J. Volumetric properties for $\{(1-x)\ CO_2+\ xCH_4\}$,$\{(1-x)\ CO_2+\ xN_2\}$, and $\{(1-x)\ CH_4+\ xN_2\}$ at the pressures (9.94, 19.94, 29.94, 39.94, 59.93, 79.93, and 99.93) MPa and temperatures (323.15, 373.15, 473.15, and 573.15) K. *J. Chem. Thermodyn.* **1996**, *28*, 521–538. [CrossRef]
65. Straty, G.; Diller, D. (p, V, T) of compressed and liquefied (nitrogen+ methane). *J. Chem. Thermodyn.* **1980**, *12*, 937–953. [CrossRef]
66. Parrish, W.R.; Hiza, M.J. Liquid-Vapor Equilibria in the Nitrogen-Methane System between 95 and 120 K. In *Advances in Cryogenic Engineering*; Timmerhaus, K.D., Ed.; Springer: Boston, MA, USA, 1995; pp. 300–308.
67. Perez, A.G.; Coquelet, C.; Paricaud, P.; Chapoy, A. Comparative study of vapour-liquid equilibrium and density modelling of mixtures related to carbon capture and storage with the SRK, PR, PC-SAFT and SAFT-VR Mie equations of state for industrial uses. *Fluid Phase Equilibria* **2017**, *440*, 19–35. [CrossRef]
68. Jaeschke, M.; Hinze, H. *Determination of the Real Gas Behaviour of Methane and Nitrogen and Their Mixtures in the Temperature Range from 270 K to 353 K and at Pressures Up To 30 MPa;* Fortschritt-Berichte VDI, Verlag R. 6 Nr; VDI-Verlag: Düsseldorf, Germany, 1991; Volume 262.
69. McElroy, P.; Battino, R.; Dowd, M. Compression-factor measurements on methane, carbon dioxide, and (methane+ carbon dioxide) using a weighing method. *J. Chem. Thermodyn.* **1989**, *21*, 1287–1300. [CrossRef]
70. Seitz, J.C.; Blencoe, J.G.; Joyce, D.B.; Bodnar, R.J. Volumetric properties of CO_2+CH_4+N_2 fluids at 200° C and 1000 bars: A comparison of equations of state and experimental data. *Geochim. Cosmochim. Acta* **1994**, *58*, 1065–1071. [CrossRef]
71. Zhang, Y.; Zhao, B.; Zhao, C.; Zhang, J.; Chen, K.; Xu, Y. Density Characteristics of a Multicomponent $CO_2/N_2/CH_4$ Ternary Mixture at Temperature of 293.15–353.15 K and Pressure of 0.5–18 MPa. *J. Chem. Eng. Data* **2022**, *67*, 908–918. [CrossRef]
72. Al-Sahhaf, T.A. Vapor—Liquid equilibria for the ternary system N_2+ CO_2+ CH_4 at 230 and 250 K. *Fluid Phase Equilibria* **1990**, *55*, 159–172. [CrossRef]
73. Al-Sahhaf, T.A.; Kidnay, A.J.; Sloan, E.D. Liquid+ vapor equilibriums in the nitrogen+ carbon dioxide+ methane system. *Ind. Eng. Chem. Fundam.* **1983**, *22*, 372–380. [CrossRef]
74. Somait, F.A.; Kidnay, A.J. Liquid-vapor equilibriums at 270.00 K for systems containing nitrogen, methane, and carbon dioxide. *J. Chem. Eng. Data* **1978**, *23*, 301–305. [CrossRef]
75. Lee, J.; Mather, A. The excess enthalpy of gaseous mixtures of carbon dioxide with methane. *Can. J. Chem. Eng.* **1972**, *50*, 95–100. [CrossRef]
76. Lee, J.; Mather, A. The excess enthalpy of gaseous mixtures of nitrogen and carbon dioxide. *J. Chem. Thermodyn.* **1970**, *2*, 881–895. [CrossRef]
77. Klein, R.; Bennett, C.; Dodgge, B. Experimental heats of mixing for gaseous nitrogen and methane. *AIChE J.* **1971**, *17*, 958–965. [CrossRef]
78. Pitzer, K.S. Thermodynamics of electrolytes. I. Theoretical basis and general equations. *J. Phys. Chem.* **1973**, *77*, 268–277. [CrossRef]
79. Akinfiev, N.N.; Diamond, L.W. Thermodynamic model of aqueous CO_2–H_2O–NaCl solutions from− 22 to 100 °C and from 0.1 to 100 MPa. *Fluid Phase Equilibria* **2010**, *295*, 104–124. [CrossRef]
80. Chapoy, A.; Mohammadi, A.; Chareton, A.; Tohidi, B.; Richon, D. Measurement and modeling of gas solubility and literature review of the properties for the carbon dioxide− water system. *Ind. Eng. Chem. Res.* **2004**, *43*, 1794–1802. [CrossRef]
81. Chapoy, A.; Mohammadi, A.H.; Richon, D.; Tohidi, B. Gas solubility measurement and modeling for methane–water and methane–ethane–n-butane–water systems at low temperature conditions. *Fluid Phase Equilibria* **2004**, *220*, 113–121. [CrossRef]
82. Darwish, N.; Hilal, N. A simple model for the prediction of CO_2 solubility in H_2O–NaCl system at geological sequestration conditions. *Desalination* **2010**, *260*, 114–118. [CrossRef]
83. Duan, Z.; Mao, S. A thermodynamic model for calculating methane solubility, density and gas phase composition of methane-bearing aqueous fluids from 273 to 523 K and from 1 to 2000 bar. *Geochim. Cosmochim. Acta* **2006**, *70*, 3369–3386. [CrossRef]
84. Duan, Z.; Sun, R. An improved model calculating CO_2 solubility in pure water and aqueous NaCl solutions from 273 to 533 K and from 0 to 2000 bar. *Chem. Geol.* **2003**, *193*, 257–271. [CrossRef]
85. Dubessy, J.; Tarantola, A.; Sterpenich, J. Modelling of liquid-vapour equilibria in the H_2O-CO_2-NaCl and H_2O-H_2S-NaCl systems to 270 C. *Oil Gas Sci. Technol.* **2005**, *60*, 339–355. [CrossRef]
86. Mao, S.; Duan, Z. A thermodynamic model for calculating nitrogen solubility, gas phase composition and density of the N_2–H_2O–NaCl system. *Fluid Phase Equilibria* **2006**, *248*, 103–114. [CrossRef]

87. Portier, S.; Rochelle, C. Modelling CO_2 solubility in pure water and NaCl-type waters from 0 to 300 °C and from 1 to 300 bar: Application to the Utsira Formation at Sleipner. *Chem. Geol.* **2005**, *217*, 187–199. [CrossRef]
88. Shi, X.; Mao, S. An improved model for CO_2 solubility in aqueous electrolyte solution containing Na^+, K^+, Mg^{2+}, Ca^{2+}, Cl^- and $SO_4{}^{2-}$ under conditions of CO_2 capture and sequestration. *Chem. Geol.* **2017**, *463*, 12–28. [CrossRef]
89. Søreide, I.; Whitson, C.H. Peng-Robinson predictions for hydrocarbons, CO_2, N_2, and H_2S with pure water and NaCI brine. *Fluid Phase Equilibria* **1992**, *77*, 217–240. [CrossRef]
90. Spivey, J.P.; McCain, W.D.; North, R. Estimating density, formation volume factor, compressibility, methane solubility, and viscosity for oilfield brines at temperatures from 0 to 275 °C, pressures to 200 MPa, and salinities to 5.7 mole/kg. *J. Can. Pet. Technol.* **2004**, *43*. [CrossRef]
91. Mao, S.; Zhang, D.; Li, Y.; Liu, N. An improved model for calculating CO_2 solubility in aqueous NaCl solutions and the application to CO_2–H_2O–NaCl fluid inclusions. *Chem. Geol.* **2013**, *347*, 43–58. [CrossRef]
92. Dhima, A.; de Hemptinne, J.-C.; Jose, J. Solubility of hydrocarbons and CO_2 mixtures in water under high pressure. *Ind. Eng. Chem. Res.* **1999**, *38*, 3144–3161. [CrossRef]
93. Qin, J.; Rosenbauer, R.J.; Duan, Z. Experimental measurements of vapor–liquid equilibria of the H_2O+ CO_2+ CH_4 ternary system. *J. Chem. Eng. Data* **2008**, *53*, 1246–1249. [CrossRef]
94. Liu, Y.; Hou, M.; Ning, H.; Yang, D.; Yang, G.; Han, B. Phase equilibria of CO_2+ N_2+ H_2O and N_2+ CO_2+ H_2O+ NaCl+ KCl+ $CaCl_2$ systems at different temperatures and pressures. *J. Chem. Eng. Data* **2012**, *57*, 1928–1932. [CrossRef]

applied sciences

MDPI

Communication

Dynamic Mechanism of Dendrite Formation in Zhoukoudian, China

Ningqiang Liu [1,*], Yinfeng He [2], Shengchao Xu [3], Lei Xiong [1], Yushuai Wei [1], Jie Li [1], Peiyu Li [1] and Qingjie Gong [1]

1 School of Earth Sciences and Resources, China University of Geosciences, Beijing 100083, China
2 Urumqi Comprehensive Survey Centre for Natural Resources of China Geological Survey, Urumqi 830057, China
3 Yunnan Institute of Geological Survey, Kunming 650216, China
* Correspondence: lnqcug@cugb.edu.cn

Abstract: Dendrite, a typical geological pattern, is developed along the bedding plane in limestone and dolomite strata in Jinzigou area, Zhoukoudian, Beijing, China, with a self-similar dendritic morphology. In order to reveal the dynamic mechanism of its formation, the diffusion-limited aggregation method, a model of fractal growth, was selected to simulate the microscopic dynamic mechanism of its formation. Take an L × L square lattice, with L = 200 lattices, 20,000 particles, and L = 250 lattices, 30,000 particles, for simulation. Obtain the simulation results of the dendritic pattern and the intermediate results with 8057 and 10,827 random particles released in the simulation process with 20,000 particles. The results show that the pattern is a typical fractal pattern formed in the process of fractal growth, with a fractal dimension of about 1.6. Its morphology is characterized by fractal geometry, and the dynamic mechanism of its formation is the fractal growth phenomenon generated by self-organizing criticality. The growth process is a nonlinear and non-equilibrium evolutionary process, which is dynamic and far from equilibrium. It is consistent with the fractal dimension of Zhoukoudian dendrite (1.52–1.78). Diffusion-limited aggregation (DLA) is a typical growth process in fractal growth. It leads to the growth of randomly branching structures that closely resemble various important systems in the earth sciences, providing a theoretical basis for revealing the nature of complex geological processes.

Keywords: dendrite; diffusion-limited aggregation (DLA); fractal growth; pattern; Zhoukoudian

Citation: Liu, N.; He, Y.; Xu, S.; Xiong, L.; Wei, Y.; Li, J.; Li, P.; Gong, Q. Dynamic Mechanism of Dendrite Formation in Zhoukoudian, China. *Appl. Sci.* **2023**, *13*, 2049. https://doi.org/10.3390/app13042049

Academic Editor: Ricardo Castedo

Received: 6 January 2023
Revised: 31 January 2023
Accepted: 3 February 2023
Published: 4 February 2023

1. Introduction

Dendrite, a typical multi-branching formation, with a bushy, or feather-like pattern, is a kind of dendritic film, much like the impression of bryophytes or algae, which is mainly produced in the bedding plane, joint, fissure or mineral surface, cleavage plane, etc., of limestone, dolomite, marble, sandstone, etc. [1]. Because of its plant-like appearance, it is often mistaken for plant fossils (Figure 1). The name comes from the Greek word dendron (δένδρον), which means "tree," since the crystal's structure resembles that of a tree [2]. It has long been recorded in the literature of the Song and Yuan Dynasties of China [3].

Dendrite samples were collected in Jinzigou area, Zhoukoudian, Beijing (Figure 1), and developed in the limestone of the Majiagou Formation and marble of the Jingeryu Formation; they are iron dendrites. Morphological observation of dendrite shows that its local pattern and overall pattern have a high degree of morphological similarity, or self-similarity, which means that the dendritic pattern of dendrite has fractal geometric morphological characteristics. Here, the similar morphology is determined by the micro dynamic mechanism. To a certain extent, it can be approximately considered as a geochemical gene [4–9], just as genes determine biological characteristics.

Since the fractal term was creatively proposed by mathematician Mandelbrot in 1967 [10–12], with the gradual growth, maturity, and development of fractal itself, it has been cited by many disciplines and departments, and, at the same time, shows the vitality of fractal application in various disciplines. This is because it can reveal the essential structure of nature and describe the actual life of human beings [13–15]. It is an intuitive geometric language to describe the motion of chaos. In fact, it is a mathematical system in closer agreement with the real world, integrating many nonlinear science contents.

Figure 1. Dendrites in Zhoukoudian, Beijing, China. JZG01, JZG02, and JZG04 are limestone; JZG03 is marble.

Earth sciences are concerned with extremely diverse sets of strongly interacting and synergetic phenomena [16–18]. In order to better understand these phenomena, it is often necessary to accurately describe complex structures and their evolution far from equilibrium. The development of fractal geometry has provided a valuable new approach towards the quantitative description of the statistical properties of various structures ranging in size from large molecules to continental coastlines [11,12]. In recent years, many simple non-equilibrium growth models have been developed [18], one of which is the diffusion-limited aggregation model (DLA), introduced by Witten and Sander [19].

As for the formation of dendrite, it is generally believed that it is the result of the infiltration and diffusion precipitation of iron and manganese solutions along the bedding surface or fracture surface after the formation of rock [1]. It is tree-like pattern of some crystal aggregates of oxide of iron and manganese, exhibits fractal morphological structural characteristics, and should be the growth pattern formed by fractal growth [14,15]. In order to investigate the dynamic mechanism of the dendrite formation, the diffusion-limited aggregation model, a typical growth process in fractal growth, was selected to simulate the micro dynamic mechanism of its formation, providing a reference for revealing the formation essence of dendrite.

As mentioned above, dendrite has only been mentioned in a few studies, and it is only a very simple introduction, without systematic discussion, especially regarding the dynamic mechanism of its formation. In fact, dendrite is a typical geological pattern, representing a large class of important systems and structures in geoscience, such as fault systems, sand dune ripples, rock cracks, mud cracks, river networks, mineral growth, ore vein morphology, and the deposit formation process. Although the characteristics of these systems or structures are very obvious, we do not know the micro-dynamic mechanism of their formation process. The study of the dynamic mechanism of the formation of dendrite provides a good example for the in-depth understanding and discussion of the micro-dynamic mechanism of the formation of many similar typical geological phenomena (or patterns).

As we know, the natural system is very complex. Specifically, it is a complex system, a dynamic system far from equilibrium, a nonlinear and non-equilibrium evolutionary system. We hope to promote an understanding of the nature of natural phenomena and deepen the understanding of non-equilibrium phenomena by elaborating the microscopic dynamic mechanism of dendrite, one of the typical phenomena in nature. After all, most processes in nature are non-equilibrium, rather than equilibrium, processes. Non-equilibrium and nonlinear processes are the essence of nature.

2. Model

Diffusion-limited aggregation (DLA) is a typical growth process in fractal growth. This model is a very convincing model of fractal growth, proposed by Witten and Sander of the University of Michigan in 1981, aiming at describing the diffusion and condensation process of coal ash, soot, or metal powder suspended in the atmosphere. It is a fractal growth process, far from the equilibrium state [19–22].

The DLA model also shows the fractional power-law behavior of correlation function [19]. This model is a variant of the Eden model, and its initial state is a seed particle at the origin of the lattice. A second particle is added at some random site, far away from the origin. The particle walks randomly until it reaches a position adjacent to the seed. Then the walking particles become part of the cluster. Subsequently, another particle is introduced at a random distance, and it randomly walks until it joins the cluster, and so on. If a particle touches the boundary of the lattices during its random walk, it will be removed and introduced into another particle [18,23].

DLA is an important and valuable model for simulating random growth process. The mathematical model describing the growth of diffusion limited aggregation is the Laplace equation. The growth probability of the surface of the growth structure is given by the scalar field (or gradient perpendicular to the surface) $\Phi(r)$, obeying Laplace equation

$$\nabla^2\Phi = 0 \tag{1}$$

with boundary conditions $\Phi(r) = 0$ at all positions r occupied by the cluster and $\Phi(r) = 1$ (or some other constant value) for $|r| = \infty$. Singularities are avoided by choosing a finite size to use the Laplace equation. In the DLA model, the probability $P(r)$ of random walk particles visiting the lattice site at position r is proportional to $\Phi(r)$. This can be easily seen by comparing the discretized Laplace equation

$$\Phi(i,j) = \frac{1}{4}[\Phi(i-1,j) + \Phi(i+1,j) + \Phi(i,j-1) + \Phi(i,j+1)] \tag{2}$$

with the equation

$$P(i,j) = \frac{1}{4}[P(i-1,j) + P(i+1,j) + P(i,j-1) + P(i,j+1)] \tag{3}$$

that describes the probability of a random walk particle visiting a lattice site (i, j), that is, the probability of visiting its nearest neighboring lattice site [18]. Here, $\Phi(i, j)$ is the value of the scalar potential associated with the position lattice site (i, j) on the square lattice, and $P(i, j)$ is the probability that a random walk particle will be found at the position of the lattice site.

In summary, the DLA process of thousands of particles, overall, forms a distribution of particle concentration (or the probability distribution of finding particles). This concentration is large away from the growth center and zero at the edge of the clustered cluster. Therefore, a concentration gradient is formed from the distance to the edge of the cluster, which can be described by the first and second equations of Fick diffusion [20].

The first Fick diffusion equation describes the diffusion particle flow j as being equal to the product of the concentration gradient $\nabla\phi$ and the diffusion coefficient D:

$$j = -D\nabla\phi \tag{4}$$

The Fick diffusion second equation shows that the change in concentration over time is equal to the concentration of the diffusion particle flow.

$$\frac{\partial \phi}{\partial t} = -\nabla \cdot j = D\nabla^2 \phi \tag{5}$$

Here, j is the diffusion particle flow, and D is the diffusion coefficient. Because j is pointing in the direction in which the concentration gradient $\nabla\phi$ is decreasing, it has a minus sign in front of it. If the particles are diffused on a large enough square lattice, and the clustered clusters are small enough, the change in the concentration of the diffused particles over time can be considered as zero for most of lattices, and thus Equation (1) can be obtained.

3. Method

As mentioned above, this model has the following properties and characteristics: this kind of fractal structure follows the Laplacian equation of a movable boundary in the formation process; in the process of condensed growth, the condensed particles exhibit irregular diffusion motion in the Laplacian concentration field; the interface of the growth clusters shows complex and unstable properties [24].

The rules of the DLA model can be summarized as follows: take a square in two-dimensional Euclidean space and divide it into many small squares to form a square lattice. A stationary particle is placed on a lattice site near the center of the lattice as a seed, and a particle is randomly generated at a distance from the seed particle. It makes a random walk on each lattice site due to Brownian motion. The result is a collision with a seed particle, in which case, the particle attaches to the seed particle and combines with it to form a cluster. The second step is to walk to the edge of the lattice, so that the particle is absorbed and disappears. Then, a second particle is randomly produced, and the process is repeated until it becomes attached to the cluster or absorbed by the boundary. After this process is repeated many times, the connected set of a square will grow outward from the original square, as shown in Figure 2. Particles exhibit Brownian motion, so when the particle is released, it is specified to move to the adjacent left, right, top, and bottom squares with a probability of one-quarter, and this process continues until the particle leaves the boundary, or reaches the cluster.

Based on the classical DLA model and MATLAB, the dendritic morphology and growth process of the dendrite are simulated.

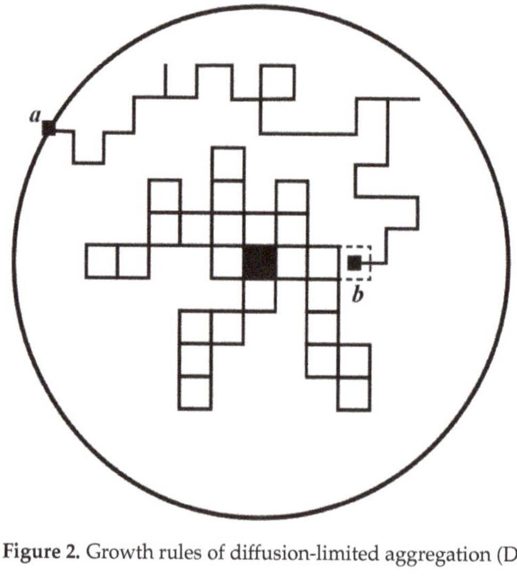

Figure 2. Growth rules of diffusion-limited aggregation (DLA) models.

Take an L × L square lattice and set a fixed particle in the center of the plane as a seed. The random function rand is used to randomly generate a particle in the plane, and the particle moves irregularly on the plane by Brownian motion. If the generated particle collides with the seed, it will be attached to the seed and form particle clusters. This process is repeated until a dendritic aggregate is formed in the lattice.

In computer simulation, first, set the size of the square grid as L = 200 or 250 and use the axis function to set the size of the square grid to L × L. Sparse function is used to generate an L × L all-zero sparse matrix, and then the seed position and seed number are set. The random function rand is used to generate random particles. Then, use the draw function to dynamically demonstrate the motion pattern of random particles. Determine the position of the random particles, count the number of "seed cluster" particles adjacent to random particles, and finally, graph these positions.

4. Result and Discussion

Figure 3 shows the computer simulation results of the DLA model, with L = 200 lattice and 20,000 particles. Figure 3a,b shows the simulated growth results when 8057 and 10,827 random particles are released, respectively, and Figure 3c shows the dendritic graph obtained after running the program (20,000 particles). From Figure 3, it can be clearly seen that the tree branches simulated by the DLA model continue to grow upward. It seems that the larger DLA cluster has more arms and fills the space more evenly than does the smaller cluster; its fractal dimension is 1.59 (Figure 4).

Figure 5 shows the computer simulation results of the DLA model, with lattice L = 250 and 30,000 random particles. This dendritic fractal pattern is relatively complex. Particles grow outward from the central seed. The dendritic pattern formed is gradually complicated. The fractal dimensions of the dendritic pattern shown in Figures 3 and 5 were calculated, using the box dimension method, to be 1.59 and 1.64, respectively (Figures 4 and 6).

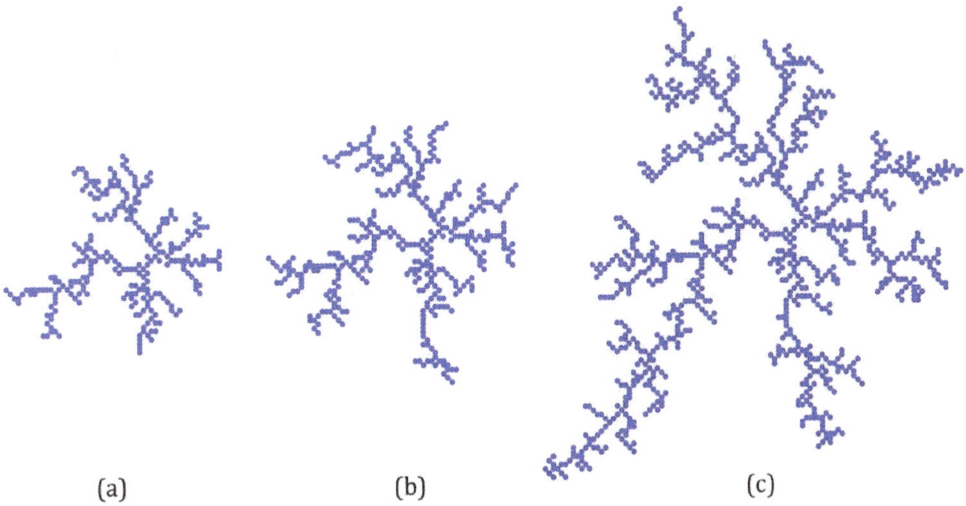

Figure 3. The dendritic pattern simulated by DLA (200 × 200 lattice, 20,000 particles). (**a**,**b**) the intermediate results of DLA simulation with 8057 particles (**a**) with 10,827 particles (**b**); (**c**) the result of DLA simulation with 20,000 particles.

In order to explore the simulation effect of the DLA model, the author selected four samples of dendrite—JZG01, JZG02, JZG03, and JZG04—in Zhoukoudian area for comparative analysis (Figure 1). The fractal dimension calculation method is the same as that of the simulated dendritic pattern, namely, the box dimension method. Through four steps:

extraction analysis location → image processing → image binary matrix data extraction → data statistical analysis, the box dimension method was used to calculate the morphological fractal dimension of the four samples in Zhoukoudian area. The results show that the fractal dimension of the four samples is 1.61, 1.67, 1.78, and 1.52, respectively, ranging from 1.52 to 1.78, with an average value of 1.65. The local fractal dimension of JZG03 is 1.77, while the overall fractal dimension is 1.78, indicating that the local pattern of the dendrite shows self-similarity to the overall pattern; that is, the dendritic pattern of dendrite has fractal characteristics. The fractal dimensions of the dendritic pattern simulated by the DLA model are 1.59 and 1.64, which are consistent with the fractal dimensions of Zhoukoudian dendrite. The simulation effect is good, which essentially reveals the microscopic dynamic mechanism of dendrite formation.

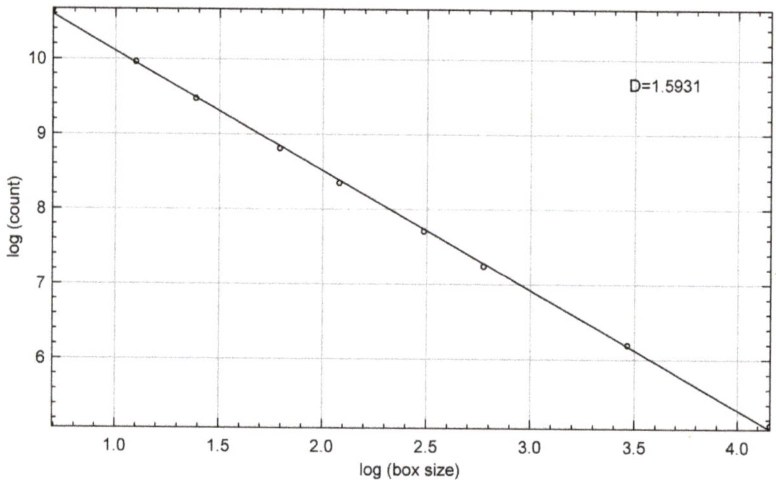

Figure 4. Fractal dimension of dendritic pattern simulated by 20,000 particles (as shown in Figure 3).

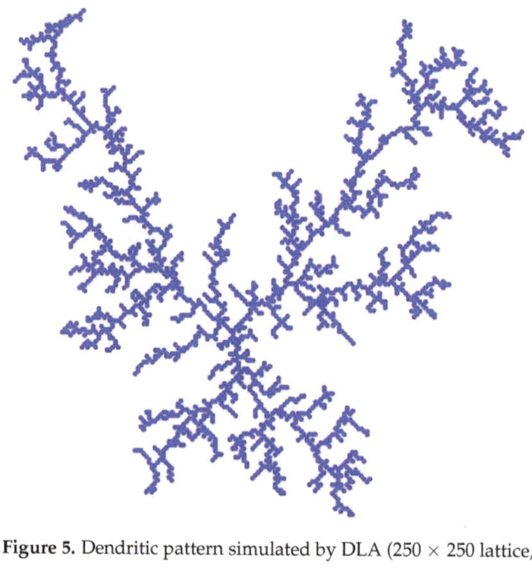

Figure 5. Dendritic pattern simulated by DLA (250 × 250 lattice, 30,000 particles).

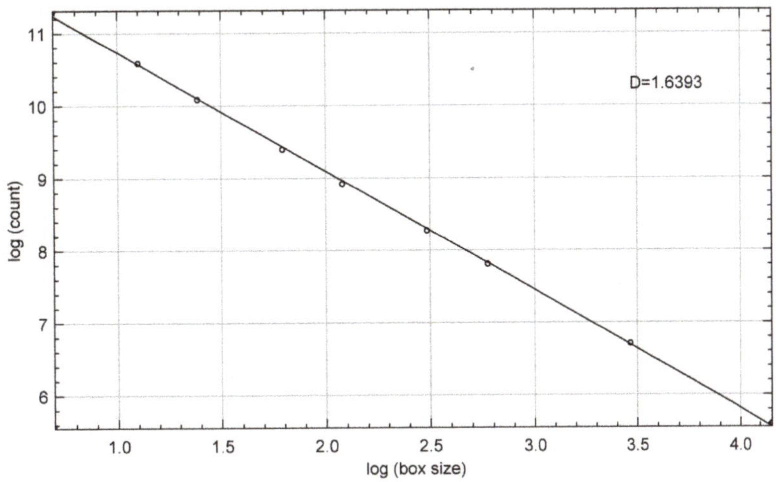

Figure 6. Fractal dimension of dendritic pattern simulated by 30,000 particles (as shown in Figure 5).

From the above, the agglomeration group (cluster) formed by the DLA model exhibits fractal characteristics. Moreover, previous studies have shown that the fractal dimension of DLA is independent of the lattice type [20]. The fractal dimension of the obtained DLA figure remains unchanged when the square lattice is changed into a triangular lattice [20], its fractal dimension does not increase with the increase in the spatial dimension, and it has a stable value [25].

DLA also has a screening effect [20]. The reason for the generation of branches with different sizes is that, due to the tortuous random motion trajectory of the particles, the branches that extend from the outside of the cluster have a greater probability of acquiring particles, which prevents the particles from intruding into the inside. This screening effect makes the clusters grow in the structure by continuously branching outward [26].

Figures 3 and 5 also show that, in the process of the random walking and outward growth of the particles, due to the high probability of obtaining particles from the branches extending outside the cluster, particles cannot invade into the interior. This screening effect makes the cluster grow continuously according to the outward branching structure, forming a complex dendritic pattern.

According to the above analysis, it is believed that the formation of dendrite is a fractal pattern formed in the process of fractal growth, that is, the microscopic dynamic mechanism of its formation.

In recent years, studies regarding fractal growth have developed rapidly [27–31]. According to the latest research results, fractal growth phenomena caused by self-organized criticality can be generally summarized into three main models: Laplace, percolation, and oscillation. For dendritic growth, these can be divided into two cases, the first being dendritic solidification, forming a solid dendritic pattern, and the second being viscous fingering, forming a fluid dendritic pattern. Under appropriate conditions, both can be studied using the DLA model.

Moreover, this dynamic mechanism reveals that the growth process is a dynamic process far from equilibrium, and it is also a nonlinear and non-equilibrium evolutionary process. It can be used to explain a large class of fractal formation processes in nature, such as fluid movement, dielectric breakdown, electrodeposition process, crystal growth in liquid film, viscous fingering, non-dendritic growth, loose rock dissolution and seismic cracking, etc. [32–37]. Therefore, it has attracted widespread attention, deepening the understanding of non-equilibrium phenomena. It has been widely used in some irreversible growth processes far from equilibrium. For example, Yu applied it to the study of mineral deposits [15,38–42], suggesting that the formation of mineral deposits is a fractal growth process, and that the dynamic mechanism of the formation of super-large deposits and ore-concentration areas constitutes the dynamics of fractal growth. In other words, super-large deposits and ore-concentration areas are realized and completed through the onset of ore formation followed by the snowball effect.

The diffusion-limited aggregation model, as well as various related models, have led to the growth of random branching structures that closely resemble various important systems in earth sciences. Although most processes in nature involve multiple mechanisms, the DLA model alone seems unlikely to provide an adequate understanding of these processes. However, the DLA model is one of the most striking examples of complex pattern generation using simple models and algorithms. It has become the dominant paradigm for pattern formation far from equilibrium, and it provides valuable examples for a wide range of natural phenomena. It gives us the first insight into the microscopic processes involved in the growth of branching structures, as well as the importance of random events or distributions to these growth phenomena. Above all, it does provide a good theoretical model for the formation mechanism of many typical geological phenomena (or patterns), such as fault systems, river networks, mineral growth, ore vein morphology and deposit formation process, etc.

5. Conclusions

The morphology of dendrite has fractal geometry characteristics, and in fact, the dynamic mechanism of its formation is the fractal growth phenomenon generated by self-organizing criticality. The growth process is a dynamic process far from equilibrium, which is a nonlinear and non-equilibrium evolutionary process. The diffusion-limited aggregation (DLA) model in the fractal growth theory can satisfactorily simulate the growth process and the formed pattern, which essentially reveals the microscopic dynamic mechanism of dendrite formation. The fractal dimensions of the simulated pattern are 1.59 and 1.64, which are consistent with the fractal dimensions of Zhoukoudian dendrite. DLA has led to the growth of random branching structures that closely resemble various important systems in the earth sciences, providing possibilities for revealing the nature of complex geological processes, and also for deepening the understanding of non-equilibrium phenomena.

Author Contributions: N.L.: conceptualization, methodology, formal analysis, data curation, and writing—original draft; Y.H.: conceptualization, data curation, and visualization; S.X.: investigation, formal analysis, and data curation; L.X.: formal analysis and data curation; Y.W.: conceptualization and investigation; J.L.: investigation and data curation; P.L.: investigation and data curation; Q.G.: conceptualization and writing—review and editing. All authors have read and agreed to the published version of the manuscript.

Funding: This work was financially supported by the Fundamental Research Funds for the Central Universities, China (Grant No. 2652018285).

Institutional Review Board Statement: Not applicable.

Informed Consent Statement: Not applicable.

Data Availability Statement: Not applicable.

Acknowledgments: We greatly appreciate the comments from the anonymous reviewers and editors for their valuable suggestions to improve the quality of this manuscript.

Conflicts of Interest: The authors declare that they have no known competing financial interest or personal relationships that could have appeared to influence the work reported in this paper.

References

1. Manutchehr-Danai, M. *Dictionary of Gems and Gemology*; Springer: Berlin, Germany, 2009; pp. 241–242.
2. Nanjwade, B.K.; Bechra, H.M.; Derkar, G.K.; Manvi, F.V.; Nanjwade, V.K. Dendrimers: Emerging polymers for drug-delivery systems. *Eur. J. Pharm. Sci.* **2009**, *38*, 185–196. [CrossRef] [PubMed]
3. Lin, J. The colorful world of dendrite. *Jewel. Gold* **2022**, *2*, 68–69. (In Chinese)

4. Gong, Q.J.; Yan, T.T.; Wu, X.; Li, R.K.; Wang, X.Q.; Liu, N.Q.; Li, X.L.; Wu, Y.; Li, J. Geochemical gene: A promising concept in discrimination and traceability of geological materials. *Appl. Geochem.* **2022**, *136*, 105133. [CrossRef]
5. Wu, Y.; Gong, Q.J.; Liu, N.Q.; Wu, X.; Yan, T.T.; Xu, S.C.; Li, W.J. Classification of geological materials on geochemical lithogenes: Illustration on a case study in Gejiu area of Yunnan Province, China. *Appl. Geochem.* **2022**, *146*, 105460. [CrossRef]
6. Gong, Q.J.; Liu, N.Q.; Wu, X.; Yan, T.T.; Fan, T.Q.; Li, X.L.; Liu, M.X.; Li, R.K.; Albanese, S. Using regional geochemical survey data to trace anomalous samples through geochemical genes: The Tieshanlong tungsten deposit area (Southeastern China) case study. *J. Geochem. Explor.* **2020**, *219*, 106637. [CrossRef]
7. Li, R.K.; Liu, N.Q.; Gong, Q.J.; Wu, X.; Yan, T.T.; Li, X.L.; Liu, M.X. Construction, test and application of a geochemical gold metallogene: Case studies in China. *J. Geochem. Explor.* **2019**, *204*, 1–11. [CrossRef]
8. Li, J.; Gong, Q.J.; Zhang, B.M.; Liu, N.Q.; Wu, X.; Yan, T.T.; Li, X.L.; Wu, Y. Construction, test and application of a Tungsten metallogene named MGW11: Case studies in China. *Appl. Sci.* **2023**, *13*, 606. [CrossRef]
9. Hou, Z.G.; Gong, Q.J.; Liu, N.Q.; Jiang, B.; Li, J.; Wu, Y.; Huang, J.X.; Gu, W.X. Elemental abundances of moon samples based on statistical distributions of analytical data. *Appl. Sci.* **2023**, *13*, 360. [CrossRef]
10. Mandelbrot, B.B. How Long Is the Coast of Britain? Statistical Self-Similarity and Fractional Dimension. *Science* **1967**, *156*, 636–638. [CrossRef]
11. Mandelbrot, B.B. *Fractal: Form, Chance and Dimension*; Freeman: San Francisco, CA, USA, 1977; pp. 1–365.
12. Mandelbrot, B.B. *The Fractal Geometry of Nature*; Freeman: San Francisco, CA, USA, 1982; pp. 1–460.
13. Zhang, J.Z. *Fractal*; Tsinghua University Press: Beijing, China, 2011; pp. 1–310. (In Chinese)
14. Yu, C.W. *The Complexity of Geosystems (Book 1)*; Geological Publishing House: Beijing, China, 2003; pp. 282–344. (In Chinese)
15. Yu, C.W. *Fractal Growth of Mineral Deposits at the Edge of Chaos (Book 2)*; Anhui Education Press: Hefei, China, 2006; pp. 105–174. (In Chinese)
16. Liu, N.Q.; Peng, N.; Gong, Q.J.; Liu, Y.S.; Yu, C.W.; Albanese, S. Spatio-temporal synchronization in complex ore-forming systems: Mesoscale case study in south China. *J. Geochem. Explor.* **2021**, *231*, 106873. [CrossRef]
17. Yu, C.W.; Peng, N. *Regional Ore Zonality of the Nanling Region*; Geological Publishing House: Beijing, China, 2009; pp. 1–256. (In Chinese)
18. Barton, C.C.; La Pointe, P.R. *Fractals in Petroleum Geology and Earth Processes*; Springer: New York, NY, USA, 1995; pp. 227–259.
19. Witten, T.A.; Sander, L.M. Diffusion-Limited Aggregation, a Kinetic Critical Phenomenon. *Phys. Rev. Lett.* **1981**, *47*, 1400–1403. [CrossRef]
20. Witten, T.A.; Sander, L.M. Diffusion-Limited Aggregation. *Phys. Rev. B* **1983**, *27*, 5686–5697. [CrossRef]
21. Bak, P.; Tang, C.; Wiesenfeld, K. Self-Organized Criticality: An Explanation of 1/f Noise. *Phys. Rev. Lett.* **1987**, *59*, 381–384. [CrossRef]
22. Sander, M.L. Diffusion-limited aggregation: A kinetic critical phenomenon. *Contemp. Phys.* **2000**, *41*, 203–218. [CrossRef]
23. Meakin, P. *Fractals, Scaling and Growth Far From Equilibrium*; Cambridge University Press: Cambridge, UK, 1998; pp. 1–674.
24. Gao, R.; Xie, S.Y.; Tao, J.D. Simulation for the fractal aggregation growth on the platform of MATLAB. *J. Southwest China Norm. Univ. Nat. Sci. Ed.* **2005**, *30*, 83–86, (In Chinese with English Abstract).
25. Satpathy, S. Dielectric breakdown in three dimensions: Result of numerical simulation. *Phys. Rev. B* **1986**, *33*, 5093–5095. [CrossRef]
26. Rosenstock, H.B.; Marquardt, C.L. Cluster formation in two-dimensional random walks: Application to photolysis of silver halides. *Phys. Rev. B* **1980**, *22*, 5797–5809. [CrossRef]
27. Stanley, H.E.; Ostrowsky, N. *Random Fluctuations and Pattern Growth: Experiments and Models*; Kluwer Academic Publishers: Dordrecht, The Netherlands, 1988; pp. 1–355.
28. Vicsek, T. *Fractal Growth Phenomena*; World Scientific: Singapore, 1992; pp. 312–319.
29. Bunnde, A.; Havlin, S. *Fractals and Disorder Systems*; Springer: Berlin, Germany, 1996; pp. 1–407.
30. Jamtveit, B.; Meakin, P. *Growth, Dissolution and Pattern Formation in Geosystems*; Kluwer Academic Publishers: Dordrecht, Germany, 1999; pp. 1–409.
31. Ben-Avraham, D.; Havlin, S. *Diffusion and Reactions in Fractals and Disordered Systems*; Cambridge University Press: Cambridge, UK, 2000; pp. 1–315.
32. Nittman, J.; Daccord, G.; Stanley, H.E. Fractal growth of viscous fingers: Quantitative characterization of a fluid instability phenomenon. *Nature* **1985**, *314*, 141–144. [CrossRef]
33. Meek, J.M.; Craggs, J.D. *Electrical Breakdown of Gases*; Wiley: New York, NY, USA, 1978; Volume 15, pp. 182–185.
34. Grier, D.; Ben-Jacob, E.; Clarke, R.; Sander, L.M. Morphology and microstructure in electrochemical deposition of zinc. *Phys. Rev. Lett.* **1986**, *56*, 1264–1267. [CrossRef]
35. Brady, R.M.; Ball, R.C. Fractal growth of copper electrodeposits. *Nature* **1984**, *309*, 225–228. [CrossRef]
36. Ben-Jacob, E.; Shochet, O.; Tenenbaum, A.; Cohen, I.; Czirok, A.; Vicesek, T. Generic modeling of cooperative growth pattern in bacterial colonies. *Nature* **1994**, *368*, 46–49. [CrossRef]
37. Sidoravicius, V.; Stauffer, A. Multi-particle diffusion limited aggregation. *Invent. Math.* **2019**, *218*, 491–571. [CrossRef]
38. Yu, C.W. Larger ore deposit and metallogenic districts at the edge of chaos. *Earth Sci. Front.* **1999**, *6*, 195–229.
39. Yu, C.W. *Fractal Growth of Mineral Deposits at the Edge of Chaos (Book 1)*; (In Chinese). Anhui Education Press: Hefei, China, 2006; pp. 1–9, 161–200.

40. Yu, C.W. Fractal growth of ore-forming dynamical systems at the edge of chaos, a new metallogeny and methodology (First half). *Earth Sci. Front.* **2001**, *8*, 9–28.
41. Yu, C.W. Fractal growth of ore-forming dynamical systems at the edge of chaos, a new metallogeny and methodology (Second half). *Earth Sci. Front.* **2001**, *8*, 471–489.
42. Yu, C.W. Fractal growth of ore-forming dynamic systems at the edge of chaos: A new metallogeny and methodology. *Bull. Mineral. Petrol. Geochem.* **2002**, *21*, 103–113.

applied sciences

MDPI

Article

Detrital Mica Composition Quantitatively Indicates the Sediment Provenance along the Subei Coast to the Yangtze Estuary

Zhicheng Dong [1,2], Lina Zhang [1,2,*] and Bingfu Jin [3,*]

1 School of Geographic Sciences and Tourism, Jiaying University, Meizhou 514015, China
2 Guangdong Provincial Key Laboratory of Conservation and Precision Utilization of Characteristic Agricultural Resources in Mountainous Areas, Jiaying University, Meizhou 514015, China
3 School of Resources and Environmental Engineering, Ludong University, Yantai 264025, China
* Correspondence: zhanglina_2005@126.com (L.Z.); bingfu_jin@163.com (B.J.)

Abstract: The influence of large rivers on the Subei littoral plain area requires more research than the results that have been available up to now. Thus, specific diagnostic indices of detrital mica are successfully applied for the first time to identify the detritus of the Yangtze River and the ancient Yellow River and to analyze their influence on the coast in the Subei littoral plain area. Based on field investigation and sample collection, detrital mica minerals within the 0.063–0.125 mm grain size fraction were selected and identified. Their content/ratio differentiations and possible origins were analyzed. Moreover, specific diagnostic indices were evaluated for detritus identification considering these two large rivers in addition to their provenance influences on the Subei littoral plain area. The results indicate that the detrital mica contents in the Yangtze River Estuary differed from those in the ancient Yellow River Estuary. The mass percentage in the former (average value of 32.2%) was much higher than that in the latter (average value of 13.1%). The former contained abundant weathered mica, with a particle percentage of approximately 50.6%, while the latter contained abundant biotite (with a particle percentage of approximately 40.9%). Differences, including but not limited to those above, could be attributed to basic geological, climatic and hydrodynamic conditions. In particular, the mica indices were clearly distinguished between these two river estuaries. These indices constitute specific diagnostic indices for differentiating river detritus and quantitative contribution analysis of detritus provenance in the Subei littoral plain area. Finally, the changes and quantitative contributions of four diagnostic indices demonstrated that in the Subei littoral plain area, northward from the Yangtze River Estuary to sample site SBY11 located in Yangkou town, Rudong County, detrital micas were mainly affected by the Yangtze River, and southward from the ancient Yellow River Estuary to sample site SBY12 located in Bengcha town, Rudong County, detrital micas were largely affected by the ancient Yellow River. The main mixing area should be located between these two towns. This study provides both a good example and an efficient approach to the application of detrital mica in detritus identification, mixed zone determination, sediment provenance analysis and transport tracing.

Keywords: mica; muscovite; biotite; muscovite; weathered mica; provenance analysis; Yangtze River; ancient Yellow River; Subei littoral plain area

Citation: Dong, Z.; Zhang, L.; Jin, B. Detrital Mica Composition Quantitatively Indicates the Sediment Provenance along the Subei Coast to the Yangtze Estuary. *Appl. Sci.* **2022**, *12*, 12653. https://doi.org/10.3390/app122412653

Academic Editor: Eduardo Ferreira da Silva

Received: 10 November 2022
Accepted: 7 December 2022
Published: 9 December 2022

1. Introduction

The Yangtze River and Yellow River play significant roles in the formation and evolution of the eastern coastal zone and continental shelf of China [1]. The identification of their river sediments represents a basic problem in provenance research [2]. The Subei littoral plain area is representative of the East China continental shelf. Sediment mixing and diffusion of the Yangtze River and Yellow River, especially their material contributions, still remain to be further studied and explained [3]. Thus, based on theories of genetic mineralogy and marine geology, numerous studies on sediment identification in these two large rivers, as well as provenance tracing across the Subei littoral plain area have been performed by evaluating the provenance significance of typomorphic minerals and their assemblage, as well as the typomorphic characteristics of minerals, and these studies have yielded numerous and substantial achievements [1,2,4–6]. For instance, the results demonstrated that differences between the sediments in these two large rivers could be found in terms of clay mineral contents [6–8], ratios [9], crystallinity [7,9], chemical indices [9], crystal shapes [10], geochemical characteristics [10], etc., including indicators of detritus identification [7,8]. Previous results also revealed differences in carbonate mineral contents [11–14], crystal shapes [12], grain size effects [12], abrasion and dissolution characteristics [15], etc., which could be used as tracing indices of the Yangtze River and Yellow River [11] to indicate the provenance of sediments on the continental shelf [12]. Other studies have suggested that indicators such as the crystal shape [16], light and/or heavy mineral assemblages [4,11,17,18], geochemical composition [5,6,19,20], magnetite content and other magnetic parameters [2,21,22] could also be applied to distinguish these two large rivers and the sediment provenance [4,5,17,23] of the Yellow Sea and East Sea. In addition, previous results indicated that Yellow River sediments were characterized by high mica mineral contents [24,25]. This finding could be considered for source identification, material diffusion, coastline changes and paleogeographic environment evolution [25]. Moreover, research has revealed that the heavy mineral assemblage of fine-grained (0.063–0.125 mm) sediments was basically characterized by a high content of schistose mica minerals (up to 60%) in the Yangtze River Estuary [26]. Compared with granular minerals, such as quartz and feldspar, schistose mica minerals, they exhibit different behaviors during migration and deposition [27–29]. Moreover, results show that mica $^{40}Ar/^{39}Ar$-dating has important implications for future provenance studies [30,31]. Thus, mica could theoretically be employed as an indicator for sediment transport and diffusion [32]. The mica content difference could be applied to distinguish between Yangtze River and Yellow River provenances [33]. However, relevant research on this topic is largely lacking. Certain questions still require further study. For example, what are the specific differences in detrital mica minerals in sediments between the Yangtze River and Yellow River? Could these differences be employed as specific diagnostic indices? Could these indices be applied to analyze detritus mixing and diffusion along the coast of the Subei littoral plain area?

Based on the above information, this study compares the differences in the contents and ratios of detrital mica in sediments between the Yangtze River Estuary and the ancient Yellow River Estuary. The possible causes of these differences were also analyzed. Consequently, reliable specific diagnostic indices of detrital mica were examined and distinguished for detritus identification between these two rivers. Then, the mixed area of detrital mica along the coast of the Subei littoral plain area was analyzed. In addition, the ranges of influence of these two large rivers were preliminarily evaluated. This study could provide both a good example and an efficient approach to the application of detrital mica in detritus identification, mixed zone determination, sediment provenance analysis and transport tracing. These efforts could help to provide new ideas and references to examine and distinguish specific diagnostic indices of sediment sources, as well as for provenance analysis in the Subei littoral plain area and even the East China continental shelf.

This work is organized as follows. In Section 2, the regional settings are reviewed and the research materials and methods, such as field investigation and surface sediment sample collection, mineral separation and identification are also described. In Section 3, the experiment results are described and analyzed. In Section 4, the implications and extensions of the results of Section 3 are discussed. Finally, Section 5 presents research conclusions.

2. Regional Settings and Methods

2.1. Regional Settings

(1) Yangtze River (Changjiang)

As shown in Figure 1, The Yangtze River (24°–35° N, 90°–122° E) is the largest river in China, with a length of approximately 6300 km and a drainage area of 1.81×10^6 km^2 [34]. The entire drainage area is controlled by temperate and subtropical climate types, with an annual average precipitation of approximately 1100 mm. The geological background in the drainage area is complex. The Yangtze River spans the South China Orogenic Belt, Yangtze Platform, Qinling-Dabie Orogenic Belt, Sanjiang Paleotethys and other tectonic units. The lithology in the drainage area is varied, comprising clastic sedimentary, metamorphic and igneous rocks. Research has demonstrated that the annual average sediment discharge reaches 0.5×10^9 t due to the high sediment content upstream and north of the drainage area [34]. Approximately 50% of the sediments are deposited near the estuary [34]. In addition, seaward sediments originating from the Yangtze River are mainly towards the southeast, with a smaller northward component. Sediment is exchanged with the coast of the Subei littoral plain area.

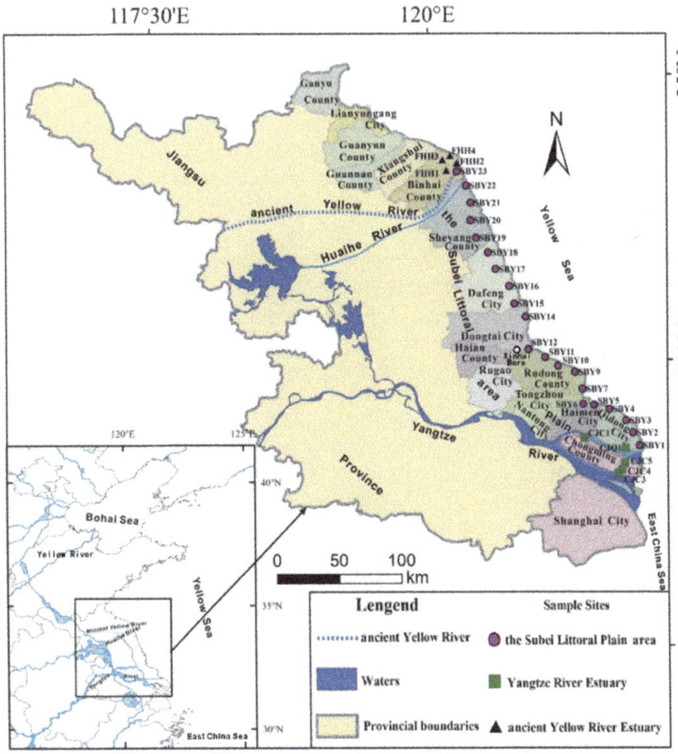

Figure 1. Study area and sampling sites. GPS point information can be found in Appendix A.

(2) Ancient Yellow River

The ancient Yellow River (Figure 1), also referred to as the waste Yellow River, is located in the northern Huaihe River drainage area. This river is an old course of the Yellow River and flows from the north of Lankao city in Henan Province toward the southeast, passing through Minquan County, north of Shangqiu city in Dangshan County in Anhui Province, north of Xuzhou city in Jiangsu Province, south of Suqian city and north of

Huai'an city; then, the river turns northeast, flowing to the south of Lianshui County and north of Binhai County, and entering the Yellow Sea at Taowan village, where the ancient Yellow River Estuary is located. Its downstream channel is also the sea channel of the ancient Huaihe River. According to historical records, the Yellow River has changed its course 11 times throughout history. During the Pleistocene and more recent historical periods, the Yellow River entered the sea in northern Jiangsu many times [35,36]. Research has indicated that the Yellow River' annual average sediment discharge in the estuary reaches 8.39×10^8 t [37] since the main provenance area is widely covered with loess [38]. Thus, the Yellow River is well known worldwide for its high concentration of fine clay and sand. As the Yellow River migrated and captured the Huaihe River, a large amount of sediments was entrained and transported. Fine-grained detritus was rapidly dominated by silty clay deposits. This change caused the land and underwater deltas of the ancient Yellow River to rapidly prograde. In particular, the coastline rapidly prograded. After 1855, the Yellow River merged into the Bohai Sea in the north. Research has revealed that approximately 90% of the detritus entering the sea by way of the Yellow River originates from the Loess Plateau in the midstream region, which is the main source of surface sediments along the northern Jiangsu coast [39].

(3) Subei littoral plain area

The Subei littoral plain area is located between the Yangtze River Delta and ancient Yellow River Delta (Figure 1). It is a wide plain formed by the development and accumulation of ancient bays under the interaction of rivers and the sea during the Quaternary Period [40]. It is generally accepted that the Subei littoral plain area was formed under the combined action of tides and seagoing rivers, such as the Yangtze River and the ancient Yellow River [40]. As the main controlling factors, the detritus carried by these two rivers are the main material sources of the Subei littoral plain area. However, before the last capture of the Huaihe River by the ancient Yellow River entering the sea, the main detritus source of the Subei littoral plain area included northward components of Yangtze River sediments. Since the amount of northward components was small, coastlines remained relatively stable for a long time. Nevertheless, the ancient Yellow River captured the Huaihe River and entered the sea in 1128. This provided a large amount of detritus for the formation of the Subei littoral plain area. A previous study demonstrated that the northern Jiangsu coast was mainly affected by the Yellow River [41]. Major element content changes suggested that northward diffusion of Yangtze River sediments was weak and ranged from the estuary to Rudong County [42]. Montmorillonite content changes indicated that the coast northward from Rudong County to the ancient Yellow River Estuary comprised ancient Yellow River detritus [42]. Yang et al. proposed that the land formation process in the Subei littoral plain area was mainly controlled by Yellow River detritus, which could affect areas as far south as the area near Xinhai Bore [43]. Li et al. suggested that sediments from the coast southward from Rudong County to the Yangtze River Estuary were dominated by Yangtze River sediments, while sediments from the coast northward from Dafeng County to the ancient Yellow River Estuary were dominated by Yellow River sediments [44]. The sediments between these two counties were mixtures of the sediments of these two large rivers [44]. Based on clay mineral assemblages, Yi et al. proposed that sediments from the coast northward from Rudong County to the ancient Yellow River Estuary were dominated by Yellow River inputs, whereas those from the coast southward from Rudong County to the Yangtze River Estuary were dominated by Yangtze River inputs [45]. As mentioned above, in the Subei littoral plain area, the ranges of influence and mixed areas of these two large rivers remain controversial.

(4) Currents Tides and Sediment Transportation

Fruitful research on tidal currents and sediment transport along the Subei coast has been performed in recent decades. The vast majority of the obtained results have indicated that under the influences of the Yellow sea coastal current (YSCC) and Subei coastal waters (SCWs) in winter, suspended sediments around the ancient Yellow River Estuary are transported to the southeast toward the radial sand ridge, even to areas near the Yangtze River Estuary, and jointly with Yangtze River sediments they are carried toward Jeju Island [46]. However, other studies have demonstrated that there is a northward flow along the Subei coast [47], and this could probably cause sediment flow from the ancient Yellow River Estuary or even from the radial sand ridge and the Yangtze River Estuary northward to Haizhou Bay [48]. Zhao et al. also proposed that the tidal residual current flowing northward along the coast could transport sediments into SCWs [49]. Xia et al. [50] also found that there exists a relatively stable northward low-frequency circulation along the Subei coast in summer, which flows northward from the north branch of the Yangtze Estuary to Haizhou Bay, turns east and then flows southeast, and this circulation could probably transport Yangtze River sediments to replenish the Subei coast. Wu et al. also determined that the direction of the coastal current in Subei is upwind in winter, and this could probably provide new ideas to explain the source-sink relationship between the Yangtze River Estuary and Subei littoral plain area, combined with the fate of materials entering the sea from the Yangtze River [51]. In summary, it could be concluded that sediment transportation along the Subei coast and the material contributions of the ancient Yellow River and Yangtze River to the Subei littoral plain area are complex and should be investigated.

2.2. Methods

2.2.1. Sampling

Sediment samples were collected via shovel sampling and were hermetically sealed in polythene bags. A total of 30 surface sediment samples were collected in March 2016. In detail, as shown in Figure 1, five sediment samples in the Yangtze River Estuary (CJC1, CJC3, CJC4, CJC5, and CJQ1), twenty-one sediment samples in the Subei littoral plain area (SBY1-SBY7, SBY9-SBY12, and SBY13-SBY23), and four sediment samples in the ancient Yellow River Estuary (FHH1, FHH2, FHH3, and FHH4) were collected from subsurface floodplains along the coast at a depth ranging from 0–10 cm. Sample sites far away from pollution sources are shown in Figure 1.

2.2.2. Mineral Separation and Identification

Mineral separation and identification conducted as follows. Approximately 100–200 g of each sediment sample were wet sieved to obtain the very fine sand fraction (0.063–0.125 mm) via nylon mesh screens. Additionally, the very fine sand fraction of each subsample was dried and weighed. Then, each subsample was placed into bromoform (CHBr3, ρ = 2.65–3.15 g/cm^3) and centrifugalized to separate the detrital micas. This was repeated until almost no mica could be separated. Then, the obtained micas were manually purified by removing other minerals under the microscope. Additionally, micas left in the very fine sand fraction subsample were manually selected under the microscope. After repeatedly rinsing with alcohol, all the obtained detrital micas were dried at 60 °C and weighed to calculate the mass percentage. Finally, the Gazzi-Dickinson method [52] was used for the mica identification under the microscope. In detail, line counts of 300–500 grains were identified under a binocular microscope with incident light. Particles of biotite, weathered mica, and muscovite were classified (Figure 2) and counted.

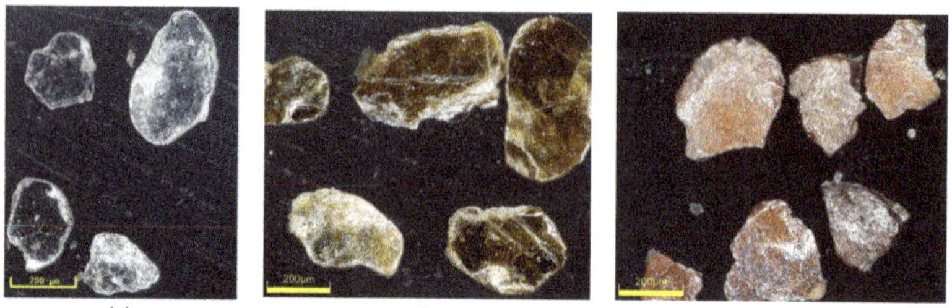

(a) (b) (c)

Figure 2. Muscovite (**a**), biotite (**b**) and weathered mica (**c**) under the microscope.

The particle percentages of biotite, weathered mica, and muscovite were separately calculated as follows: particle percentage of biotite or weathered mica or muscovite = 100% * particle number of biotite or weathered mica or muscovite/total particle number of mica. Additionally, the mass percentage of mica was calculated as follows: mass percentage of mica = 100% * total mica mass/total mineral mass.

2.2.3. Multivariate Statistical Analysis and Calculation of Provenance Contribution

Multivariate statistical analysis and the charts were conducted by using the Statistica Software v.6.0 (Palo Alto, CA, USA).

Based on quality conservation, countless sediment provenances and the mathematical model of nonlinear programming [53], we believe that detrital micas in the very fine sand fraction of sediments in the Yangtze River, the ancient Yellow River, and other unknown sources, all contribute to the Subei littoral plain area. Additionally, there is a certain linear mathematical relationship between them. This relationship can be calculated by the following mathematical model:

$$Y_i = a_1 Y_{1i} + a_2 Y_{2i} + \varepsilon_i \quad (1)$$

where Y_i is the value of mica-specific diagnostic index *i* in the very fine sand fraction of the Subei littoral plain area sediments, Y_{1i} is the value of mica-specific diagnostic index *i* in the very fine sand fraction of the Yangtze River sediments, Y_{2i} is the value of mica-specific diagnostic index *i* in the very fine sand fraction of the ancient Yellow River sediments, ε_i is the contribution of mica-specific diagnostic index *i* in other unknown sources, a_1 is the contribution percentage of the Yangtze River, a_2 is the contribution percentage of the ancient Yellow River, i is the serial number of the mica-specific diagnostic index (i = 1, . . . , n).

3. Results

3.1. Mica Contents in the Very Fine Sand Fraction of Yangtze Estuary Sediments

The mass percentage of mica, the particle percentages of biotite, weathered mica and muscovite significantly differed among the samples of the very fine sand fraction collected in the Yangtze River Estuary (Figure 3). Specifically, the mass percentage of mica was high, with an average value of 32.2% and a maximum content of 57.3%. The particle percentage of weathered mica was the highest, with a value of approximately 50.6%, and the highest content reached 65.7%, followed by muscovite, with an average particle percentage of 37.2%. The particle percentage of biotite was the lowest, with a value of only approximately 12.3%, and the highest content reached only 19.8%.

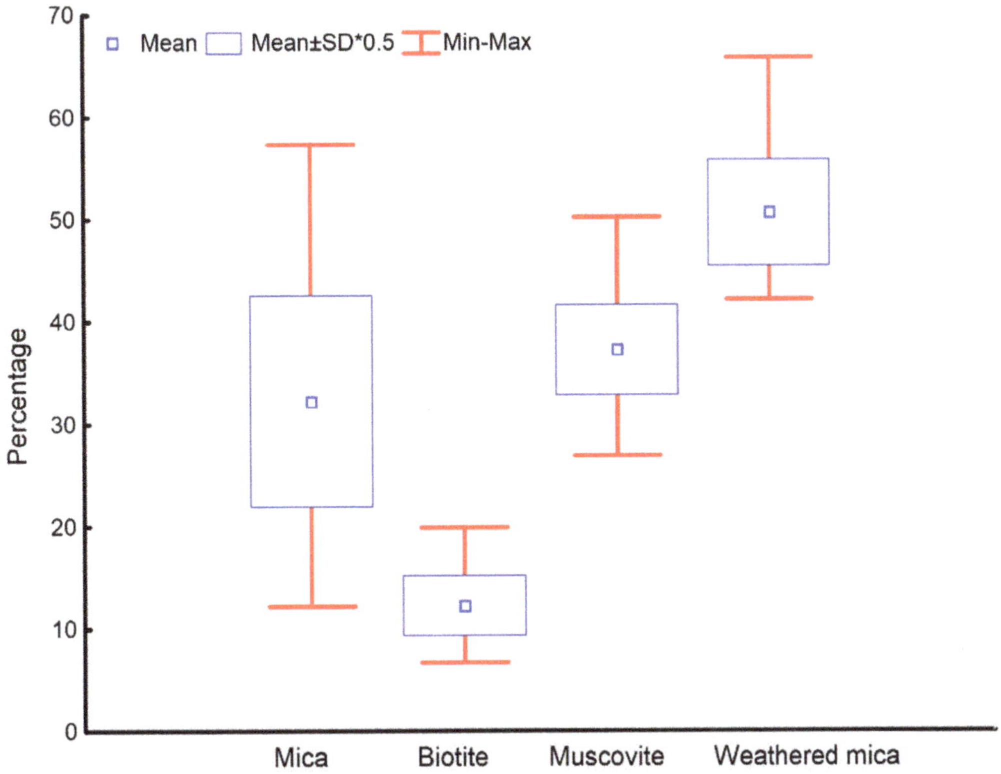

Figure 3. Mass percentage of mica, particle percentages of biotite, weathered mica and muscovite in the very fine sand fraction of the collected Yangtze River Estuary sediment samples (mass percentage of mica = 100 * total mica mass/total mineral mass. Particle percentage of biotite or weathered mica or muscovite = 100 * particle number of biotite or weathered mica or muscovite/total particle number of mica).

3.2. Mica Contents in the Very Fine Sand Fraction of Ancient Yellow Estuary Sediments

The mass percentage of mica and the particle percentages of biotite, weathered mica and muscovite obviously varied among the samples of the very fine sand fraction collected in the ancient Yellow River Estuary (Figure 4). In detail, the mass percentage of mica was low, with a mean value of only 13.1%. The mass percentages in most samples were low, ranging from 1% to 5%, except for sample FHH3, which exhibited a higher value of 47.5%. Comparison and analysis of the particle percentage differences among biotite, muscovite and weathered mica revealed that biotite was the main mica type in the very fine sand fraction of the sediment samples, with a particle percentage of 40.9%, followed by muscovite, with an average particle percentage of 32.3%, slightly lower than that of biotite. The particle percentage of weathered mica was the lowest, with a value of only approximately 26.8%.

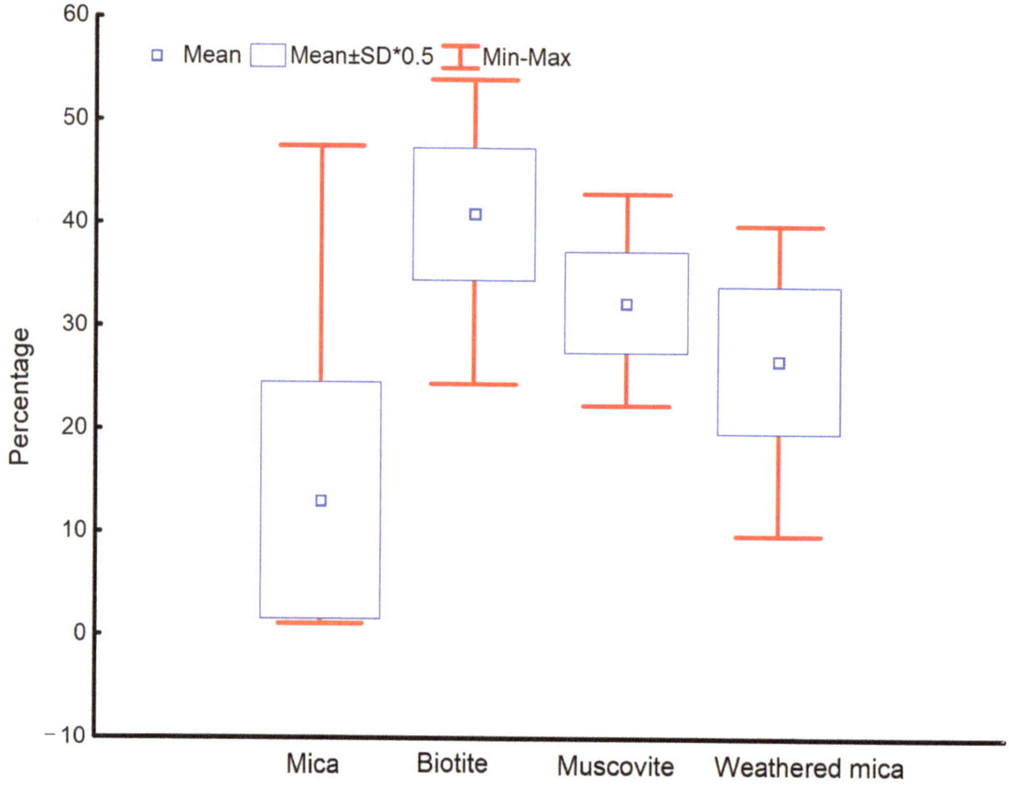

Figure 4. Mass percentage of mica, particle percentages of biotite, weathered mica and muscovite in the very fine sand fraction of ancient Yellow River Estuary sediments (mass percentage of mica = 100 * total mica mass/total mineral mass. Particle percentage of biotite or weathered mica or muscovite = 100 * particle number of biotite or weathered mica or muscovite/total particle number of mica).

3.3. *Mica Contents in the Very Fine Sand Fraction of Subei Littoral Plain Area Sediments*

The mass percentage of mica, the particle percentages of biotite, weathered mica and muscovite obviously differed among the various samples of the very fine sand fraction of coastal sediments of the Subei littoral plain area (Figure 5). More specifically, the mass percentage of mica was very high, with an average value of up to 43.3%. The dispersion of the mass percentage data was very high, with the standard deviation reaching 24.3. By comparing and analyzing the particle percentage differences among biotite, muscovite and weathered mica, the results indicated that muscovite was the main mica type in the very fine sand fraction of the sediment samples collected in the Subei littoral plain area, with an average particle percentage of 40.9%. The average particle percentage of weathered mica was 33.0%, which is slightly lower than that of biotite. The particle percentage of biotite was the lowest, with a value of only approximately 26.2%.

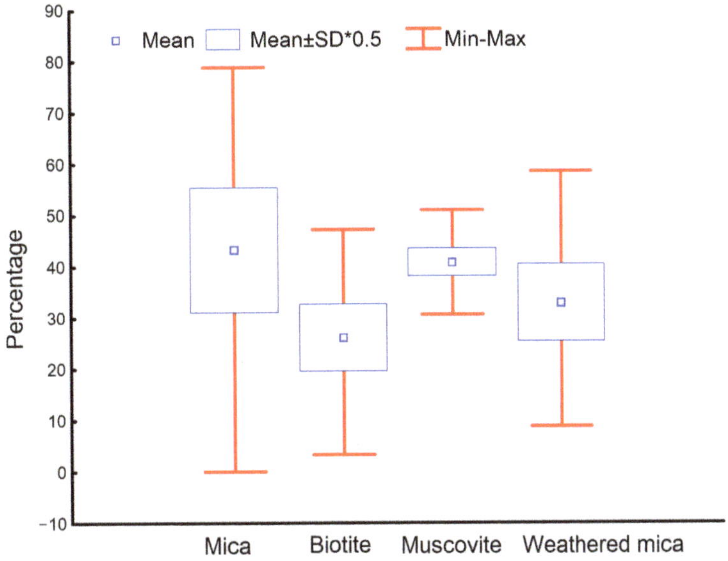

Figure 5. Mass percentage of mica and particle percentages of biotite, weathered mica and muscovite in the very fine sand fraction of Subei littoral plain area sediments (mass percentage of mica = 100 * total mica mass/total mineral mass. Particle percentage of biotite or weathered mica or muscovite = 100 * particle number of biotite or weathered mica or muscovite/total particle number of mica).

4. Discussion

4.1. Differences in Detrital Mica Contents in Sediments between the Yangtze River Estuary and Ancient Yellow River Estuary and the Causes of these Differences

Detrital minerals in sediments differ with the original rock, weathering degree, tectonic activity, climate change and other supergene environmental conditions [2,7], and micas are no exception. Their contents in large river sediments differ with watershed environments [7].

As shown in Figure 6, the contents and ratios of detrital mica in sediments between the Yangtze River Estuary and ancient Yellow River Estuary significantly differed. Specifically, the mass percentage of mica, particle percentage of weathered mica, particle percentage of muscovite, and particle percentage ratio of weathered mica to the sum of biotite and weathered mica in the very fine sand fraction of Yangtze River Estuary sediments were 2.47, 1.89, 1.15 and 2.06 times higher, respectively, than those in the very fine sand fraction of ancient Yellow River Estuary sediments. However, the particle percentage of biotite, particle percentage ratio of biotite to muscovite, and particle percentage ratio of the sum of biotite and weathered mica to muscovite in the very fine sand fraction of the ancient Yellow River Estuary sediments was 3.33, 4.05 and 1.28 times higher, respectively, than those in the very fine sand fraction of Yangtze River Estuary sediments. All of these results indicate that the mass percentage of mica and the particle percentage of weathered mica in the very fine sand fraction of the sediments in the Yangtze River Estuary were significantly higher than those in the very fine sand fraction of the sediments in the ancient Yellow River Estuary. The weathering degree of mica (the particle percentage ratio of weathered mica to the sum of biotite and weathered mica) was much higher than that in the ancient Yellow River Estuary. All of these results also suggested that the particle percentage of biotite and the particle percentage ratio of biotite to muscovite in the very fine sand fraction of the sediments in the ancient Yellow River Estuary were significantly higher than those in the very fine sand fraction of the sediments in the Yangtze River Estuary, although the weathering degree of mica was very low. Moreover, the particle percentage ratio of easily weathered mica (sum of biotite and weathered mica) to difficult-to-weather mica (muscovite) in the very fine sand fraction of the sediments in the ancient Yellow River Estuary was also higher than that in the very fine sand fraction of the sediments in the Yangtze River Estuary.

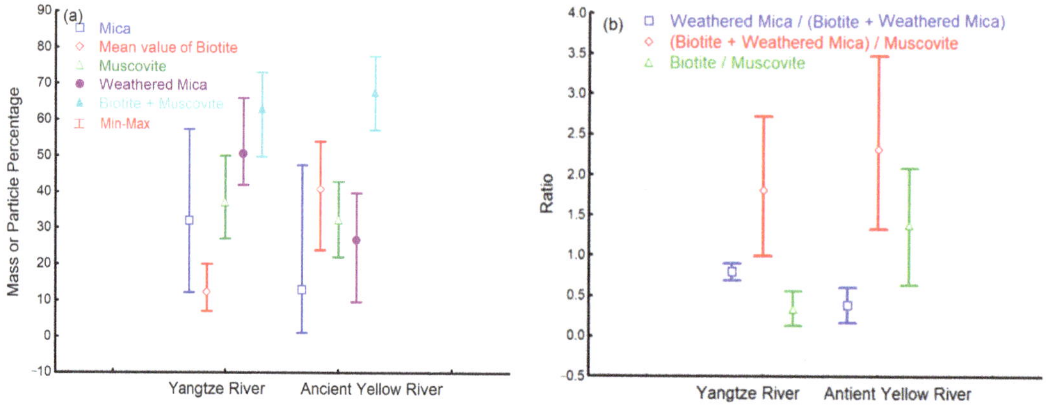

Figure 6. Comparison of the detrital mica contents (**a**) and ratios (**b**) in the very fine sand fraction of the sediments between the Yangtze River Estuary and ancient Yellow River Estuary. (**a**) shows the differences of mass percentage of mica (in bule) and particle percentages of biotite (in red), muscovite (in green), weathered mica (in purple) and sum of biotite and muscovite (in cyan). (**b**) shows the differences of particle percentage ratio of weathered mica to the sum of biotite and weathered mica (in blue), particle percentage ratio of the sum of biotite and weathered mica (in red), and particle percentage ratio of biotite to muscovite (in green).

Researchers have previously reported similar characteristics, such as high mica and muscovite contents in the very fine sand fraction of Yangtze River Estuary sediments, a high biotite content and high particle percentage ratio of biotite to muscovite in ancient Yellow River sediments. For example, Lv found that the content of schistose mica minerals in the 0.063–0.125 mm fraction of sediments in the Yangtze River Estuary was very high, with a maximum value of up to 60% [26]. This value was thought to represent a basic feature of the heavy mineral assemblages in the very fine-grained (0.063–0.125 mm) sediments of the Yangtze River Estuary [26]. Zhang and Meng also proposed that mica is one of the dominant minerals in Yangtze River Estuary sediments [33]. The highest mica content reached 32.4%, with a content of 17.1% in the silt fraction. Wang et al. noted that muscovite is one of the characteristic minerals of underwater delta sediments in the Yangtze River [54]. It was found that muscovite is widely distributed with moderate contents ranging from 5.7% to 2.5%, while biotite contents were lower, with the highest value of only 1.5% in the silty fraction. In addition, Lin et al. proposed that Yellow River materials were characterized by abundant mica minerals [25]. Biotite is one of the main minerals with high contents of up to 64.7% in underwater deltas. Muscovite is a secondary mineral and its content could reach approximately 5%. They also suggested that a high particle percentage ratio (value of 8.97) of biotite to muscovite could serve as a mineralogical indicator of Yellow River materials [25]. Wang et al. also found that the biotite content in Yellow River sediments (up to 23.36%) was much higher than that in Yangtze River sediments (very low) [55]. It was further suggested that mica in the 0.063–0.125 mm fraction of Yellow River Estuary sediments was the main dominant heavy mineral because its particle percentage reached 39.2% [32]. They also found that the muscovite content (17.6%) was higher than that of biotite (16.3%) and hydrobiotite (5.3%) [32].

In river basins, geological conditions, climate types and hydrodynamic conditions notably impact minerals in sediments [7,56], including detrital minerals. Thus, the causes of detrital mica differences in sediments between these two large river estuaries should be related to these factors (Figure 7). First, compared to the Yellow River drainage area, the exposed rocks in the Yangtze River drainage area are richer in mica. In the Yangtze River drainage area, granite, schist and gneiss are widely distributed in the middle-to-lower stream sections. This leads to a high content of detrital mica in Yangtze River sediments. However, in the Yellow River drainage area, loess widely covers the midstream area and is the main provenance of Yellow River detritus [35]. The mica content is approximately 18.4% in the >20 μm fraction of loess paleosol, with a maximum value lower than 26% [57]. This indicates that the mica content in the very fine sand fraction is not overly high in Yellow River sediments. Hence, the difference in geological conditions between provenance areas is an important reason why the mass content of mica in the very fine sand fraction of Yangtze River Estuary sediments is significantly higher than that in the very fine sand fraction of ancient Yellow River Estuary sediments. Second, compared to the Yellow River, the climatic conditions in the Yangtze River drainage area are more favorable for weathering. These climatic conditions include abundant precipitation and a high temperature in most areas of the Yangtze River drainage area, except for the upstream area. However, the region is dry and cold, with a lower annual precipitation and poor hydrothermal conditions in the Yellow River drainage area. Research has demonstrated that the chemical weathering rate (61.58 $t/km^2 \cdot a$) in the Yangtze River drainage area is significantly higher than that in the Yellow River drainage area (39.29 $t/km^2 \cdot a$) [58]. Strong chemical weathering in the Yangtze River drainage area inevitably leads to the release of a large number of mica minerals in igneous and metamorphic rocks, such as granite, into the river. Moreover, strong chemical weathering in the Yangtze River drainage area inevitably leads to the transformation of a large amount of biotite into weathered mica. Thus, the difference in weathering conditions is another important reason why the mass percentage of mica in the very fine sand fraction of the sediments in the Yangtze River Estuary is much higher than that in the very fine sand fraction of the sediments in the ancient Yellow River Estuary. This is also the main reason for the higher particle percentage of weathered mica in the very fine sand fraction of Yangtze River Estuary sediments and largely explains both the higher weathering degree of mica and the higher particle percentage of biotite. Third, in the Yangtze River Estuary, the flow velocity suddenly declines due to the low open flat trumpet-shaped terrain [59]. This terrain shape leads to the deposition of a large number of detritus [59]. Coupled with the controlling effect of seawater in the estuary and the disturbance of coastal currents, detrital mica easily affected by hydrodynamic forces also accumulates in this location. This is the third important reason for the higher mica content in the very fine sand fraction of the sediments in the Yangtze River Estuary. In contrast, mica originating from the Loess Plateau is resorted under the influence of stronger hydrodynamic forces in the estuary area of the ancient Yellow River. Moreover, due to the large differences in the particle size, density, shape, volume, and diameter-thickness ratio, the depositional velocity of mica is much lower than that of other minerals with the same particle size, such as quartz and feldspar. Thus, the particle size of mica settling in the very fine sand fraction is usually larger than that of other minerals, such as quartz and feldspar [28]. Research has demonstrated that the particle size difference between mica and other minerals in the same size fraction, such as quartz and feldspar, ranges from 1Φ to 1.5Φ [27]. This is also an important reason for the lower mass percentage of mica in the very fine sand fraction of ancient Yellow River Estuary sediments.

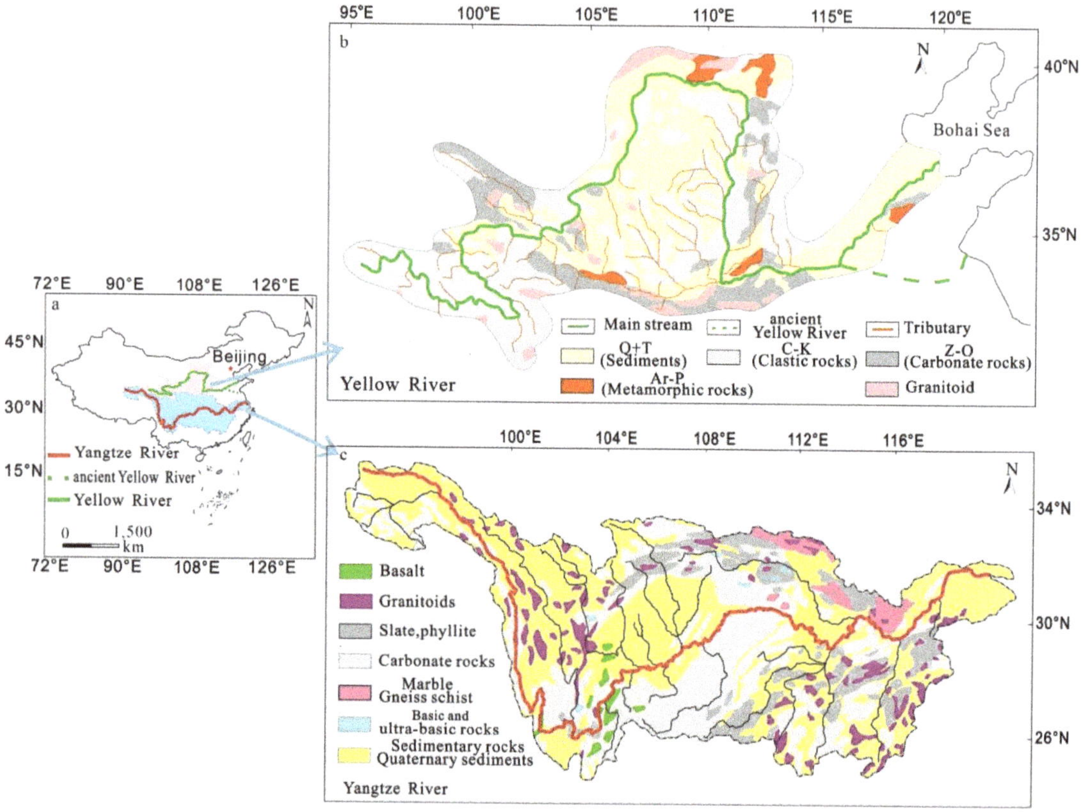

Figure 7. Geological map of the drainage basins in this study (modified based on Hongfei [60] and Wang [18]).

4.2. Specific Diagnostic Indices to Effectively Distinguish detritus between the Yangtze River Estuary and Ancient Yellow River Estuary

Micas in detrital sediments are divided into muscovite and biotite. Muscovite exhibits the most stable chemical properties and a high erosion resistance [61]. Biotite with unstable chemical properties is easily weathered [61]. Therefore, the differences and changes in mica indicators, such as the content and/or ratio, provide a certain significance to indicate provenance conditions, such as the watershed climate type and hydrothermal conditions.

Under the influence of the basic geology, climate and hydrodynamic forces in the source area, the detrital mica content and ratio in the very fine sand fraction of the sediments of the Yangtze River Estuary differ from those in the very fine sand fraction of the sediments in the ancient Yellow River Estuary. These differences make it possible to determine specific diagnostic indices for detritus to distinguish between these two large river estuaries.

As shown in Figure 8, four mica indices, including the particle percentage of biotite, particle percentage of weathered mica, particle percentage ratio of weathered mica to the sum of biotite and weathered mica and particle percentage ratio of biotite to muscovite, significantly differ between the Yangtze River Estuary and ancient Yellow River Estuary. Specifically, in the very fine sand fraction of Yangtze River Estuary sediments, these mica indices ranged from 6.67% to 19.85%, from 42.14% to 65.71%, from 0.69 to 0.90, and from 0.13 to 0.56, respectively. However, in the very fine sand fraction of ancient Yellow River Estuary sediments, these indices ranged from 24.41% to 53.93%, from 9.74% to 39.81%, from 0.17 to 0.60, and from 0.64 to 2.09, respectively. Thus, these specific diagnostic indices could be effectively used to distinguish detritus between these two river estuaries. These results are more detailed and specific than the existing research results. For instance, based on the characteristic of a high mica content in Yellow River sediments [24], Lin et al. proposed that the mica content could be used to distinguish the source and diffusion of marine sediments, identify coastline changes and determine the evolution of the paleogeographic environment [25]. They also suggested that a high particle percentage ratio of biotite to muscovite could be used as a mineralogical tracer parameter to distinguish the provenance of Yangtze River detritus [25]. In addition, Wang KS et al. proposed that mica minerals could be used as indicators of sediment transport and diffusion [32].

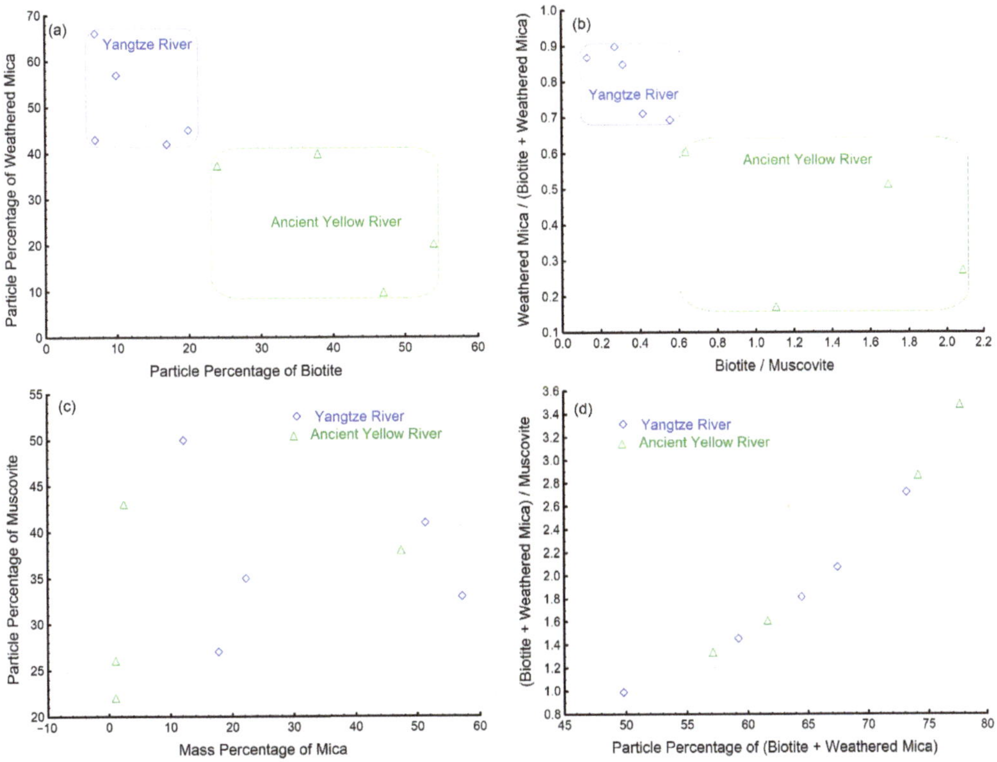

Figure 8. Index scatter diagrams of detrital mica in the very fine sand fraction of the sediments of the Yangtze River Estuary and ancient Yellow River Estuary; (**a**) particle percentage of biotite; (**b**) particle percentage ratio of weathered mica to the sum of biotite; (**c**) particle percentage of weathered mica; (**d**) weathered mica and particle percentage ratio of biotite to muscovite, significantly differ between the Yangtze River Estuary and ancient Yellow River Estuary.

4.3. Variation in the Mica-Specific Diagnostic Indices for the Very Fine Sand Fraction of Coastal Sediments in the Subei Littoral Plain Area and Provenance Significance

As previously mentioned, the four mica-specific diagnostic indices for effective detritus discrimination between the Yangtze River Estuary and ancient Yellow River Estuary include the particle percentage of biotite, particle percentage of weathered mica, particle percentage ratio of weathered mica to the sum of biotite and weathered mica, and particle percentage ratio of biotite to muscovite. Their numerical changes in the very fine sand fraction of sediments at different locations along the coast of the Subei littoral plain area are shown in Figure 9. These changes could effectively indicate the influence range of the Yangtze River and the ancient Yellow River on the coast of the Subei littoral plain area. These changes could be helpful to better explain the mixing area of these two sources at this location.

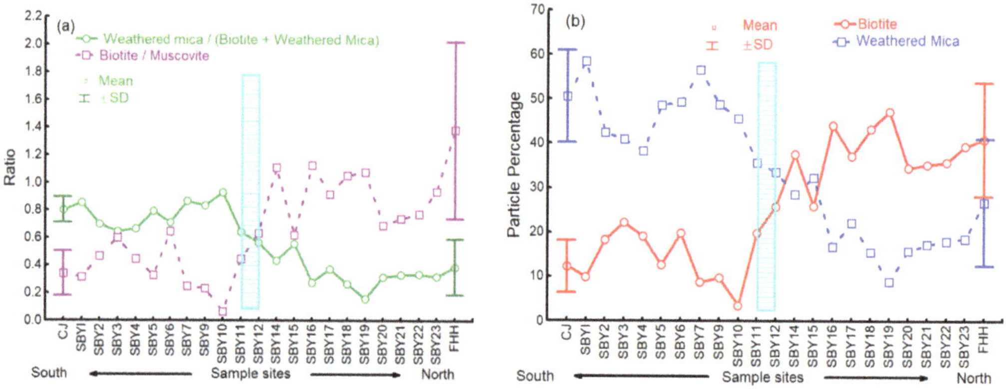

Figure 9. Variation in the mica-specific diagnostic indices in the very fine sand fraction of coastal sediments between the Yangtze River Estuary (CJ) and the ancient Yellow River Estuary (FHH) together with the Subei littoral plain area. (**a**) shows the variation of paticle percentage ratio of weathered mica to the sum of biotite and weathered mica (in green), and the variation of paticle percentage ratio of biotite to muscovite (in purple). (**b**) shows the variation of paticle percentage of biotite (in red) and weathered mica (in blue).

As shown in Figures 9 and 10, northward from the Yangtze River Estuary to Yangkou town in Rudong County (SBY11), the particle percentage of biotite and the particle percentage ratio of biotite to muscovite were low, while the particle percentage of weathered mica and the weathering degree of mica (the particle percentage ratio of weathered mica to the sum of biotite and weathered mica) were high. These values were close to those in the Yangtze River Estuary. This result indicates that detritus in the region along the coast northward from the Yangtze River Estuary to Yangkou town in Rudong County (SBY11) were mainly affected by Yangtze River detritus. This relationship is generally consistent with existing understandings. Li et al. suggested that the sediments southward from Rudong County to the Yangtze River Estuary could be dominated by Yangtze River detritus [43]. Changes in major element contents indicated that the northward diffusion range of Yangtze River sediments was smaller thanthe Yangtze River Estuary to the coast near Waya Port on the north side of Xiaoyangkou in Rudong County [42]. This area is close to the region of interest of this study. In addition, based on the characteristics of clay mineral assemblages, Yi et al. suggested that sediments from the coast southward from Rudong County to the Yangtze River Estuary were dominated by detritus inputs from the ancient Yangtze River [45].

Moreover, as shown in Figures 9 and 10, northward from Bencha town in Rudong County (SBY12) to the ancient Yellow River Estuary, the particle percentage of biotite and the particle percentage ratio of biotite to muscovite significantly increased, while the particle percentage of weathered mica and the weathering degree of mica (the particle percentage ratio of weathered mica to sum of biotite and weathered mica) significantly decreased. These values were close to those in the ancient Yellow River Estuary. This result indicates that detritus in the region along the coast northward from Bencha town in Rudong County (SBY12) to the ancient Yellow River Estuary were mainly affected by ancient Yellow River detritus. This relationship is also basically consistent with existing research results. For example, Zhao considered the area along the coast northward from Jianggang Port to the ancient Yellow River Estuary (close to the SBY13 sample site in Dongtai city in this study) to mainly be affected by the ancient Yellow River [41]. Based on the variation in the montmorillonite content, Zhang proposed that detritus along the coast northward from Rudong County to the ancient Yellow River Estuary originated from the ancient Yellow River [42]. By applying element geochemistry and heavy mineral methods, Yang et al. suggested that the land-forming process in the Subei littoral plain area was mainly controlled by the ancient Yellow River, with the southern boundary of influence near Xinhai Bore (near sample site SBY11 in this study) [43]. In addition, based on the characteristics of clay mineral assemblages, Yi et al. proposed that sediments from the coast northward from Rudong County to the ancient Yellow River Estuary were dominated by detritus inputs from the ancient Yellow River [45].

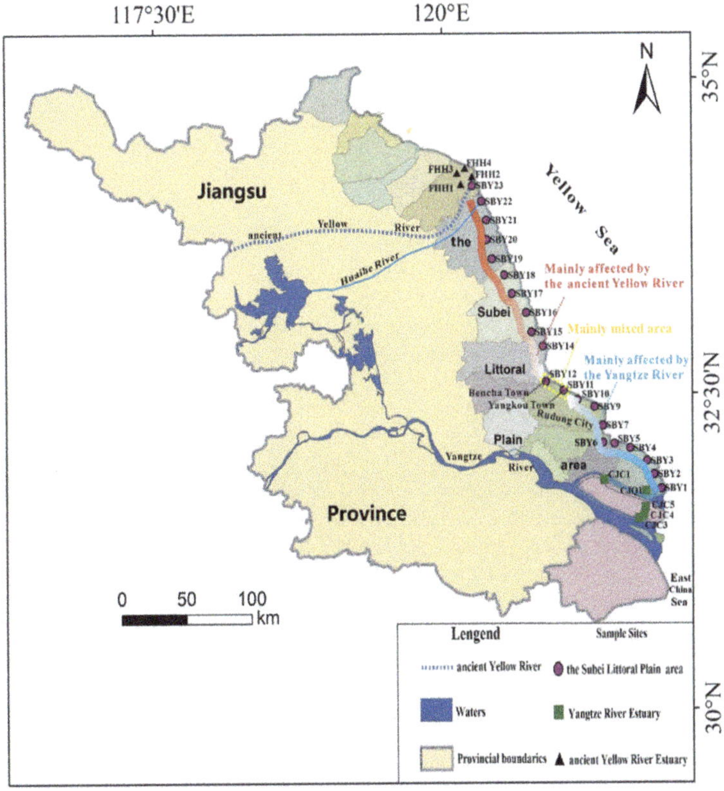

Figure 10. Ranges of the influence of the Yangtze River and the ancient Yellow River on detrital mica in the very fine sand sediments in the Subei littoral plain area.

In addition, as shown in Figures 9 and 10, compared to the four mica-specific diagnostic indices of the samples southward from SBY10 to the Yangtze River Estuary and northward from SBY14 to the ancient Yellow River Estuary, the index values at sample sites SBY11 and SBY12 were moderate. These results indicate that the main mixed area occurred between these two sites, i.e., SBY11 and SBY12. Detritus were mainly affected both by the Yangtze River and ancient Yellow River at this location. Yang et al. also proposed that between Dongtao Bore (near sample site SBY14) and Xinhai Bore (near sample site SBY11), the surface sediments at Sancang Bore (near sample site SBY12) were mainly mixed Yangtze River and ancient Yellow River sediments [43].

4.4. Quantitative Contributions of the Yangtze River and the Ancient Yellow River to Detrital Micas in the Subei Littoral Plain Area and Indicative Significance

The quantitative contributions of the Yangtze River and the ancient Yellow River to detrital mica in the very fine sand fraction of the sediments of the Subei littoral plain area are shown in Table 1. The coefficients of determination (R^2) are all more than 0.783 (Table 1). All of the variants explained are close to 100 (Table 1). Additionally, these quantitative contribution data are reliable (Figure 11). Thus, the mathematical model of provenance contribution based on mica-specific diagnostic indices for the very fine sand fraction of sediments is reliable. As indicated in Table 1, southward from sample sites SBY11 to SBY1, where SBY11 is located near Yangkou town in Rudong County and SBY1 is located close to the Yangtze River Estuary, the quantitative contributions of the Yangtze River (a_1) are all higher than 50%, while those of the ancient Yellow River (a_2) are lower than 50%. However, northward from SBY12 to SBY23, where SBY12 is located near Bencha town in Rudong County and SBY23 occurs near the ancient Yellow River Estuary, the quantitative contributions of the ancient Yellow River (a_2) are all higher than 50%, while those of the Yangtze River (a_1) are lower than 50%. In addition, it could be deduced from Table 1 that the mixed area of these two large rivers occurs between the SBY11 and SBY12. This deduction further confirms the correctness of the previous understanding obtained in this study.

Table 1. Quantitative provenance analysis results for the very fine sand fraction of the sediments in the Subei littoral plain area (a_1 is the contribution percentage of the Yangtze River, a_2 is the contribution percentage of the ancient Yellow River, $\varepsilon$is the contribution other unknown sources).

Samples	Regression Coefficient			Test Indices of the Regression Model			
	a_1	a_2	ε	Final Loss	R	R^2	Variance Explained
SBY1	1.00	0.00	1.39	61.6	0.987	0.973	97.3
SBY2	0.72	0.23	−0.03	0.01	1.00	1.00	100
SBY3	0.62	0.36	−0.05	0.01	1.00	1.00	100
SBY4	0.60	0.29	−0.04	0.03	1.00	1.00	100
SBY5	0.95	0.02	0.00	0.00	1.00	1.00	100
SBY6	0.90	0.10	1.53	14.7	0.995	0.991	99.1
SBY7	1.00	0.00	0.59	47.0	0.989	0.978	97.8
SBY9	0.97	0.00	−0.62	3.30	0.999	0.998	99.8
SBY10	0.92	0.00	−2.20	43.4	0.985	0.970	97.0
SBY11	0.53	0.33	−0.05	0.04	1.00	1.00	100
SBY12	0.39	0.51	−0.08	0.03	1.00	1.00	100
SBY14	0.10	0.89	−0.07	0.01	1.00	1.00	100
SBY15	0.36	0.53	−0.08	0.04	1.00	1.00	100
SBY16	0.00	0.99	−1.59	95.6	0.961	0.924	92.4
SBY17	0.00	0.90	−0.40	3.20	0.998	0.997	99.7
SBY18	0.00	0.96	−1.70	107.4	0.955	0.911	91.1
SBY19	0.00	0.99	−2.87	324.0	0.885	0.783	78.3
SBY20	0.00	0.80	−1.00	30.5	0.980	0.961	96.1
SBY21	0.00	0.82	−0.86	21.3	0.987	0.974	97.4
SBY22	0.00	0.84	−0.82	19.3	0.989	0.977	97.7
SBY23	0.00	0.91	−1.03	34.9	0.983	0.966	96.6

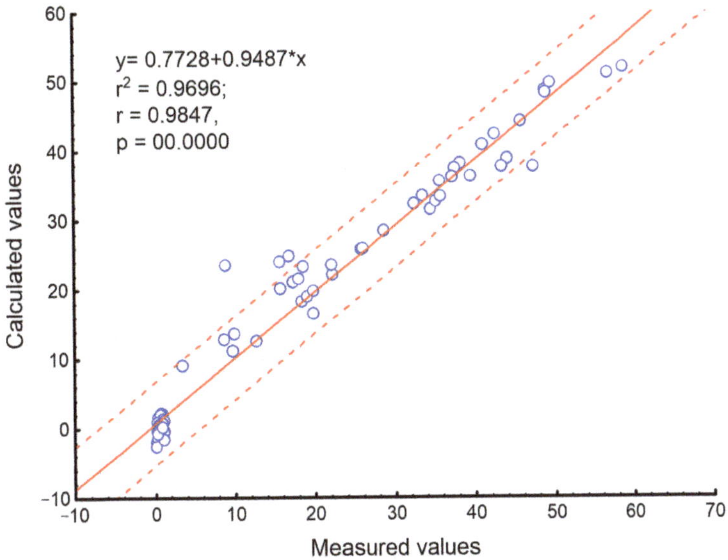

Figure 11. Scatter diagram for calculated values versus measured values of specific diagnostic indexes of detrital mica in the very fine sand fraction from sediments of the Subei littoral plain area (95% confidence).

5. Conclusions

Detrital mica contents were interestingly displayed and studied to identify two large rivers, namely the ancient Yellow River and the Yangtze River. Micas indices were selected and applied as provenance indicators to determine sediment contribution from the two rivers to the Subei coastal plain.

The contents and ratios of mica minerals in the very fine sand fraction of the sediments in the Yangtze River Estuary differed from those in the very fine sand fraction of the sediments in the ancient Yellow River Estuary. This difference could be attributed to a combination of different factors, such as basic geology, climate and estuarine hydrodynamics, in these two drainage area.

Four diagnostic indices were selected and used to effectively distinguish detritus in the Yangtze River Estuary and ancient Yellow River Estuary; these indices include the particle percentage of biotite, particle percentage of weathered mica, particle percentage ratio of weathered mica to the sum of biotite and weathered mica, and particle percentage ratio of biotite to muscovite. These indices ranged from 6.67% to 19.85%, 42.14% to 65.71%, 0.69 to 0.90, and 0.13 to 0.56, respectively, in the very fine fraction of Yangtze River Estuary sediments and 24.41% to 53.93%, 9.74% to 39.81%, 0.17 to 0.60, and 0.64 to 2.09, respectively, in ancient Yellow River Estuary sediments.

In the Subei littoral plain area, northward from the Yangtze River Estuary to SBY11 in Yangkou town, Rudong County, detrital micas were mainly affected by the Yangtze River. Moreover, in the Subei littoral plain area, southward from the ancient Yellow River Estuary to SBY12 in Bengcha town, Rudong County, detrital micas were mainly affected by the ancient Yellow River. In addition, the main mixing area of the Yangtze River and the ancient Yellow River occurred between these two sampling sites. The demarcation line between these areas could also be located in this region.

The above specific diagnostic indices of detrital mica could be employed for quantitative analysis of the provenances of detritus and their contributions.

Detrital mica in certain grain size fractions of sediments could be used for detritus identification, mixed area determination and provenance analysis.

Author Contributions: Conceptualization, Z.D. and L.Z.; Writing—Original manuscript Preparation, Z.D. and L.Z.; Writing—Review and Editing, L.Z. and B.J.; Ideas and experimental funds, L.Z. and B.J.; Data processing and Figures, Z.D. and L.Z.; Sampling and Experiments, L.Z. and B.J. All authors have read and agreed to the published version of the manuscript.

Funding: This study was supported by National Natural Science Foundation of China (41576057), Guangdong Basic and Applied Basic Research Foundation (2020A1515011077), Scientific Research Projects of Jiaying University (2020KJY05, 2019KJY05), Yantai Key Research and Development Plan (2019XDHZ103).

Institutional Review Board Statement: Not applicable.

Informed Consent Statement: Not applicable.

Data Availability Statement: It and all the data presented in this study are available on request from the corresponding author.

Acknowledgments: The authors would like to thank editors and all anonymous reviewers for their constructive suggestions and comments that helped to improve the quality of this paper.

Conflicts of Interest: The authors declare no conflict of interest.

Appendix A

Appendix A is the GPS locations of collected samples. It can be found online at https://data.mendeley.com/datasets/9f9y33rkm5/draft?a=c0bf25a2-f419-4bb9-acfb-b2564a9917df (accessed on 1 November 2022).

References

1. Wang, F.; Zhang, W.G.; Nian, X.M.; Andrew, P.R.; Zhao, X.; Shang, Y.; Ge, C.; Dong, Y. Magnetic evidence for Yellow River sediment in the late Holocene deposit of the Yangtze River Delta, China. *Mar. Geol.* **2020**, *427*, 106274. [CrossRef]
2. Zhang, W.G.; Xing, Y.; Yu, L.Z.; Feng, H.; Lu, M. Distinguishing sediments from the Yangtze and Yellow Rivers, China: A mineral magnetic approach. *Holocene* **2008**, *18*, 1139–1145. [CrossRef]
3. Zhang, W.G.; Ma, H.L.; Ye, L.P.; Dong, C.Y.; Yu, L.Z.; Huang, F. Magnetic and geochemical evidence of Yellow and Yangtze River influence on tidal flat deposits in northern Jiangsu Plain, China. *Mar. Geol.* **2012**, *319–322*, 47–56. [CrossRef]
4. Wang, K.S.; Shi, X.F.; Jiang, X.L. Sediment provenance and province of the southern Yellow Sea: Evidence from light mineral. *Chin. Sci. Bull.* **2003**, *48*, 30–36. [CrossRef]
5. Zou, L.; Dou, Y.G.; Hu, X.h.; Hu, B.Q.; Lin, X. Provenance analysis for surface sediments in different sepositional environments of the middle-south Okinawa Trough. *Mar. Geol. Quat. Geol.* **2021**, *41*, 115–124. (In Chinese with English Abstract)
6. Lu, J.; Li, A.C.; Zhang, J.; Huang, P. Yangtze River-derived sediments in the southwestern South Yellow Sea: Provenance discrimination and seasonal transport mechanisms. *J. Asian Earth. Sci.* **2019**, *176*, 353–367. [CrossRef]
7. Fan, D.J.; Yang, Z.S.; Mao, D.; Guo, Z.G. Clay minerals and geochemistry of the sediments from the Yangtze and Yellow rivers. *Mar. Geol. Quat. Geol.* **2001**, *4*, 7–12. (In Chinese with English Abstract)
8. Yang, Z.S. Mineralogical assemblages and chemical characteristics of clays from sediments of the Huanghe, Changjiang, Zhujiang Rivers and their relationship to the climate environment in their sediment source areas. *Oceanol. Limnetica Sin.* **1988**, *19*, 336–346. (In Chinese with English Abstract)
9. Zhang, Z.P.; Chu, Z.X. Modern variations in clay minerals in mud deposits of the Yellow and East China Seas and their geological significance. *Holocene* **2017**, *28*, 386–395. [CrossRef]
10. He, L.B.; Liu, Q.Y. Chemical characteristics of clay minerals in the sediments from the Yellow River and the Changjiang River. *Chin. Sci. Bull.* **1997**, *42*, 488–491. [CrossRef]
11. Zhao, J.S.; Zhou, J.; Chen, Q.; Zhen, K.G. Identification of Yangtze River and Yellow River Paleochannels in South Yellow Sea Shelf. *Adv. Mater. Res.* **2013**, *664*, 21–27. [CrossRef]
12. Yang, Z.S.; Fan, D.J.; Guo, Z.G.; Mao, D. Distribution of the carbonate clast size and the provenance analyses of the surface sediments in the northern East China Sea. *Acta Sedimentol. Sin.* **2002**, *20*, 1–6. (In Chinese with English Abstract)
13. Chen, J.; Chou, G.; Yang, J.D. Sr isotopic composition of carbonate in loess and identification of primary and secondary carbonate. *Prog. Nat. Sci.* **1997**, *6*, 731–734. (In Chinese with English Abstract)
14. Liu, D.S. *Loess and the Environment*; Science Press: Beijing, China, 1985; pp. 1–251. (In Chinese)
15. Yang, Z.S.; Wang, H.C.; Qiao, S.Q. Carbonate minerals in esturay sediments of the Changjiang and Huanghe: The content, morphology, and influential factors. *Oceanol. Limnetica Sin.* **2009**, *40*, 674–681. (In Chinese with English Abstract)
16. Zhang, J.Q.; Li, C.X.; Cong, Y.Z. Hydrodynamic environment and source of the old tidal sand body in the coastal plain of the northern Jiangsu. *Acta Oceanol. Sin.* **1998**, *20*, 82–90. (In Chinese with English Abstract)

17. Jin, B.F.; Wang, M.Y.; Yue, W. Comparative analysis of heavy mineral characteristics of sediments from the Huanghe River and the Changjiang River based on the multiple-window grain size strategy. *Cont. Shelf Res.* **2021**, *216*, 104326. [CrossRef]
18. Wang, Z.-B.; Li, R.-H.; Yang, S.-Y.; Bai, F.-L.; Mei, X.; Zhang, J.; Lu, K. Comparison of detrital mineral compositions between stream sediments of the Yangtze River (Changjiang) and the Yellow River (Huanghe) and their provenance implication. *China Geol.* **2019**, *2*, 169–178. [CrossRef]
19. An, Y.H.; Liu, J.; Zhang, J.Q.; Chen, B.; Chen, L.L.; Zhang, X.; Sheng, S. Comparative researches on the provenance indicators of Huaihe River, Yangtze River and Yellow River sediments. *Quat. Sci.* **2020**, *3*, 837–850. (In Chinese with English Abstract)
20. Yang, S.Y.; Jung, H.S.; Choi, M.S.; Li, C.X. The rare Earth element compositions of the Changjiang (Yangtze) and Huanghe (Yellow) River sediments. *Earth Planet. Sci. Lett.* **2002**, *201*, 407–419. [CrossRef]
21. Yang, S.Y.; Li, C.X.; Zhu, J.C.; Zhang, J.L. Provenance indicator of chemical fingerprint of magnetite in the Yangtze and Yellow river sediments. *Geochimica* **2000**, *5*, 480–484. (In Chinese with English Abstract)
22. Wang, Y.H.; Shen, H.T.; Zhang, W.G. A preliminary comparison of magnetic properties of sediments from the Changjiang and the Huanghe Estuaries. *Acta Sedimentol. Sin.* **2004**, *22*, 658–663. (In Chinese with English Abstract)
23. Lu, K.; Qin, Y.C.; Wang, Z.B.; Huang, L.; Li, G.X. Heavy mineral provinces of the surface sediments in central-southern East China Sea and implications for provenance. *Mar. Geol. Front.* **2019**, *35*, 20–26. (In Chinese with English Abstract)
24. Sun, B.Y. Detrital mineral assemblages in the Huanghe, Changjiang and Zhujiang Delta sediments. *Mar. Geol. Quat. Geol.* **1990**, *10*, 23–34. (In Chinese with English abstract)
25. Lin, X.T.; Li, W.R.; Shi, Z.B. Characteristics of mineralogy in the clastic sediments from the Yellow River provenance, China. *Mar. Geol. Quat. Geol.* **2003**, *23*, 17–21. (In Chinese with English Abstract)
26. Lv, Q.R. Mineral characteristics of fine-grain sediment and its sedimentary differentiation in Changjiang estuary. *Shanghai Geol.* **1992**, *43*, 18–25. (In Chinese with English Abstract)
27. Fan, S.M.; Jin, B.F.; Wang, X.; Yu, H.Y. Mica shape factor and its equivalent sedimentation in the sediment of the Yellow River Estuary. *Mar. Geol. Front.* **2021**, *5*, 31–38. (In Chinese with English Abstract)
28. Doyle, L.J.; Carder, K.; Steward, R.G. The Hydraulic Equivalence of Mica. *J. Sediment. Petrol.* **1983**, *53*, 643–648.
29. Sun, X.; Kuiper, K.F.; Tian, Y.; Li, C.; Gemignani, L.; Zhang, Z.; Wijbrans, J.R. Impact of hydraulic sorting and weathering on mica provenance studies: An example from the Yangtze River. *Chem. Geol.* **2019**, *532*, 119359. [CrossRef]
30. Gemignani, L.; Kuiper, K.F.; Wijbrans, J.R.; Sun, X.; Santato, A. Improving the precision of single grain mica 40Ar/39Ar-dating on smaller and younger muscovite grains: Application to provenance studies. *Chem. Geol.* **2019**, *511*, 100–111. [CrossRef]
31. Thierry, B.B.; Lebogang, M.; Chris, M.; Kelebogile, P.; Tebogo, K. Multistage gold mineralization events in the Archean Tati greenstone Belt, northeast Botswana: Constraints from integrative white mica Ar/Ar, garnet U-Pb and sulfides Pb/Pb geochronology. *Precambrian Res.* **2020**, *339*, 105623.
32. Wang, K.S.; Shi, X.F.; Cai, S.W.; Qiao, S.Q.; Jiang, X.L. Distribution and provenance of the surface sediments of the Yellow River Mouth and Laizhou Bay deduced from heavy minerals. *Mar. Geol. Quat. Geol.* **2010**, *30*, 1–8, (In Chinese with English Abstract). [CrossRef]
33. Zhang, F.Y.; Meng, Y. Heavy mineral distribution and magnetic characteristic of surface sediments in the north branch of the Changjiang River. *Mar. Geol. Quat. Geol.* **2011**, *31*, 31–41. (In Chinese with English Abstract) [CrossRef]
34. Hong, Q.Y.; Shi, M.D.; Cheng, H.T. *Changjiang Water Resources Commission. The History of Yangtze River*; Encyclopedia of China Publishing House: Beijing, China, 2007; pp. 25–77. (In Chinese)
35. Liu, J.P.; Milkman, J.D.; Gao, S.; Chen, P. Holocene development of the Yellow River's subaqueous delta North Yellow Sea. *Mar. Geol.* **2004**, *209*, 45–67. [CrossRef]
36. Xue, C.T.; Zhou, Y.Q.; Zhu, X.H. The Huanghe River course and delta from end of Late Pleistocene to the 7th century BC. *Acta Sedimentol. Sin.* **2004**, *26*, 48–61. (In Chinese with English Abstract)
37. Ren, M.E. *China's Three Deltas*; Higher Education Press: Beijing, China, 1994; pp. 56–73. (In Chinese)
38. Dai, Y.S. Basic characteristics of geological structure in the Yellow River Basin. *Yellow River* **1984**, *3*, 20–26. (In Chinese with English Abstract)
39. Ren, M.; Shi, Y. Sediment discharge of the Yellow River (China) and its effect on the sedimentation of the Bohai and the Yellow Sea. *Cont. Shelf Res.* **1986**, *6*, 785–810. [CrossRef]
40. Wang, Y.; Zhang, Z.K.; Zhu, D.K.; Yang, J.H.; Mao, L.J.; Li, S.H. River-sea interaction and the north Jiangsu plain formation. *Quat. Sci.* **2006**, *26*, 301–320. (In Chinese with English Abstract)
41. Zhao, Q.J. Influence of river on development of Jiangsu coast. *Mar. Sci.* **1992**, *3*, 53–55. (In Chinese with English Abstract)
42. Zhang, Y. A study of characteristics and sources of clay minerals of sediments in coastal areas of Jiangsu province. *Mar. Sci.* **1990**, *4*, 34–42. (In Chinese with English Abstract)
43. Yang, S.Y.; Li, C.X.; Zhang, J.Q. Palaeogeographic evolution of coastal plain and provenance study of postglacial sediments in north Jiangsu province. *J. Palaeogeogr.* **2000**, *2*, 68–75. (In Chinese with English Abstract)
44. Li, C.X.; Zhang, J.Q.; Fan, D.D.; Deng, B. Holocene regression and the tidal radial sand ridge system formation in the Jiangsu coastal zone, east China. *Mar. Geol.* **2001**, *1731*, 97–120, (In Chinese with English Abstract). [CrossRef]
45. Yi, S.Q.; Chen, B.B.; Wang, S.H. Numerical classification of clay minerals in beach soil of Jiangsu. *Acta Sedimentol. Sin.* **1998**, *25*, 349–355. (In Chinese with English Abstract)

46. Guo, Z.G.; Yang, Z.S.; Zhang, D.Q. Seasonal distribution of suspended matter in the northern East China Sea and barrier effect of current circulation on its transport. *Acta Oceanol Sin.* **2002**, *5*, 71–80. (In Chinese with English Abstract)
47. Liu, Z.L.; Hu, D.X.; Tang, X.H. Tidal current observation in the southern Yellow Sea in the summers of 2001 and 2003. *Chin. J. Oceanol. Limnol.* **2008**, *26*, 121–129. [CrossRef]
48. Chen, B.; Zhou, L.Y.; Liu, J.; Wang, K. The relationship between the suspended sediment movement and tidal current dynamic characteristic in Old Yellow Delta. *Mar. Sci.* **2011**, *5*, 73–81. (In Chinese with English Abstract)
49. Zhao, B.R.; Fang, G.H.; Cao, D.M. Characteristics of tidal residual currents and their relations with coastal current transports in the Bohai Sea, Yellow Sea and East China Sea. *Stud. Mar. Sin.* **1995**, *36*, 5–10.
50. Xia, C.S.; Qiao, F.L.; Yang, Y.Z.; Yuan, Y.L. Simulation of double cold cores of the 35° N section in the Yellow Sea with a wave-tide-circulation coupled model. *Chin. J. Oceanol. Limnol.* **2004**, *22*, 292–298.
51. Wu, H.; Gu, J.H.; Zhu, P. Winter Counter-Wind Transport in the Inner Southwestern Yellow Sea. *J. Geophys. Res. Ocean.* **2018**, *123*, 411–436. [CrossRef]
52. Ingersoll, R.V.; Bullard, T.F.; Ford, R.L.; Grimm, J.P.; Pickle, J.D.; Sares, S.W. The effect of grain size on detrital modes: A test of the Gazzi–Dickinson pointcounting method. *J. Sediment. Petrol.* **1984**, *54*, 103–116.
53. Fan, D.; Sun, X.; Yang, Z.; Guo, Z. A mathematical model on the quantitative provenance identification: Take the identification of the surface sediment sources from ECS as example. *Acta Sedimentol. Sin.* **2002**, *20*, 30–33. (In Chinese with English Abstract)
54. Wang, K.S.; Wang, G.Q.; Cai, S.W.; Dou, Y.G.; Shi, X.F.; Cheng, Z.B.; Jiang, X.L. Heavy mineral characteristics of surface sediments in the subaqueous Yangtze River Delta. *Mar. Geol. Quat. Geol.* **2007**, *1*, 7–12. (In Chinese with English Abstract)
55. Wang, L.C.; Chen, X.L.; Chu, T.Q. A contrast analysis on the loads character of the Changjiang River and the Yellow River. *Geogr. Res.* **1997**, *16*, 71–79. (In Chinese with English Abstract)
56. Weltje, G.J.; von Eynatten, H. Quantitative provenance analysis of sediments: Review and outlook. *Sediment. Geol.* **2004**, *171*, 1–11. [CrossRef]
57. Zheng, H.H.; Theng, B.K.G.; Whitton, J.S. Mineral composition of loess-paleosol in the Loess Plateau of China and its environment implication. *Geochimica* **1994**, *23*, 113–123. (In Chinese with English Abstract)
58. Li, J.Y.; Zhang, J. Chemical weathering processes and atmospheric CO_2 consumption of Huanghe River and ChangJiang River basins. *Sci. Geogr. Sin.* **2005**, *15*, 16–21. [CrossRef]
59. Chen, J.Y.; Yun, C.X.; Hu, H.G. The model of development of the Changjiang Estuary during the last 2000 years. In *Estuarine Comparisons*; Kennedy, V.S., Ed.; Academic Press: New York, NY, USA, 1982; pp. 655–666.
60. Hongfei, Z.; Yunhong, L.; Claudio, O.D.; Yue, M.; Jie, Z.; Hongming, H. Contribution of soil erosion to the evolution of the plateau-plain-delta system in the Yellow River basin over the past 10,000 years. *Palaeogeogr. Palaeoclimatol. Palaeoecol.* **2022**, *601*, 111133.
61. Pal, D.K.; Srivastava, P.; Durge, S.L.; Bhattacharyya, T. Role of weathering of fine-grained micas in potassium management of Indian soils. *Appl. Clay Sci.* **2001**, *20*, 39–52. [CrossRef]

applied sciences

Article

Classification and Provenance on Geochemical Lithogenes: A Case Study on Rock–Soil–Sediment System in Wanquan Area of Zhangjiakou, North China

Yonglong An [1,2], Xiulan Yin [3], Qingjie Gong [1,*], Xiaolei Li [4] and Ningqiang Liu [1]

1 School of Earth Sciences and Resources, China University of Geosciences, Beijing 100083, China
2 Beijing Institute of Ecological Geology, Beijing 102218, China
3 China Institute of Geo-Environment Monitoring, Beijing 100081, China
4 Center for Development and Research, China Geological Survey, Beijing 100037, China
* Correspondence: qjiegong@cugb.edu.cn

Abstract: Geochemical lithogenes have been successfully applied as an innovative concept in the field of composition classification and source traceability of geological materials recently. This paper introduces the background of the development of geochemical genes and the construction and application of LG01 and LG03 lithogenes. Based on LG01 and LG03, the LG_CR classification and provenance are applied and verified on a weathering profile, ten gully sedimentary profiles and regional stream sediments in the Wanquan area of Zhangjiakou city, Hebei province, China. The geochemical lithology of the weathering profile shows a gradual variation from basic-like in the bottom rock to acidic-like at the upper soils compositionally with heterogeneity. The classification results on 10 sedimentary gully profiles (each with five samples) indicate that soils at the bottom of the gully system are dominated with 11 types of LG_CR materials, while the top materials are made up of 21 types, reflecting the mixing of the upstream soils. The results of stream sediments from a regional geochemical survey with a scale of 1:200,000 in this area illustrate that the classification results of LG_CR on stream sediments are basically consistent with the petrological results derived from regional geological mapping. Therefore, LG_CR can be used not only as an effective tool for classification and traceability of geological materials but also has great potential in lithological mapping in petrological-overburdened areas.

Keywords: LG_CR; geochemical classification; geochemical traceability; mapping in overburdened area; weathering

Citation: An, Y.; Yin, X.; Gong, Q.; Li, X.; Liu, N. Classification and Provenance on Geochemical Lithogenes: A Case Study on Rock–Soil–Sediment System in Wanquan Area of Zhangjiakou, North China. *Appl. Sci.* **2023**, *13*, 1008. https://doi.org/10.3390/app13021008

Academic Editor: Dibyendu Sarkar

Received: 13 December 2022
Revised: 3 January 2023
Accepted: 5 January 2023
Published: 11 January 2023

1. Introduction

Geochemical gene is a new technique that can be used for composition classification and source traceability of geological samples, and the proposal of lithogene has initiated the study of geochemical lithogenes in recent years [1]. The advantage of geochemical lithogenes is that they express trends among chemical elements in geological materials, such as the elemental spider diagram [2,3], and are applicable to rocks, soils, sediments, and plants, etc. Thus, it is a key link between geology and ecology using the relationship of elements rather than their absolute concentrations and overcomes the limitations of the applicability of graphical tracing methods and isotopic tracing methods in the traditional study of geochemistry [4–7]. Two metallogenes (named gold metallogenes MGAu and tungsten metallogene MGW) and two rare-earth elemental genes (named REEG01 and REEG02) have been proposed recently [8–10] and the tungsten metallogene MGW11 is also presented now [11]. During subsequent practice and application, Gong et al. [10] and Li et al. [12] proposed LG01 and LG03 lithogenes (Table 1) after the LG02 lithogene [13], respectively. The spectra lines of LG01 and LG03 genes of the ideal rock samples in China are shown in Figure 1 [1]. Gong et al. [1] reviewed the above seven geochemical genes (except the MGW11) and their applications recently.

Table 1. Elemental sequences and their reference values of LG01 and LG03 geochemical lithogenes.

Gene	Sequence No.	1	2	3	4	5	6	7	8	9	10	11
LG01	Gene elements	Zr	Ti	Al_2O_3	TFe_2O_3	SiO_2	P	Pb	Mn	Th	Nb	U
	Reference values	147	4016	14.8	6.4	60	756	19	940	5.72	14.5	1.2
LG03	Gene elements	Nb	Ti	Zr	Cr	La	V	Pb	Co	U	Ni	Th
	Reference values	14.5	4016	147	81	35	130	19	24	1.2	32	5.72

Notes: The units of reference values of major oxides are % and others are μg/g.

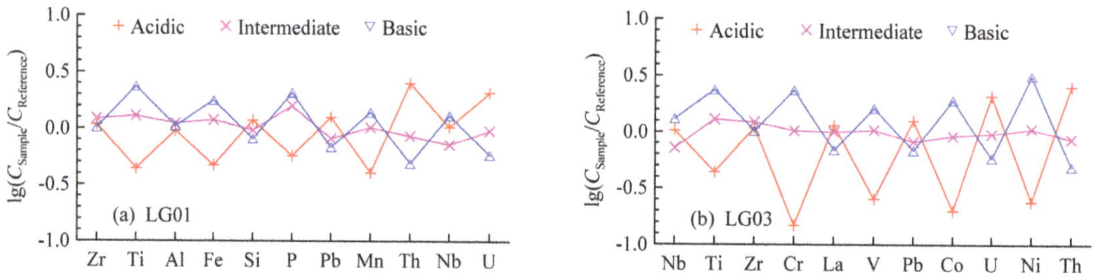

Figure 1. Spectral lines of LG01 (**a**) and LG03 (**b**) lithogenes for the ideal rocks in China. Al, Fe, and Si are the abbreviations of Al_2O_3, TFe_2O_3, and SiO_2 on the horizontal axis. Elemental abundances of ideal rocks in China are from Chi and Yan [14] and listed in Table 2.

Table 2. The elemental abundances of rocks in China.

Rocks	Zr	Ti	Al_2O_3	TFe_2O_3	SiO_2	P	Pb	Mn	Th	Nb	U	Cr	La	V	Co	Ni
Acidic rock	160	1770	14.20	3.00	70.85	430	24	380	14.5	15	2.5	12	40	33	4.8	7.7
Intermediate rock	180	5200	16.42	7.62	57.79	1200	15.5	960	4.9	10.4	1.15	83	35	135	22	34
Basic rock	150	9470	15.54	11.33	48.68	1570	13	1310	2.8	19	0.7	190	24	210	46	100

Notes: The units of major oxides are % and others are μg/g.

The advantage of geochemical lithogenes is that they can not only classify geological materials (rocks, weathered debris, soils, stream sediments, etc.) compositionally, breaking through the technical bottleneck that rocks, debris, soils, and sediments cannot be classified uniformly due to different criteria, but also can establish a uniform classification method. The ideal acidic rock in China is a virtual rock sample represented by the elemental abundances of acidic rock in China (Table 2), whose LG01 and LG03 lithogenes are both coded as 10202020202. The gene similarity between a sample and the ideal acidic rock is called the acidic similarity of the sample, which is labelled as R_{Acidic}. The R_{Acidic} of samples can be used as a tool to classify geological materials into three types compositionally, namely acidic-like ($R_{Acidic} \geq 80\%$), intermediate-like ($25\% \leq R_{Acidic} \leq 75\%$), and basic-like ($R_{Acidic} \leq 20\%$) components.

In order to further integrate the classification results of LG01 and LG03 lithogenes and make the sample classification results more accurate, Wu et al. [15] proposed the concept of LG_CR (classification results on lithogenes). Firstly, samples were classified into three types: acidic-like component with $R_{Acidic} \geq 80\%$ labelled as 1-type, intermediate-like component with $75\% \geq R_{acidic} \geq 25\%$ labelled as 2-type, and basic-like component with $R_{acidic} \leq 20\%$ labelled as 3-type on LG01 and LG03, respectively. Subsequently, the classification results were expressed as double-digit numbers on the sequence of placing the classification results of LG01 in the first digit and LG03 in the second digit. Therefore, a total of 9 types (or LG_CR types) could be classified theoretically as 11, 12, 13, 21, 22, 23, 31, 32, and 33 type, although 13 type and 31 type may rarely occur in nature. The advantage of this classification method is that it is applicable to geological materials, such as fresh and weathered rocks, debris, soils, and sediments on a uniform criterion.

In this paper, the classification results of LG_CR were applied and tested on a combined weathered profile in the Wanquan area of Zhangjiakou city, Hebei province, China firstly. Then, 10 vertical sediment profiles were applied along or across a gully to reveal the material's migration in horizontal directions. Finally, the regional geochemical survey data of stream sediments were used to classify their LG_CR types in this area.

2. Geographical and Geological Settings

The study area is located in the northern part of Wanquan district, Zhangjiakou city, Hebei province, China (Figure 2a), with an area of about 1080 km^2 ranging from E 114°16′33″ to 114°38′36″ and N 40°44′14″ to 41°04′07″ (Figure 2b) and is located in the transition zone between the North China Plain and the Inner Mongolia Plateau, with high topography in the northwest and low topography in the southeast, undulating hills, and a mainly shallow-cut landform type. The landform type is mainly shallowly cut stripped-erosion low hills, with altitude between 1000 and 1300 m. The northern part is adjacent to the Zhangbei Dam Plateau. The area has a temperate semi-humid continental monsoon climate, with an average precipitation of about 400–500 mm. The soil type is mainly chestnut brown soil and brown soil [16], and the mountainous land is covered by larch, white birch, and mountain poplar, etc. [17], while bulk crops and vegetables grow on the plains.

The strata in the study area belong to Archean, Sinian, Jurassic, Cretaceous, Neogene, and Quaternary periods, respectively, of which petrological descriptions are illustrated briefly in Figure 2b as notes [18,19]. The spatial distribution has the following characteristics: the northern region is dominated by basaltic rocks of Hannuoba Formation (N_3), the central and southeast region is dominated by Jurassic, Cretaceous, and Quaternary rocks or sediments, and the southwest region is dominated by Archean and Sinian rocks. Faults mainly trend northwest and northeast. Intrusions in the study area are less developed, except diabase stock in the northwest (Figure 2b).

3. Materials and Methods

3.1. Materials

A weathering profile was collected, with 16 samples (including 3 rock samples, 5 weathered debris samples, and 8 soil samples), which included 2 sub-profiles labelled as PM-1 and PM-2 (Figure 2c–e). The specific descriptive information and analytical data of the 16 samples are shown in Table 3 and Table S1 in Supplementary Materials. The sampling length or regolith depth of PM-1 is ca. 7.5 m and that of PM-2 is ca. 7.6 m. There is a boundary or platform between the two parts and the total depth of the weathering profile is ca. 15.1 m (Figure 2c–e). The profile samples are divided into three parts from the top to the bottom sequentially as soil, debris, and rock. When collecting soil or debris samples from the weathering profile, the lateral exposed surface soil should be removed at a depth of about 10–20 cm, while rock samples should be collected by removing the external weathering surface and taking the fresh part. The location of this weathering profile is just located near the boundary between the first section of the Lower Cretaceous Tujingzi Formation (K_1t^1) and the upper Neogene Hannuoba Formation (N_3) (Figure 2b).

In order to trace soil migration scientifically according to the topography of the terrain, which can be initially recognized as two pathways, it is necessary to determine the main direction of migration firstly. In total, 10 vertical sediment profiles were laid out along these two migration directions. The first pathway profile CJPM-1 along the primary channel from N-S, with a vertical elevation difference of about 260 m and a transverse migration distance of about 5 km, includes 7 profiles of TP1, TP2, TP3, TP4, TP5, TP7, and TP8, which were spaced almost equally except the distance between TP5 and TP7. The second pathway profile CJPM-2 includes 4 profiles, TP14, TP15, TP16, and TP4 (used repeatedly), along the E-W tertiary channel, which were spaced almost equally with an interval of ca. 2 km and with a height difference of ca. 150 m. With respect to these 10 profiles, 5 samples in each profile were collected sequentially from the surface soil to the bottom soil. Each sample is collected continuously within a depth of 0.2 m and, therefore, the depth of each soil profile is 1 m. Thus, 50 soils samples in these 10 profiles were collected (Table S2 in Supplementary Materials).

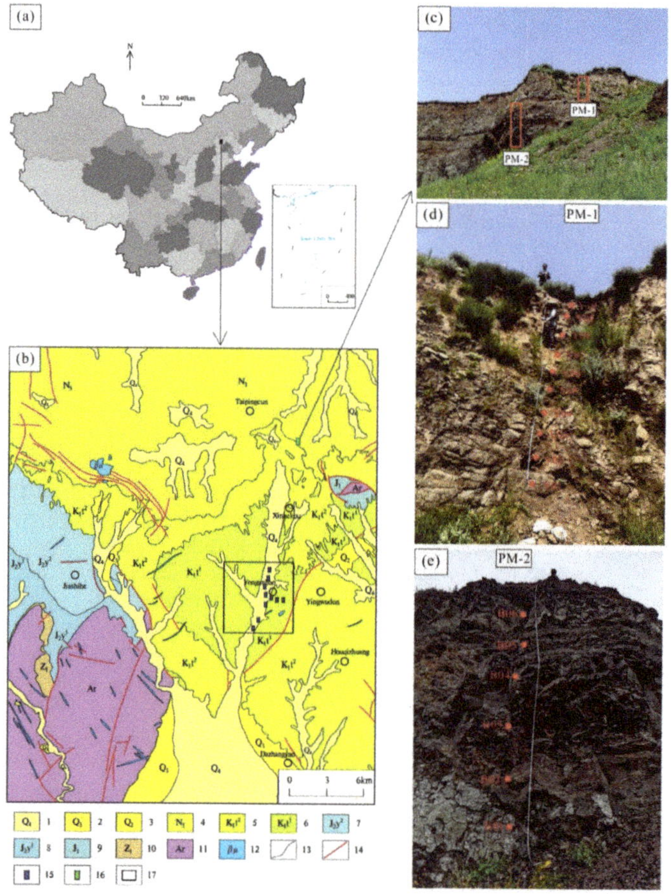

Figure 2. Location of the study area in the Chinese mainland (**a**) and its geological map (**b**) after the K5025 geological map with a scale of 1:200,000 in which a weathering profile (**c**) is located and composed of sub-profiles of PM-1 (**d**) and PM-2 (**e**). Notes in (**b**): 1—Holocene sub-clay, sub-sand, silt with gravel; 2—Upper Pleistocene sub-clay, sub-sandstone, gravelly layer; 3—Middle Pleistocene gravelly sandstone, sub-clay; 4—Upper Neogene basalt with clay and shale in the middle and upper part; 5—The second section of lower Cretaceous Tujingzi Formation siltstone, mudstone, conglomerate sandstone; 6—The first section of lower Cretaceous Tujingzi Formation conglomerate; 7—The second section of middle Jurassic Yanjiayao Formation sandstone, sandy shale; 8—The first section of middle Jurassic Yanjiayao Formation gravelly coarse sandstone, sandstone, shale; 9—Lower Jurassic sandy shale, siltstone, conglomerate sandstone; 10—Lower Sinian quartzite, dolomitic sandstone, shale, dolomite; 11—Archean hematite, striped mixed rock; 12—Diabase; 13—Petrological boundary; 14—Fault; 15—Locations of vertical profiles; 16—Location of the weathering profile illustrated in (**c**–**e**); 17—Range of the pathway profiles.

In the study area of Wanquan with an area of about 1080 km^2, 278 geochemical records (or samples) of stream sediments were retrieved from the database of the RGNR (Regional Geochemistry-National Reconnaissance) project [20]. In this project, stream sediment is the sampling media with a scale of 1:200 000 and was analyzed with 10 major components and 29 trace elements [21].

3.2. Methods of Analyses

Soil samples were put into clean white cotton bags after removing gravel, grass roots, animal dung, insect shells, etc., in the field. After collecting on the same day, they were placed in a ventilation room for air-drying to avoid breakage or mold caused by prolonged wet accumulation and then sent to the laboratory in time to complete pre-processing, such as grinding and sieving (200 mesh). The weight of bedrock and weathered debris samples was ca. 500 g. The field collection and processing of the samples were in accordance with the requirements of the Specification for Geochemical Evaluation of Soil Quality (DZ/T 0295-2016).

Rocks, weathered debris, and soils were analyzed for the major oxides of SiO_2, Al_2O_3, TFe_2O_3, K_2O, Na_2O, CaO, MgO, TiO_2, P_2O_5, and MnO and trace elements of Zr, Nb, Th, U, La, Pb, V, Cr, Co, and Ni. The major oxides were determined using a wavelength dispersive X-ray fluorescence spectrometer (ARL Advant XP + 2413) with detection limits of 0.05%, except Al_2O_3 of 0.03% and MgO, CaO of 0.02%. The trace elements were determined by high-resolution plasma mass spectrometry (X Serise2/SN01831C) where the detection limits were 5 for Zr, 2 for Nb, Th, V, Cr, 1 for La, Ni, 0.2 for Co, and 0.1 for Pb, U in μg/g. The accuracy and precision of the analytical method were controlled by the national standard substances (GSB-1, GSB-5, GSS-20, GSS24, GSS34) by adding 10% blank samples and parallel samples. The accuracy of the analysis of the first-grade standard substances was more than 98%, the repeatability of the sample test was more than 100%, and the relative standard deviation was less than 5%. The analytical methods, precision, accuracy, and detection limits were all in accordance with the requirements of the specification for multi-purpose regional geochemical survey (DZ/T 0258-2014) [22].

3.3. Methods on Weathering Indices

The weathering degree of a sample is commonly depicted on weathering indices [23–27]. The commonly used indices are CIA (chemical index of alteration) and WIG (weathering index of granite). The CIA was developed by Nesbit and Young [28] in reconstructing paleoclimate from Early Proterozoic sediments and the WIG (weathering index of granite) was proposed by Gong et al. [29] to describe the weathering degrees of granitic weathered products in the absence of CO_2 contents. Their calculation methods used here were detailed by Wu et al. [7] and briefly illustrated as

$$\mathrm{CIA} = [\mathrm{Al_2O_3}/(\mathrm{Al_2O_3} + \mathrm{CaO}^* + \mathrm{Na_2O} + \mathrm{K_2O})] \times 100 \quad (1)$$

$$\mathrm{WIG} = [\mathrm{Na_2O} + \mathrm{K_2O} + (\mathrm{CaO}\text{-}10/3\mathrm{P_2O_5})]/(\mathrm{Al_2O_3} + \mathrm{TFe_2O_3} + \mathrm{TiO_2}) \times 100 \quad (2)$$

where the oxide content is expressed in moles, CaO * represents CaO in silicates (i.e., removing CaO in carbonates and apatite), and (CaO-10/3P_2O_5) is taken as a non-negative value (i.e., 0 when its value is less than 0). It has been shown that CIA values are divided into <60, 60–80, and >80 [30], and WIG values are divided into >60, 60–20, and <20 [7,10], which represent the incipient, intermediate, and extreme weathering degree, respectively. Values of CIA increase with the weathering degree, while WIG values decrease with the weathering degree according to their definitions (Equations (1) and (2)).

Table 3. Information and analyzed results of samples from Wanquan area of Hebei province, China.

No.	ProfileNo.	SampleNo.	SampleInfo	Sample Description	Depth m	SiO_2 %	Al_2O_3 %	TFe_2O_3 %	K_2O %	Na_2O %	CaO %	MgO %	TiO_2 %	P_2O_5 %	MnO %	Ti μg/g	P μg/g	Mn μg/g	V μg/g	Cr μg/g	Co μg/g	Ni μg/g	Pb μg/g	Nb μg/g	Th μg/g	U μg/g	Zr μg/g	La μg/g
1	PM-1	Y10	Soil	Dark brown loamy soil with small amount of weathered debris, containing humus, plant root development	0.1	52.8	12.3	7.10	1.80	1.20	2.36	2.35	1.10	0.273	0.100	6620	1192	776	108	70.2	29.2	74.5	17.0	25.9	10.5	1.99	318	33.8
2		Y09	Soil	Brownish yellow chalky loam with a few plant roots visible	0.3	54.5	11.8	5.97	1.92	1.35	2.09	2.09	1.01	0.238	0.091	6066	1038	702	99.1	60.7	22.6	56.2	19.4	27.4	8.90	2.18	355	31.5
3		Y08	Soil	Brown clay, with obvious rainwater drainage marks visible on the external surface	0.6	59.4	12.4	4.87	2.34	1.34	1.14	2.00	0.66	0.135	0.084	3931	590	647	82.5	59.7	14.7	33.9	22.7	17.0	11.2	2.14	250	35.0
4		Y07	Soil	Brownish chalky soil, a little weathered debris, easy to crush by hand	1.3	59.2	12.1	4.80	2.26	1.43	1.39	2.02	0.74	0.146	0.097	4429	637	752	86.7	66.4	16.4	36.6	23.2	19.9	10.3	2.35	388	34.5
5		Y06	Soil	Brownish yellow clayey sandy soil with occasional mixed gravels	2.0	59.1	12.1	4.82	2.31	1.61	1.57	1.97	0.81	0.162	0.076	4847	707	590	89.7	76.2	15.4	32.6	22.0	28.3	10.9	2.29	535	47.7
6		Y05	Soil	Light yellow sandy soil, a large number of gravels can be seen, the grain size is 0.4–5 cm, the gravels are poorly rounded and sorted	2.8	52.1	14.7	9.63	2.31	1.01	1.89	2.48	1.64	0.375	0.155	9814	1637	1200	105	71.6	34.0	78.6	11.7	51.0	10.1	2.17	454	57.2
7		Y04	Soil	Light gray clayey soil	3.9	59.4	11.9	4.68	2.26	1.42	1.33	1.71	0.71	0.189	0.064	4246	825	498	81.6	59.0	14.6	31.4	22.2	17.6	10.9	2.36	324	38.5
8		Y03	Soil	Brownish gray loamy sandy soil, a large number of debris can be seen, the debris composition is mainly strongly weathered basalt, particle size varies	4.4	54.7	13.4	7.38	2.24	1.43	2.11	2.23	1.16	0.312	0.125	6936	1360	969	108	65.6	27.5	55.4	17.6	34.5	11.1	2.41	486	46.0
9		Y02	Weathered debris	Strongly weathered basalt, weathered debris to gravel approximately 1:2, residual original rock structure	5.6	46.8	14.1	11.5	2.10	2.58	5.23	3.78	1.94	0.701	0.160	11631	3059	1242	131	72.0	39.5	82.3	6.82	72.6	7.22	1.86	427	54.5
10		Y01	Weathered debris	Weakly weathered basalt, W-S oriented joints developed, hard	6.8	45.8	14.3	11.9	1.93	2.54	5.74	3.81	2.03	0.754	0.182	12189	3291	1413	135	55.4	46.9	85.2	6.51	81.1	6.84	1.56	479	53.6
11	PM-2	B06	Weathered debris	Strongly weathered basalt, mainly coarse debris, grain size 0.3–1.8 cm, containing more gravel	9.0	48.0	13.9	14.9	1.50	0.41	2.05	2.50	2.90	0.305	0.086	17371	1330	663	227	140	51.3	115	18.2	60.3	8.06	4.07	305	42.5
12		B05	Weathered debris	Moderately weathered basalt, mainly small gravels, 1–6 cm in size, broken by hammering	9.9	44.9	12.6	12.3	1.42	1.14	6.62	4.86	1.92	0.757	0.202	11517	3302	1566	201	115	53.6	168	5.24	60.3	5.10	1.18	312	43.6
13		B04	Weathered debris	Weakly weathered basalt with layers of 210–250 cm	10.7	43.6	12.4	12.4	1.24	1.87	7.11	6.11	1.94	0.772	0.179	11622	3371	1390	185	116	48.5	164	3.87	59.0	4.87	1.27	336	44.8
14		B03	Basalt	Fresh basalt, hard, weathered surface yellow-green	11.9	49.2	15.5	11.7	2.26	3.30	6.42	4.37	2.34	0.741	0.123	14018	3232	955	132	60.2	43.5	73.1	3.40	85.4	9.90	1.77	388	43.1
15		B02	Basalt	Fresh basalt, hard, weathered surface grayish white	13.2	49.1	15.1	12.2	2.81	3.10	6.29	4.85	2.39	0.677	0.134	14353	2956	1039	138	65.9	45.2	76.3	4.20	84.5	9.00	1.59	376	43.8
16		B01	Basalt	Fresh basalt, hard, weathered surface gray-black	14.5	51.4	15.2	10.1	1.24	3.26	7.01	4.89	1.58	0.382	0.117	9454	1666	903	139	113	47.7	126	4.00	27.5	3.80	0.57	151	21.6

Notes: The unit of depth is m (or meter). The units of major oxides are % and others are μg/g.

4. Results and Discussion

4.1. Weathering Profile

The results on weathering indices of CIA and WIG of the weathering profile are shown in Figure 3. The values of CIA in the profile vary in a range of 44.6 to 74.0, and WIG values vary from 19.5 to 78.3, which indicates an incipient to intermediate weathering degree mostly. Although the weathering degree is increasing gradually from fresh bedrock at the bottom to the weathered debris in the middle parts and then to topsoil, an abrupt variation at the boundary of PM-1 and PM-2 is recognized at the platform.

The geochemical lithogenes of LG01 and LG03 of samples from the weathering profile were coded on GGC (Geochemical Gene Coding) software [1], and then the acidic similarities (R_{Acidic}) were calculated and are illustrated in Figure 3.

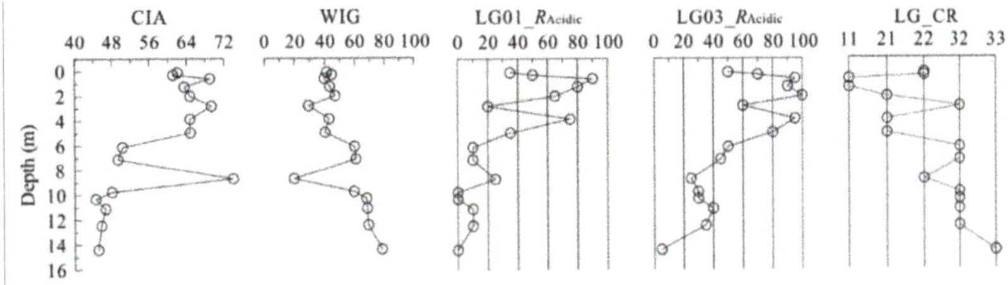

Figure 3. Weathering indices, acidic similarities of lithogenes, and the LG_CR results in the weathering profile.

With respect to the bottom rock, the R_{Acidic} values of LG01 and LG03 are all ≤20%, which indicates that the bottom sample is the 33 type of LG_CR compositionally. With respect to the other rock and debris (below 5 m in profile depth), they are basic-like materials on LG01 classification and intermediate-like on LG03 classification; therefore, they belong to the 32 type of LG_CR compositionally, except the top material in the sub-profile of PM-2, which is the 22 type of LG_CR and is located near the boundary of the platform or sub-profiles, while the soils (above 5 m in profile depth) are 11, 21, 22, or 32 types of LG_CR, which indicates the lithology of the weathering profile is heterogeneous compositionally or soils were mixed with different sources compositionally. The lithological variation in the upper soils in the profile may be explained by its location near the petrological boundary of the conglomerate (K_1t^1) and the basalt with clay and shale in the middle and upper part (N_3) (Figure 2b).

In a word, the geochemical lithology of the weathering profile shows a gradual variation from basic-like in the bottom rock to acidic-like at the upper soils compositionally with heterogeneity.

4.2. Gully Sediment Profiles

The LG01 and LG03 lithogenes of the 50 soils in CJPM-1 and CJPM-2 pathway profiles were coded by GGC software [1], and then the acidity similarity (R_{Acidic}) of each sample was calculated. The LG_CR results are derived based on the acidic similarities and illustrated in Figure 4.

In Figure 4, there are only 2 types of LG_CR recognized in the pathway profiles as 11 and 21 types compositionally. In the CJPM-1 profile, the seven sediment profiles are distributed in the Quaternary strata along the N-S trending gully (Figure 4a). Therefore, residual soils in the alluvial gully are prone to be mixed with migrated soils. If the residual or background soils in the pathway profile are the 11 type of LG_CR, as illustrated in Figure 4b,c, and the migrated soils are the 21, 22, and even 32 types, as illustrated in Figure 3, the mixing result will be the 21 type of LG_CR, which is consistent with the facts in Figure 4b. In the CJPM-2 profile, only the TP4 profile is located in the N-S trending gully and the other three profiles are located in the Cretaceous strata area with conglomerate petrology. Therefore, only the topsoil in the TP4 profile is the 21 type, which is mixed with the upstream soils, and the others, far from the gully, are all the 11 type of LG_CR.

In summary, soils from the CJPM-1 profile in the N-S trending gully are mixed with the upstream soils and soils from the CJPM-2 profile have not undergone mixing with other lithological components, except the gully soils. These results indicate that LG_CR can be viewed as a useful tool to recognize and trace geological materials.

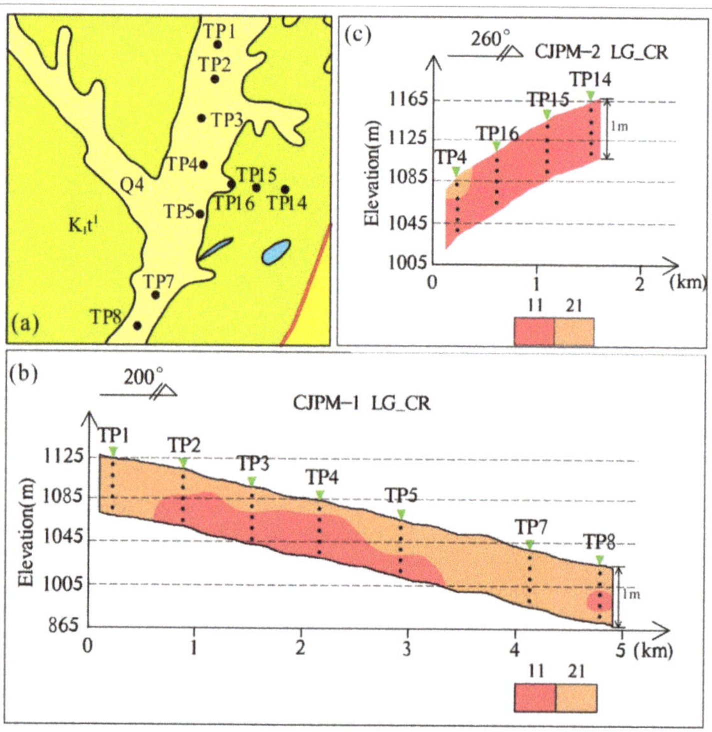

Figure 4. Locations of the pathway profiles (**a**) and LG_CR results of soils from the CJPM-1 (**b**) and CJPM-2 (**c**) profiles. Legends in (**a**) are the same as in Figure 2b.

4.3. Stream Sediments from RGNR Project

Based on the 278 stream sediments' data retrieved from the RGNR project in the study area of Wanquan district of Zhangjiakou city in Hebei province (Figure 2b or Figure 5d), the codes and acidic similarities of LG01 and LG03 lithogenes are calculated and the LG_CR results are derived. The geochemical maps of R_{Acidic} of LG01 (Figure 5a), R_{Acidic} of LG03 (Figure 5b), and LG_CR values (Figure 5c) are contoured and classified compositionally like the method of the geochemical map [31].

By comparing Figure 5a,d, we can find that the red areas with $R_{\text{Acidic}} \geq 80\%$ in LG01 are mainly Jurassic and Cretaceous strata in the central part, the orange areas between 25% $\leq R_{\text{Acidic}} \leq 75\%$ are mainly Archean and Sinian strata in the southwest and Quaternary strata in the north-central part, and the blue areas with $R_{\text{Acidic}} \leq 20\%$ are mainly Hannuoba Formation (N_3) with petrological basaltic materials. In conclusion, the classification results of the stream sediments on the LG01 lithogene are generally consistent with the petrological results derived from the regional geological survey.

By comparing Figure 5b,d, the results are similar to those from the comparison between Figure 5a,d. The notable difference is that the basic-like components are also recognized in the southwest on the LG03 lithogene. Overall, the classification results on LG03 are also basically consistent with those derived from the regional geological survey.

Although nine types of LG_CR can be classified theoretically on double-digit numbers based on the acidic similarities of LG01 and LG03 lithogenes, only six types are recognized in the Wanquan area as lacking the 12, 13, and 31 types (Figure 5c) on the geochemical data of 278 stream sediments, each representing 4 km^2.

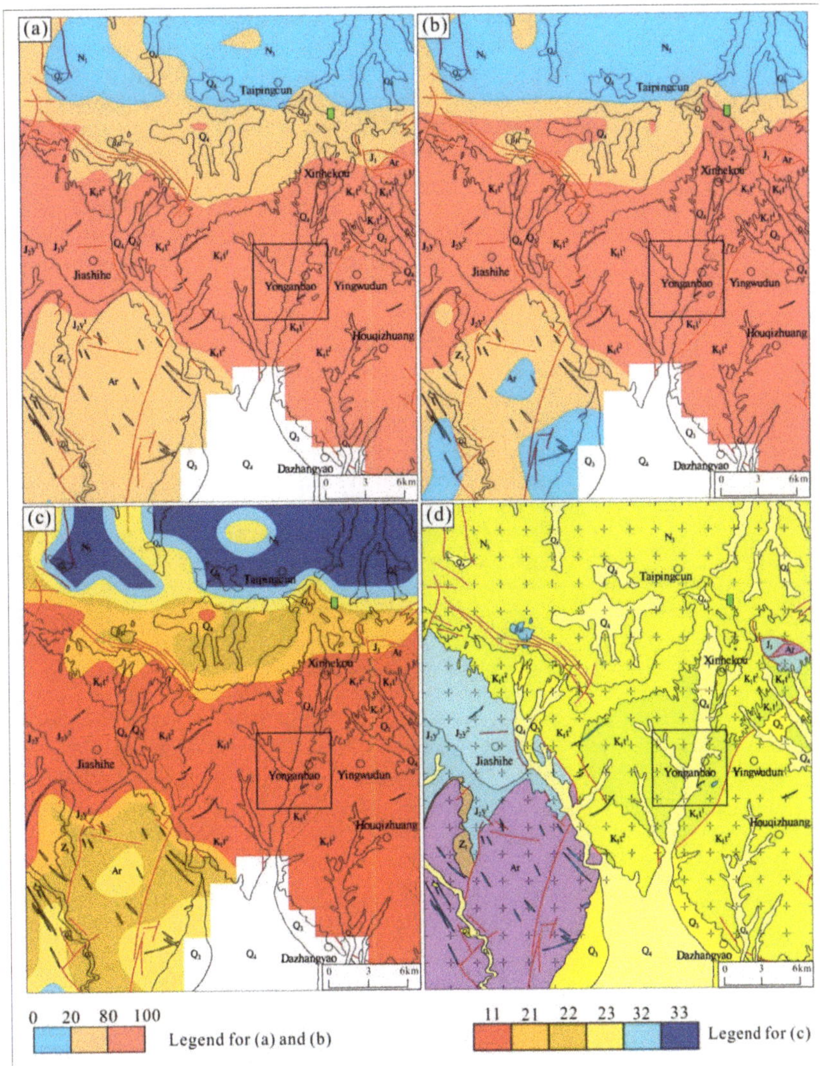

Figure 5. Geochemical maps of R_{Acidic} of LG01 (**a**), R_{Acidic} of LG03 (**b**), LG_CR values (**c**), and the geological map (**d**) in the study area.

A comparison of Figure 5c,d shows that the red areas in the 11 type are mainly in the Jurassic and Cretaceous strata in the central part. The dark-yellow areas in the 21 type are mainly in the Jurassic and Quaternary strata in the central and southern part, occurring as the transition zone between the 11-type and 22-type areas. The orange areas in the 22 type are mainly in the Jurassic and Quaternary strata in the central and in the Archean and Sinian strata in the southern part.

The light-yellow areas in the 23 type are mainly in the Archean strata in the southwest part and as the transition zones between 22-type and 32-type areas in the Hannuoba Formation (N_3) in the north part. The light-blue areas in the 32 type are also as transition zones between 23-type and 33-type areas in the north part, while the dark-blue areas in the 33 type are mainly distributed in the Hannuoba Formation (N_3) with petrological basaltic materials.

Furthermore, the 10 sediment profiles are located in the 11 type of LG_CR (Figure 5c) area determined on the stream sediments with a scale of 1:200,000, which is basically consistent with the results derived on the soils from the two pathway profiles (Figure 4b,c).

In summary, the main types of LG_CR of stream sediments in the Wanquan area are 11, 22, and 33 types. The lithological results of LG_CR on geochemical lithogenes are basically consistent with the petrological results derived from the regional geological survey. However, the LG_CR method is applicable to stream sediments, soils, debris, and rocks in wider geological materials, rather than only rocks in petrology. Therefore, the LG_CR method will be a useful tool for lithological mapping in the petrological overburdened areas.

5. Conclusions

(1) The geochemical lithogenes are applied in the Wanquan area of Zhangjiakou city in Hebei province, China, on samples from a weathering profile, 10 sediment profiles, and 278 stream sediments, covering an area of ca. 1080 km^2 to classify geological materials.

(2) The soils in the gully have undergone mixing with the upstream soils and the lithological results on LG_CR of stream sediments are basically consistent with the petrological results derived from the regional geological survey.

(3) The LG_CR method on geochemical lithogenes can be viewed as a useful tool to recognize and trace geological materials. Furthermore, it will have great potential in lithological mapping in petrological overburdened areas.

Supplementary Materials: The following supporting information can be downloaded at: https://www.mdpi.com/article/10.3390/10.3390/app13021008/s1, Table S1: Sample information, analytical data, weathering indexes (CIA and WIG), LG01 and LG03 codes, their acidic similarities, and LG_CR of samples from Wanquan area of Hebei province, China.; Table S2: Sample information, analytical data, weathering indexes (CIA and WIG), LG01 and LG03 codes, their acidic similarities, and LG_CR of Sedimentary profile samples from Wanquan area of Hebei province, China.

Author Contributions: Y.A.: Conceptualization, Data curation, Writing—original draft. X.Y.: Conceptualization, Data curation, Formal analysis. Q.G.: Conceptualization, Methodology, Writing—review and editing. X.L.: Data curation, Formal analysis. N.L.: Methodology, Formal analysis, Data curation. All authors have read and agreed to the published version of the manuscript.

Funding: This work was financially supported by the Ecological Geological Survey and Risk Assessment of Heavy Metals in Soil of Pinggu District, Beijing (11000022T000000439569).

Institutional Review Board Statement: Not applicable.

Informed Consent Statement: Not applicable.

Data Availability Statement: Not applicable.

Acknowledgments: We greatly appreciate the comments from the anonymous reviewers and editors for their valuable suggestions to improve the quality of this manuscript.

Conflicts of Interest: The authors declare that they have no known competing financial interests or personal relationships that could have appeared to influence the work reported in this paper.

References

1. Gong, Q.; Yan, T.; Wu, X.; Li, R.; Wang, X.; Liu, N.; Li, X.; Wu, Y.; Li, J. Geochemical gene: A promising concept in discrimination and traceability. *Appl. Geochem.* **2022**, *136*, 105133. [CrossRef]
2. Sun, S.S.; McDonough, W.F. *Chemical and Isotopic Systematics of Oceanic Basalts: Implications for Mantle Composition and Processes*; Geological Society: London, UK, 1989; Volume 42, pp. 313–345.
3. Hou, Z.; Gong, Q.; Liu, N.; Jiang, B.; Li, J.; Wu, Y.; Huang, J.; Gu, W. Elemental abundances of moon samples based on statistical distributions of analytical data. *Appl. Sci.* **2023**, *13*, 360. [CrossRef]
4. Yan, T.; Gong, Q.; Li, J.; Chen, J.; Zhou, W.; Li, R. $A1_2O_3$/Ti: Protoliths tracer in the process of weathering and alteration. *Acta Petrol. Sin.* **2016**, *32*, 2425–2432, (In Chinese with English abstract).
5. Costa, L.; Mirlean, N.; Johannesson, K.H. Rare earth elements as tracers of sediment contamination by fertilizer industries in Southern Brazil, Patos Lagoon Estuary. *Appl. Geochem.* **2021**, *129*, 104965. [CrossRef]
6. Zhang, Y.; Han, R.; Wang, L.; Wei, P. Zn–S isotopic fractionation effect during the evolution process of ore-forming fluids: A case study of the ultra-large Huize rich Ge-bearing Pb–Zn deposit. *Appl. Geochem.* **2022**, *140*, 105240. [CrossRef]
7. Wu, Y.; Li, X.; Gong, Q.; Wu, X.; Yao, N.; Peng, C.; Chao, Y.; Wang, X.; Pu, X. Test and application of the geochemical lithogene on weathering profiles developed over granitic and basaltic rocks in China. *Appl. Geochem.* **2021**, *128*, 104958. [CrossRef]
8. Li, R.; Liu, N.; Gong, Q.; Wu, X.; Yan, T.; Li, X.; Liu, M. Construction, test and application of a geochemical gold metallogene: Case studies in China. *J. Geochem. Explor.* **2019**, *204*, 1–11. [CrossRef]
9. Gong, Q.; Liu, N.; Wu, X.; Yan, T.; Fan, T.; Li, X.; Liu, M.; Li, R.; Albanese, S. Using regional geochemical survey data to trace anomalous samples through geochemical genes: The Tieshanlong tungsten deposit area (Southeastern China) case study. *J. Geochem. Explor.* **2020**, *219*, 106637. [CrossRef]
10. Gong, Q.J.; Wu, X.; Yan, T.T.; Liu, N.Q.; Li, X.L.; Li, R.K.; Liu, M.X. Construction and test of geochemical genes: Case studies in China. *Geoscience* **2020**, *34*, 865–882, (In Chinese with English abstract).
11. Li, J.; Gong, Q.; Zhang, B.; Liu, N.; Wu, X.; Yan, T.; Li, X.; Wu, Y. Construction, test and application of a tungsten metallogene named MGW11: Case studies in China. *Appl. Sci.* **2023**, *13*, 606. [CrossRef]
12. Li, J.; Liu, N.; Gong, Q.; Wu, X.; Yan, T. Construction and test of a geochemical lithogene based on trace elements: Case studies on weathering profiles in China. *Geoscience* **2021**, *35*, 1459–1470, (In Chinese with English abstract).
13. Yan, T.; Wu, X.; Quan, Y.; Gong, Q.; Li, X.; Wang, P.; Li, R. Heredity, inheritance and similarity of element behaviors among parent rocks and their weathered products: A geochemical lithogene. *Geoscience* **2018**, *32*, 453–467, (In Chinese with English abstract).
14. Chi, Q.; Yan, M. *Handbook of Elemental Abundance for Applied Geochemistry*; Geological Publishing House: Beijing, China, 2007; pp. 1–148, (In Chinese with English abstract).
15. Wu, Y.; Gong, Q.; Liu, N.; Wu, X.; Yan, T.; Xu, S.; Li, W. Classification of geological materials on geochemical lithogenes: Illustration on a case study in Gejiu area of Yunnan Province, China. *Appl. Geochem.* **2022**, *146*, 105460. [CrossRef]
16. Wang, Y.; Dong, Y.; Liu, M.; Wang, Y. The spatial distribution of soil properties and their GW correlation: A case in Zhangjiakou City. *Sci. Geogr. Sin.* **2020**, *40*, 1191–1201.
17. Huang, L.; Zhang, Y.; Shao, F.; Yu, X. Soil ecological stoichiometry and its influencing factors in natural secondary forest, North Mountain of Hebei Province. *Acta Ecol. Sin.* **2021**, *41*, 6267–6279.
18. Yang, H.; Liang, R.; Xu, C.; Zhao, J. Prospecting for the north-easterly periphery of Damaping peridot ore in Wanquan County, Hebei Province. *Miner. Resour. Geol.* **2017**, *31*, 935–940, (In Chinese with English abstract).
19. Cui, X.; Su, S.; Song, C.; Jiang, J.; Hei, H.; Wu, Y. Origin and source of the Hannuoba alkaline basalts. *Ti Hsueh Ch'ien Yuan* **2019**, *26*, 257–270, (In Chinese with English abstract).
20. Xiang, Y.; Mu, X.; Ren, T.; Ma, Z.; Liu, R.; Gong, Q.; Wang, M.; Gong, J.; Yang, W.; Yang, Y.; et al. *Application of Geochemical Survey Data on Potential Evaluation of Mineral Resources in China*; Geological Publishing House: Beijing, China, 2018; pp. 1–445.
21. Xie, X.; Cheng, H. Sixty years of exploration geochemistry in China. *J. Geochem. Explor.* **2014**, *139*, 4–8. [CrossRef]
22. Li, M.; Xi, X.H.; Xiao, G.Y.; Cheng, H.X.; Yang, Z.F.; Zhou, G.H.; Ye, J.Y.; Li, Z.H. National multi-purpose regional geochemical survey in China. *J. Geochem. Explor.* **2014**, *139*, 21–30. [CrossRef]
23. Nesbitt, H.W.; Young, G.M. Prediction of some weathering trends of plutonic and volcanic rocks based on thermodynamic and kinetic considerations. *Geochim. Cosmochim. Acta* **1984**, *48*, 1523–1534. [CrossRef]
24. Zhang, J.; Zhao, Z.; Li, X.; Yan, Y.; Lang, Y.; Ding, H.; Cui, L.; Meng, J.; Liu, C. Extremely enrichment of ^{7}Li in highly weathered saprolites developed on granite from Huizhou, southern China. *Appl. Geochem.* **2021**, *125*, 104825. [CrossRef]
25. Xiong, Y.; Qi, H.; Hu, R.; Xiao, Y.; Wei, L. Lithium isotope behavior under extreme tropical weathering: A case study of basalts from the Hainan Island, South China. *Appl. Geochem.* **2022**, *140*, 105295. [CrossRef]
26. Duzgoren-Aydin, N.S.; Aydin, A.; Malaps, J. Re-assessment of chemical weathering indices: Case study on pyroclastic rocks of *Hong Kong Eng. Geol.* **2002**, *63*, 99–119. [CrossRef]
27. Gong, Q.; Deng, J.; Jia, Y.; Tong, Y.; Liu, N. Empirical equations to describe trace element behaviors due to rock weathering in China. *J. Geochem. Explor.* **2015**, *152*, 110–117. [CrossRef]
28. Nesbitt, H.W.; Young, G.M. Early Proterozoic climates and plate motions inferred from major element chemistry of lutites. *Nature* **1982**, *299*, 715–717. [CrossRef]

29. Gong, Q.; Deng, J.; Wang, C.; Wang, Z.; Zhou, L. Element behaviors due to rock weathering and its implication to geochemical anomaly recognition: A case study on Linglong biotite granite in Jiaodong peninsula, China. *J. Geochem. Explor.* **2013**, *128*, 14–24. [CrossRef]
30. Fedo, C.M.; Nesbitt, H.W.; Young, G.M. Unravelling the effects of potassium metasomatism in sedimentary rocks and paleosols, with Implications for weathering conditions and provenance. *Geology* **1995**, *23*, 921–924. [CrossRef]
31. An, Y.; Yan, T.; Gong, Q.; Wang, X.; Huang, Y.; Zhang, B.; Yin, Z.; Zhao, X.; Liu, N. Chromium (Cr) geochemical mapping based on fixed-values' method: Case studies in China. *Appl. Geochem.* **2022**, *136*, 105168. [CrossRef]

MDPI
St. Alban-Anlage 66
4052 Basel
Switzerland
Tel. +41 61 683 77 34
Fax +41 61 302 89 18
www.mdpi.com

Applied Sciences Editorial Office
E-mail: applsci@mdpi.com
www.mdpi.com/journal/applsci

www.ingramcontent.com/pod-product-compliance
Lightning Source LLC
Chambersburg PA
CBHW040811250926
51850CB00007BA/1137
9783036583464